The Combat History of

GERMAN TIGER TANK BATTALION 503
IN WORLD WAR II

EDITED BY
FRANZ-WILHELM LOCHMANN,
RICHARD FREIHERR VON ROSEN, AND ALFRED RUBBEL

WITH CONTRIBUTIONS BY FORMER MEMBERS
OF TIGER TANK BATTALION 503

STACKPOLE
BOOKS

Published in paperback in 2008 by
STACKPOLE BOOKS
5067 Ritter Road
Mechanicsburg, PA 17055
www.stackpolebooks.com

www.jjfpub.mb.ca

Cover design by Wendy A. Reynolds

Printed in the United States of America

10 9 8 7 6 5 4 3 2 1

Library of Congress Cataloging-in-Publication Data

Combat history of Schwere Panzer-Abteilung 503
  The combat history of German Tiger Tank Battalion 503 in World War II / [edited by]
Franz-Wilhelm Lochmann, Richard Freiherr von Rosen, and Alfred Rubbel. — 1st ed.
     p. cm.
  Originally published: Combat history of Schwere Panzer-Abteilung 503. 2000.
  ISBN-13: 978-0-8117-3484-4
  ISBN-10: 0-8117-3484-6
  1. Germany. Heer. Schwere Panzer-Abteilung 503. 2. World War, 1939–1945—Regimental histories—Germany.
3. World War, 1939–1945—Campaigns—Europe. I. Lochmann, Franz-Wilhelm. II. Rosen, Richard, Freiherr von.
III. Rubbel, Alfred. IV. Title.
  D757.58503rd .L63 2008
  940.54'1343—dc22
                          2007036078

TABLE OF CONTENTS

FOREWORD

Since the end of the war we have talked about attempting to write a history of our battalion. The fact that more than 250 former members regularly get together after forty-five years is a clear indication that a better form of record needs to be created than that which is preserved in our memories.

The Kleine/Kühne book, *Tiger: The History of a Legendary Weapon*, whose German edition came out in the mid 1970s, presented a comprehensive picture of all of the Tiger battalions. It was a remarkable attempt to present their history. That book, which was well received, and not only by former Tiger men, consisted largely of contributions and illustrations from them. Unfortunately, the authors did not always hit their targets, and the presentations in the book did not always meet the expectations of those who had provided the information. The portion devoted to Tiger Tank Battalion 503 was, of necessity, limited in its scope. That was another reason for us to proceed in our plans for our own account. Given those starting points, we went to work two years ago. This book is particularly notable for giving the greatest possible number of our comrades a chance to speak.

What is presented here should not be evaluated as a historically documented report, but as the sum of more or less subjective accounts. These are based on facts and experience, but written down as experienced by the individual authors.

The editors did not consider checking the contents of the accounts to be part of their task, that lying beyond both their mission and capabilities. The authors vouch for their reports by the use of their names. Furthermore, one must consider that, after forty-five years, our memories are not entirely reliable. It need not be mentioned that the comrades who have put their contributions into this book gave it their best effort. It is unavoidable that there will be discrepancies regarding dates, place names, and persons. Such discrepancies occur even in the most rigorous military histories. That is why we replaced the common term—battalion history—in the German edition with the less exacting *Erinnerungen an die Tiger-Abteilung 503* (*Recollections of Tiger Battalion 503*).

In spite of an abundance of records, there are still holes in the source material that could not be eliminated by inquiry. Therefore, the companies could not all receive equal emphasis, nor have individually important wartime events all received the emphasis they deserve in our account. On the other hand, some events are described several times from differing viewpoints.

Our book is no replacement for the battalion war diary that was lost at the end of the war. Nor does it make literary or historical pretenses in presenting the wartime experiences of our unit. The editors set themselves the task of putting together a suitable collection from available, comprehensive, but exceedingly varied sources, from the literature as well as new accounts that would present a portrait of Tiger Tank Battalion 503 as it exists in our memories.

Our book is intended primarily for reading, rather than looking. It was not written for the individual companies, but, rather, for the entire battalion. We took pains to present factual reports instead of emotional presentations. Personality cults were avoided. However, it lies in the nature of things that some individuals received extensive mention, others less, and the majority none at all.

We, the authors, have to give manifold thanks. First in line are the comrades who have encouraged us in the project and who helped with advice and deed during the two years of work that went into its production.

Without the many contributions in form of text, pictures, documents and assistance, the book would never have reached completion. For that, we offer special thanks. As is well known, nothing takes place without money. Those whose timely contributions supported the project financially, in good faith that the project would succeed, receive our heartfelt thanks.

We present our comrades with these recollections. We hope it meets their expectations. This book is a tribute to Tiger Tank Battalion 503. We are proud to have belonged to it. We also wish to honor our dead.

Dr. Franz-Wilhelm Lochmann
Richard Freiherr von Rosen
Alfred Rubbel
Rolf Sichel
May 1990

INTRODUCTION
by the Last Commander of the Battalion

It is not easy, forty-five years after the German collapse, to prepare a greeting to the surviving members of a military unit, men who courageously performed their duty—disciplined and conscious of their responsibility—to the bitter end. Today, if one uses words like courage, comradeship and fulfillment of duty, one runs the danger of being categorized by the media as a warmonger, cold-war fighter or potential murderer. The molders of public opinion prefer to label as "heroes," those who did not fulfill their duties, who committed acts of sabotage, who deserted. Those are the ones for whom monuments are erected, holidays celebrated. Those who disfigure or destroy memorials are honored as "true friends of peace." It is notable that, in Europe, only the Germans engage in this form of self-reeducation. One has only to compare such behavior with that of the French, who, after conquering almost all of Europe and, then, after the collapse of Napoleon, still honor and count as heroes of the *Grande Nation* their soldiers who were badly beaten in the battles on the Beresina, at Leipzig and at Waterloo.

So, in this place, I offer a word of recognition to the soldiers of Tiger Tank Battalion 503, whom I had the honor to command during the difficult final five months of the Second World War. This was a unit that had, for three years, enjoyed a reputation for performance above that of the average soldier. From the beginning, it was no group of "wild warriors," no "bloodthirsty conquerors" or "fanatical Nazis striving for world conquest." It was, rather, a sworn comradeship whose efforts were based on personal values and courage, on unconditional comradeship and on matter-of-fact fulfillment of duty. The obvious bond between officers, noncommissioned officers and men was universal, but especially so among the armored force, where tank crews operated within the closest of quarters and there were no distinctions as to burdens, dangers faced or common fate.

The time of the rapid assault and successful offensive operation had already gone by the time I led this unit. It had become a matter of defending against an enemy who was superior in manpower and equipment and of throwing him back in local counterattacks so as to enable our own army, the wounded and the civilian population to withdraw. There was no room for grand language, for exhortations to success and promises of ultimate victory. There were no great laurels to be won. It was only daily, grinding, costly defensive combat with inadequate supplies and replacements.

In that depressing phase of the war, the strength and discipline of this courageous unit shone forth in exemplary fashion. No one sought to shirk action, never was a wounded comrade left in the lurch. Even in the most hopeless situation, each placed his life on the line for his fellow soldiers as the obvious and only thing to do. The unit would never have been such a reliable bulwark and "fortress in the storm" to the last days without the successful activities of the logistical units which—day and night—fought their way through, often between the lines, or without the self-sacrificing technical helpers from the maintenance company and the maintenance sections which, in the midst of the fighting and under enemy fire, repaired our tanks or towed them to the rear. Just as vital were the motorcycle messengers with their dare-devil journeys in the battle lines.

Until the very end, the radio operators, motor-cycle drivers and liaison officers of the battalion enabled us to have a seamless overview of the situation while attached to a panzer corps—despite the holes in the defensive front. It was an extremely heavy burden for our battalion that we had to bury so many especially reliable and successful comrades in the last weeks of the war.

Thus, this has become a eulogy for Tiger Tank Battalion 503. We were unable to do that at the end of the war. For those who were members of the battalion, it went without question they would fulfill their duties to the end—in the midst of the collapse of the leadership and the desperate war situation, which, for many, was tied up with loss of homeland, many family members, their homes and all of their belongings. There, once again, the true value of soldierly conduct was proven, and I wish for us and for all the family members of those who were in Tiger Tank Battalion 503 that this memory—in contrast to the "modern" attacks on the values of the honorable soldier—may live on into the future. That is also the purpose of this small account of the battalion and of the long-lasting bonds of our comradeship.

Dr. Nordewin von Diest-Koerber
June 1989

PART ONE

ORGANIZATION OF THE BATTALION

CHAPTER 1

In Review

Alfred Rubbel

The battalion was dissolved at Dobrusch, west of Budweis, on 10 May 1945. The main body of the battalion—around 450 men—had moved there with its vehicles. Within a few hours the battalion had dispersed to the four winds, headed towards the west.

In the numerous discussions with members of the battalion that took place during the preparation of this record, it was obvious that our memories had become unreliable. Because of that and because many of the peripheral occurrences related to the battalion's existence might not be known, a little "review" will be offered here.

The threatening superiority of the Russian KV-1 and T-34 tanks over the German Panzer IIIs and Panzer IVs accelerated the development of the follow-on model that had been underway since 1939. Within twelve months that resulted in an experimental model that resembled the Tiger. At first, preference went to the technically interesting VK 4501 (P), which led to the Porsche Tiger. Because that model was not yet fully developed, the VK 3601 (H), which had been in parallel production by Henschel, went into production, resulting in the Tiger I.

The 1st Company, Tiger Tank Battalion 503, was the only unit of the army that received the Porsche Tiger I, if only temporarily. The company was later re-equipped with the Henschel Tiger.

Another controversial question at the higher levels was where the Tiger was to be placed in field organizations. In 1941 Hitler had demanded that each Panzerdivision should have twenty of them "for the spearhead of the armor formation." Various tactically and technically important reasons led to the decision to concentrate the Tigers in separate units as army-level troops (*Heerestruppen*) at the disposal of OKH (*Oberkommando des Heeres*, or Army High Command). That had both advantages and disadvantages. The advantages were that OKH had direct interest in its Tiger battalions and our commanders were able to use that "connection" in order to forestall tactically false employment of the Tiger by corps and divisions. The disadvantage was that, because we did not organically belong to them, the corps and divisions occasionally used the Tigers recklessly and ignored the technical needs of these very special armored formations. All of us experienced that. The booklet that Guderian issued, *Merkblatt über Tiger-Einsatz* (*Guidelines for Employing the Tiger*), which was primarily intended for the higher levels of command, helped little in that respect, if the essentials of armor, and, especially, of Tigers were not known or were ignored.

Of the ten separate Tiger battalions, Tiger Tank Battalion 503 was the oldest. It existed for three years and reached its full strength very early

(April 1943: 3 combat companies = 45 Tigers). It had the good fortune, apart from a few exceptions, of always being employed in its entirety, under its own command structure.

Its combat strength and good reputation guaranteed that it had a very eventful existence, with hard operations, always at the hot spots. In its 36 months of existence, our battalion had twenty-seven months of service at the front. The battalion reported its 1,500th tank destroyed in October 1944. By the final capitulation, that total may have risen to 2000, since the battalion still had an estimated twenty Tigers in March 1945. There were more than enough enemy tanks and the companies were committed uninterruptedly from October 1944 to the last day. In accord with the ongoing employment, losses were also very high. They will be reported in a special chapter.

From the first operations in December 1942 to the end of the war in May 1945, percentage losses (killed) by rank were 53 percent officers, 26 percent noncommissioned officers, and 21 percent enlisted men.

CHAPTER 2

Summary of the Employment History of Tiger Tank Battalion 503

Alfred Rubbel

Our employment was limited to the theaters of war in the Kalmuck Steppe and the Ukraine, Normandy, and Hungary, Austria, and Czechoslovakia.

Because of missing records, it is not possible to give a seamless sketch of the wartime events. I have prepared a tabular outline of the battalion's employment, indicating dates and locations. That may help in keeping track of the details of time and location.

Although it certainly would have been interesting to name all the divisions to which the battalion was attached, that information was not available in most instances. Therefore we had to limit ourselves to the higher level of command (army and corps). As a rule, the battalion was attached to a division that fought as the main effort (forming the *Schwerpunkt*, or spearhead). On occasion, the battalion was split up into companies. Starting in 1944, the tanks were assembled into battle groups (*Kampfgruppen*) without reference to their company affiliation.

The data provided on the next few pages is based on soldier pay book (*Soldbuch*) entries, published accounts and personal notes. There may be errors.

Period	Area of Operations / Activity	Command Relationship

4 May 1942 to end of December 1942	Germany
	Organization, equipping and training of the
	    Headquarters, the Headquarters Company, two tank
	    companies and the Maintenance Company at
	—Neu-Ruppin
	—Fallingbostel (3rd Company, Tiger Tank Battalion 503)
	—Döllersheim
	(1st Company, Tiger Tank Battalion 503, received the
	    Porsche Tiger)
	Kalmuck Steppe: Army Group Don (von Manstein)
		Responsible military district
		
		4th Panzer Army

30 December 1942 to 11 February 1943	Offensive operations and defensive fighting on the Manytsch, east and west of the lower Don Ukraine: Army Group Don (von Manstein)	

Period	Area of Operations / Activity	Command Relationship
17 February to 4 March 1943	Defensive fighting in the Donez region.	Army Detachment Hollidt (6th Army)
5 March to 10 April 1943	Defensive fighting in the Mius-Donez position.	
11 April to 4 July 1943	Army Group Don, renamed Army Group South (v.Manstein) Transfer to Kharkov area. Reorganized under the 1943–44 tables of organization. Preparations for Operation "Zitadelle": —Boguduchow —Kharkov —Tolokonoje —Türkenübung (The "Dog and Pony" Show)	Army Detachment Kempf (8th Army)
5–16 July 1943	Operation "Zitadelle" —Bjelgorod —Rasumnoje —Jastrebowo —Werchne Olchanez	Army Detachment Kempf III Panzer Corps (6th, 7th, and 19th Panzer Divisions)
17 July to 23 August 1943	Fighting withdrawal west of the middle Donez; defensive fighting at Kharkov	XI Corps
	Defensive fighting west of Kharkov; fighting withdrawal	8th Army
14 September 1943	East of the Dnjepr (changing command and control relationships; units farmed out to different commands)	
Until on/about 31 December 1943	Defensive fighting on the Dnjepr —Army reserve at Snamenka —Commitment as a battle group at Kiew, Krementschug, Pawlisch, Glinsk and Tschigrin	8th Army
1 January to 25 February 1944	Defensive fighting west of Kiew and in the southern Ukraine	8th Army
(5–18 January 1944)	Defensive fighting near Kirowograd	
(24 January to 25 February 1944)	Attack in opening the Tscherkassy pocket while attached to III Panzer Corps Tiger Tank Regiment Bäke —Oratoff —Frankowka —Tschessnowka Army Group South, renamed 30 March 44 as Army Group North Ukraine (Model/Harpe)	
4–16 March 1944	Defensive fighting in the Winniza, Jampol and Proskuroff areas of operations III Panzer Corps	
17 March to 10 April 1944	Operations to break through at Kamenez-Podolsk	XXXXVI Panzer Corps
10–27 April 1944	Offensive operations on the Upper Dnjestr and east of Carpathian Mountains	

Period	Area of Operations / Activity	Command Relationship
28 April to 5 May 1944	Positional warfare on the Upper Dnjestr and in the Carpathian Mountains	
March to April 1944	Employment of Battle Group Mittermeier at Tarnopol	XXXXVIII Panzer Corps
May to June 1944	Refitting at Ohrdruf Training Area; 1st Company, Tiger Tank Battalion 503, received the Königstiger	Wehrkreis-Kommando IX
July to August 1944	Normandy Army Group B (Rommel) Defensive fighting in the Caen and Cagny areas of operations; fighting east of the Orne	LXXXVI Corps (21st Panzer Division and 16th Luftwaffe Field Division)
September to October 1944	Germany Refitting in the Paderborn area	Wehrkreis-Kommando VI
October to December 1944	Hungary, Austria and Czechoslovakia Heeresgruppe Nordukraine, renamed Army Group South (Frießner/Wöhler) Defensive fighting in Hungary: —Operation "Horthy" —Fighting between the Theiß and the Danube in area of Budapest and near the Plattensee	IV Panzer Corps, III Panzer Corps, and LVII Corps
January to May 1945	Army Group South renamed April 45 as Army Group Ostmark (Austria) (Wöhler) Incorporation into Panzer Corps "Feldherrnhalle" Defensive fighting between the Plattensee and the Danube: —Stuhlweißenburg —Zamoly —Vertes Mountains	Panzer Corps "Feldherrnhalle," III Panzer Corps, and other attachments (among them: 1st, 23rd, and 24th Panzer Divisions; 4th SS Police Division; & 4th Cavalry Brigade)
	Attack out of the Gran bridgehead Fighting withdrawal from the Lesser Carpathian Mountains —Verebely —Neutra —Tyrnau Defensive fighting north of Vienna —Zistersdorf —Poysdorf —Mistelbach Withdrawal of the battalion through Czechoslovakia to the German border (Böhmer Wald and Bayrischer Wald): —Znaim —Budweis	Div. "Hoch und Deutschmeister" Panzer Corps "Feldherrnhalle"
9–10 May 1945	Capitulation west of Budweis to elements of the U.S. Third Army and U.S. XII Corps; battalion disbanded	

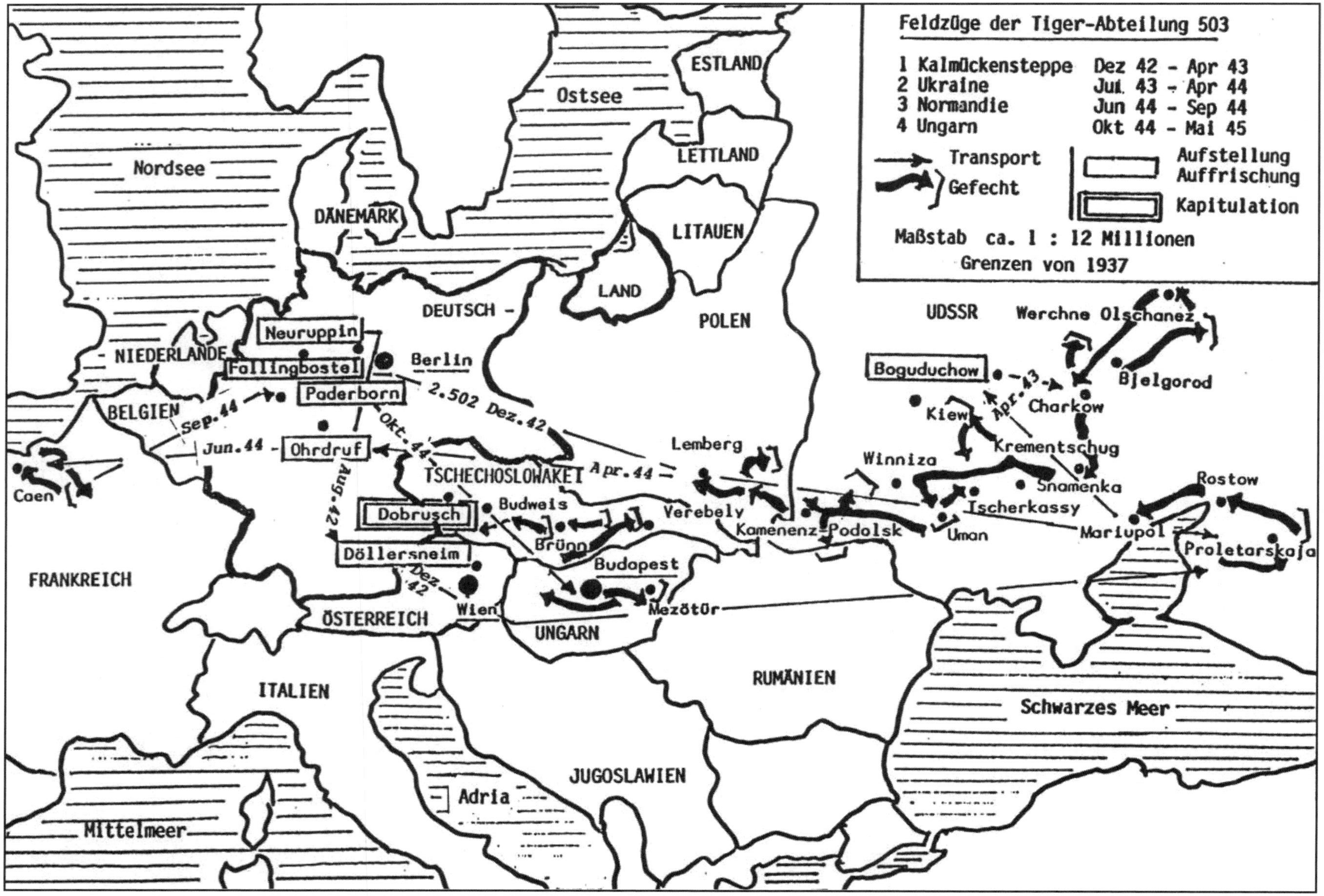

Feldzüge der Tiger-Abteilung 503
1 Kalmückensteppe Dez 42 - Apr 43
2 Ukraine Jul. 43 - Apr 44
3 Normandie Jun 44 - Sep 44
4 Ungarn Okt 44 - Mai 45
Transport
Gefecht
Aufstellung
Auffrischung
Kapitulation
Maßstab ca. 1 : 12 Millionen
Grenzen von 1937
Nordsee
Ostsee
ESTLAND
LETTLAND
LITAUEN
LAND
DÄNEMARK
NIEDERLANDE
BELGIEN
FRANKREICH
DEUTSCH -
POLEN
UDSSR
TSCHECHOSLOWAKEI
ÖSTERREICH
UNGARN
RUMÄNIEN
ITALIEN
JUGOSLAWIEN
Adria
Mittelmeer
Schwarzes Meer
Neuruppin
Fallingbostel
Paderborn
Ohrdruf
Berlin
Dobrusch
Döllersheim
Budweis
Brünn
Wien
Budapest
Mezötür
Verebely
Lemberg
Kamenenz-Podolsk
Winniza
Kiew
Boguduchow
Charkow
Werchne Olschanez
Bjelgorod
Krementschug
Snamenka
Tscherkassy
Uman
Mariupol
Rostow
Proletarskaja
Caen
Sep.44
Jun.44
Okt.44
Aug.42
Dez.42
2.502 Dez.42
Apr.44
Apr.43

CHAPTER 3

Roster of Senior Positions in Tiger Tank Battalion 503, 1942–45

Various Contributors

COMMAND AND STAFF
Battalion Commanders
Oberstleutnant Post
Oberstleutnant Hoheisel
Hauptmann Graf Kageneck
Hauptmann Fromme
Hauptmann Dr. von Diest-Koerber

Adjutants
Oberleutnant Prillwitz
Oberleutnant Smend
Oberleutnant Dr. Barkhausen
Oberleutnant Heerlein

Orderly Officers (*Ordonnanzoffiziere*)
Leutnant Smend
Leutnant Linden
Leutnant Heerlein
Leutnant Rollik
Leutnant Rubbel

Maintenance Officers
Major (Ing.) Fichtner
Leutnant (Ing.) Gille
Leutnant (Ing.) Schenk

Battalion Surgeons
Stabsarzt Dr. Sprockhoff
Oberarzt Dr. Schramm
Ass. Arzt Dr. Büri

Signals Officers
Oberleutnant Reichel
Feldwebel Berger

HEADQUARTERS COMPANY (*STABSKOMPANIE*) AND SUPPLY COMPANY (*VERSORGUNGSKOMPANIE*)
Company Commanders
Oberleutnant Spremberg
Hauptmann Fest
Hauptmann Wiegand (later Supply Company)
Oberleutnant Brand
Oberleutnant Dr. Barkhausen

First Sergeants
Hauptfeldwebel Richter (later Supply Company)
Hauptfeldwebel Schad

Major Clemens Graf Kageneck, June 1943 to January 1944.

Graf Kageneck received the Oak Leaves to the Knight's Cross while commanding Tiger Tank Battalion 503. He received the award on 17 February 1944. He had received the Knight's Cross 7 August 1943.

Reconnaissance Platoon (*Aufklärungszug*) Leaders
Leutnant Bussenius (KIA 1943)
Leutnant Haß
Leutnant Koppe
Oberleutnant Ohnesorge

Scout Platoon (*Erkundungszug*) Leaders
Leutnant Haß
Leutnant von Hagemeister

Engineer Platoon (*Pionierzug*) Leaders
Leutnant Brodhagen
Oberfeldwebel Rîmhild

Antiaircraft Platoon (*Fla-Zug*) Leaders
Leutnant Fürlinger
Leutnant Vieten

Supply Section (*Versorgungsstaffel*) Leaders
Leutnant Bielefeld
Leutnant Koppe
Leutnant Witt
Leutnant (W) Schulz (W = ordnance officer)

Civil Officials in Administrative Services (*Intendanten*)
Oberzahlmeister Rohde
Stabsintendant Kretteck

1ST COMPANY
Company Commanders
Hauptmann Kaphengst
Oberleutnant von Foerster
Hauptmann Burmester
Oberleutnant Adamek (KIA 1944)
Oberleutnant Reutemann (KIA 1944)
Oberleutnant Oemler
Leutnant Fürlinger (KIA 1945)
Leutnant Piepgras

First Sergeants
Hauptfeldwebel Schmitz
Stabsfunkmeister Nega
Stabsfeldwebel Schmidt (KIA 1945)
Oberfeldwebel Wendt
Oberfeldwebel Haase

Platoon Leaders
Oberleutnant von Foerster
Oberleutnant Oemler
Leutnant von Koerber, Detlef (KIA 1943)
Leutnant Meller (KIA 1943)
Leutnant Jammerath (KIA 1943)
Leutnant Linsser
Oberfeldwebel Fendesack (KIA 1943)
Leutnant Labut
Leutnant Witt
Leutnant Piepgras
Leutnant Topel
Leutnant Schröder (KIA 1944)
Leutnant Hamann
Leutnant von Koerber, Achim

2ND COMPANY
Company Commanders
Hauptmann Heilmann
Hauptmann von Eichel-Streiber

Hauptmann Rolf Fromme, February to December 1944

First Sergeants
Hauptfeldwebel Bachmann
Hauptfeldwebel Hänsen

Platoon Leaders
Oberleutnant Hansen
Leutnant Cüsow (KIA 1943)
Leutnant Bielefeld (KIA 1943)
Leutnant Haß
Leutnant Witt
Leutnant Armbruster (KIA 1944)
Leutnant Beyer
Leutnant Linkenbach (KIA 1945)
Leutnant Günther
Leutnant Wagner

**3RD COMPANY (FORMERLY 2ND COMPANY,
TIGER TANK BATTALION 502)**
Company Commanders
Hauptmann Lange
Hauptmann Scherf
Oberleutnant Freiherr von Rosen
Leutnant Koppe

First Sergeants
Oberfeldwebel Rondorf
Stabsfeldwebel Kisseberth
Hauptfeldwebel Schad
Hauptfeldwebel Müller

Platoon Leaders
Oberleutnant Scherf
Leutnant Dr. Taubert (KIA 1942)
Leutnant Forkel
Leutnant Weinert (KIA 1943)
Leutnant Freiherr von Rosen
Oberfeldwebel an der Heiden
Leutnant Koppe
Leutnant Rollik
Leutnant Rambow
Leutnant Rubbel

**MAINTENANCE COMPANY
(*WERKSTATTKOMPANIE*)**
Company Commanders
Hauptmann Fest
Oberleutnant (Ing.) Diekamp
Oberleutnant (Ing.) Groß
Oberleutnant (Ing.) Theiß
Oberleutnant Dr. Barkhausen
Leutnant (Ing.) Gille

Hauptmann Fromme received the Knight's Cross on 29 January 1941. He was also mentioned by name in the Wehrmacht Report of 5 November 1944 while serving as commander of Tiger Tank Battalion 503.

Hauptmann Dr. Nordewin von Diest-Koerber, February to December 1944. Hauptmann Dr. von Diest-Koerber received the Knight's Cross on 1 May 1945. He was also the recipient of the German Cross in Gold, which was awarded to him on 17 February 1944.

First Sergeants
Stabsfeldwebel Bittkowski

Platoon Leaders
Oberwerkmeister Bahl
Werkmeister Neubert
Werkmeister Scheerbarth
Technischer Inspekteur Rathje
Technischer Inspekteur Frohmüller
Werkmeister Späth
Ingenieur Aust
Leutnant König (Bergezug = recovery platoon)
Leutnant (Ingenieur) Schenk
Leutnant Eilers (KIA 1945)

Notes
This list makes no claims to completeness and accuracy. Official records are not available. The battalion commanders, company commanders and first sergeants are listed in chronological order. It was attempted to list the others in the same sequence.

Roster assembled by Ullrich Koppe (1990)

Sources: contributed information, notes of Dr. Barkhausen, Dr. Lochmann, Niemann, Freiherr von Rosen, and Rubbel.

CHAPTER 4

Recipients of High Military Decorations in Tiger Tank Battalion 503

Tiger Tank Battalion 503	Oak Leaves	Knight's Cross	German Cross	Honor Roll Clasp	Mention in the Wehrmacht Report	Panzerkampfabzeichen (Level 4 = 75 Engagements)
Headquarters Company / Supply Company						
– Hauptmann Graf Kageneck	26 Jun 1944	7 Aug 1943				
– Hauptmann Fromme		29 Jan 1941			5 Nov 1944	
– Hauptmann von Diest-Koerber		1 May 1945	17 Feb 1944			
1st Company						
– Hauptmann Kaphengst			Apr 1944			
– Hauptmann Burmeister		2 Sep 1944	1943			
– Oberfeldwebel Fendesack			11 Oct 43			
– Feldwebel Knispel			20 May 1944		25 Apr 1944	
– Feldwebel Berger						1945
– Unteroffizier Lochmann						1945
– Unteroffizier Schmidke						1945
2nd Company						
– Leutnant Cüsow			4 Feb 1944			
– Leutnant Linkenbach				Feb 1945		
– Feldwebel Bialkowski				1944		
3rd Company						
– Hauptmann Lange		13 May 1944				
– Hauptmann Scherf		23 Feb 1944	7 Oct 1943	5 Feb 1945		
– Oberleutnant Freiherr von Rosen		Feb 1945				
– Feldwebel Seidel			15 Dec 1944			
– Unteroffizier Gärtner			Jul 1944			
– Oberfahnenjunker Rondorf			20 May 194			
– Leutnant Weinert			16 Jan 1944			
Maintenance Company						
– Werkmeister Neubert		1944*				

*Knight's Cross of the War Service Cross
Note: Because of gaps in source material, mistakes are unavoidable

CHAPTER 5

Organization and Strength of a Tiger Tank Battalion

Alfred Rubbel and Wolfgang Schneider

The organizational diagrams come from *Tigers in Combat I* by Wolfgang Schneider.

The organizational diagram for December 1942 shows the battalion as it was initially structured with a so-called mixed organization of late model, short-barrelled Panzer IIIs and the Tiger I. There were only two companies until the 2nd Company, Tiger Tank Battalion 502, was incorporated into the battalion as the 3rd Company, Tiger Tank Battalion 503, in early 1943.

By July 1943 when the battalion was employed at Operation Citadel, it only had the Tiger I in its organization. The authorized strength was fifty-four tanks.

During the fighting in Normandy, the battalion had already started to received the Tiger II. These were only present in the 1st Company. Even in that company, there were still two Tiger Is. The authorized strength of the battalion remained at fifty-four tanks, with seventeen each in the tank companies and three in the battalion headquarters.

The final organization of the battalion is indicated in the last chart. By September 1944, the battalion was equipped entirely with Tiger II's. The overall authorized tank strength was reduced from fifty-four to forty-five, however. Despite that, the battalion may have had several extra "floats." The personnel strength of the battalion under that organization is indicated below:

The wheeled vehicles of trains (*Troß*), combat trains 1 and 2 (*Gefechtstroß*), and baggage trains (*Gepäcktroß*) were removed from the tank companies and placed in the newly formed Supply Company (*Versorgungs-Kompanie*). That streamlining of personnel led to the reduction of the tank companies from 113 soldiers to 88. The personnel strength of the battalion dropped from 1,093 to 897.

Unit/Personnel Strengths (September 1944)	Officer	NCO	Enlisted	Aggregate
Headquarters and Headquarters Company	9	37	130	176
Supply Company	5	55	188	250
Maintenance Company	3	37	162	207
1st Company	4	46	38	88
2nd Company	4	46	38	88
3rd Company	4	46	38	88
Totals	29	267	594	897

Of the totals above, seven were civilian officials.

December 1942

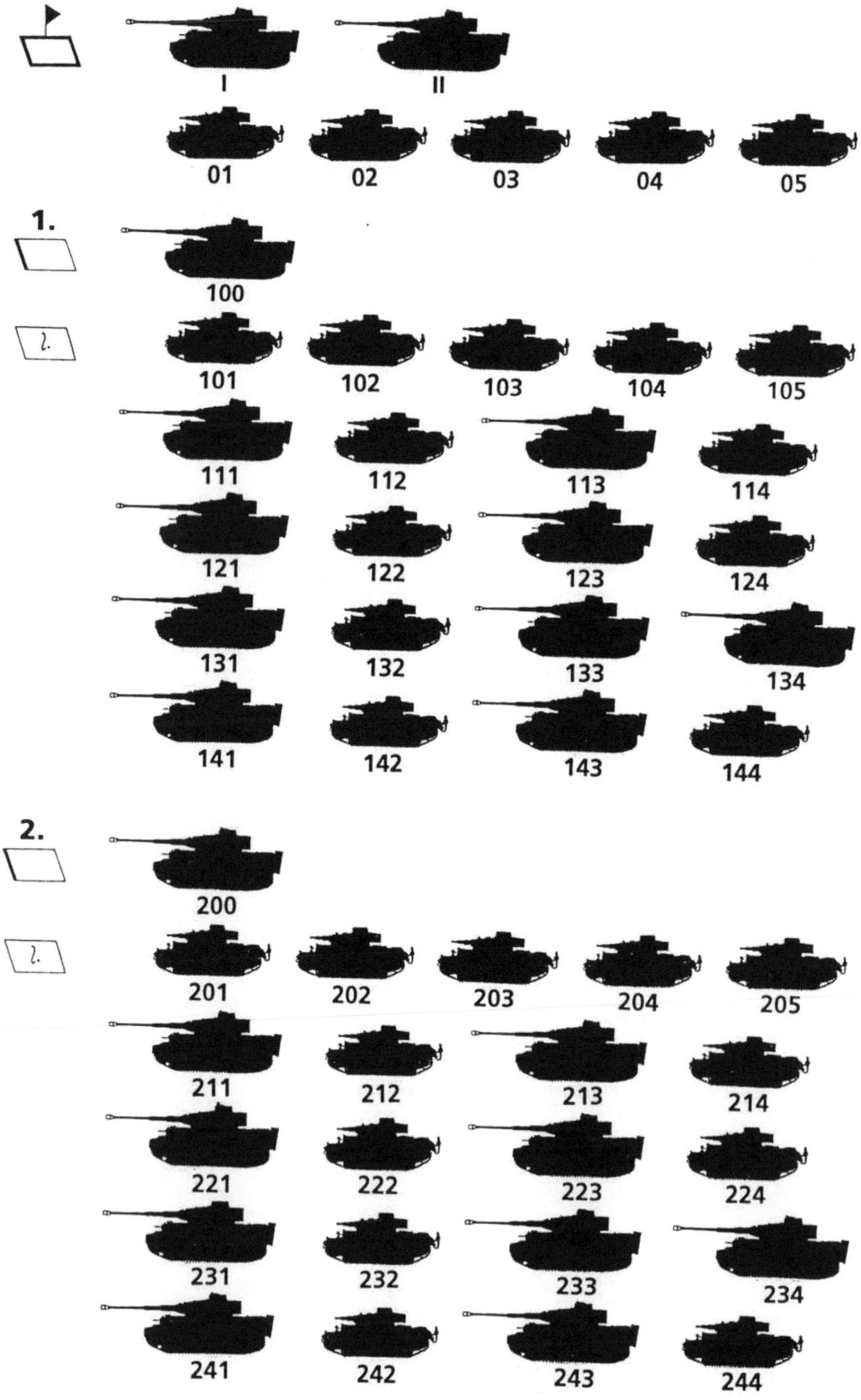

I
II
01
02
03
04
05
1.
100
2.
101
102
103
104
105
111
112
113
114
121
122
123
124
131
132
133
134
141
142
143
144
2.
200
2.
201
202
203
204
205
211
212
213
214
221
222
223
224
231
232
233
234
241
242
243
244

July 1943

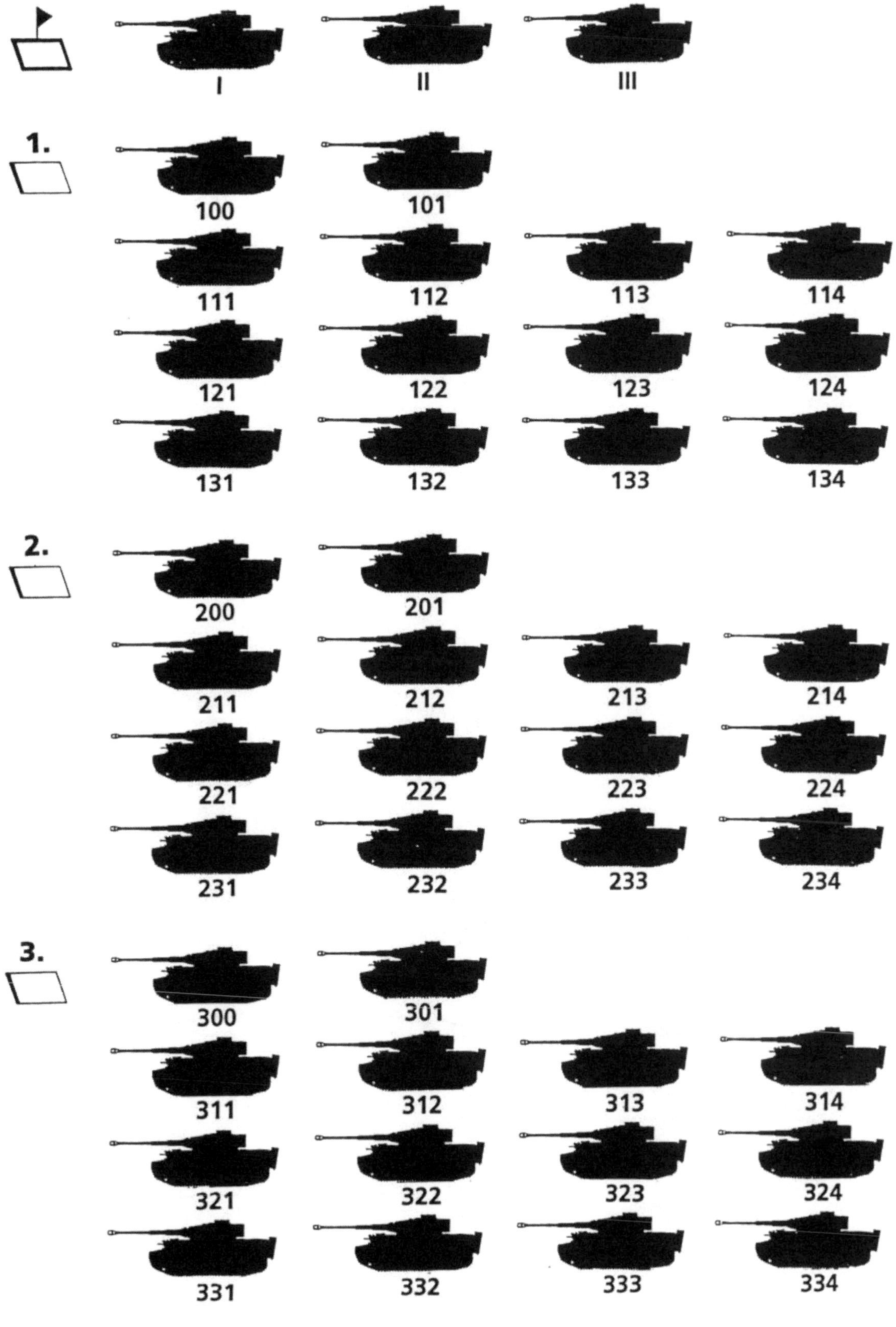

I
II
III
1.
100
101
111
112
113
114
121
122
123
124
131
132
133
134
2.
200
201
211
212
213
214
221
222
223
224
231
232
233
234
3.
300
301
311
312
313
314
321
322
323
324
331
332
333
334

June 1944

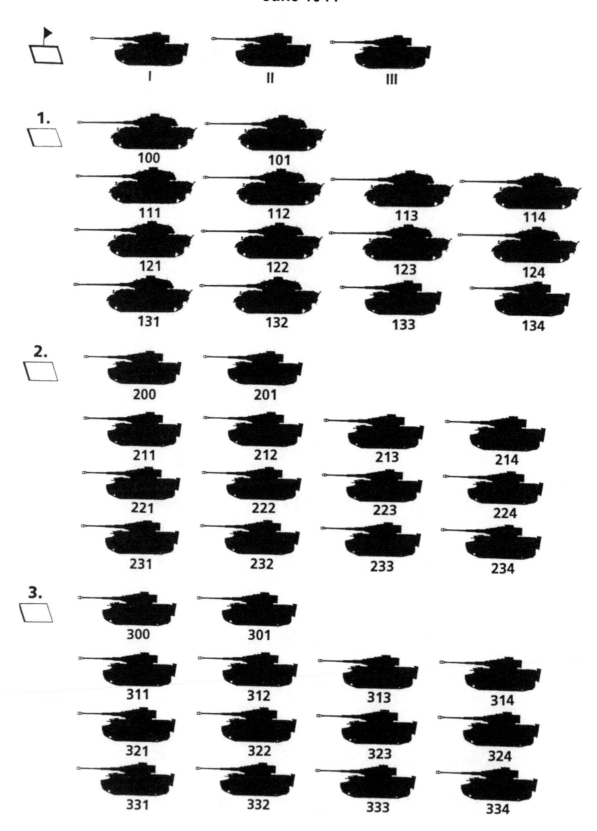

September 1944

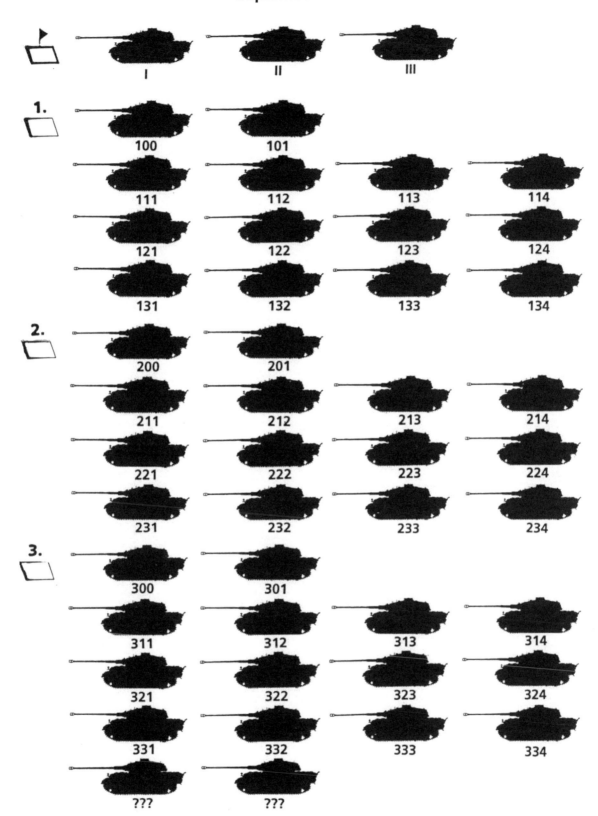

CHAPTER 6

A Tank Commander Remembers

Alfred Rubbel

January 1943 in Putlos. The cadre unit (*Personaleinheit Schober*) had received home leave in several installments. I returned from leave, late at night. The next morning, at breakfast in the squad room with Hannes Rippl, Herbert Petzka and Heino Kleiner, the conversation turned to the first Tigers that had arrived the day before. Although I had not yet seen one, I had heard many wonderful things about them. When I asked Heino, who had already seen them, how they looked, the following memorable dialogue took place:

> Heino: "Imagine a very long cannon. Got that?"
> Myself: "Yes."
> Heino: "It is even longer!"

Soon I, too, saw the wonder. I was impressed, but also a bit disappointed. I had expected a tank with an elegant shape, something like the Russian T-34. And there stood a vehicle that, in shape and proportions, resembled no tank known to us—a dinosaur rather than a miracle weapon of the future.

Sennelager, March 1943. The first Tiger Is to be assigned to Company Schober had arrived at the railroad station and had to be guarded until they were unloaded on the following morning. I

was detailed for that. There was no guard house and it was cold, so I sat in the driver's seat of a tank. Everything was new and strange—and it got boring during the course of the night. The key was in the ignition. I had already figured out the function of several switches. Would the engine start easily? True, I did not have a tank driving license, but I had often illegally moved tanks which drove with steering levers. Curiosity quickly shoved inhibitions aside—the motor ran!

What I did not know at that time was that a gear was always engaged! As I then played around with the steering wheel there was a jerk to the side, which I strengthened by giving it gas. What had happened? The chock blocks that secured the Tiger had been forced away and the front and rear stuck far out over the edges of the SSYMS-Wagen (special heavy-load capacity railroad cars). For fear of further mishaps I did not make any attempt to straighten the tank out. I do not know what the unloading party thought of the situation. There was no investigation. The "optical" surprise the Tiger had offered me at Putlos was now joined by a "physical" one as well. After that, I took the Tiger seriously and learned the basics so as to avoid further serious consequences. That paid off!

Our "114" and its crew first saw action on 5 July 1943 as part of Operation Citadel (*Zitadelle*) at

Bjelgorod. We had been prepared well: The *"Türken"-Übung* ("Turkish" exercise); a live-fire exercise on the Donez at Tschugujew; recovery exercises in marshy terrain; and, weapon and equipment training. All had familiarized us with the tank. The equipment had proven itself as durable. Our comrades who had already had experience with Tigers confirmed the pronouncement in the *Tigerfibel* (Tiger primer): "It can stand up to anything . . ." The Tiger had won the race between armor protection and armor-piercing rounds. Not much could get at the Tiger man. The hard fighting during Citadel proved to us that

- the armor was capable of standing up to enemy weapons. The weak point was the smoke stack-like commander's cupola. A hit from a 7.62cm gun would shear off the cupola, complete with the commander's head
- the firepower of the 88mm main gun was fantastic in the certainty with which it guaranteed hits, and in its rate of fire, penetration and destructive power
- the maneuverability of the Tiger was seriously inadequate. The most significant contributor to that deficiency was the low power to weight ratio of 10 horsepower/ ton (T-34 = 18 hp/ ton.) The immediate consequence of that deficiency was a very low march speed (a theoretical 38 km/hr, which was never actually attained in practice). Ten km/hr was the rule in driving cross country.

The engine did not take well to overloading. Its longevity in service was limited. Assuring availability for operations demanded a great deal of technical understanding and hard work from our drivers. The maintenance sections and the workshop were constantly in demand. I remember how I always kept one ear free to listen to the engine when road marching as a tank commander. Overheating led to destruction of the seals around the cylinder liners, allowing coolant water to get into the cylinders. The only remedy for that was removing the spark plugs to get the water out. After that, the Tiger would never be a fast mover. Overheating could also burn up the cork in the cylinder-head gasket and the engine would lose oil. Whenever the maintenance section or the workshop were not available, our driver, Walter Eschrig, had us chew away at *Kommißbrot* (the standard army hard bread), and, with the bread pulp, achieved a temporary seal for the cylinder-head gasket.

Additional weak points were the transmission, final drive and running gear. All of us remember how often we had to make an emergency gear change to the adjacent gear and creep home that way. The hydraulic system had not yet overcome its teething problems. The final drive was as delicate as an egg in its shell if any undue load was put on it. That frequently occurred in conjunction with throwing a track, usually as a result of inadequate track tension along with backing up and turning. I learned to fear that as the worst kind of damage. Nevertheless, although avoidable, it did happen to us once. There was no alternative but to cut the track, disconnect the final drive from the transmission at the flange and wait for the recovery vehicle, sometimes with the hope that it would appear sooner than "Ivan." A "pleasure" of a special sort was the care of the interleaved roadwheels of the Tiger I. Everybody knows there were sixteen roadwheels on eight torsion-bar arms on each side. Hopefully, at the start of the march, all sixteen roadwheels were there. The four outer roadwheels, starting with the front one, gradually freed themselves. Movement of the torsion bars and bending loads resulted in the loosening of the connection of the entire road wheel to the flange. That, in turn, increased the load on the remaining roadwheels and led to the destruction of the rubber rims. The amount of work involved in changing the center-most inner roadwheel was mind-boggling. Eight roadwheels had to be removed first.

My sketch of the intensive material maintenance is an opportunity to also gratefully remember the constant, painstaking major commitment of labor by our comrades of the maintenance sections and the maintenance company. And how often was this the result of neglect by the crew!

The superiority of the Tiger I and Tiger II in weapons performance and armor protection in comparison with all enemy tanks—which continued right up to the end of the war—allowed us to remain without a care in the face of the enemy. When pulling security—even during combat operations—we often remained stationary for hours at a time, exposed in open terrain without cover or concealment—and, indeed, nothing happened to us!

The result was that we dispensed with the doctrinal behavior that we had all learned. Young soldiers and tank commanders who lacked front experience picked up on our poor conduct. With our practice of exposing ourselves for hours at a time like targets on a shooting range, we gave up the opportunity to surprise the enemy. When the Russians spotted us, as a rule, they attacked elsewhere with their tanks. The result was that penetrations or breakthroughs took place at other locations, where we would then clean them up as "fire brigade."

A better alternative would have been to keep the Tigers hidden under cover and concealment behind the main line of resistance, and then, when the direction of the attack and its Schwerpunkt were clearly identified, strike hard and by surprise. That approach would have brought us more successes at less cost. I fully realize, however, that it was necessary to have tanks immediately behind the battle line as "corset stays" for the hard-fighting infantry formations that had been bled white, so as to stabilize their fighting morale. That requirement interfered with the tactically correct commitment. We often had the experience that the withdrawal of individual Tigers for refueling and resupplying with ammunition was a signal for the infantry to abandon their positions and pull back along with the tanks.

On the Eastern Front, nearly up to the end of the war, there was no real threat from the air. That resulted in a relaxation of all the passive means of protection, such as camouflage and spotters keeping watch over the air space until, on the Western Front, the total domination of the air by the enemy air forces taught us a fearful lesson.

It was considered the right thing to do in the Panzer forces and, naturally, among us, too, for the tank commander—whether company commander or platoon leader—to switch to the next-available tank and carry on if his tank were disabled. Unfortunately, that dangerous maneuver in combat caused a high casualty rate among commanders. There was an especially impressive ritual when Hauptmann Burmester, commander of the 1st Company, nicknamed "Hein Mück," switched tanks. First the map board and binoculars were more-or-less roughly transferred from the commander's cupola to the rear deck. The box with the "Wilhelm II" brand cigars followed, with great care. The commander came out with

a dive toward the rear, definitely no delicacy there. After collection of the "combat utensils" came the dash to cover behind the new command tank. The remounting process followed the same sequence and the same gradations of tender care. To the best of my memory, that unique procedure always succeeded without a scratch to the person or the objects.

Many of my comrades in the combat elements would agree with me, at this point, in finding words of praise for the leader of our recovery platoon, Oberfeldwebel, later Leutnant, Kînig and his men. Whether we had been knocked out by gunfire, broken down, overturned or bogged down, and in nearly impossible situations, his recovery platoon with its nearly four-meter high 18-ton prime movers were on the spot to recover our Tigers. With a combination of technical knowledge and cool thinking, even the most difficult cases were dealt with and, if the enemy did not prevent it, the Tiger was somehow recovered, towed and loaded. Leutnant Kînig had a nose for where the most difficult situations were and where he, himself, was most needed. His arrival and that of his prime movers—later we also had Bergepanthers—followed a well established pattern.

First, he arrived on the scene by himself with his VW-Kübelwagen. At a suitable distance he got out of his VW-Kübel, armed with a gnarled walking stick. Escorted by a soldier with a machine pistol, he approached the disabled vehicle in a manner appropriate to the situation and took what measures he deemed suitable. As a rule, that was to call up the prime movers that he had waiting in a covered location. It might also be that the first measure was a mighty storm of wrath, that poured upon the crew if they had not carried out the necessary preparations, such as disconnecting the final drive and clearing away obstructions.

Our tank was more than just a means of combat to us. It was our transportation, it was where we spent our free time and found recreation, where we lived and slept. It protected us from more than just the effects of enemy weapons. Therefore the crew had a very close relationship with its tank. Keeping it in impeccable condition was the foremost task of all five men. In my experience, the tank driver felt that he, above all others, was responsible for the overall maintenance condition. His training at the Tiger training courses at Paderborn went well beyond the service requirements and technical understanding of the functioning of the engine and drive train. He directed the other members of the crew in the technical servicing of the equipment in the hull, chassis and running gear, which called for the greatest share of the work. In our battalion, it was standard procedure that every crew member lent a hand with the work. In combat, the driver's task was not just to move the tank in a tactically correct manner, but to also keep an eye on the progress of the fighting. Our long-time driver, Walter Eschrig, exceeded all expectations in his quiet but determined way.

In my opinion, the next most important man was the gunner. He was the one whose understanding determined whether the full potential of the weapon was developed in a firefight or whether only bungling fireworks resulted. Full of respect, I remember our outstanding gunner, Walter Junge, who is no longer with us. In the thirteen months we spent together in "114"—which were particularly lucky in that we went through two Tigers, as a result of enemy action, without losing any of the crew largely due to him—he mastered his tasks beyond anything we could expect, which many did not think he was capable of initially. In addition to lightning fast reactions and instant comprehension of his commander's intentions, his fellow crew members found him always ready to help and always a cheerful companion. I ask the forgiveness of all tank commanders, loaders and radio operators, when I rank their importance below that of the drivers and gunners.

Thirty-seven months of experience at the front taught me to see things that way. Nevertheless, I must state a truism, that, without good functioning of the other crew members—the loader and the radio operator—the tank was incomplete as a weapon.

Judging by his reticence in conversation, one would never have expected our loader in "114," Johann Strohmer, to be a man of rapid action. Quite otherwise in action! Johann developed such speed in loading that the gunner rarely had to wait to fire—not an easy task with the nearly 20-kilogram weight of the 88mm round. Frequently, it was beyond my comprehension where the ammunition came from in an engagement. Only once did he have to take a bye. That was at Merefa, in August 1943, when, after we cleared out of Kharkov, instead of the reserve ammunition that was meant to be stored under the turret floor, there were only flasks of the famed Kharkov "hair tonic".

The radio operator had a special status among the crew. Because, if necessary, the fight could temporarily go on without him, they made the crews dependant on them for other things. Since the radio operator continually listened to the radio traffic, he had an "informational head start," which he utilized. The radio operator also earned a high reputation as the on-board quartermaster. Since he also had both need and opportunity to take note of the achievements and failures of his own and other crews, the knowledge so gained served as a kind of unofficial "war diary," which could be presented, when called for, with appropriate commentary. As I write this I have in mind our radio operator, Alfred Peuker, who will read and, I hope, confirm this.

The unit spirit and comradeship that were so remarkably good in the battalion and in its companies is repeatedly spoken of in these "recollections." That could not be taken for granted in a body of nearly 1,000 men. The coming together of these men after the war and their cohesiveness to this day affirms that bond. I intend to pursue the question of how that could result in such a young formation that only existed for three years—the tank regiments that were formed in peacetime existed for ten years.

I consider the most important and fundamental prerequisite was that we were brought to full battalion strength relatively quickly. As a result of that, we were committed successfully in combat as a complete unit. Thus, the soldiers could see and evaluate themselves beyond company boundaries. This also provides opportunity to refute the proposal that was put forward in 1942 in an after-action report of forming separate companies rather than battalions. On organizational grounds alone, the companies could not exist on their own. The most probable approach would have been to integrate them into existing tank regiments. That would have led to the result that the peculiarities of the Tigers would have received inadequate consideration. It must be conclusively stated that the form of organization as separate army-level Tiger battalions was the right choice.

The next prerequisite for good unit spirit was the separate-unit status that elevated us a bit above the "normal" tank formation through preferential selection of personnel and equipment and, accordingly, led to a reinforced self-awareness as a formation. The fact that decisive positions for command and leadership were filled with good officers and noncommissioned officers contributed to the cohesiveness that held the organization together without any signs of dissolution right up to the final day of its existence. Of course, it must be stated, that corrections were required in the first months after the unit was organized.

CHAPTER 7

The 2nd Company

Various Contributors

It is unfortunate that, in contrast to the truly comprehensive pictures of the 1st and 3rd Companies, practically no accounts for our book came from the ranks of the former 2nd Company. The editor had the thankless task, with respect to the other two companies, of having to select from the wealth of materials provided. For the 2nd Company, however, the short account that follows stems from all that is available, the accounts given by comrades Willibald Krakow and Martin Burmester, who died during the year this book was assembled.

The 2nd Company, along with the 1st Company, was organized in May of 1942 in Neuruppin. In the three years of its existence, there was only one change in company command. Hauptmann von Eichel-Streiber succeeded Hauptmann Heilmann. In that same time period, company command changed eight times in the 1st Company and four times in the 3rd Company.

Martin Burmester wrote that the 2nd Company had the misfortune on 5 July 1943 during Operation Citadel to move into a minefield. It caused severe damage to all twelve vehicles. As a result, the company did not get reemployed as a complete unit until its refitting at Ohrdruf in May of 1944. Its employment in Normandy in 1944 and in the final phase of the war in 1945 were again as a complete unit.

The following is an excerpt from the company newsletter published 10 December 1944.

The original newsletter contained a list of those killed and missing in action up to the time of its publication.

Headquarters 22 402
Russia, 10 December 1943

Dear Comrades!

As we celebrate Christmas in a few days, our thoughts will turn to our loved ones and to all of you who have had to leave the company prematurely due to wounds or illness. We picture you in the hospital, in the replacement unit or with your loved ones at home by the Christmas tree and we know that, at this moment, you wish to be with your old comrades, your company. You do not know where it is at the moment and, nevertheless, would like to partake in its joys and sorrows.

Therefore, we are using this means to pass on to you a few things that have happened and are now happening and tell you about some things you might not have heard.

We do not need to say much about the fighting. You can well imagine that it was hard. Wherever things were hot, the company has been in action and has attained splendid successes. Among other things, about 175 tanks and more than 200 antitank guns have been knocked out. On a single day, nineteen Russian T-34s were knocked out; on another day, seventeen T-34s were put out of commission. Unfortunately, in the recent past, we also had several painful losses.

Killed: Stabsfeldwebel Hammrich, Unteroffizier Schälicke, Gefreiter

Williard and small Gefreiter Beckmann, who was loved by everyone.

Wounded: Feldwebel Plum, Unteroffizier Schumacher, Gefreiter

Rabeneck and Gefreiter Mallon.

By way of joyful events, in the last 3 months there were several noteworthy promotions:

to Feldwebel: Unteroffiziere Plum, Moorkötter and Heinl

to Unteroffizier: Obergefreite Hösek, von Knobelsdorff, Keller, Leibe

to Gefreiter: Dilly and Kloosick.

The company went through hard times when Hauptmann Heilmann gave up command of the company and Leutnant Cüsow went on convalescent leave in Germany as a result of his wounds. Therefore, the rejoicing was all the greater when Leutnant Cüsow returned and took over command of the company. Hopefully, that situation will continue.

Our "company mother" is Oberfeldwebel Hänsel—well known to all—who took over the job immediately after his return from the hospital.

At the moment, the company is again in action.

We do not know whether we will be granted the opportunity to have a little Christmas celebration. That will depend on the situation.

However, you should know that you always have your place with us and that, especially during these days, our thoughts are with you. May you be given the opportunity to celebrate this holiday with your family or with your parents and siblings. To those of our comrades who are still in the hospital, we wish you a speedy recovery and hope that we will soon be able to greet you anew here in the company.

We wish you all the best for the Christmas celebration and the New Year.

(signed) Hänsel   (signed) Cüsow
Hauptfeldwebel   Leutnant and company
                     commander

2nd Company, Tiger Tank Battalion 503
In the field, Christmas 1944

Dear Comrade!

You should know that you have not been abandoned by us. Therefore, we want to give you a general outline of what has taken place since January during this year of 1944.

Despite moments of temporary crisis, the company has, in general, had notable successes. The battalion was twice mentioned with praise in the Wehrmacht reports, and we are all proud of the fact that those honorable mentions also praised the accomplishments of the 2nd Company. In that recognition we see inspiration for new deeds and, as before, commit our entire strength to the attainment of final victory.

In March of this year we had to begin the withdrawal out of Galicia from Grzymalow. That was a very difficult time for the company. We had to leave behind several loyal comrades who had been killed, captured or were missing. In the course of several weeks we moved through Rumania, Hungary and Slovakia to the assembly point at Lemberg. Hauptmann von Eichel-Streiber took over command of the company there. After a short stay there, we loaded up and, in May, moved for refitting at Ohrdruf [Thuringia]. We only remained there for a short period but, nevertheless, two-thirds of the company was able to take twenty-one days of home leave.

Soon we received new tanks, wheeled vehicles and equipment. Shortly thereafter we were again on rail cars. No one knew where the march would take us until we crossed the Rhine. Then it was clear to us that we were going to France. The general rejoicing at that was very great. Soon, however, we realized that our celebration had been premature and that our mission was difficult and serious. The commitment at the invasion front demanded the utmost in ultimate self sacrifice and fulfillment of duty from everyone of us, since the enemy airforce played a dominant role to a degree that we had never experienced. Because of the total unsuitability of the terrain for Tigers, the company's success there was not satisfying and bore no relationship to the losses of combat vehicles. In August we had to take part in the withdrawal from there to the homeland. We passed through Belgium and Holland and into the Reich. Unfortunately, we lost several very competent and exemplary comrades during those operations.

Because of lack of space, we were billeted at Sande near Paderborn for reorganization. Those weeks in good quarters were very pleasing and restorative for the comrades. While the remaining third of the company took its home leave, the new Tiger IIs arrived for upcoming operations.

At the beginning of October, we set out for Hungary. On 15 October we took an active part in putting down the Putsch in Budapest. Because of the extraordinarily good success of the operations in Hungary, a large number of company personnel have been awarded decorations. At the time, the company is spread over 300 kilometers in individual section-sized elements. One element is conducting operations; vehicles with minor maintenance problems are located at a forward repair point; vehicles with more serious damage are attended to at the Werkstätte II and III in the rear. Supply, in these circumstances, is somewhat difficult but, nevertheless, we have so far been able to enjoy a pleasant situation (particularly as regards the good, heavy Hungarian wine).

Below is a short report of our successes, decorations awarded, announced promotions and losses since the company has existed.

The company has knocked out or destroyed: 305 tanks, 234 antitank guns, 42 heavy guns, 1 airplane, and at least 750 other light weapons of all sorts.

The following decorations have been awarded: 63 Iron Crosses, Second Class; 7 Iron Crosses, First Class; 36 War Merit Crosses with Swords, Second Class; and 2 War Merit Crosses with Swords, First Class.

Since our records were lost in the East, we can only list promotions since the spring of this year. From that point in time, 32 of our comrades were promoted to Obergefreiter, 24 to Unteroffizier, 7 to Feldwebel and 6 to Oberfeldwebel.

Christmas is now at hand and at this point we do not yet know whether we shall be able to celebrate this holiday together.

In the name of the entire 2nd Company, we wish you a truly joyous celebration and an equally salutary year for 1945. We hope that we will be able to welcome as many of you as possible back after your convalescence. Above all else, we hope that 1945 will bring a victorious end to the war and that our beautiful Germany will rise again in full bloom and greater than before from the

wreckage and the ashes—in spite of all the devastation from the terror attacks.

Above all things, however, we hope and wish that our brilliant and beloved Führer and Feldherr (military commander), Adolf Hitler, remains in good health.

With heartfelt greetings for Christmas and the New Year, we remain your comrades of the 2nd Company.

(signed) Hänsel   (signed) von Eichel
Hauptfeldwebel   Hauptmann and
          company commander

[Editor's Note: At this point, all of the KIA, WIA, MIA and other casualties of the company were listed.]

2nd Company, Tiger Tank Battalion "Feldhernhalle"
Location classified, 17 January 1945

Excerpt from the Special Order of Tiger Tank Battalion "Feldhernhalle," 15 January 1945

I offer my thanks and recognition to all tank crews that took part in the attack south of Zamoly on 11 January 1945 for their exemplary spirit in the attack. In spite of significant losses of tanks and of numerous comrades, the company accomplished the mission that had been ordered. In so doing, it made possible the capture of Zamoly to the rear of the battalion.

The extraordinarily spirited conduct of Leutnant Linkenbach and his crew—Unteroffizier Burmester, Obergefreiter Kopp, Gefreiter Schülgen, and Gefreiter Treiber earned special recognition. On 11 January, the crew was an example to the entire battalion.

The battalion's success on 11 January 1945 consisted of a successful breakthrough of the enemy main line of resistance with destruction of 21 tanks and assault guns, 3 aircraft, 1 Stalin Organ, at least 28 light and medium antitank guns, and numerous infantry weapons.

signed von Diest-Koerber
Hauptmann and Battalion Commander

for the accuracy of the copy:
(v. Eichel)
Hauptmann and Company Commander

CHAPTER 8

My Time with the 3rd Company

Gerhard Niemann

[Editor's Note: This section covers all of Gerhard Niemann's service with the battalion. We thought it enlightening to place it at this point in the text in order to give the reader a broad overview of the operations of the battalion and the campaigns it participated in.]

1943

24 May: Transferred, effective 26 May 1943, to Tiger Tank Battalion 503.

3 June: Arrived at Kharkov. Unteroffizier Jäckel, Unteroffizier Dolk and I were assigned to the 3. company. A chilly welcome there. Company commander needed drivers not gunners; applied to have us transferred back.

Mid-June: Still no assignment in a tank. Instead, we constructed a sand table scale model of terrain in the Donez sector south of Bjelgorod.

27 June: As motorcycle sidecar rider to field-training exercise near Kharkov for Field Marshall von Manstein and high Turkish officers.

28 June: Ordered to report to the company commander—application for transfer denied. That afternoon I got my place in a Tiger. I joined Leutnant Weinert's crew in Tiger 311.

OPERATION CITADEL

1 July: Approach march to assembly area at Tolokonoye.

5 July: Crossed Donez at Ssolomino. Attacked Rasumnoje and Generalowka. Received serious hit and damage to chassis from mines. Knocked out two T-34s and four 9.2 cm antitank guns.

6 July: Continued attack against the collective farm at Batratzkaja Datscha. The defensive fire was heavier than on the previous day. The Tiger was taken out of the attack formation after additional severe hits. Leutnant Weinert took over Tiger 313. Oberfeldwebel Rondorf took ours to the workshop.

7 July: Tawrowo. The damage to our Tiger was beyond the capabilities of the maintenace personnel. The vehicle was written off and cannibalized for parts.

23 July: Artillery barrage on the Werkstatt area. Gefreiter Pichler was killed right beside me.

End of July: Back to the old quarters at Kharkov. The crews were, in part, redistributed. I joined Feldwebel Weiland's Tiger 332.

Defensive Fighting West of Kharkov

OPERATIONAL AREA MAXIMOFKA (ABOUT 25 KM NORTHWEST OF KHARKOV)

5 August: Alarm! Prepare for a new operation. We still had the night for our commander's bachelor party, however.

6 August: Feldwebel Weiland was married— long distance, by proxy—in a hurry. In the after-

noon we moved toward Merefa. We were quartered several kilometers outside of Kharkov. During the night a *Nähmaschine* ["sewing machine," a Russian nighttime nuisance bomber] demolished our billets—otherwise, no injuries.

7 August: March direction changed to Bogoduchow. Commitment as battle groups.

8–10 August: Battle Group Leutnant Weinert (= four tanks) at Maximofka; attached to the 2nd SS Panzer Division "Das Reich." Calm sector. Employed in no more than small harrassing actions. Knocked out three T-34s and destroyed one enemy supply column.

11 August: battalion assembled at the Feski collective farm = 13 Tigers.

12 August: Fighting at Maximofka.

13 August: Attack on Chrutschtschewo-Nikitowka. Heavy tank fighing. During the two days, Tiger 332 destroyed three T-34s, two KV-Is, one SU-122 and five antitank guns. Leutnant Weinert was wounded.

Through 17 August: Defensive fighting in the Maximowka area.

18 August: Attack on Hill 228.1, northeast of Maximowka. We took a hit from a Russian antitank rifle on the gun barrel. Cannon unserviceable. Nevertheless, in action until noon, then back to the Werkstatt at Walki.

31 August: Rear-area elements and Werkstatt transferred to Krasnograd.

MEREFA-TARANOWKA AREA OF OPERATIONS

10 September: After ten days in the infirmary (jaundice) I was assigned to Feldwebel Bormann's crew. The battalion had been employed in the Merefa sector since the beginning of September.

11 September: Trip to the front.

12 September: Defensive fighting south of Taranowka. Steady rain, terrain turned to mud, unceasing attacks by Russian motorized rifle formations with strong artillery support. Our line of defense was weak, with great gaps. Unteroffizier Weigel's tank broke down due to damage to the transmission during reconnaissance in front of our lines. It was recovered during the night.

13 September: Fighting north of Taranowka. Weather conditions unchanged. Kampfgruppe Oberfeldwebel Rondorf (= four tanks) and a company-strength infantry battalion spent the entire day in bitter combat with superior enemy forces

for the possession of a commanding hill position. When darkness fell, we disengaged. We joined up with Battle Group Oberleutnant Scherf (= three tanks). Tiger 334 (Unteroffizier Rieschel) was blown up. Withdrawal to Krasnograd.

WITHDRAWAL BEHIND THE DNJEPR

14 September: Krasnograd. Maintenance work.

15 September: Ordered to evacuate Krasnograd. While preparing for the move, our tank dropped out because the final drive was torn off.

16 September: Towed to loading. Major congestion in the city. The steady rain had turned the roads into muddy wastes. Everything was at a standstill. The column of prime-movers that was towing us could only move forward with difficulty. Loading the immobilized tanks lasted right up to morning.

17 September: The rail movement with the damaged tanks (= eight Tigers) left Krasnograd. In Poltawa in the afternoon.

18 September: Krementschug. The transport was side-tracked because of "improper loading of the Tigers."

19 September: Checked over the loading of the railroad cars again with *Zollstock* ("official" railroad measuring stick for checking clearance).

20 September: Snamenka. We were supposed to detrain there. But how, and with what? There was no end-ramp and no means of towing. The railroad officials had no advice. After a number of telephone calls the transportation commander in Lemberg made the decision: Continue to march!

Next stations: Perwomaisk, Slobodka, Shmerinka and Proskurow.

24 September: On arrival at the Tarnopol railroad station, a Tiger that stuck out too far to the side shattered a wooden bridge pillar. By evening we were on a siding in Berozowiza, eight kilometers from Tarnopol.

25–30 September: Daily inquiries with the commander of the railroad station at Tarnopol produced nothing regarding our further fate. It seemed that the battalion no longer existed. When not assigned guard duty, we spent our evenings in Tarnopol, at the *Soldatenheim* [soldier's club] at the nurses' home of the German Red Cross or at the local command's officers' club where we were allowed in by an engineer belonging to the Organization Todt.

1 October: At last the battalion was located. It was at Snamenka.

We traveled through Shmerinka, Winniza, Berditschew, Fastoff and Bobrinskaja, until, finally, on . . .

4 October: . . . we reached Snamenka.

20–25 October: Bombing attacks on Snamenka, with advance warning to the civilians by air-dropped leaflets. Only limited damage in our billeting area.

30 October: We went with Battle Group Leutnant Weinert (= four tanks) by rail transport to Pavlish, southeast of Krementschug, then into corps reserve at Uspenskoje.

3 November: I fractured an ankle jumping from the tank and rode back to Snamenka with a supply truck.

13 November: With Battle Group Cüsow in Tiger 323 to Kirowograd. City defense, but no action up to the time I was relieved on . . .

21 November: . . . because the injury to my foot had not yet healed.

23 November: Leave in Germany.

22 December: *Frontleitstelle* (forward directing station for personnel in transit) at Kowel.

24 December: *Frontleitstelle* at Pomoshnaja, south of Novo Ukrainka.

25 December: Directed on to Kirowograd. However, the train arrived in Bobrinskaya, south of Tscherkassy. The railroad station was under artillery fire. No information available. Soldiers were being impressed into units. I slipped onto a damaged-vehicle train that was standing by with steam up.

26 December: Christinowka, then on to Monastyrishche.

27 December: Arrived at the company in Zybulew. No more tanks available.

TIGER TANK REGIMENT BÄKE, 1944

1 January: Road march in trucks to Shmerinka in the Rumanian Sector of the Ukraine.

3 January: The company received new tanks. Maintenance service, breaking them in, sighting in the guns. Oberleutnant Scherf went on leave. Leutnant Beier led the company.

4 January: The battalion, along with the 2nd Battalion of the 23rd Panzer Regiment (Hauptmann Euler's Panther detachment), was attached to the local area commander at Shmerinka for defending the city.

16 January: The 3rd Company was placed under the operational control of the 371. Infanterie-Division for the elimination of the Russian bridgehead at Ssutiski. Snow mixed with rain and onset of thick fog complicated the operation. First contact with the enemy came just outside of Shmerinka. Shukowzy captured by noon. Two SU-122s were knocked out. The attack was renewed at 1400 hours with Pantherabteilung Euler, a grenadier company and two combat engineer platoons from the 371st Infantry Division. Nowo Petrowsk was captured and secured shortly before night fell. Feldwebel Weiland's Tiger 332 dropped out with engine trouble. Then back to Shmerinka.

19 January: Transport by rail to Winniza. We were billeted in a former Red Army barracks. Oberleutnant Scherf rejoined the company.

23 January: Formation of Tiger Tank Regiment Bäke (Tiger Tank Battalion 503, the 2nd Battalion of the 23rd Panzer Regiment, an artillery battalion, a combat engineer battalion, and a mountain troop [*Gebirgsjäger*] battalion). March to the assembly area.

24 January: Breakthrough through the Bila position to Ocheretnaya.

25 January: Armored fighting in the Ssosoff area. The village was taken after hard fighting.

26 January: Defensive fighting in the Ssosoff area. The supply elements were delayed in arriving so, for a while, the fighting went on without us.

27 January: Armored engagements south of Ocheretnaya in the direction of Rososhe. Tiger 332 was put out of action en route back to the regiment's command post by a round fired by a Panther from the 1st SS Panzer Division "Leibstandarte" that hit the left final drive. Tiger 332 had just finished executing a special mission.

During the past four days, Feldwebel Weiland destroyed ten T-34s, two SU-122s, six antitank guns, and two trucks towing guns.

28 January: Maintenance facility at Winniza.

After the conclusion of the fighting around Oratow-Balabanowka, Tiger Tank Regiment Bäke moved to the area of operations north of Uman.

6 February: Rail movement from Winniza to Potash.

10 February: Road march by the company to the assembly area at Rubany Most.

11 February: At precisely 0700 hours, after a strong artillery preparation, we started the attack

on the encirclement around Korsun [Tcherkassy Pocket]. We attacked toward Bushanka–Frankowka. In spite of extremely difficult ground conditions the tanks made good progress forward, reaching Frankowka by noon. The enemy fled Frankowka after relatively limited resistance. Swiftly pursuing Panthers took possession of the bridge over the Gniloi Tikitsch and formed a bridgehead. Tiger 332 destroyed four T-34s, one antitank gun, and a Stalin Organ. In all, the 3rd Company destroyed eleven rocket launchers. Shortage of fuel and ammunition precluded further advance by the tanks.

12 February: Three Tigers (Oberfeldwebel Rondorf, Feldwebel Weiland, and an unknown commander), four Panthers and Panzeraufklärungsabteilung 16 set out in thick fog to attack the high ground east of Daschukowka. After negotiating several small hills, we ran into defensive fire from an unknown number of tanks and antitank guns. The four Panthers went up in flames. The Tigers took heavy hits and had to set out for the maintenance facility at Potash as nearly total losses.

17 February: Conclusion of the fighting at Tscherkassy.

23 February: Oberleutnant Scherf awarded the Ritterkreuz.

24 February: Schweres Panzer-Regiment Bäke dissolved.

2 March: The 3rd Company transferred to Proskurow area. Our crew along with four others remained with a maintenance section and an 18-ton prime mover to load the 21 Tigers that had been left at the maintenance faility at Potash. Leutnant(W) Schulz was in charge of the party.

6 March: Russian forces broke through at Buki.

7 March: Defensive fighting at Potash. That day the battalion lost all of the tanks that had been left behind; one after a vain attempt at the local defense of Potash, and two more after an attempt at a nighttime defense of Pomoynik in crossing over the Revukha.

8 March: Feldwebel Weiland and three crews reached Uman after an adventurous march on foot. Then, on to Shmerinka in an armored train. There we encountered the rear party of the battalion—led by Leutnant Ohnesorge—getting ready to depart.

Transport by rail through Mogilew/Dnjestr, Tschernowitz, Snyatin, Stanislau, Stryi to Lemberg. No contact with the battalion. Attempted to reach Proskurow by land route. Intercepted at Pomorczany by the XXXXVIII Panzer Corps and directed onward through Brzezany to Kozowa. Appropriated two Tigers that had been allocated to Panzer Grenadier Division "Großdeutschland." With those, we continued on to . . .

26 March: . . . Teofipolka. Reported there to . . .

TIGER BATTLE GROUP MITTERMEIER

. . . which was engaged there, fighting defensively and offensively in the Kozowe area.

30 March: Attack on Sloboda Zlota. Heavy snow squalls led to cancellation of the operation. Unteroffizier Rothemann killed.

31 March: Attack successfully remounted.

4 April: Tank fighting at Hill 371. Our tank dropped out with track damage. An Obergefreiter who was with the Tigers taken from "Großdeutschland" was killed.

7–8 April: Attack on and capture of Uswie. The 9th SS Panzer Division "Hohenstaufen" took over the Kozowa sector.

16 April: Kampfgruppe Mittermeier dissolved.

17 April: Rail transport with two damaged tanks to the army repair depot at Sanok.

22 April: To Lemberg, then to the company at Stanislau.

Battalion went to Germany for refitting. The 3rd Company transferred to Nadworna and, as of . . .

6–14 May: . . . reorganized under the designation 1st Tiger Demonstration Company, 1st Panzer Demonstration Group North Ukraine, training Hungarian soldiers on the Tigers taken over from Battle Group Mittermeier.

14 May: Turned over the Tigers to Tiger Tank Battalion 509. The company proceeded to Germany for reorganization at Ohrdruf. Went on leave.

FRANCE—INVASION FRONT

12 June: "Rejoin unit immediately."

13 June: Accepted new tanks.

22 June: Generaloberst Guderian inspected the battalion.

26 June: Journeyed from Ohrdruf through Mainz, Homburg, Saarburg, Luneville, Nancy . . .

28 June: . . . Pagny on the Meuse. Bomber formations flew over the transport. Onward through Bologne, Chaumont, Melun.

30 June: Past Paris toward Versailles. The railroad facilities were completely destroyed with only one track passable.

2 July: Unloaded at Houdan. Road march through Verneuil, Argentan, Falaise. As a rule, we only marched at night.

6 July: Tiger 323, (Feldwebel Seidel) collapsed a road bridge at Canon by Mezidon, southeast of Caen, onto a railroad track.

Until 16 July: At the field hospital in the fortress of Canon, then joined the trains.

22 July: Advance party sent to accept new tanks. Two days in Paris.

25 July: *Truppenübungsplatz* (troop training grounds) Mailly le Camp. Quartered in the village of Sompuis.

29 July: The company arrived at Mailly le Camp—a training area in the woods.

31 July: The first new tanks—Tiger II—arrived. Usual maintenance work. Propaganda team filmed *Day in the Life of a Tiger Company in Action*, in the course of which the tanks of Feldwebel Seidel and Unteroffizier Jäckel dropped out with transmission problems.

11 August: The company moved to its new employment—without us.

16 August: A work group from the Organization Todt made an unsuccessful attempt to fix the transmission.

23 August: To Troyes by Volkswagen. Clothing supply dump cleared out. "Appropriated" leather jackets.

24 August: Leutnant von Rosen returned from the hospital in Reims. He concerned himself with getting us moved out.

25 August: To the railroad station at a snail's pace. Attack by low-flying aircraft. Locomotive disabled with shot-out boiler, blocking the rail line.

26 August: The rail line was cleared. Our train set out again with a new locomotive after many hours.

In Epernay, Reims and Charleville there were difficulties with the local commanders and the railroad authorities. The reason: With twenty axles, the train was under utilized. Feldwebel Seidel was able to get approval to continue to travel at the first two stations. At Charleville, however, the locomotive was uncoupled to take over a train-

load of wounded. Hopeless confusion at the railroad station. The dispatching of trains was stoped. Feldwebel Seidel took advantage of the still-intact telephone switchboard and, after several calls, managed to arrange for a locomotive to be sent from Sedan.

28 August: Through Givet and Namur to the army repair depot at Tilleur by Liege. Repair of the tank was not possible because of lack of replacement parts or a new transmission.

3 September: Through Aachen and Cologne to Paderborn.

9 September: The company arrived without tanks at Paderborn. The two "rescued" Tigers had to be given up. We rejoined the company. Billeting in private quarters at Hîvelhauf. Reorganized anew.

30 September: Hauptmann Scherf bid farewell. Oberleutnant von Rosen took over the company.

CAMPAIGN IN HUNGARY

9 October: We loaded the tanks at Sennelager in the pouring rain. Where to? The direction of travel was clearly to the east: Halberstadt, Halle, Eger, Pilson, Prague, Brünn, Preßburg.

14 October: Budapest. Detrained at the east railroad station. Drove south through the city towards Taksony. Warmly greeted by the local population. Good quarters—in the tavern with the locals until late at night.

15 October: 0600 hours—Alarm! Back to Budapest. The 3rd Company quartered in a park in the suburb of Budakeszi. Street control and disarming Hungarian troops.

16 October: Horthy's resignation. The tanks remained in the city, ready to be employed in case of a popular uprising.

17 October: Loaded tanks for employment at the front.

18 October: Unloaded at Cegled. Tiger 321 (Leutnant Rambow) disabled by steering gear problems.

21 October: To Szolnok. Security at the Theiß bridgehead.

23–26 October: Battle Group Leutnant Rambow (= three tanks) in the Theiß bridgehead at Szolnok. Security assignments, no enemy contact.

28 October: Defensive fighting on the west bank of the Theiß at Toszek. Tiger 321 out of

action with damage to radiator and coolers due to a mortar hit.

29 October: In the maintenance facility at Jaszladany.

1 November: Jaszladany evacuated. Damaged tanks were towed or inched along to Cegled—if they were still drivable. Direct route through Abony was under artillery fire.

2 November: 2300 hours. Departure of the damaged tanks—about twelve, some of them in tow—marched off under command of Leutnant Rambow toward Budapest. Shot up by a low-flying aircraft between Alberti and Pilis. At Ullö, about 15 miles outside of Budapest, we ran into a Russian antitank blockade. Where did they come from? Our tank was shot into flames while withdrawing. We had been providing cover. All the other Tigers were saved and taken to the maintenance facility.

5–17 November: With the trains in either Gödöllo or Koka.

18 November: Transported by truck to the maintenance facility; headed toward Vagselly (nowadays: Sala) following the railroad line Preßburg-Neuhäusel. In Tiger 314.

16 December: Transport by rail to Lake Platten.

18 December: Balatonkenese.

22 December: Nadasladany. Attack on Urhida. Leutnant Koppe, who was the temporary commander of the 3rd Company, transferred to Tiger 314 after his tank was disabled. I took his tank to the maintenance facility at Varpalota. Ran into Oberst Rudel, the commander of Ground-Attack Wing (*Schlacht-Geschwader*) "Immelmann," at Varpalota. He let me brief him on the Tiger. His reaction: "If the Russians had such a tank, we would have to have a more powerful on-board cannon."

24 December: The maintenance facility moved to Dudar. Prime mover broke down after 3 kilometers with transmission problems.

26 December: Towed to Szapar. Motor replaced on the open road.

29 December: To Balinka (battalion command post). Then on to Mor to Battle Group Oberleutnant von Rosen.

30 December: Reconnaissance in force to Pusztavam with the 5th Cavalry Regiment "Feldmarshall von Mackensen" (Rittmeister Bullinger?).

31 December: Mortar fire on Mor. Billets destroyed by a direct hit.

1945

1 January: Aircraft attack on Mor. Successful attack on Hill 128, five kilometers north of Mor. Security duty, in conjunction with the attack, with the 2nd Company of the 5th Cavalry Regiment 5 at Felsödopuszta.

3 January: Night attack on Pusztavam. Two Tigers, one Jagdpanzer IV , two Panzerflak on self-propelled mounts, elements of the 4th Cavalry Brigade with three Panzer IIs. The Russians were surprised. Many hand-held weapons, vehicles and eleven antitank guns were captured, along with a great many prisoners.

4 January: The tanks were ordered to Bakonyszombathely for changing the turret traversing ring and tracks.

5 January: Announcement of the redesignation of the battalion to Tiger Tank Battalion "Feldherrnhalle."

6 January: Bakonycserny–Bodaik–Fehervarcsurgo.

7 January: Attack on Zamoly. Six Tigers, ten Sturmgeschütze of the 4th Cavalry Brigade. Heavy snow squalls. Massed defensive fire forced the operation to be broken off. Feldwebel Gärtner killed by a round that penetrated the side of the turret.

9 January: Attack on the hilly terrain east of Sarkeresztes. Leutnant Rambow's tank put out of action by a burst barrel, but it still stayed in action for two more days.

12 January: Company to Magyaralmas. Leutnant Rambow's Tiger 321 sent to the maintenance facility at Sur.

16 January: With the trains at Papateszer.

24 January: Bakonyszombathely.

13 February: Road march to Tardosked, north of Neuhäusel. Combat elements at the Gran bridgehead.

7–31 March: Feldwebel Tomforde (2nd Company) took a detail to Vienna to pick up new tanks. Vienna had not been advised of anything like that. Directed on to Znaim to the organizational staff of Panzer Grenadier division "Feldhernhalle." There, too, nothing was known about new tanks. We were quartered in Lechwitz.

31 March: Ordered to return to the battalion. Last known location: Tardosked.

1 April: In Lundenburg, where red flags were already flying, we rolled past a Tiger rail transport on the siding. We learned the transport was headed

for Nikolsburg. On that same evening, Feldwebel Tomforde reported the return of the detail.

Because of the terrible tank situation, a march company was formed on 24 March 1945 from the crews with no tanks. The march company was to push through to "Army Wenck." Tomforde's detail joined the march company. But it was not possible to depart from Bratelsbrunn (5 April) Neu Serowitz at Mährisch-Budwitz (9 April), Petrowitz at Klein Wartenberg (12 April) or Ratibor at Neuhaus (20 April). In one instance, there was no rail line; in another instance, a bridge had been blown up somewhere. Finally, the transport vehicles that had been alleged to have been sent failed to arrive.

20 April: The march company was dissolved. We proceeded back to our companies.

5 May: Neuhaus

7 May: Wittingau. Czechoslovakian militia tried to block passage for the march column, but were dispersed by two Vierlings-Flak (four-barreled 20mm antiaircraft guns).

8 May: Budweis. Endless columns of vehicles were moving through the city, mostly at a snail's pace with many traffic jams.

9 May: An assembly point for the battalion was announced in the afternoon.

10 May: Waited in vain for the combat elements at the assembly point. *Wehrpässe* [soldier's military record books] were distributed and the company's store of worthless Czechoslovakian Kronen was distributed. After the fall of darkness, we marched to the west. After a few kilometers, the column split apart after a rear-end collision. We, the rear portion, joined up with a different column. There were several incidents with the Czechs who were, in part, supported by French and Polish workers.

INTO CAPTIVITY

At about noon on 11 May we encountered the first American sentries. We were required to surrender our weapons, but not otherwise searched. The vehicles were not searched either. Therefore we hung onto our pistols. The second group of sentries was a hundred meters farther on: Inspec-

tion of our *Soldbücher* [soldier's pay books]. Germans and Austrians were free to go south. All others were held back.

Late in the afternoon, the column came to a halt. The terrified cry, "The Ivans are coming!" spread like wildfire. Shots could be heard from farther ahead. Then the word was, "The SS has knocked out two tanks." The Americans had hoodwinked us.

Since there was no way that the tightly packed vehicles could turn around on the very narrow road, we grabbed our personal belongings and made the vehicles unusable. Then into the woods to the right of the road. There were about thirty men from the battalion, including Unterarzt Dr. Büri with a portion of the medical echelon. When it got dark, a war council was held. One group argued for going cross-country, directly to the west. Others wanted to go by the more passable routes. I was among the latter. I was in the minority. At midnight we took a rest. We managed to get one or two hours of sleep. When I woke up again, we were only four of us left.

We marched on through the woods until midday. Then we came to an open field and, in the distance, vehicles were driving. We approached the road carefully. It was a column of the 24th Flak Division. A little later we were "prisoners of war" and in either Camp Nesselbach at Rosenheim or Camp Rosental in the Böhmer Woods. There we encountered another little group from our battalion under Oberarzt Dr. Schramm.

By agreement between the commander of the 24th Flak Division and the American camp commander, the camp was declared an "internee camp." That enabled us to escape the clutches of the Red Army.

On 16 May the discharge process began. On 22 May, after surrendering my Soldbuch and the pistol that I had kept to this point, I was in an American truck that unloaded its cargo on a road at the German border. The American escort officer said farewell to us as "free citizens" and wished us a good homecoming.

On 3 June I made my entry into Hamburg.

CHAPTER 9

Technical Services and Supply/Logisitics

Alfred Rubbel

CONCEPT AND PRACTICE IN TIGER TANK BATTALION 503

Maintenance of combat readiness in a separate formation like a Tiger battalion required a major commitment of personnel and technical expertise within the framework of the formation. The battalion could depend on

- The organic maintenance sections of the companies for keeping the equipment in good condition,
- The organic maintenance company of the battalion for light and medium repairs, and
- General headquarters maintenance units for heavy repairs.

All that meant that maintenance support at division, corps or army level was not programmed.

Logistical support, which included the supply of—ammunition, bulk petroleum products, rations, and other expendable materials—was, as a rule, supplied by the major formations to which the battalion was attached or supported. The battalion could support itself temporarily though its organic short-haul capacity of 400 tons. Despite that, bottlenecks occurred repeatedly. We must not forget, however, that higher echelons of command were concerned with assisting. Tank

engines were frequently flown in. Similar treatment was also given to the priority resupply of ammunition and fuel by air to hot spots.

Someone came up with the rule of thumb that "one hour of tank operation requires ten hours of technical service." That relationship seemed appropriate at the time. The examples in the table below, although they are hypothetical, are reasonably realistic examples and demonstrate how repair and maintenance were actually carried out:

Times given are approximate and depended on availability of replacement parts.

Maintenance of the approximately 250 other vehicles was second in priority to that of the tanks. In summary, one could say that, in spite of the imponderables of war, the conceptual framework for the maintenance of materiel was optimally conceived and functional.

The supply of expendable items was—with some exceptions and not looking at everything under a microscope—set up in such a manner that the battalion was able to carry out its missions, aside from the period when it was at the invasion front. In order of importance, supply items included bulk petroleum products (without fuel the Tigers could not move); ammunition (without ammunition, the Tigers could not fight, even though they could still move out of harm's way); and rations (as a rule, rations could be brought forward by the companies, even though it was frequently at ungodly hours).

It can be said that, thanks to the system and the activities of the soldiers concerned, the logistic system generally performed its mission in spite of the conditions of combat.

After these "introductory remarks," it should be obvious that the combat readiness of the equipment was a central concern to the battalion's leadership in terms of the significance it had and the expenditure of resources devoted to it. The Schwerpunkt in this effort was the responsibility of the battalion's maintenance company. Those who were members of the combat elements need to remember them and their performance. As we recognize their accomplishments, we also need to include the maintenance sections of the tank companies, the medics and the supply services. These include, among others, the many truck drivers, the field kitchen personnel and the technicians. More than half of the battalion's personnel were employed in logistical or technical work. There were 207 men in the maintenance company, 250 in the supply company, and about 30 more in each of the tank companies.

It in no way diminishes the respect due to the many unnamed comrades if two of their number are selected for special mention due to the importance of their activities. The first of these was the leader of the recovery platoon, Oberfeldwebel, later Leutnant, Kînig. At some time or another, he had every one of our Tigers "on the hook" of his prime movers and brought it back to safety. Unfortunately, nothing is known of his own fate, so it must be assumed that he, himself, will not have the opportunity to read this appreciation of his performance.

Equally well known to us was our motor transport specialist (*K-Werkmeister*, or *Offizier des Kraftfahrwesens*) Späth—a true Swabian—and a well known engine specialist. He did not limit himself to the workplace of his maintenance platoon. He showed up where the fighting was most intense. If a Tiger crept back from the battle line, gasping and coughing on only half its cylinders, Späth and his forward-support specialists took charge of it, repairing or improvising, often under enemy fire. In April 1945 he was awarded the Iron Cross, First Class for his personal bravery. This was a very rare award for someone in his position, a civilian who had been detailed to the front from the Maybach

factory. After the war, we encountered him at the battalion and company gatherings and were able to make known to him our respect for the manner in which he understood and performed his duty. Unfortunately, he is no longer with us.

ORGANIZATION OF THE MAINTENANCE COMPANY OF TIGER TANK BATTALION 503

This is an attempt to outline the organization of the maintenance company of Tiger Tank Battalion 503. As with any unit, the maintenance company had a command and a supply element (company command group with the commander, the first sergeant, the supply sergeant and others) and the sub-elements for maintenance services (maintenance platoons, recovery platoon, communications and weapons maintenance sections and replacement parts element).

The maintenance services were directed in technical matters by civilian technical officials with nominal rank as officers, usually on the technical war advisory board (*technischer Kriegs-Verwaltungsrat*). The perception that we had only two maintenance platoons, since one platoon had been transferred to Paderborn in March 1943 to the 500th Replacement Battalion, does not appear to be correct. In January 1943 when the 2nd Company, Tiger Tank Battalion 502, was incorporated into Tiger Tank Battalion 503, it had two maintenance platoons. That then gave a total of four maintenance platoons, one more than the table of organization authorized.

The maintenance company, according to its 1945 table of organization, had a personnel strength of 207 soldiers. By way of heavy equipment, it had one (perhaps two?) portable bridge-cranes (*Strabo-Portalkräne*) for removing the Tiger turrets. The maintenance company started out with six 18-ton prime movers for recovery operations. By the end of the war, that number had increased to three Bergepanthers and eleven 18-ton prime movers (according to the strength reports of the battalion as of 15 December 1944).

DIARY NOTES OF HERMANN RÖPSCHER OF THE MAINTENANCE COMPANY OF TIGER TANK BATTALION 503

From 12 June 1942 until 1 March 1944 I belonged to the communications repair section of the maintenance company. Then I was transferred to the 1st Company as the communications sergeant. In the spring of 1945, when the battalion had to "slim

Maintenance Company of *schwere Panzer–Abteilung 503*

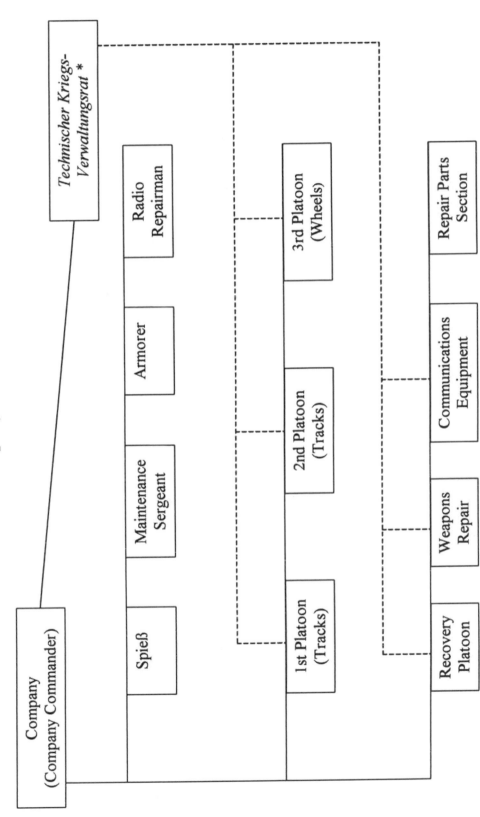

* Civilian official with nominal officer rank who was entrusted with providing the command technical advice concerning maintenance and repair issues. He had no command authority but was in daily contact with the maintenance section and platoons, hence the dotted lines.

down," I was transferred to the 211th People's Grenadier Division along with other comrades from the 1st Company of Tiger Tank Battalion 503, among them Stabsfeldwebel Schmidt. At the time, I was shaken by the measure. Schmidt was killed at Zistersdorf. I was wounded at Laa on the Thaya River. That saved me from the Russians. Unfortunately, my notes are incomplete.

June 1942

12 June 1942: Arrived at Neuruppin from the replacement unit at Meiningen (signals section of the 81st Rifle Replacement Regiment).

15 June 1942: Assigned to the communications repair section.

19 June 1942: Company formation with the company commander, Leutnant Bielefeldt.

22 June 1942: Started work in the communications repair section.

23 June 1942: Battalion formation with the battalion commander Oberstleutnant Post.

July 1942

9 July 1942: Assignment of maintenance Platoons.

14 July 1942: Company formation with Hauptmann Fest, the new company commander.

18 July 1942: Hauptmann Fest transferred to the headquarters company.

23 July 1942: Oberleutnant (Ing.) Diekamp, new company commander.

24 July 1942: Company formation with the new company commander (introduction).

27 July 1942: Oberfunkmeister Benecke transferred to Regensburg.

August 1942

1 August 1942: Oberleutnant (Ing.) Diekamp left the maintenance company. Oberleutnant (Ing.) Groß new company commander.

8 August 1942: 1st Company transferred from Neuruppin to Döllersheim.

11 August 1942: Company formation, greeted by Oberleutnant (Ing.) Groß.

15 August 1942: Oberfunkmeister Endreß transferred to the maintenance company. The 2nd Company also left Neuruppin.

29 August 1942: Maintenance company transferred from Neuruppin to the training area at Döllersheim (Lower Austria) in several rail transports.

September 1942

Maintenance service.

October 1942

16 October 1942: First round of handball ended. Three games, three wins for the maintenance company.

30 October 1942: I received my Class II truck license. Examiner: Technical War Advisor Hallerberg.

November 1942

16 November 1942: Loading exercise, etc.

17 November 1942: Leutnant von Koerber awarded the Handball Challenge Trophy to Oberleutnant (Ing.) Groß. Promotions included, among others, Feldwebel König to Oberfeldwebel.

December 1942

Maintenance service. Rumors circulated about where the battalion would go into action (Africa, Iran, Iraq, Russia?). Medical fitness-for-tropical-duty examinations (Africa?). Soldiers who were not suitable for service in the tropics were sent back to the replacement unit. That came to a sudden end with the issue of winter gear. Therefore, the East was our "travel destination."

The first units rolled out by rail on 20 December 1942. One of the entraining stations was Göpfritz. The Christmas season was spent on the railroad, traveling east through Prague, Slovakia etc. Destination: Rostow on the Sea of Asov. The battalion was to relieve Stalingrad from the south.

For us, 1942 ended in the East!

January 1943

1 January 1943: In Rostow.

2 January 1943: In Salsk. Final destination for the maintenance company was Proletarskaja, near the Manytsch dam.

3 January 1943: Technical service at Proletarskaja. It was already dark by 1500 hours.

5 January 1943: According to a report, our Tigers had their first contact with the enemy.

6 January 1943: First reported success. Much work for the maintenance company.

8 January 1943: Armored vehicles assembled at Proletarskaja.

13 January 1943: Company formation. Oberst Thomale, from the staff of the panzer troops at

the Führer headquarters, made a speech offering us thanks and recognition.

14 January 1943: The situation became critical. The enemy advanced toward Manytsch. Enemy aircraft alarm. We took down our crane during the night—the same went for the maintenance platoons.

15 January 1943: We marched off early in groups toward Salsk. New billets near the railroad. Temperature -25 Celsius degrees [-13 degrees Fahrenheit]!

16 January 1943: Impending change of positions.

17 January 1943: Departed towards Cilina. There are a lot of sweet things to eat. The maintenance platoons were dispersed with the First Platoon at Gigant and the Second Platoon (with the communications repair section) and armorers at Jegorlyskaja!

18 January 1943: Temporarily working in former automobile plant.

19 January 1943: Lost the field bakery. For some time there was only hardtack and sweet things but no bread.

20 January 1943: Moved on to Kagalinsk, spending the night there.

21 January 1943: On to Bataisk, spending the night there.

22 January 1943: On to Rostow. Quartered there in the industrial district for 14 days.

23 January 1943: Technical service, etc.

24 January 1943: Thaw. Technical service.

26 January 1943: The commander visited the maintenance company. Air attack on the factory facilities and railroad station.

February 1943

1–2 February 1943: Technical service, etc.

4 February 1943: The LVII Panzer Corps, to which our battalion was attached, was mentioned in the OKW (Oberkommando der Wehrmacht) report.

5 February 1943: Change of positions to Awrosiewka except for the 1st Maintenance Platoon, which remained in Rostow.

12 February 1943: Our tanks involved in the fighting for Rostow.

18 February 1943: Division order of the day regarding the fighting at Rostow included special thanks to Tiger Tank Battalion 503.

19 February 1943: Preparation for change of position.

20 February 1943: Departure towards Stalino.

21 February 1943: Objective for the day—Wolnonache. Heavy snow drifts. Our battery truck was in tow (transmission problems).

22 February 1943: Our journey continued toward Mariupol, arriving there at 1500 hours. We were billeted at the Iljitsch Works and the hotel of the same name.

23 February 1943: Change of position for the armorers—to Federowka.

24–25 Feb 1943: On to Federowka, along with the First Platoon. At about 1000 hours a Panzer III exploded because of carelessness in welding; one soldier from the 1st Maintenance Platoon was killed, two from another unit. Our equipment truck also was hit in two places (roof and radiator housing).

26 February 1943: Return to Mariupol.

27 February 1943: Leutnant Bielefeldt read out a Führer order to the 16th Infantry Division (mot.) and the 4th Air Fleet (*Luftflotte*).

March 1943

4 March 1943: With the Third Maintenance Platoon at the Iljitsch Works.

5 March 1943: Technical service, etc. The Iljitsch Works was a major Russian tank factory, with a monthly production capacity of about 700 T-34 tanks! Many German industrial machines, as well as a large bridge-crane (made in Germany) with a capacity of 100/300 tons.

19 March 1943: Teletype from the Commander-in-Chief of Army Group South, von Manstein, to the new 6th Army, under General of Infantry Hollidt.

22 March 1943: Leutnant Bielefeldt was transferred to the headquarters company.

31 March 1943: The 3rd Maintenance Platoon left Mariupol for Germany for a new assignment. Parts of the 1st and 2nd Maintenance Platoon went with it.

April 1943

Technical service and other duties at Mariupol.

5–10 April 1943: Trip to communications depot at Dnjepropetrowsk to get electrical parts for the communications maintenance section.

26 April 1943: Change of position, headed for Kharkov by rail.

28 April 1943: Unloaded at Kharkov and continued the journey to Tolokonoie.

May 1943

4 May 1943: Oberwerkmeister Bahl was promoted to Hauptwerkmeister. Werkmeister Neuberth was awarded the War Service Cross, First Class.

13 May 1943: The Second Maintenance Platoon and replacement parts section changed position to Kharkov, along with the communications repair section.

15 May 1943: Billeted at Kharkov at the edge of the city in a workers' housing project; the maintenance sections were located in the former "Hammer and Sickle" Works.

16 May 1943: Technical service, etc.

18 May 1943: General of Panzer Troops Breith visited the maintenance company.

19 May 1943: Oberfeldwebel Nest and Feldwebel Fromm were killed in an accident as they left the factory grounds in a Kübelwagen. They collided with a freight train that was backing up while switching.

21 May 1943: Both were interred at the military cemetary at Kharkov. Technical service, etc.

June 1943

1 June 1943: Took pills (Atebrin) as protection against malaria. Technical service alternated with drills. Instruction.

18 June 1943: Battalion commander, Oberstleutnant Hoheisel, was given his farewell.

19 June 1943: New battalion commander, Graf (Count) Kageneck.

July 1943

4 July 1943: 1st Maintenance Platoon at the front. The battalion was committed in the Bjelgorod area. The battalion commander was wounded at the end of July. Hauptmann Burmester assumed temporary command. Technical service, etc.

August 1943

War advisor Hallerberg was transferred to Tiger Tank Battalion 508 on 1 August 1943. Oberleutnant (Ing,) Groß was promoted to Hauptmann (Ing.).

13 Aug. 1943: Change of position to Walki. Battle lines: Kharkov-Jewgeniwka. Heavy aerial attacks!.

30 Aug. 1943: Heavy work load for the entire maintenance company, due to damaged tanks. Occupy an alternate position since Kharkov had been evacuated in the middle of the month.

September 1943

2–3 September 1943: Change of position toward Krasnograd. Billeted at Dechtsjansk.

9 September 1943: Hauptmann Graf Kageneck received the Ritterkreuz.

12 September 1943: Change of position to Krasnograd.

15 September 1943: Another change of position to the Poltawa area. Roads terrible; mud. Spent the night at Kalowka, then on to Meserowka.

19 September 1943: 2nd Maintenance Platoon remained in Poltawa (for the time being).

22 September 1943: Change of position toward Krementschug.

25 September 1943: In Krementschug, then on to Pawlisch.

26 September 1943: Destination Snamenka. Technical service, etc.

October 1943

12 October 1943: Hauptmann (Ing.) Groß was bid farewell.

13 October 1943: Oberleutnant (Ing.) Theiß was the new company commander. Strong air attacks on Snamenka at night and in the late afternoon.

Technical service, etc.

November 1943

10 November 1943: Company formation. War Service Cross, First Class to Hauptwerkmeister Bahl and Gefreiter Strittmarder.

11 November 1943: Internal move of the maintenance company in Snamenka.

20 November 1943: Night shifts for both platoons until further notice.

27 November 1943: First Maintenance Platoon transferred to Nowo-Ukrainka.

December 1943

2 December 1943: 2nd Maintenance Platoon transferred to Nowo-Ukrainka.

3 December 1943: Communications repair section transferred to Nowo-Ukrainka.

5 December 1943: Our Tigers engaged at Dimitrowka. Leutnant Weinert, 3rd Company, killed.

6 December 1943: Maintenance elements of Panzer Grenadier Division "Großdeutschland" also in Novo-Ukrainka.

Technical service, etc.

New Year's 1944 at Nowo-Ukrainka.

January 1944

In Nowo-Ukrainka until 5 January 1944

6 January 1944: Second Maintenance Platoon transferred to Winniza. Technical service, etc.

February 1944

Until 27 February 44: "Home leave," then back to Snamenka. Communications repair section back from the front. Oberfunkmeister Endreß let me know that I was going to be transferred to the 1st Company.

March 1944

19 March 1944: End of my assignment to the maintenance company. Set off to join the 1st Company and reported there to Oberleutnant Linden.

TANK MAINTENANCE ACTIVITIES

Activity	Performed By	Time Required
Engine oil change	Tank crew	About 4 hours
Damage to turret traversing gear	Tank crew	About 2 hours
Mine damage to running gear	Tank crew and company maintenance section	Depending on damage, about 12–24 hours
Engine change	Tank crew and battalion maintenance company	About 24 hours
Battle damage to final drive	Battalion maintenance company	Depending on damage, about 12–24 hours
Penetration of hull with destruction of transmission	Army-level repair facility at the Vienna arsenal	2–4 weeks

COMMAND POSITIONS IN THE MAINTENANCE COMPANY OF TIGER TANK BATTALION 503 (JUNE 1942–OCTOBER 1943)

June 1942	Company Commander	Hauptmann Fest
	First Sergeant	Oberfeldwebel Bittkowski
	Supply Sergeant	Oberschirrmeister Jungmann
	Communications NCO	Oberfunkmeister Benecke
	Armorer	Oberfeldwebel Nest
	Platoon Leader	Leutnant Bielefeldt
	Platoon Leader	Oberwerkmeister Bahl
	Platoon Leader	Werkmeister Scheerbarth
	Recovery Platoon	Oberfeldwebel König
	Replacement Parts Section	Oberschirrmeister Rukop

**COMMAND POSITIONS IN THE MAINTENANCE COMPANY OF TIGER TANK BATTALION 503
(JUNE 1942–OCTOBER 1943)**

23 July 1942	Company Commander (no other changes at this date)	Oberleutnant (Ing.) Diekamp
21 October 1942	Company Commander Communications NCO Replacement Parts Section (no other changes at this date)	Oberleutnant (Ing.) Groß Oberfunkmeister Endreß Stabsfeldwebel Frohmüller (Stabsfeldwebel Müller)
1 April 1943	Company Commander Supply Sergeant Platoon Leaders (no other changes at this date)	Oberleutnant (Ing.) Groß Schirrmeister von Blottnitz (Schirrmeister Seidelmann) Kraft-Werkmeister Neuberth
1 September 1943	Company Commander	Hauptmann (Ing.) Groß
15 October 1943	Company Commander Recovery Platoon (no other changes at this date)	Oberleutnant (Ing.) Theiss Leutnant König

Note: Werkmeister = Shop foreman, civilian official ranking as a master sergeant.
(Ing.) = Ingenieur: Civilian official with nominal military rank serving in a technical capacity.

Pass-in-review on the occasion of German Memorial Day on 15 March 1942. These soldiers are from the 6th Company, Panzer Replacement Battalion 5, which provided many of the soldiers who would form the nucleus of Tiger Tank Battalion 503.

Neuruppin, the garrison town where Tiger Tank Battalion 503 was formed. In this view, we see the train station near the base.

The billets of Panzer Regiment 6 in Neuruppin where the soldiers who helped form Tiger Tank Battalion 503 were housed.

Tank storage areas at Neuruppin.

Lake Neuruppin, which was the designated swimming spot for Panzer Regiment 6, as evidenced by the stencilling on the life preserver.

Panzer Replacement Battalion 5 conducts training on Panzer IIIs and IVs at Neuruppin in 1942.

The instructors from Panzer Regiment 6 who were responsible for the young soldiers of Tiger Tank Battalion 503. On the far left is Hans von Hagemeister, who would later become an officer and served as the leader of the battalion's scout platoon and the reconnaissance platoon.

A boat ride on Lake Neuruppin in 1942 for soldiers and family members of the cadre of Tiger Tank Battalion 503. (Neuruppin is located about 50 kilometers from Berlin.)

The "Swiss" area of Saxony toward the end of August 1942 as viewed during the trip to Döllersheim.

The Fourth Platoon of the 1st Company, Tiger Tank Battalion 503, during an excursion to Vienna from Döllersheim. In the background is Schönbrunn Castle. Leutnant Meller, killed in action on 9 January 1943, is wearing the peaked cap. On the left in the front row is Feldwebel Hörnke; on the right is Unteroffizier Tessmer.

October 1942. The battalion marched from Neuruppin to Döllersheim in Austria. In this photograph, we see a maintenance halt of the motorcycle section of the scout platoon.

Döllersheim, east of Vienna, in October 1942. Döllersheim had been a training area for the Austrian Army.

Unfortunately, the only billets available were these barracks. The terrific wine helped make up for the meager accommodations.

Spieß Rondorf at mail call, Fallingbostel, autumn 1942.

The 2nd Company of Tiger Tank Battalion 502 (later the 3rd Company of Tiger Tank Battalion 503) at clothing inspection in front of its billets at Fallingbostel, December 1942.

Company formation. In front of the formation are Oberleutnant Scherf and Unteroffizier Fuhrmann.

En route to the Eastern Front in 1942.

PART TWO

FIRST EMPLOYMENT IN THE KALMUCK STEPPES, 1942–43

CHAPTER 10

The Senior Tiger Battalion— Tiger Tank Battalion 503

Alfred Rubbel

If Georg Tessin, the author of the twelve-volume documentary series on the formations and branches of the German Armed Forces (*Verbände und Truppen der Deutschen Wehrmacht und Waffen-SS*) is correct in his research, our battalion was the first organized and, thus, the senior Tiger battalion. The period of seniority over the other "senior battalions" was not large—one week! The battalions were organized in 1942 in the following order:

Tiger Tank Battalion 503: 4 May 1942
Tiger Tank Battalion 501: 10 May 1942
Tiger Tank Battalion 502: 25 May 1942
Tiger Tank Battalion 500: 20 December 1942
Tiger Tank Battalions 504–509: 1943.
Tiger Tank Battalion 510: 1944.

The activation of our battalion began in Neuruppin—the peacetime garrison location of the 6th Panzer Regiment—located west of Berlin. A large portion of the command and cadre personnel in the first stage of organization came from the 5th and 6th Panzer Regiments. We also received young, inexperienced tankers.

First organized were the headquarters company, maintenance company, and 1st and 2nd Companies of Tiger Tank Battalion 503.

After completion of basic and specialty training, which were very thorough, the battalion was transferred to Döllersheim in Lower Austria in August 1942. The heavy equipment was sent there. Because the *Oberkommando des Heeres* [OKH, or Army High Command] had not yet decided which of the competing models of the Tiger, the Henschel or the Porsche ones, would be chosen for final issue, the 1st Company was temporarily issued Porsche Tigers and was trained in them. After the Army decided to adopt the Henschel Tiger, the Porsche Tigers were turned in.

At the beginning of December 1942, the first Henschel Tigers were issued. A total of sixty Henschel Tigers were completed by the end of December. The critical situation on the Eastern front, especially in the south, forced premature commitment of the Tigers. The first three battalions each received only twenty Tigers, the balance of the armor consisting of twenty to twenty-five Panzer IIIs with the KWK 7.5cm main gun. Obviously, with that kind of mixed equipment, it was scarcely possible to follow Guderian's fundamental precept for commitment of armor, "*Klotzen, nicht kleckern*" [roughly, "Strike with a fist, not an open hand!"]

Transportation to the southern sector of the Eastern Front began on 21 December 1942. Detraining from the railroad transports which had been routed for express movement took place at Proletarskaja. The war began for Tiger Tank Battalion 503 in the early days of January 1943 along the Manytsch River.

Tiger Tank Battalion 502 had also been organized at nearly the same time as Tiger Tank Battalion 503. It also had only two tank companies. In the fall of 1942 it had been committed to action in the northern sector of the Eastern Front with a headquarters company, a maintenance company and only one tank company. The 2nd Company of Tiger Tank Battalion 502 had been held back at Fallingbostel. In December of 1942, that company was loaded on rail for transport to Heeresgruppe Don. On arrival, it was attached to the 17th Panzer Division and saw its first employment in the Kalmuck Steppes southeast of Rostow under its company commander, Hauptmann Lange.

The 502's 2nd Company possessed a fairly good capability to operate on its own. In order to be logistically self-sufficient, it had been provided with the requisite additional elements. The 2nd Company would have liked to keep that status. For reasons of practicality and necessity, the 2nd Company was consolidated with Tiger Tank Battalion 503 as the 3rd Company at the beginning of January 1943. Tiger Tank Battalion 503, of course, was also employed in the Kalmuck Steppes at the time. That OKH decision was not greeted with a lot of enthusiasm by the company.

With that addition, Tiger Tank Battalion 503 became the first Tiger battalion to be brought to full strength according to the 1943 standard of organization.

In April 1943, in the Bogoduchow area, the battalion matured into a formation with extraordinary combat strength, with forty-five Tigers and an array of vehicles and equipment in which nothing was left to improvisation, an outfit that the old and proven panzer regiments could only dream of.

CHAPTER 11

Organization of the 3rd Company, Tiger Tank Battalion 503 (formerly the 2nd Company, Tiger Tank Battalion 502) and Its Initial Employment with Army Group Don

Richard Freiherr von Rosen

AT FALLINGBOSTEL

The 2nd Company of Tiger Tank Battalion 502 under Hauptmann Lange had been attached to the Tiger Tank Battalion 503 since 16 January 1943. It was consolidated with the battalion at Rostow and redesignated as the 3rd Company of Tiger Tank Battalion 503. That ended the separate unit status and the unique position of the company. Although it had only a brief period of operating on its own, that experience continued to influence the company for the entire period of the war and is still perceptible, even today, when the company gets together. For that reason I will report on the activation and initial employment of the 2nd Company, Tiger Tank Battalion 502 which took place outside of the framework of the battalion.

The 2nd Company was organized within the framework of Tiger Tank Battalion 502 in May 1942 at Bamberg. The 35th Panzer Replacement Battalion assisted in the unit's activation. The battalion was formed from men who came from the 35th Panzer Regiment, as well as the 1st and 10th Panzer Regiments. On 28 July 1942 all of the ele-

ments of Tiger Tank Battalion 502 transferred to the Fallingbostel training area, where the organization was continued. On 23 August 1942, the 1st Company of Tiger Tank Battalion 502 along with the battalion staff, the Headquarters Company and half of the Maintenance Company loaded for transport to the northern sector of the eastern front and detrained in Mga. At that point in time, the 1st Company had four Panzer VIs and a few Panzer IIIs equipped with the short-barreled 75mm main gun. The four Tigers were employed the same day they detrained.

The 2nd Company remained at Fallingbostel and was to have been shipped off to join the battalion as soon as it received its tanks. On 25 September 1942, the company got its first two Panzer VIs (Tigers). However, on 13 October 1942, it had to relinquish both of them to the 502's 1st Company on the Eastern Front. At that point, priority in the issuance of the Tigers had gone to the 1st Company of Tiger Tank Battalion 502 and also to Tiger Tank Battalion 501, which had been organized at the same time at Fallingbostel and, in

November 1942, had been loaded, fully equipped, for transport to Tunis.

In October 1942, the commander of Tiger Tank Battalion 502, Major Märker, ordered the 2nd Company rail loaded from Fallingbostel to the battalion in the Krasnogwardeisk area—prior to the company being issued with its tanks. In preparation for the movement, the company was ordered to send an advance party under Leutnant Pech to the battalion's assembly area in order to construct winter quarters there for the company. After several interventions by the company commander, Hauptmann Lange, the battalion commander's order was rescinded by the panzer troop branch of OKH. The party that had been detailed never returned to the company, however.

The 2nd Company remained at Fallingbostel. The training was, perforce, limited to theoretical instruction based on instructional displays on the new Panzer VI which the company made for itself, as well as general weapon and terrain training. In order to conduct training for at least the technical personnel on actual equipment, the maintenance elements and Panzer VI drivers of the company, as well as the specialists of the maintenance platoon who had remained with the company, were detailed to go to Tiger Tank Battalion 503 at the beginning of December 1942. That detachment order came to a surprise end on 21 December 1942.

DEFENSIVE FIGHTING IN THE KUBERLE SECTOR AND IN THE ROSTOW AREA

Without any advance notice, on 21 and 22 December 1942, the company was provided with one Panzer VI on each day. Two more Tigers followed on 25 December, three on 26 December and, finally, on 28 December 1942, yet another two Tigers arrived. All of the tanks were unloaded and conducted initial firing, even though the order stated that the last two were to be left on the Ssyms railroad cars so as not to delay their transport on to the company. In the evening of 23 December 1942 the teletype brought the order placing the company under the operational control of Army Group Don. That made it clear the company would be separated from Tiger Tank Battalion 502 and go into action in the southern sector as a separate company.

In order to guarantee that the company would be supplied with ammunition and fuel, rations

and replacement parts, additional trucks were requested, which were picked up by the company at the army motor transport parks by December 26. The additional drivers needed arrived from various replacement units in the morning hours of 27 December. Numerous couriers and parties from the company traversed Germany to assemble the materiel that was still lacking. For example, none of the Panzer VIs had arrived with bore brushes. They had to be obtained from Krupp or Wegmann. The same applied for the ice cleats for the tracks. A detail under Leutnant von Rosen got them on 24 December in Saarbrücken.

On 27, 28 and 29 December 1942 the company—fully equipped with personnel and materiel—left Fallingbostel on three transport trains and headed for the Don Front. The drama of Stalingrad was in high gear. The company knew why it was being sent so precipitately in express trains to that hot spot. As far to the rear as the railroad station at Rostow, it was overflowing with thousands of Rumanians and Italians who were fleeing. It was obvious that a catastrophe was in progress. From there on, the tanks were manned so that they could open fire to either side from the train in the event enemy forces that had broken through were able to advance as far as the railroad line.

On 5 and 6 January 1943 all three transports were unloaded at Proletarskaja. On 7 January 1943 the company was placed under the operational control of the 17th Panzer Division and sent on to Ssungar in the Kuberle sector. The company covered the 107-kilometer road march in piercing cold temperatures in a ten and a half hour march with no mechanical losses.

At that point, the company had nine Tigers and ten short-barreled 75mm Panzer IIIs. It was organized as follows: company headquarters section with one Panzer VI, two platoons with four Panzer VIs each, and two platoons with five Panzer IIIs each. The company officers were: Hauptmann Lange (company commander), Oberleutnant Scherf, Leutnant Dr. Taubert, Leutnant Forkel, Leutnant Weinert and Leutnant von Rosen. The company First Sergeant was Oberfeldwebel Rondorf.

After leaving the city of Kuberle, the railroad line ran through steppe that was only cut by a few streams through Simowniki-Kommissarow-Kutjelnikowa for more than 200 kilometers to

Stalingrad. The railroad ran thus through the very area which the Rumanian and Italian soldiers had abandoned in headlong flight. There just weren't sufficient forces to close the existing gaps or to open a relief attack on Stalingrad from there. The 2nd Company, Tiger Tank Battalion 502, just like everyone else, could serve as no more that a breakwater in the storm flood.

On 8 January 1943 the unit was employed for the first time. After an attack against an enemy that had advanced westward from Ilowaskij, the company was directed to turn around across the Kuberle sector by radio from the 17th Panzer Division. It then smashed an attack by two Russian regiments supported by armor from the direction of Osserskij. In the course of that action, two Russian tanks, eight antitank guns and about a thousand Russian soldiers were destroyed, for the most part by running over them. The company had its first losses. Gefreiter Zahn was killed, and Oberfeldwebel Gerrels and his Panzer III crew were missing (Unteroffiziere Runge, Werner Jürgensen, Karl Wiebscher and Sigmund Rummel). Unteroffizier Gericke was so severely wounded that his leg had to be amputated.

On 9 January 1943 the company attacked in the morning hours and cleared the village of Ilowaskij. During that operation, five antitank guns, two field guns and a weak Russian battalion were destroyed. At about 0900 hours the company was assigned a new task by radio: "Fifteen enemy tanks are approaching at Bratskij. Engage and destroy them." The enemy tanks, however, pulled back toward Ssalk before we arrived. After that, the company was ordered to attack the village of Osserskij. In the course of that attack, twelve more antitank guns were destroyed. However, the company suffered further losses. Leutnant Dr. Taubert was killed on the rear deck of his tank as he was checking the engine, which had been set on fire by an antitank round. Leutnant Ferkel broke his arm. After two days of action, the company was down to only four officers.

On 10 January 1943 the company smashed an enemy armored attack northwest of Budjenny, destroying eleven tanks, two antitank guns and a Russian infantry battalion in the process. It suffered no losses. By order of the corps, all serviceable tanks were placed under the operational control of the 16th Infantry Division (motorized). Three Tigers and six Panzer IIIs were sent. Oberleutnant Scherf led the unit. The Tigers remained until 15 January 1943 and the Panzer IIIs until 24 January 1943, where they took part in many operations. On 14 January the three Tigers were given the task of securing the withdrawal of the 16th Infantry Division (motorized) toward the west, three kilometers north of Nowo Ssadkowskij. On completion of that task, they were to proceed on their own to the company at Proletarskaja. Several bridges that were unable to bear the heavy weight of the Tigers prevented the Tigers from following the 16th Infantry Division (motorized). However, the six Panzer IIIs remained attached to that division.

All three Tigers had mechanical problems during the withdrawal and had to stand out on the steppe for up to thirty hours until they could be recovered. An icy storm blew up and the temperature dropped to 40 degrees Celsius below zero. No human being could withstand that temperature without frostbite. It was fortunate that the Russians did not pursue energetically.

The tanks that had dropped out, along with the remainder of the company at Ssungar, were ordered to pull back to Proletarskaja on 10 January. The Russians had already captured a portion of the former supply route, which complicated the movement. All of the equipment could be recovered. Provisionally drivable tanks towed the unserviceable vehicles. On 16 and 17 January, the elements that had been restored to serviceability were committed to a covering force mission at Stalinski-Pud. The damaged tanks that were in tow were brought to Ssalsk. By 20 January four Tigers and three Panzer IIIs had been loaded for transport to Rostow.

Tiger 200 broke through the ice in driving around a wooden bridge that was too weak to bear its weight. The recovery was not completed until 20 January and tied up six 18-ton prime movers and two Tigers that were urgently needed for evacuating the remainder of the damaged equipment. On 21 January the company crossed the bridge at Bataisk and was in Rostow on 22 January, where every bit of energy went into repairing the vehicles by the maintenance elements which had, in the meantime, been brought forward. The company heard the news about the end of the fighting at Stalingrad while at Rostow. It also learned it would be integrated into Tiger Tank Battalion 503 as its 3rd Company.

At the end of January, the enemy pressure increased daily on Rostow. At night the hard-pressed city was afflicted with aerial attacks. For those reasons Tiger Tank Battalion 503 moved to new and more dispersed billets. On 28 January 1943 the battalion commander was bid farewell. Oberstleutnant Hoheisel became the new commander.

Oberleutnant von Foerster took over temporary command of the 1st Company on 1 February, since Hauptmann Kaphengst returned to Germany by teletype order of OKH. One of the first orders of the new commander was to consolidate the remaining available tanks of the 1st Company with the other two companies. As a result, there were only two companies available and fit for action for the time being. In the meantime, Tiger Tank Battalion 503 had been placed under the operational control of the 23rd Panzer Division, which had the mission of holding Rostow for as long as possible.

In the course of the reorganization of the companies, Leutnants von Koerber and Jammerath (formerly of the 1st Company, Tiger Tank Battalion 503) each took over a light platoon of Panzer IIIs. On 7 January 1943 they were employed as security at the outskirts of Rostow. Two days later, Leutnant von Koerber was killed by a head wound

he received as he was rescuing wounded comrades from a Panzer III that belonged to his platoon and had been set afire. The 3rd Company was also committed on the western edge of Rostow on 8 February. From that point on, the 3rd Company participated in the heavy defensive fighting that was carried on with great intensity after the Russian breakthrough in the Donez basin.

The front was pulled back to the Mius, where the situation stabilized. The battalion moved to Prolowskoje, where it remained until 11 April 1943. After those operations, the Iron Cross, First Class was awarded to the following members of the company: Feldwebel Müller, Unteroffizier Wunderlich, Unteroffizier Miederer and Unteroffizier Gärtner. Heinrich Baschek and Alfred Brunswieck were killed on 21 February.

In the meantime, the Maintenance Company had moved to Mariupol and taken advantage of the period of relative calm to overhaul the equipment and restore the tanks to combat readiness. Hauptmann Lange was transferred to Germany on 12 March 1943. Oberleutnant Scherf took over the 3rd Company. Leutnant Weinert led the First Platoon and Leutnant von Rosen the Second Platoon.

After its first employment, which had cost the company heavy casualties—nine killed—the battalion was ordered to prepare for entraining.

CHAPTER 12

Recollections of a Panzer Soldier of the 1st Company

Dr. Franz-Wilhelm Lochmann

ORGANIZATION

The "chronicler" of this section belonged to a small group of very young tankers from the headquarters company of the 5th Panzer Replacement Battalion who were sent at the beginning of April 1942 to an intensive course for radio operators. The course was conducted by the communications officer, Oberleutnant Reichelt. The training schedule comprised nothing but training in radio practice and theory from morning until evening. Several hours a day were dedicated to practice in keyed communication.

At the end of the training, about half of the soldiers were assigned to radio-controlled tank units (Goliath). The training cadre and the remaining ten soldiers went to another building of the replacement battalion where Tiger Tank Battalion 503 was being organized under its first commander, Oberstleutnant Post. Oberleutnant Reichelt became the communications officer for the battalion. Oberfeldwebel Rebitzki and Unteroffizier S. formed the nucleus of the battalion's communications platoon. The tank radio operators were assigned to the 1st and 2nd Companies of Tiger Tank Battalion 503.

In the days that followed there was a beehive of activity. Soldiers steadily arrived from the 5th Panzer Replacement Battalion, but also from other garrisons in the Berlin area. In all, it was a mixture of trainees from replacement units, convalescents and recruits. The complement of com-

pany officers was already on hand. The officers checked on the men's skills in the various specialties and assigned them to the combat elements or to the trains, as appropriate. Most of the soldiers with combat experience came from the 5th and 6th Panzer Regiments. In 1943, contingents came from the 4th and 29th Panzer Regiments. I, myself, had long discussions with Leutnant Detlef von Koerber and, later, with Leutnant Meller. I then had to report briefly to Hauptmann Kaphengst, the company commander of the 503's 1st Company, and was then assigned as platoon leader's radio operator in the fourth platoon of the company.

We stayed at Neuruppin for three months. During that time, we heard rumors we were to be equipped with a new and completely unknown kind of tank. All that was clear was that the armament would probably be an 88mm gun. As far as equipment went, there were only a few wheeled elements during this period. The morning hours at Neuruppin were filled with tough infantry work in the field and tactical instruction.

Leutnant Oemler, platoon leader of the Second Platoon, took care of most of the infantry work. The instruction for the combat elements followed, by squads. It was conducted by the company officers; in my case, Leutnant Meller. In the afternoon there were always sports. They were led by Leutnant Detlef von Koerber. In addition, there was driving instruction, exercises for the wheeled units, and occasional firing practice on the "vibrating stand" with carbines. However, for those us who were radio operators there were repeated radio-net exercises in communicating with the Communications Platoon of the Headquarters Company. Armored vehicles such as the Maybach command vehicle were not available at that time, except for training exercises. We had no knowledge of the existence of Tigers until August of 1942.

On 10 August the battalion moved to the wooded area of the training grounds at Döllersheim (Austria). By then there was a Headquarters Company, a Maintenance Company and two tank companies, for which quite large company trains had been established.

From that point on, the training began on the Porsche Tiger. It was quite a tank, and it impressed me immediately. The two sides of the running gear were each driven by a separate gasoline engine, generator and electric motor. The vehicle drove like a street-car. The drives for the two sides of the running gear were separately started. Two levers governed forward and reverse direction, as well as the desired speed. The running gear seemed to us to be unquestionably superior to that of the Henschel Tiger that we later became familiar with. The 88mm gun was the last word for us.

The turret was set very far to the front, so that the driver and radio operator had no hatch above them. That meant that the entire crew usually had to enter and exit through the turret. It very quickly became clear to us that, in the event of trouble, the driver and radio operator had drawn very bad cards; although both had the possibility of also leaving the vehicle through escape hatches in the bottom. I got to know that tank relatively well, since I was continually doing radio-net exercises in it.

Unfortunately, the technology of that brilliantly designed tank had not yet developed to the point of being ready for serial production. Complications developed daily during our exercises. I particularly remember vehicles bogged down in difficult terrain and abundant engine fires.

During the weeks that followed, the maintenance sections and the drivers were continually detailed to duty at the factories. First they went to St. Valentin; later, predominantly Kassel and Friedrichshafen. The level of secrecy was so great

that I, myself, had no suspicion of the existence of a Henschel Tiger. While this was going on, the combat elements of the battalion moved to Putlos for live ammunition firing (Panzer IVs). We, who almost never got out of Döllersheim, learned only slowly that we probably would not be equipped with the Porsche Tiger.

At the beginning of December 1942, things went crazy. The first Henschel Tigers were delivered and portions of the combat elements accepted Panzer IIIs from Magdeburg. Now we got an idea of the planned organization of vehicles. The company had four platoons. The platoon leader and section leader (at that time one officer and one Feldwebel) were outfitted with a Tiger. Both had a Panzer III N with the 7.5 cm short-barrel gun. The company commander also had a Tiger. In addition, there was a light platoon with five Panzer III Ns. The leadership positions of the company were occupied as follows:

> Company Commander: Hauptmann
>   Kaphengst
> Light Platoon: Leutnant Jammerath
> First Platoon: Oberleutnant von Foerster
> Second Platoon: Leutnant Oemler
> Third Platoon: Leutnant Detlef von Koerber
> Fourth Platoon: Leutnant Meller

In all, the company had nine Tigers and thirteen Panzer IIIs. The light tanks didn't have skirts on either the turrets or the hull sides.

Shortly before Christmas the soldiers were totally confused. One knew the "time had come". Both tropical uniforms and winter gear were issued at different times. What did they have in mind for us? After we had been outfitted with winter coveralls, things suddenly happened on 21 December. We were ordered to Proletarskaja in the Kalmuck Steppes. We went by way of Brest, Kharkov and Rostow. The new weapons were to prove themselves in Russia.

MOVEMENT TO RUSSIA

Traveling by so-called *Blitztransport* [lightning train], we reached Gomel in the darkness. It was bitterly cold. The Tigers still had their rail-transport tracks mounted. From that point on, the Wehrmacht had reduced the former Russian wide-gauge railroad track system to the width of the European standard gauge. That conversion produced an increase in the distance between adjacent sets of tracks. Thus, the extremely wide Tigers could be transported on the Russian rail system with their full-sized march-tracks. Our Tiger crews had to exchange tracks on their vehicles for the first time. That turned out to be expecting the virtually impossible of the crews. In addition to their own inexperience, they were confronted with exasperating failures in planning. The march-tracks were not on the Ssyms railroad cars that transported the tanks, as would have made sense. Instead, they had been loaded in boxcars. It took tremendous amounts of time in the icy cold to get the tracks on the tanks. However, we learned quickly. Later, such a change of tracks would be no problem for us. In any case, it was clear to us that we would have no pause for rest there. We were committed immediately.

We reached Rostow. The tension grew. Whenever the train stopped, we had an opportunity to talk to other soldiers. We heard really bad things. Trains with men returning from leave and equipment and supplies were no longer advancing northeast toward Stalingrad. The Russians had encircled the city. Others came from the Caucasus. Everything was going in only one direction—to the rear. In the immense sector stretching from the encircled 6th Army in Stalingrad to the Caucasus, there were only a few German units. We met soldiers from the 17th and 23rd Panzer Divisions, the 16th Infantry Division (motorized) and the 5th SS Panzer Grenadier Division "Wiking."

The trains that rolled past us from the east were filled with fleeing Rumanians. They hung on the railroad cars like burrs. They wore remarkable, tall fur hats that reminded me of the busbies worn by the English soldiers of the guard. It made one think. The Italian and Hungarian formations were no longer able to hold their positions either. The situation grew increasingly uneasy. Will it turn out well!

We detrained at Proletarskaja and immediately proceeded to the Manytsch position. The first Tigers dropped out due to mechanical failure on that first road march. On New Year's Day, the crews that lacked vehicles pulled security between the tanks. The weather was still relatively mild. Snow had not yet fallen. There was only an unpleasant wind.

I stood watch in the night with Obergefreiter Leitzke, who was quite tall. We could not see the adjacent sentries. Leitzke philosophized about the war. It did not sound good: "How could our Führer attack Russia? What the Swedes and Napoleon could not do, he will not succeed at either."

Something resembling a kind of barn door emerged from the darkness in front of us. I poked Leitzke in the ribs. "What is that? Are the Russians pushing a truck at us?" That was what I was thinking. Then everything became clear. It was Kalmucks with a pair of camels. My greatcoat was much too large. I stepped on it continually. It was too heavy for me. I had a backache.

The follow-on transports reinforced our security at the Manytsch bridge. The Russians were still holding back. On 5 January things really started happening. We were continuously in action. There wasn't much sleep. In the meantime, it had also gotten very cold. Our first men were killed.

WESSELY

On 9 January we headed out into the steppes from Proletarskaja. We tanked up with fuel. Prepare for operations! The covers were removed from the machine guns and main guns. Everything was checked out one more time. Then the battalion rolled. A village emerged, far in front of us: Wessely! Cleared for combat! The radio was on. The battalion rolled to the east in inverted wedge formation; the light tanks leading, the Tigers following. A few enemy tanks moved out of the southern part of the village. To my total surprise, an "echelon right" was ordered. Leutnant Meller was cautious. He only traversed the turret a bit. The Russian tanks disappeared into a Balka [Editor's note: a defile, usually with a stream bed, which cut into the steppe] and were almost on our flank. The order came to open fire. Two or three T-34s were set alight immediately.

Then all hell broke loose. A vast number of antitank guns opened fire on us from the village. Right away, I could see one of our light tanks on fire in front of us. Then it was our turn! Our Tiger 141 was continuously pounded by impacts of various caliber. All the vehicles then halted. While I peered intently through the optics, something hit me like a knock-out blow. I fell back on the radio-operator's seat. I slowly regained consciousness. It was remarkably calm. Only occasional hits on our vehicle. I mechanically registered them as harmless small calibers. Then the Tiger was literally knocked to its knees. Aha: 7.62cm! Gradually I came to myself a bit and felt more secure. My God! This crate really couldn't be penetrated! But what was happening? I no longer heard the familiar noise of the intercom in my headphones. It dawned on me slowly. The electricity was out. I looked over at the driver. Unteroffizier Timpke lay collapsed in the driver's seat. He was pale and seemed totally lifeless. I stared at him in horror. At that instant he turned his head toward me. "Damn!" I thought, "We've got to do something!" Then I got an idea: The fuses! Carefully, we opened the covers of the fuse boxes. All of the fuses fell out. I put them back in place. The intercom worked again. Timpke tried the starter. The Tiger fired up. Then we were told to pull back. The battalion attack had failed. We rallied about two kilometers outside the village. We looked over Tiger 141. In addition to many 7.62cm hits, our vehicle was badly damaged by smaller caliber hits and, especially, by high-explosive rounds.

The exterior looked completely bare. Neither axe nor tow cable were there. The track guards and the antenna were gone. I found a 7.62cm hit in the ball-mount of my machine gun. The armor plate around the ball mount was torn in a star-shaped pattern. That explained why I was knocked out! That same day the vehicle went back to Proletarskaja and was displayed for Oberst Thomale. It was then loaded for shipment back to Germany. On the next day I ran into my comrade from Hamburg, Herbert Ritscher, at the maintenance facility. He told us about his Panzer III being knocked out at Wessely. His commander, the likeable Unteroffizier Scheele, had been killed. Herbert had tears in his eyes. With circumspection, he let me know that my platoon leader, Leutnant Meller, had also been killed in the second assault on Wessely. I was totally done in; somehow I was unable to comprehend it all.

Two Panzer IIs of the 5th SS Division "Wiking" stopped beside us. They had a third vehicle in tow. They had a dead man with them and two wounded. They stared at our tank in amazement. "What a life-insurance policy!" they said. I came back to myself and cracked a joke: "We also don't get a pay-bonus for service at the front!"

The SS men reported on their action. They had been in an attack on a village on the steppe. They thought it was Wessely. "You can't approach it during the day. We did it at night. We moved around the village and got interspersed in the Russian columns. We then stirred things up inside the village."

Was that really Wessely? We still had a lot to learn!

A little later, our commander, Oberstleutnant Post, was replaced by Oberstleutnant Hoheisel. At the same time, our company commander, Hauptmann Kaphengst, was transferred to the OKH and Oberleutnant von Foerster took over the 503's 1st Company. The battalion moved to Rostow.

A short period of apparent calm set in, if one disregarded the Russian bombing attacks. The company commander let the specialists keep the company busy. There were formations and practical jokes. The company commander's radio operator, Unteroffizier Matthies, went to officer candidate school. Later, he became communications officer in the 500th Panzer Replacement Battalion at Paderborn.

I became the company commander's radio operator. Politely and a bit self-consciously, I checked in with the crew. Pan Vogel was the gunner; Walter Martach the driver. Walter was an Unteroffizier and former driver for the battalion commander. Wolfgang Speckin—nicknamed Specker—completed the crew as the loader. Walter Martach told me how things went. "And when everything turns to shit, or you have problems, then you come to me. You can always feel free to talk to Uncle Walter." I was happy and proud to be accepted by such a crew. I then participated in the initial defensive fighting for the city in Tiger 101, the commander's tank.

A few days later the "Great Mufti"—pardon me, our company commander—made his 111 the command tank. I had to transfer over and we rolled back into action.

During that period the tanks of the company were apportioned, in part, to the 2nd Company and, in part, to the 3rd Company. The former 2nd Company, Tiger Tank Battalion 502, coming from Fallingbostel, had been attached to Heeresgruppe Don. That company had detrained at Proletarskaja. It was then attached to the 17th Panzer Division and was employed in the Kuberle sector. It was then consolidated with our battalion as the 3rd Company, Tiger Tank Battalion 503. That made us the first fully outfitted Tiger battalion to see action. Tiger 111 was assigned to other groups attached to the companies. The commander was Unteroffizier Günter Tessmer. We pulled security on the outskirts of Rostow.

WE DESTROY A RUSSIAN BATTERY

Tiger 111 occupied a good position on a sandy ridge. Below us was the Don; the landscape on the other side was flat. Snow lay in between. We watched the Russians as they brought four heavy artillery pieces into position on the other side. Trucks brought up ammunition. The ammunition was piled beside the guns. Our gunner, Bieske, was squirming in his seat, but Gènter Tessmer held back: "Wait a bit; the payoff will be greater."

Suddenly a Russian scout car appeared, moving across our front and approaching the battery. Bieske no longer waited for the commander's order. The range was extreme. He had set the optics as far out as it would go. The high-explosive round howled on its way. The shell impacted, but way too short. The deflection was perfect. The round was at least 400 meters short. Our gunner was an artist. The second round wiped out the scout car. And it went on. One after another, the four guns were hit by our high-explosive rounds. The ammunition burned.

I got along well with this crew, too. Günter Tessmer was a very calm and level-headed commander. Bieske was an outstanding gunner, but terribly nervous. Our loader, Heinz Mundry, who was one of the fastest I have ever seen, was much too slow for Bieske's temperament. The two were always shouting at each other in combat. It was a good thing that Günter Tessmer always remained calm during it all. From time to time, he leaned forward, grabbed the gunner and loader and knocked their heads together. Then things would go smoothly for a while. Our driver, Unteroffizier Otto Mewes, was also a master of his trade, but he could not resist giving a running commentary during engagements.

The next day there was a problem with a tank from the 2nd Company during a local attack. The radio was transmitting and the operator had turned on the intercom. That messed up the frequency and made it a nearly impossible to control the other vehicles in the fighting. I swore to myself I would never let that happen, even if the tank were burning up.

SAPATNI

It was now 9 February 1943. I was still in Tiger 111 and Unteroffizier Tessmer was our tank commander. The Russians had penetrated into Rostow from several sides. We moved to relieve Sapatni.

Two light tanks under Leutnant Detlef von Koerber failed to come back out of Sapatni again. All we could learn over the radio was that one of them was on fire and that the lieutenant had been killed. We started the attack, rapidly reaching the central square. We drove in the middle, as lead tank. Behind us, Oberfeldwebel B. secured the entrance to the square. He still had a few light tanks available behind him. We were greeted with aggressive fire from the Russian antitank rifles. Under those circumstances, it would have been lethal for the light tanks to advance.

There were two bundles of furs on the rear deck of our tank. Tracer ammunition set them on fire. The flames were drawn into the engine compartment and into the hull of the tank by the engine air intake. A fire developed. Since the houses surrounding the square were heavily occupied by Russian infantry and our own infantry was not available, we asked Oberfeldwebel B. to move forward to where we were to give us cover so we could get rid of the furs. But the Oberfeldwebel only radioed: "It is not your tank that is on fire, only the furs." When the Oberfeldwebel finally ordered the light tanks to move forward to our location, that was too much for us: "Light tanks halt! That's insane!" While I again asked the Oberfeldwebel for help, our loader, Heinz Mundry, was already outside and disposed of the furs. He was lucky and got away with it.

After the vehicle fire had been put out, the Oberfeldwebel ordered us to advance further into the village by ourselves. While we were doing that he would secure the empty square. Yeah, he had it hard. He had to bear all that responsibility! Slowly and cautiously we moved farther into the village, following the main street to the right. We were all alone in the midst of the Russians. Suddenly, as the nose of our tank approached a side street, I saw it—an antitank gun! It was only a few meters away from us. "Otto, move right!" And then it happened—Bieske's high-explosive round hit home. Otto couldn't control himself, he drove right over the antitank gun. Then we got back to our original direction and continued forward. After a 100 meters we discovered what had happened to our light tanks. We were right in front of them. Russian infantry swarmed everywhere. One of the light tanks was burnt out. The second had broken tracks. We saw three dead crew members. There was nothing to be done there. We reported the situation and were ordered back.

That evening we were supplied by the 3rd Company. Spieß Rondorf came forward. What a difference in the service we got compared to our functionaries! We were given the best of food. The fuel truck pumped the fuel into our tanks. The ammunition vehicle crew passed the shells into our turret. The machine gun ammunition was already belted. My God, were we pampered!

SARTANA

At that point there were only small battle groups employed. One after another, the companies were moved to Sartana near Mariupol. Spieß Nega acted insane. Shaves and haircuts were constantly inspected. In addition, there were weapons and uniform inspections. To vent our feelings we prepared a company fest where we could let out all our frustrations. Our old songs had become obsolete. For example:

> The weekend and sunshine,
> and we're alone at Döllersheim.
> What more do you need to be happy.
> Once upon a time at Neuruppin,
> We all got to go to Berlin.
> Now the Spieß's off to Vienna by himself
> and we are all allowed to go to Göpfritz.

We had new material. Our sick Tigers were the main theme:

> Engine cover off, engine cover on.
> That's our very favorite song.
> Tanks to the front, tanks to the rear.
> Early in the morning or late into the night.
> Do you have some free time?
> Then you can lift the rounds up.
> No need to wait.
> Engine cover off, engine cover on,
> That's our very favorite song.
> Tanks to the front, tanks to the rear.
> Early in the morning or late into the night.

Or . . .

> Our Tigers go "klipp-klapp,"
> as the road wheels take off every few meters.
> The torsion bars broke; it was a magnificent sight.
> And everything was fixed in Rostow.
> It was a rip-roaring company fest, and the
> alcohol flowed in streams.

The tank crews took advantage of the time and puttered around their vehicles. Tiger 111 also had a bit that needed looking after. Since the maintenance section could not fix the damage on its own, we drove to the maintenance facility at Mariupol. Our tank was overhauled in the Ilytsch Works. The crew had to stand guard day and night. It was cold. We built stoves in the corners of the great halls out of 200-liter fuel drums. Someone swiped my pistol. Now it was my turn!

From Mariupol we then drove Tiger 111 to Pokrowkoje on the Mius. It was mainly our light tanks that had been in action in that sector. First and foremost were Leutnant Linser and Leutnant Cüsow who, along with other formations, had smashed a Russian mechanized corps. During those engagements, one of our light tanks broke through the ice on the Mius. We did not find the commander, Unteroffizier Dunkel. Obergefreiter Gronau, Gefreiter Wolfgang Schult and Panzerschütze Großman were laid to rest in the military cemetery at Pokrowskoje. The gunner was the only one who had been able to save himself.

At night, when it was quiet, we heard the Russian loudspeakers calling on us to defect. I was totally infested with lice. I cleaned my uniform in a bucket of gasoline and, in the first spring sunshine of March, I took a full bath in front of our billets. As a result of that, I had to report to my company commander in steel helmet and got the obligatory three days confinement to quarters. I was confined for three days in a Russian hovel and had enough time to hunt out the rest of the lice.

CHAPTER 13

Diary Entries of Leutnant von Koerber, Platoon Leader of the 1st Company (1 January to 7 February 1943)

Detlev von Koerber

Introduction: Our heavy tank company had been formed at the beginning of May at Neuruppin. It was transferred at the beginning of August to the troop training grounds at Döllersheim, 100 kilometers north of Vienna. The entire battalion followed. The company command consisted of the commander, Hauptmann Kaphengst and the company officers, Oberleutnant von Foerster, Leutnant von Koerber, Leutnant Meller and Leutnant Jammerath. The company first sergeant was Hauptfeldwebel Schmitz.

At Döllersheim, where we stayed for nearly five months, a colorfully assembled group became a unit. Hours of training, terrain exercises, road marches by the trains, sports and fests gradually welded us together. Details to the factories at St. Valentin and, later, to Kassel and Friedrichshafen, as well as a trip by the tank platoons to Putlos for firing practice also played their part.

In September, the 1st Company received the Porsche Tigers with the 88mm main gun, the first unit in Germany to do so. That started intensive training for the drivers and the entire crews. Unfortunately, the Porsche Tigers still had too many teething problems from a technical standpoint. Thus, in November, we suddenly converted

to Henschel Tigers and—after a short "African" episode, during which we had to prepare for tropical service—we then had to prepare for Russia in a single week. In four rail loads—21, 22, 23 and 24 December—the company rolled to the Eastern Front, happy to finally be on its way.

1 January: New Year's Day! Our battalion and, with it, our company were rolling East (Göpfritz-Lundenburg-Oderberg-Deblin-Brest-Minsk-Gomel-Kharkov-Slawjansk-Rostow-Proletarskaya). A portion had already arrived at its destination and unloaded. The advance party, formed from our company (Oberleutnant von Foerster), arrived simultaneously with the first train. For the New Year, Oberleutnant von Foerster, who had already met with Generaloberst Hoth, had already taken over security of the Manytsch sector (two bridges). Each arriving train transport reinforced it.

The company commander arrived in the evening with the third train at Proletarskaja. It immediately unloaded and moved out (in the process, the first Tiger—133—dropped out with engine problems!)

2 January: The security force at the Manytsch bridges kept getting stronger. The company and the battalion were in the village of Manytsch.

Together with elements of the Luftwaffe Field Division, Covering Force Post [*Sicherungsgruppe Post*] was formed under our commander, Oberstleutnant Post. It provided security toward the Kalmuck steppes to the east. An advanced security detachment was sent out to the east beyond the bridge security with a section of tanks and a platoon of Luftwaffe infantry under Leutnant von Koerber.

The winter got off to a good start. The temperatures were bearable, hovering right around the freezing point, but an icy wind (up to force ten) forced the tank crews, housed in their home made earthen bunkers, to don winter clothing. Livestock was slaughtered and everyone was cooking. Technical problems were attended to. The last transport arrived.

3 January: The battalion moved forward to Proletarskaja, where the 2nd Company had already arrived. Our company again secured at the Manytsch. All sorts of Sunday roasts simmered in diverse pans. There was a lot of housekeeping, the billets were improved and pressing work done on the vehicles. Repeated commanders conferences with the battalion commander, who discussed the overall situation in the sector of the 4th Panzer Army. It was intended for us to fend off the Russian attack at this location (if they advanced that far). The Russians were streaming through the gaps created by the fleeing Rumanians. From here we would initiate the counterattack towards Stalingrad as soon as enough forces had assembled. A variety of rules for conduct and orders went round.

4 January: All sorts of inspections, necessary repairs to the tank and such. Lots of roast geese prepared for the company. Our quarters had become quite homey. Missing equipment, replacement parts and tools continued to arrive. Unfortunately, only a portion of what was needed. The order came from the battalion that afternoon that by noon of the following day everything would have to be ready to move. By evening the order was changed so that march readiness was to be established by 0900 hours. As a result, the pace of work and preparation reached fever pitch. For several tanks, trucks and other wheeled vehicles there were suddenly maintenance problems. But everything was ready in time. Indeed, for most of us, it was even possible to get a little sleep.

5 January: We started from Manytsch at 0500 hours. Beyond the bridge, the security elements integrated themselves among the line units. The march continued through Proletarskaja, from which the 2nd Company had departed an hour and a half earlier. It continued south to its first engagement. The trains remained at Proletarskaja under Leutnant Jammerath. The 2nd Company, which was the lead company, took the first Russian prisoners, ran into strong enemy resistance outside of Nikolajewski and had its first losses (one Panzer III and two killed). We did not yet get into the fight. The battalion withdrew a bit and set up a hedgehog in the village of Krasnij Skotorot where, in the course of the evening, a battalion of panzer grenadiers (2nd Battalion, 126th Panzer Grenadier Regiment) arrived by way of reinforcement. It was cold, and a very sharp southeast wind was especially vile. The supply unit was brought forward in the evening and everything was refueled. Two Tigers and one Panzer III had to go to the maintenance facility because of mechanical problems along the way.

6 January: Awoke at 0430 hours, all the tanks of the battalion moved out at 0500 hours in a wild snow squall. Enemy tanks had been reported. The mission of the 1st Company was to attack and take the village of Konartal from the front while orienting on the right side of the road. The 2nd Company enveloped the village from the left. In spite of the poor visibility due to the weather, that first operation was quite successful for us: nine Russian T-34 tanks, one T-60 tank, one armored car and five guns were destroyed. The village was taken by storm and the fleeing Russians pursued and scattered as far as the Ssalonka ravine (Leutnant Oemler's platoon) until the fuel situation forced him to turn back. Unfortunately, the commander of Tiger 100, Unteroffizier Bleß, was killed during the attack while bailing out after an artillery hit. Three men were wounded. In spite of many hits, there were no total losses of tanks, though there were dropouts due to mechanical problems. The 2nd Company had heavier losses. After refueling and resupplying with ammunition at Nikolajewski, the battalion formed a hedgehog for the night two kilometers to the east at Stepnoje. The supply units came forward.

7 January: Leutnant von Koerber moved out during the night on orders from the battalion. He had two Tigers (one of which, however, dropped out after traveling a few kilometers toward Stawropol and had to be recovered in the morning) and four Panzer IIIs from the battalion's Light Platoon (Leutnant Cüsow) . Its mission was to block the lines of communication for a Russian withdrawal at Lake Goloje.

After difficulty in orienting itself in the morning dawn, the unit succeeded in destroying several enemy trucks and bringing back eighteen prisoners. However, the pursuit of enemy vehicles to the high ground east of Lake Goloje ran into such strong enemy defense—antitank guns, artillery and Russian tanks—that it had to pull back. The battalion, which was following von Koerber's group during the morning hours and which had been joined by the division commander, could not attack the heights. It pulled back to Stepnoje in order to spend the night. It hedgehogged in the old positions and took care of all sorts of mechanical problems and refueling. The company had only ten tanks still in service. The others were in the maintenance facility.

8. January: At 0500 hours in the morning, the battalion moved out—the 1st Company in the lead—back to Proletarskaja again, where warm billets in permanent structures were occupied. All the tank commanders were assembled to meet with the commander of the 4th Panzer Army, Generaloberst Hoth, at 1030 hours in the morning. Generaloberst Hoth spoke of his appreciation for the battalion and of impending missions of great importance. (The battalion had been mentioned in the Wehrmachtbericht the previous day.) In the afternoon we conducted motor stables (armored and wheeled elements). After that, the men all had another opportunity to properly wash up, get their affairs in order and write home, all of which was really necessary. After our billets had been set up to our comfort and everything had quieted down, the company commander came back from the battalion at 2230 hours with an alert message: Get ready to move out immediately! One hour later, the company minus the trains was on the move back to Krasnyj Skotorot with ten tanks, including six Tigers. Hauptmann Schmidt was detailed to the company that day.

9 January: (I remained at Proletarskaja as officer reserve and "overseer," since Tiger 131 was in the maintenance facility.) After a three-hour march, the battalion got to Krasnyj Skotorot, where it refueled. At about 0630 hours it mounted the attack on Wesselij from there. Bad orientation by the battalion staff! The battalion was turned

along the defensive positions of the village when the place was finally found. As a result, Tiger 144 was knocked out, although without casualties. The 2nd Battalion, 126th Rifle Regiment, failed to advance. After the 2nd Company had also lost some tanks, the battalion withdrew after knocking out three Russian tanks. The company moved under the leadership of Oberleutnant von Foerster while Hauptmann von Kaphengst arranged for supplies in Krasnyj Skotorot. Leutnant Oemler was then committed with five tanks against Wesselij. He was able to get close to the village but not into it. Leutnant Meller was severely wounded and died that very night in Proletarskaja. Therefore, back again to Krasnyj Skotorot, where the riflemen had remained. During the move back Unteroffizier Scheele was wounded. While that was going on, Hauptmann von Kaphengst arranged for the return of the battalion to Proletarskaja. The vehicles gradually arrived there, the last getting in by 2400 hours.

10 January: Again, no chance to sleep one's fill. The mission-capable tanks of the battalion were advanced towards Budenowskaja to stop an enemy advance. (Ambush!) The company commander moved out with the combat elements, the section leaders and several supply vehicles at about 0600 hours, while the rest of the trains remained in quarters at Proletarskaja, near the railroad station. That day, the combat elements did not see action. (There were actually only two Tigers and three Panzer IIIs from our company and two Tigers and two Panzer IIIs from the 2nd Company, Tiger Tank Battalion 502.) The combat elements returned to its billets area at about 2130 hours, where everything rapidly calmed down.

The new battalion operations order arrived during the night for the next day, for which three Tigers and four Panzer IIIs were ready for action.

The decision was made in the maintenance facility to send Tigers 121 and 141 back to Germany. They could not be repaired there due to damage caused by the enemy.

January 11: Early in the morning the battalion's combat elements (our contribution still consisting of two Tigers and three Panzer IIIs) headed north to Romanow. They were led by the battalion commander and once again contained the maintenance sections. Late in the afternoon, a counterattack was launched against the village of Nikolajewski from the west. That time things went well; all branches worked together well: Stukas, artillery, Nebelwerfer, Sturmgeschütze, SS riflemen and us! The attack succeeded for us without losses and we destroyed heavy enemy opposition. Even mechanical problems remained within normal limits and were promptly taken care of by the maintenance services. After temporarily providing cover there the combat elements returned to Proletarskaja at 2100 hours—in a first-class mood. After brief food and drink, came the necessary rest, while the maintenance crews worked through the night to put the tanks back in shape.

12 January: A day of rest. All units of the company were billeted at the former site (school) at the railroad station. Everything was checked out and put in order. At 1020 hours, in biting cold, the burial of Leutnant Karl Meller was carried out at the Proletarskaja Military Cemetery. The service was organized by Leutnant von Koerber; the fourth platoon provided a squad as honor guard. All of the officers of the battalion were there. The company commander spoke first, then the battalion commander. At 1130 hours Oberst Thomale from the FÅhrerhauptquartier spoke to the combat elements of the battalion regarding our mission and great responsibility.

In the evening the company commander held a company formation, where all pressing and important affairs were discussed. Praise and blame. After that, *Marketenderwaren* [roughly equivalent to American PX items, referred to as "personal demand items," but handled through the Spieß] were distributed. Most everyone was tipsy. Calm, except for individual bombs that fell nearby during the night.

13 January: Still in the billets area. Preparations for combat readiness and maintenance. At noon, Leutnant von Koerber was given a scouting mission from the battalion regarding bridges at Nowy Manytsch and Barraniki for Battle Group Heilmann, which set out at 1300 hours with three Tigers and six Panzer IIIs. The battle group reached Jekaterinowka that evening. The divisional commander was already there. An attack was prepared against two Russian battalions that had infiltrated over the Manytsch east of Barraniki. The crews (under command of Leutnant von Koerber, who had already returned) rested or pulled security in the village.

The remainder of the company continued in policing and maintenance work. Biting east wind, intense cold.

14 January: The tanks of Battle Group Heilmann reached Nowy Manytsch in the gray light of dawn after a night march. While the battalion's five Tigers were given the task of securing the village (against scattered Russian units!), all of the Panzer IIIs crossed the bridge to Baraniki. They fought there, along with riflemen from the division, against Russian units that had already penetrated that far. Unteroffizier Jochen Griewaldt was shot in the head and killed during the fighting in the village. The fight ended successfully (but with few results!) as night fell. The Tigers withdrew almost sixty kilometers (!) under Leutnant von Koerber. During the night, all of the Panzer IIIs also returned to the billets area where the rest of the company had remained.

Tiger 113 slid off an embankment into the marshy ground in the dark shortly before reaching its destination. It was only after much work with the battalion engineer platoon and seven prime movers that it could be pulled out at 1000 hours the following morning.

15. January: The company combat elements had to move out early again with two Tigers and six Panzer IIIs (under Leutnant Jammerath). Along with the rest of the battalion—Battle Group Kaphengst—and units of the 5th SS Panzer Grenadier Division "Wiking," the company attacked a collective farm on the road ten kilometers east of Proletarskaja. It cleaned up the farm in tough fighting until there were only small remnants of the enemy left. Only a few mechanical problems; no losses. Everyone returned to quarters in the evening—very important to warm up, since Siberian cold and wind ruled outside!

The maintenance sections have completed their work in the meantime.

Unteroffizier Meinert, the supply sergeant, was removed from his position because of negligence of duty. Feldwebel Hübner replaced him for the time being.

16 January: Things gradually heated up in Proletarskaja, our once so peaceful billeting area. Enemy artillery shelled it and it was bombed. More and more troop elements were withdrawn. Schwere Panzer-Abteilung 503 and the 5th SS Panzer Grenadier Division "Wiking" covered the retreat, for which purpose the first platoon under Leutnant Jammerath was pre-positioned at the eastern outskirts of the city. Immobile Tigers were towed over the Manytsch toward Ssalsk. Since an irreparable Tiger of the 2nd Company had to be destroyed at

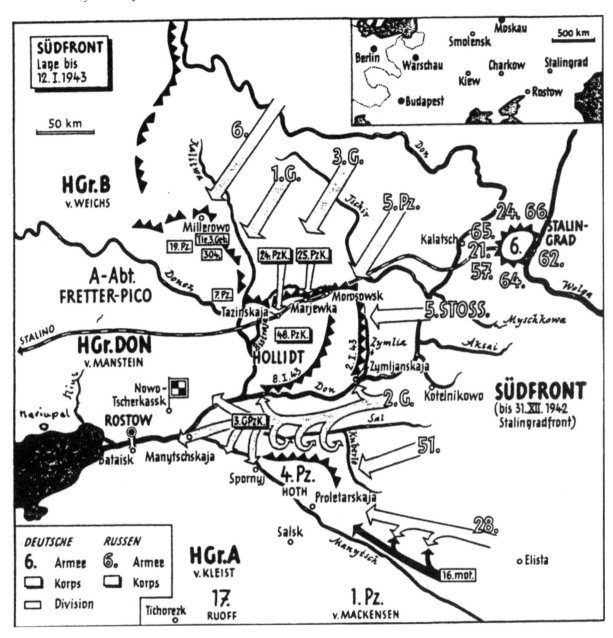

the railroad station, we had to clear out of our quarters at the school and move further into the city into the large building of the former hospital. We set up our new billets. Leutnant Oemler was sent ahead with the greater part of the trains to recon for new billeting areas on the other side of the Manytsch. By order of the battalion, Leutnant von Koerber scouted the river crossings—difficult due to snow and ice! Repair and maintenance work ran far into the night; tea with rum in the evening, then, soon, deep sleep, even though our own artillery (heavy field howitzers) opened fire outside our door and enemy bombs fell.

17 January: Sunday. We still held the place. The rest of the trains was sent back early. Leut-

nant Jammerath's covering force platoon (in radio contact with the company) exchanged fire from the outskirts of the city with enemy attacking from the direction of Krassny Skotorot. It knocked out a Russian scout car. The company's new quarters proved short lived, as the roof started burning around noon. It could not be extinguished, so we had to move out slowly. Since the order arrived to move out at nightfall, no new quarters were sought. On battalion orders, Leutnant von Koerber moved by motorcycle to Stalinskij Ret to the 2nd Company, bringing it the order to pull out. Finally, by 1600 hours, Tiger Tank Battalion 503 left Proletarskaja, where it had once arrived with such high hopes. The combat units broke contact with the enemy, crossed the Manytsch by 1745 hours and, after a four-hour march, arrived at Budennoje (the state-owned estate of Marshall Budenny). The entire battalion found quarters in a large, hopelessly overfilled building.

18 January: After a good, if brief, sleep, everything was untangled again and put in order during the morning. Mechanical problems in the vehicles were fixed, weapons cleaned and so forth. Hauptmann Schmidt, who had been temporarily detailed to us—he was a mountain trooper—went back to the corps headquarters, where he became the intelligence officer. Then our quarters were cleaned (the previous occupants had been Rumanians!). Rooms were assigned to us, and we set up for the long haul. The consequence of all that was that the order arrived that afternoon from the army headquarters for us to move out the next morning and pull back further to the west! In the evening, Leutnant Oemler, with one platoon of Panzer IIIs (four vehicles), was detailed to provide security for the divisional staff. During the night and the following morning, sometimes alone, sometimes in conjunction with SS Panzer Grenadier Regiment "Nordland," he and his platoon had two intense engagements at Jekaterinowka, during which Panzer III 134 took an antitank rifle hit in its ammunition storage and burnt out. The tank commander, Unteroffizier Dürrlich, and the loader, Gefreiter Buck, were killed; the gunner, Gefreiter Schato, was wounded.

19 January: Early in the morning, at 0500 hours, the entire battalion got moving. The companies drove in close order. The tanks helped clear the way through the snowdrifts. It was a long and difficult march as far as Ssalsk, from where the wheeled units then preceded the tracked vehicles. The march continued to Zelina and beyond. The "priority route"—along which everything withdrew to the rear, in orderly fashion!—was completely jammed with columns as far as Jegorlikskaja, a totally overcrowded hole in the wall. It was good that the Russian air force put in so few appearances, quite in contrast to our own! Leutnant von Koerber's advance party had already set up a provisional billeting area there. Late and tired, but with no one missing, the company elements arrived there. By the early morning everyone had found at least a few hours of sleep.

20 January: We started out between 0500 and 0600 hours in two march groups (tanks and wheeled elements, then the leadership elements and the commanders of the 1st Company, Tiger Tank Battalion 503, and of the 2nd Company, Tiger Tank Battalion 502). The advance party was led by Stabsfunkmeister Nega (?). He was serving as the field first sergeant. There was a lot that had to be towed—especially tanks—that was quite difficult to do given the jammed roads, weak bridges and occasional steep inclines. Thank God that the steppe was mostly level and, accordingly, the road's width was a matter of preference. In addition, we were blessed with mild winter weather. By noon we had made twenty-five kilometers to Metschedinskaja, and then again as far to Kayalnickaja. There the company benefited from a rations depot that had to be cleared out. It "procured" marmalade, meat, hard fruit candies, and cooking oil, among other things. While that was happening, the Panzer IIIs that had been detailed from Leutnant Oemler's platoon (down to three tanks) arrived and took their place in the column. A great mass was flowing to the rear, including great herds of horses and cattle, but we made more-or-less good progress. Then in quarters in K. (individual houses). *Marketenderwaren* were sold and rum issued. Fuel in short supply. Rest.

21 January: We were off quite early, at 0440 hours, in fog and damp cold. The battalion formed five march groups (with the battalion commander leading the advance party!). The route led twenty-five kilometers farther to Bataisk over terrible roads. We arrived there about noon without losses. We were shown to our quarters and settled in (an entire block lined with houses for the company). Further distribution of Marketenderwaren. Everyone washed themselves and their underclothes thoroughly, for once. The first lice were reported in the company—and killed! Unfortunately, there was still no mail for us, but everyone used the free time to briefly write home.

The maintenance section worked through the evening, attending to various mechanical problems. Otherwise, it was soon quiet.

22 January: Off early in two march groups (wheeled units under Heilmann, armored vehicles led by von Kaphengst), but we could only slowly work our way into the traffic columns on the main road through Bataisk. Then on to Rostow. Between 1200 and 1800 hours, the 1st Company gradually crossed the valley of the Don and the river itself with the battalion over long causeways and bridges (especially difficult for Tigers). It reached the city and went into a previously scouted billeting area in a large school at the outskirts of the city near the railroad station. The 2nd Company and the headquarters Company were also billeted there. The Maintenance Company established itself nearby in several large production halls of the "Rostow Works" (empty and partially destroyed).

The weather was pleasantly mild. The dilapidated quarters first had to be cleaned and then made livable and heated.

On the Don bridges, we encountered the 11th Panzer Division (Sagan), which was covering the enemy.

23 January: Finally we got an opportunity to sleep until 0700 hours. Then a fundamental cleaning and arranging of the quarters. The vehicles were inspected; all of the tanks went to the maintenance facility for that. All of the immobile tanks trickled in there, either towed behind the prime movers of the Recovery Platoon or transported by rail through Ssalsk. On battalion orders, Leutnant von Koerber again went to Bataisk with a Volkswagen to find and direct the units that were trickling in.

The weather kept getting milder—thaw weather!

The official routine returned in full force, with training schedules, delegation of responsibilities and all the attendant official nonsense!

24 January: More repair and maintenance on all of the vehicles. Every day the tank crews were at the maintenance facility in the morning, returning in the evening. There was a lot of work and there was no break for Sundays. That morning, in wild and rainy weather, our two dead whom we had brought with us, Unteroffizier Griewaldt and Gefreiter Buck, were buried at the military cemetery. A Wehrmacht chaplain said a few words and, in closing, Leutnant von Koerber spoke briefly for the company.

There were several theater and movie passes for the company, which, of course, were a great hit. The company had not been allowed on pass up to that point in time; up to then it hadn't mattered.

25 January: As on the previous days, maintenance and repair duties, complicated by a sudden savage outbreak of cold—within three hours the temperature dropped by almost 30 degrees Cel-

sius! The maintenance sections worked as a group almost constantly on the tanks in the maintenance facility, but it still went very slowly. There was a lot of pressure from above, particularly given the critical overall situation.

In the afternoon, at 1600 hours, all of the officers were assembled at the battalion. We got a new commander (thank God!)—Oberstleutnant Hoheisel—who briefly introduced himself. He made a very energetic impression.

In the evening, the company finally got its first mail from home, about fourteen days old. Hopefully that will function better from now on.

26 January: Maintenance duty and work by the maintenance sections on the vehicles in the billeting areas. A lot of sentries were posted, especially at the Rostow-Works to protect the maintenance facility. Company briefing by the company commander at midday in our quarters. He discussed the general situation and awarded the first *Panzerkampfabzeichen* [armored combat badge, awarded to members of armored units after three separate armored engagements]. Attendance at movies and theater was interfered with early: The "Ivan on duty" arrived right after darkness fell and dropped his bombs!

The combat elements were reorganized based on the changed vehicle situation: Company headquarters section, a light platoon with five Panzer IIIs and two heavy tank platoons, each with three Panzer VIs.

There were no rations on 26 January since the truck had not arrived with them. Was that due to the Russians . . . ? Soon things settled down, at least, if there was not a maintenance detail.

27 January: Work at the maintenance facility was pushed hard, day and night in two shifts of six hours for each of us. The mechanics and the crews were with the Tigers, getting them ready for action again. It was very important, especially for the time consuming work on the running gear and with the extremely heavy demands that were being made on the maintenance facility itself at that time. Things took their course. Two vehicles were done, completely checked and repaired. Then the others were taken in hand.

On orders from above, the battalion organized an alert company with the combat vehicles that were ready. It was led by Hauptmann Lange (2nd Company, Tiger Tank Battalion 502) whom the commander wasted no time in putting through his paces. Our contribution consisted of two Tigers and four Panzer IIIs led by Leutnant Jammerath. Russian bombs fell close to the school during the night. Windows and, in some places, walls were destroyed, so it immediately got very cold. For two and a half hours the company moved from our second story down to the ground floor and waited for morning in the orderly room of the Headquarters Company.

28 January: This situation of having three companies in one building was untenable. Ivan was not to be trusted. This day's bombs caused fifteen casualties and a great deal of damage to the 2nd Battalion, 15th Panzer Regiment, which was only 200 meters from us. Therefore we moved to a new billeting area. It was farther from the maintenance facility, to be sure, but there were friendly people and clean quarters. It was at the outskirts of town in a group of widely-separated houses, approximately one crew per house. Leutnant von Koerber had scouted out the area.

In the evening, all of the officers assembled at the battalion command post for the assumption of command of the battalion by Oberstleutnant Hoheisel and the departure of Oberstleutnant Post. There was a short conference there. Back at the billets, Leutnant von Koerber received the first Iron Cross, Second Class from the company commander. Two more were awarded to Unteroffizier Tessmer and Panzerschütze Vogel. Our nighttime peace was undisturbed.

29 January: After settling into the new quarters, the normal duties resumed, particularly work on the vehicles. Our company commander had his birthday. Stabsfunkmeister Nega presented best wishes in the name of all the company at noon. He had also set up a nice little table with presents laid out on it.

The alert company—our portion under Leutnant Jammerath—remained in our former quarters at the school. It had not yet seen action.

In the evening, we celebrated our company commander's birthday with invited guests (the other company commanders) and the company officers. The company received tea with rum.

30 January: Normal duties. The fuel situation was tight. Continuation of many sentry and work parties. Göring gave a speech on 30 January, which was listened to by some. General situation unchanged. We will probably go into action in the general line of defense east of Rostow, for the for-

mation of which our comrades in Stalingrad were sacrificed. For the time being, we saw little of the war other than the nightly three or four bombs, which dropped more-or-less close to us. Mail came fairly regularly and quickly and one gradually became a human again.

In the meantime, the entire battalion was placed under the operational control of the 11th Panzer Division.

31 January: The pleasant life seemed too much for some people to bear. Inspection of quarters turned up all sorts of slackness, so that punishments and disciplinary sentry duty were called for. Also painful for the idlers were repeated inspections and exclusion from being able to purchase *Marketenderwaren*. Along with that, the repair and maintenance work continued. Missing replacement parts that were not available from our Maintenance Company were obtained by cannibalizing from the army transportation motor pool [*Heereskraftfahrpark*]. There was a lot of work.

1 February: Starting early in the morning, there was concentrated motor stables for all of the company vehicles—wheeled units and available tanks—in the open square. It was intended to get them inspection-ready. Weapons cleaning and inspection were emphasized.

In the afternoon, the officers of the battalion went to a conference which, however, did not take place. Our commander, Hauptmann von Kaphengst, received a teletype from the OKH summoning him back to Germany. Oberleutnant von Foerster took over temporary command of the company. However, in the event of operational commitment, the combat units of the company—the Alarm Platoon with Leutnant Jammerath had returned to the company—would be divided between the 2nd Company, Tiger Tank Battalion 503, and the 3rd Company, Tiger Tank Battalion 503 (the former 2nd Company, Tiger Tank Battalion 502). Everyone was somewhat depressed.

2 February: The maintenance was carried on as rapidly as possible in clear, frosty weather. It was good that we could be in our quarters there and did not have to spend those cold nights outside in the open without quarters. But that would soon change. Leutnant Oemler took off in a Volkswagen 200 kilometers to the west as an advance party to scout out a new billeting area for the wheeled units of our company as well as for the Headquarters Company and the Maintenance Company.

In the afternoon, Generalleutnant Balck showed up in the company area and inspected one of our Tigers.

Unfortunately, our attachment to the good 11th Panzer Division was terminated.

3. February: Continued repair and maintenance of the vehicles. Adequate fuel has arrived. All officers were called to a conference with the new commander at the old school. A reorganization of the combat elements was ordered: Two each Tiger platoons and two each light platoons.

On our arrival at noon, our former company commander, Hauptmann von Kaphengst, took leave of his company and handed it over to Oberleutnant von Foerster, after he had read the order of the day from the new commander on taking over the battalion. He also awarded several *Panzersturmabzeichen*. The mood was slightly depressed.

The work and duties continued. It was important to make all vehicles ready for service. Our company had the largest number of serviceable wheeled vehicles and tanks in the entire battalion. Despite that . . . !

4 February: Leutnant Oemler returned for a short time from his advance party mission during the night. Things had not worked out there yet. However, he was off again in the morning. The clear winter cold had strengthened. The cutting wind was especially unpleasant. Nevertheless, the technical work continued, including the work in the maintenance facility which, at the time, was starting to break down for moving again.

In the morning, Hauptmann Kaphengst finally got started back to Germany by way of Taganrog, accompanied by the company's best wishes.

The outcome was that now—when the battalion was divided into two operational companies—our company, having the junior commander, was split and attached to the other two. The wheeled elements went back with the Maintenance Company about 200 kilometers to Ambrosiewka. Two platoons, each with two Tigers and four Panzer IIIs under Leutnants von Koerber and Jammerich went, respectively, to the 2nd Company of Tiger Tank Battalion 503 (Hauptmann Heilmann) and the former 2nd Company, Tiger Tank Battalion 502, which had been consolidated with our battalion as the 3rd Company, Tiger Tank Battalion 503 (Hauptmann Lange). Final preparations for separation, and then, in spite of the nightly bombing, rest.

5 February: Early in the morning, at 0700 hours, the tank elements that had been detached reported to their new commanders. At 0930 hours the main body of the company under Oberleutnant von Foerster, along with the attached trains elements, moved out to the other companies. The officers who went to the other companies, Leutnants von Koerber and Jammerich, were each given a light platoon and gave up their Tigers.

The five remaining crews (Tiger 131 was added to that a day later!) stayed in the billeting area, moving closer to one another and waiting to be employed. The rest of the maintenance duties carried out. Rations and supply with the 2nd Company, Tiger Tank Battalion 503. All of the tank commanders gathered there at 1700 hours for a situation briefing with Hauptmann Heilmann. We were again to play the role of firemen. Rostow was to be held as long as possible. We were attached to the 23rd Panzer Division.

That night there were major fireworks in the direction of Bataisk. Quiet.

6. February: Contrary to our expectations, things did not start happening that night. We kept on waiting. The Russians had taken Bataisk during the night. Many railroad trains did not get away, and the tanks that were on them were blown up.

Tiger 131 came back from the maintenance facility, ready for action. Feldwebel Schönberg climbed into Tiger 131 and Leutnant von Koerber took over Tiger 122 as his vehicle. More waiting. Weapons cleaning and camouflaging vehicles. The maintenance section of the 2nd Company, Tiger Tank Battalion 503, inspected our tanks. In the afternoon an officer conference with the battalion commander was cancelled at the last minute. Instead, Hauptmann Heilmann came from the battalion, bringing a requirement for increased combat readiness. We were to figure on moving out for an operation during the night. Preparations for moving out; sleep.

7 February: Alert at 0030 hours. Twenty minutes later we were moving out and infiltrating the march column of the 2nd Company, Tiger Tank Battalion 503. All then proceeded to the old school quarters, near which the entire battalion took an alarm position for the night.

Note: Leutnant Detlef von Koerber was killed on 9 February at the western outskirts of the city of Rostow fighting against the Russians who had penetrated into the city from three sides. He was shot in the head while attempting to save wounded comrades from a burning Panzer III that was under his command.

Leutnant Detlef von Koerber was the youngest brother of Leutnant Achim von Koerber, who was the acting commander of the 1st Company (following the death of Oberleutnant Adamek) when he was seriously wounded in January 1944 at Winniza and of the last commander of the battalion, Hauptmann Dr. von Diest-Koerber.

CHAPTER 14

First After-Action Report of the Company Commander of the 2nd Company, Tiger Tank Battalion 502

This report concerns itself with the activation of the company, its first operations east of the lower Don and with technical details of the Tiger. The 2nd Company, Tiger Tank Battalion 502, later became the 3rd Company, Tiger Tank Battalion 503.

After-Action Report

Hauptmann Lange
In the Field, 29 January 1943
2nd Company, Tiger Tank Battalion 502

I. Unit Activation:
The company was activated within the framework of the battalion in May of 1942. The first two Tigers were issued on 25 September 1942 and had to be turned over to the 1st Company, Tiger Tank Battalion 502 (Wolchow), on 13 October 1942. During that time, the drivers were certified by Ingenieur Hering and tank training was started. Both Tigers spent most of the time in the maintenance facility. Until the final issue of equipment, the training had to be limited to theoretical instruction from instructional tables we had procured and general weapons and terrain training.

On 21 and 22 December 1942, one Tiger was issued each day. Three Tigers were issued on 26 December and two Tigers on 28 December 1942. Training time was limited to a few hours on those days since the components of end item, basic-issue items and field modifications had to be accounted for or applied. In addition, all of the work that remained in the maintenance facility had to be completed. Starting at the beginning of December and running through 21 December 1942, the maintenance sections and the Panzer VI drivers of the company, along with the specialists, foremen and the Inspektor of the maintenance platoon were detailed to Tiger Tank Battalion 503. All of the Tigers' guns were sighted in at Fallingbostel, though there were orders that the last two Tigers were to be left on the Ssyms railroad cars. Nevertheless, all three transports rolled out on the dates ordered: The first train left Fallingbostel at 2000 hours on 27 December 1942; the second train at 0500 hours on 28 December 1942; and, the third train at 1100 hours on 29 December 1942.

The difficult situation was exacerbated because of the fact that it was not until the evening of 23 December 1942 that the order first arrived by teletype that the company was to be placed under the operational control of Army Group Don. It was not until then that it was known the company would be separated from the battalion. In the meantime, however, all of the consolidated supply elements were with the Headquarters Company with the battalion in Wolchow. In order to assure supply for the company, trucks were requested, which were immediately provided through the General Army Office [*Allgemeines Heeresamt*] and picked up by the company by 26 December 1942. Drivers arrived

79

from the replacement battalion during the morning of 27 December 1942. In addition, all of the Panzer VIs, for example, arrived without main gun bore brushes (for the KWK 36), which had to be provided by special couriers from Krupp or Wegmann.

No time at all was given for battalion-level training. It would be advisable for Tiger units to be given a minimum of three weeks total time for battalion-level training after receiving the last tank. In addition it would be advisable to provide experienced officers as advisers on a temporary basis, who could pass on to the troops the benefits of their experience throughout the training. Any hasty actions lead to inadequate success when employed and to the premature loss of Panzer VIs as a result of lack of knowledge. It is recommended that the tank battalions of established regiments be equipped with Tigers, since they already have solid grounding with respect to the basics of tactical and technical matters.

II. Employment:

On 5 and 6 January 1943 the three trains were unloaded at Proletarskaja. On 7 January 1943 the company was attached to the 17th Panzer Division and proceeded to Ssungar (Kuberle sector). The 107 kilometers were covered without mechanical losses in ten and a half hours of continuous road marching. A short maintenance halt was called every 20 kilometers.

8 January 1943:

Mission:

The company was placed under the operational control of Panzer Battalion 39. Together with Panzer Company Sander, it attacked six villages on the left flank and in front of the left wing of the Division with its spear point at Osserskij and Nish-Sserebjakowka. The enemy was destroyed wherever he appeared. After the first village, twelve miles west of Ilowaskij, had been set on fire with gunfire, the Division radioed: "Immediately cross through the Kuberle sector and attack and destroy two Russian regiments with armored support coming from the direction of Osserskij."

In the course of that operation, the company destroyed two tanks, eight antitank guns, and about 1000 Russians, mostly by overrunning them. In addition, many antitank rifles and light infantry weapons were captured or destroyed. As a result,

the attack in front of our own lines was ruthlessly smashed.

That day a total of 65 kilometers was covered.

Losses:

one Panzer VI due to transmission damage,
two Panzer III's lost to enemy gunfire.

Casualties:

one killed,
five missing,
three wounded.

Weather:

heavy snow squalls in the morning with icing, later, good visibility.

9 January 1943:

Mission:

Together with Panzer Company Sander, clean out the southwest portion of Ilowaskij.

The attack began at dawn and ended with the destruction of five 7.62cm antitank guns, two light field guns and one weak Russian battalion.

After the mission was completed, the company assembled in the northern portion of Ilowaskij.

At 0900 a new mission was assigned: Engage and destroy in Bratskij fifteen enemy tanks approaching.

Since the Tiger Company could not cross the bridge across the Kuberle at Bratskij, the attack was carried out as a pincers movement. The company crossed the Kuberle embankment east of Ilowaskij by itself and advanced to the north. A strong enemy antitank concentration was encountered about 1000 meters in front of our own lines. It was destroyed by attacking it. Part of the attack used artificial smoke. In that attack eight antitank guns were destroyed.

On completion of that, the company turned toward Bratskij in order to join with Panzer Company Sander. In the meantime, the Russian tanks turned toward Ssal. After joining up with Panzer Company Sander, an attack on Osserskij was ordered. Parts of the village were set alight by gunfire after eliminating four flanking antitank guns. After that was completed, the company conducted its return march, escorting tanks that had dropped out.

Distance driven: on that day, 48 kilometers

Losses:

one Panzer VI. A 7.62 cm round lifted up the commander's cupola. The weld seam and cupola bolts were broken. Temporary damage to the elevation mechanism, apparently from the hit,

one Panzer VI due to shifting difficulties,

one Panzer VI through engine compartment fire which was extinguished by the automatic fire extinguisher

one Panzer VI with its right drive sprocket shot off.

Casualties:

one killed (Leutnant Dr. Taubert was killed while inspecting the engine after a fire caused by an antitank gun hit on the rear.)

Weather:

cloudy, good visibility.

10 January 1943:

Mission:

Attack enemy tanks northwest of Budjenny along with Panzer-Kompanie Sander.

In so doing, the company destroyed eleven tanks (three T-34s, one KV-I, and seven T-60s), two antitank guns, one Russian battalion.

Losses and casualties:

none.

By order of the corps, all mission-capable tanks were to be placed under the operational control of the 16th Infantry Division (motorized) immediately. Three Panzer VIs and six Panzer IIIs were sent. The Panzer VIs remained with the 16th Infantry Division (motorized) until 15 January 1943 and the Panzer IIIs until 24 January 1943, where they took part in several operations. For the most part, however, they had to cover a lot of ground. On 14 January, three Panzer VIs received the mission of covering the withdrawal of the 16th Infantry Division (motorized) to the west toward Kamarow, starting three kilometers north of Nowo-Ssadkowskij. On completion of that, they were to head toward Proletarskaja to the company. The Panzer IIIs remained under the operational control of the division. All three Panzer VIs dropped out during the rearward march due to mechanical problems. Due to the shortage of prime movers, they had to remain on the steppes for thirty hours until they could be recovered.

On 10 January 1943 the remainder of the company and the immobile tanks in Ssungar were ordered to pull back to Proletarskaja. The march to the rear ran into serious difficulties since the recovery elements could not be turned around in time and the Russians held a portion of the former supply route. In spite of that, everything was recovered. For the most part, it was with tanks that had been made provisionally mobile and withdrew in part with the rear guard.

On 16 January and 17 January the operational units were committed to a covering force mission at Stalinski Pud and took part in the repulse of a Russian infantry attack. When darkness fell, the 2nd Company, Tiger Tank Battalion 502, was ordered to pull back. The company had been attached to Tiger Tank Battalion 503 in the meantime. The march to Rostow was carried out in stages and lasted until 22 January 1943. Four Tigers and three Panzer IIIs were rail loaded at Ssalsk. The others were brought back in a road march, for the most part towed by two serviceable Tigers. The four prime movers had been needed for rail loading or had been damaged themselves. The withdrawal and the towing were particularly complicated by embankments, deep ravines and heavy ice conditions.

III. Evaluation:

There must be strict orders that, under no circumstances and at all levels of command, Tiger units must never be committed at less than company strength and that Panzer VIs and Panzer IIIs are not to be committed separately. The Tigers must be used as the battering ram as the attack advances and remain as a bulwark at the Schwerpunkt of the defense. Soldiers, in general, are of the opinion that the Tiger can do anything and everything. They do not understand that a newly developed weapon system has deficiencies and weaknesses that first need to be remedied as a result of increased experience and further development.

Because of that, the danger exists that Tiger units may be assigned tasks that normal tank companies can perform without difficulty. As a result of continual movement and the resultant increased demands placed on running gear and power plants and lack of time allowed for technical service, damage occurs that results in Tiger units having mechanical problems when they are used. The maintenance facility must be able to work as long as possible at a single location, preferably a railroad station. When locations are changed, they have a particular need to know the final destination. The Tiger unit must, for the present, be kept as the unit commander's last reserve, waiting in readiness behind a key sector so that it can force a decision when all other means fail.

The Road March:
The winter cleats offer inadequate protection against sliding sideways, which is a particular problem at present due to the many ice-covered ravines and embankments. The road-march speed meets requirements in every respect.

Effects of Enemy Fire:
Gunfire from enemy 7.62cm antitank guns did not achieve any penetrations of the company Tigers or cause severe damage. In one case, a hit on the top of the front of the commander's cupola raised it somewhat because the weld broke and the cupola bolts shot inside the tank.

The Russian Model 42 antitank rifle penetrated up to 17mm, measured on the driver's front slope. The antitank rifle was encountered frequently; it was easily identifiable by its sizeable muzzle flash. In one case, a round hit the forward vision slot of the commander's cupola at an angle, broke out one corner, ricocheted and made the vision block unusable. If it had been a direct hit, it probably would have penetrated. Most of the hits from the antitank rifles were close to the vision slits. A hit on the outer jacket tube of the 8.8 cm main gun, probably from a 45mm antitank gun, caused a sizeable indentation of the outer tube and a very slight indentation in the inner tube. Since the crew did not suspect a hit in that location, the firefight was carried on without any problem.

Conduct of Fire:
The main gun reliably achieved hits at up to 1500 meters with a well bore-sighted weapon. The effect and penetration performance of the 8.8cm gun against all targets up to now leaves no room for improvement.

The ammunition basic load should be a 1:1 ratio between armor-piercing and high-explosive

rounds. As a minimum, they have to be delivered to the supply units in this ratio in order to balance out the daily requirements of fighting. During the last few engagements, only armor-piercing rounds were available. Some of the bases of the shell casings were thicker, which resulted in blockages because the breech-block jammed on them.

The mechanism for securing the main gun during vehicle movements must be operable by hand. The readiness of the weapon to fire suffered from the present locking system, resulting in delays of at least a minute. Driving without travel locking the weapon during operations cannot be done since the weapons loses its elevation boresight after a short period of time.

Firing observation is adequate for the tank commander, but the gunner's vision is severely hindered by the smoke from the discharge. In any case, the optics need a wiper. At this time, a device of our own construction has proven itself well.

Desired Changes:
Tank commander:
The commander's cupola must be lower. The vision slits must be adjustable. As proposed earlier, the cupola hatch must open to the side. The cable for the earphones and microphone is too short. The commander's emergency hand wheel for the traversing mechanism must be provided with a neutral setting. Vision blocks would be good for the commander's cupola.

Gunner:
The seating arrangement twists the hips. The hand wheel for the elevating gear should be higher and provided with a knob. The optics froze when it got very cold so that the cross-hairs slipped and it was impossible to determine the range. The mechanism for securing the turret in place needs to function from top to bottom, since it comes loose in the present form. An additional turret travel lock is needed for the 6 o'clock position since, when towed, the turret wandered to the side.

Loader:
The machine gun is too close to the main gun, which interferes with feeding ammunition belts. The machine gun jams a lot because the sear breaks or bends easily. The ammunition stowage for the 8.8cm main gun is impractical, especially

the lower stowage. The emergency escape hatches have to open like doors. Hinges should be like the radio operator's hatch (completely inside). Presently, the emergency escape hatch can only be opened but not closed from within. The hatch is not just so that the crew can bail out in an emergency, but also for evacuating wounded, for communication with infantry, for throwing out empty shell cases and for extinguishing engine fires in combat by turning the turret to three o'clock. It also is used for getting outside to prepare for towing damaged tanks in combat.

Driver:
The vision slit jams easily. Side-vision optics (vision blocks for the driver and radio operator) need to be moveable. The inspection hatch between the fighting compartment and the engine compartment needs to be larger to improve capability to work. The rear marker light needs armor protection because it is continually destroyed. Tool boxes need to be placed inside the vehicle or inside the stowage box. Otherwise they regularly get lost.

Radio Operator:
There is serious interference in the tank. Medium-wave apparatus would be effective for use as a command tank and for the company commander so as to be able to stay in constant communication with the division. That lack was felt as a serious hindrance during operations with the 17th Panzer Division.

IV. Organization:
With two heavy companies, the Tiger battalion constitutes a very strong fighting force. Reinforcement with a third Tiger company, as some propose, is considered unnecessary. At the present time, massing that many Tigers at one location is not possible. The result is that the battalion is split up, resulting in correspondingly increased difficulties in supply. There is the additional danger

that the battalion will become too unwieldy and no longer be able to properly perform its missions. Already, during a unit move, the terrible condition of Russian roads gives rise to difficulties in the march and blockages caused by a battalion that is heavily equipped with vehicles.

The following organization of the company is considered practical and has been used since its activation:

Company headquarters section: two Panzer VIs (both equipped as command vehicles. The second, serving as a reserve vehicle for the company commander, is presently lacking.)
Two platoons, each with four Panzer VIs
Two platoons, each with five Panzer IIIs (with the 7.5cm short gun)

Rationale:
The two Tiger platoons combine strong firepower and can be employed rapidly by the company commander. In the event of losses, each platoon retains sufficient combat power. Fire control is firmly in the platoon leader's hand at all times.

The two Panzer III platoons can be used either for reconnaissance to the front or flank or to protect the Panzer VIs from close-in attack, as well as in combat against infantry and massed targets at any time.

Equipping the unit with supply and logistical elements and the exact table of organization [*Kriegststärkenachweis*] and table of basic allowances [*Kriegsausrüstungsnachweisung*] must be established in coordination with officers who can report on their experiences during operations.

In summary, it can be stated that, after correction of its developmental teething problems, the Tiger completely fulfills all the requirements for a heavy tank in combat.

Of the nine Tigers in the company, most have reached a kilometer reading of about 800 kilometers.

In the Kalmuck Steppes in January 1943. Local forms of transportation are impressed into service.

Left to right: Gefreiter Biermann, Unteroffizier Bandt, Gefreiter Reis, Panzerschütze Hoffmann (H.).

Left to right: Unteroffizier Bandt, Unteroffizier Nobel, and Unteroffizier Diener.

Wheeled vehicles of the battalion in the Kalmuck Steppes.

A factory in Rostow that served as the location for the Maintenance Company from January to February 1944.

Workplace of a maintenance platoon of the maintenance company at Proletarskaja, January 1943.

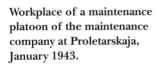

A Panzer III belonging to the light platoon of the 2nd Company, Tiger Tank Battalion 502 (later 3rd Company, Tiger Tank Battalion 503). Tank commander Unteroffizier Mieder and his crew in March 1943 in the area between the Don and the Mius. For additional protection against rounds, the tank had spaced armor added to the front surfaces. A hit can be seen on the front slope above the driver's vision slot. Had the additional armor not been there, the round might have penetrated.

The turret of a Tiger I hangs from the *Portalkran* (portable bridge crane). Apparently, the barrel (barrel lining) of the main gun had been replaced. The barrel has white winter camouflage. It might have come from the turret with white camouflage which is in the background.

Supplies roll to the front over the military bridge across the Don near Bataisk, January 1943.

Oberleutnant Scherf, the commander of the 3rd Company of Tiger Tank Battalion 503, briefs the battalion commander, Hauptmann Graf Kageneck, on the situation. Leutnant Bielefeld stands next to Scherf. Possibly at Oratoff, January 1943.

January 1943 in the Kalmuck Steppes at Ssalsk. Tiger crews view Russian prisoners.

January 1943 in the Kalmuck
Steppes between Ssalsk and
Kuberle. A T-34 has been
knocked out by a Tiger.

Refueling a Tiger of the 2nd
Company, Tiger Tank
Battalion 503 from 200-liter
fuel drums in Anastasijewska,
February 1943.

After the battalion
commander was wounded,
Oberleutnant Scherf assumed
temporary command of the
battalion and led it during the
Tscherkassy Operation.

The battalion will eat well tonight. Left to right: Obergefreiter Daubitz, Schütze Kluge, Unteroffizier Plenge, and Gefreiter Städing. Anastasijewska, February 1943.

Gefreiter Werner Reis in
Rostow at the end of January

Left to right: Gefreiter Neubert, Gefreiter Philipps, Gefreiter Fischer (W.), Gefreiter Kielke, Unteroffizier Heier, Gefreiter Riedel (with the two children), Unteroffizier Plenge, Gefreiter Baumgart, and an unidentified soldier. Anastasijewska, February 1943.

Unteroffizier Heier and Unteroffizier Plenge in Anastasijewska, February 1943.

The local populace at the 503's billets in Barischnas.

In February 1943, as the last in a line of ten or eleven tanks moving forward, Panzer III 103 broke through the ice while crossing the Mius and sank. With the exception of the gunner, Gefreiter Ringleb, the other four members of the crew drowned. When the river became free of ice at the end of March, the tank was recovered. Three of the drowned crew—Obergefreiter Gronau, Gefreiter Schult, and Panzerschütze Großman—were recovered. They were buried in the military cemetery at Prokowskoje. The tank commander, Unteroffizier Dunkel, was not found. Presumably, he had been carried away by the current. The following five photos illustrate that tragic event.

In the foreground is Panzer III 103, which belonged to the Light Platoon. Prokowskoje is in the background. The vehicles are bunched up at the Mius crossing. There was a bridge for light vehicles, but the tanks had to cross on the ice.

Divers connected the recovery cable of the prime mover to the sunken tank. The Mius bridge is in the background.

Three 18-ton prime movers of the recovery section of the battalion's maintenance company were hitched up. Oberfelwebel König, the leader of the Recovery Platoon, directed the recovery from his position on the hood of the lead prime mover, where he was visible to his drivers.

Panzer III 103 finally emerged from the water after a month of being submerged.

The recovered vehicle is brought ashore. On the left is the company commander, Oberleutnant von Förster, along with Oberfeldwebel König.

Gefreiter Kempe and Gefreiter Rogall.

Gefreiter Hirlimann of the ammunition section has a "slight" accident at Rodionowski, April 1943.

The ammunition section appears to be taking a maintenance halt while in march column, Rodionowski, April 1943.

Feldwebel Kurt Fischer and Unteroffizier Heier next to an ammunition truck, Rodionowski, April 1943.

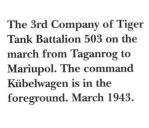

The 3rd Company of Tiger Tank Battalion 503 on the march from Taganrog to Mariupol. The command Kübelwagen is in the foreground. March 1943.

A maintenance halt. The Tiger in the foreground carries the unit insignia of Tiger Tank Battalion 502—the mammoth—on the left side of the front armor in front of the radio operator's position. When the company was incorporated into Tiger Tank Battalion 503, that insignia was removed. 503 did not carry any recognition markings. March 1943.

Hauptmann Fichtner (left), the battalion maintenance officer, and Oberleutnant von Förster, March 1943.

Left to right: Oberleutnant von Förster, Stabsfunkmeister Nega, and Oberfeldwebel König, spring 1943.

Tigers of the 3rd Company, Tiger Tank Battalion 503, on the move. To the right of the bridge is the vehicle of the company commander, a Kfz. 15. March 1943 in the southern Ukraine.

Two photos showing repair work on the engine of Tiger 324 of the 3rd Company, Tiger Tank Battalion 503, in Mariupol, March 1943.

The Ilitsch steel plant at Mariupol. Tiger Tank Battalion 503's maintenance company was located there in March 1943.

The 1st Company, Tiger Tank Battalion 503, preparing for a road march. Tiger 101 will lead the column.

The following soldiers from the 3rd Company, Tiger Tank Battalion 503, received the Iron Cross, First Class: (left to right) Unteroffizier Wunderlich, Leutnant Jammerath, Unteroffizier Miederer, Unteroffizier Gärtner, an unidentified soldier, Feldwebel Müller, and, sitting, Hauptmann Lange, the company commander. (Jammerath and the unidentified soldier had been temporarily attached from the 1st Company.)

Hauptmann Lange says farewell to the 3rd Company. Left to right: Oberleutnant Scherf, Hauptmann Lange, and Leutnant Freiherr von Rosen. Scherf and von Rosen later served as company commanders in the battalion. Prokowske, March 1943.

Panzer III with the short-barreled 7.5 cm gun. Leutnant Jammerath, leader of the Light Platoon of 503's 1st Company.

These photos and those on the following page originate from an ammunition sergeant in the battalion's logistics section. They show various views of rail-loading operations in April 1943 at the Sartana train station.

The above photo shows Unteroffiziere Mertens and Asch (foreground) and Obergefreite Sohr and Albrecht on the rail car.

Another view of rail-loading operations at the Sartana train station in April 1943. Tiger 323 of the 3rd Company stands by to be loaded on the train. Note the narrow transportation tracks on the Tiger.

Rail transport to Bogoduchow. Tiger 101 of the 1st Company is pictured. Note the additional bracing materials employed to ensure the tank does not shift during the rail movement.

Unteroffiziere Heier, Diener, Bauer, and Nobel of the battalion's ammunition section.

The thaw sets in at Rodionowski.

Gefreiter Perschner and Gefreiter Reis with the local populace.

All the conveniences of home: an example of "plumbing" in the Ukraine.

Unteroffizier Mertens, Unteroffizier Asch, and Gefreiter Rogall.

Gefreiter Biermann, Gefreiter Hoffmann (H.), Gefreiter Reis, Gefreiter Perschner, and Unteroffizier Plenge.

Stabsfeldwebel Kisseberth, Unteroffizier Würke, and an unidentified soldier.

PART THREE

IN THE UKRAINE, 1943–44

CHAPTER 15

With Army Group Don in the Ukraine from April 1943 to May 1944

Alfred Rubbel

The battalion had its baptism of fire behind it. The fighting between the Manytsch and the Mius, measured against later and more difficult operations of the battalion, had been very costly. In December 1942, the primary operational objective for Army Group Don—later renamed Army Group South—was to hold open a corridor on the lower Don at Rostow for the units of Army Group A that were fighting their way back from the Caucasus. That was a success, if only for the 1st Panzer Army. Our battalion, committed with Army Battalion Hollidt, contributed its part. Later, when I came to the battalion in March of 1943, it was clear to me that the 13th Panzer Division, where I had served at that time, had made it back safely thanks to the defense at the Manytsch.

The experiences up to that point had emphatically proven that it was not practical to link the light Panzer IIIs with the Tigers in a single platoon or within a single company. When transferred to the area of operations of Army Battalion Kempf in the Kharkov area, we were given a "pure fleet" of forty-five Tigers. A shakeup of personnel corrected additional areas of weakness.

The reorganization in the Bogoduchow area, and later at Kharkov, also brought us several weeks of quiet before the beginning of July when we moved into an assembly area at Tolokonoje, north of Bjelgorod. Operation Citadel (*Zitadelle*) started from there.

The battalion spent the following eleven months in unbroken, difficult operations. The well-known fact that there are always a number of tanks that are out of action because of enemy action or technical deficiencies, however, blessed the tankers with an occasional pause to catch their breath.

During that time period, we were involved in
* Operation Citadel in the Kursk-Orel area: July 1943,
* The fighting retreat from the Donez to the Dnjepr: August–October 1943,
* The defensive fighting in the southern Ukraine: January–May 1944
* Defensive fighting and containment operations at Oratoff and Tscherkassy in Tiger Tank Regiment Bäke
* Defensive fighting at Winniza and Proskuroff,
* Containment operations at Kamenez-Podolsk
* Offensive operations and positional warfare on the Dnjestr and in the Carpathians.
* Operations with Battle Group Mittermeier at Tarnopol.
* Withdrawal of the battalion and refitting at Ohrdruf: May–June 1944.

The significance and intensity of the fighting during Operation Citadel and at the Tscherkassy Pocket stand out among the actions in the

Ukraine. Citadel proved to be a failure and had to be called off. Of all its operations, that was where the battalion suffered the heaviest casualties. At Tscherkassy, where we attempted to save two encircled corps with a total of about 50,000 men, the battalion was to play a decisive roll as part of Tiger Tank Regiment Bäke. It was possible for about half of the encircled men to break out. It was heartening that the battalion itself suffered very few losses of personnel and material, even though it was committed for seventeen days straight.

During the withdrawal of Army Group South from the Donez to the Dnjepr, the battalion was split up and committed across the entire width of the 8th Army. As a result, we lost many Tigers due to mechanical problems. Because recovery means were lacking, they had to be abandoned. Unfortunately, there are scarcely any accounts of those operations, which lasted all of September 1943 and ended with us assembling at Snamenka.

The period of fighting that extended from Tscherkassy until the withdrawal of the battalion in May cost us heavy losses. The actions often contradicted the basic fundamentals for the commitment of Tigers. That was of secondary importance, however, because the Heeresgruppe, under the brilliant command of Generalfeldmarshall von Manstein, had to do its utmost to prevent the collapse of the front. That succeeded, but, in the process, our battalion was worn threadbare. We turned over the remaining Tigers, along with the other equipment, to Tiger Tank Battalion 509, led at that time by the former commander of the 1st Company of Tiger Tank Battalion 503, Hauptmann Burmester. We went from the assembly point at Lemberg for refitting at Ohrdruf.

A portion of our battalion which had been detached from us and had received new Tigers from Germany fought with Battle Group Mittermeier at Tarnopol. It was led by Leutnant Piepgras.

Up to that point in time, the battalion had the following soldiers killed in action:

- 1st Company: 57 killed
- 2nd Company: 40 killed (estimated)
- 3rd Company: 32 killed
- Headquarters Company: ?
- Support Company: ?
- Maintenance Company: ?

According to the tank situation report on 30 April 1944 there were still seven Tigers in service; twenty-two were awaiting repair in various categories of damage; and sixteen had been lost since 31 December 1943.

CHAPTER 16

Recollections from My Time as Commander of Tiger Tank Battalion 503, June 1943–January 1944

Clemens Graf Kageneck

When, today, forty-five years after the events, I attempt to make a contribution to a book of Tiger Tank Battalion 503, I must first make some prefatory remarks. Unfortunately, my relatively sparse diary notes taken down in the hectic days at the front were lost later on. Therefore I cannot provide precise dates or name specific places. However, the totality of major events, as seen from my personal viewpoint, naturally, has been so indelibly stamped in my memory that I can dare hope that most of my comrades will agree with my presentation based on their own perceptions. Therefore I will attempt to sketch the events from my arrival at the battalion at Kharkov in the middle June of 1943 until I left, due to wounds, at the end of January 1944.

On the day before the final day of the battalion commander's course in Paris, the class advisor, Oberst von Waldenfels, called me to his office and informed me that I should immediately pack my bags and hasten by the fastest route to Kharkov in order to take over command of a Tiger battalion. It would be the legendary Tiger. The most any of us at the course knew about it was from a speech by Herr Goebbels. According to Goebbels, this new weapon system was far superior to anything the enemy had.

At the Kharkov airport, I was met by an Oberleutnant (Smend), who appeared to be somewhat older than the average lieutenant. He told me on the way to visit the commanding general—

Breith—he had formerly been a diplomat at the German Embassy in Rome. Breith had invited us to dinner. Smend proved himself, in any event, to be a most circumspect adjutant and organizer. His special strength was in composing diplomatic letters to General Thomale (the Inspector General of the Panzer Troops) when it was important to get speedy replacements for vehicles that had been lost.

General Breith, who commanded the III Panzer Corps at the time, knew me from his time as commander of the 3rd Panzer Division during the great raids to the Caucasus during the summer of 1942. I had led a company in the 6th Panzer Regiment. He told me that a great mission awaited me and indicated the powerful weapon would play a decisive role. Then I was off to where my new comrades were quartered. The Headquarters Company and the three tank companies had already assembled. Oberstleutnant Hoheisel said his farewells and I gave a short "arrival speech."

For a while, the situation remained quiet for us. Only much later did I discover—for example, from von Manstein's memoirs—how the higher levels of command had already struggled with Hitler for the earliest possible execution of Operation Citadel. That would have denied Ivan additional time to reinforce the salient around Kursk in great depth. We would soon feel the consequences of that delay of more than seven weeks.

During the period of peaceful "garrison service" at Kharkov there was, nevertheless, one exciting day. Under the direction of Field Marshal von Manstein, Commander in Chief of Army Group South, a "dog and pony" show was staged for very high Turkish military leaders. It was intended to impress them with the power of our army. Turkey, at the time, was wavering in deciding whether to support the Allies or the Germans. Our Tigers had the honor of advancing at the head of a strong battle group of the 7th Panzer Division through a deep Balka. We would then break through strong enemy defensive positions located on the far slope of the defile. Since everything was taking place with live ammunition and, in addition, our own Stukas were hurling their "cargo" against the "enemy" directly in front of our battalion, the whole affair was a display of fireworks such as scarcely anyone of us had ever experienced. The Turks were enormously impressed and, after Manstein had departed with his guests, we celebrated for a long time at the dinner table in the Balka. At the end, Oberst Schulz—commander of the 25th Panzer Regiment and, later, commander of the 7th Panzer Division and recipient of the diamonds to the Knight's Cross—and I passed out at the table and were hauled off in a Kübelwagen.

On 4 July the battalion marched to an assembly area northeast of Bjelgorod, near the Donez. We were attached directly to Army Detachment Kempf. After I had arrived, it was clear to me that Kempf would ignore Guderian's maxim of *klotzen, nicht kleckern*. He had distributed our three tank companies on a broad front among his three attacking divisions. I immediately reported to General Breith and asked him to persuade higher levels of command to undo that folly. He did exactly that, and was successful, but it took several days before the battalion was reassembled.

And so I experienced the beginning of Citadel more or less as a spectator with the comrades of the Headquarters Company. I stood on the bank of the Donez in the gray light of dawn on 5 July to watch the crossing of our tanks into the bridgehead. The engineers had worked feverishly during the night and the bridge was 80 percent completed. Then, suddenly, a "red sunrise" arose on the far side as hundreds of Stalin organs hurled their rockets exactly onto the crossing site. The bridge was totally demolished and the engineers, unfortunately, suffered heavy losses. Never had I

hugged the dirt so tightly as when those terrible shells sprayed their thin fragments just above the ground. That barrage first brought to light the unbelievable defect in the plans that had been totally overlooked during the preceding weeks: The enemy positions at the southern edge of our bridgehead had to be eliminated, since those positions gave the enemy perfect observation into our location from a distance of about two kilometers (we could see the high ground). Thus, the attack in this sector was delayed at the onset.

Kempf's detachment, with our Tigers in the lead, had the mission of covering the main northward thrust of Army Group South toward Kursk. We covered to the northeast. That soon meant an open right flank, of course. We didn't notice that at first, since the daily fighting occupied us completely. Never before had a major German offensive operation had to master such a deeply echeloned and imaginatively organized defensive system. (In 1940 Rommel penetrated the Maginot line with the 7th Panzer Division in a single night!) What Manstein and Kluge had feared since May— that, with every week's delay, the Russians would create a nearly impenetrable fortification—was what we now had to face. We found letters from German prisoners who had been captured at Stalingrad at several locations in the abandoned positions. The Ivans had used the prisoners in the construction of more and more new positions.

Every day we had to crack at least one defensive barrier that included an ingenious system of flanking antitank positions. At one point, my tank was positioned right on top of an occupied trench. It was only from on high that you could look down into it—the machine gun was helpless at that angle—and I saw how the brown figures were laughing as they passed Molotov cocktails to one another. The only solution was "step on the gas" and move on. After eight days, in spite of constant threats to the open right flank, we (still at the head of Detachment Kempf) had won our way to high ground that had to be held for a while. We had to hold it because our neighbors to the left had been held up. We had already penetrated a good forty kilometers.

Naturally, a lot of tanks had dropped out along the way, probably fewer due to enemy action than to the frequent transmission problems of the initial Tigers. Mine, too, was soon in the maintenance facility for repair, so I had to use a Steyr

Kübelwagen to visit the 1st Company, which was securing somewhere to the northeast. I thought I would take a shortcut on the return trip—one orientated by the sun—through a Balka that curved half-right. So my driver and I dashed off down the defile. Conspicuously heavy artillery fire was coming down about a kilometer away on the far slope and I thought to myself "what a heavy caliber Ivan was using." At the bottom of the depression we had to make a gentle curve to the right, and then both of us felt our hearts drop: In front of us stood a group of about ten Russian soldiers, mostly officers, talking in the middle on the sandy path. I shouted, "Step on the gas!" The Russians leaped to the side and, ducking low as the machine guns above us fired along the ravine, we constantly expected to run into the next Russian position. Suddenly, I saw a German steel helmet just above the ground and, a few meters farther, we were in the foremost unit of the panzer grenadiers of the neighboring division—safely home again.

Citadel reached its high point after about ten days, a battle of attrition such as we had never previously experienced. When Generaloberst Model's 9th Army (in Field Marshal Kluge's Army Group Center) attacking from the north (Orel) came under severe pressure from heavy enemy attacks and had to break off its attack, we also had to start pulling back. We suffered a particularly deplorable loss during an evening operation. Apparently the commanders involved had not coordinated effectively. In any case, several of our own assault guns appeared about 800 yards ahead of us—clearly recognized as such by us—but one of them opened fire and achieved a clean penetration with his long-barreled 7.5cm gun at the radio operator's position in one of our vehicles. That was an indication of how easily the lines can blur at the turning point of an operation.

While we had been the "spearhead" up to that point, it was the role of "fireman" that fell to us now. Our neighbors pulled back under the growing Russian pressure and Ivan advanced with strong armored forces. On one such action I was able to hastily assemble eight tanks and we attacked across a swampy sector, behind which an alder-covered slope rose to high ground. Then we saw an amazing picture. Riflemen from our neighboring division were withdrawing—still in a half-organized fashion—and in between them rolled Russian tanks, firing wildly around in all direc-

tions. We were already in an ideal position and, in a short time, knocked out more than twenty of the Russian tanks that were moving in front of us like targets on a range. Once again the weakness of the T-34 showed up—the tank commander in the turret could not see around him. Therefore none of them noticed how the neighboring tanks were going up in flames, and new targets kept coming over the hill.

It was probably 14 July when we reached the Bjelgorod-Kursk road with the last ten intact tanks. The main effort had started there at the beginning of Citadel. Now there was nothing but withdrawal—very few orders were coming from the higher levels of command—and we were soon left all alone to the right and left. As long as it stayed light, we advanced here and there into the steppe. At night we had to stay awake since we were lacking infantry support—an all too common experience for us tank men. My tank was positioned right next to the road. The night was pitch black, and a closed up company of Russians marched directly toward us. There wasn't even any feeling of sporting fairness. It was simply a matter of keeping them in the searchlight beam at short range.

The next morning I finally had radio contact with the 7th Panzer Division and reported we were still holding on with a few tanks but that the enemy pressure was constantly increasing. Our own forces had, in the meantime, withdrawn a good five kilometers farther to the south. When a tank off to my left stopped dead (hit in the running gear), I moved over to it in order to rescue the crew. All around us the steppe swarmed with Russians, whose antitank rifles were as good as invisible. When I was barely ten meters away from the other tank I gave the signal to bail out from my open turret hatch, at which point I was suddenly hit by shrapnel from the turret in the hand and lower arm. I only came to briefly from my unconsciousness (an hour later?), lying in a roadside ditch. A general (I only saw red and gold) emphatically wanted to question me about the situation at the front. However, due to the shock and the major loss of sleep from the previous nights, I immediately passed out again. Only three days later, in the hospital in Kharkov, did I discover from Smend, the adjutant, that the crew of the other tank had been rescued and the entire battalion had rejoined the lines. Our fighting all by ourselves had, without a doubt, given major relief to the entire sector. General Breith recommended me for the Knight's Cross [*Ritterkreuz*].

My wounds—a number of fragments had to be removed by surgery—healed in Germany on the Mosel. I returned to the battalion at the beginning of September. At that time, unfortunately, I no longer ended up in Kharkov, but at Proskuroff. Von Manstein's entire army group had withdrawn to the southern bank of the Dnjepr after heavy fighting at Kharkov.

My staff was in the Snamenka area. I was angry to discover that the commanding general of the infantry corps—General Stemmermann—had assigned a tank company to each of his three divisions. He probably had in mind Goebbels' pronouncement that, "wherever there is a Tiger, no enemy gets through," more than the wise maxims of Guderian. Therefore I made haste to the next higher command post, the staff of General Wöhler's 8th Army in Kirowograd, thirty kilometers distant. There I was received by the chief of staff, a general who seemed more of a philosopher than a type-A personality.

It was General Speidel, who later led Field Marshal Rommel's staff during the invasion, and, many years later, was one of the founders of the Bundeswehr. I told him of my concerns and soon discovered that he was in full agreement with me regarding the fundamental of tank commitment—*klotzen, nicht kleckern*. Within three days, our three tank companies were assembled at Snamenka. And not a day too soon, for the Russians suddenly assaulted from a bridgehead farther east on the Dnjepr with strong armored forces and rolled right over the headquarters of General Stemmerman. He and his entire staff passed by us helter-skelter. Our Tigers were able to clean up the situation with an immediate counterattack. We then had some quiet in our sector to work on the tanks and look after our own health. There was also an officer's shooting competition, of which I still have a few pictures.

I still remember something that happened from our time in Snamenka. Shortly before we were withdrawn from that area for commitment elsewhere, an extremely young infantry lieutenant showed up and told me that, as leader of a hastily thrown together unit, he was to occupy a defensive position in that area and wanted me to brief him on the terrain. The situation had apparently reached a point where convalescents returning to the front were being yanked off trains, hastily thrown together into local defense groups and entrusted to any available officer. I then led the agitated young comrade around the sector, when an Oberstleutnant suddenly appeared, whose battalion held the immediately adjacent position. He closed his "remarks" with the pithy remark, "Here you can either earn the Knight's Cross or a court martial." After that hardcore gentleman departed, I was at pains to calm down the poor Leutnant. It helped to assure him our Tigers would still be nearby.

In any event, however, our tanks had become a wandering fire brigade. Even for the brilliant strategist, von Manstein, "the blanket was too short." On one of those short raids something unusual happened that easily could have brought about a "hero's death" for the fatherland. The only way our tanks could get to the designated area led across a stream with steep embankments and the bridge looked damned shaky. There was no other way, so we had to take the risk of crossing it with our thirty tanks, each weighing sixty-two tons. The crossing did, in fact, succeed although at less than a walking pace. The ensuing operations—containing a minor penetration—was wrapped up after three hours. Unfortunately, the return led back over that same bridge. My tank was riding point. It moved cautiously onto the bridge. The upper half of my body was clear of the cupola. Then things went so fast that there was no time for me to react at all. All of a sudden everything turned around and I found myself standing on my head, directly over the stream. The long cannon of our Tiger had saved me. When the colossus turned over so rapidly, the long barrel had dug into the bank and stopped the sixty-two-ton monster from turning totally topsy-turvy. Otherwise I would have been crushed to a pulp.

The winter weeks passed in continuous, mobile defensive fighting against an enemy who was perpetually superior in weapons. It was only in mid-January that von Manstein, our commander-in-chief, glimpsed a chance to take advantage of the deep enemy breakthrough in the Winniza area and turn it into an encirclement. Two panzer corps—one from the Uman area to the east, the other coming from the west—would encircle the Russian army that had advanced to Winniza from the north. In addition to the commanding generals of the two corps, I was also summoned to the issuance of orders at the field marshal's head-quarters. Our battalion was to form the spearhead of the western attack wedge as part of Battle Group Bäke.

In the gray light of dawn on the morning of 28 January 1944 we set out over the endless snow-covered steppe. The first radio message from the 1st Company, which was committed on the right, was painful to me: Oberleutnant Adamek, who had just come to us from my former Panzer Regiment 6, had been killed by a head wound.

My memory gives no clearer contours than the monotonous white steppe and occasional duels with enemy tanks, mostly at about 2,000 meters. Back then we still used "Kentucky windage" and left it up to our excellent gunners and the high velocity of our 88mm guns. We usually hit the enemy with the second or third round. My tank achieved that kind of a hit, apparently setting off the enemy's ammunition. In any case, when the powder smoke cleared, the T-34 had vanished. When we got to its location, the remnants were scattered over a broad area.

A few years ago, when I visited the Panzer Demonstration Battalion in Munster where my son served, he and his young comrades proudly showed me the technical marvels of their "Leo" and explained that there was no more "Kentucky windage." A laser range-finder determined the range immediately and adjusted the gun sites on the target. The turret was, of course, stabilized, and this amazed veteran learned that you had a greater than 80 percent chance of hitting the target with the first round while firing on the move against a moving target. There was no question about the fact they had the best night-vision sights. I had to think back to the "firing halts" that we had to make if we were to use the main gun, and what a good target we then made for the 7.62cm antitank guns.

But back to our fighting. In a situation we had become accustomed to at Citadel and as sung in the tanker's song—"All alone during the fight"—we were all on our own during the rapid attack. We formed hedgehog defensive positions at night. The objective of our attack, the Oratoff railroad station was at least ten kilometers to the east. We were to meet the spearhead of the panzer division that was coming to link up with us there. A radio message reached me from Battle Group Bäke stating that the corps had ordered us to immediately set out for Oratoff.

Some sort of instinct told me that danger was building in that area from the north, that the enemy, aware that we were closing a pocket around the army that had advanced on Winniza, would certainly mount a relief attack. The gap between our battalion and Battle Group Bäke was already large enough so that Ivan could simply push into the vacant space, if we were to follow the order and roll farther to the east. Therefore, I resolved to wait out the balance of the darkness and immediately reconnoiter the high ground to the north.

As it turned out, as first light dawned, enemy armor rolled forward on a broad front. We were in a nearly ideal position and knocked out thirty-seven Russian tanks, whereupon the others pulled back. Our successful engagement there was later evaluated as having been decisive for the success of the encirclement. At that point we could again advance at high speed and link up with the other units as if on maneuvers. The commander of the panzer regiment that made contact with us was Oberst von Colin, whom I had met nine months earlier in Paris as the class advisor to our course of instruction. There was, accordingly, a joyful vodka salute.

When I then moved back to my own vehicle and asked the gunner for some bread for my stomach, which had gone empty for six hours, something hit me a series of hard blows to my right leg. I rolled right in front of the tracks of the tank next to mine and saw a motorcycle-sidecar combination with two men drive off at high speed into the pocket. It remains an open question whether that was the action of men from the so-called National Committee for a Free Germany [*Nationalkomitee Freies Deutschland*] or whether (improbably) it was a couple of Ivans who had remained hidden in some hole. In any case, I then found myself in a Russian hut with two shots clean through my right knee. Our excellent battalion surgeon applied a sort of emergency splint. Only then did the pain and the high fever set in. The old Matka brought warm milk. Of more concern than the pain was our few tanks, which were all alone and might have had to ward off an attack at any time. The panzer regiment that we had linked up with had already advanced to the south in order to clean up the pocket.

At about midday a radio message arrived from the corps headquarters asking whether a Fieseler

Storch could land—answer: "Ja!" The slow bird soon arrived and took me on board. I was only able to take my leave of a few of the comrades. The tanks had already occupied various positions. The flight seemed endless to me—over enemy-occupied territory and in a slow-moving target for enemy fighters. We finally landed at the airfield at Winniza. Since Hitler's headquarters had been at Winniza during the summer months starting in 1941, that air strip must have experienced many more distinguished guests than me. I was immediately taken on to Tarnopol and, three days later, to Breslau, where I spent seven excruciating weeks in a cast from shoulder to toes. My last official act was recommending Oberleutnant Walter Scherf for the Ritterkreuz.

My convalescence lasted much longer than at first expected, so it was soon clear to me that it had been my final departure from my battalion. One day in March 1944, to my immense joy, Oberleutnant Smend showed up at my room in Breslau and reported to me about what had happened with my comrades since I had left them, especially about the great battle of Tscherkassy. Our Tigers had again played a decisive role there. Smend had now also bade his farewells and been called back to the diplomatic service in Italy by his former boss, Ambassador Rahn.

I cannot close my recollections without thanking the man who kept up my physical strength with his incredible skill at cooking. After hours of operations in the tank, I could always count on a meal in my tent, prepared by that good man, Heinz Kieckers. There were even "straw-potatoes," thin strips of potatoes baked in sunflower oil. I remain eternally grateful for the pains that he took at the most difficult of times.

I could never have wished for a better adjutant than Wolfgang Smend. Clever and circumspect, extremely accomplished in dealing with high levels of officialdom, he always understood how to get replacement Tigers for us in a short time when we had losses. Therefore, both I and the battalion were sorry when he left.

Unfortunately, the period of time during which I had the honor to command such a unit as Tiger Tank Battalion 503 no longer belonged to the offensive heydays of the years 1941 and 1942. Instead it belongs to the period of difficult defensive fighting after the "turning point" at Stalingrad. However, it was exactly that which demanded the utmost from officers and men. My old comrades can be proud that they continually fought at the hot spots and join with me in loyal remembrance of our brave comrades who were killed.

CHAPTER 17

Recollections of a Panzer Soldier (Part 2)

Dr. Franz-Wilhelm Lochmann

BOGODUCHOW

Our tanks were loaded on 14 April and we went to Bogoduchow, about sixty kilometers south of Kharkov. All of the light tanks were then turned in. The company was outfitted with a total of fourteen Tigers and we received three complete additional crews that already had experience in Russia—Oberfeldwebel Fendesack and Unteroffiziere Ribbel and Rubbel. Integrating those three crews was decisively important for the 1st Company. It was only then that it bonded into an intense comradeship. At the same time we received a new company commander, Hauptmann Burmester, nicknamed *der lange Hein* ["the tall Hein"].

Most important for the company at that time, however, was the replacement of the Spieß [first sergeant]. Stabsfunkmeister Nega had been anything but a "top" sergeant to the company. He certainly understood how to torment the young soldiers with petty harassment. Granted, it had been a long time since we took him seriously, but we were still glad when he was finally relieved. I saw him once more in 1944 during the Normandy invasion. During an attempt to "find" something alcoholic in a neighboring village, I walked in broad daylight along a ditch beside the road. Then I saw him approaching on the other side. His stride was typical. He fixed his gaze on me promptly and expected a proper greeting. Sud-

denly he was quite bewildered: "Jesus, Lochmann, you sack of shit, who made you an Unteroffizier?"

Before we were sent to Kharkov, all of the Tigers were made combat ready. From that time on, the company consisted of three platoons, each with four Tigers. In addition, we had a command tank and a commander's back-up tank. The command tank then bore the turret number "100" and the back-up was numbered "101." The crew of Tiger 100 consisted of Pan Vogel, Walter Martach, Wolfgang Speckin and myself.

KHARKOV

Soon we arrived at Kharkov, where we had a very good time, almost as if we were on leave. From then on we lived together as crews. Our main concern was to look out for our common welfare. We always had something good cooking and there was always something to drink. We celebrated, and anyone who desired could even go to the opera. Obviously, we also arranged for a first-class company party while we were there.

The period of rest at Kharkov was interrupted by three events. First, at Easter we moved our Tigers to the lines at Tschugujew on the Donez, where we boresighted in the guns on our new vehicles. Prior to doing that we had been provided with first-class aerial photographs where the Russian bunkers were easy to make out. Each tank knew its target and executed its assignment in-between the fortified positions of the infantry. It was just like being at the range.

The second diversion was the visit of the Turkish generals that blessed us with the so-called *Türkenübung* [a slang term roughly equivalent to "dog and pony show"]. As part of a larger formation we simulated the great event that was approaching, Operation Citadel. The exercise was executed with unheard of realism and demonstrated a precise cooperation among various army branches and with the Luftwaffe. As the spearhead, the battalion moved so close to the Stukas' target box that any imperfection in their aim could have led to a catastrophe for us.

The third event that enlivened the peaceful routine of our stay in Kharkov was the most important. A few days after we had occupied our quarters, we were blessed with our new commander. He was Hauptmann Graf Kageneck. He would lead Tiger Tank Battalion 503 during its most successful period. Hauptmann Graf Kageneck as well as his later successors, Hauptmann Fromm and Hauptmann von Diest-Koerber, were typical "line" soldiers, who worked well with troops.

In Kharkov we were quartered in the "Plechanowski" district. The 1st Company was in the Starobelska, a street in that industrial district. In our immediate neighborhood there was a schnapps distillery, a sports stadium and the Schewschenko theater. The latter presented both performances of local character and also operatic productions in the Viennese style. One who first visited the schnapps distillery and then attended the opera had a burned out T-34 as a landmark right on the way home between the theater and our quarters. Anyone who ventured into the relatively intact inner city certainly remembers the Red Square and the orthodox cathedral. We also remember that the city electric system was still functioning. It was so peaceful that, in June 1943, there was even an entertainment troop that made it as far forward as us.

CITADEL

At that point, the battalion was moved to its assembly area in the forest at Tolekonoje, where we spent the last peaceful days.

Everything that our commander, Hauptmann Graf Kageneck, wanted to prevent, happened. The three tank companies were each assigned to a different division. The 1st Company came to a halt under heavy antitank gun fire in the midst of a minefield in front of an antitank ditch. The combat engineers (70th Engineer Battalion) who advanced suffered fearsome losses. They were decimated before our eyes while they cleared entire belts of mines. One tank company of the neighboring panzer regiment on our right attempted an attack. It was not troubled by mines. However, that attack was brought to a halt by heavy antitank gun fire. Most of the tanks of that company (Panzer IV) burned. The company commander of that unit was Oberleutnant Reutermann. We would get to know him later as our company commander.

The next night I had to pass on a supply report to the responsible corps by keyed transmission. Since I could not, of course, keep up with the rapid tempo of a trained staff radio operator, it turned into a joke. Only after I requested he go more slowly was I able to carry out the task in a more-or-less satisfactory manner.

On the third day we fought our way through the antitank positions. The enemy pulled back. The company only had four vehicles in service. When the crew of Tiger 100 was standing behind its vehicle, it was surprised by a heavy mortar (17.2cm). We all tried to dive under the vehicle at the same time, but our loader, Wolfgang Speckin, Pan Vogel and I were wounded. We took Speckin to the closest medical clearing station, where he was cared for immediately and sent on to a hospital in Germany. Pan Vogel and I, each of us with a fragment in our butt, were driven to a rear-area dressing station where we were cared for and then taken back to Kharkov. When they then put us on a hospital train we blew our tops. We got off again, took our uniforms and went back to Bjelgorod. We spent a few days at the company trains recuperating and then were back in our Tiger.

Citadel went badly. We were engaged in fighting for days on end. Although we knocked out all sorts of targets, we kept duking it out with those terrible defensive belts of antitank guns. At that point I came down with a stubborn case of diarrhea. There was the heat in the tank, the constant thirst, and then, every half hour, I had to go. At first I used the oh-so practical muzzle-brake cover, but then nothing mattered to me any more. I climbed out to squat behind the tank. I just didn't notice enemy fire. I didn't get healthy until we visited Kharkov again during the march back.

Walter Martach did the cooking. The aroma of Sauerbraten was seductive. An entire bucket of vanilla pudding was an outstanding success. My mouth watered. All day long I'd had nothing but tea and the hard tack from the emergency rations. I devoured the Sauerbraten—and that was the end of the diarrhea. My mineral balance was normal again. I regained my strength and could handle the sledgehammer. At that point I tipped the scales at less than 110 pounds.

DERGATSCHI

We were detailed to the 6th Panzer Regiment with Oberleutnant Oemler and an additional Tiger. We were located in the Dergatschi area between the 6th Panzer Regiment's 6th (Leutnant Sorge) and 7th (Oberleutnant Taulin) Companies. While Oberleutnant Oemler personally went to get us supplies as soon as possible, Unteroffizier Willy Roth joined our crew. For several days it was the same game. Sudden tank noise, and the endless field of corn in front of us would be set to swaying. Then, all at once, the Russians would be right in front of us. We knocked out T-34s daily, with an occasional T-60 as well. Leutnant Sorge got really angry and repeatedly tried to get his own company to move forward. We wondered why. The poor swine had it a lot harder than we did. What was sport for us was deadly serious for them. It was remarkable that in a pure fight with other armor we felt like hunters: We had no fears, we knew the superiority of our weapon and relied on the heavy armor. All that we needed was a little common sense and to avoid being foolish.

Three days later a damned antitank gun, which we had not spotted in time, shot off one of our tracks. Our second Tiger towed us back with a great deal of effort. Our track was left lying out in front of the Russian lines for a while. While we were making ready to go and haul the track back with our second tank, it was already on its way back to us, brought by the battalion surgeon in his tank. Those boys were first class. They had pushed forward and taken our track in tow. Our vehicle was quickly put back in shape. Jochen Oemler was back with us again the next day. We had to move on with our two tanks during the night. We got to a patch of woods. Suddenly there was industrious activity all around us. We had driven into the midst of a Russian tank assembly area. Since all they had was diesel fuel and we did not care for

their rations, we decided discretion was the better part of valor and got out of there as quietly as we could.

DEFENSIVE FIGHTING ON THE HIGH GROUND AT MEREFA

This was not the kind of game we liked to be involved in . . . we were positioned all day long with one or two tanks on the high ground with no infantry protection. We were providing security against the Russians. Again and again they tried armored assaults. Our field of fire, however, was superb. The Russians tried to weaken us with artillery. Every day they started their game early in the morning and did not run out of ammunition until evening. If the Russians had advanced during the night with infantry, they would long since have thrown us off of the high ground. We were able to complete our mission, however, the objective was bitterly contested. Feldwebel Lehmann, Unteroffizier Neumann, Obergefreiter Krüger, Gefreiter Jockwer and Gefreiter Hornberger were killed on our hill.

Then we pulled back. By winter, at the latest, a prepared position at the rear had to be constructed on the Dnjepr. The crew of Tiger 101 had been newly assembled. The gunner was now Unteroffizier Heino Kleiner, the loader, Herbert Ritscher and the driver, Piepel Grasse.

"SCORCHED EARTH"

We were in the sector of SS Cavalry Division Fegelein. The company was billeted in a village; the acting commander was Oberleutnant Oemler. Around us were vast pumpkin and melon fields. Everyone was sitting in the garden at the company commander's quarters. The alcohol was flowing freely. Suddenly, an excited staff officer appeared and showed his disapproval of our undisciplined behavior. Twenty five Russian tanks had penetrated the main lines. The company was to deploy immediately. "What?" asked our commander. "Twenty-five enemy tanks—and you want the entire company?—No way! That calls for my 1st Platoon."

We set out with four tanks. One had already dropped out with mechanical problems by the time we got to the next village. In Tiger 100 we had Oberfeldwebel Fendesack, along with Heino Kleiner, Piepel Grasse and Herbert Ritscher. Günther Tessmer and his crew followed us, as did Feldwebel Hörncke.

As we moved through the next village, we ran into the commander of the 3rd Company, Hauptmann Scherf. He heard about what we were intending to do and joined our group with his tank. Unfortunately, his vehicle also dropped out, so we made it to the lines with only three tanks. We had all gotten pretty lively. Only Heino, our gunner, still lay on the rear deck in deep sleep, fighting with the alcohol in his bloodstream. We decided what we were going to do behind the last high ground. Günther Tessmer on the left, Feldwebel Hörncke on the right, and us in the middle—that was how we would engage the bastards. The Oberfeldwebel adjusted the sights. He placed the gunner in his seat and then it began.

Günther Tessmer had some problems with his engine and only appeared a bit later on the high ground. One of our own Pak also managed to get into position. The terrain favored us so we were the first to be able to spot the enemy below us. Feldwebel Hörncke showed up a little later to our right. We were the lucky ones and were able to open the festivities. The Russians were fully occupied with their own problems. Several of them had driven into a marshy spot and gotten stuck. Others tried to pull their comrades out. Only a few were immediately able to defend themselves against us. At a range of between 400 and 600 meters, we had knocked out nine Russian tanks in a few minutes. Franz Hörncke polished off another six. Günther Tessmer had to content himself with one. Even the Pak scored. It accounted for the last of the Russian tanks, which was in the process of making tracks out of there.

A FEW DAYS LATER

Günther Tessmer was now our tank commander. A few days later we were in a village on the steppe in a battle group with the crews of Unteroffiziere Ribbel and Rubbel, again with SS Cavalry Division Fegelein. Our tank was ordered a few kilometers east to pull security, while the SS prepared the village for defense and Ribbel and Rubbel stood ready in reserve.

Night slowly fell and it got dark. Nothing stirred near us in the landscape. Everything was peaceful. About an hour later, horse-drawn vehicles drew near us. They were not Russians, but soldiers of the Waffen-SS who had become separated from their units.

As midnight approached, we were ordered back into the village to ward off an expected armored attack. We were positioned on the road at the outskirts of the village. Ribbel and Rubbel were posted to our left. It was a strange night. A light ground fog lay over the broad steppe, which was cut partially by Balkas. Overhead, at our position, the stars shone in the heaven. As a result, we could barely perceive the noises approaching us. Perhaps the small amount of alcohol in our bloodstream had something to do with our inability to recognize the sounds. Everyone was awaiting the arrival of attacking Russian tanks. Only Günther Tessmer and I thought it could be something else. We thought it was the sound of prime movers. Besides, it could be our own units, especially since we had had the experience a few hours earlier with the horse-drawn vehicles. Günther and I sat on the turret. He had the flare pistol in his hand. Only when the vehicles that were approaching were very close would he illuminate the scene and, if need be, start the engagement.

The time had come; a green flare climbed on high (white would blind our own gunners). Santa Claus had come to town. The T-34 moving out front had its gun aimed directly at our Tiger. Behind it were the silhouettes of a great number of enemy tanks. I found it a very impressive picture. The T-34 looked like it was crouched to spring, and the brilliant light of the flare tinted everything a surreal green that shone, muted, through the ground fog. Then things started happening—fast! Günther Tessmer leaped behind the turret. I jumped inside through my radio operator's hatch. At the instant that I disappeared inside there was a blow against our turret. While the other two tanks took care of the enemy, we were unable to take part in the fight. Our turret was jammed and we had to drive back to the rear that night. The radio-operator's hatch was jammed and could no longer be opened. After their first surprise, the Russian tanks pulled back and attacked the village again. It did not turn out well for them. Rubbel and Ribbel made good work of it.

On the next few days we moved westward through the steppe. The company's tanks were dispersed everywhere.

At some point we developed technical problems. The only gear that would engage in the transmission was fourth gear, and the worst thing was that the main gun would not work. When we got to Poltawa, it was already burning. And despite that they still could not decide to distribute the contents of the giant ration dump to the troops without following the book. Everything had to be done in proper military fashion, orderly and by the book. That was when Heino turned out to be our man. Properly uniformed and with correct, impeccably soldierly bearing, he officially received rations for a major battle group of the battalion. Yes, it was certainly important to have a proper soldier in the crew. We were able to meet our needs for weeks through that opportunity. We set off calmly toward the Dnjepr. The German columns flowing to the rear rolled on to Krementschug.

We moved cross-country through the steppe alongside those columns. The clear water of a little stream gave no hint of its actual depth. There was a fearful bow wave that nearly swept our driver from his seat. As the tank climbed the bank on the far side of the little stream, an opened can of marmalade tipped over onto the driver's head. You can imagine the words coming out of Piepel's mouth! And, of course, it was all my fault.

Our move to the rear in fourth gear was later halted by a Fieseler-Storch. Oberst U. materialized—a notorious dragooner of soldiers. He ordered us to take over security on the road. We, of course, had no idea how we were to be effective as route security with no more armament than our bow machine gun. The only matter of importance to us was to get our tank back in combat-worthy condition. Our mission was to get beyond Krementschug to the battalion. After the Oberst had flown off again, we resumed our journey to Krementschug by night. When we got to the Dnjepr, the first thing we did was to carefully hide our tank. We then reconnoitered for crossing sites across the river.

One option was the railroad bridge, which had already been prepared for demolition. If we had possessed any way to get loaded [on a railroad car], that would certainly have been the best way. We quickly forgot about the railroad bridge and turned our attention to a group of engineers, which was ferrying individual Panzer IVs over the river on rafts. We were certain that we could have persuaded the young engineer to attempt the same for us, specially since we did not have to let them know the actual weight of our tank. However, we were afraid that we would put them in unnecessary danger. We decided against that as well. That left only the approximately 1.5-kilometer-long "Rundstedt bridge." The pontoon bridge had been constructed during the advance by the engineers and appeared extraordinarily stable. Even though we passed our vehicle off as a Panzer V (Panther), the crossing-site commander was not about to allow any experiments. When the good man finally headed back to Krementschug that evening, we tried one more time and were lucky. We infiltrated the endless column and were careful to maintain the proper spacing fore and aft and drove very slowly over the Dnjepr. Once in Krementschug, we ran into "Tall Hein" and soon rejoined the company, which was billeted at Snamenka.

THE KIEW BRIDGEHEAD

In Snamenka, the crew was separated. Heino went on leave and Herbert Ritscher took over as driver for a vehicle that was in the maintenance facility for lengthy repairs. Tiger 100 was quickly put back in service. Within three days it was ready for action again. Piepel Grasse and I had worked at a fevered pace. Soon I was headed off on leave. I had a large duffel bag and filled it with the precious items from the army ration dump at Poltawa. I pictured it all in my mind: I would be received at home like Santa Claus. The sack was packed full with cigarettes, alcohol, chocolate, coffee, tea, soap—even pudding powder and marmalade. I stowed yet another valuable in the sack that I had removed from a T-34. The Russian tank had a kind of periscope in the commander's cupola, and that was to be the foundation for my "Hamburg Tank Museum."

My celebration was premature. With somewhat excessive haste, the combat-ready vehicles were thrown together into a battle group. Werner and I rolled to the railroad station and received a bitter shock. The leader of that battle group was not "Tall Hein," as we had expected, but Hauptmann Scherf. To be sure, the upcoming operation would be in the best of hands, but we were concerned about how the crew would be rounded out. I no longer knew who joined us as loader. Obergefreiter Ringleb joined us as gunner. He had been the sole survivor to escape when one of our light tanks had broken through the ice on the Mius. He was a singularly nice young man and had, until then, mainly been employed with the fuel and ammunition section, where he had always seemed to me to be especially helpful. For tank commander, we got Leutnant Günter Grünwold. I knew Günter well. Back at Döllersheim he had been the senior occupant in our barracks room, after a bit of prior experience with Rommel in the Afrika Korps. We had been together at Döllersheim in an officer-candidate course taught by Leutnant Detlef von Koerber.

I remember the course well. At that time I was faced with the question: Who or what was Bucephalos?—and I could not answer it. It was terrible! The name of Alexander the Great's war horse had slipped my mind. At the end the "pre-selection" course we were tested in our ability to give an extemporaneous speech to the assembled soldiers. Each of us was to talk for ten minutes within the overall theme of "The Eastern Area" on a topic of his own choosing. I spoke on the historical movements of populations, of the battles between the Germans and Slavs and, finally, of the mixed population that had resulted. Then I got to Prussia, the state that had been so important in the later founding of the Reich and its army. There were the soldiers who had been trained to such unconditional obedience, and the officers, their brave leaders. By listening carefully, one could detect in what I said that the Prussian population, as a product of its history, was composed of a melting pot of various races, predominantly Slavs and Germans.

That evening I had to report to Leutnant von Koerber. He talked for about half an hour, without getting into my morning presentation. As the conversation drew to an end and I was ready to go, he merely said, "One more thing, Lochmann, that I want to say to you. Your presentation today was very interesting. However, I want to give you some good advice. You should never say such things openly again."

Several tankers from that group later became officers. I remember Unteroffizier Mathies, Unteroffizier Lewandowski, Gefreiter Hans-Martin Müller, and Gefreiter Günter Grünwold. And with that last one, Leutnant Grünwold, we would then head north on the railroad, where the Russians had formed a major bridgehead at Kiev.

THE ASSEMBLY AREA

During the night we rolled from the railroad into a totally shell-torn patch of woods. Spectral splintered trunks of trees strove toward the heavens. It was pitch black and strangely still. Only four tanks from our train had made it that far. Our mood was depressed, nor did the assembled foot soldiers show any sign of optimism. They were members of the veteran 70th Engineer Battalion. Their memory of the first day of Citadel remained fresh, a day that had ended in catastrophe for those courageous men.

A bottle of schnapps made the rounds, followed by a macabre conversation. "I expect nothing but a shitty situation here—heads must roll for victory." Feldwebel Hörncke came later, bringing further bad news about the three Tigers that had not yet linked up with us. Two of them would not be ready for action before the following noon. His own tank had engine problems and had to go back to Snamenka. In closing, Franz told me that I was the next one who would get to go on leave and I should drive back to Snamenka with him. Franz wanted his own radio operator, good old "Schorsch", to get the third combat engagement he needed for the *Panzerkampfabzeichen*. I declined. I could not leave Werner Grasse alone with Tiger 100, since the crew was just a bunch that had been thrown together. Moreover, we did not know whether Günter had done well on his "homework" at officer candidate school. In leaving, Franz wanted to take my duffel sack with him, which I also turned down. I could look after my stuff on my own.

THE UNSUCCESSFUL ENGAGEMENT

Our artillery opened fire with the first light of dawn. It was a murderous barrage. We began our attack. First it led through one of our own anti-tank ditches. Then came the outposts of our infantry, who had constructed the system of trenches. Then it crossed a gently rising plain. We advanced at a good pace, with Feldwebel Wolf alongside us. We followed hard on the heels of the impacting rounds of our own artillery. Next came a steep climb. We got into a deeply echeloned Russian trench system. Our artillery had churned things up frightfully. I saw scarcely any living Russian soldiers. We continued to follow the rolling barrage. The terrain was incised with bizarre, deep cuts, until we reached a terraced slope leading up to the high ground. We entered a broad, flat piece of terrain, about 100 meters wide. Again, the picture was the same. In front of us lay a massive system of Russian trenches and, again, one could scarcely see a living Russian. By then, we had covered about two and a half kilometers.

Just before the next terrace was when it happened. Both of us drove onto mines at practically the same time. We still had luck in our misfortune. Werner promptly brought our rig to a halt. The tracks were still on, and we had relatively good cover. However, we had only a very narrow field of fire. Feldwebel Wolf, who was about fifty meters to our left, and a little behind us, was worse off. His tank had been moving forward at a good clip when his tracks were ripped off by the mines. His tank was positioned in the open without tracks. Our own artillery ceased its fire at about that moment. It had used up its ammunition.

Soon thereafter the other side started its own barrage. The Russian artillery fired without pause and gave special attention to Feldwebel Wolf's tank. At the same time, an extremely large number of Russian antitank guns started their target practice. The tanks were hammered.

We were able to silence the Russian antitank guns in our own narrow field of fire, but that didn't do much to help our neighboring crew. They continued to be hit and could not defend themselves. Their main gun had been hit. During a break in the fire, the crew bailed out. Several members of the crew were severely wounded in the process. The radio operator did not make it. Werner supported me by talking me into targets, so that we could drive out the Russians who were lying in front of us. If only we had a better field of fire! A panzer regiment arrived beside us on the right. I heard the dramatic radio conversations of its commander—he, himself, was wounded—as he repeatedly tried to rally his crews. But they couldn't get through there either. The deeply echeloned Russian antitank defenses and the lack of adequate cover brought the attack to a standstill. The tanks from the panzer regiment pulled back later.

Werner and I couldn't hear the tank commanders talking to one another. On both sides of our tanks the Russians brought forward infantry reinforcements. They reoccupied their trench system and their own artillery helped them advance to the trenches that were far behind us. We had missed out on the fact the crew in the turret had bailed out. We had been totally involved in combating the Russians attacking in front of us. The escape hatch had been opened in the turret. We were all alone in the tank. It was high time that we found out what was going on behind us. Two of our tanks were immobilized not far from our own antitank ditch. The German infantry had been swept away by the Russian artillery. We were all alone out there in the midst of those Russian bastards, about two and a half kilometers in front of our lines, and Russian infantry reinforcements had again infiltrated its own system of trenches.

The hope that the two tanks that were sitting behind us could be put back in action and help us turned out to be wishful thinking. It was a really difficult decision to abandon our tank. With covering fire from one or two tanks, we could have stayed in our relatively well-concealed position and fixed the tracks—if the Russian artillery left us in peace. The other option—waiting until dark and then clearing out—was overcome by events.

When there were too many Russian infantry already behind us for our own comfort, we decided that we would also bail out. For reasons of safety, we chose to use our own hatches, which we cautiously opened. We then played a lively game with the Russian infantry. Constantly alternating, we set a cap on a machine gun barrel and shoved it above the hatch. Each time it was greeted with furious infantry fire. We kept that maneuver up until there was only an occasional Russian reaction. Then we both leaped out simultaneously. We crept into a shallow depression behind the tank and agreed that, since we were only armed with a pistol, we would attempt to get back to our own lines separately.

Werner went around to the right and had a lot of luck. He crossed an open, flat piece of terrain, took advantage of a Balka to leave a section of the Russian system of trenches behind him on the left and made it to an unoccupied system of Russian trenches. For my part, I had to get past a shorter bit of open terrain on the left, but I quickly landed in the Russian trenches. I slowly, cautiously worked my way along the left flank of the trench system. As I made it past a corner in the trench, an Asiatic type with short-cropped hair suddenly stood in front of me. He stared at me, totally aghast, and took to his heels. I needed a lot of time to cover 500 meters. Again and again I had to steer clear of Russian infantry. Finally, at the left-hand anchor position of the trench system, I had a good view of a Balka and I could not believe my eyes. There, below, was a Panzer IV. Two of its crew had apparently just fixed the track and were climbing back inside. I exulted internally: "That looks like my ticket back to the company!" At that moment the tank started up, setting out to drive around some high ground. I threw caution to the winds and ran for my life. As I got to the rearward base of the high ground, the Panzer IV crossed my path.

The vehicle had side skirts. On the run, I leaped at the side of the vehicle, around the loader's hatch. I held tight to the upper edge of the skirts, from which I then pulled myself up and into the loader's hatch. Totally exhausted, I landed on the floor of the tank. A young, smiling Leutnant bent down from the turret, saying only, "He needs a schnapps." I made it back in this tank to our own positions behind the tank ditch unharmed. It dropped me off right by our unit. The first person I saw was my driver. Werner had also made it back. My comrades had already given me up. Only Alfred Peuker had known: "Wilhelm will wangle a way through."

Hauptmann Scherf tried another attack on the high ground in the early afternoon with three Tigers. At the very least, he wanted to try to recover the two vehicles that had been left behind. There was no way to get there. A third tank had to be temporarily abandoned. There was only one thing left to do. If we wanted to save our vehicles, we would have to make a nighttime attempt to recover one or another. Werner Grasse and I were detailed to brief the artillery forward observer. The area around our vehicles would be secured against the Russians with occasional shelling by the artillery.

We were really lucky. The night was pitch black. Whether the Russians had gotten tired, or whether they were lulled into a feeling of security, whether they were licking their wounds or were busy with their resupply, I do not know. In any case, supported by a handful of infantry, we were able to slowly work our way forward to our vehicles with our crews. Two 18-ton prime movers from our recovery platoon followed us. Without any exchange of fire we were able to get to the Tigers. Feldwebel Wolf's tank had to be abandoned. We were able to repair the tracks on our rig and then slowly make it back to our own positions. An additional Tiger could also be recovered. At the start of the next day, we bogged down again trying to cross the antitank ditch. The prime movers had to head for safety when heavy artillery fire began, so it was not until the next night that our Tiger was freed. In the end, we had to knock out Feldwebel Wolf's Tiger with our own gunfire.

When we finally got back to the company at Snamenka, my leave papers were already in the orderly room. Unfortunately, my beautiful duffel bag filled with goodies had been left behind during the operation described above. The Russian bastards had taken it from our Tiger, and I mourned for my lost treasures. However, I did not return home empty handed. Fritz Riemer, the mess sergeant, packed me a bag full of precious goodies and, to top it all off, he gave me a twenty-liter canister of sunflower oil. On about 10 November I was deloused at Kowel and left from there for home for the first time in a year and a half.

OBERLEUTNANT ADAMEK

I got back from leave just before Christmas of 1943. The journey on the leave train had not gone without problems. The company was in the little village of Zibulew. The village was surrounded by extensive forest, which was massively infested with partisans. Everything was covered with deep snow and the air was clear. I was in a depressed frame of mind. I felt an ongoing queasiness in my stomach. "Damn! Can one really allow oneself the luxury of melancholy?" I knew the proper therapy. "Action" was called for, and a little alcohol would also do some good—then one would be back into the swing of things.

The first person I ran into was Unteroffizier Willy Roth and a part of my tanker comrades. There was vodka, and it helped. Then there was something to eat on the table. I was back to myself again. "You bums! Have you forgotten everything I ever told you about fine dining? Here I am, gone only a few weeks, and everything has already fallen apart." We "found" some ducks and had a choice meal.

In the meantime, we got a new company commander. He was Oberleutnant Adamek. He made an excellent first impression. It took a while to get to know him. He seemed to me to be introverted and thoughtful. He carried some sort of burden around with him. Two evenings later I was able to suspect what it was. His appointment to the company was actually a promotion for him. He saw it otherwise, at least in part. There was something wrong. When his old unit was withdrawn from the mess, he was immediately given a new assignment. He needed to, or more likely, wanted to prove himself. I was able to understand at that point. A few days later he gave me a letter to keep for him, a letter to his family, the duplicate of a letter of farewell. For a while I was worried. I was afraid I was watching someone destined for suicide. In the mood I was in, that was something I didn't want to deal with.

I needed a change. For a few days, I went with two other soldiers in a horse-drawn Panje cart and sled to a distant collective farm to "procure" some milk. The fresh winter air and the permanent state of alertness did me good. The woods were full of partisans. We kept constant watch and paid attention to the fresh sled tracks. Any sled was suspicious. Machine pistols and machine gun were constantly ready.

We moved to Shmerinka, a village somewhat south of Winniza. Aside from guarding against partisans, it was quiet. To the best of my knowledge, the 3rd Company had an engagement with Russian tanks during that time. On 14 January 1944 our maintenance section went to Winniza unescorted. Our people were killed in a partisan ambush. Only Gefreiter Ernst Kaplan survived. He spoke Czechoslovakian and was taken prisoner by the partisans, ending the war in adventurous fashion on the other side. Ernst was lucky. He drove in the last truck in the column, together with Alex, our *Hiwi* [short for *Hilfswilliger*, an East European or Russian prisoner of war who volunteered for non-combat service with the German Army]. Alex made it back to the company with our captured Dodge. He told us about the massacre. All of the other comrades were killed by the partisans and laid out in a row along the road. I still remember the names: Unteroffizier Öls, Obergefreiter Heider, Gefreiter Mineck, Gefreiter Djuba, Gefreiter Minck, Gefreiter Wiesenfarth, and Panzerschütze Barton.

On about 20 January the tank elements moved to Winniza. A substantial body of troops were assembled. I remember the breakthrough through the Bila position as follows: The company set out very early in the morning. It was a clear winter day. Everything was under deep snow. The Waffen-SS prepared for the attack in the next village. It seemed to be the third wave. We moved on. In the next village were armored vehicles. I saw *Hummels* and *Hornisses* ["bumblebees" and "hornets," nicknames for, respectively, a self-propelled 15cm howitzer on a Panzer III/IV chassis and a self-propelled 88mm PaK 43/I L/71 antitank gun on a Panzer III/IV chassis].

The battalion led the attack. Our company moved out in wedge formation. Tensely, I surveyed the flat terrain in front of our tank. Suddenly, right in front of us, I saw little heaps of snow, quite symmetrical and echeloned in depth. I thought: "Even the most industrious mole isn't that tidy in his work." Without hesitation, I raked a few of those little hummocks with my machine gun. Splinters of wood flew up. "Halt!" I shouted. "Mines!" The company halted. The vehicle on our left had already moved a bit in front of us, but things went well for us again this time. The minefield had been spotted in time.

Don't count your chickens before they're hatched! Our quick reaction had only partially ruined Ivan's surprise. He hoped to shell us when we were helpless in the minefield, but even on the edge of it we were not exactly in a good position. The company was subjected to murderous antitank gun fire. Tiger 100 took an bad hit. An 85mm armor-piercing round ricocheted off the lower part of the gun barrel and penetrated the upper deck of the hull, right between the driver and the radio operator positions. I stared at the hole in disbelief. My radio had packed it in. The driver, Werner Grasse, looked at me in horror. I became aware of an unnaturally warm feeling in the area of my lower abdomen. I was terrified. A stomach wound? I mechanically worked my way in through the winter coveralls and uniform. In my underwear I found a big fragment, almost a cubic centimeter in size. I was relieved. Nothing had happened to the crew.

The company started to engage the antitank positions. For us, however, the turret would not move. It was jammed. Oberleutnant Adamek leaned down from the commander's cupola into the fighting compartment and called to me: "Come with me. We're going to 131." I said something to the effect that, "You can't do that. That is Oberfeldwebel Fendesack's tank. We have to use another one." The Oberleutnant, however, was already out of the tank. I caught up with him on the rear deck of Tiger 131. He sent me back to our own vehicle for his maps, which he had forgotten. I ran back. As I was standing behind the rear of Tiger 131 with the maps, the Oberleutnant stood next to the turret beside the tank commander in order to tell him and the radio operator to go to our tank. At that moment, a high-explosive round struck the turret of Tiger 131. Oberleutnant Adamek was killed instantly.

While the attack continued, we rolled back toward the rear. We ran into Spieß Haase. He was all ready to climb aboard as tank commander. It was only with difficulty that we got him to understand that we had been penetrated by a shell, that our turret was jammed, and that the damage could only be repaired at the maintenance facility.

During the next few days, the battalion fought its way on to Oratoff. If one thinks of what massive opposition the Russians put up, the success was striking. Our commander, Graf Kageneck, was wounded at Oratoff. Spieß Haase, who had received another tank, was also seriously wounded. He lost one eye and was flown out in a Fieseler-Storch. Leutnant Wilfried von Koerber also was hit. He was severely wounded. Karl Kubin was killed while rescuing him. Another tank suffered the same fate as ours—only the crew wasn't as lucky as we were. A shell ricocheted along the gun barrel and penetrated the roof of the hull. Wolfgang Bürger, the radio operator and the son of a pastor from Anklam in Pomerania and a good friend of mine, was killed. I had a chance to look over that vehicle at the maintenance facility. I climbed in and sat in the radio operator's seat and realized how much good fortune I myself had had.

TSCHERKASSY

Our company occupied an assembly area in almost knee-deep mud, as we and our battalion got ready to relieve the two corps that were encircled in the Tscherkassy Pocket. We were part of schweres Panzer Regiment Bäke. The battalion, at that time, was led by the commander of the 3rd Company, Hauptmann Scherf. It was not until a strong frost set in and it started snowing lightly that we were able to begin that difficult operation.

Oberfeldwebel Fendesack was our tank commander, and we were in intense action daily. The village of Frankowa was captured and we were able to exact a substantial toll in tanks from the Russians, who were operating cleverly. At that time, the overall situation—especially on our flanks—was wholly confused. We had to stand up to repeated Russian surprise attacks. When our spearhead got very close to the encircled formations, our vehicle had to be towed back to the maintenance facility at Potasch with a mechanical problem. As we were towed back, I got the impression that our unit had only opened a small corridor. The flanks continued to be threatened by the Russians.

We were quickly repaired. Along with several other vehicles that had been put back in service, we set out to make our way back to the battalion. We were led by Hauptmann Wiegand. In the middle of the narrow corridor I described above, we found one or our own Tigers that had been towed back. It was immobile and was positioned on the road. There was a village about one and a half kilometers away. The crew of the damaged tank had already fended off a Russian infantry attack from that direction. Strong enemy forces were expected. Evidently, they didn't have any antitank weapons available at the moment. We attacked that village from late in the afternoon until evening and drove off the Russian infantry. Hauptmann Wiegand left two of our tanks to stay on the road at that critical point, while he continued on to the battalion with the rest of the vehicles.

While we secured that critical sector and the damaged tank, the Russians were completely quiet for a while. We became careless. The next day, sheltered from the wind between the tightly clustered vehicles, we made our coffee. At about midday I had an uncomfortable feeling and took a look forward of the tanks to observe the village. I must have had quite a look on my face before I shouted, "Alarm!" Widely dispersed, the Russians had worked their way unnoticed to within 100 meters of our tanks. Our carelessness had almost been severely punished. We jumped into the two operable vehicles and threw the battalion of Russian bastards back into the village.

In the afternoon the battalion slowly drew back to our position. The Landser who had been freed from the pocket wee streaming back. The operation had been successful, but at what cost. To be sure, a large number of German soldiers had escaped out of the pocket, but they had lost practically all their weapons and equipment and, what was worse, they had left behind the majority of their wounded comrades. At that point our new commander, Hauptmann Fromme, arrived at the battalion from Germany.

Once again, our tank rolled back to the maintenance facility at Potasch. There was a big celebration. Officer candidates Hans Lewandowski and Alfred Rubbel had been posted to officer candidate school. Unteroffizier Alois Trnka, in charge of the orderly room, was made a Feldwebel. Gerald Höppner and I became Unteroffiziere. Even today I can still see my unforgettable loader, Erich Walter, grinning as he said, "That's like setting the fox to guard the hen house!" Somehow, I was a bit offended. Why hadn't I been promoted to Obergefreiter? My comrades put an end to my regrets. I was named an honorary member of the Obergefreiter's mess.

Our celebration in Potasch was not only a binge, it was also a lot of fun. I was still unable to fully realize the wish that I had nurtured for so long—to even the score with the orderly-room Unteroffizier who had harassed me so long. Now he had advanced past me in rank. I was only allowed to extract partial revenge. I grabbed a large cooking pot and asked him to drink a toast to bury the hatchet. While Alois Trnka still thought there might be something with alcohol in it, I poured the kettle full of pea soup over his head. It was great.

The weeks that followed—right into April—were filled with more than just work for the tank elements. We fought in vain to hold the Russian pincer movements at bay that eventually led to the formation of the Kamenez/Podolsk pocket. We could knock out as many of them as we wanted. The T-34s seemed to multiply like rabbits. Eventually we, too, had to fight our way through to the south as part of what was also called the Hube Pocket. We took over the spearhead toward the west until, finally, thanks to the commitment of the 9th SS Panzer Division "Frundsberg" and the 10th SS Panzer Division "Hohenstaufen," we succeeded in getting out of that hell.

OBERLEUTNANT REUTERMANN

The operations outlined above began for us in Proskuroff. We had a new company commander, Oberleutnant Reutermann. After we had gotten to know him at Bjelgorod when he was operating with Panzer IVs in an adjacent regiment, we in the crew did not mince words with him: "Don't do things like that with this company. If you lose that many Tigers in a fight, you will be facing a court martial. But be reassured, you dontt need to do that." He would soon see for himself.

The battalion attacked north under the new commander, Hauptmann Fromme. On 8 March the village of Frydrychowka was captured. Oberleutnant Reutermann was amazed. One platoon of the company opened the night operation with a flank attack from the east. The village burned. The tanks which were employed to the front hardly had to get involved. We were practically spectators as our comrades knocked out the fleeing Russian tanks. We would only have endangered our own side if we had become involved in that engagement. During that engagement we lost Feldwebel Erdmann. As a result, the bottle of champagne that the Oberleutnant had coughed up tasted flat to us.

At that time, Unteroffizier Mundry was gunner. Obergefreiter Schmidtke was driver, and Obergefreiter Walter was our loader. Heinz Mundry knew how to do his work well, having spent a long period as a loader. Erich Walter was a armorer by trade, so we were, in that respect, completely self sufficient. Summing up, Joachim Schmidtke was a very experienced driver, with a lot of action already behind him.

Our battalion's advance to Frydrychowka had gone sensationally deep into the Russian flank. Elements of the trains and additional tanks that had been repaired at the maintenance facility could not be brought forward very rapidly by Hauptmann Wiegand. It was still night as we moved many kilometers in the direction of the trains in our tank with Oberleutnant Reutermann. We came to a marshy, broad riverbed and reconnoitered three relatively widely separated crossings. Then we moved farther south in order to link up with the trains in a village.

After we had linked up, our engine went on strike. The Oberleutnant took the gunner with him and drove off toward Frydrychowka in the command Kübelwagen (driver: Obergefreiter Krause), together with the trains. One man from the maintenance section was supposed to repair the problem. I would then link up with the Oberleutnant. The repair work took several hours. Finally, we could follow our unit. In the meantime, light snow had started to fall. Again and again we saw fresh track marks in the ground where Russian tanks had crossed our direction of travel. I was extremely cautious. We drove with the intercom turned on. The Gefreiter from the maintenance section had to be ready to fill in as loader, while Erich Walter took the gunner's place.

As we drew nearer to the marshy lowland, I had to decide which of the three crossings we had scouted I would use. At that point, there was no radio contact with the unit. The distance was too great. I decided to use the middle crossing. A defile led down in a curve to it. At the end of the extremely long embankment that led over the marshy terrain were three Waffen-SS trucks that had been plundered. Nothing had happened at that location last night. I was wide awake. The

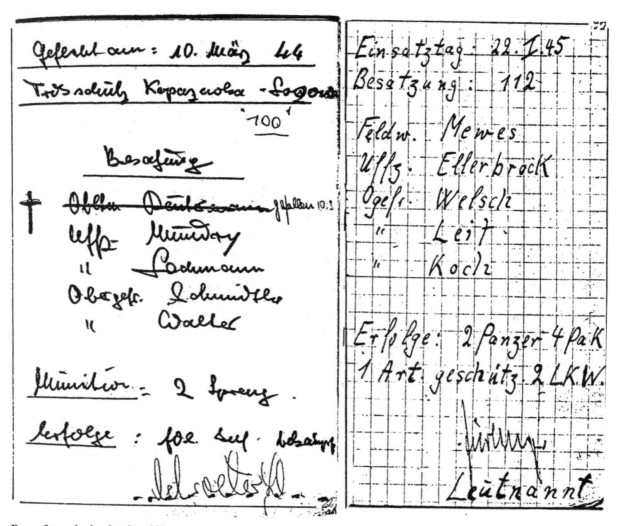

Pages from the log books of Tigers 100 and 112. The entries have been verified by the platoon leaders and tank commanders for the respective tanks. The left-hand entries are from Leutnant Schröder; the right-hand entries from Leutnant Fürlinger.

causeway that stretched before us was about 300 meters long. At the other end there was a sort of sandy ridge on which a village was built.

Laundry flapped in the wind in front of every house. There was no doubt about it. A Russian unit was quartered there, but we had not yet been spotted. I thought about it. There was no way we could move in reverse since, in that terrain, we would lose our tracks in any sort of turning movement. Could we turn around in that small area? We would have made so much noise that any antitank weapons in the village would be alerted to our presence. If we then went and turned our vulnerable rear armor toward them? No way! That was not an option. Well, then, forward and through!

We headed down the narrow causeway at full speed. The driver, Jochen Schmidtke, understood

his work perfectly. While advancing, we placed a high-explosive round in the midst of those bastards to create a little confusion. At that moment I heard a cry from our replacement loader. The dumb fool had activated the safety with his right hand and his left hand was still on the gun shield as the barrel recoiled. In spite of smashed fingers, he shoved the next round into the barrel and we fired that one, too, as we drove on at full speed. It all went very fast. We were in the village, the Russians fled and then we were through. We moved on over some flat high ground and, about 500 meters beyond, I found a position that was suitable for transmitting over a long distance to reach our own troops. Oberleutnant Reutermann had chosen the western crossing. Our tanks had already nearly completed escorting the fuel and ammunition trucks past that sector. We then assumed rear-guard duties.

Oberleutnant Reutermann had left our gunner, Heinz Mundry, behind as a guide at that location. The Oberleutnant had gone ahead with Obergefreiter Krause to bring the happy news about the arrival of the trains to Frydrychowka. He was fired on from a village on the western flank while heading there. We reconstructed what then happened, after the fact. The village, into which the Oberleutnant had driven so as to scout it out, was occupied by partisans. Obergefreiter Krause was killed with a round to the head. Our company commander, Oberleutnant Reutermann, however, was beaten to death.

MEMORIAL DAY [*HELDENGEDENKTAG*]

We then moved predominantly to the south or the southwest behind the Russian pincers. It was 13 March. We were located in some small village with Tiger 100, securing the trains elements of our battalion. A motorcycle messenger brought Unteroffizier Höppner to us as tank commander to complete our crew. Infantry in the next village requested our assistance because the Russians had infiltrated. We went there and threw the Russians out. From there we were able to observe how a group of Russian tanks was approaching the village where we had just left our trains. Behind the tanks we saw endless columns of Russian infantry. Since we were all by ourselves, we resolved to fool the Ivans with a trick.

Between the two villages was a patch of woods. We moved around it in a wide arc and maneuvered so we would were on the flank of the Russian infantry columns and moving behind their tanks. Everything went exactly as we had thought it would. The Russians did not notice it was a German vehicle. They greeted us cheerfully. The seven Russian tanks that were moving in front of us were T-34s of the latest type. Before the poor guys had noticed what was happening, we had knocked out four of them. And, to our general edification, we had to play a few more measures of the march music that was so popular that day .Two T-34s turned and fled. The last one was suddenly in front of us, cowering in a Balka. His gun barrel was aimed directly at us. But Mundry was faster. There was a great jet of flame that shot up from the turret. I am sure that I saw that tank commander sitting on top of the flame. Along with

the antitank gun we had eliminated in the other village, we had done enough for the day.

The battalion rolled on. We were advancing more or less to the south, in the direction of Skalat. The crew was now a smoothly functioning team. On 15 March 1944 we took the village of Skalat. We fought our way onward toward the Hube pocket. The battalion's adjutant, Oberleutnant Linden, joined us on 20 March. He became the acting commander of the 1st Company. We duked it out with the Russians at Hill 401 northeast of Skalat. Due to the lack of an adequate supply of high-explosive rounds, we were having to engage field positions with armor-piercing rounds—it improved morale more than anything else. While bypassing a patch of woods the next day, we ran onto mines. However, we were soon back in action and, by the following day, we were able to participate in some heavy tank engagements, when the battalion was involved at Grzymalow. Thank God, we had almost nothing but armor-piercing rounds on board.

The Russians attacked with very large armored formations. The battalion no longer had many tanks available. Widely dispersed in hilly terrain, we accepted the Russian challenge. After we knocked out the first few tanks, the Russians scattered in general disorder. They tried to get away from our armor-piercing rounds by scattering in every direction. All of the T-34s carried two drums of diesel fuel with them on the back of the vehicle, so even high-explosive rounds were a disaster for them.

Oberfeldwebel Rondorf of the 3rd Company moved to our left. That day he seemed to have all kinds of success. If an enemy tank appeared in front of us, it was gone before you knew it. Rondorf had scored a hit. It was unbelievable how he was cleaning up. We were downright envious, though we were not exactly idle. We still managed to get seven T-34s. As the fighting went on and we ran out of high-explosive rounds, we had to engage trucks and other enemy vehicles with armor-piercing rounds. By evening, we had used up a total of forty-five armor-piecing and eighteen high-explosive rounds. Oberleutnant Linden had got off to a good start. (See the vehicle log book elsewhere.)

We were off to the southwest again and reached Touste the following day. The village was behind a small river we had to cross. The battalion was down to only a very few vehicles by then. The majority of the Tigers provided cover to the northeast and held off strong enemy formations. We were ordered into the village and filled our fuel tanks. In the process, Mundry, our gunner, was wounded by an artillery fragment. He had recently been promoted to Unteroffizier. Feldwebel Mertens temporarily joined us. He was from the Headquarters Company.

We were instructed to follow the river a little bit to the west with our vehicle to scout out the situation. About three kilometers from Touste we encountered horse-drawn artillery. It was in the process of crossing the river to the southwest at a ford in order to continue toward Husatin. We heard from those soldiers that there was a tank located in the steppe to the north of the crossing point. We moved to the spot and found Unteroffizier von Borries' crew with an immobile Tiger. The driver was my former loader, Herbert Ritscher. We reported the situation to the battalion and were ordered back to Touste. The situation there very quickly became serious.

The Tigers had to cross the river, since the Russians had not only started to attack with major reinforcements, but the main body of the Ivans had already gone around our flank to the east and threatened to cut us off. In addition, we heard that Husatin was already in Russian hands. Thus, the horse-drawn artillery was heading directly toward the Russians, and our comrades on the steppe would no longer get through either. We continued the withdrawal and repeatedly took over securing the withdrawal route. For once, on 28 March, we did not have any contact with the enemy. On 29 March we advanced to Skala and took it. We were convinced that we would soon reach the Hube pocket.

EVENING AT SKALA

The civilians had cleared out of the village. We quartered ourselves in an apothecary's house and cooked a big batch of chicken soup. Then we sat down. "Bon Appetit to all," said Obergefreiter Walter, our loader. He was first to stick his hand into the pot of soup. Obergefreiter Berger and Schmidtke and I followed his example. Oberleutnant Linden watched us, disapprovingly: "Just like in Bavaria." He stood up and left the room. We kept on eating ravenously. By that time, we knew Hannes Berger liked being part of our crew. He was one of the most experienced soldiers in the

company. First as a radio operator, then as gunner, he had been in a vast number of armored engagements. By the end of the war he could tally more than a hundred armored engagements. He also had the great good fortune of never being wounded. Hannes was a quiet type with a sunny disposition. He liked playing chess. When he had to, however, he could attack any job forcefully.

While we were still sitting next to the chicken soup, the door opened suddenly and our commander, Hauptmann Fromme, appeared. "What do you have to chow down on?" He was already sitting down with us. He dipped his hand into the soup and grabbed a drumstick. "Where is Hannes Linden hiding?" he inquired, while he chewed.

Erich Walter opined, "He is too well-mannered to eat with us."

The commander laughed. Vodka followed the meal. "Man, oh man," said the commander. "You're pulling out all the stops."

"That we are," answered Walter.

"What's the occasion?" asked the commander. "Is someone celebrating a birthday?"

"No, Herr Hauptmann. We our celebrating our radio operator's fiftieth tank operation. And, of course, we are also celebrating the scout car and airplane that we bagged today."

Our forces consisted of the remains of the 7th Panzer Division, the remains of the 1st SS Panzer Division "Leibstandarte" and a freshly constituted infantry division from Germany—nothing but young guys who didn't have a clue. They were thrown against the Russians and, for the most part, immediately decimated. In addition, there was also a wonderful separate Heeres-Flak-Abteilung. By that point, the battalion was down to only three tanks. There was Tiger "II" of the battalion, Feldwebel Seidel's tank from the 3rd Company, and our Tiger 100. Fuel and rations were in short supply. Every time, at critical moments, He 111 formations showed up and supplied us with the requisite fuel and emergency rations by air drop.

Oberst Mauß commanded our battle group, which slowly made its way to join the Hube pocket. On one occasion we found time to prepare a delicious meal in a village. It seems our quarters were selected for a situation briefing. All the officers were sitting together. We passed out "hors d'oeuvres"—as befitted the situation. The door opened and our loader, Erich Walter, appeared. Granted, he had not "found" any canned goods, but he had found a top hat. He burst into our quarters wearing it. Confused, he removed his headgear when he saw what a distinguished gathering had assembled. "Praise be to Jesus, gentlemen. This is what I like, everybody is chowing down with the crew of Tiger 100." Peals of laughter.

During the final breakthrough to the southwest on 31 March we knocked out three more T-34s. We had finally reached the Kamenez/Podolsk pocket and then moved with our three Tigers as its spearhead toward the west.

It happened as we were crossing the Sereth on a massive bridge. The construction had too little decking. It got to shaking and, without any fanfare, we slid into the river. It was a long time before we could get Tiger 100 out again. Hannes Linder, the company commander, was fatally injured. In the end, the river was crossed at a ford. At that point, Tiger 100 gave up the ghost. The damage was only minor, but there were no replacement parts. We were forced to blow it up.

One day later there was a new misfortune. Feldwebel Seidel's tank also had to be abandoned. On 6 April the commander turned over the last of the battalion's tanks, Tiger "II," to the battalion orderly, Leutnant Heerlein. The driver, Gefreiter Lange and the medium-wave radio operator, Gefreiter Spann remained with the vehicle. We replaced the balance of the crew. I took over the ultra-short wave radio in the turret and had to share the space with our loader, Walter. Our gunner, Hannes Berger, took his accustomed position. When the pocket finally broke out of the encirclement, we formed the rear guard. Tiger "II" looked pretty bad. The running gear had been shot up, but it still ran. Ammunition was in extremely short supply. We had six armor-piercing

rounds left. In the end, we stayed without infantry in a shell-torn village and waited for the Russian armored attack. In the best case scenario, we could earn some respect by knocking out six tanks and then get out of there intact. And, as it turned out, that is how it went. We were able to withdraw across the river. We had been fortunate enough to survive the Hube pocket. After a few kilometers, we encountered Major Burmester, our former company commander. He was then the battalion commander of Tiger Tank Battalion 509. We had to turn over the only tank left in the battalion to him. As a result, we could not make a "grand" entry into Lemberg, where our battalion had already assembled.

As we wearily removed our meager belongings from Tiger "II," Hein asked the obligatory question: "Have you also unloaded the gun?" My God! When had we ever unloaded the weapon during the recent weeks? We had to check it out. Walter climbed back into the vehicle one more time. He attempted to open the breech of the gun. Nothing moved. Shit! There was still a round in the tube. We traversed the gun toward the east and sent a final salute to Ivan. The breech still refused to open. The gun was defective. What if . . . ? We didn't want to think about it.

What had only been heard as rumors in the pocket became fact in Lemberg. Group Mittermaier had been renamed as Tiger Tank Battalion 503 (new). It had been formed from battalion soldiers who had not been in the Hube pocket. Group Mittermaier was employed in the Tarnopol area. We, however, were withdrawn from the East and returned to Germany, where we ended up at the Ohrdruf training grounds. The battalion was reorganized. I was fortunate and, after a relatively short wait, received three weeks of home leave.

CHAPTER 18

Fendesack's Platoon

Alfred Rubbel

Platoon Fendesack was the contingent of five crews and Tigers which had joined the 1st Company of Tiger Tank Battalion 503 in March 1943. Oberfeldwebel Hans Fendesack had led the contingent from Panzer Replacement Battalion 500 in Paderborn. In addition to Fendesack were tank commanders Petzka, Rippl, Rubbel and Seidel and their crews. Fendesack, Rippl and Rubbel were assigned to the 1st Company; Petzka went to the 2nd Company; and, Seidel was assigned to the 3rd Company.

We didn't stay together in the 1st Company either. In the course of reorganizing the battalion according to the 1944 tables of organization and equipment—the Panzer IIIs were turned in—we were distributed among all three platoons of the company. I landed in the first platoon with Leutnant Jammerath and commanded Tiger 114. My companions in the tank were Walter Junge (gunner), Walter Eschrig (driver), Alfred Peuker (also as driver) and the quiet Johann Strohmer (loader). But let's start at the beginning . . .

Christmas 1942: After almost ten days of travel by rail, we were assembled as Personaleinheit Schober (cadre unit), along with the remnants of the 3rd Battalion of the 4th Panzer Regiment. We were coming from the Ordshonikidse area in the East Caucasus to the gunnery school at Putlos. We were to receive new-equipment training on the Panzer VI (Tiger).

The very pleasant period at Putlos did not last long. We were transferred to Panzer Replacement Battalion 500 at Paderborn and, later, at the end of the training, to the training area at Sennelager. The training was thorough and concerned itself exclusively with the Panzer VI (Tiger). The personnel of the unit mostly came from the 4th and 29th Panzer Regimenter, southern Germans and Austrians from the 4th Panzer Regiment and northern Germans from the 29th. We had been formed into a company. All of soldiers had gained sufficient front experience during a year and a half of action on the Eastern Front.

Those of us in Platoon Fendesack had gotten to know each other quite well during the time we were employed in the central sector, on the northern front and in the Caucasus with the 29th Panzer Regiment. Judging by the preparations for personnel and tanks, we were headed toward service in the tropics. Company Schober formed the nucleus for the reorganization of Tiger Tank Battalion 504. It was intended to use it with the Afrika Korps and was initially sent to Sicily. The surrender of the Afrika Korps and the critical developments in the winter of 1942–43 on the Eastern Front changed the situation for us, too.

At Padeborn and Sennelager we were in a comfortable situation. The duties were pleasant, the superiors understanding, the war far away. We asked ourselves what employment might be planned for us. We would soon get the answer. It was in the middle of March, at the morning formation of the company. As was the norm, the tank crews formed up by crew. It was announced to the company that five crews, with tanks, would be detailed for service at the Eastern Front. The company command was faced with the difficult task of sending twenty-five men to the Eastern Front while the main body would remain in the rear. No one knew how long it would stay or whether it would be sent for service at some other, less difficult theater of the war. In the search for solutions, it was also considered whether the "Eastern Front" contingent should be selected with equal numbers of northern Germans and southern Germans or, indeed, just be chosen by lot. The company command apparently did not consider volunteering an option.

The ensuing chain of events is among the strongest impressions I ever had during the war. I still remember them as if they were yesterday. We stood at ease. Spieß Gruber had explained the situation to us. What was I thinking? I would have liked to spend some more time in Westphalia. While all were generally somewhat non-plussed— that was how I perceived it—Fendesack turned from his position at the right side of the first rank, in which the tank commanders stood, looked left along the row of tank commanders, nodded, hesitated a moment, and, without a word, stepped five steps forward. That was unusual, as was what followed. Without haste, indeed, somewhat hesitantly, four additional commanders stepped forward. They were the four who came from the 29th Panzer Regiment. They had been in action in the central sector at Minsk, Witebsk and Wjasma, in the northern sector at Tschudowo, Schlüsselburg, and Tichwin and in the Caucasus at Maikop and Ordschonikidse. Some of them had even fought with the same crews in formation with them that morning.

Only those who were on the parade ground in front of Block 9 at Sennelager that morning can grasp the special nature of what happened. The five commanders who spontaneously decided to voluntarily go to the Eastern Front in response to Fendesack's example, needed crews for their tanks. We looked back to our former crews. In the blink of an eye twenty-five tankers had closed ranks with us and volunteered freely for the Eastern Front. I still remember the magnificence of

that gesture. We wanted to stay together. Even though we already had enough experience at the Eastern Front and knew what was awaiting us there, we chose to stay together over all the other possibilities, including more pleasant prospects. And thus it was that we came to Tiger Tank Battalion 503.

It was Easter in 1943 when we and our brand new Tigers arrived at the billeting area of the 1st Company at Bogoduchow, about 60 kilometers northwest of Kharkov. Right off the bat, we were somewhat irritated by what we experienced during the days and weeks that followed in the company. We were dismayed at the composition of the personnel and the mood of the company.

The most advanced tank of the day had been turned over to soldiers, most of whom, at the enlisted level, had scarcely any experience at the front. That says nothing about their qualities of character. On the contrary, we found an overwhelming number of close friends among those men. As for the noncommissioned officers, we couldn't help but notice there were four Stabsfeldwebel in the company. Three of them did administrative duties. Only one of them, the "Staber" Ehrentraut mounted up in a tank and had a respectable amount of combat experience. We later learned to respect him a lot. We were also very put off by the Spieß's decision to billet tanks commanders separately from their crews in the billeting area Boguchow. Thanks to the authority of our "Little Hans" Fendesack, we were able to remain with our crews. Such an action was not the norm at that time in the 1st Company.

We were fortunate that Fendesack knew Oberleutnant Oemler, who was the acting company commander at the time. As a result, there were no repercussions against our decision to stay with the crews. For example, as the youngest commander, it was intended for me to turn over my tank to someone who was older but who had no frontline experience. That did not happen. We also found it unacceptable that the Unteroffiziere had priority in line at the field kitchen or had their food brought to them. We consciously fought against that bad practice. When the tank commanders were due for their food, they closed their mess tins with a loud snap and took a place in the enlisted line at the field kitchen without regard to their rank. That did not fail to make an impression.

One more experience that depressed me: It concerned the medical care within the battalion. Seidel's driver, Schmidt, had an attack of malaria. Since I was familiar with the course of tertian Malaria—like Schmidt, I had caught it in the Caucasus—I brought Schmidt to the battalion's medical section. Since the medics were unfamiliar with the symptoms of malaria, they called the battalion physician. That doctor's therapy: 1) a sharp dressing-down for both of us and, 2) an order to maintain discipline and not bother the doctor with such bagatelles. Schmidt survived the malaria, but was later killed.

Fendesack's platoon quickly integrated itself into the company—and without any harm to the company! We found a comradeship that still holds firm today. I am convinced that Hans Fendesack, more than any other, and perhaps without even being aware of it, was responsible for the good way the company turned out. He toned down the brash and encouraged the modest. His task was to lead a platoon, but, unintentionally, he accomplished far more. Today one would label what he did with the high-brow term of "inner leadership." Hans Fendesack, decorated in 1943 with the German Cross [*Deutches Kreuz*] in Gold, was killed on 18 August 1944 in the Falaise area of the invasion front. He was thirty-one years old. He left behind his wife, but no children, in Breslau. Like all of us, he was not free of human weakness. He was a particularly fortunate combination of soldier, comrade, superior, friend and human being. Without in any way diminishing the respect due others in the battalion for those qualities, Oberfeldwebel Hans Fendesack was an exemplary soldier in both war and peace to me. In addition to me, many members of the 1st Company remember him with gratitude and respect.

CHAPTER 19

The Dog and Pony Show

Alfred Rubbel

It is no secret that, aside from the 503's 3rd Company (the former 2nd Company, Tiger Tank Battalion 502)—things were somewhat better there—the personnel of the 1st and 2nd Companies were composed to a large extent of personnel who had not had any experience in Russia or with "shots fired in anger." In the "script" for the "Dog and Pony Show," the 2nd Company was chosen to execute a live-fire exercise during one portion of the demonstration. The higher-ranking officers were not entirely satisfied with the way it went, particularly Field Marshal von Manstein. I ask my honored former commander, Graf von Kageneck, to pardon me for presenting private details of the battalion here, but he had only just taken over the battalion and certainly could not be held responsible for its state of training—my supposition being that my "reliable sources" have reported accurately to me. Further, I am not at all certain whether the 1st or 3rd Companies would have fired any better.

The consequence: The battalion was ordered to carry out a wide-ranging training program that included weapon and equipment training, breaching obstacles and live-fire exercises at the main lines on the Donez in the Tschugujew area.

The companies road marched from Kharkov, either closed up or by platoons, to the previously noticeably quiet infantry positions on the western bank of the Donez. Our appearance made it difficult for the Russians on the far bank, since we shot their bunkers to pieces. That put an end to the period of quiet for both sides, since the Russians answered with their artillery. I doubt if the infantry who were holding the positions were very enthusiastic about our arrival.

Our period on the Donez also served as a "morale boost". We were sent to the rear elements of the units holding the positions with individual Tigers to demonstrate the new "wonder weapon." I was at a regimental headquarters company with Tiger 114. After the demonstration was completed, there was a fearful amount of booze flowing. Someone, hopefully it was the regiment's commander, doubted that the Tiger could smash down a house. It came to a test, which turned out positive. It turned out, however, that the "test object" housed the regiment's telephone switchboard. It was a good thing that we could head back to Kharkov the next day.

The Turkish delegation views the "Dog and Pony" Show on 25 June 1943 at Kharkov. The senior officer of the Turkish delegation, Colonel General Toydemir, can be seen at the scissors scope on the left. Generalfeldmarschall von Manstein, the commander-in-chief of Army Group South, is observing through the second set of optics.

CHAPTER 20

Citadel

Richard Freiherr von Rosen

On 11 April 1943 the battalion moved to Mariupol. Three days later it was rail loaded to Bogoduchow, seventy kilometers southwest of Kharkov. The 3rd Company was given billets in Ssemenjof-Jar. New tanks arrived. There was little duty and soccer was played. On Easter Monday things started happening again. The battalion road marched along the Kharkov-Bjelgorod road. The 3rd Company set up in a patch of woods at Tolokonoje, thirty kilometers behind the front at Bjelgorod. The company received combat engineer training from Oberfeldwebel Baumann. In particular, it learned how to remove and defuse the notorious wooden-cased mines. Additional Tigers arrived, as did personnel replacements from the replacement battalion. The company turned in the remaining Panzer IIIs and then had fourteen Tigers, organized into a company headquarters section with two Panzer VIs, and three tank platoons, each with four Panzer VIs. Oberfeldwebel an der Heiden became the platoon leader of the newly formed third platoon. Oberfeldwebel Rondorf, the company Spieß, became a tank commander in the first platoon. Stabsfeldwebel Kisseberth became the new company first sergeant.

On that day Tiger Tank Battalion 503 achieved its authorized strength of forty-five Panzer VIs. As a result, it consisted of three complete tank companies.

At the beginning of May 1943 the intended attack against the Kursk salient (Operation Citadel) was postponed. Hitler wanted to delay starting the offensive until the first production batch of several hundred Panthers had arrived at the front.

On 10 May the entire battalion moved to Kharkov. At Kharkov, intensive training was initiated, particularly driver training and practical gunnery training. For that purpose, the 3rd Company was moved in platoon increments to the front at the Donez River. Once there, the platoons engaged Russian bunkers, antitank gun positions and mortar dug-outs that had been previously identified on the far bank of the Donez.

At the beginning of June the 3rd Company took part in a major exercise within the framework of the 7th Panzer Division. The exercise was near Kharkov and took place in front of higher-ranking commanders of Army Group South. A similar exercise, likewise with live ammunition, was carried out on 27 June in front of Field Marshal von Manstein and a group of Turkish generals whom Hitler had invited to inspect the Eastern Front. At about that time, the second commander of the battalion, Oberstleutnant Hoheisel, left command to later become commander of the Tiger training courses at Paderborn. Hauptmann Graf Kageneck became the new commander.

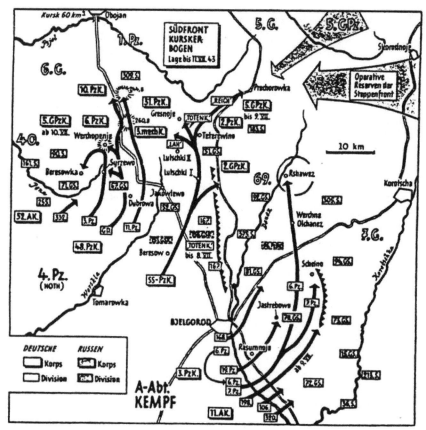

The Southern Sector of the Kursk Salient through 11 July 1943.

Tiger Tank Battalion 503 was placed under the operational control of the III Panzer Corps (Breith) for Operation Citadel. The corps consisted of the 6th, 19th, and 7th Panzer Divisions. In spite of spirited objections by the battalion commander, Tiger Tank Battalion 503 was split up and attached to the three panzer divisions for the attack. The commanders of those divisions saw the attachment somewhat differently from their viewpoints: They wanted to form a battering ram or a strong armored spearhead so they could better break through the enemy's strong defensive front. The Tiger could do that far better than the inadequately armored Panzer III and Panzer IV.

As a result, the 1st Company went to the 6th Panzer Division, the 2nd Company to the 19th Panzer Division, and the 3rd Company to the 7th Panzer Division.

The 3rd Company was placed under the operational control of the 25th Panzer Regiment, whose commander was Oberstleutnant Schulz, later Generalmajor and recipient of the diamonds to the Knight's Cross.

Within the 3rd Company, Leutnant von Rosen's second platoon was placed in front during and after crossing the Donez, which formed the front line. Days preceding the attack, Leutnant von Rosen had already reconnoitered a ford for the tanks. He had conducted the reconnaissance in a night patrol together with the combat engineers and the grenadiers who were at the front. The streambed was good, but the banks were too steep on both banks and would have to be reduced by the engineers using explosives. Accordingly, the plans were laid out so the grenadiers would first form a bridgehead so the engineers could start their activities.

The 3rd Company moved on 1 July 1943 from Kharkov to the assembly area at Tolokonnoje on the Kharkov-Bjelgorod road. During the evening of 4 July the company moved to the jump-off position that had been reconnoitered for the attack. The second platoon, in advance of the company, moved to a point directly west of the intended crossing point at Ssolomimo with a good field of fire on the enemy positions.

On 5 July at 0230 hours the German artillery opened its barrage and the infantry crossed the Donez in rubber assault boats. The 2nd Platoon rushed to the bank with the combat engineers, the demolition charges were brought forward and both banks were blown in short order. At that point, the enemy counterfire opened up. Artillery and mortar fire concentrated on the crossing site. The platoon-leader's tank, Tiger 221, moved into the river and disappeared in the water up to the mud guards. The tank waded through the river and started to climb the far bank. However, the tracks could not gain a grip on the soft earth where the bank had been blown, so the river crossing failed. The towing cable had to be attached to the tank underwater and then lengthened. This was done under heavy artillery and mortar fire. After hard work—under continuous fire—it succeeded and Tiger 221 was towed back and pulled up onto the firm bank.

It was then necessary to wait until the engineers had built a bridge capable of bearing the weight of a Tiger at the same place. The Tigers were positioned on the river banks—widely dispersed—while the infantry fought their way forward without armor protection. In a superhuman performance, disregarding gunfire and losses, the engineers readied the bridge after five hours of work. Early in the afternoon of 5 July, the second platoon was finally able to cross the Donez and make it to the front. At long last it was able to bring some relief to the infantry that had shed so much blood in holding the bridgehead for hours.

On 6 July the attack of the 3rd Company and the 25th Panzer Regiment continued along the Rasumnaja stream in the direction of the destroyed village of Generalowka. Antitank guns, artillery pieces, tanks and infantry were destroyed. But our own losses were also heavy. Oberleutnant Scherf, commander of the 3rd Company was put out of action. Leutnant von Rosen then led the units that had been attached to the 25th Panzer Regiment. He was then also severely wounded five days later. In the 1st Company, Leutnant Jammerath was killed.

The 3rd Company battered its way straight through Krutoj Log, Batrazkaja Datscha, Mjassojedowo and Scheino, breaking through one Russian defensive system after another. The company had four total losses by July 12 and almost all the tanks had suffered heavy to very heavy damage from the deeply echeloned minefields and antitank positions. In just a few days, ten veteran tankers were killed. Among them were Feldwebel Wunderlich, Oberfeldwebel Tröger, Unteroffizier Miederer, Unteroffizier Angerer, Unteroffizier Clas, and Unteroffizier Petzka.

Tiger Tank Battalion 503 gained bitter experience during the fighting in Operation Citadel. The Russians had learned how to set up defenses in any line they held. They held in great depth, well dug in. "Walls of artillery" and "antitank fronts" were set up facing every breakthrough point. Tanks in unheard of numbers and the newly introduced Russian assault guns repeatedly blocked the way. The battalion encountered for the first time the heavy KV-85 tank and the SU-152 assault gun with its 152mm howitzer. Thus, the enemy succeeded in bringing our attack to a halt and, finally, in completely shattering it.

Carell writes of the fighting on 7 and 8 July:

As soon as they had crossed the Donets south of Razumnoye, the regiments were involved in heavy fighting by Soviet armored forces. The grenadiers of 7th Panzer Division heaved a sigh of relief when the 25th Panzer Regiment from Erlangen at last arrived. Heading the long columns of tanks was Lieutenant-Colonel Adalbert Schulz in his command tank.

Lieutenant-Colonel Adalbert Schulz, generally known as "Panzer Schulz," spread confidence wherever he went. The grenadiers knew that wherever he was nothing went wrong. They now watched him prepare for action. Fan out. Batten down hatches. Advance in a broad wedge. And already the first tank guns were opening up.

Schulz had got right into a Soviet tank assembly position. The enemy commander clearly lacked combat experience. He led his unit nervously, losing the overall view. As darkness fell on the battlefield thirty-four T-34s, a curious play on numbers, were littering the ground around Razumnoye, in flames or smoldering.

But a strong enemy was well established and brilliantly camouflaged in the thick forests on the ridge of high ground. The division was caught in enfilading artillery fire. The Panzer Regiment was unable to help.

But the corps had to move on, move forward, unless the whole plan was to be upset. Manteuffel regrouped. On 8th July he succeeded by means of concentrated forces in breaking through the Russian barrier on the ridge of high ground behind the Donets.

General Breith immediately exploited this success. Since 6th Panzer Division was clearly encountering difficulties in crossing the Donets bridges at Belgorod to schedule, he did not hesitate long. "The main effort has got to be made wherever the front is moving forward," he said to Colonel Merk, his chief of staff. In consequence, he also moved 6th Panzer Division into the zone of attack of 7th Panzer Division.

The two divisions now burst forward towards the northeast. To their left, 19th Panzer Division was moving forward. Along the Donets, 168th Infantry Division was punching its own way ahead; its task was to provide cover for the open flank of the Berlin Panzer Corps.

Over a broad front the tank regiments cleared the way for the grenadiers, Panzer-Schulz on the right, Colonel von Oppeln-Bronikowski with his Paderborn 11th Panzer Regiment on the left. Between them was Count von Kageneck's Tiger Battalion 503. An armada of 240 tanks was sweeping towards the enemy positions.

But east of the Donets too the Russians were established in well-built defensive zones echeloned in depth. Anti-tank gun emplacements, minefields, antitank ditches were everywhere. Moreover, there were some tricky swamps.

Breith, an experienced and shrewd commander of armored forces, realized that in the circumstances he would never be able to thrust sufficiently fast or sufficiently far to the east to keep to the timetable. He therefore made the only correct decision and on 8th July wheeled towards the north.

In a small ravine near Yastrebovo Breith met the commander of 6th Panzer Division. The two command tanks halted alongside.

The maps were spread out on the floors of these mobile armored signals stations. The corps commander's hand brushed towards the top of the map: "Hünersdorff, you will make a thrust to the north and break through. You will cause the enemy's main defensive zone to collapse!"

And Walter von Hünersdorff, one of the boldest and most experienced tank commanders in the Wehrmacht, moved off. He toppled the Soviet defensive positions. He repulsed an attack by Soviet armored forces near Melekhovo. Together with 19th Panzer Division he encircled two Soviet rifle divisions.

Forward! Without halting, 6th Panzer Division raced on to the upper Donets. Would it get to Prokhorovka in time?

The Soviet High Command realized the danger threatening from this massive thrust along the flank of the operation. Stalin ordered his strategic reserves from the distant Steppe Front to move towards Prokhorovka in forced marches. Would they arrive in time?

Lieutenant Podgorbunskiy jumped out of the way, saluted, and stared after the general in amazement.

No one had ever seen the chief of staff in such a state. He was normally a calm, stolid person whom nothing could upset. But now he was running through the little ravine that housed the advanced headquarters of First Tank Army, panting, his face purple, and without his cap. He stormed up the slope toward a little wood. He disappeared in the thick undergrowth.

Up there was an artillery observation post. General Katukov and Nikita Sergeyevich Khrushchev had gone up there an hour previously.

But when Major-General Shalin burst into the command post through its camouflage of branches and foliage, there was only Khrushchev left. Katukov had gone on to the HQ of VI Tank Corps.

"What's up?" Nikita Sergeyevich asked suspiciously on seeing Shalin in a state of utter consternation.

The chief of staff, still trying to recover his breath, wordlessly handed him a piece of paper—a signal on a printed form. It came from General Cherniyenkov's XXXI Tank Corps.

Khrushchev read: "Defenses penetrated. Troops in flight and not to be stopped. Usychov." Disaster! Disaster recorded in eleven words.

"Who is that?" Khrushchev asked, his finger excitedly tapping the signature.

"Lieutenant-Colonel Usychov is chief of signals of XXXI Tank Corps," Shalin replied.

"If his report is correct then nothing can stop the Germans from striking across the Psel at the rear of the First Tank Army," Kruschev muttered.

And what he thought, although he did not utter it, was this: If the Germans strike at the rear of First Tank Army, then the Russian defense must collapse along the southern front of Kursk. That would be the end of the battle for Kursk. That would mean victory for the Germans.

Regarding the breakthrough on 10 and 11 July, Piekalkiewicz wrote:

In the early hours of that night, the German 6th Panzer Division (Major General von Hünersdorff) was moved to the heavily fortified Rzhavets. In a surprise attack they were supposed to seize a bridgehead over the northern Donets and then advance to Provorot. The bulk of this division and the 19th Panzer Division (Lieutenant General G. Schmidt) were ordered to continue pursuing the defeated Soviet formations and simultaneously attack the left flank of Fifth Guards Tank Army (Lieutenant General Rotmistrow) and Sixty-ninth Army (Lieutenant General Kryuchenkin). The 11th Panzer Regiment (Colonel von Oppeln-Bronikowski) and his two armored companies, one panzer grenadier battalion, and the rest of Tiger Tank Battalion 503 started on their night march on Rzhavets. They were led by two captured T-34s at the head of the column under strict silence and no-fire orders. The combat group moved toward the town ten kilometers away. After

bypassing Kurakovska village, they were behind Soviet lines. The column threaded into the busy traffic on the main road and fell in line with Soviet units heading in the same direction. During a short rest, German and Red Army soldiers were sitting almost side by side without suspicion. One of the captured T-34s unexpectedly stopped because of engine trouble and a Panzer IV pushed it into a ditch. At 0400 the head of the column reached the edge of Rzhavets and looked for the way to its bridge in the darkness between marching Soviet infantry and truck columns. In the village the combat group missed the turn to the bridge in their excitement and rolled past a column of twenty-two Soviet T-34s. Apparently the Soviet tank drivers had become suspicious, because they suddenly fell out of line and followed the Germans. Major Bäke and Lieutenant Zobel were able to knock out three of them in close-range combat with magnetic antitank charges, but now a batch of flares went up and machine guns began to rattle from all directions.

The combat group had not as yet reached its objective when a tremendous detonation blew up the bridge. The grenadiers and engineers, however, were able to reach the northern bank of the Donets over a footbridge and establish a bridgehead there. The surprised Red Army soldiers hardly put up a fight.

CHAPTER 21

Tiger 311 on the First Day of Citadel

Gerd Niemann

TIGER 311

Tank commander	Leutnant Weinert
Gunner	Unteroffizier Niemann
Driver	Unteroffizier Kuhnert
Radio operator	Obergefreiter Lehner
Loader	Gefreiter Stühler

5 July 1943: At 0200 hours the tanks were ready to depart; the crews assembled for the orders session. By flashlight, Oberleutnant Scherf read the order of the day for the attack on the Russian positions east of the Donez between Bjelgorod and Orel. Thirty minutes later, simultaneously with the first artillery and rocket-launcher strikes, the Tigers rolled through a narrow defile in the woods onto the plain of the Donez. The river crossing was to be by a ford, not far from the village of Ssolomino.

We had run through that phase of the operation several times on the sand tables at Kharkov: 2nd Platoon in the lead, then the command tank, followed by the 1st Platoon and then the 3rd Platoon. We approached the crossing in that order on this morning as well. Leutnant von Rosen's Tiger 321 approached the ford directly. The others remained a bit to the side in covered positions. Tensely, we followed the crossing. Slowly, until the water rose over the track guards, the Tiger made its way through the Donez, apparently without any problems. Just a few meters more and the next tank could follow. But that was not to happen.

Tiger 321 remained stuck on the far bank. In spite of repeated approaches, it could not get firm ground under its tracks. It had to return. The fording operation was scuttled.

What was to be done? A bit farther upstream was a provisional bridge. At the moment, the 25th Panzer Regiment was crossing it. Why couldn't we just follow it? No passage for vehicles over thirty tons! A new crossing would have to be arranged for the Tigers. Instead of "Tanks to the front!" the cry was now, "Engineers get to work!" In the meantime, the Russian artillery had found the range of the crossing. The shells burst everywhere, as did the unpredictable salvoes of the Stalin Organs. The combat engineers did not let that faze them. They dragged the heavy bridging materials forward, drove piles into the riverbed and laid planks on timbers.

The Tigers remained widely dispersed on the open Donez plain. The sun blazed down mercilessly on the steel armor. In the fighting compartment it was as hot as the inside of an incubator. Wounded infantry, returning from the fight, could not understand that the Tigers were unable to move forward. Again and again they called to us, "Move on forward! Move on Forward! Your comrades are waiting for you!"

Finally we had reached the point of no return: "Company, march!" After a few hundred meters we were in contact with the enemy. "Two o'clock, bunker—high explosive!" I went "automatic." My feet pressed forward on the pedals of the power turret traversing mechanism, my left hand set the range on the optics, then reached for the wheel of the gun's traversing mechanism, my right cranked the elevating gear. "Identified!" Safety off! "Fire when ready!" I pulled the trigger. The target disappeared in a cloud of smoke. Was it a hit? Leutnant Weinert gave me no time to observe. The tank was already rolling on. In the optics I then saw another picture.

And so it went several times: discharge—smoke cloud—onward. The Tiger was constantly in motion, first swinging to the left, then to the right, moving forward or moving back. Soon I had no idea of what direction we had come from. Red soldiers appeared in front of the tank. We drove directly into a defensive position. "Coax!" The brown-clad figures rose in masses, kneeling and standing, firing with their machine-pistols and rifles against our steel armor. A few pulled back. Others sought cover in a depression in the ground. They could not stop us. Those who were not cut down by the bursts of our machine gun fire were run over.

To the right was a grain field. Watch out for antitank guns! Leutnant Weinert was given the mission of destroying any enemy there. Short swing to the right. "One o'clock—fifty meters—high explosive—safety!" We moved forward very cautiously, my forehead pressed hard against the head-protector of the optics. All I could see were stalks of grain. An uncomfortable feeling. There, a flash—a dull impact against the armor. At that same instant a fountain of earth spouted up at a range of thirty to forty meters.

"Bravo, direct hit!" I was not consciously aware I had fired the gun. That made no difference. The loader, in any case, shoved a fresh round into the breech.

The Tiger received additional hits. The shots came from the depths of the grain field. The enemy was not to be seen. Nevertheless, the loader had to work without a break. I followed Leutnant Weinert's instructions exactly. Fire, fire again! Ivan must not feel that he is safe!

A heavy impact shook the tank. Unteroffizier Kuhnert called out something about "penetration!"; Obergefreiter Lehner shouted something

about "wounded!" Leutnant Weinert took it very calmly. "Anything else?" "Nein, Herr Leutnant." "Then keep going, Kuhnert."

Calmly, as if on the training ground, Leutnant Weinert directed the Tiger through the field of grain towards an antitank gun. Left, right, left. The tracks caught the gun. Under the weight of our sixty tons it broke apart. I wiped out the next antitank gun. Then another clattering for us. The electrical system went out; the humming tone went dead in the headphones. The tank kept on moving, however. Half-right, another antitank gun barely fifty meters away. The crew took to its heels. Machine gun fire. At that moment there was movement at the gun; a flash, an impact against the Tiger. A fearsome blow resounded through the fighting compartment. Before I knew what was happening, Unteroffizier Kuhnert had already turned around on the gun position. The fourth gun was put out of action. But we did not get away scott-free. A hit in the rear stopped the engine. We stood there, unable to move. The starter was no longer functional. I tried to traverse the turret by hand. At that instant Leutnant Weinert shouted, "Stop!" "What about the antitank gun?" I asked. "Oberfeldwebel Rondorf got it." So we were not alone. Operation "Grainfield" came to an end. Time for a cigarette and, finally, fresh air.

But it did not end with that. Enemy tanks were reported. We started the engine with the hand crank. As we withdrew from the grain field we ran onto a mine. Fortunately, we only suffered minor damage to the running gear which was quickly fixed. Then we arrived at a burning village (Rasumnoje?). The enemy tanks were easy to identify. Range 1,200. I needed two rounds to knock out the first tank.

The next T-34 moved into our line of fire. It was moving at speed. That time the loader had to shove three rounds into the breech.

After that, it settled down. The company set up security for the night. Two days later, Tiger 311 was in the maintenance facility. It was written off and cannibalized. The damage to the hull and drive train that had occurred on 5 July and during the continuation of the attack on 6 July could not be repaired with the means available to the maintenance facility.

CHAPTER 22

Tiger 332 in Action from July 1943 to the End of January 1944

Gerd Niemann

TIGER 332

Commander	Feldwebel Weiland
Gunner	Unteroffizier Niemann
Driver	Obergefreiter Mangels
Radio operator	Unknown
Loader	Gefreiter Einecke

Maximofka area, about twenty-five kilometers northwest of Kharkov

At the end of July, the battalion moved to Kharkov for reconditioning and issuance of tanks. Operation Citadel had cost the 3rd Company ten dead, an unknown number of wounded and four Tigers as total losses. In addition, several more Tigers were in the maintenance facility with technical problems or battle damage.

On the evening of 5 August, the order was issued: Prepare to move out. We were kept waiting until the afternoon of the following day for the movement order. As a result, the long-distance marriage by proxy that had been planned for Feldwebel Weiland could take place as planned.

We spent the night of 7 August in a village southwest of Kharkov. It was said we would be employed at Merefa. That plan was overcome by events in the morning. Things were hot north of Kharkov. New direction of march: Bogoduchow.

Battle Group Weinert reached its area of operations at Maximofka with three of its four Tigers. Leutnant Weinert's vehicle dropped out with drive problems. Feldwebel Weiland had to give up his

place to the Leutnant. We were placed under the operational control of the 2nd SS Panzer Division "Das Reich." During the three days from 8-10 August, the battle group was only employed twice for short periods of time. On 8 August, it worked with an SS grenadier batallion, advancing the main line of resistance about 500 meters on to key high ground and, on 10 August, on reconnaissance-in-force suggested by Leutnant Weinert. Three T-34s and an enemy truck column with ammunition and fuel were destroyed during the raid. On 11 August the battle groups assembled at the Feski collective farm. In the afternoon the battalion occupied an assembly area near Maximofka with twelve or thirteen Tigers.

After an artillery preparation on the morning of 12 August, we assembled for a counterattack. Tiger 332 had a track knocked off in its first contact with the enemy. Leutnant Weinert transferred into another vehicle. Feldwebel Weiland came back to us.

Repair of the damage took longer than expected. Far and wide, nothing more was to be seen of the combat elements. The sound of battle could only be heard in the distance. Feldwebel Weiland asked over the radio where the company was. The answer: "Move along the woods and you will soon find us." And that was what we did.

Suddenly there was a flash, off to the left in the woods. A round struck a few meters in front of the tank. Halt! Transmit! Feldwebel Weiland reported that we had been fired upon and wanted to know who was there in the woods. To our surprise, we were informed, "Not us. Return fire!"

In the meantime, I had aimed the gun at the wood line, but could not make out any movement. Thick undergrowth prevented any observation into the woods. Driver, move out! The moment we moved there was another muzzle flash, right at the right-hand edge of the optics, barely visible. Again, the impact was just in front of the tank. I aimed at the suspected position—and got no more than a chilly silence. Isn't that why we had machine guns? Right after the first burst of fire came another impact on the tank. That time the muzzle flash was farther to the left, but well in my field of view. My first round swept the underbrush away. Almost in the center of the space I had cleared stood an antitank gun. It was ready to fire again, and then bits of gun spun through the air. Now the wood line came alive. Flashes came from several locations at the same time. We cleared the way free with machine guns and cannon. Five antitank guns were destroyed.

Feldwebel Weiland tried in vain to report our successes to the company. No more contact. So on we went along the wood line. A small rise in front of us. Feldwebel Weiland was able to see behind it from his elevated position.—Halt! Driver, back up!—A little later we were told what he had seen: "Four Russian tanks—two T-34s, two KV-1s—broadside to us." Still in the reverse-slope position, I traversed the turret as instructed. Then it was Obergefreiter Mangels' turn. Very delicately he moved the Tiger just far enough up the rise until the target appeared in my optics. Thanks to Feldwebel Weiland's excellent instructions, I scored a direct hit with the first round. The other three Russian tanks pulled back without turning their turrets. I knocked out two of them. The fourth disappeared into a hollow, from which a cloud of smoke soon arose. While we were still pondering what might have been going on, two Tigers suddenly came into view from the right, emerging from behind a point of woods. We had found the combat elements.

Instead of praise for our successes, Feldwebel Weiland got a dressing down from the commander because he had not responded to the latter's radio messages. We had, indeed, moved directly in front of the barrels of a Russian tank assembly area. The fact that we discovered the cause of the loss of radio contact—we no longer

had any radio antenna, it had been shot off right at the base—seemed to make no difference.

For the next few days, the combat elements were occasionally engaged in heavy defensive fighting in the Maximofka sector of the front.

Leutnant Weinert was wounded on 13 August in armored fighting at Chrutschtschewo-Nikitowka. On that day the 5th SS Panzer Grenadier Division "Wiking" relieved the 2nd SS Panzer Division "Das Reich," to which we had been attached up to that point.

The history of the 5th SS Panzer Grenadier Division "Wiking" reported the 18 August attack on Hill 228.1, northeast of Maximofka, as follows:

The artillery barrage began in the gray of dawn. The enemy initially attacked Hills 228 and 209 on a broad front. After an hour he had advanced to 209.5 with tanks and follow-on infantry. The 5th SS Panzer Battalion mounted an immediate counterattack. A Tiger company (503) was speedily sent forward by the corps. Intense armor engagements developed along the entire front. The Schwerpunkt [spearhead] of the enemy attack was on Hills 228 and 209.5. Eighty four out of about a hundred enemy tanks were knocked out.

The operations officer of headquarters, 8th Army, sent the following teletype on 20 August 1943:

During the last few days, the corps has two major successes to recognize:

1. The defensive success of SS Panzer Grenadier Division "Wiking," which knocked out a total of 84 Russian tanks after commitment of a Tiger battalion.
2. . . . My thanks and my full appreciation to the leadership and the troops.

signed Woehler
General der Infanterie

I am pleased to pass on the above message of recognition from the Commanding General of the 8th Army to its attached divisions and corps units.

signed Breith
General der Panzertruppen and Commanding General of the III Panzer Corps
(Strassner, *Die 5. SS-PzDiv. WIKING*, pp. 216 ff.)

Tiger 332 (Feldwebel Weiland) dropped out of the fighting on 18 August with damage to its main gun and had to go to the maintenance facility at Walki.

According to the German Red Cross list of those killed in action, the 3rd Company lost the following:

20 August	at Maximofka	Herbert Bierig
30 August	at Scharowka	Heinz Riedel
31 August	at Goluboff	Heinrich Legath
		Peter Schilling
2 September	at Goluboff	Alfred Will

As I recall, two Tigers of our company were knocked out by our own assault guns. One radio operator was killed, one loader severely wounded (? Franz Roth died 4 September in Military Hospital 13/X.)

On 31 August the rearward echelon of the battalion and the maintenance facility moved from Walki to Krasnograd.

(At that time—until 9 September—I was in the infirmary with jaundice. Since Tiger 332 was already back in service, I joined Feldwebel Bormann's tank on 10 September.)

During the first half of September the great change in the weather came. It rained in buckets. The roads turned into bottomless streams of mud; the open country became a landscape of morasses. Even tracked vehicles had trouble moving.

At that time, the combat elements were in the Merefa-Taranowka sector of the front. Attacks were only mounted to clean up penetrations. Otherwise it was a matter of putting up a delaying action until, somewhere, a new defensive position was established. And then that did not hold because the forces were inadequate.

Again and again contact was lost with adjacent units, leading to kilometer-wide gaps between formations, through which the Russians could continue their assaults unimpeded.

12 September: As night fell, the routine "withdrawal" began. First the grenadiers, by squads, then the tanks. Our departure was delayed. We were still waiting for Unteroffizier Weigel's tank, which had been detailed with a squad of grenadiers to secure the gap with the neighboring battalion. It was already dark. Still no trace of Unteroffizier Weigel. Then came the report by radio: immobilized by transmission problems! Feldwebel Borman was given the task of recovering the Tiger.

While the combat elements orientated themselves toward the rear, we moved perpendicular to the front, without really knowing whether the Russians had already infiltrated into the gap. The tension was very great, because we could hardly see anything and the directions for getting to the location of the breakdown were only vaguely given in terms of kilometers and direction. We had radio contact with Feldwebel Weigel. He directed us by listening. Halt—Stop the engine—Start the engine—Good, move out!—We followed that procedure several times. Feldwebel Bormann was getting uncomfortable, since we had already gone beyond the number of kilometers that had been given. He wanted Unteroffizier Weigel to send up a flare. Unteroffizier Weigel refused, for fear of betraying the location of the breakdown. Then, at last, we were there. The way back stretched endlessly before us. We proceeded at a walking pace. With sixty tons in tow, the soft ground permitted no faster pace. And then there were the swampy pits that we could not make out in the darkness. Twice the towed vehicle bogged down. When that happened, we had to unhook the towing cable, pull the inert Tiger out backwards, and then hook up the tow again! The Russians seemed to be asleep.

Long after midnight, Feldwebel Bormann reported to the commander, "Mission accomplished."

13 September: Rain. Nothing but rain. We waited for the arrival of the supply elements. They did not come. Instead, we received the next operations order. As best we could, we filled the holes in the ammunition racks and put in the fuel tanks what fuel we could transfer in a hurry from the Tigers that were being towed by the recovery platoon because of mechanical problems.

In the action that followed, we were committed as battle groups. Battle Group Rondorf, with the tanks of Oberfeldwebel Rondorf, Feldwebel Bormann, Feldwebel Blume and Unteroffizier Meinert, along with a grenadier battalion, was assigned to win back some high ground that had been given up the previous evening and hold it until evening. The combat strength of the battalion amounted to little more than a company of tired and burnt-out grenadiers, who only hesitantly followed our attack. The Russians cleared out of the position without offering significant opposition. But, scarcely had the grenadiers settled down between the tanks when it started to liven up in front of our lines.

Suddenly it was alive with earth-brown figures. They didn't seem very impressed by our defensive fire. Then they were a good 200 meters away. Suddenly they all dropped to the ground—and a howling approached: Artillery. The grenadiers abandoned their inconspicuous foxholes in flight. As the final rounds burst, the human steamroller started moving forward again. Our fire was unable to bring it to a halt. The first Russians were already pushing in between our four tanks. There was nothing left for us but to reverse gear. The hill had changed owners.

After a short break to regroup, we mounted a counterattack. Our high explosive rounds had the same effect as the Russian artillery fire. The position belonged to us. But then the human steamroller returned, supported by artillery and mortars.

We lost the hill again. And, again, the counterattack followed. Our ammunition count shrank rapidly. In the afternoon we were on the hill—without the grenadiers. They hadn't followed us on the last counterattack, having disappeared from the picture without a trace. Oberfeldwebel Rondorf reported the incident and asked for further orders. The answer did not please us at all: We were to hold the position until 1800 hours!

A while after the withdrawal of the grenadier battalion, two assault guns showed up. Our joy at having some more firepower on our side proved to be wishful thinking. The reinforcements turned out to be as toothless as we were. They also had no ammunition. Someone had intercepted them en route from the maintenance facility to their unit and ordered them into action. After a good half hour, we were alone again. Fortunately, the Russian infantry didn't undertake any more major attacks, and the Russian artillery did not fire.

We pulled out at 1800 hours sharp. We linked up with the three tanks of Battle Group Oberleutnant Scherf at the former battalion command post. Unteroffizier Rieschel's Tiger had to be blown up: Radiator and fan damage from an artillery hit. The general shortage of fuel in all of the other tanks meant that a tow was out of the question. Soon it was dark, pitch black and still raining. Hand grenades detonated a short distance away and rifle fire flashed. It didn't phase us.

After a few kilometers, Oberleutnant Scherf called the tank commanders over to him. What he had to say was already common knowledge: Situation uncertain, but not hopeless. It made us think, however, when he allowed us alcohol—"for inner warmth." Then we went on, and always past burning cottages and haystacks—hallmarks of a retreat.

As midnight approached we reached German lines in the vicinity of Krasnograd. Was that the new main line of resistance? A little stream almost sealed our fate there. The bridge we had to cross had already been cleared for demolition.

14 September: Krasnograd. Technical service.

15 September: Army Group South began its retreat to the near side of the Dnjepr. The order went out to the battalion to prepare to move out. The immobile tanks were supposed to be brought back by rail.

Still 15 September: While we were still in the area where we had been quartered, Feldwebel Bormann's tank dropped out of action due to driver carelessness with a shorn-off final drive. It had to be loaded on the train.

The recovery platoon started evacuating vehicles to the railroad station that afternoon. The route to the station led through the city and was one horrible traffic jam. Innumerable wheeled vehicles had mired themselves in the viscous masses of paste that were called streets. The prime movers made no more than slow progress. Whenever possible, they made their way alongside the road. As darkness fell, the towing operations had to cease by order of the military police. There was no more movement in the city.

16 September: The evacuation was resumed, though the situation in the city had scarcely improved. At the railroad yard there was also crowding and confusion. The Tigers could not be loaded. It wasn't until noon that the first one was towed over an end-loading ramp onto a Ssyms-railroad car. There was no locomotive available for shunting the hitched-up prime mover. The railroad officials had no idea where the loaded Ssyms-cars were to go to assemble the transport train. The railroad lines were just as jammed as the streets. Hours passed before a solution was found. In the meantime, we kept ourselves very busy, clearing out a giant rations depot.

The loading dragged on endlessly. No Tiger could just have its tracks changed and be pulled right up over the ramp and correctly loaded. Painstaking sideward corrections had to be made, and that during a dark and rainy night with no more than flashlights for illumination.

17 September: Eight Tigers were loaded. Three more stood in front of the ramp without tracks. By order of the railroad station commander, those would have to be loaded by daylight. It was feared that in the darkness one might slide to the side and block the adjoining track. But it was too late. There was total confusion at the railroad station. The Reichsbahn [German railroad] took away the switching engine. The train that had been put together up to that point was hitched to a locomotive and, within a few minutes, left Krasnograd. One train after another rolled through to Poltawa with little space between them.

18 September: Railroad siding at Krementschug. The oversize Tigers were a thorn in the side of the railroad command. It took twenty hours before the transport got a green light.

19 September: Snamenka. According to the transport papers, that was our final objective. However, there were no facilities to unload, no end-loading ramp, no means of towing. The railroad station and supervisor were agreed on one thing: For want of a railroad siding, the transport would have to keep moving. After several telephone calls to the movement control command at Lemberg we were provided with new papers late that afternoon that did not specify a destination. We were sent on a wild-goose chase.

21–23 September: Perwomaisk-Slobodka-Shmerinka-Proskurow.

24 September: Tarnopol. Our journey came to an end after a wooden bridge pillar was shattered by a Tiger. Great head-scratching at the railroad command. No one knew what to do with the train. There was a lot of telephoning, but it did not produce any results. As evening approached, the transport was moved to the Berozowica railroad station, which was about eight kilometers distant. We stayed there until 1 October. Then back to Tarnopol, which we left on 2 October. On through Shmerinka, Winniza, Berditschew and Fastow until, on 4 October, we arrived at Snamenka. That evening all of the Tigers were in the maintenance facility.

20–25 October: Bombing attack on Snamenka. The billets received a severe hit. There were no casualties.

30 October-4 November: Battle Group Weinert was assigned as corps reserve in Uspenskoje, southeast of Krementschug.

13–22 November: Battle Group Cüsow in Kirowograd.

23 November–24 December: On leave.

27 December: Reported to the company at Zybulew (between Winniza and Uman). No more tanks available. Oberleutnant Scherf went on leave. Leutnant Beier was given temporary command of the company.

1944

1 January: Road march by truck from Zybulew to Shmerinka (Rumanian Sector).

3 January: Received a new Tiger. Maintenance service, breaking it in and sighting in the guns.

9 January: The company was placed under the operational control of the local area commander at Shmerinka for local defense. Through "rumor control" we learned that the Russians had crossed the Bug and threatened the Winniza-Shmerinka-Slobodka railroad line.

During the night there was wild shooting in the city. The Rumanian patrols fired on anything that moved. It was extremely dangerous for our sentries to cross the street.

10 January: Early in the morning we received the operations order. The objective of the attack was the enemy bridgehead at Ssutiski, twenty kilometers east of Shmerinka.

The weather was rain mixed with snow and development of rapidly thickening fog. The ground conditions were bad.

We headed out of Shmerinka toward the southeast. There were preparations for defense throughout the city. Field positions were constructed and antitank guns positioned on the approach streets. Just past the the outskirts of the city—the German Red Cross sisters at the Soldiers' Home had just waved to us—we were fired on from the left flank, catching us completely by surprise. There were four rounds fired. The tank in front of us was hit in the running gear, the other shots landed to the right on the railroad embankment. Presumably it was a nervous Rumanian antitank gun crew that had fired at the sounds of armor. There was nothing to be seen. Visibility was barely 100 meters. So we kept on moving.

The history of the 23rd Panzer Division describes the rest of the attack:

In Shukowzy the [Tiger company] succeeded in bringing units of the 371. Infanteriedivision into position for local defense. . . . From there, at 1400 hours, the 2nd Battalion of the 23rd Panzer Regiment and a Tiger company, a company of grenadiers and two platoons of combat engineers advanced through Nowo Petrowsk to the Bug at Woroschilowka. Nowo Petrowsk was captured and secured shortly after dusk after knocking out two enemy tanks.

On the next day, Tiger 322 (Feldwebel Weiland) was already back in the maintenance facility as the third factory-new tank that had broken down with engine problems.

19 January: Transport by rail from Shmerinka to Winniza.

23 January: By order of Army Group South, Tiger Regiment Bäke was formed from Tiger Tank Battalion 503 and the 2nd Battalion, 23rd Panzer Regiment. Its first mission was to clean up the Soviet area of penetration that existed east of Winniza by attacking to the east and destroying the enemy forces that had penetrated southward to the Bug. (Rebentisch)

24 January: Breakthrough at the Bila position.

25 January: Armored engagements in the Ssossoff area.

26 January: Defensive fighting in the Ssossoff area.

27 January: Armored engagements south of Otscheretnya (Ocheretnya).

From the Wehrmacht report of 31 January 1944:

During offensive fighting in the area south of Pogrebitsche from 24 to 30 January 1944, more than ten Soviet rifle divisions and several armor corps were destroyed by formations of the army and Waffen-SS under command of General of Panzer Troops Hube. They were effectively supported by elements of the Luftwaffe. The Bolsheviks lost more than 6,500 prisoners and 8,000 dead during that time period. 700 tanks and assault guns as well as numerous other weapons and equipment were either destroyed or captured. The 16th Panzer Division (from Westphalia), under the command of Generalmajor Back, and a Tiger regiment, under the command of Oberstleutnant Bäke, especially distinguished themselves during the operation.

CHAPTER 23

From the Donez to the Dnjepr in September 1943

Alfred Rubbel

Citadel had failed. None of the objectives, neither cutting off of the Kursk salient that jutted so far to the west and whose elimination would have shortened the main line of resistance from about 400 kilometers to 200 kilometers nor smashing the Soviet forces of two "fronts" [equal to German army groups] that had there grown to threatening proportions had succeeded. Our southern attack group, the 4th Panzer Army and Army Detachment Kempf, had penetrated the strongly fortified defensive positions after heavy and costly attacks. The breakthrough seemed almost within grasp when the German Army High Command canceled the operation after fourteen days (5 July–17 July 1943). There were two reasons for that:

1. The attack of the northern attack group of Army Group Center, Model's 9th Army, did not advance because the Russians preempted the German attack and forced the German troops onto the defensive. That eliminated the second arm of the pincers for the envelopment.
2. United States forces had landed on Sicily and the Italian army pulled back almost without a fight. Based on that, the Oberkommando der Wehrmacht (German Armed Forces High Command) had to assume that the Italian forces would respond in similar fashion to a landing on the Italian mainland. German

forces had to be withdrawn from the Eastern Front, with the major portion coming from the formations that had been committed to Citadel. They were sent in march to the Mediterranean theater.

The Soviets who were concentrated in the Orel-Kursk area—in places with a six-fold superiority—had operated in the best "Manstein manner." After first parrying the northern half of the German attack, they went over to the offensive "on the backhand." Their operational objective was the capture of Kharkov, outflanking the German forces between the Donez and Dnjepr, gaining the Dnjepr line and smashing Army Group South east of the Dnjepr. Kharkov was evacuated in mid-August of 1943. Army Group South began its withdrawal on a broad front on 2 September. The initiative had finally been lost and it had gone over to the Red Army. So much for the larger picture.

Tiger Tank Battalion 503 had to take part in a fighting retreat from the middle of July until the end of September 1943. It was committed piecemeal. From that period we remember place names such as Kowiagy, Merefa, Maximowka, and Achtyrka. It was a wearisome fight. In small groups, often less than platoon strength, we were split up and farmed out to regiments and divisions. Generally, there was no communication with the company. We could find rations for ourselves, but ammunition and fuel were scarce. The worst part of the situation was the lack of recovery vehicles and repair services. Masses of the civilian population, herds of cattle, transport columns and goods being evacuated trekked along as one giant army "worm" on designated movement routes. It was the same across the entire width of the 8th Army sector where our battalion was employed. And it was no different for the 4th Panzer Army of Army Group South.

We were in action with Tiger 114. It was the second Tiger 114. The first had received several hits from 7.62cm antitank guns. There was a hole in the front hull. The left-hand final drive was shot up and the transmission was out of action. The crew was still the same one we had started with in the spring of 1943. During the weeks from the end of August until the end of September 1943, our task in that almost unique withdrawal to the "Ostwall" at the Dnjepr was varied. At one point, we provided an escort for the remnants of an infantry division. At another time, we served as rear guard and held a village long enough for there to be some distance between the withdrawing troops and the pursuing Russians. We also created some breathing room by launching local counterattacks. Due to a lack of recovery vehicles, we also had to tow our damaged Tigers. As a rule, we provided cover during the days and linked up with the retreating elements at night.

During those types of operations we scarcely got any rest. The equipment could not be maintained. We often had to take wide detours because bridges could not carry us. Whenever the situation demanded it, we also withdrew at night. We were then pulled in close to the units. One Tiger took the point and also established the orientation. Another Tiger, its main gun at six o'clock, moved at the rear of the column, which stumbled along through the night at a walking pace. I particularly remember an operation with two Tigers—the other commander was Hannes Rippl—with the 8th SS Cavalry Division. The division was commanded by SS-Brigadeführer Fegelein (related by marriage to Hitler and shot in Berlin at the end of April 1945 by a firing squad). I drove point because I had a map. We set out as night fell. Hannes Rippl drove at the tail end of the column. The distance between the two tanks was so great that radio contact was sometimes lost. It started raining; the visibility was only a few meters. At some point we lost our way. Decision: Get the

compass, head west! The gunner, Walter Junge, was outfitted with a machine pistol, flare gun and flashlight. We fastened a white towel on his back with safety pins—the towel could hardly have been very white!—and he marched cross-country, about five to ten meters in front of the tank. Because visibility was so bad, the idea was he would be able to warn the driver, Walter Eschrig, about terrain problems, trenches, marshy ground and obstacles. During the night, we changed "pilots" every hour.

The division followed us on horse-drawn vehicles, mounted on horseback, on foot and in a few motor-driven vehicles. We were lucky: No insurmountable obstacles, no enemy contact, no breaks in the column. When dawn broke we reached the objective of our march, a village on the Psiol with a wooden bridge over the medium-sized river. Because we were not sure we would be able to cross the river with our un-tested and non-maintained deep-wading equipment (up to four meters depth), the division crossed the bridge first. Then came the tense moment to find out whether the bridge could carry the sixty-ton weight of the Tigers. Everyone but the driver dismounted. Walter Eschrig, a master of his craft, drove, no, crept over the bridge, which yielded on its piles. Rippl's driver decided on the "full throttle" approach. The bridge did not stand up to that. The tank broke through, pushing the bridge decking together in front of it, and landed with its rear end in the water. However, even that mishap worked out with the same good fortune as the rest of the undertaking. We hitched our Tiger on in front and helped the derelict to claw its way out.

Alongside the positive circumstances of how that mission turned out, there was a negative aspect in the behavior of the SS officers of that formation. Up to that point, I had always had a high regard for the discipline, concern for their men and bravery of the Waffen-SS. During that night's raid, our Tiger was crowded to capacity wherever there was room with SS officers—on the turret floor, at the crew positions and on the rear deck (to the point the air intakes for cooling the engine were covered). They made themselves comfortable and drank freely of alcohol. They increasingly got in our way instead of being concerned about their men. We were glad to be rid of that unit the next morning.

At some point in time we also reached the Dnjepr. The river was supposed to function as the "Ostwall," behind which we would spend the approaching winter. We had no idea where the battalion or company with the command and trains elements were. In spite of the radio, from which you could figure out a little, the flow of information that got to a tank was scanty.

The next requirement was to get across the Dnjepr, which reached a breadth of up to three kilometers in places where it was not regulated. The railroad bridge at Krementschug, a giant, wooden military bridge that the engineers had constructed was one possibility. We were, apparently, the last ones on the east bank. I figured that the heavy equipment had been taken over on the railroad. For Tigers, the only possibility was to be rail loaded across the bridge. However, for that we required the special Symss rail cars, and there were no more of those east of the river. For weeks we had brought our tank through all hazards. Was this to be the end? Necessity is the mother of invention...and it increases one's readiness to take risks.

Since there was no more than a small detail at the bridgehead to provide security for the demolition preparations, there was no crossing-area commander to interfere with us. We found an open railroad flatcar with a twenty-four-ton capacity. We also found a ramp. We managed to roll the railroad car to the ramp by hand. We did not have much time. The bridge would be blown at 2400 hours. We then moved our Tiger onto the 24-ton flatcar. The springs took on a reversed curve and the longitudinal beams sagged, but the Tiger was positioned in the center of the flatcar and the flatcar had remained on the rails. At that point, twenty to thirty men shoved the railroad car by hand—complete with the Tiger—over the nearly 1,000-meter-long bridge. There has probably never been a tank movement quite like that! The crossing-area commander grabbed us when we reached the west bank and incorporated us into the bridge security detail. At midnight, a column of flame shot high into the night sky. The bridge collapsed, its components falling into the Dnjepr. Operations Citadel and Scorched Earth (*Verbrannte Erde*) were over for us. At that point, the orderly hand of the Army took hold again. We were then loaded, provided with transportation orders and landed at Snamenka for a short but intensive period of rest, which restored our senses and blessed us with happiness and, for some, even home leave.

According to the proven principle that the soldier should be given no more knowledge of an operation in which he takes part than he needs to have to carry out his mission, we knew little regarding the withdrawal of Army Group South from the Donez to the Dnjepr. It wasn't until serious studies about the eastern campaign appeared after the war that the extent of the uniqueness of the planned and accomplished movements of the withdrawal of an army group in the face of the enemy were revealed. It was obviously the command skill of Field Marshal von Manstein that made possible the impossible, in spite of all untoward events, sometimes resulting from the enemy, sometimes released by the highest levels of command.

The withdrawal from the Donez to the Dnjepr was the greatest withdrawal movement ever executed that ran according to the way it was planned.

It was necessary to withdraw four armies consisting of twelve corps (a total of forty-two divisions) with about a million soldiers. March movements on a front with a width of 1,000 kilometers and depth of 300 kilometers had to be coordinated across six bridges over the Dnjepr. Additionally, 200,000 wounded had to be evacuated. Likewise, important war materiel had to be brought across the river.

After crossing the river, the units had to immediately fan out and occupy 800 kilometers of river position and prepare for defensive operations. At that point, the Russians had succeeded in establishing several bridgeheads on the west bank. Those had to be crushed or blocked off. That did not always work.

As for the "Ostwall," there was hardly anything there, other than the naturally elevated west bank of the river. Hitler had forbidden timely construction of planned positions because he did not want to encourage a "bolt to those positions." Thus it came about that the value of the river as a barrier was not developed to the extent that the situation demanded.

It has been said that Field Marshal von Manstein considered that task to have been the most difficult that ever faced him. It succeeded because

- the strategic commander was able to effectively apply superlative skill without hindrance,

- men of extraordinary ability at the tactical level (corps and divisions) knew how to translate the plans into action and
- it could be taken for granted the troops could be relied on to react properly and selflessly in the situation.

Rubbel, Alfred: Personal experiences
Carell, Paul: *Verbrannte Erde*
Haupt, Werner: *Die Schlachten der Heeresgruppe Süd*
Von Manstein, Erich: *Verlorene Siege*
Zhukov, G. K.: *The Memoirs of Marshal Zhukov*

CHAPTER 24

Tscherkassy

Alfred Rubbel

I would like to dedicate this section concerning the efforts of the battalion to free the encircled troops of the IX and XXXXVI Army Corps in the early part of 1944 in the Tscherkassy area to my former battalion commander, Clemens Graf Kageneck, who was respected by all of us in the battalion. He was severely wounded in the fighting. He was an expert and a cavalier. Every tanker could see that. I am obligated to thank him since he allowed me to return "home" to the battalion after I was selected to become an officer and had completed my training and was promoted. This dedication comes with my congratulations on the occasion of his eighty-sixth birthday.

IN THE SOUTHERN SECTOR OF THE EASTERN FRONT, 1943

The writers of history have seen the surrender of the 6th Army at Stalingrad in 1942 as the obvious turning point in the German conduct of the war. The soldier on the Eastern Front—the combatant in the foxhole or the tank—had only his personal impressions of the events in his immediate vicinity, if he thought of the end of the war. For me, it was the failure of Operation Citadel in the summer of 1943 that first made it clear to me that the war was lost for Germany. In spite of the commitment of large amounts of troops and equipment, only local successes were achieved. At the time, we were not aware the concentration had only been achieved by irresponsibly thinning out other sec-

tors. When Operation Citadel bogged down after initial successes and the Red Army began to drive us back "on the backhand," that could only result from a German inferiority that could never be redressed.

The overall result was that, starting with the summer of 1943, the German army in the east had lost the initiative and could only react. That meant that the war with the USSR could not be won. At that point in time, the invasion of the European continent by the Western Allies had not yet begun. The costly war in the east and the conquest and occupation of almost all of Europe had exhausted German personnel and equipment.

We were almost entirely dependant on our own sources for production of armaments. There were an increasing number of bottlenecks. The supply of aircraft, tanks and motor vehicles no longer covered our losses. During 1943 the number of German divisions in the east sank from 214 to 190. Only the elite formations had their full combat strengths. The Red Army could increase the number of its divisions from 442 to 512 and solve chronic shortages of equipment with U.S. equipment, primarily tanks and trucks.

By the end of August 1943, the U.S. had provided 6,207 aircraft, about 10,000 tanks, 138,000 motor vehicles, 1.5 million tons of food supplies—a total of almost 5 million tons of goods. We experienced that intimately starting in the summer of 1943. Almost every third tank and about half of the trucks that the Red Army employed against Army Group South were of American manufacture.

The following situation existed for Germany in 1943. In the Teheran Conference in November 1943, it was agreed that

- there would be no conditional peace agreements,
- the war would be carried through to unconditional surrender,
- Germany would be totally occupied by the Allies,
- measures would be taken to make sure that there would never again be an autonomous German political entity and
- an international court would punish German war criminals.

The German government at the time made sure that the German people knew those intentions. By doing that, support from the populace was deprived to the growing opposition movement. The Allied belief that those threats and the terror bombing campaign against the civilian population would lead to an early end to the war proved to be a miscalculation. The endurance of the German soldier to the bitter end was no irrational Nazi fanaticism but, rather, the desire to go on fighting, whether voluntarily or forced by the above circumstances. Most of us could not imagine the consequences of the Teheran Accord because there was no historical precedent. Also, there was always a kernel of hope that, in the long run, it would turn out to be impossible for the western world to work together with the communists. That the later course of history confirmed our hopes might make us feel good but, unfortunately, the political change came too late for us.

For soldiers on the Eastern Front, the immediate experience of the front was more decisive in our attitudes than the political background outlined above. The tank raid of the 1st Panzer Army to the Caucasus in 1942 was, in retrospect, no more than an "armed excursion."

The 6th Army had perished at Stalingrad. Citadel turned out to be a mistake. The retreat to the Dnjepr position took place in orderly fashion. Holding that position through the winter of 1943–44 was rendered illusory by breakthroughs and outflanking maneuvers.

The Red Army—here we are talking about the Second Ukrainian Front—was numerically superior to our formations in both personnel and equipment. Our own superiority lay in the capability of our command and control, starting at the level of the squad leader or tank commander and fully developing at the tactical and operational levels. It was the tragedy of the German military that the highest levels of German leadership often did more to hinder this tactical and operational leadership capability and force it into disastrous operations than did the enemy. By that I mean Hitler's interference in the operations of the higher commanding officers at the front. It would be false to claim the war would have turned out differently without Hitler's dilettantism. The Eastern Front existed in the winter of 1943–44, however, primarily because of the confluence of the following: The bravery of the German soldiers, the initiative that rose to the occasion and the outstanding quality of the leadership. Both leaders and led were bound together right up to the last day by a mutual trust that grew in spite of the worsening situation, perhaps, indeed, because of it.

At that time, the Eastern Front stretched approximately 2,240 kilometers from the Baltic Sea to the Black Sea. The spearhead was in the south. That was where we fought. One should remember the psychological situation in which the soldier found himself on the Eastern Front in addition to the political and military situations. For many soldiers, the original conviction that it was a good thing to serve in the war for the Fatherland had begun to develop internal conflicts. Germany had become the prize of an increasingly irresponsible, indeed criminally acting Nazi dictator, as we now know. I think that something like an internal emigration began to materialize in many of us. We found refuge with our good comrades, with the tank crew, with the company and with the battalion. We felt ourselves to be sheltered in that military sphere; decency and humanity had not been lost there. We thought—perhaps later inquiry will even confirm these opinions—that we had to fight against an enemy that had threatened our country and our way of life.

We had come to know the enemy as cruel, which forced us to adapt to something that was foreign to us in order to survive.

The long years of war had distanced us from our civilian life style and, above all, from our families, which had formerly provided us with security and shelter. Now we found security in our military fellowship. It was not a total replacement, but it was the center of our existence in carrying out our daily military duties. Practical concerns played a major part, but there was also moral support. Something was displayed there that was not to be found in any other army. The superiors, particularly the officers, lived without "privileges" among their men and under the same conditions. They were a role model and had been trained to be the same when it came to taking risks as well.

The objectives of our operations were

- in attack, to destroy the enemy forces or to capture enemy-held territory,
- in defense, to ward off enemy attacks and
- in retreat, to fight delaying actions so as to hold the enemy at a distance and slow him down.

Although the completion of the mission was always of primary importance, the responsible leader also had to ensure that the combat strength of the unit was preserved. If the losses rose disproportionately or if the destruction of the unit was feared, the officer had to refuse to carry out the mission, possibly having to accept personal consequences in the bargain. That was the way that our company commanders and battalion commanders had led and, in so doing, protected us from senseless losses. At that point, we were assigned as spearhead of an attack group with Tiger Regiment Bäke. Bäke's unit had been formed to penetrate the encirclement around two army corps with about 50,000 men west of Tscherkassy and prevent the destruction of those large formations. That mission would take on a whole new meaning apart from anything we had experienced previously.

THE SITUATION OF ARMY GROUP SOUTH (VON MANSTEIN) IN THE WINTER OF 1943–44

Although this section of the book is about Tiger Tank Battalion 503 and its employment at the Tscherkassy pocket, it should also seek an answer to the question: How did two army corps manage to get encircled? Hadn't the German Armed Force High Command learned anything from the catastrophe at Stalingrad, where the 6th Army per-

ished with about 250,000 men? Or, in this case, was it the superiority of the Red Army and the weakness of the German army in the east that had such fateful consequences?

This must be stated at the outset: Everything mentioned above played a role. In addition there was the following:

- Hitler's general lack of insight, along with utopian plans for operations,
- the nearly exhausted personnel and equipment resources (although a division might be indicated on a map, it really only had about one third of its strength, that is, a regiment),
- the lack of adequate reserves and
- the increasing strength of the Red Army, in part due to aid from the U.S.

The German leadership at the front was, as it had been earlier, far superior to that of the Soviets. The Soviets could partially offset that weakness with numerical superiority. The Oberkommando des Heeres, that is, Hitler, often helped them in that he often interfered with operational command and control on the Eastern Front, preventing it from doing the right thing and what the situation demanded.

In this case, the period of winter calm that the Germans had hoped for while the Red Army prepared for its spring offensive after crossing the Dnjepr did not materialize. Based on that rather shaky assumption, the intention was to stabilize the front line behind the Dnjepr, when the opportunity presented itself in 1943. At the same time, one wanted to create the prerequisite for being able to operate offensively at the local level. Above all, one wanted to establish contact with the Crimean Peninsula where the 17th Army had been left.

However, the First Ukrainian Front, with the Sixth and First Guards Tank Army, had succeeded by the end of January 1944 in forcing the left wing of Army Group South south of the Pripjet Marshes far to the west. The right wing of Army Group South was far to the east, echeloned forward to the Dnjepr. In that situation, OKH decided that the operations of Army Group A (von Kleist) to reestablish contact with the 17th Army on the Crimea would be postponed and that an attack north along the Dnjepr from the Winniza-Korsun area by the forces of Army Group

South would be launched to establish contact with Army Group Center and encircle both of the Russian armies west of the Dnjepr. With that objective in mind, OKH ordered both of the army corps at Tscherkassy-Korsun to stay put.

During the final ten days of January, the German attack forces started the approach march to the Uman area. In addition to the XI and XXXXII Army Corps at Tscherkassy and Korsun, the XXXXVII, VII and LII Army Corps and the III Panzer Corps, were to carry out the attack that would have crossed more than 200 kilometers. A total of between fifteen and eighteen divisions would have participated.

We in Tiger Tank Battalion 503 were incorporated into schweres Panzer-Regiment Bäke and belonged to Breith's III Panzer Corps. The corps also consisted of the 1st Panzer Division, the 16th Panzer Division, the 17th Panzer Division, the 1st SS Panzer Division "Leibstandarte," and the 198th Infantry Division. From the planner's point of view, that represented a powerful tank armada. Presumably, Führer headquarterse was as far removed from reality as Hitler was and had not considered the strengths of these formations. The attacking units hadn't been in the locations the planners thought they were for a long time. Instead of a normal winter with hard frozen ground, alternating frost and thaw, the spring mud season, the feared Russian *rasputiza*, took us fully in its grip.

One must remember that there were hardly any paved roads in the western Ukraine. The fertile soil, a mixture of loam, loess and humus, made roads that were hard as asphalt when dry and, when wet, turned to mud that pulled the boots right off of the infantry and held the vehicles fast. Only tracked vehicles could move, and that movement was slow and involved enormous fuel expenditures. The Russians had the same problem that we did, only they knew better how to deal with it and were never at a loss at improvising. When Russian trucks were unable to get through, the Russian inhabitants were ruthlessly used to carry the loads. And, in contrast to us, the motor vehicles with which the Red Army was equipped were better, thanks to the United States lend-lease shipments. When you have a lot of trucks, it is easier to accept the loss of several vehicles stuck in the mud.

Disregarding the development of the situation west of the Dnjepr in the Tscherkassy-Korsun area,

where the IX and XXXXII Army Corps had clearly been in the process of being encircled by the mechanized formations of the Russian Sixth and Fifth Guards Tank Armies since 20 January, the attack troops were laboriously brought forward and scattered for the advance north to Medwin. They were committed without forming any kind of spearhead. We recall place names like Oratoff and Balabanowka from that period. On the "Days in Combat" pages of our pay books, the following places are indicated:

- 24 January 1944: Pentration of the Bila position
- 25 January 1944: Engagement at Ssosnoff
- 26 January 1944: Defensive fighting at Ssosnoff
- 27 January 1944: Armored engagement at Otschertnja
- 28 January 1944: Breakthrough to Oratoff
- 29 January 1944: Defensive fighting at Oratoff
- 30 January 1944: Defensive fighting at Oratoff
- 31 January 1944: Defensive fighting at Oratoff

From 21 to 31 January we battered away in that useless, costly assault north toward Medwin, even though the encircling forces of the Fifth Guard Corps and the Twentieth Tank Corps had already joined hands at Swenigorodka. In addition, Hitler's layman's concept of "holding strongpoints" and, in so doing, "fixing the enemy's forces" may have won the day in contrast to the intention to carry out mobile operations as Army Group South had done previously. Only when the people at the *Wolfsschanze* [the Führer Headquarters in East Prussia] finally grasped the seriousness of the situation were we redirected south over more than 20 kilometers to the original jump-off position. In doing so, we had to tortuously cross our way through the mud again. We then set off with the III Panzer Corps to the east to open the pocket. The Oberkommando des Heeres seemed only then to realize that there, after the start of the New Year, a new catastrophe was looming.

TIGER TANK BATTALION 503 IN THE SMERINKA-UMAN AREA AT THE END OF 1943 AND THE BEGINNING OF 1944

Our battalion had laboriously assembled at the start of January 1944 at Smerinka. It had been pretty well picked over in the "skirmishing" during the last three months of withdrawal from the

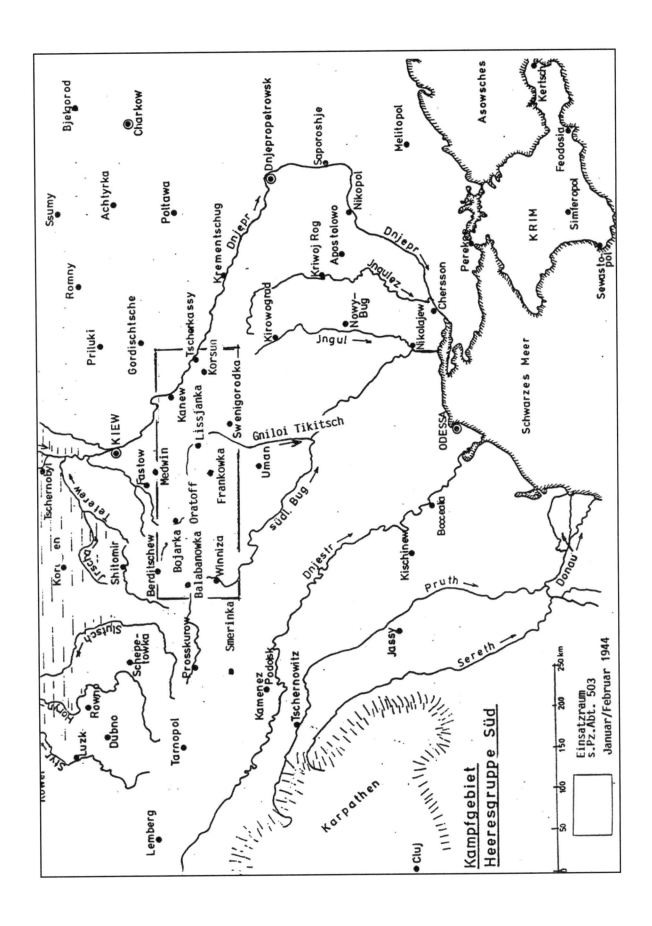

Kampfgebiet
Heeresgruppe Süd

Einsatzraum
s.Pz.Abt. 503
Januar/Februar 1944

50   100   150   200   250 km

Dnjepr to the Bug. We wanted to replenish our sizeable losses in personnel and equipment, especially in Tigers. We were the reserve of the 1st Panzer Army. Smerinka was a little country town in Transnistria, between the Dnjestr and the Bug. It was also intended to give the troops a period of rest. The battalion and company leadership would have an opportunity to "get their houses in order" after the long period during which they had been scattered to the winds in tiny battle groups of two to three Tigers and continually changing command and control relationships. Only four of the forty-five Tigers were still on hand. About twenty had been lost; the others had all been sent off for depot-level repairs. We expected the arrival of new Tigers. In January, thirty-five factory-new Tigers were issued. We, the crew of Tiger 114 received a new Tiger with the flat commander's cupola. That eliminated the danger to the tank commander that a single round from a 7.62cm antitank gun might take off the former smokestack-like cupola, complete with his head. Further, you no longer had to expose the upper half of your body in order to close the new swinging hatch-cover as had formerly been the case.

Smerinka was under Rumanian administration. The shrewd Rumanians offered wares in the bazaar that we had not seen in a long time—even beer. As a footnote, on the Eastern Front, beer was an absolute rarity, and not because it was being withheld from the soldiers as a form of prohibition. Beer—*piwo* in Russian—just was not available, and transport of beer from the homeland was just out of the question, given the perpetually over-stressed supply situation. Therefore, Smerinka continues to hold a pleasant spot in our memories because of the availability of beer. We imagined ourselves to be far behind the front and thought we would enjoy an opportunity for rest and refitting. I had private quarters with a Rumanian dentist. Granted, I did not have a bed. I had not known such a bourgeois pleasure since July of 1943 in Kharkov, but I did have an oilcloth-covered sofa. A loudspeaker droned on all day and part of the night in my quarters. It could be heard all over the village. It was controlled centrally and could not be shut off other than by cutting off the power. We thought that, with the arrival of the new tanks, we would have time for a bit of well-earned rest. The stowage of the on-board gear, the application of the speckled camouflage, the numbering of the turrets and the introduction of new crew members was not done at a hectic pace.

One night—it was the night of 10–11 January 1944—we were roused from our sleep by the sound of fighting, in which heavy weapons also took part. Mechanized enemy formations, albeit weak, had broken through to the west north of us. Command and control on the German side had apparently dissolved. The advance of those enemy forces through Winniza to the south as far as our position in Smerinka had either gone unnoticed or the lines of communication to us had temporarily been broken. We were alerted, but there was no fighting. By morning the commotion was over. We were ordered to be ready to road march or be rail loaded. We reached Winniza by rail. Following our arrival, Tiger Regiment Bäke was formed. It included Tiger Tank Battalion 503, with about twenty Tigers, under Hauptmann Graf Clemens Kageneck, and the 2nd Battalion of the 23rd Panzer Regiment with about twenty-five Panthers under Hauptmann Euler. The weather was not very wintry, with fog, wet snow and occasional temperatures below freezing.

As we set out from Winniza on our march to the north, we still knew nothing of what awaited us during the upcoming weeks.

TIGER TANK REGIMENT BÄKE

This formation was unique. Panzer regiments were generally firmly integrated into the structure of panzer divisions. A panzer regiment consisted of two or three battalions. Tiger Regiment Bäke was a provisional formation assembled for a specific mission in the winter of 1944 in the Winniza and Tscherkassy area. The commander of this extremely powerful formation was Oberstleutnant Dr. Bäke, regimental commander of the Westphalian 11th Panzer Regiment. The regiment existed for around two months in January and February 1944. It was dissolved after the conclusion of its mission—the Tscherkassy pocket—on 25 February 1944. The units then returned to their original command and control relationships.

Organization:

- Tiger Tank Battalion 503 with 20 Tigers combat ready out of 34
- 2nd Battalion, 23rd Panzerregiment (Panther), with 25 Panthers combat ready out of 46
- 1 self-propelled artillery battalion

- 1 combat-engineer battalion with bridging equipment
- 1 mountain regiment

These pages are primarily written to honor the memory of the regimental commander, Dr. Franz Bäke, and the regiment named in his honor. Dr. Bäke, a reserve officer and dentist from Hagen (Westphalia) who was born in 1898, was forty-six years old (!) in 1944. He was an outstanding and beloved armor commander.

He possessed a natural authority and decisiveness. He did not spare himself. He exhibited personal bravery. He was concerned about those who were placed under his command. Above all else, he had a sort of "seventh sense" for developing the situation. He was never at a loss for improvising and, what was very important, was that he understood something about the employment of armor.

I consider him the most capable commander of armor at the level where the formation commander still also acts as a tank commander, leads from a tank and also participates in tank combat. We first met him in the summer of 1943 during Citadel. He was the commander of the 2nd Battalion, 11th Panzer Regiment. At that time he led a brilliant night attack in which our battalion also took part. We called that operation the "Attack through the Seven Villages." As battlefield deception, Bäke had placed two captured Russian T-34s at the head of the attack in order to deceive the Russians with their characteristic engine noise. It succeeded. At daybreak, when we were deep into the enemy, the German crews of the T-34s took off the blankets that covered the German crosses on the turrets and opened fire.

Here is a short military biography of Dr. Bäke [from Will Fey, *Armor Battles of the Waffen-SS*]:

During the heavy fighting in the defense and retreat to the Dnjepr that followed the failed Operation Citadel, one man took command over the 11th Panzer Regiment who, although not a professional soldier, is linked to the 11th Panzer Regiment. The former commander of the 2nd Battalion, 11th Panzer Regiment, Major of Reserves Dr. Bäke, became the new commander of the regiment.

He participated in the First World War from the time he volunteered in 1915 to its end. He was discharged as an acting Feldwebel and officer candidate after being wounded twice. On completion of his studies in medicine and dentistry, Bäke settled down as a dentist in Hagen. The Wehrmacht had barely been reborn when he reported for reserve exercises and was assigned to Tank Battalion 65 as a Leutnant of Reserves.

As an Oberleutnant, he commanded a tank company of that battalion in the Western Campaign in 1940. Shortly thereafter he was promoted to Hauptmann of Reserves and, in 1942, took over as commander of the 2nd Battalion, 11th Panzer Regiment, during the regiment's refitting in France. As a Major he led his newly equipped battalion to Russia. He prevented a breakthrough by vastly superior Soviet armored forces between the Don and Donetz and was awarded the Knight's Cross for that operation in January 1943.

In July 1943, northeast of Bjelgorod, he formed a bridgehead deep in enemy territory in a bold night-time coup de main, passing by an enemy armored column. [The so-called "ghost march" described above.] For that deed he received two *Panzervernichtungsabzeichen* [tank destruction badges] for destroying tanks on his own and the Wound Badge in Gold for having received his fifth wound. The Oak Leaves to the Knight's Cross soon followed.

During the fall of 1943 he was promoted to Oberstleutnant. As commander of Panzer Regiment 11, he never lost his composure or his head. He always led from the front of his dwindling tank and brought the men who had been entrusted to him through all dangers. With the newly formed schweres Panzer Regiment Bäke, which consisted of a Tiger battalion and a Panther battalion, along with other forces, he enabled German forces to break out of the encirclement at Tcherkassy. His forces knocked out 268 enemy tanks in the process. For that, Dr. Bäke was awarded the Swords to the Oak Leaves of the Knight's Cross.

In July of 1944, he was named commander of the newly formed 106th Panzer Brigade. In the meantime, he had been promoted to Oberst.

After being mentioned in the Wehrmacht Report on numerous occasions and having been wounded seven times, he took over the 13th Panzer Division in Hungary in 1945 and was promoted to Generalmajor. In all, he had been knocked out in his tank thirteen times.

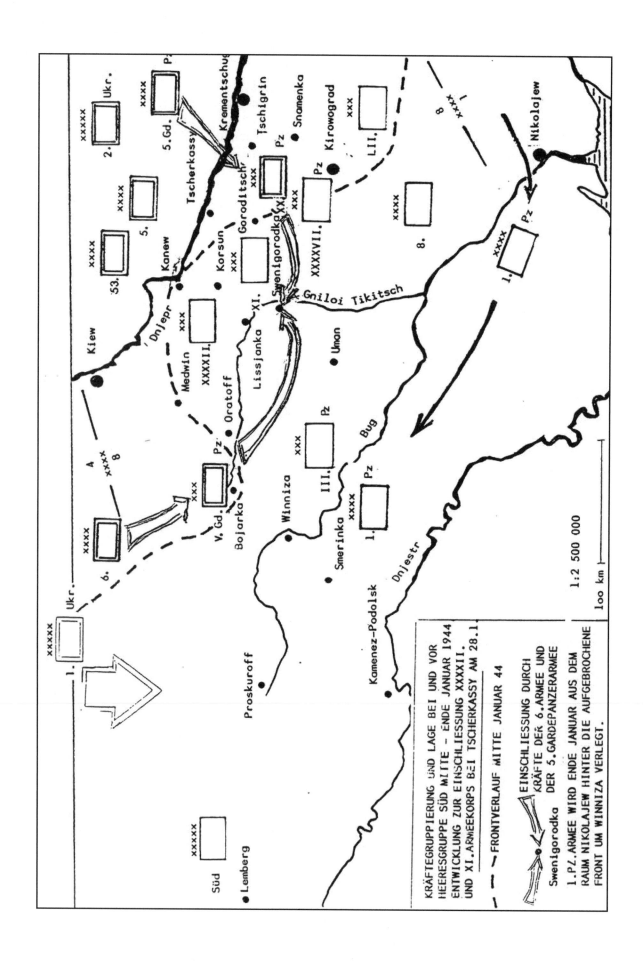

KRÄFTEGRUPPIERUNG UND LAGE BEI UND VOR
HEERESGRUPPE SÜD MITTE - ENDE JANUAR 1944
ENTWICKLUNG ZUR EINSCHLIESSUNG XXXXII.
UND XI.ARMEEKORPS BEI TSCHERKASSY AM 28.1.

——— FRONTVERLAUF MITTE JANUAR 44

EINSCHLIESSUNG DURCH
KRÄFTE DER 6.ARMEE UND
DER 5.GARDEPANZERARMEE

Swenigorodka

1.PZ.ARMEE WIRD ENDE JANUAR AUS DEM
RAUM NIKOLAJEW HINTER DIE AUFGEBROCHENE
FRONT UM WINNIZA VERLEGT.

1:2 500 000

100 km

After the war, General a.D. Dr. Bäke, who had taken part in more than 500 armored engagements, returned to dental practice. He died on 12 December 1978 and the age of eighty as the result of an auto accident.

The following text, which comes from the papers he left behind, concerns itself with the operations of Tiger Tank Regiment Bäke in January and February 1944. Dr Bäke wrote:

The Balabanowka Pocket, 25 January–30 January 1944

In mid-January 1944 I was the commander of the 11th Panzer Regiment of the 6th Panzer Division. I received the order from Army Group South (Field Marshal von Manstein) to immediately report to General Hube at the forward command post of the 1st Panzer Army at Pritzkoje. General Hube informed me that I would take over a Tiger regiment (one battalion of Tigers and one battalion of Panthers) for a special mission. The situation briefing revealed the following:

The enemy had advanced east of Winniza and had created a broad salient protruding into our defensive positions east of there. That salient was to be surrounded and destroyed. That, however, was of secondary importance.

Five enemy armored corps had been identified about 100 kilometers north of Winniza. Their attack in a southwest direction through Winniza could be expected any day.

The army group had no units with which to intercept that feared advance. The encirclement of the enemy units that had pushed forward was intended to draw those five armored corps from the north and destroy them.

That was the primary mission of the Tiger Tank Regiment. The Tscherkassy pocket had not been formed at that time. The attack was to begin the following morning at 0600 hours. Attack east. Objective: Oratow. Link up there with units advancing from the east. The 101st Jäger Division had the mission of securing the north flank.

The attack began punctually at 0600 hours. It succeeded in drawing the five Russian armored corps from the north away from the pocket that was forming at Balabonowka. Tiger Tank Regiment Bäke was presented with a new armored

corps to deal with each day. Each was destroyed in heavy fighting.

In all, during those five days, 267 enemy tanks were destroyed. Our own losses consisted of one Tiger and three Panthers.

On the third day, the attack by the infantry divisions on the right wing bogged down at Ssossow. Manstein already wanted to call off the attack. General Wenck (Chief of staff of the 1st Panzer Army) wanted to wait for further radio contact with Bäke before doing so. Bäke confirmed the attack was not making progress at Ssossow.

On his own initiative, Bäke started the Panther battalion towards Ssossow, even though it was not in his own attack sector. Falling on the enemy's rear, he smashed the enemy resistance. That cleared the way for the infantry. It was intended for the 1st SS Panzer Division "Leibstandarte," 15 kilometers outside of Oratow, to execute the breakthrough to Oratow after the enemy tank corps that had come from the north had been destroyed. The 1st SS Panzer Regiment of the division had pushed forward but then brought to a halt waiting for fuel. Since the area between the regiment and its logistical elements was held by the enemy, supplies were not able to get through.

The enemy armored attack on the supply elements of the Leibstandarte was smashed and twenty enemy tanks were destroyed by Tiger Tank Regiment Bäke which, fortunately, arrived at the opportune moment. Without further ado, Tiger Tank Regiment Bäke took over the fuel supplies for the regiment—reporting that fact to the divisional commander, SS-Brigadeführer Wisch—and thrust on forward to SS Panzer Regiment 1, bringing fuel to it.

The next morning, Tiger Tank Regiment Bäke, on its own initiative, again took the point. In a heavy snowstorm, it overran the strong Russian antitank defensive system, destroying twenty-five heavy antitank guns in the process. The Panther and artillery battalions crushed an attempt by the enemy to break out of the pocket.

At that point, Tiger Tank Battalion 503 advanced east to Oratow and established contact with the 16th Panzer Division that was coming from the east. It arrived at Oratow at the same moment.

[See the 1st Panzer Army order of the day and mention in the Wehrmacht Report on 31 January 1944 for Tiger Tank Regiment Bäke.]

Tscherkassy, 3–20 February 1944
Advance Northeast toward Medwin,
3–9 February 1944

Tiger Regiment Bäke took the lead in advancing with the 16th Panzer Division. Further assaults followed on the third day. The attack began at 0600 hours. The Russian defensive front was massed between two Balkas which ran in the direction of the attack of Tiger Tank Regiment Bäke. There was a distance of about 800–1,000 meters between the two Balkas. Since heavy losses would have been expected in a frontal attack, a feint was launched against the enemy around 0600 hours to fix him. At daylight, the Panther battalion advanced in a large arc around the right-hand Balka until it was possible to cross over in the enemy's rear.

At about 0830 hours, the Panther battalion attacked in the rear of the completely surprised enemy. Thereupon the main body of Tiger Tank Regiment Bäke attacked, along with the reconnaissance battalion of the 16th Panzer Division. In that narrow sector alone, eighty enemy tanks were knocked out (without counting numerous antitank guns or other weapons). An attack by the reconnaissance battalion was intended at 0600 hours. However, as the situation showed, such an attack would have been impossible without sacrificing the battalion. Higher levels of command were angry that the attack had not started at 0600 hours. Once the situation was explained, the matter was settled.

Advance East after Regrouping on
10 February 1944

In the meantime, muddy conditions prevailed and it was difficult to advance. There were many mechanical problems due to the weather. Order: Capture the bridge over the Gniloi-Tikitsch at Bushanka. Since it was open to question whether that bridge was still intact, a coup de main by the Panther battalion was directed at the bridge at Frankowka. That bridge had already been mined and prepared for demolition, but it was captured

at the last minute. It was not in our sector of attack. (Decision made on own initiative.) As assumed, the bridge at Buschanka had been destroyed. Thirty enemy tanks were knocked out on the far bank. The weather caused additional losses. Supplies were completely held up by the mud. Resupply by air was inadequate. Chizinzy was captured and contact established with the 1st Panzer Division. First contact was made with the encircled units on 17 February as they broke out from the pocket. Advance towards Dshurzhenzy and Hill 239 on 17 February was impossible due to shortage of fuel.

Only on 18 February, after some fuel was brought forward, was mobility sufficient enough for the assault south of Dshurzhenzy to Hill 239 to succeed. (It was not a hill, merely a point on the ridge.)

One Russian column after another moved westward in front of us to Frankowka. We halted 200 meters next to the Russian march columns until a gap suddenly appeared in the march formation. With a "Panzer march!" we infiltrated into the column and marched westward with them. Shortly outside the small bridgehead at Frankowka, the Russians turned off to the right and left. At that moment Tiger Tank Regiment Bäke swept past the Russian columns: "Button up and enage at will!" The surprise was complete. The German bridgehead had been informed of our intentions. We fired the agreed on recognition flares and made it without loss into the bridgehead through the completely confused Russians. There we fended off additional Russian attacks. The bridgehead was recaptured, the bridge destroyed. In the meantime, the Russians had closed ranks again behind us.

In the gray light of dawn the next morning, we also succeeded in breaking through the enemy lines without losses. We then had to break through the enemy lines one more time before reaching the German ones. That also succeeded.

So much for Dr. Bäke's account; here's an excerpt from the Wehrmacht Report from 31 January 1944 and the order of the day for the 1st Panzer Army on 25 February 1944:

In offensive operations in the area south of Pogrebischtsche from 24 to 30 January 1944, units of the army and the Waffen-SS under the command of General of Panzer Troops Hube—effectively supported by formations from the Luftwaffe—destroyed more than ten Soviet rifle divisions and several armored corps. The Bolsheviks lost 6,500 prisoners and more than 8,000 killed in that period. Seven hundred tanks and assault guns, 680 guns, 340 antitank rifles, several hundred motor vehicles and numerous other weapons and equipment were destroyed or captured. The Westphalian 16. Panzerdivision, under command of Generalmajor Back, and a Tiger regiment, commanded by Oberstleutnant Bäke, particularly proved themselves.

Here's an excerpt from the order of the day for the 1st Panzer Army on 25 February 1944:

Copy!

Commander in Chief   Command Post,
1st Panzer Army   25 February 1944

ORDER OF THE DAY!

As of today Tiger Tank Regiment Bäke is dissolved. The various elements are to return to their units. With this action ends a period of great accomplishment for the regiment. Created for the relief operation that began in the middle of January, with the mission of forming the heavy attack wedge after the infantry had broken through the forward-most enemy positions, the regiment moved out from Britskoje and hurled back the enemy.

It then defeated the superior enemy armored forces that hastened to the scene from the north and made possible the further breakthrough of the infantry divisions. During the days that followed, the regiment took over the spearhead of the attack and advanced boldly. In so doing, the regiment established the first contact with friendly armor advancing from the east. With that, the enemy forces located to the south were cut off and struggled against their destruction. However, not satisfied with that and acting on his own initiative, the courageous commander then advanced into the newly arrived Russian armored forces that were in assembly areas north of the Oratoff railroad station. The regiment dislodged them as well, inflicting heavy losses.

A few days later, after successful reorganization, the regiment's mission was to break through to the encircled units of the XI and XXXXII Army Corps.

In that action, Tiger Regiment Bäke formed the spearhead once again. In an audacious surprise attack it broke through the enemy and rolled up the enemy as far as Kutschowka. Then, two days later after reorganizing again, the regiment advanced to Guschanka. Laboriously struggling forward through the mud, continuously weakened by weather-induced losses, the regiment forced a crossing over the Gniloi Tikitsch River. It maintained its position as the spearhead of the attack despite having only a few tanks and facing ever increasing enemy superiority.

Approaching to within eight kilometers of the encircled units, the regiment made it possible for the encircled units to break out in its sector.

In recognition of that outstanding achievement which was decisive to the battle on many critical days, our Supreme Commander has awarded the Diamonds to the Oak Leaves of the Knight's Cross to the regiment's courageous commander, thus honoring him and his entire regiment.

I, myself, remember the achievements of the regiment with gratitude. They will remain indelibly etched in the history of the 1st Panzer Army. I offer my best wishes for the future to the courageous commander and all the members of Tiger Tank Regiment Bäke.

signed Hube
General of Panzer Troops and Commanding
General of the 1st Panzer Army

THE ENCIRCLEMENT OF THE XI AND XXXXII ARMY CORPS

The situation that preceded the encirclement must be described first. Generalleutnant von Vormann, the commanding general of the XXXXVII Army Corps, examined and evaluated the events of that period with unique clarity in his book, *Tscherkassy*. The XXXXVII Army Corps was employed south of Swenigorodka to the right of the III Panzer Corps. His evaluation of the divergence in opinion between OKH and the army group regarding many points concerning the execution of the operation is extensive. He also puts to rest the accusation that the 1st Panzer Division failed to do everything in its power to avert the catastrophe of Tscherkassy. Once again, the omissions and errors found their source at OKH. The inexcusable, elementary mistake: "Too little and too late." Just as at Stalingrad, it was the soldiers who had to pay the price.

Von Vormann wrote:

The III Panzer Corps thrust like a sharp knife deep into the enemy. To the west, the weak flank guard provided by the 34th Infantry Division provided only very dubious protection. To the east, the flank and rear were wide open. An additional thirty kilometers still separated the corps from the pocket, which had, in the meantime, been compressed around Gorodischtsche and Korsun-Schewtschenkowskij. It was now exactly due east. As had been foreseen from the beginning, the operation north had been a serious error. Blood and combat power had been squandered to no avail.

In East Prussia the pointlessness of a further advance on Medwin had been recognized. The III Panzer Corps was ordered to call off the attack to the north and advance from the Winograd area [15 kilometers south of Bojarka] to the east through Bushanka-Lissjanka [villages on the Gniloi Tikitsch] to Kwitki. That meant nothing less than starting the relief attack by the shortest and most direct route. However, five precious days had gone by in the meantime and the regrouping cost yet another two days. The ground that had been so painfully won on the Gniloi Tikitsch was evacuated and the reinforced 16th Panzer Division pulled back to the south, a difficult operation under increasing enemy pressure. General Breith again used the 17th and 16th Panzer Divisions as his battering ram in the middle, with the 1st Panzer Division aggressively covering the south flank and the 1st SS Panzer Division "Leibstandarte" covering the north flank.

The eleventh of February brought a promising success. There had been a light frost, so the ground had hardened and the new direction of attack seemed to have taken the enemy by surprise. Pressing far forward, the 1st Panzer Division had made a good start in capturing Bushanka on the Gniloi Tikitsch and the 17th and 16th Panzer Divisions were engaged in forming small bridgeheads over the stream to its left.

The Sixteenth Tank Corps pressed energetically to the south, obviously encouraged and driven on by the withdrawal movements on 9 and 10 February. The 1st SS Panzer Division "Leibstandarte," which had to cover a continually lengthening north flank, pulled back. Elements of the 17th Panzer Division—that is, elements from the actual spearhead—were therefore forced to turn in that direction.

The 16th Panzer Division overcame all difficulties, bridged the half-frozen Gniloi Tikitsch and set out anew to the east. In spite of the standing threat to its open north flank, it captured Daschukowka. The 1st Panzer Division made no use of the bridgehead that had been captured at Bushanka. It advanced south of the river to Lissjanka.

That move may have been for tactical reasons as a result of enemy pressure, but that route did not lead toward Komarowka and the pocket. Lissjanka was on the north bank and the Gniloi Tikitsch, which could only be crossed by bridge, offered a sizeable barrier. It was twenty to thirty meters wide and its depth was greater than a man's height. Sheets of ice projected from the soft, swampy banks into the river in whose center great ice floes were slowly driven by the current. The encircled XI and XXXXII Corps were later to pay dearly for the lack of favorable access to the southern bank in that sector.

The Thirteenth and fourteenth of February brought no real results. The 1st Panzer Division forced it way into Lissjanka and was dislodged from the village in hard fighting. The 17th Panzer Division sought in vain to open a crossing over the stream for its neighboring division by launching an attack south from the area east of Daschukowka. The unfortunate operation launched on 12 February by the 1st Panzer Division could no longer be made good. The 1st Panzer Division was unable to cross the Gniloi Tikitsch. At that same time, the Sixteenth Tank Corps thrust from Bojarka into the rear of the 16th Panzer Division, which was advancing toward the east. The Russians forced it to divert substantial units to the west and north. Nevertheless, Oberstleutnant Bäke succeeded in advancing into Chishinzy. Barely ten kilometers separated him at that point from the encircled comrades. But he could not hold out alone in the village

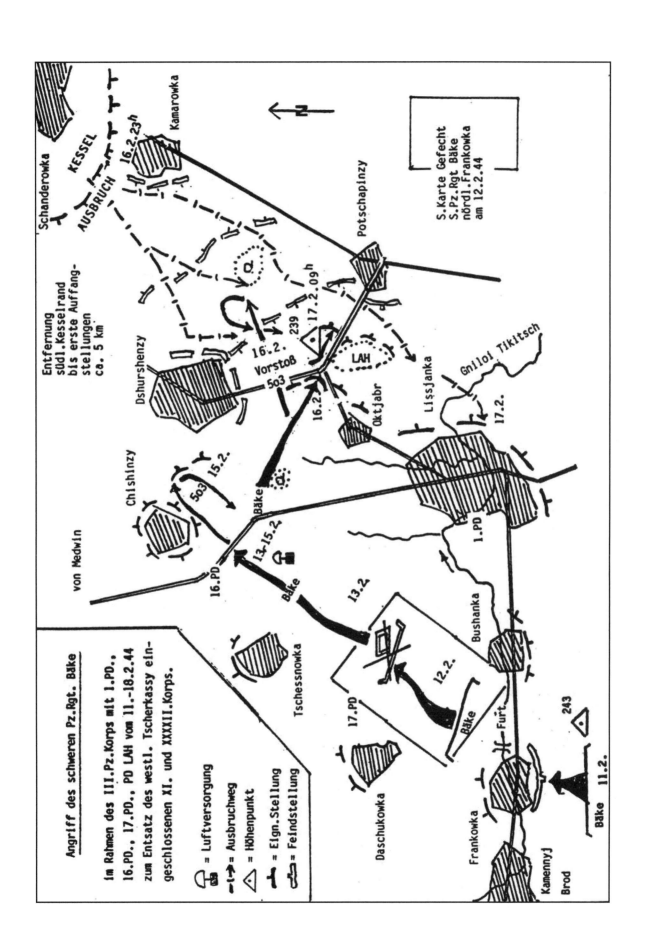

Angriff des schweren Pz.Rgt. Bäke

Im Rahmen des III.Pz.Korps mit 1.PD., 16.PD., 17.PD., PD LAH vom 11.–18.2.44 zum Entsatz des westl. Tscherkassy eingeschlossenen XI. und XXXXII.Korps.

= Luftversorgung
= Ausbruchweg
= Höhenpunkt
= Eign.Stellung
= Feindstellung

S.Karte Gefecht
S.Pz.Rgt Bäke
nördl.Frankowka
am 12.2.44

N

Schanderowka

KESSEL
AUSBRUCH

Kamarowka

16.2.23ʰ

Potschapinzy

Entfernung
südl.Kesselrand
bis erste Auffang-
stellungen
ca. 5 km

Dshurshenzy

16.2.
Vorstoß
5o3

239

17.2.09ʰ

16.2.

LAH

Oktjabr

Lissjanka

Gnilol Tikitsch

17.2.

Chishinzy

von Medwin

5o3 15.2.

Bäke

13–15.2

Bäke

16.PD

1.PD

Bushanka

Tschessnowka

13.2

17.PD

12.2.

Bäke

Daschukowka

Frankowka

Furt

243

Bäke 11.2.

Kamennyj
Brod

with his tanks against the concentric attacks of the Fifth Guards Tank Corps. He was forced to pull back again to the west.

The III Panzer Corps tried yet again to break through on 15 and 16 February. With the 16th Panzer Division providing protection from the rear and the north flank against Bojarka and Medwin, the 1st and 17th Panzer Divisions were supposed to advance from Lissjanka over the commanding high ground of Hill 239 south of Dshurshenzy. Panzer Group Bäke would thrust through Chishinzy to Komarowka. The bridge at Lissjanka collapsed. The entire attack failed to develop and came to nothing. The troops had been pushed beyond their capabilities and the equipment used up.

In the meantime, the XI and XXXXII Corps (Stemmerman and Lieb) had been ordered to break out to the southwest during the night of 16–17 February. During the evening of the portentious 16 February, the most advanced units of the III Panzer Corps were firmly held in the line Lissjanka-Oktjabr-Chishinzy. It was simply beyond human capacity to cover the last ten kilometers. Oberstleutnant Bäke set out again on 17 February and, with his tanks, actually reached Hill 239 south of Dshurshenzy. His regiment thus pinned strong enemy units in Potschapinzy. But he, too, was unable to effect any more changes in the fate of the encircled comrades. The help came too late and was too weak.

The Breakout by Gruppe Stemmermann on 16–17 February 1944

The decision had been made on 15 February. Relief could no longer be expected by an attack of the III or XXXXVII Panzer Corps (Breith and von Vormann). The 8th Army gave the order by radio at 1105 hours:

The ability of the III Panzer Corps to conduct operations is limited by the weather and the supply situation. Group Stemmermann must carry out the decisive breakthrough to Dshurschenzy-Hill 239 (up to two kilometers south) on its own. It will link up with the III Panzer Corps there. The breakthrough assault force, under command of Generalleutnant Lieb, XXXXII Army Corps, must force the breach. It will concentrate all its attack forces, in particular the 5th SS Panzer Divi-

sion "Wiking," supported by the main body of the artillery. No separate attacks!

The plan for the attack had already been worked out. At 2300 hours on 16 February, the breakout force would move out with no fire preparation from the line Chilki-Komarowka. It would employ three assault groups, all deeply echeloned. They would silently work their way forward and fall on the enemy in a rush with cold steel and "Hurra." They groups would advance to the Dshurshenzy–Hill 239.0 line in order to conduct a passage of lines through the III Panzer Corps (Breith).

The attack groups were assigned assembly areas and attack zones as follows:

Right: Corp Detachment B at Chilki. Axis of advance: Over the high ground south of Petrowskoje (Point 234.1)–Dshurshenzy south.

Center: 72nd Infantry Division in the low ground 1.5 kilometers southeast of Chilki. Axis of advance: North edge of woods southeast of Dshurshenzy–north of Point 239.0–Oktjabr.

Left: 5th SS Panzer Division "Wiking" at Komarowka. Axis of advance: Parallel to the 72nd Infantry Division past Point 239.0 to the south.

The VIII Air Corps was to screen the flanks, beginning at daybreak. The III and XXXXVII Panzer Corps were also to draw as many Soviet forces as possible and pin them by carrying on their attacks in the former direction.

The divisions were organized with three waves:

First wave: Bayonet wave (infantry assault force)
Second wave: Heavy weapons
Third wave: Artillery and trains

The rear guard, composed of the 57th and 88th Infantry Divisions, had to cover the rear of the breakout groups by occupying a shallow arc around Schandorowka. The rear guard forces were to withdraw on receipt of a radio code word. The 57th Infantry division would follow in the wake of the 5th SS Panzer Division "Wiking"; the 88th Infantry Division following the 72nd Infantry Division.

Artillery, tanks, assault guns and other heavy weapons were to be employed and brought along in relation to their mobility and ammunition supply. Everything else was to be destroyed.

The order stated that about 1500 wounded were to be left in Schandorowka with doctors and requisite medical personnel for their own possible salvation. The later course of events proved that measure to have been justified.

In the northeast, the Russians had attacked into the withdrawal movements of the intended rear-guard divisions (the 88th and 57th Infantry Divisions). It was only with difficulty that the dangerous penetration could be successfully sealed. However, that pushed the front line back closer than intended to Schandorowka—within three kilometers—into which the troops were massed. All traces of command and control threatened to vanish there.

In the southwest, where the 5th SS Panzer Division "Wiking" was located, the smoldering fighting flared up at Komarowka on 16 February. Apparently, the Russians could not accept the loss of that village. During the morning hours, it changed hands for the fourth time. The front line was forced back there to within barely three kilometers of Schandorowka. The assembly areas that had been planned in the village were lost. The decision to forego an immediate counterattack was difficult, but it was necessary to avoid premature ignition of a hot spot. The danger of drawing in additional new Russian forces was too great. The moment of surprise at 2300 hours might have been endangered. It appeared preferable, in spite of all concerns, to move the assembly area farther back. Countermanding orders to the formations following behind were necessary. Not all of them got through. "Order, counterorder, disorder . . ." Napoleon was right again.

The pocket was in a pressure cooker and all the safety valves were closed. Any break in the circle of protection would lead to an explosion which, in this case, meant panic and chaos. Fifty thousand men and all their equipment were in a 50-square-kilometer area [approximately 18 square miles]. Such compressed masses can no longer maneuver; they can no longer be controlled. The release could only take place at the appointed hour and in the appointed direction. That was the only hope for freedom.

The hours dragged on in grueling tension, far too slowly for the excited nerves and far too quickly—apparently—for the regrouping that

had been ordered. It went on and on, seemingly without end. Every unit commander knows that period of time during which he dare not intervene. Any interference from him can only cause confusion in the precisely measured course of the movements, in the orders of his subordinates that he is not aware of. Those are hours of inactive waiting in which heart and mind continue to be tortured with the constant questions: Have you done all that is humanly possible, can you justify what is happening here?

Under ordinary circumstances, those hours are an ordeal. There at Chilki the responsibility exerted a gigantic pressure since there was no other alternative. Preparing for the attack on 15 and 16 February brought extraordinary difficulties and the friction of war to the surface. The only route for the approach marches of three divisions, all of the trains and rear services of both corps led through Schandorowka. In the deep mud, the movements crept on at a torturously slow pace. Since they could not be hidden from enemy observation, observed fire from artillery, Stalin-organs and mortars continuously pounded the congested masses.

Vehicles that had broken down, burning ammunition vehicles, collapsed walls and burning houses blocked the single narrow road. Smoke, screams, the moaning of the severely wounded and the barking crash of the defending Flak filled the air. In the midst of all that thundered the discharges of friendly artillery. The guns that had to be blown up fired off their remaining ammunition. Attacks by low-flying aircraft, dropping bombs and strafing, completed the vision of hell in the village. In spite of everything, new formations kept pouring in from the north, east and south. There was no way around, and only to the west was there any chance for freedom. "Freedom" [*Freiheit*] was also the official password of the day.

All telephone connections had been torn up for some time. The radio sets, which had been placed on Panje carts, only functioned irregularly. To the extent that reports from the front reached General Stemmerman at Chilki, they indicated an attempt to squash the pocket with concentric attacks. It had shrunk to a frightfully small dimension.

Breakthrough as ordered. At any price! All bridges to the past had been broken. Along with

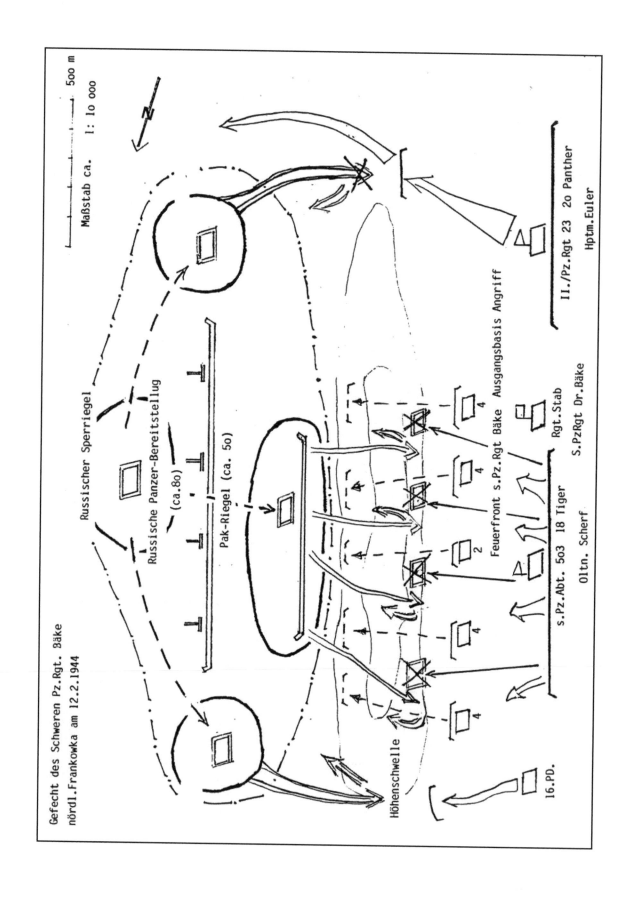

Gefecht des Schweren Pz.Rgt. Bäke
nördl.Frankowka am 12.2.1944

Maßstab ca. 1 : 1o 000   5oo m

Russischer Sperriegel

Russische Panzer-Bereitstellug
(ca.8o)

Pak-Riegel (ca. 5o)

Höhenschwelle

16.PD.

Feuerfront s.Pz.Rgt Bäke Ausgangsbasis Angriff

Rgt.Stab

S.PzRgt Dr.Bäke

s.Pz.Abt. 5o3 18 Tiger

Oltn. Scherf

II./Pz.Rgt 23 2o Panther

Hptm.Euler

the superfluous weapons and equipment, all papers and files, even the personal effects, had been burned. The parting with the treasured everyday things, memorabilia to which the heart clung, all that one owned—that parting was hard. All that was left was what one needed for close combat and could carry.

The early onset of darkness, arriving with frost and snow squalls, came as desired. The worse the weather, the greater the probability that the surprise would succeed. The enemy still seemed oblivious. His fire became more and more irregular and weak. Even in Schandorowka the situation worked itself out and, one after another, the attack groups reported the completion of their preparations. The hour of decision could arrive.

At about 2300 hours, the first wave of the three attack groups set out without fire preparation. The completely surprised enemy was overrun, his resistance was limited. The ring was broken and, by any normal standard, the breakout seemed assured of success, assuming that the III Panzer Corps (Breith) was positioned at Dshurshenzy, on Hill 239 and in Potschapinzy.

The final radio message as of 1500 hours read: Oktjabr captured. With that, all command and control by Gruppe Stemmerman came to an end; indeed, Group Stemmermann ceased to exist. Since the prerequisites for success of the desperate operation had not been met by the III Panzer Corps (Breith), what followed was a individual race against death, in which all military formations dissolved. The influence of the officers only extended as far as their voices carried. The elemental flow of the masses was uncontrollable.

As a result, the course of events during the hours that followed is difficult to reconstruct. The only sources are the confused and contradictory individual accounts of the survivors. Unit staffs and command organs no longer existed. The departure of the second and third waves from the assembly positions took place according to plan, under the impression that the first wave had succeeded in breaking through. In a steadily growing stream, about 40,000 men flowed to the west. One only had to make it another few kilometers in order to get to the comrades of the relief force who were rushing forward!

The disillusionment and horror was horrendous when murderous tank, antitank gun and artillery fire tore into the crowded mass of human beings as the day dawned outside of Dshurshenzy-Potschapinzy. The troops had dragged all of their heavy equipment with them through the deep, snow-filled Balkas. Everything was smashed up then in the hail of Russian fire. Guns and assault guns were left behind after firing off the last of their ammunition. The wounded whom the units had brought along met their fate.

Then the masses of men picked themselves up—left to their own devices and the weapons they carried in their hands. With the courage of desperation, they sought a way out of the chaos. Packs of hundreds of soldiers, thrown together from every branch of service and formation, pushed on to the west, led by the first officer they could find. Russian infantry was swept aside with cold steel. Even Russian tanks turned away. However, the Russian fire beat without hindrance into the blind and uncontrolled mass of unprotected men. The losses mounted.

The Russians were positioned for the defense in the line Dshurshenzy-Potschapinzy, not Breith's III Panzer Corps. Its divisions were fighting at Chishinzy, Oktjabr and at Lissjanka for a crossing back over the Gniloi Tikitsch.

Only scattered , small groups were fortunate enough to break through under the protection of darkness and snow squalls. They ran into German tanks at Oktjabr and were saved.

As day broke, individuals turned south in their desperation, since the noise of combat seemed weaker there. The mass followed in a stampede. The Russian infantry fled from the eastern portion of Potschapinzy before their wild rush. The way was free. The enemy river defenses along the banks of the Gniloi Tikitsch were scattered from the rear. However, there was no bridge, and the ice on the river was broken. Forced onward by gunfire from tanks, artillery, and continually strengthening Russian infantry, the mass of men that had been driven together finally leaped into the icy flood, leaving their last handheld weapons behind. Many drowned. Those who reached the far bank were not yet saved. Even there, the fire from the T-34s and artillery pursued the half-frozen men up the long, open high ground southeast of Lissjanka. Those who were not hit and did not collapse from the cold, were received by the 1st Panzer Division in the southern portion of Lissjanka.

Many hundreds of men of the rear guard fought their way back to the German lines during the night of 17–18 February. They had stood against the enemy in exemplary fulfillment of duty. Half frozen, starving, weaponless and doubting their own sanity, about 20,000 to 25,000 men found themselves assembled in the intended passage-of-lines assembly area north of Uman. They found no answers to their rapid flow of questions about the meaning of the entire operation. Those who had escaped the hell of that twenty-one-day battle were, physically speaking, no longer fit for action. The damage that the morale of the troops had suffered was irreparable. They had lost confidence in their leadership.

The XI and XXXXII Corps (Stemmermann and Leib) had ceased to exist. Their disappearance from the front prepared the way for the Russian breakthrough in March over the Bug and Dnjestr to the Pruth.

So much for what von Vormann had to say.

As part of the overall evaluation of the Tscherkassy operation, it is also interesting to hear from the other side. Field Marshall Zhukov, at that time Deputy of the Supreme Commander [Stalin], presents a very one-sided view of the events of the Battle of Korsun-Schewchenkowski [the Russian name for the Tcherkassy fighting] in his book, *The Memoirs of Marshall Zhukov*. As with all Soviet presentations, the ideological viewpoint, which interferes with historical veracity, is obvious. The Soviet soldier is always a hero; mistakes were never made. The German soldier is cowardly, traitorous and stupid. Nevertheless, if one knows how to read between the lines, one can discover factual events among the circumlocutions and distortions. However, there is always exaggeration. Manipulation of information is a well-known weapon of psychological warfare, which is as much directed at one's own people as at the enemy.

Zhukov's remarks are striking in their exemplification of the archaic hate of the enemy that insists that even his honor must be taken away. In truth, there were no German generals flown out of the pocket. General Stemmermann was killed in the pocket; Generalleutnant Lieb became a prisoner of war. Likewise, there were no officers or SS people who broke out of the pocket with armored vehicles. Not a single armored vehicle came out of the encirclement.

The Red Army hoped to destabilize the German front by employing the National Committee for a Free Germany [*Nationalkomitee Freies Deutschland*]. The "committee" was composed of German soldiers who had been captured or who had crossed the lines and changed sides. Air-dropped leaflets, speeches over loud-speakers, radio broadcasts and even armed involvement were all fruitless. For example, our battalion commander, Graf Kageneck, was severely wounded by soldiers wearing German uniforms who were riding in a motorcycle-sidecar combination at Oratoff.

Now for several excerpts from Zhukov's book, *Erinnerungen und Gedanken* [translator's note: The differences between the text of the German edition that the author quotes and the English-language edition of *The Memoirs of Marshal Zhukov* are substantial enough that I have chosen to translate the German version into English for the following passages]:

In order to ward off the inevitable defeat of the encircled troops, the German high command began to concentrate forces against our outer front. On 27 January the 3rd, 11th, and 4th Panzer Divisions reached the Nowo-Mirgorod area. Two days later the 13th Panzer Division also advanced there. The 16th and 17th Panzer Divisions were then concentrated in the Risino area.

All of us who had carried out this operation of encircling the units of the enemy's 1st and 8th Armies knew full well that the German command would undertake to save the encircled units with a blow from outside. The Sixth Tank Army of the First Ukrainian Front, which had been reinforced with the 47th Rifle Corps, and the Fifth Guards Tank Army of the Second Ukrainian Front, which had been reinforced with the 49th Rifle Corps and the Fifth Engineer Brigade, were committed to stabilize the outer front and guarantee the destruction of the encircled units. The flanks of the external front were covered by the 40th and 53rd Armies.

In contrast to the enemy forces that had been encircled at Stalingrad and defended themselves in expectation of salvation from outside, hoping that von Manstein's group would advance to them from the Kotelnikowo area, the units that had been encircled at Korsun-Schewtschenklowski attempted to break out of the encirclement on their own, advancing toward the assault group that was to bring them relief from outside.

During the first days of February, the enemy units attempted in vain to break through the sector of the outer ring of encirclement that was held by the Second Ukrainian Front at Nowo-Mirgorod. They used a portion of their armored forces. The enemy then regrouped in front of our First Ukrainian Front, striking us two heavy blows at Risino and at Tomatsch-Iskrennoje, where he committed three additional tank divisions.

At Risino he succeeded in wedging his way into our positions. The German command was convinced the breakthrough would succeed this time. General Hube, the commander of the 1st Panzer Army, did not spare the promises. We intercepted a radio message saying, "I will get you out! Hube." He did not give up the intention of breaking through our outer ring of encirclement. He brought in another armor division, a battalion of heavy tanks [Tiger Tank Battalion 503] and two assault gun battalions. He moved a large group of armor divisions to the Jerki area and launched a fierce attack. On 9 February I sent an encoded radio message to the Supreme Commander [Stalin] in which, among other things, I said:

"According to interrogations of prisoners, the enemy has suffered great losses in the pocket. At the present time, confusion can be felt among soldiers and officers. In isolated cases it amounts to panic.

"According to information from our reconnaissance forces, the encircled enemy has concentrated the major portion of his forces in the Steblew-Korsun-Schewtschenkowski area. He obviously prepares to launch a final attempt to break through to the armored group that is advancing toward Malaja Bojarka. In order to secure this area we are committing a tank brigade from Rotmistrow and, in the Krasnogorodka-Motajewka area, the 340th Rifle Division from Schmatschenko. The Armies of Korotejew, Ryschow and Trofimenko will start their offensive on 9 February.

"On 8 February at 1550 hours our parliamentary handed our ultimatum regarding the encircled enemy to the German Oberst Fucke [Oberst Fouquet] who commands the Steblew sector. The parliamentaries have returned and passed on the information that the German command would answer on 9 February at 1100 hours. Zhukov."

On 9 February at 1200 hour General Stemmerman's staff informed us that our ultimatum had been declined.

At the same time, the Germans began a bitter attack on the inner front as well as on the outer front. On 11 February extremely intense fighting flared up. Our troops fought with extraordinary steadfastness. The enemy's armor divisions [in actuality, only the 1st Panzer Division was employed] succeeded in advancing into Lissjanka with great losses. However, having accomplished that, his strength was exhausted and he went over to the defense.

During the night of 12 February the encircled group concentrated in a narrow sector and attempted to break out through Steblew to the armor divisions that were in Lissjanka. That, however, did not succeed. The enemy was brought to a halt. The distance separating the encircled group and the relief forces had narrowed to 12 kilometers, but we felt that the enemy lacked the strength to bridge the gap and link up. During the night of 12 February 1944, I reported to Supreme Headquarters:

"The enemy is positioned outside of Krawtschenko with about 160 tanks [editor's note: the entire 1st Panzer Army did not have 160 tanks] and motorized infantry and is attempting to force his way forward along the line Risino-Tschemeriskoje-Tarassowka in the direction of Lissjanka. He has broken through the first defensive line of the 47th Rifle Corps and driven a wedge ten kilometers into our positions."

On 14 February, units of the 52nd Army of the Second Ukrainian Front captured the city of Korsun-Schewtschenkowski. The ring drew ever tighter. The soldiers, officers and generals of the German units clearly realized that the promised help would not arrive and they were thrown entirely on their own resources. Prisoners reported that the troops were quite desperate, especially when they discovered that a number of the division commanders and staff officers had been flown out.

During the night of 16 February a snowstorm arrived. The visibility was only about 10 to 20 meters. The Germans renewed their hope that, with the protection of the storm, they would be able to slip through to Lissjanka and link up with Hube's forces. That breakout attempt was quashed by the 27th Army, under S. G. Trofimenko, and by the Fourth Guards Army of the Second Ukrainian Front. The cadets of the Non-commissioned Officer's Academy from the training battalion of the 41st Guards Rifle Division of Major General K. N. Zwetkow fought with particular heroism. A fierce struggle raged during the morning of 17 February with the German columns attempting to break out, most of which were either wiped out or taken prisoner. Only a portion of the tanks and armored vehicles with generals, officers and SS people succeeded in escaping the encirclement. As we had expected, we were finally through with the encircled group on 17 February. According to reports of the Second Ukrainian Front, 18,000 men were taken prisoner and the combat equipment of the group was captured.

So much for what Zhukov had to say.

The German Wehrmacht Report of 20 February 1944 reported:

The Wehrmacht High Command elaborates on the liberation of the German battle group that had been encircled west of Tscherkassy:

The passage of lines by the divisions that were freed has been completed. The units of the army and the Waffen-SS that had been cut off since 28 January have heroically stood off the assault of far superior enemy forces. Under the command of General of Artillery Stemmerman and Generalleutnant Lieb, they broke through the encirclement in furious fighting. Officers and troops provided another shining example of heroic steadfastness, audacious, aggressive spirit and self-sacrificing comradeship for the history of the German military.

The formations of the army and the Waffen-SS that took part in the relief of that battle group, established the conditions that made the breakout possible. Commanded by General of Panzer Troops Breith, in cooperation with the units commanded by Generalleutnant von Vormann, every individual soldier exhibited exemplary conduct in the severest weather and terrain conditions. The Soviets suffered serious and bloody losses and, between 4 and 18 February, lost 728 tanks and assault guns. Eight hundred guns were captured and several thousand prisoners brought in.

The VIII Air Corps, commanded by Generalleutnant Seidemann, provided outstanding support to the hard-fighting army troops in the spirit of combined arms operations. Transport and combat formations supplied the encircled forces under serious weather conditions and, in spite of heavy enemy fighter and antiaircraft defenses, brought them ammunition, rations and fuel. They also brought back more than 2,400 wounded. In the process, thirty-two transport aircraft were lost. Fifty-eight enemy aircraft were shot down in aerial combat and by flak.

On 22 February, the Wehrmacht Report had the following to say:

General of Artillery Stemmerman, commander of the battle group that was encircled west of Tscherkassy and which then broke out, was killed on the final day of the breakout by an artillery round which hit his vehicle. He deserves a large share of the credit for the unshakeable behavior and the breakout of the battle group. The Army has lost an especially good, veteran troop commander.

Research after the war has shown that the Wehrmachtsberichte were free of actual false statements, which seems amazing in a war in which everything appeared to be allowed. It may well be, however, that political or military developments that were inopportune were passed over in silence or presented with an altered bias. Despite that, one can assume the information presented in the Wehrmacht report from 20 February was factual. What was not officially mentioned was that 30,000–50,000 soldiers had been encircled. Also left out was that 20,000–25,000 were saved. No one knew exactly how high the death rate had been during the fighting in the pocket or during the breakout. Zhukov's figures of 18,000 prisoners must be doubted, given the Russian practice of exaggerating successes. If, however, the numbers were to agree, then the total deaths would have been between 2,000 and 7,000.

The German side estimated that Tcherkassy had cost about 10,000 soldiers. For Tiger Tank Battalion 503, it was the most difficult operation of its existence.

CHAPTER 25

The Operations of Tiger Tank Battalion 503 in Opening the Tscherkassy Pocket

Alfed Rubbel

OUR SITUATION AT THE END OF JANUARY AND BEGINNING OF FEBRUARY 1944

On 20 January 1944 the battalion reached Winniza by rail. Although we received several factory-new Tigers during the refitting at Smerinka, we had only thirty-five Tigers on hand as compared with the forty-five allotted according to our table of organization. Twenty-five of those were fully operational. That number varied continually due to gains and losses as a result of mechanical problems and tanks repaired. The number of trucks had been similarly decimated. Only 68 out of 111 cross-country vehicles were ready for service, which meant that only 119 tons out of our total 234 tons of transport carrying capacity was available. That would lead to logistical problems, since there were no paved roads available in that operational area and supplies would have to be transported long distances over soft ground.

The personnel situation did not look good either. The battalion was short seven out of twenty-eight officers, including two company commanders and three tank platoon leaders. Thirty-four of the 274 noncommissioned officers were lacking, mostly from the tank crews. Since 1 January 1944, three officers had been killed and four wounded. Twelve noncommissioned officers had been killed and sixteen wounded. The complement of enlisted men was at full count, with 694 soldiers. It is interesting that, of the ninety *Hiwis*, we had been short fifty to sixty of them for a number of months. The inclination toward a relatively generous existence, mostly as a driver or assistant driver instead of the deprivations of a prisoner-of-war camp had declined. The rapidly worsening German situation was having its effect.

In the monthly situation report for January 1944 the state of training and health for the battalion was indicated as good. In February, the battalion reported "morale is outstanding as a result of major achievements."

That was the condition of our battalion as we joined Tiger Tank Regiment Bäke, which had been formed for a specific operation. The regiment was meant to be committed as a concentrated armored striking force—it would form the Schwerpunkt of the operation.

At first, the regiment's commitment had nothing to do with the Tscherkassy pocket. It was intended for the III Panzer Corps to advance north in the direction of Medwin to intercept and destroy three Russian corps. Tiger Tank Regiment Bäke was placed under the operational control of the corps. That effort miscarried due to the threefold Russian superiority. While that fruitless operation wasted time, strength and energy, the impending encirclement of the XI and XXXXII Corps was completed on 28 January 1944. The III Panzer Corps was then pulled back thirty kilometers in order to prepare to open the pocket. It was under extreme time pressure. The battalion assembled in the Schubenny Staw area. The Maintenance Company was ready for operations at Mankowka. The company combat trains and maintenance sections were held close at hand and quartered at Rubany Most. On 28 January 1944 the battalion commander, Hauptmann Graf Kageneck, was wounded. Oberleutnant Adameck, company commander of the 1st Company, was killed on 24 January 1944. In the attack to the north, the entire maintenance section of 1st Company was killed by partisans in the Oratoff area in a most cruel fashion.

TIGER TANK BATTALION 503 WITH TIGER REGIMENT BÄKE FROM 21–25 FEBRUARY 1944
Preparations
19 January: Loading at Smerinka, rail transport

20 January: Unloading at Winniza

21 January: Formation of Tiger Tank Regiment Bäke

Attack on Medwin
22 January: Preparations for the attack on Medwin at Balabanowka

23 January: Attack on the Bila position

24 January: Breakthrough at the Bila position

25 January: Armored fighting at Ssosoff

26 January: Defensive fighting at Ssosoff

27 January: Armored fighting south of Otscheretnja

28 January: Armored fighting and breakthrough at the Oratoff railroad station

29 January: Fighting at Oratoff

30 January: Defensive fighting at Oratoff

31 January: Defensive fighting northwest of Oratoff

Attack on Tscherkassy
1 February: Movement to new area of operations

2 February: Movement to new area of operations

3 February: Attack on Pawlowka

4 February: Breakthrough at Pawlowka

5 February: Attack on Wotylewka

6 February: Defensive fighting at Wotylewka

7 February: Defensive fighting at Wotylewka

8 February: Attack on Repki

9 February: Fighting in the Repki area of operations

10 February: Preparations for the attack on Frankowka

11 February: Attack at Frankowka and formation of bridgehead

12 February: Enlargement of the bridgehead at Frankowka

13 February: Armored fighting at Tschessnowka

14 February: Defensive fighting at Tschessnowka

15 February: Offensive and defensive operations south of Dshurshenzy

16 February: Attack on Hill 239

17 February: Covering force on Hill 239; passage of lines by the pocket units

18 February: Covering force on Hill 239; passage of lines by the pocket units

19 February: Fighting withdrawal to the Gniloi Tikitsch

20 February: Ready reserve at Bossowka

21 February: Road march to Uman

25 February: Deactivation of Tiger Tank Regiment Bäke

There were no more officers in the battered 1st Company. The few Tigers—there might have been five or six—were led by Oberfeldwebel Hans Fendesack. At the time, I was a Fahnenjunker-Feldwebel, about to leave for officer-candidate school. I was the tank commander of Tiger 114.

I no longer remember what the tank situation was like in the 2nd Company. The 3rd Company was the only company that was still commanded by its company commander, Oberleutnant Walter Scherf. It had the most tanks. Of the approximately twenty-five Tigers with which we had set out on 21 January, there were eighteen to twenty ready for action as we went into the Tscherkassy operation on 3 February.

In light of the personnel and tank situation, Scherf dissolved the companies and distributed the tanks among four platoons. The platoons were led by Oberfeldwebel Fendesack, Oberfähnrich Rondorf, Oberfeldwebel an der Heiden and Oberfeldwebel Sachs. With the exception of Oberfeldwebel Fendesack, all of the platoon leaders were from the 3rd Company. In that situation, Oberleutnant Scherf became the acting commander of Tiger Tank Battalion 503. A battalion of mountain troops from the 4th Mountain Division with about 200 soldiers and 15 SPWs were placed under the operational control of the regiment. That was a good addition to the regiment's combat power, especially since there was always a shortage of infantry. Half of the mountain troopers came to the battalion. Leutnant Haß, the special-duty staff officer [*Ordonnanz-Offizier*] of the battalion, was responsible for the forwarding of supplies and maintaining liaison with the regiment. There were only three officers at the "front": Oberleutnant Scherf, Leutnant Haß and the battalion surgeon, Dr. Schramm.

The III Panzer Corps, commanded by Generalleutnant Breith, along with the 1st Panzer Division, 16th Panzer Division, 17th Panzer Division, 1st SS Panzer Division "Leibstandarte," 198th Infantry Division, and Tiger Tank Regiment Bäke was assigned the mission of opening the Korsun-Tscherkassy pocket with the forces that were encircled there, the XI and XXXXII Army Corps. To fulfil that mission, the III Panzer Corps ordered the attack as follows:

- 16th and 17th Panzer Divisions and Tiger Regiment Bäke were to attack in the center toward the northeast over Hill 239-Buschanka-Frankowka and to cross the Gniloi Tikitsch River, capturing the high ground northeast of Frankowka and securing there.
- 1st Panzer Division, on the right, was to follow the attack and cover the southern flank.
- 1st SS Panzer Division "Leibstandarte" was to follow the attack on the left and cover the northern flank.

The attack was to start at 0730 hours on 11 February 1944.

11 February 1944: The battalion set out in the first wave while it was still dark. The ground was lightly frozen on the surface and there was scarcely any snow. As it got light, the Tigers encountered several Russian T-34 tanks and antitank guns in position on the Bossowka-Bushanka road. Seven Russian tanks were knocked out, the others withdrew.

In order to capture the important village of Frankowka with its bridge across the Gniloi Tikitsch, the battalion was ordered to support the Panthers and grenadiers attacking Frankowka on the right with fire. Frankowka was captured by noon. Unfortunately, because of their great weight, the Tigers were unable to use the bridge and, for the time being, had to remain south of the river at Frankowka. We found a ford and took up positions for the night on the high ground north of the village. Unfortunately, our rejoicing

at having the mountain troopers for night security was premature. We had to take care of it ourselves. We formed a hedgehog position, arranging the Tigers in an oval with their guns pointing outward. Most of the tanks faced toward the front, a few on the sides and to the rear. The tanks were close enough together so that one could see both adjoining tanks in the darkness. The hatches were buttoned up. The person pulling guard in the commander's cupola had only his head sticking up above the rim of the open hatch. He had a machine pistol, a flare pistol and hand grenades in front of him. The watch changed every hour. The crew did their best to sleep inside the tank. The night remained calm, if one disregarded the noise of the fighting around us.

12 February 1944: The Fifth Guards Tank Corps and Twentieth Tank Corps, which had linked up on 28 January 1944 at Swenigorodka and completed the encirclement, were of the opinion that they had surrounded the entire 1st Panzer Army. Expecting German attacks to open the pocket, the enemy held strong forces—estimated at eighty tanks and fifty antitank guns—ready for either defense or counterattack. That grouping of forces, which had moved north of Frankowka against our attack, had to be promptly and effectively eliminated in order to advance our attack toward the pocket. The objective of the battalion, which was employed on the left of the regiment, was the road east of Tschessnowka. German dive-bombers supported the attack, which began at 0900 hours. The aerial attack was particularly successful against the unprotected antitank guns. Because those guns were difficult to spot until they fired their first round, they were extremely dangerous to tanks.

Our attack broke all the way through. We destroyed about twenty or twenty-five Russian tanks. The regiment and the 16th Panzer Division that was attacking along with us had destroyed about seventy tanks and forty antitank guns by evening. The ground gained was a wedge about five kilometers deep and barely three kilometers wide. The 1st Panzer Division and the 1st SS Panzer Division "Leibstandarte" had to cover the deep flanks while operating offensively. The farther the attack group—Tiger Tank Regiment Bäke, the 16th Panzer Division, and the 17th Panzer Division—penetrated into the area of the break-in, the weaker its combat power became, since the two flanking divisions were no longer able to work their way forward. In addition, the III Panzer Corps had two enemy tank corps in front of it that were less attrited than it was. I estimate the German formations had less than half of their combat strength left.

In the evening the battalion formed a hedge-hog about one kilometer south of Tschessnowka, which was still in enemy hands, and waited for resupply. Because of danger from the enemy in the rear area and miserable road conditions, the supplies could not be brought forward by trucks. Instead, they were supposed to be air-dropped during the night. The battalion had lost five tanks due to enemy action: Four of them complete losses and one capable of being repaired. Unfortunately, we had four killed and several wounded.

The aerial resupply failed to show up during the night. Three fires in a triangle marked the drop site. The night was undisturbed. A light snow-fall had started and the temperature dropped, but the ground still was not hard enough. Our tanks left deep track marks and the heavy wheeled vehicles had to struggle laboriously through the barely frozen ground that did not yet bear their weight.

13 February 1944: At daybreak we launched our attack from the northeast, turning east on the Medwin-Lissjanka road. We knocked out six out of the seven Russian T-34/85s and U.S.-built Sherman tanks approaching from Medwin. Upon reaching the road, our twelve Tigers provided cover to the north and east for a while. It seemed that uncoordinated, small Russian tank attacks in company strength were the rule. Enemy tanks could appear anywhere and at any time.

The 1st Panzer Division had bitten off more than it could chew at Lissjanka. Strong local defense and the Gniloi Tikitsch River held the division back, which was supposed to provide flank guard for the operation. There have been unjustified aspersions cast at the 1st Panzer Division, claiming that it frittered itself away in fighting in the village. It thus lost the battle against time, time that was running out for the encircled troops. The corps had put the main effort on the left. A badly battered armor division that lacked tanks and, even more important, that lacked infantry forces, was in no position to swiftly eliminate the villages of Lissjanka and Oktjabr.

It was at least ten kilometers to the western edge of the encirclement. Those ten kilometers formed a wall consisting of heavily armored Russian formations. A tank formation could

and should ignore open flanks during the rapidly changing situations in a war of movement but, in the deeply echeloned and strong defenses surrounding the pocket, open flanks had to be attended to and avoided. Several times enemy tanks emerged in front of the Tigers of Fendesack's platoon and Rondorf's platoon. About ten were knocked out. The villages of Chischinzy and Dshurshenzy were chock full of Russian tanks and infantry. At long last, the promised airdrops that had taken off from Uman arrived with fighter escort. Right on target, and flying at extremely low altitude—scarcely more than ten meters off the ground—they dropped the fuel drums, fuel pumps and ammunition for the tanks. Unfortunately, many of the supplies were lost to breakage. Our tanks moved individually to the drop sites, fueled up and resupplied with ammunition.

Unfortunately, there were no rations, which had become extremely short. The emergency rations had long since been consumed. The "eating off the land" that was usual in such situations was impossible, since we hardly got into villages. Besides, they were empty of people.

It was decided that Tiger Tank Regiment Bäke would attack as far as the Chishinzy-Dshurshenzy road and hold there until the 16th Panzer Division had taken Chishinzy and the 1st Panzer Division had captured Lissjanka. Then we would turn to the southeast and capture the village of Kamarowka, about six kilometers away. The only tanks that were in action from the 1st Company were those of Fendesack, Erdmann and me.

14 February 1944: The 16th Panzer Division captured Chishinzy. We remained in our positions on the road to Dshurshenzy and had to ward off at least four attacks by groups of five to seven Russian tanks, each attack thus approximating a weak tank company. At least twenty tanks were knocked out in the process. Increasingly, we also had to fight off infantry. In the meantime, our own infantry closed up and we were a bit more secure against hunter/killer teams. Snow squalls and fog dampened the noise of the fighting; due to poor visibility enemy tanks did not emerge into sight until they were extremely close.

The operations order was changed, presumably because our forces were insufficient for the advance to Kamarowka. The 1st Panzer Division was still fighting in Lissjanka. The capture of Dshurshenzy and Kamarowka would have taken

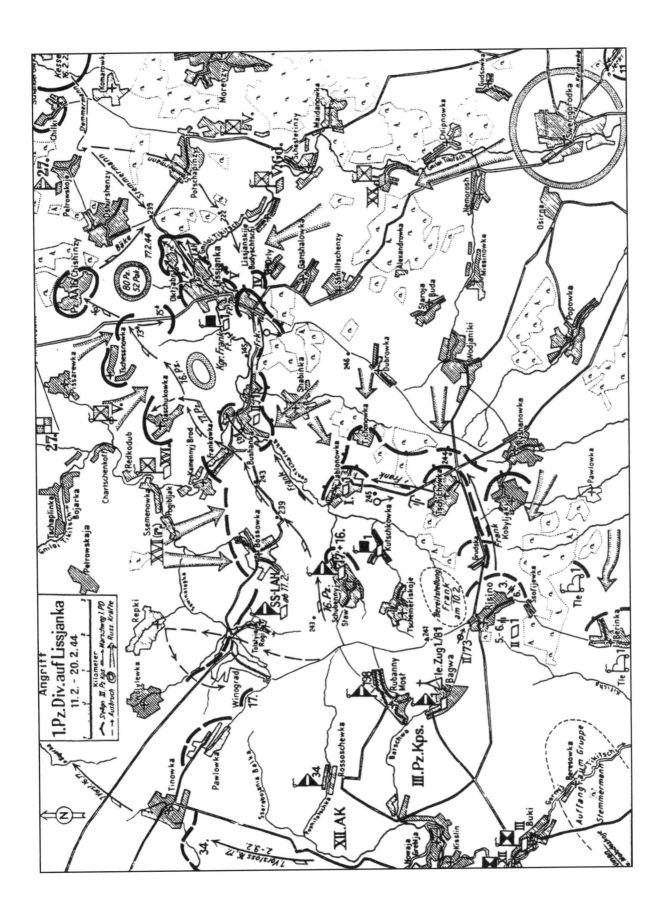

Angriff
1.Pz.Div.auf Lissjanka
11.2. - 20.2.44

too much time and consume too much combat power. The situation of the encircled forces, which was dramatically worsening by the hour as they were forced to repulse ceaseless attacks on all sides and suffered extremely heavy losses, demanded speedy operations. At that point it was either do something or nothing!

The new objective was to capture and hold the terrain around Hill 239 between the enemy-held villages of Dshurshenzy and Potschapinzy. The encircled forces were to break out on their own to the west past Kamarowka to the passage points on both sides of Hill 239. Those passage points were about eight kilometers from the southern edge of the pocket. That choice was a risk. It rested on the assumption that there was still adequate combat strength within the pocket to realize that plan. There was no alternative. The battalion had nine Tigers left.

15 February 1944: A great number of Russian tanks were said to be in a assembly areas in front of our positions, which were still on the road from Dshurshenzy. While it was still dark, we attacked to the northeast, where the enemy tanks were believed to be.

The visibility was very poor in places. We were just as surprised as the Russians when we encountered tanks and engaged them at close range. We were able to confirm that Dshurshenzy was packed with enemy tanks and infantry. We knocked out a total of fourteen Russian tanks in our attack. Unfortunately, one Tiger was a total loss and two men were killed. It is probable that the main objective of the attack was to convince the Russians that the main effort to open the pocket would take place here, between Chishinzy and Dshurshenzy. The Russian concentration of forces there could have been seen as proof that the deception was a success. We returned to our assembly positions before the fall of darkness and prepared that night for the new attack against the area around Hill 239 on 16 February. Seven Tigers were still combat ready.

16 February 1944: In the rear area of the III Panzer Corps—the slice of terrain was no wider than five kilometers—vehicles, even ambulances, could only move in convoys escorted by tanks. Our battalion surgeon, Dr. Schramm, had tanks placed under his control from the regiment that were no longer capable of fighting but were still mobile.

The fighting then entered the decisive phase in establishing the prerequisite conditions for the breakout. We were given the limited objective of attacking south of Dshurshenzy, advancing to a patch of woods. The terrain was incised by ravines and did not allow good observation. The Gebirgsjäger who were accompanying us had just combed through the patch of woods when several T-34s attacked. All of the T-34s were immediately knocked out. Additional Russian tanks continued to appear, in an apparently uncoordinated fashion. Presumably those were tanks that had been employed as infantry support. Almost all of them were knocked out. By evening there were probably about twenty of them. But we also had a loss. Oberfeldwebel Fendesack's Tiger was hit on the side of the hull by a round from a T-34, resulting in an engine fire. The crew was not injured.

That was one of the rare cases in which a T-34, presumably one with the 8.5cm main gun, knocked out a Tiger. At short range—less than 500 meters—the eight centimeter side and rear armor could be penetrated. Our attack was supported by dive-bombers attacking targets well behind the lines. We could only see columns of smoke from the fires. The regiment began its attack in the morning with eight Tigers, nine Panthers and twelve SPWs. That was the final offensive measure toward the pocket. The increasing opposition which the regiment had been able to penetrate heretofore in its role as spearhead then amounted to an insurmountable barrier. The other units of the III Panzer Corps had to exert maximum possible effort to maintain the flanks of the wedge and prevent a second pocket from being formed.

Elements of the 1st SS Panzer Division "Leibstandarte" were ordered to support the 1st Panzer Division on the right. Up to then, it had been employed on the left. Finally, on 16 February, it was possible to capture the villages of Lissjanka and Oktjabr, from which the entire operation had been threatened for days. The battalion was ordered to pull back to a line about two kilometers to the rear so as to establish contact on the left with units of the 16th Panzer Division and, on the right, with units of the 1st SS Panzer Division "Leibstandarte" and the 1st Panzer Division. The highly visible Hill 239 then became the fateful point that would be decisive in the salvation of the encircled elements—various formations, corps troops, and five divisions or, more accurately, what was left of them, about 40,000 soldiers. The gap between the two villages of Dshurshenzy and

Potschapinzy was the door which the regiment had to hold open.

On 16 February 1944 at 2300 hours the breakout to the west began!

17 February 1944: The army high command was still under the impression the breakout would be conducted and led as an disciplined military operation. For the worst-case scenario, particularly with respect to the enemy situation, about which only the sketchiest information was known, the command considered a hasty attack on Kamarowka. It would be conducted by all of the units that were on the northeast front of the relief wedge to link up with the units that were breaking out.

It had been coordinated that, starting at midnight, our foremost units would fire off white signal flares at short intervals so as to indicate our positions to those breaking out. The breakout units were to reply in similar fashion. The sounds of fighting could be heard throughout the entire night coming from the direction of the pocket with varying degrees of intensity. The Russians had occupied fronts facing in two directions: The ring encircling the pocket facing toward the east and the other, the defensive front, facing westward toward us, the attackers.

We could only hope that the forces breaking out would make their way out in a narrow sector through which the mass of the troops in the pocket could then follow. We also operated on the assumption that the Russians had concentrated their forces on the two fronts and that the space in between the fronts would be weakly held. We would be able to assist in the breakout through the second front facing our positions. Our expectation of how the situation would develop turned out to be illusory since, right at the start in the pocket, there was scarcely any operational freedom due to lost ground. After a more-or-less orderly start to the operation, the movement west degenerated into a disordered, leaderless and extremely costly mass flight.

With hardly a sound, at 0400 hours, footsteps approached the Tigers. Footsteps! Were they Russian of German soldiers? They were Germans! Mostly on foot, exhausted, mostly without weapons. The acting battalion commander had the ones who had trouble walking moved to the regimental command post in SPWs. By the time the day dawned, about 500 to 600 men had made the passage of lines near the Tigers and been forwarded to the regimental command post. On our right we could hear vehicle sounds. Were they Russian or German? They were German. The battalion surgeon, Dr. Schramm, had moved forward to the regimental command post with the medical section. He supervised the first aid and evacuation of the wounded who had come out of the pocket. Unfortunately, the limited capacity of the medical section meant it was only of limited assistance in dealing with the masses of soldiers. A reception camp was set up in the Buki area. At least the comrades from the pocket were safe behind our positions.

It was astonishing that the enemy was so quiet. It would have been a catastrophe if the Russians had followed closely, mixed in with the Germans fleeing from the pocket. By daylight, two large groups of about 500 to 600 soldiers each had passed the regiment's position, with its eight Tigers and six Panthers. With daylight, the Russians became active. Our positions were repeatedly shelled by artillery. Russian tanks appeared in small groups in front of our positions. The same took place west of Potschapinzy, where the regiment ordered an attack with limited objectives. We got to within about one kilometer of the village when five T-34s approached us. Three were knocked out. We returned to our jump-off positions near Hill 239 without any losses.

Although individual soldiers and small and large groups continued to come out of the pocket throughout the entire day, most of them to the south of us, the enemy did little to interfere. The breakout had confused him. He had enough units available to have dealt with the westward movement or to have hunted down the leaderless and defenseless troops. Our tankers were deeply moved by the appearance of those apathetic soldiers who had barely escaped death or capture.

18 February 1944: The stream of those who had been saved continued throughout the night. We remained in our positions at Hill 239 throughout the day without being disturbed. There again the weakness in Russian leadership was evident—to our good fortune! Individual initiative and mission-oriented operations were unwanted, indeed, forbidden. Their mission should have been: Eliminate the troops in the pocket! Such concepts were in direct contrast to German leadership training. It was thanks to that mentality that about 20,000 to 25,000 German soldiers made it to freedom. The Russian units in Dshurshenzy appeared to be the first to have overcome the shock of the breakout. There were several advances by tanks

which were repulsed. After it had been determined that everything which could still walk or move had reached the German lines, preparations were made for a fighting withdrawal, first to the Gniloi Tikitsch River, then to the jump-off positions south of Frankowka.

19 February 1944: With six Tigers and five Panthers—the remnants of the regiment—we withdrew southwest according to plan and under the leadership of Oberleutnant Scherf. The 1st SS Panzer Division "Leibstandarte," the 16th Panzer Division, and the 17th Panzer Division were also part of these withdrawal movements. They were able to repulse the pursuing enemy by means of a fighting withdrawal and local counterattacks. The remnants of the regiment were to be relieved the following night and, for the time being, were a ready reserve in the Bossowka area. Subsequently we were to be transferred to Uman.

20 February 1944: For Tiger Tank Battalion 503, which had only 10 percent of its tank strength left, that was the end of the Tscherkassy operation. Hauptmann Rolf Fromme, the new battalion commander, arrived on the battlefield, replacing the severely wounded Hauptmann Graf Kageneck. Oberleutnant Scherf received the Knight's Cross and was promoted to Hauptmann.

21 February 1944: The battalion moved to Uman with its tracked and wheeled elements.

Along with the report from the battalion level, the events of the Tscherkassy operation are presented here from the viewpoint of the tank crew. Hans-Joachim Thaysen, radio operator in the 1st Company writes of his experiences on behalf of all of the members of the combat elements, who probably experienced similar things.

24 January: The night was spent refueling and loading up ammunition. At 0600 hours the attack started toward the northeast. Just as the attack began, Tiger 100 was hit on the main gun. The shell ricocheted and penetrated the hull between the driver and radio operator without wounding anyone. Oberleutnant Adamek was shot in the head and killed while climbing into another tank. Leutnant von Koerber took over command. After crossing a minefield, the attack continued. The enemy resisted us with antitank guns and infantry

but was thrown back. We reached the village at noon. The attack came to a halt in front of a small river with marshy banks, the Gniloi Tikitsch.

Leutnant von Koerber's tank got stuck and was recovered under mortar fire by ours. As evening approached the attack continued along the river. An additional village was captured during the night in spite of very heavy fire from antitank guns. Leutnant von Koerber was shot in the head and severely wounded while making contact with the infantry. Oberleutnant Kubin was killed while rescuing the Leutnant. We withdrew from the village during the night to resupply with ammunition and fuel.

25 January: We crossed the Gniloi Tikitsch River at 0200 hours in the morning in the bridgehead the engineers and the 3rd Company had formed. We were immediately met by an intense barrage from a variety of weapons. It was a miracle that no one was hit. We moved out in the gray light of dawn. During the night the enemy had put together a defensive position studded with a tremendous number of antitank guns. It exacted a fairly high toll of blood and equipment, particularly among the Panthers, before they broke through to the north. Oberfeldwebel Fendesack boarded our tank as commander. The center of the defensive front was in a village with both flanks resting on wooded areas. A bypass was not possible. We moved out against the village once again at noon. Just as hopes grew that the enemy was finally on the run, we suddenly found ourselves in a minefield in which several tanks were immobilized.

By the time we had breached the obstacle, a heavy barrage from antitank guns and tanks set in, leaving several more tanks disabled along the way. Ours was the first vehicle to make it past the barrier, taking up the battle along with the other vehicles of the platoon. After we had knocked out no less than eight antitank guns and twenty enemy tanks and assault guns, the Russians withdrew. In the pursuit that followed, we captured a railroad station and the adjacent village. We had to capture another enemy line in the evening. We captured the village of Ssosoff with the last of our fuel and ammunition.

26 January: We remained in Ssosoff under heavy fire from enemy antitank guns, tanks and artillery until noon, unable to defend ourselves due to ammunition shortage. Finally, at about 1300 hours, the supplies made it through and we

moved out immediately. However, after darkness fell, the attack had to halt in the open area since our losses would have been too high in the heavy ground fog.

27 January: In the morning the attack continued until we were outside a village. Several tanks were knocked out along the way. Shortly before we got to the village, the enemy unexpectedly opened fire from well-constructed positions.

The attack halted and a duel began on both sides that continued for several hours with neither side gaining any significant results. As we moved out again, several hits knocked out our right track. We had to pull back and were towed from the battlefield by another tank. Several other tanks turned back with hits. The enemy attacked with tanks on the right flank and was thrown back after most of his tanks had been knocked out. We fixed our track and moved to the company maintenance section, since the right-hand drive sprocket was unserviceable. On the route back, several enemy tanks that had been knocked out were "investigated."

28 January: The day was fully occupied with changing the drive sprocket and repairing other damage. Our work was interrupted by several aerial attacks.

29 January: During the most recent fighting, Tigers 112 and 132 were left lying behind the Russian lines after the crews disabled them by making the main guns unserviceable. We tried to recover the vehicles during the evening of 29 January with our Tiger 100, a tank from the 3rd Company and several assault guns. The Russians had anticipated the attempt and covered both of the tanks with mines and barriers of antitank guns. It was impossible to get close to the vehicles. We received several antitank gun hits. This time Tiger 100 lost its left-hand drive sprocket and had a round penetrate. At that point the operation was called off, and we returned to the old position.

30 January: We attended to our running gear and began the march back to the battalion in the evening. The Volkswagen belonging to the company maintenance section happened to get under the track and hull of a Tiger and was squashed flat, killing Gefreiter Wollmann and Gefreiter Wilke. Gefreiter Donath was rescued from the wreckage of the Volkswagen, severely wounded.

31 January: The march continued to Gaisin. There, at long last, we got mail. Gefreiter Bürger was killed on that day when a shell penetrated

Tiger 111. On the previous day, the battalion commander, Hauptmann Graf von Kageneck, and Hauptfeldwebel Haase were severely wounded.

In January the following members of the 1st Company were killed:

1. Oberleutnant Adamek
2. Unteroffizier Oels
3. Gefreiter Mink
4. Gefreiter Schuber
5. Gefreiter Mynik
6. Gefreiter Wiesenfath
7. Gefreiter Wilke
8. Gefreiter Bürger
9. Panzerschütze Hayder
10. Panzerschütze Barton
11. Obergefreiter Kubin
12. Gefreiter Wollmann

1 February: Marched back to the battalion. Damage to the idler wheels while under way, which we were able to fix with a lot of work. We reached the battalion, which was ready for loading at a railroad station, by evening.

2 February: The tanks were loaded at about noon. During the loading, Unteroffizier Scharff received the Iron Cross, First Class, as did Hauptfeldwebel Haase, who lay wounded in the hospital. In the evening the train proceeded to Potasch, which was 30 kilometers northeast of Christinowka.

3 February: We arrived at Potasch at about 0400 hours. We looked for a billeting area. After that was found, we spent the day cleaning weapons and sleeping. At about 1700 hours the march resumed to Buki, where we refueled again. From there we moved to the assembly area, which was reached at 0400 hours the next day.

4 February: At 0600 hours the attack began to relieve the XXXXII Corps, which had been encircled at Tscherkassy. We moved as point vehicle and ran into heavy fire from antitank guns within the first few hundred meters. After knocking out various antitank guns and tanks, the attack ground to a halt in terrain that did not permit observation and in misty weather that made it barely possible to see the defensive lines. After a minefield had been cleared, the concentrated attack speedily rolled over the enemy lines. The final resistance was crushed after we overcame a railroad embankment that had been made into an antitank obstacle. We then advanced as far as a

major Russian transportation route and blocked it. Long columns of wheeled vehicles—trucks, guns, Panje carts, etc.—fell into our hands. An enemy tank attack was smashed after we knocked out a number of tanks. Later on, our tank and Tiger 114 took a village by surprise. (Tiger 114, commanded by Rubbel, was the only tank besides ours left from the company.) When we took the village, a few trucks were captured and a Sherman was knocked out.

The village was occupied until darkness. In the evening, we withdrew from the village and moved back to our jump-off positions.

Resupply was supposed to take place there. A few Russian trucks were "inspected."

5 February: Fendesack's platoon set out in the morning in a fresh attack with support from infantry and Sturmgeschètze to capture the village of Wotylewka. During the night the Russians had dug in. However, they were thrown out of the northeast part of the village in a rapid assault, losing several of their heavy tanks in the process. In the course of the day, several tank attacks were repulsed, during which a number of enemy tanks were knocked out.

6 February: Three of us provided cover in Wotylewka. Because the terrain did not allow good observation and there was thick fog both day and night, the watch required the highest level of alertness. For days, neither rations nor other supplies had made it to us, since the perpetual rain had turned every path into a sea of mud. Again and again, Russian tanks and infantry were shot to pieces in various attacks. Our basic load had been reduced to a few rounds. A fourth tank brought us fifteen rounds for the three Tigers. While one tank was called away to the 2nd Company and we were taking on the ammunition that had been brought up, Rubbel was attacked by several Russian tanks and had to break off the battle. He pulled back because he was out of ammunition. We saved the situation by knocking out three Russian tanks, including one T-34 that was polished off at a range of six meters.

The security mission continued for the entire day and also, again, through the night.

7 February: In the morning we finally set out to clean up the rest of the village of Wotylewka and the terrain around it. The attack proceeded in landscape criss-crossed by defiles. In the course of the attack a series of the super-heavy Russian assault guns (SU-152) were knocked out. For the

remainder of the day and the night that followed we again secured the village.

8 February: In the gray dawn of 8 February, the enemy attacked Wotylewka with strong forces and numerous tanks and assault guns. At 0700 hours we moved out to counterattack. The enemy withdrew. When the fog suddenly lifted, the enemy was identified and an intense firefight developed at a range of about 2,000 meters. Five enemy tanks were knocked out. Since the range at which the fighting took place constantly increased, the action was broken off and we attacked the village of Pawlowka to the southwest. However, we were halted by lack of fuel before we reached the village.

As evening approached, the enemy attacked once again from the southeast with strong armored forces. It cost him a large number of fighting vehicles. We knocked out seven tanks on our own during that engagement. Late in the evening, we received fuel and moved into the village of Pawlowka, which had already been captured by the Panthers. The tank was readied for further action and then, for the first time, we caught forty winks. The sentries at the security posts whiled away the time trying to irritate the nighttime nuisance bomber with machine-gun fire, with the result, however, that they got bombed for their troubles.

9 February: The day was occupied with slaughtering swine and roasting them; except for artillery and bombers, the day was quiet. As evening approached, we were suddenly told to get ready to move out. I had to report to the command post as a messenger. We lined up at 2200 hours. The departure was delayed until 0200 hours. To crown it all off, we had to tow a field kitchen.

10 February: With ceaseless refueling and resupply with ammunition—every few kilometers there was a heap of ammunition—the night passed. It was another whole day before we reached the new assembly area, about thirty kilometers away.

11 February: In the morning we got the first mail in weeks. At about 0800 hours a new attack began to relieve the XXXXII Corps. The first anti-tank gun positions were overrun. Several Stalin organs fell into our hands.

At noon we reached a village (Frankowka) that was set deep in a valley. At the same moment lots of enemy tanks appeared on the opposing high ground and a firefight opened at 1,800 to 2,000 meters range. About twenty Russian tanks were knocked out. Our tanks also took some hits. Rubbel's track was shot off. Several Panthers burned up. Feldwebel Erdman and our tank secured the village to the west well into the night. Then we had the pleasure of maintaining a beacon fire for the resupply aircraft. However, the "birds" failed to come.

12 February: Finally the Junkers brought us ammunition and fuel. The night passed without incident.

13 February: Early in the morning we moved into the bridgehead at the village of Frankowka. At 0800 hours the attack began anew in the direction of the encircled corps. A village—Bushanka (?)—was captured in hard fighting. The village was studded with antitank guns and tanks and taking the village exacted a heavy toll. The Russians had constructed a defensive front in a depression behind the village with about fifty dug-in tanks and innumerable antitank guns. Erdmann's tank and ours took over the point. When we came over the high ground, heavy defensive fire tore into us. We succeeded in knocking out two tanks. Then we ourselves took a hit on the commander's cupola. It knocked out all of the vision blocks and also knocked the gun out of adjustment. We moved back to the jump-off position, made emergency repairs and then moved forward to the battalion. Eighty tanks were knocked out that day by the battalion and the attached Panthers. We got to the company about midnight and then pulled security duty together with Tiger 132 (Erdman).

14 February: Early in the morning our two tanks, along with five Panthers, were ordered to clear a village—Dshurshenzy (?). Elements of the encircled corps were supposed to already be there. Instead of running into our own people, the enemy gave us a right proper greeting. Two Panthers were knocked out. The infantry suffered heavy losses since they bunched up behind our tanks like grapes. We were dealing with the "Stalingrad" division, a Russian elite troop. Since the enemy kept bringing up more heavy weapons and our losses were something fearful, the attack was called off and we held the line we had reached. Although another company came as reinforcements in the evening, the situation still remained critical, since the enemy blocked the route of the approach march with strong units.

15 February: According to conservative estimates, the enemy brought up forty tanks during the night. We were in the center of the village of Chishinzy (?), and the Russians held the other part. There was obviously no point in holding the village in that impossible situation, the more so since the enemy could get in our rear at any time with his tanks. So we moved out of the village in the direction of our own troops in the gray of morning. Erdmann's tank and ours covered the retreat, during which we had the bad luck of an overheated engine. We could only move at a walking pace. Thank God that the enemy did not catch on to the situation. We made it back to the battalion, with a two-hour delay and only pursued by infantry.

There it turned out that the tank was ready for the maintenance facility. The same went for Erdmann's tank, so we both moved back toward the maintenance facility. That evening we set up our billets. On the way we ran into five tanks that were being sent to the front, including Tigers 100, 123, and 121. The tanks got lost and moved into a village held by the Russians. They ran onto mines and had to be blown up since there was no possibility of recovering them. Only Tiger 121 was towed back for a bit. It was expected it would also have to be blown up. Leutnant Linden was in command of that bunch. He got sick the following day and vanished.

There ends the Thaysen notes on the Tscherkassy fighting. Alfred Rubbel continues in the following.

I took part in that fighting from 24 January to 14 February. I was still in Tiger 114. It was the third Tiger. We had lost two to enemy action since July 1943. Except for one new man, it had always kept the same crew. That much luck was unusual! Several experiences and impressions from that period will be reprinted here, since they were typical of the fighting...

The accusation has sometimes been made against the III Panzer Corps and, more frequently, against the 1st Panzer Regiment of the 1st Panzer Division, that it had not done its utmost to save the encircled troops. Specifically, the division had allowed itself to get bogged down too long at Lissjanka. That accusation is not tenable:

First of all, consider the force ratios! Five Soviet tank armies against two German panzer corps [the Russian tank Army is about the same size as a German panzer corps]. Then there was the weather which put the German attacker at an inconceivable disadvantage due to terrible ground conditions. The Germans had to struggle through the mud while the Russians could generally fight from positions.

Ammunition and fuel, for the most part, had to be flown in from the Uman airfield and air dropped.

Rations were almost non-existent. The maintenance services were unable to deal with the mounting vehicle repairs. Those equipment bottlenecks could not be offset by strength of will nor by bravery!

The relief units knew very well the significance of what was up and did not spare themselves. A supporting example comes from the experience of our own battalion. We began the advance north toward Medwin with thirty-four Tigers on 24 January. After reorganizing for the attack on Frankowka on 12 February, only nineteen Tigers were available. Fifteen had been knocked out. On 19 February we had only six left.

The personnel losses were similarly high. The battalion commander was severely wounded, the company commander of the 1st Company was killed and seven officers were wounded. For the start of the attack toward the pocket, the battalion had only two line officers, one with the combat elements and one in charge of logistics.

The following details remain in my memory of the fighting, which was marked by unusual circumstances:

- The corridor that we cleared was so narrow we could see the Russians on both sides with the naked eye.
- Rations were so scarce that I instructed my gunner, Walter Junge, to aim at the turrets of Russian tanks in hopes that the vehicles would not burn so we could capture their bread. Once we captured a great big can of US corned beef and, in one truck, we found a half-full 200-liter drum of vodka. Unfortunately it tasted of gasoline!
- For the first time, I experienced psychological warfare. On the ultra-short-wave radio frequencies for the tanks, and also with long-range loudspeakers, we were flooded with speeches from our "comrades" on the National Committee for a Free Germany. These were supported by air-dropped propaganda leaflets. Those efforts were poorly prepared and totally ineffective.
- The airmen who brought us supplies in the corridor earned our highest respect. Some of them flew in the good, old Ju 52. They corrected the general picture of fliers that was held by the typical lousy, filthy army soldier in Russia. Two crew members of a Ju 52, an Oberleutnant and a Feldwebel, made it safely to us from their aircraft. It had been shot down in no man-s land. They drank their first shot of liquor with pleasure with us—vodka from a gasoline drum. We presented it to them, even though they were accustomed to better.
- During the twenty-two days, from 24 January to 14 February 1944, my crew and I never saw the inside of a house, even for an hour. We slept on our crew stations in the Tiger. The driver and radio operator had comfortable seats that were almost up to the standard of today's reclining seats in cars. The loader had no comfort at all, but did have room—namely, the right side of the turret floor. It was hard, but he could stretch out. The gunner and commander had it rough on their narrow seats. If the situation permitted, I preferred the warm motor cover on the tank's rear deck. Despite all that, we were certainly much better off than the infantry during those days.
- On 15 February I took leave of my Tiger 114, where I had served as tank commander without a break for eleven months. I went to the 500th Panzer Replacement Battalion at Paderborn, where I attended the three-month-long officer candidate school. My recollections of the school, which represented a break with everything else, are no longer as clear to me as everything else. What could have been the cause of that?

The battle of Tscherkassy was reaching its high point. The 1st Company had five Tigers as total losses since the start of the year—many of the losses could have been avoided—and we had sixteen killed. We, the crew of Tiger 114, had made it through the last eleven months with singular good fortune. We had run up a score of fifty-seven enemy tanks knocked out. When we lost our own Tiger, it had been shot out from under us. We never had to abandon or blow up a single one. I thought at the time and I still think today, that we had an optimal relationship among all five crew members in "our war," the war in which we had taken part, performed our duty and assisted each other.

At that point, I departed. I left my crew to go back into the climax of the battle, and I went home to Germany, where mortal danger, unrest and disorder were not the focal points of ones existence. I must confess that I gladly traded my tank commander's seat for a seat in the classroom at the academy at the time. I didn't have too bad a conscience with regard to the comrades who had remained behind. According to my wishes, I was promised I could come back to the battalion. And that was, indeed, the way it turned out.

Corps Headquarters,   17 February 44
    III Panzer Corps
Ia (Operations)
to 1st Panzer Army High Command

Daily Report

1.) III Panzer Corps captured Hill 239.0 in an attack.

By 1300 hours about 6,000 soldiers from the encirclement had been passed through the lines by the leading elements of the attack. Approximate estimates lead to the expectation that about 10,000 to 12,000 men of the previously encircled forces will be passed through the lines by the III. Panzerkorps by this evening. The troops arrive without heavy weapons and without vehicles; unit integrity has been lost. Battle Group Bäke is currently attacking energetically from the vicinity of Point 239.0 toward Potschapinzy, to assist the breakout of additional encircled units.

The Luftwaffe has supplied our own attack units and the battle groups that have broken out under most severe weather conditions.

Command and control of the attack groups has been markedly complicated by the failure of most of the radio stations.

1st Panzer Division: Numerous assaults on Oktjabr and the area northeast of it and toward the east brought essential relief to the previously encircled battle groups that were arriving from that direction. Point 239.0 was reached by 1130 hours. After Oberstleutnant Frank was wounded, Oberstleutnant Bäke assumed command of the battle group in Oktjabr. Since 1545 hours Battle

Group Bäke has been attacking toward Potschapinzy against strong enemy resistance. At present, a counterattack is in progress against enemy that has advanced into the eastern portion of Oktjabr from the east at 1615 hours.

1st SS Panzer Division "Leibstandarte": In the Oktjabr area an advanced guard of the division has become involved in the fighting and supporting Battle Group Bäke in offensive and defensive operations. Additional battle groups are on the way to Lissjanka.

16th and 17th Panzer Divisions: No particular activity.

198th Infantry Division: Two enemy groups, each of about regimental strength, that had broken into the north and northwest sections of Winograd were thrown back with high losses for the enemy. The village was again brought firmly into our own hands.

6.) Will be reported later.

7.) Freeing additional units by offensive operations.

8.) 2 prisoners, 133 verified enemy dead, 28 tanks, 2 assault guns, 1 antitank gun, 14 machine guns, 10 antitank rifles, 59 machine pistols, 2 trucks.

9.) Snowstorm, roads and lanes rough, at times drifted with snow, still passable with difficulty for wheeled vehicles.

Ia (operations officer)
Reviewed for Correctness
[illegible signature]
Hauptmann

Corps Headquarters   18 February 1944
    III Panzer Corps
Ia (Operations)
to 1st Panzer Army High Command

Daily Report

1.) III Panzer Corps was able to pass additional strong, formerly encircled German forces through the lines in the Oktjabr area of operations while defending against strong enemy attacks under extremely difficult weather conditions and as the result of advances towards the south. The passage continues. The arriving battle groups were escorted to the rear, organized and, on being received at Buki, were led to the predetermined divisional assembly areas.

According to rough estimates, about 30,000 soldiers had arrived by this evening.

The corps does not have sufficient means to supply those elements and evacuate the wounded. Above all, cross-country vehicles are missing.

For statistics on the corps' operations 4-18 February, see the separate report.

The enemy stepped up his pressure on the northern front and carried out several attacks in up to regimental strength.

1st Panzer Division: Strong enemy armor attacks, especially from the north, were repulsed in heavy fighting in Oktjabr and at the northeast outskirts of Lissjanka; the former main line of resistance was reestablished.

1st SS Panzer Division "Leibstandarte": The forward-most battle groups supported the offensive and defensive operations of the elements of the 1st Panzer Division committed in the Oktjabr—Lissjanka area of operations.

16th Panzer Division: Local weak enemy advances were repulsed in the divisional sector and Daschukowa was taken over after the division was relieved.

17th Panzer Division: An enemy attack from the direction of the woods directly east of Bossowka in approximately regimental strength was intercepted near the collective farm south of Bossowka and eliminated in a counterattack with heavy losses for the enemy. So far, about 100 enemy dead have been verified and 60 prisoners taken. At this time, the depressions southeast of Bossowka are being cleared of the remaining scattered enemy groups.

At this time the enemy is still in the woods at Bossowka.

198th Infantry Division: Generally, the day was quiet. Two reconnaissance-in-force missions by weak enemy combat groups against Winograd were repulsed.

4th Mountain Division: The following units arrived by rail:

Main body 13th Mountain Regiment,
Elements of 94th Anti-Tank Battalion,
Elements of the 94th Nachrichten Battalion.

They are currently moving to their assembly areas. The liaison party has arrived at corps headquarters.

5.) 1st Panzer Division: Schubennyj Staw

6.) Will be reported later.

7.) Defense.

8.) 73 (2) prisoners, 100 verified enemy dead, 7 tanks destroyed, 10 machine guns, 4 antitank rifles, 15 machine pistols.

9.) Snowstorm, roads only useable for horse-drawn vehicles, numerous snowdrifts.

(2000 hours)

Ia
Reviewed for Correctness
[illegible signature]
Hauptmann

Annex to Daily Report
Results of the Operation

Opposing the corps at the start of the attack to relieve the encircled German units on 4 February were four Russian rifle divisions and one mechanized corps as well as elements of two tank corps still in their approach march.

Because of the onset of a thaw and mud-inducing conditions prior to 4 February—which turned the roads to bottomless mud for the course of the operation—the initial successes could not be exploited rapidly and enlarged. The enemy was therefore able to introduce new units right up to the time that the encircled divisions were rescued, to the extent that the III Panzer Corps had to break an opposition that totaled 10 rifle divisions or guards air-landed divisions, as well as 5 armored or mechanized corps.

The tally for the corps, in particular, the high number of destroyed or captured tanks, assault guns and guns testify to the heavy losses that the enemy suffered as a result of our attack.

From 4–18 February, the reports to date show 606 tanks and assault guns, 336 antitank guns, 71 guns, including 16 multiple-rocket launchers destroyed or captured, 1346 prisoners were captured and heavy, bloody losses inflicted on the enemy.

CHAPTER 26

Battle Group Mittermeier (Tiger Tank Battalion 503 "new")

Various Contributors

In the spring of 1944, the 1st Panzer Army, which included our battalion as part of the III Panzer Corps, had been able to break out of the "wandering Hube pocket" to the west in costly fighting. It had been bled white as far as equipment was concerned. According to the battalion status report as of 1 March 1944—at that time we belonged to the 4th Panzer Army—we had only twenty-four Tigers. Ten were being repaired. The fighting and the terrain had taken their toll on the other vehicles; 85 percent of them were no longer serviceable and the vehicle complement had shrunk to 64 percent of what the table of organization authorized. OKH ordered twelve new tanks issued to the battalion from the March production of Tigers.

The development of the situation in Army Group South—after Field Marshall von Manstein was relieved in March 1944 and replaced by Field Marshall Model, the army group was renamed to Heeresgruppe Nordukraine—as well as the danger of an invasion in the West, brought us new employment. Before that happened, we spent a few weeks at Ohrdruf in Germany refitting.

However, the special detail that had been sent to pick up the twelve new Tigers was still en route to the western Ukraine with them. It would no longer link up with the battalion, which was preparing to transfer back to Germany. Those Tigers and their crews were "confiscated" by the XXXXVIII Panzer Corps. Since we only had vague

information about what was happening to the detail, the rumors flourished. As a result, we wanted to try to shed some light on the subject. The evidence is sparse.

Günter Piepgras wrote the following concerning this episode:

On 15 February 1944, the battalion sent a detail to Königsborn at Magdeburg to fetch new Tigers. At that time the battalion was at Potasch (Ukraine). In addition to myself, the detail included tank commanders Tessmer and Schwarzmann (1st Company), Övermann (2nd Company), Kitzmann (?) and others from the battalion. The railroad journey through Breslau to the depot at Königsborn at Magdeburg took about eight days. After the Tigers were loaded, the train rolled to Lemberg.

The deep Russian breakthrough in the Army Group South area of operations to the Lemberg area prevented the Tiger transport from continuing to the battalion, which was employed in the Proskuroff area. Our Tigers were placed under the operational control of General Balck's XXXXVIII Panzer Corps. On 8 March 1944, we were set in march from Lemberg to the east for employment at Tarnopol.

Major Mittermeier, the commander of the battle group, joined us during the approach march. The approach to Tarnopol was only possible along an approximately 5-kilometer-long causeway which was under direct Russian artillery fire from both sides. Therefore the breakthrough did not succeed in reaching Tarnopol until it got dark. We reported to the local-area commander, General von Neindorf, at midnight. We suffered no losses in that operation.

On 9 March 1944 the battle group moved southeast to free German forces that had been encircled in the Smykowce area. During a Russian counterattack from the area east of Tarnopol, we knocked out several enemy tanks. We then broke through to Smykowce and brought the encircled forces back to Tarnopol. The area around Tarnopol had to be given up. In the aftermath, a fighting retreat developed to the west.

We were then placed under the operational control of Generalleutnant Arndt's 359th Infantry Division. The division command post was in Helenkow. During the defensive fighting on the Strypa in the Koslow-Horodyce-Plostysza area, we crossed the Strypa at Denisov in a night attack. After the first Tiger had crossed, the bridge collapsed, and we were all alone on the east side of the river. Major Mittermeier gave us the mission of continuing the attack. We slugged it out with the enemy until we had expended all of our ammunition. Thereupon we received orders to look for a crossing over the river and withdraw to the west. We succeeded in doing that, with the help of snow squalls. We reported back to the command post.

On March 26 we successfully attacked the enemy in positions at Teofipolka and to its east. Unteroffizier Rothermann was killed in the bitter fighting. The battle group command post was in Kozowa. We found ourselves continually in action. At the beginning of April we attacked Soboda-Zlota. After initial success, the attack continued against enemy positions in Kalne. After those had been destroyed, the attack continued against Uwsie, which was captured in conjunction with Pionier-Bataillon Haase. There we found cruelly mutilated corpses of German soldiers and the local inhabitants.

The defensive fighting in the Kozowa area lasted from the end of March to the beginning of April. Our Tigers were temporarily directed to support a Hungarian cavalry formation (division?). I was wounded in an attack on Malowody and brought to the dispensary at Brzenany and from there to the military hospital at Roszlocz.

On 30 May I was released from the hospital to the battalion, which had, in the meantime, arrived at Ohrdruf.

So much from Günter Piepgras (1st Company).

1ST TIGER DEMONSTRATION COMPANY OF THE 1ST PANZER DEMONSTRATION GROUP NORTH UKRAINE (1944)

Soldiers from the 503's 3rd Company trained Hungarian tankers on the Tiger at Nadworna, near Stanislau (south Poland) during the time period from 6-14 May 1944. Equipment shortages never did allow the issuance of Tigers to the Hungarians. They were later equipped with the Panzer IV with the long-barreled 75mm gun.

The award recommendations that follow were recently found in Hungarian archives. They were written for five soldiers of the 3rd Company. The political situation may well have prevented the decorations from being handed out. The original Hungarian text contains the justification for the award of a decoration to Feldwebel Großmann as well four other soldiers.

Großman, Fritz, Feldwebel: The Golden Cross of the Order of the Hungarian Holy Crown with War Decorations and Swords

On 8 May 1944 he was an instructor at the armor school at Nadworna. Within the framework of the instruction, he constantly discussed small-unit tactics. In simple terms, he explained solutions that would lead to the attainment of the desired objective and the mutual support of the tanks. He also drew attention to the density and the location of possible enemy antitank defenses so that means could be taken in advance to avoid superfluous losses. In passing on knowledge of the German equipment, he particularly stressed the advantage that came from quality, preparing the students to use it to their own later advantage and the advantage of the fatherland.

Schünrock, Herbert, Feldwebel: The Golden Cross of the Order of the Hungarian Holy Crown with War Decorations and Swords

On 8 May 1944 he was an instructor at the armor school at Nadworna. He functioned as a section leader at the demonstration exercises. He demonstrated great military expertise and knowledge in the demonstration of the equipment by the instructors. He had a large share in the fact that the course achieved its objective in a short time. By his personal commitment, he developed the basis for a great bond of comradeship and instructed the students in an extremely knowledgeable fashion.

Reinhardt, Ernst, Obergefreiter: The Silver Cross of the Order of the Hungarian Holy Crown with War Decorations and Swords

On 8 May 1944 he was an instructor at the armor school at Nadworna. He readily imparted his great technical knowledge to the students. He particularly excelled in explaining and teaching the mechanics of the radio equipment. He laid great emphasis on the practical benefits of learning communications. He was constantly sympathetic in his instructions to the Hungarian students, particularly when difficulties arose from linguistic misunderstandings.

Wunderlich, Gotthold, Obergefreiter: The Silver Cross of the Order of the Hungarian Holy Crown with War Decorations and Swords

On 8 May 1944 he served as a tank driver at the armor school at Nadworna. As a very experienced tank driver, he willingly shared his experience with the trainees. During the hands-on training, he continually executed his task with great zeal. He skillfully instructed the trainees on the teamwork needed between the tank driver and the remainder of the crew during operations. He also explained how tank-driver duties were most easily performed, using examples from real life at places where these duties required extra attention. As a result, he contributed significantly to the success of the course.

Bartels, Hans, Gefreiter: The Bronze Cross of the Order of the Hungarian Holy Crown with War Decorations and Swords

On 8 May 1944 he was an instructor at the armor school at Nadworna. Based on his technical knowledge, he gave practical instruction in the handling, maintenance and repair of weapons. He exhibited a superior level of commitment in teaching his Hungarian comrades about the weapons. Further, he stressed the importance of always having a tank's weaponry capable of functioning properly. He demonstrated the problems that arise in combat and how to deal with them, using examples from experience. He worked with all his zeal to train those who had been assigned to him so they could handle the weapon in a short time.

In the Tolokonoje Woods around 20 May 1943. This was the assembly area for the preparations for Operation Zitadelle. Left to right: Hauptfeldwebel Kiseberth, Oberleutnant Scherf, Leutnant von Rosen, and Hauptfeldwebel Haase. With the exception of Haase, who was from the 1st Company, the remaining soldiers were assigned to the 3rd Company. Note the custom-made camouflage tunics the officers are wearing. HAASE

Another view from the Tolokonoje Woods around 20 May 1943. Left to right: Unteroffizier Zeidler, Leutnant Scherf, unknown (probably Leutnant von Rosen, based on the camouflage material), and Hauptfeldwebel Rondorf. These soldiers were all assigned to the 3rd Company. HAASE

The company band of the 3rd Company, Tiger Tank Battalion 503, at Tolokonoje Woods. Left to right: Unteroffizier Fuhrmann, Hauptfeldwebel Haase, Hauptfeldwebel Kisseberth, and Hauptfeldwebel Rondorf. At the drum set is Unteroffizier Zeidler; on the accordions are Gefreiter Werkmeister and Gefreiter Rothschild. May 1943.

High-rise buildings on Red Square (renamed "Leibstandarte SS Adolf Hitler" Square after the successful counteroffensive to retake the city) in Kharkov.

Unteroffizier Seredsußt, Gefreiter Düring, Unteroffizier Diener, Gefreiter Dörschel, Gefreiter Döbert, Obergefreiter Brückmann, Unteroffizier Heier, Gefreiter Ohrdorft, Gefreiter Siebert, and Gefreiter Pieger.

The battalion ammunition section in Kharkov, May-June 1943. Among the soldiers are Obergefreiter Brückmann, Obergefreiter Farnleitner, Gefreiter Düring, Gefreiter Döbert, Unteroffizier Seredsußt, Gefreiter Hoffmann (H.), and Gefreiter Dörschel.

This photo shows a rare event: All fourteen Tigers of the 1st Company, Tiger Tank Battalion 503, closed up during a maintenance halt during the road march to Tschuguje for gunnery training. Left to right: unknown, Loh, Eschrig, Strohmer, Mewes, Tesmar, Hörnke, Rubbel, Peuker, and Junge.

The crew of Tiger 114. Left to right: driver Walter Eschrig, radio operator Alfred Peuker, tank commander Alfred Rubbel, gunner Walter Junge, and loader Johan Strohmer. The crew is taking a break guring the gunnery training at Tschugujew in June 1943. Note the unique camouflage tunic Rubbel is wearing.

Gefreiter Heinz Philipp in the billeting area at Kharkov.

Additional views of soldiers from the ammunition section enjoying a few moments of levity.

Tiger 213 of the 2nd Company undergoing backbreaking running-gear work. Standing behind the drive sprocket is Gefreiter Polzin. Kharkov, 1 June 1943.

Tiger 213 is road-worthy again. The tank commander was Unteroffizier Groß, and the loader was Gefreiter Polzin

Tiger 311. The tank commander, Leutnant Weinert, was also the platoon leader of the 1st Platoon. Also shown are Obergefreiter Schneider, Gefreiter Rotschild, and possibly Unteroffizier Petzka.

Motorcycle messenger of the 3rd Company, Tiger Tank Battalion 503, Gefreiter Reichmann, and Alex, one of the six Hiwis (Russian volunteers) who had signed on with the company at Prokowskoje. Kharkov, June 1943.

The crew of Tiger 321 at Tolkonoje Woods in June 1943. Left to right: Gefreiter Spiekermann, Gefreiter Werkmeister, Leutnant von Rosen, Unteroffizier Fuhrmann, and Unteroffizier Ziegler.

June 1943. The assembly area around Kharkov was used prior to Operation Zitadelle to familiarize the battalion even better with the Tiger. In this picture, the capability of the vehicle to negotiate marshy ground is tested. If the hull touched bottom, the tracks would turn, but the vehicle was stuck firmly to the ground. By placing a ditching beam in front of the tracks, the Tiger was able to free itself under its own power. This exercise was conducted with Tiger 114 of the 1st Company.

After tank exercises, the crew shares breakfast. Left to right: Johann Strohmer (loader), Walter Eschrig (driver), and Alfred Rubbel (tank commander).

Additional views of Tiger 114 undergoing troop-initiated testing.

Field Marshall von Manstein and his entourage with the Turkish delegation in June 1943 at a live-fire exercise with participation by armor, panzer grenadiers, panzer artillery, and dive bombers.

The commanding general of the III Panzer Corps, General Breith, at the "Dog and Pony Show."

Field Marshall von Manstein still had a peaceful countenance near the positions of the Tigers before the firing. According to those who were on the scene, however, his countenance—wrinkled nose, drawn down corners of the mouth—reflected the results as the firing progressed.

Tiger 300, the command tank of Oberleutnant Scherf, during the "Dog and Pony Show" in June 1943.

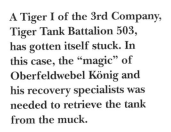

A Tiger I of the 3rd Company, Tiger Tank Battalion 503, has gotten itself stuck. In this case, the "magic" of Oberfeldwebel König and his recovery specialists was needed to retrieve the tank from the muck.

Turkish officers get briefed on the Tiger by Leutnant Jammerath of the 1st Company, Tiger Tank Battalion 503. At the far left is General of Panzer Troops Kempf. June 1943.

As a result of its lackluster firing, the battalion was ordered to carry out a wide-ranging training program which included weapon and equipment training, breaching obstacles and gunnery practise along the lines on the Donez River in the relatively quiet Tschugujew area.

The companies road marched from Kharkov, either closed up or by platoons. The battalion's appearance made it difficult for the Russians on the far bank, since it shot their bunkers to pieces. That put an end to the period of calm for both sides, since the Russians answered with their artillery. It is doubtful if the German infantry who were holding the positions were very enthusistic about the tanks' arrival on the scene.

Gunnery practice with the 2nd Company, Tiger Tank Battalion 503, during the "Dog and Pony Show."

View from the high west bank of the Donez. Across the river that formed the main line of resistance were the Russian positions that the 503 engaged.

Another view of Tiger 213. Here it occupies a firing position in order to engage Russian bunkers on the far side of the Donez on 19 June 1943.

Additional views taken of the gunnery training around Kharkov in June 1943.

The 3rd Company road-marching back to its billeting area after the "Dog and Pony Show."

The 3rd Company demonstrates how to negotiate an antitank ditch with a Tiger as part of the "Dog and Pony Show."

In the bivouac area at Tolokonoje, prior to Citadel, June 1943. Right to left: Leutnant Cüsow and Oberfeldwebel Röder.

A Tiger of the 1st Company, Tiger Tank Battalion 503, at Belgorod in July 1943.

Stabsfeldwebel Kisseberth, Stabsfeldwebel Krech, and Oberschirrmeister Hartmann in the Tolokonoje Woods just prior to the battalion moving out for Operation Citadel.

Stabsfeldwebel Kisseberth and Oberschirrmeister Hartmann.

Unteroffizier Hans von Hagemeister is transported to the hospital. Kharkov, July 1943.

An unknown crew in a brand-new Tiger. The lack of battle damage and the completeness of the basic-issue items outside the tank are the tell-tale indicators that this is a new tank. It would look much different in a few weeks.

The Tiger of Unteroffizier Vogel, who was known as "Pan" in the company.

The Tiger of Feldwebel Lehmann a few days before he was killed. Lehmann is standing behind the turret.

Tigers of the 1st Company, Tiger Tank Battalion 503, in the middle of a firing halt during Operation Citadel. Because of the intense heat, the turret hatches are open.

Operation Citadel, east of Belgorod, July 1943. Tankers of the 1st Company gather around Tiger 122.

A Tiger crew checks out a knocked-out T-34 during Operation Citadel.

Tank maintenance during a break in the fighting during Operation Citadel. In the foreground (from the left): Leutnant Linsser, Hauptfeldwebel Haase, Hauptmann Burmester, and Unteroffizier Lewandowski. On the tank (from the left): Hans Thome, Heinz Quast, and Rolf Sichel.

During the deep penetration that the 6th Panzer Division made with Tiger Tank Battalion 503, German forces were able to destroy a whole series of enemy tanks. Rshawez area, 10 July 1943.

Loading ammunition into Tiger 211. All of the crew was necessary . The number 1 man took the round from its shipping container and handed it to the number 2 man on the tank. He in turn passed it to the number 3 man on the turret. The number 4 man received the round in the turret through the commander's or loader's hatch and then passed it on to the number 5 man, who placed the round in its storage rack.

All's well that ends well. Turret hit on Tiger 101, commanded by Feldwebel Guse.

The crew of Tiger 114 (left to right): Alfred Peuker, Walter Junge, Alfred Rubbel, Walter Eschrig, and Johan Strohmer.

Spieß Haase and his driver, Hebenstreit, move through an assembly area that has been vacated by the combat elements. The first sergeant is bringing supplies up front to the troops in the Ukraine, July 1943.

Another view of Spieß Haase and soldiers of the headquarters section of the company.

Crew members and maintenance personnel address mine damage on Tiger 211. Left to right: Feldwebel Nestler, Unteroffizier Krefting, unknown, unknown, unknown, unknown, Gefreiter Völz, and Oberleutnant Hansen.

A Soviet SU-85 assault gun that was knocked out and set on fire. One hit can be seen on the casemate, upper left. Citadel, July 1943. [Editor's note: There are numerous references in German literature concerning the Battle of Kursk claiming the SU-85 was deployed there. In fact, the SU-85 did not enter service until 1944. Some SU-122s and SU-152s were employed operationally at Kursk.]

July 1943. Tiger 213 was commanded by Obergefreiter von Knobelsdorf. That was unusual inasmuch as Tigers were usually commanded by noncommissioned officers. Von Knobbelsdorf came from a famous military family that had provided generals and officers to the army of Frederick the Great. Von Knobbelsdorf is second from the left.

July 1943. Combined-arms operations. Here Tigers of Tiger Tank Battalion 503 advance with Panzer IVs (possibly of the 6th Panzer Division) and panzer grenadiers. The mechanized infantry moved in front of the tanks or behind them depending on the terrain and the enemy situation.

Vehicles of the scout and reconnaissance platoon of the battalion in the summer of 1943 at Belgorod. Fahnenjunker-Feldwebel Hans von Hagemeister is driving the Zündapp Ks 750. Behind the motorcycle is a Sd.Kfz. 250, which also belongs to the platoon.

Tigers of the 1st Company,
Tiger Tank Battalion 503,
at the time of Operation
Citadel in July 1943. Since the
terrain offered no cover or
concealment, a weak attempt
was made to conceal the
Tigers using stalks of wheat.
Gefreiter Welsch can be seen
in the middle of the card
players.

The photos here come from Gefreiter Schley, who was the radio operator on Tiger 213. Tiger 213 received several hits from 7.62 cm antitank guns during Operation Citadel, as can be seen clearly in two of the pictures. Although the maintenance team was called forward, it verified that Tiger 213 was still operational. From the expression on Gefreiter Schley's face, it appears that the enemy's activities have not phased him.

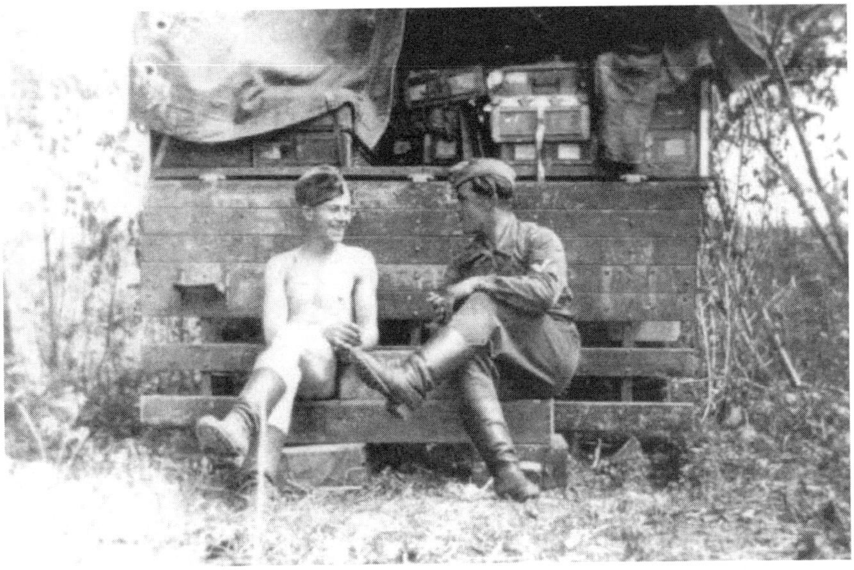

Ammunition truck with ammunition shipping containers on board. Obergefreiter Biermann and Obergefreiter Schmidt share a lighter moment.

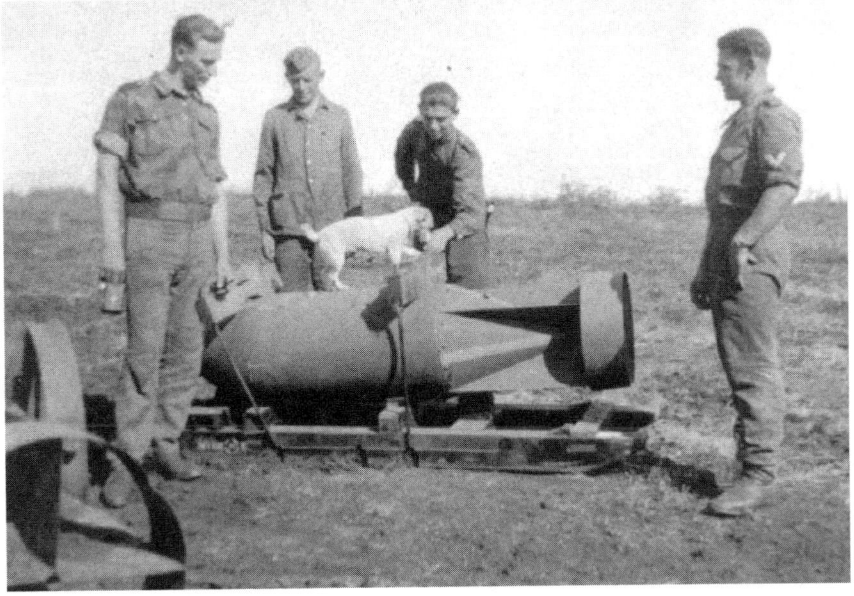

Gefreiter Hoffmann (H.), Soldat Kleine-Langhorst, Gefreiter Dörschel, and Obergefreiter Schmidt (A.) inspect a Russian bomb found on a captured Soviet airfield south of Belgorod in July 1943.

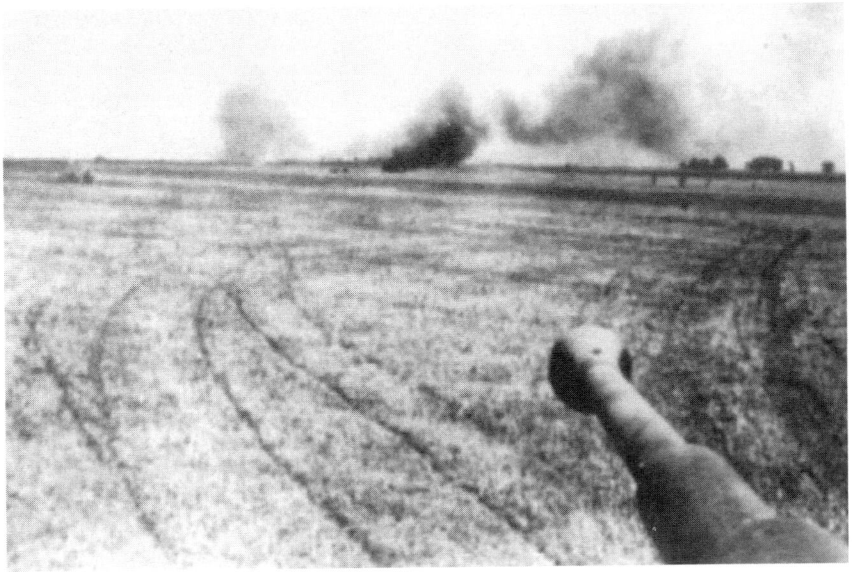

A T-34 knocked out by Martin Burmester's Tiger west of Kharkov in August 1943.

Work on the running gear of a Tiger was intense. These three photos were taken in August 1943 in the Ukraine.

Tigers from the 2nd Company, Tiger Tank Battalion 503, on a road march in the Ukraine in the summer of 1943.

Damage from mines was even harder to repair. On-board means could provide only conditional assistance; provisional measures were often required. (See the wood blocks under the hull of the Tiger next to the drive sprocket.)

The sixth member of a crew takes a snooze while his comrades work.

FAMO 18-ton prime movers
attempt the recovery of a
disabled Tiger.

Tiger 334 undergoes repair
work to its running gear. Note
the removed idler wheel next
to the vehicle.

The ammunition section at
Ssneschkoff Kut in August
1943. From the left: Gefreiter
Döring, Gefreiter Pieger,
Gefreiter Schewzyk,
Obergefreiter Farnleitner,
Unteroffizier Nobel, Gefreiter
Hoffmann (H.),
Oberfeldwebel Laden, and
Hiwi Pascha.

Soldiers of the fuel section of the battalion during a formation. These soldiers were kept very busy satisfying the "thirst" of a Tiger, which consumed 500 liters of fuel for 50 kilometers of cross-country movement.

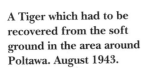

A Tiger which had to be recovered from the soft ground in the area around Poltawa. August 1943.

Another view of the recovery operation near Poltawa.

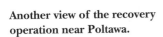

A Tiger turret is suspended from a portal crane in order to exchange or repair an important component. The operation has been skillfully camouflaged against observation from the air.

Withdrawal from Kharkov, August 1943. Feldwebel Krakow of the 2nd Company, Tiger Tank Battalion 503, sports the head bandage; to the right of the Waffen-SS officer is Leutnant Cüsow.

An image from the withdrawal between the Donez and the Dnjepr in September 1943.

Unteroffizier Siefert of the ammuntion section sits atop a disabled Tiger at Krasnograd in September 1943. The strain of the retreat seems to be etched upon his face.

Personal comfort items—usually alcohol and tobacco products—have arrived. Of the six soldiers pictured here, none survived to see the end of 1943. Right to left: Unteroffizier Thome, Feldwebel Binder, Gefreiter Woisin, Feldwebel Lehmann, Unteroffizier Scharf, and Unteroffizier Leitzke.

Another image from the withdrawal operations during September 1943. Identified soldiers: Unteroffizier Heier, Obergefreiter Farnleitner, Gefreiter Pieger, and Gefreiter Städing. Several infantryman have stopped to check out this Tiger from the 3rd Company, Tiger Tank Battalion 503.

Tiger 213 has suffered additional running-gear damage through enemy fire in the area around Krasnograd, 12 September 1943.

The battalion crossed the "Field Marshall von Rundstedt" Bridge over the Dnjepr at Krementschug on 24 September 1943.

Scenes from the withdrawal in September 1943. Columns en route to the Dnjepr pass through burning villages.

Battalion shooting competition. Left to right: Fahnenjunker-Feldwebel von Hagemeister, unknown, Oberleutnant Smend, Oberarzt Dr. Schramm, Hauptmann Graf Kageneck, Hauptmann (Ing.) Groß, Oberwerkmeister Neubert, unknown, and Oberleutnant Haß. Snamenka, September 1943.

Eight of the fourteen tank commanders of the 1st Company, Tiger Tank Battalion 503. Left to right: Hörnke, Rippl, Fendesack, Knispel, Kleiner, Tessmer, Rubbel, Junge, Erdmann, Guse (Buse?), Wolf (?), and Binder. Snamenka 1943.

Helmut Michaelis of 1st Company leads the "meat on the hoof" to pasture. Knowing him, he would have chosen Walter Flex or Goethe for his reading. Between the Donez and the Dnjepr, September 1943.

A welder attempts to repair the early-model commander's cupola that had been knocked off a Tiger. Based on input from the field, this type of cupola was later replaced with a lower-profile one. Tank commanders did not like it because it tended to get knocked off the tank by antitank rounds—frequently taking the commander's head with it.

The fuel section in Snamenka in September/October 1943. Standing, left to right: Gefreiter Döbert, Hiwi Wassili, Gefreiter Neubert, Gefreiter Ohrdorft, Hiwi Pascha, Gefreiter Schewzyk, Obergefreiter Wächter, Hiwi Mischa, and Obergefreiter Brückmann. Foreground, left to right: Obergefreiter Biermann, Unteroffizier Bandt, Gefreiter Schlonsock, and Gefreiter Hoffmann (H.).

Another view of soldiers from the fuel section. Left to right: Obergefreiter Biermann, Soldat Klingelhiller, Obergefreiter Schmidt (A.), Gefreiter Schlonsock, and Obergefreiter Brückmann.

A march unit composed of the 2nd Company, Tiger Tank Battalion 503, in the spring of 1943. The Tigers take a maintenance halt. Maintenance halts were proscribed for every two hours of march and lasted thirty minutes. The crew checked the running gear, and the vehicles were topped off. The Tigers at the beginning and end of the march unit provided security and air guards for the formation.

The German military cemetery at Snamenka, September 1943.

Obergefreiter Biermann and Hiwi Wassili.

October 1943. Oberfeldwebel Fendesack of the 1st Company, Tiger Tank Battalion 503, receives the German Cross in Gold from the acting battalion commander, Hauptmann Burmester. The battalion adjutant, Leutnant Schmend, is in the background.

October 1943. The withdrawal of the 8th Army from the Donez and the Dnjepr. Tiger 133 has changed externally from a fighting vehicle to a transportation asset. Besides the crew, we can see a rabbit hutch, a calf, several containers with sunflower oil, and a 200-liter barrel of fuel. The visible crew, left to right: "Piepel" Böhme, Hannes Rippl, "Bimbo" Binder, and Helmut Michaelis.

Sisters Hala and Musja from the theater troop try out a ride in the motorcycle-sidecar combination. Let us hope this "indiscretion" was not misinterpreted by the Russians after the retreat.

In October 1943, the battalion enjoyed a brief respite as the army reserve after the operationally difficult but successfully completed withdrawal to the Dnjepr. The Ukrainian populace was not unfriendly to German soldiers. There were theaters offering cultural events for both the locals and the soldiers. The non-fraternization order was not obeyed. Here are the female members of the theater troop.

Starting about October 1943, the battalion also started to receive massive aerial attacks, the likes of which it had never experienced before. Hans von Hagemeister measures the depth of the crater—approximately 7 meters. A 2,000-pound bomb created the crater but did not cause any damage.

Tiger formations had a great deal of technical requirements. As a result, the Tiger crews held the maintenance and other support personnel in high esteem since they allowed the combat elements to execute their missions. Here, two unidentified support personnel are seen during the relatively quiet time at Snamenka in late 1943.

Gefreiter Walter Junge, the proven, experienced gunner of Alfred Rubbel. Junge was awarded the Iron Cross, First Class, after his fifty-seventh kill.

One of those responsible for keeping the tanks and other vehicles operational was Oberschirrmeister Wagner of the 1st Company, Tiger Tank Battalion 503.

It was the maintenance personnel of the company and the battalion who were able to make the tanks operational over and over again, even though they frequently had only very modest means and manpower to do so. In this photo, they have to work outdoors in bitterly cold conditions.

Spieß Hänsel of the 2nd Company, Tiger Tank Battalion 503, next to an unidentified soldier and his means of transportation, the indestructible Volkswagen Kübelwagen.

Christmas 1943 at Zybulew for the battalion ammunition section. Left to right: Gefreiter Döbert, Gefreiter Schlonsock, Gefreiter Hoffmann (H.), Hiwi-Gefreiter Pascha, Gefreiter Tapetto, and Gefreiter Klingelhöller.

Panthers of Tiger Tank Regiment Bäke top off with fuel in January 1944 in the Oratoff area of operations.

Gefreiter Schlonsaok of the battalion ammunition section came from upper Silesia in present-day Poland.

Gefreiter Klingelhöller of the battalion ammunition section.

Several Panthers and other tanks line up to join the attack of Tiger Tank Battalion 503 at Oratoff in January 1944.

The battalion commander, Hauptmann Graf Kageneck, issuing orders for an operation with Tiger Tank Regiment Bäke in February 1944. Left to right: Leutnant Haß, unknown, and Hauptmann Graf Kageneck.

The battalion moves out to attack in the Tscherkassy area. The companies have deployed in a double column since that allowed maximum flexibility in the open terrain for developing the situation upon enemy contact.

A combined-arms operation with infantry.

A photograph for the armor recognition experts. Maintenance work being performed on what appears to be a Pz Kpfw 35(t) with the barrel of its 37 mm KwK 34(t) L/40 missing. This is possibly a Rumanian or Slovakian vehicle.

The crew of Tiger 100: Piepel Grasse, driver; F. W. Lochman, radio operator; Herbert Ritscher, loader; and Heinz Mundry, gunner.

A T-34 that bogged down and was abandoned by its crew. Feldwebel Erdmann admires the "booty."

Tiger 101 has recovered the T-34. Werkmeister Späth (fourth from left) was indispensible for such operations. Unteroffizier Ritscher, of the 1st Company, Tiger Tank Battalion 503, can be seen on the T-34's driver position. Oratoff area, February 1944.

The company commander's radio operator in Tiger 100: Franz-Wilhelm Lochmann at his station. Tarnopol area, March 1944.

Leutnant Linsser and Fritz Riemer of the 1st Company, Tiger Tank Battalion 503, are clueless about the fate that will soon befall them.

Leutnant Linsser gets clobbered by his men in a barrage of snow balls.

Leutnant Piepgras of the 1st Company signs passes for his soldiers. He was the leader of a detail sent to pick up tanks in Germany. March 1944.

Feldwebel "Fritze" Riemer, who was responsible for the material well-being of the company. He never let them down.

March 1944. A Maultier precedes a Tiger of the battalion. The Maultier proved itself reliable as a supply vehicle in both snow and mud.

March 1944 in the western Ukraine. Soldiers of the 1st Company, left to right: Schirrmeister Wagner, Feldwebel Riemer, Oberfeldwebel Fendesack (leader of the 3rd Platoon), Fahnenjunker-Feldwebel Rubbel (commander of Tiger 114), Leutnant Linsser (leader of the 2nd Platoon), and two unidentified soldiers. Oberfeldwebel Fendesack appears to have found some contraband.

A track gets mounted at the maintenance company. The tank crews were responsible for doing that. That helped to "moderate" the crews—when they had to fix what they broke, they tended to be more careful with their equipment.

The noncommissioned officer corps of the 1st Company, Tiger Tank Battalion 503. This photo was taken in April 1944 at Lemberg after the battalion had turned in all of its equipment and was headed to Ohrdruf for refitting and issuance of the first King Tigers. Left to right: unknown, Moscardini, Markus, Hänsel, Ehrentraut, unknown, unknown, Graumenz, Tessmer, unknown, Knispel, Höppner, Fendesack, unknown, Kück, Michaelis (?), Wagner, Riemer, unknown, and Vogel.

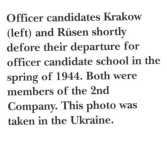

Officer candidates Krakow (left) and Rüsen shortly defore their departure for officer candidate school in the spring of 1944. Both were members of the 2nd Company. This photo was taken in the Ukraine.

The Spieß takes time to enjoy a cigar. Spieß Hänsel of the 2nd Company stands next to an unknown noncommissioned officer and Fahnenjunker-Feldwebel von Hagemeister from the headquarters company. The Ukraine, spring 1944.

While the remainder of the battalion entrained for Ohrdruf, elements of it were employed as Battle Group Mittemeier. Battle Group Mittemeier assembled at Teofipolka to assist in the relief effort directed at Tarnopol in March 1944 and the follow-on defensive efforts in April 1944.

Various elements of the relief force assemble at Teofipolka.

A happy Hannes Kück receives home leave.

The first Russian Joseph Stalin tanks were knocked out by the 1st Company, Tiger Tank Battalion 503, at Tarnopol in April 1944. This tank was a dangerous opponent when it could engage Tigers since it could penetrate the Tiger's armor anywhere on the tank. Its disadvantage was the slow rate of fire of its 12.2 cm main gun (separate shell and cartridge case) and its limited ammunition supply (only twenty-eight rounds).

Rail movement to Lemberg in 1944. Tigers of the battalion are rail-loaded with Panthers and other tracked vehicles from an unidentified unit.

At Brzezany, 11–15 April 1944. A late-production Tiger I with steel-rimmed road wheels.

Tigers and personnel of the 1st Company, Tiger Tank Battalion 503, during the fighting around Lemberg.

Stanislau, 17–20 April 1944, with its "very modern" maintenance facilities.

War and peace.

Vehicles and personnel of
Battle Group Mittermeier,
26–30 April 1944.

These tankers from the 3rd Company, Tiger Tank Battalion 503, enjoy a lighter moment.

From 6–14 May 1944, soldiers of the 3rd Company, Tiger Tank Battalion 503 (Battle Group Mittermeier), trained Hungarian soldiers on the Tiger at Nadworna, southeast of Stanislau in southern Poland. During that time, it temporarily bore the designation of 1st Tiger Training Company of 1st Panzer Training Group North Ukraine. The Tigers came from Battle Group Mittermeier. In this picture, we see Unteroffizier Gärtner providing instruction on the components of the turret. The turret has been removed from the tank and is suspended from a crane.

Feldwebel Weiland provides training on the radio sets of the Tiger.

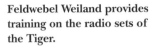

The Wehrmacht report of 25 April 1944 reported that Kurt Knispel knocked out 101 tanks between July 1943 and March 1944. Yet he only won the German Cross in Gold, a relatively modest award. The Tiger was considered to be such a superior weapon that tank engagements were not considered dangerous. Knispel was mortally wounded as a tank commander on 29 April 1945 at Stronsdorf. He died at the military medical facility at Urbau and was buried there in the community cemetery. Knispel was the most successful gunner of the Wehrmacht. In March 1945, the battalion reported his 162nd kill to Panzer Corps "Feldherrnhalle."

The Kolomea Front, training
Hungarian soldiers in
southern Poland in May 1944.

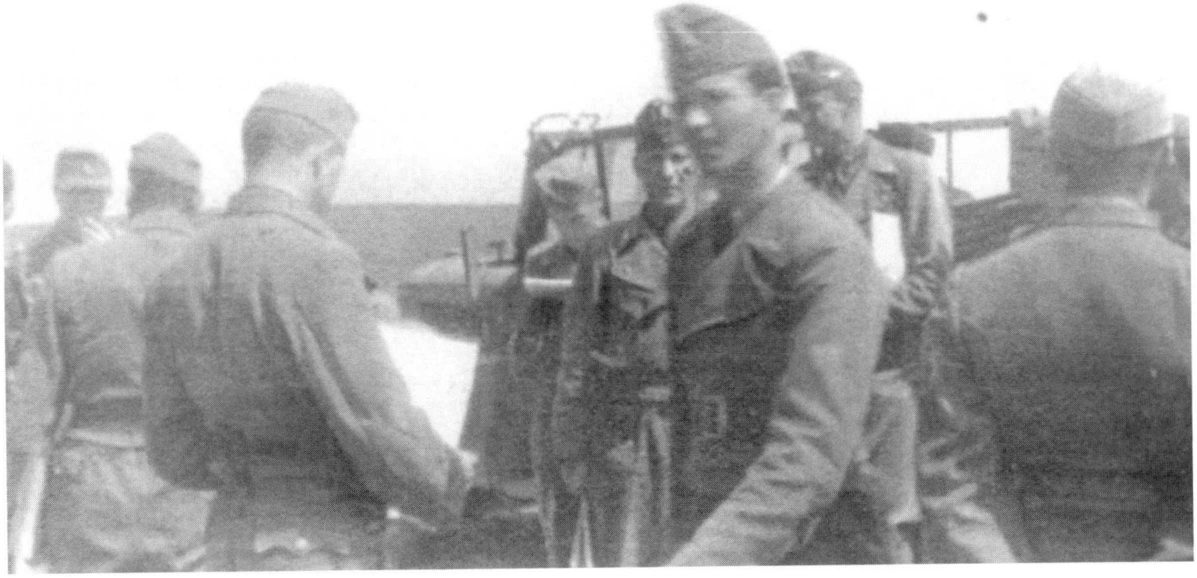

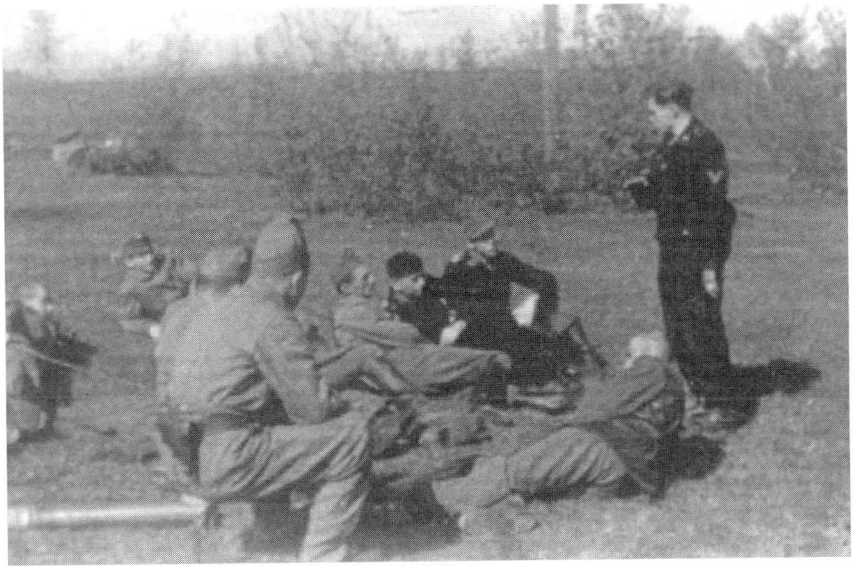

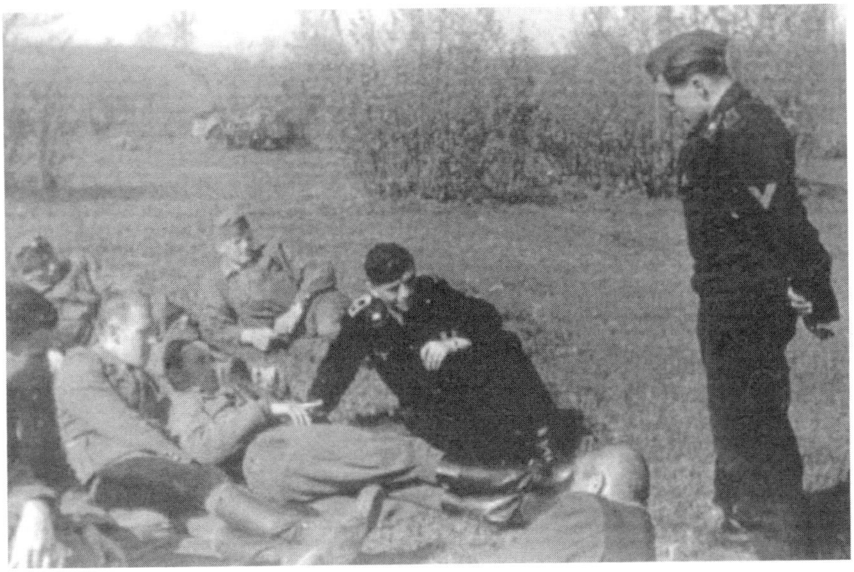

The final excercise with the Hungarians. Despite these efforts, the Hungarians never received any Tigers. On 23 May, the 503 also got to head back home.

PART FOUR

NORMANDY, 1944

CHAPTER 27

The Battalion Receives the King Tiger

Alfred Rubbel

After giving up all of our equipment, much of which was, in any case, no longer on hand, to Tiger Tank Battalion 509 in the Kamenez Podolsk area, the companies were transferred to the Ohrdruf training area in Thuringia as personnel units. An exception was the 3rd Company of Tiger Tank Battalion 503, which was training Hungarian tankers on the Tiger I near Stanislau in southern Poland. It arrived at Ohrdruf at the end of May. The goal of the complete refitting was to complete the replenishment of personnel and equipment as rapidly as possible. We were to be ready to rail load within two weeks of the arrival of the tanks, by 14 July 1944 at the earliest.

The command group of the battalion staff as well as the 1st Company of Tiger Tank Battalion 503 received the new Tiger II. For the time being, the 2nd and 3rd Companies of Tiger Tank Battalion 503 received the Tiger I. Their re-equipping with the Tiger II was planned for a later time, since the Tiger II had just gotten into full production. The first tanks had the "Porsche" turret. The battalion's organization as a so-called "open organization" [*"freie Gliederung"*] was based on the former one, with a headquarters, a headquarters company, three tank companies and a maintenance company. A supply company was not yet organized, since the tank companies had their own supply elements. The supply company would be added later.

It was planned that the battalion would be committed in western Europe, where the OKW expected the invasion. The battalion commander was Hauptmann Fromme. Hauptmann Wiegand commanded the headquarters company. Oberleutnant Oemler led the 1st Company of Tiger Tank Battalion 503, Hauptmann von Eichel-Streiber the 2nd Company, and Hauptmann Scherf the 3rd Company. Oberleutnant Groß was in charge of the maintenance company. We knew that the battalion, a proven and strong tank formation, would only be allowed a short time of rest. In 1944, the fifth year of the war, the duration of that rest depended on the development of the war in the west. Responsible leaders do everything in their power to grant their soldiers as much free time and relaxation as possible, commensurate with the upcoming mission. There again, the reciprocal trust between the leaders and the led that had developed in hard combat proved itself anew.

Early summer in Thuringia, the green heart of Germany! Ohrdruf was right next to the Thuringian Woods, a wooded range of low mountains with picturesque small cities and resorts: Eisenach, Erfurt and Weimar were nearby. The company commanders were able to guarantee a modest measure of home-leave to the Russian vets and yet receive and integrate the new personnel into the crews and, at least for the 1st Company, train with the new Tiger II.

The most pleasant task was "breaking in" the new vehicles we received. "Breaking in" was done, at that time, partly to accustom the driver to the new vehicle and also to verify the builder's specifications. Naturally, we did not drive around on the training area at Ohrdruf. Instead, we tested the vehicles on road marches to Oberhof or Erfurt or the like. At that time, I was in the hospital at Ohrdruf getting over a bout of malaria acquired in the Caucasus. One day my comrades appeared suddenly in front of the hospital and a sympathetic medical officer gave me permission for an excursion in the new Kettenkrad to Suhl to pick up rubber-stamps for the company. The Kettenkrad was new to us. We thought its cross-country capabilities were highly suited for Russian conditions. However, the total lack of spring suspension was a torture on paved streets. Nevertheless, it was a wondrous trip.

On 6 June the invasion began in the Seine bay between Cherbourg and Le Havre. The battalion's days at Ohrdruf were numbered. Company festivities, to which family members were also invited, are a lasting memory. At that time, the battalion was not ready for a rail load, let alone combat.

On 16 June the first King Tigers (*Königstiger*) were unloaded at the Ohrdruf railroad station. The station's facilities and access ramps were not suited for those 70-ton tracked vehicles. The movement to the North Camp, where the battalion was set up, led through the adjoining fields. That special event—the first issue of the Tiger II to a unit—was marked by having the Inspector General of the Armored Forces, Generaloberst Guderian, complete the issuance of the vehicles at a battalion formation in Ohrdruf.

After the officer candidate school for the armored forces had been moved by the OKH, from Wünsdorf to Ohrdruf, the inspector general took advantage of his presence at Ohrdruf to look into the state of the training of the Fahnenjunker (officer-candidates) of the panzer troops. What will now be sketched can only be compared with the probability of a major win in

the lottery, only in reverse. The school had three instruction groups (armor, mechanized infantry and armored reconnaissance/antitank), each with three groups of officer candidates. Each candidate group was further divided into three sections. The armor instruction group was practicing battle drills in tanks on the training ground. That aroused more attention than did the activities of the Panzergrenadier—or Panzeraufklärer/Panzerjäger—instruction groups. That the inspector general decided to visit the first group with Hauptmann Matthias and then go into Leutnant Barbist's section was a dark turn of fate. That training session was studying "the lead platoon of a tank company." Fahnenjunker Feldwebel Alfred Rubbel was sitting in a Panzer IV—a fairly unworthy piece of armored equipment—as tank commander. After three years at the Eastern Front, he was not a novice at the business of tanks. Fate took its course as the inspector general mounted that particular tank, had himself provided with a communications headset, and became tied in with the combat exercise on the radio net.

The inspector general could now listen in on the conduct of the fighting. As targets then appeared on the armor battle run and I, the commander, assigned targets and gave firing commands in a very uniquely personal, but proven-successful, fashion, the Generaloberst Guderian's patience came to an end. Bellowing loudly—and he could do that well—he ordered me to dismount and sent me packing to the barracks on foot—a terrible fate for a tanker. I thought that marked the end of my career as an officer. That was not the case. But it was an impressive enrichment to my repertoire of educational training measures. Much later, if tankers were guilty of flagrant violations against the hallowed standards, I ordered them home "on foot," well knowing that "a tanker lost his self-esteem in proportion to the amount of kilometers he had to walk."

On 26 June the battalion left Ohrdruf by rail to the invasion front in France. The detraining station lay west of Paris. The war there forced us into another dimension that we had not yet known and in which we were inferior. We were crushed in battle by an unimaginable material superiority against which courage and experience at the front were unable to prevail.

OKH ORDER FOR TIGER TANK BATTALION 503 TO PREPARE FOR EMPLOYMENT IN NORMANDY

The order alluded to in the section heading reached us in Ohrdruf. As of 18 June 1944 we were supposed to be ready for employment, which meant "ready for action." At that point, we had the first two Tigers. On 26 June the arrival of the bulk of the tanks was completed and rail transport started to France.

It can be seen in the copy of the order how Hitler, as "supreme commander of the armed forces," interfered in the affairs rightfully belonging to subordinates. Thus the order states: "1.) By order of the Führer, the Tiger Tank Battalion (Tiger) 503 is to be prepared for operational commitment by 18 June."

CHAPTER 28

Employment on the Invasion Front, July–August 1944

Richard Freiherr von Rosen

At the beginning of May 1944 the battalion—temporarily minus its 3rd Company—moved to the North Camp of the training area at Ohrdruf in Thuringia. Under the designation 1st Tiger Demonstration Company of the Panzer Demonstration Group North Ukraine, the 503's 3rd Company was training Hungarian soldiers on the Tigers received from Battle Group Mittermeier. That assignment was completed in the second half of May and the 3rd Company also arrived at Ohrdruf.

Roster of officers as of 1 June 1944 (incomplete):

Commander
    Hauptmann Fromme
Adjutant
    Oberleutnant Barkhausen
Ordonnanzoffizier
    Leutnant Heerlein
1st Company
    Oberleutnant Oemler
    Leutnant Piepgras
    Leutnant Schröder
2nd Company
    Hauptmann von Eichel-Streiber
    Leutnant Beyer
3rd Company
    Hauptmann Scherf
    Leutnant von Rosen

    Leutnant Koppe
    Leutnant Rambow
Headquarters Company
    Hauptmann Wiegand
    Leutnant Schulz
    Stabsarzt Dr. Schramm
Flak platoon
    Leutnant Fürlinger
Reconnaissance Platoon
    Leutnant Brodhagen

Hauptfeldwebel Neubert, the leader of the second maintenance platoon, received the Knight's Cross of the War Service Cross with Swords at Ohrdruf on 19 May. At the beginning of June, Unteroffizier Gärtner, tank commander in the 3rd Company, received the German Cross in Gold.

On 6 June 1944: the Allied invasion began on the coast of Normandy. The men were ordered back from leave, as were the special details to the Henschel works at Kassel. In mid-June the battalion received its new tanks. The 2nd and 3rd Companies received the Tiger I; the 1st Company was the first company of the army to be equipped with the new Tiger II (*Königstiger*, or King Tiger).

On 15–16 June: Generaloberst Guderian, Inspector General of the Armored Forces, visited the battalion. At the officer's night at the mess, he discussed with us how serious our impending mission in the expected operational area at the invasion front would be. "If we are not successful in eliminating the enemy beachhead in the next fourteen days, then we will no longer be able to win the war."

On 26 and 27 June: The battalion was loaded on eight trains headed for the invasion front. As a result of the systematic Allied air attacks on the railroad network, especially in France, the trains frequently had to be rerouted and only reached the planned destinations at the railroad stations at Houdan and Dreux, about 70 kilometers west of Paris, on 2 and 3 July. The companies moved in several nighttime road marches through Verneuil-L'Aigle-Argentan-Falaise to the future area of operations east of Caen. The enemy fighter-bomber activity made it impossible to march by day. Therefore, every night we marched from 2300 hours to 0300 hours, then took cover in woods. We then moved another increment the following night. During the final march segment on 6 July, the 3rd Company lost its first tank. While crossing a bridge over a rail line in an embankment near the village of Canon at Mezidon, the bridge collapsed under the weight of the tank. Tiger 323 (commanded by Feldwebel Seidel) fell through to the railroad tracks below, suffering so much damage that, even though it was recovered, it was beyond repair. In so doing, the company suffered its first tank total loss and casualties at the Normandy front.

On 7 July, Tiger Tank Battalion 503 was placed under the operational control of the LXXXVI Army Corps and, for the time being, directed to support the 16th Luftwaffe Field Division. The Luftwaffe division had taken over the sector of the 21st Panzer Division on the previous day. After the heavy losses the 16th Luftwaffe Field Division suffered on the following day in the fighting at Caen, the entire sector was again taken over on 8 July by the 21st Panzer Division; the remnants of the 16th Luftwaffe Field Division were placed under the operational control of that division.

Tiger Tank Battalion 503 was then attached to the tank regiment of that division, the 22nd Panzer Regiment. The 22nd Panzer Regiment consisted only of a Panzer IV battalion at the time. The commander of the regiment was Oberst von Oppeln-Bronikowski. Hauptmann von Gottberg commanded the 22nd Panzer Regiment's 1st Battalion. Together with Tiger Tank Battalion 503, that formed the armored operational reserve of the 21st Panzer Division. Our battalion was assigned an area east of Troarn for its assembly area. Our battalion commander was ordered to report each evening to the regimental commander in Troarn for a situation briefing.

The situation at the invasion front had developed as follows up until the arrival of the battalion: With mounting losses, twenty-one divisions of the Wehrmacht defended a front stretching 140 kilometers between the mouth of the Orne and the west coast of the Cotentin peninsula. East of the Orne, the British had held a bridgehead of about 25 square kilometers since the invasion began. A fixed front line and well-built positions were not available. Because of an abundance of isolated attacks, defensive successes, and pinning operations by both sides, the front line was in a constant state of flux. The Allied forces had not, however, achieved a decisive breakthrough. It was clear to everyone that they would make that attempt.

On 8 July the battle of Caen began. The German forces evacuated the city, as ordered, during the night of 10 July. The front was pulled back to the east bank of the Orne. The southeast suburbs remained in German hands and blocked further Allied advance on the plain of Falaise.

The enemy artillery activity, which increased during the days that followed—and to which the battalion was also subjected—and the attempt to broaden the Orne bridgehead indicated an imminent British attack. Where would it occur? An enemy attack from Caen itself was considered improbable since it would require a contested crossing of the Orne. The most likely direction appeared to be an attack to the south or southeast from the Orne bridgehead.

On 9 July, by order of Panzer Group West, the 1st Battalion of the 22nd Panzer Regiment and Tiger Tank Battalion 503 were brought forward into the main lines. This was contrary to the recommendations of the battalion commanders, the 21st Panzer Division and the LXXXVI Army Corps. From that point on, the battalion was located only a few kilometers behind the main line of resistance in the eastern Orne bridgehead. The battalion staff moved to Emieville. The 503's 1st Company and the 1st Battalion of the 22nd Panzer Regiment were southeast of that village. The 503's 2nd Company was northeast of Emieville and its 3rd Company was in a patch of woods on the land of the Maneville stud farm, 2.5 kilometers from the battalion command post.

In the second week of July, the battalion commander, Hauptmann Fromme, had to go to a hospital in Paris because of an inflammation of his eye, which had been injured in the war. Hauptmann Scherf assumed temporary command of the battalion in his absence and Leutnant von Rosen led the combat elements of the 3rd Company. The companies reconnoitered the future area of operations with all of the tank commanders so that they would be prepared for any eventuality. One company at a time was detailed for twenty-four hours as the "ready" company. During that time it had to remain immediately operationally deployable. However, for the time being, the front remained calm.

On 11 July at 0530 hours, the 3rd Company was alerted. After short, heavy artillery fire, the enemy forces—British tanks and Canadian infantry—had penetrated our main line of resistance between Cuverville and Colombelles and taken possession of the high ground north of the factory complex at Colombelles. The 32nd Luftwaffe Rifle Regiment, which had been in position there, pulled back to Cuverville. The way was then open for the enemy to Giberville and into the area east of Caen. An immediate counterattack of the 503's 3rd Company from Giberville to the north was able to reestablish the former main line of resistance without German losses. Eleven Sherman tanks and four antitank guns were destroyed. Two undamaged Sherman tanks were captured and moved to the rear. After the 32nd Luftwaffe Rifle Regiment had reoccupied its position in the late afternoon, the 3rd Company was withdrawn and returned to its assembly area at Maneville.

LEUTNANT VON ROSEN'S REPORT ON THE OPERATIONS OF THE 3RD COMPANY ON 11 JULY 1944

On 11 July 1944 a battalion messenger woke me up at 0500 hours: Prepare for immediate employment! I was ordered to the battalion command post. I rapidly issued my orders, briefed Leutnant Koppe and had the motorcycle take me to the command post. There Hauptmann Scherf gave me a quick briefing on the situation: Enemy tanks and infantry had succeeded in overrunning the lines at Collombelles that had been held by a battalion of the 16. Luftwaffenfelddivision. The most recent report from the front stated that the

enemy was already three kilometers northwest of Giberville. A strong massing of armor had been observed. The greatest possible speed was needed. I received the following mission: "The 3rd Company is to eliminate by counterattack the enemy forces that have broken through, reestablish the former main line of resistance and hold that position until further orders are received."

In the meantime at the company, engines had been warmed up and the tank commanders were waiting for my return at the command tank. Briefing the tank commanders went quickly and, within thirty minutes of the initial alert, the company rolled at top speed toward Giberville. I led the company to the front, established contact at the outskirts of the village with the unit that was there and had good observation of the attack terrain from a roof gable. It was easy to make out several of the enemy tanks that were at a farmyard about two kilometers away.

I returned to the company, brought it up to date on the new situation and then ordered: "Panzer marsch! Move out!" The first tank (Leutnant Koppe) had barely reached the northern outskirts of the village when it received heavy fire from enemy tanks. That resulted in a brief halt, but then the company deployed. The first platoon, under Feldwebel Sachs, sheared off to the left, the second platoon (Leutnant Koppe) to the right. I stayed even with both platoons. The third platoon (Leutnant Rambow) remained behind me. During that maneuver the tanks took a significant number of hits. However, at that range, they could not do us much harm.

I then gave the order over the radio to advance by alternating bounds. That meant one platoon would provide cover and fire while the other platoon advanced. However, there was no reaction to my order. I repeated it over the radio, but nobody stirred. Instead, my tanks were engaging the enemy. At that great range, there was little that could happen to our tanks. It was easy to observe the effect of our fire on the enemy, however, thanks to the resulting clouds of dark smoke. After nothing had stirred on our side, I threatened over the radio to traverse my turret to six o'clock and open fire to the rear if people didn't move out immediately.

At the same time, enemy tank rounds continually struck my tank. At that point I saw through the vision slit of my command cupola that the

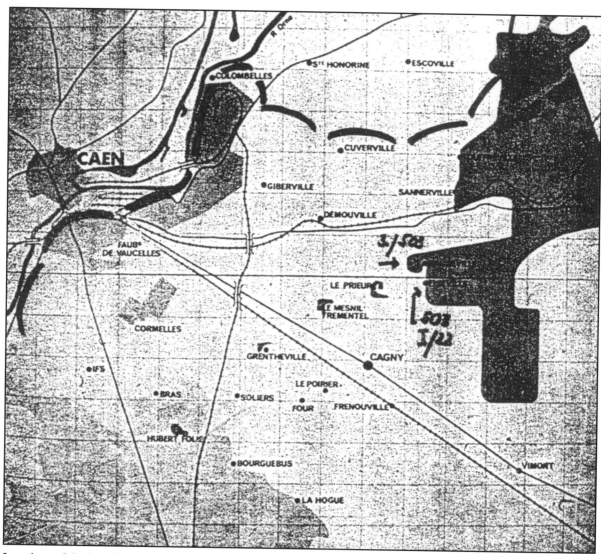

Locations of the battalion headquarters of Tiger Tank Battalion 503 and its 3rd Company in the Caen area of operations (9–10 July 1944). The battle for Caen began on 8 July 1944. On the night of 9–10 July, German forces evacuated the city to establish new lines east of the Orne River. As a result, the southeastern suburbs of the city remained in German hands, thus blocking the Allied advance on Falaise. The increasing artillery activity as well as the attempts to expand the bridgehead on the Orne in the days leading up to 11 July had indicated a British attack was imminent. Where would it take place? It was unlikely the enemy would attack from Caen itself, since the Orne would then be a contested crossing in a built-up area. It appeared more likely that an attack would be launched from the south or the southeast out of the Orne bridgehead.

antenna had been shot off my tank, resulting in the loss of radio contact. At that point it became clear why my orders had not been carried out. I had my tank move forward 300 meters in a single bound and, as I looked around me, I saw, to my relief, that the first platoon followed me while the second and third platoons kept firing. We then conducted the entire attack with no radio communication. All the maneuvers were automatic. One platoon secured and provided covering fire, the other moved forward in a single bound. Little

more was to be seen of the enemy tanks, since the farm where they had taken position was then only a dark cloud of smoke.

The enemy infantry then withdrew with the aid of a smokescreen. As the smoke cleared somewhat, I spotted several enemy tanks. At that extremely short range, every round from our gun sent another Sherman up in flames. The crews bailed out of their yet undamaged tanks in terrified panic. We received no more fire and covered the final 200 meters in a single bound. We were in

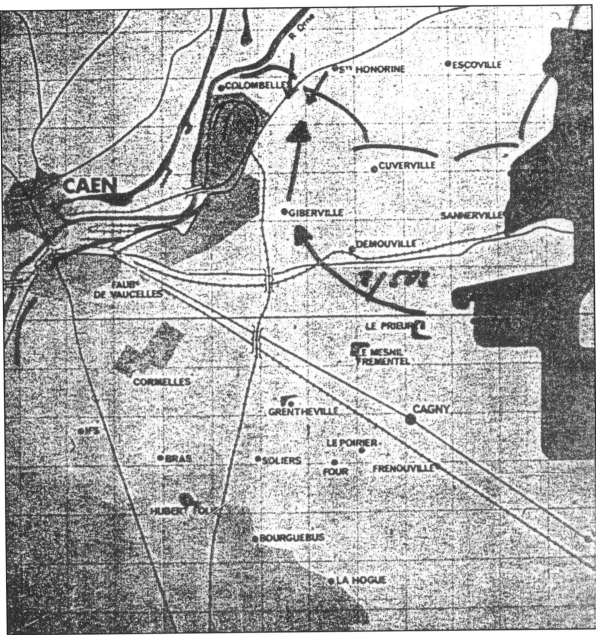

Mission: "The 3rd Company, Tiger Tank Battalion 503, destroys enemy forces which have broken through in an immediate counterattack. It restores the front lines and holds it positions until receipt of further orders."

the farmstead and had regained the former main line of resistance. All of that had taken about thirty minutes.

I then regrouped the company for security in that open terrain. Scarcely had we more-or-less completed that movement when an artillery observation plane appeared overhead and we were pounded with a sudden barrage of artillery that overwhelmed the senses. That lasted for about two to three minutes. Then calm returned. We changed positions from time to time, some-

times 500 meters forward, sometimes 500 meters to the rear so as to avoid the artillery fire, which opened up with the next salvo about twenty minutes later. That's what we did, positioned like targets on a range, for eight hours until the infantry came forward and again occupied its former positions. My tank had taken a direct hit from the artillery. Thank God the English were using superquick fuses and, thank God, shortly before we left Germany the turret armor had been reinforced with a second armor plate. Inside the tank we received quite a blow. The lights went out and we were dazed for several moments. Several welded seams were broken in the armor, so that I had to switch to another tank.

During a long pause in the shelling, I took a somewhat closer look at the enemy tanks. Twelve Sherman tanks sat there, burned out. Most of them had 75mm guns, but several had the more modern 17-pounder (Sherman II Firefly). Four 57mm (6-pounder) antitank guns were knocked out. Then I spotted two undamaged Shermans among the houses of the farmstead. They had run into each other in the attempt to turn and had been abandoned by their crews. One of those tanks was a command tank. Inside it I found a whole handful of annotated maps, radio documents, orders etc. I moved back by the fastest route to the battalion command post, which had been temporarily located at the railroad line at Demouville. During the course of the morning, Hauptmann Fromme had arrived there, returned from the hospital in Paris. When I reported there, he gave me the mission, if possible, of bringing back both Shermans. I moved back to the front and got there just as the infantry arrived and relieved us. Leutnant Koppe led the company back to the old assembly area at Maneville, where everyone disappeared into the same position they had occupied previously. I stayed at the front with my tank and two drivers from the company maintenance section. After a bit of experimentation, we got both Shermans running and disentangled.

In plain view of the English, who could watch all that from a modest distance, we moved back with the two Shermans, escorted by a Tiger. We felt that was a triumph. But the triumph did not last long. On the following day, which, aside from German artillery barrages, was quiet, there were increasing signs of an impending major British attack. After the success on 11 July, we really believed we could deal with it. However, we had no idea of what was actually about to happen.

END OF REPORT: OPERATION "GOODWOOD," 18 JULY 1944: THE DARKEST DAY FOR TIGER TANK BATTALION 503

The overall situation on the invasion front was relatively positive in the middle of July. The Allies had made three unsuccessful attacks. Their attempt to attack across the Odon had been repulsed by panzer divisions. On 8 July the British

and Canadian units were unable to reach the southeastern portions of the city in their attack on the city of Caen from the north. Finally, the U.S. attempt to break out at St. Lô had failed. All of those were positive indicators.

The British wanted to force a change at any price, to break out of the bogged-down front and gain ground in depth. They had to get their armored formations out of the hedgerow country that was so favorable for defense and unfavorable for armor and get into the plains around Falaise that was so congenial for armor. The fulcrum and hinge for that large-scale plan was possession of the Bourgebus ridge. That key position for the operation was eight kilometers east of the British Orne bridgehead. That was where the British intended to engage, pin and destroy the German tank formations and their reserves in battle. That would open the route to Paris. The result of those British considerations was the operation that was given the codename "Goodwood," named for the famous British race track.

On 18 July 1944 the British VIII Corps attacked out of the bridgehead east of the Orne with the 11th and 7th Armored Divisions as well as the Guards Armored Division—a total of 877 tanks.

The left flank of the attacking divisions was covered by the British I Corps, the right flank by the Canadian II Corps. The offensive was prepared by 2,077 bombers, which dropped 7,800 tons of bombs, and 720 medium and heavy field pieces, which had 250,000 shells at their disposal.

From 0545 to 0630 hours, 1,056 heavy bombers of RAF Bomber Command attacked (targets A, H, M). From 0700 to 0730, hours 529 bombers of the US Army Air Corps attacked (targets C, D, E, F, G). From 0800 to 0830 hours, 482 Bombers of the US Army Air Corps attacked (target P).

That fire preparation hit the villages of Emieville and Cagny, as well as Maneville, the assembly area of the 3rd Company, particularly hard. Maneville lay in the target zones of both the British and American heavy bombers and was the target of murderous attacks, with only short breaks, from 0545 to 0745 hours. That was a black day for Tiger Tank Battalion 503. Never before had such an armada of bombers been employed. In comparison, in the attack on Dresden in February 1945, "only" 1,084 aircraft of the RAF and U.S. Army Air Corps were employed, dropping 3,425 tons of ordnance.

At 0800 hours the British 11th Armored Division crossed the line of departure with its 29th Armored Brigade and 159th Infantry Brigade. They ran into almost no opposition, since the battalions of the 16th Luftwaffe Field Division that had been committed forward had been totally wiped out by the carpet bombing. At 0830 hours the British spearhead had already crossed the Caen-Troarn railroad line. Thus, there were no longer any German units in front of the assembly areas of Tiger Tank Battalion 503. And what a sight at the location of Tiger Tank Battalion 503!

The battalion staff survived the carpet bombing in the tower of the old villa where the command post was located. The staff had no losses but, on that morning of 18 July, there was no communication with the staffs of the 22nd Panzer Regiment or with the 21st Panzer Division. The 1st Company of Tiger Tank Battalion 503 in Emieville had lost tanks but no personnel were killed. Just as was the case with the neighboring 1st Battalion of the 22nd Panzer Regiment, it was in the midst of a sea of craters. The tanks had to be dug out through intensive manual labor.

There was no report from the 2nd Company. It appeared that it had been hit least by the carpet bombing. The 3rd Company seemed to be in the worst shape. Unteroffizier Westerhausen's tank had taken a direct hit and was thoroughly shredded. Oberfeldwebel Sachs' tank lay upside down, on its turret. The air pressure had blown over the 58-ton colossus. The three members of the crew that were inside the tank survived. There was a giant crater in front of my Tiger 311 and the tank's engine cover was pushed in.

There was also a direct hit on the contact team from the company maintenance section. In their case, there were also only craters and no traces of the vehicles. A number of tanks had such severe damage, especially to the running gear, that they were immobilized. Several had been pushed as much as a meter sideways by the air pressure. All of the tanks were buried in dirt and had to be dug out. They stood in the midst of a field of craters. It seemed nearly impossible to get them out of that and onto solid ground. Hauptmann Fromme had personal contact with Leutnant von Rosen, who went by foot to the battalion command post at about 0900 hours and reported on the situation at the company. Leutnant von Rosen was given the mission of immediately going into position with all available tanks directly south of Maneville, securing toward Le Prieure and preventing an enemy breakthrough between Maneville and Vagny. At that point the battalion commander had no communication with the 1st and 2nd Companies.

The 3rd Company was able to get to the designated position with six tanks by 1000 hours. All those tanks were actually ready for the maintenance facilities, but whatever could still creep along in some fashion and could make its way out of the sea of craters at Maneville was brought into position. Two tanks had engine fires during the march and could only follow slowly. A little later, the headquarters tank of the battalion headquarters showed up with the battalion commander. Hauptmann Scherf and his Tiger 300 also appeared. He had remained with the battalion staff after Hauptmann Fromme had returned from the hospital.

A reconnaissance in force by a company of the 5th Guards Armored Brigade was repulsed there at about 1100 hours. It was only then that it became clearly evident what hitherto unseen damage the tanks had received during the carpet bombing. The worst result was that all of the tanks' guns were completely out of alignment with the sights. We needed three rounds now where only one would have been adequate before. The field of fire was obstructed by hedges and brush so that the company could not take effective action. Loud tank noises could be heard from the direction of Le Prieure.

Leutnant von Rosen ordered a change of positions forward in order to get a better field of fire. Rounding a small patch of woods, the company moved toward the southwest toward Cagny for a while, so as to then turn to the west toward Le Prieure. During that movement two sharp detonations came, one right after the other, and Feldwebel Schönrock's tank immediately caught fire, penetrated by a round from the front. The same happened to Feldwebel Müller's tank. We rescued the wounded and brought them to the forward aid station at Maneville. Unteroffizier Matthes died there as a result of his severe burns.

Shortly thereafter, at the battalion command post, Tiger 300 took a hit on the gun mantlet—probably a ricochet—that had no penetrating power. By order of Leutnant von Rosen, the 3rd Company pulled back about 200 meters and took up a new position there. It was not possible to

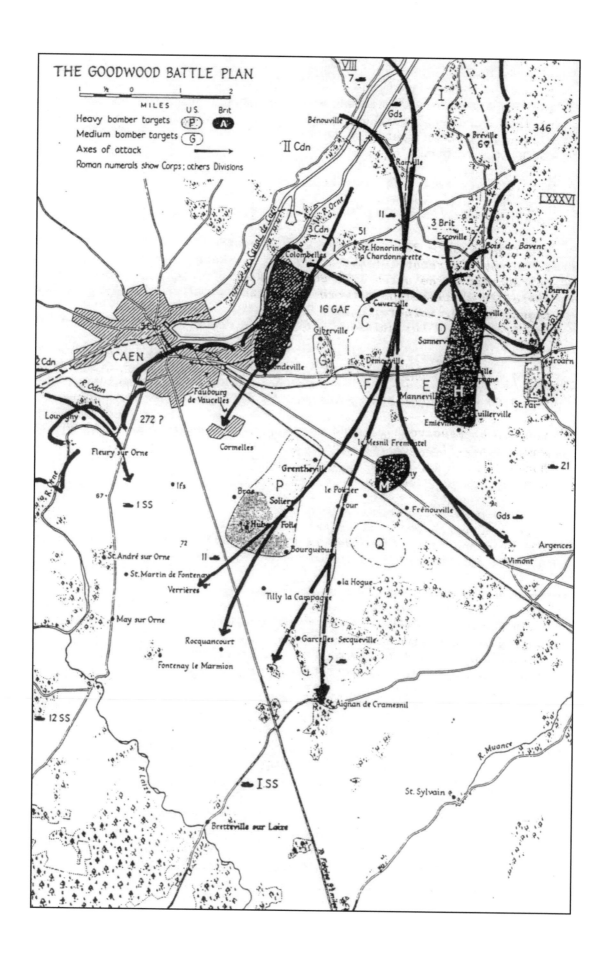

THE GOODWOOD BATTLE PLAN

MILES

Heavy bomber targets
Medium bomber targets
Axes of attack

Roman numerals show Corps; others Divisions

determine where the rounds had come from. Since both tanks had been penetrated from the front, the rounds must have come from the direction of Cagny, which was 1,200 meters distant. However, at that point in time, Cagny was still in our own hands. Only in 1966 was it discovered that a Luftwaffe 88mm flak battery that had been employed in a ground role as an antitank battery. It had apparently mistaken our Tigers for British tanks and was responsible for the frontal penetrations of the two Tigers.

English reports attributed the fact that Cagny could not be captured by British troops until late afternoon, far later than the British had planned, due to the action on the left flank of the attack sector of six Tigers of Tiger Tank Battalion 503 that had miraculously escaped the carpet bombing.

At 1600 hours, the 3rd Company had only one tank that could be considered combat ready. Some of the others could still move, but they could not fire. Hauptmann Fromme ordered the 3rd Company to withdraw and recover those tanks that were repairable with its own means. As a result, the remnants of the 3rd Company assembled that evening in Rupiere with the combat trains. It had succeeded in towing two more tanks out of the sea of craters at Maneville. It had also rescued alive Feldwebel Sachs and two men of his crew from Tiger 313, which was upside down, resting on its turret.

LEUTNANT VON ROSEN'S REPORT ON THE CARPET BOMBING OF 18 JULY 1944

I was in the position we had dug out under my Tiger 311 with Unteroffizier Werkmeister. It was, indeed, a bit cooler there and, as a result, more comfortable than in the tank. The remaining three members of the crew were sleeping in the tank. On 18 July I was awakened at about 0600 hours by the intense noise of engines in the air. Still half asleep, I heard the sound of falling bombs. They hit about 200 meters in front of us, but the concussion was so strong that the tank shook. It was immediately clear to me that the attack was aimed at us, but there was no time to think about it. The air was filled with the rushing of the falling bombs, and I instinctively pressed firmly against the ground. Then came the ear-bursting crash of the detonation, the earth heaved, but I was not yet hit. I was still alive. And then, again, I heard the rush of the falling bombs and again the detonations. I felt completely helpless against that power, there

was no escaping, I could not think of anything at all. I have no idea how long that lasted. All conception of time was lost.

Suddenly, Unteroffizier Werkmeister and I were thrown into a corner by the concussion. I was completely covered with earth and lay, unconscious, for a while, until the slow return of consciousness and the realization I was still alive. But then the next bombs came and with them, the realization that this was not all a bad dream, but that, at that instant, I truly had no choice but to let that firestorm engulf me again. As I remember, it lasted—with short pauses—a good two and a half hours. It is hardly possible to describe that period of time with words. I only know that I lay under my tank, held my ears and bit the blanket so as not to scream. Finally the attack seemed to come to an end. As I crept out from under the tank...what a picture!

Of that once so beautiful park, all that were left were splintered trees that lay every which way, plowed up meadows and gigantic bomb craters that were so numerous that they overlapped each other. It was a gray, hostile moonscape enveloped in an impenetrable dust cloud that made it hard to breathe. Trees were on fire, as were the fields of grain, and one saw the red reflection of the fires in the thick clouds of smoke. I went to the tank beside me, Unteroffizier Westerhausen's tank. It had taken a direct hit and tongues of flame played in the wreckage. There was no trace left of the crew. I worked my way through the craters and over giant trees, through a true primeval forest, and then got to Oberfeldwebel Sachs' tank. In front of it there was a giant crater. The tank had been tossed by the concussion and lay on its turret, the running gear in the air. We found two of the crew, dead, and no trace of the others. Two excellent men of the company maintenance section had been killed. They, too, had sought refuge under that tank.

I immediately had the tanks readied for action. First they had to be shoveled free, since they were covered in earth right up to the turrets. Trees had been toppled onto them, tracks torn off—how were we to ever get the company ready for action? The work had to be broken off frequently, because the naval artillery began to register on us with heavy 42cm [16-inch] rounds. At that point I also noticed that, 15 meters in front of my tank, there was a 6- or 8-meter-deep crater in which the Tiger could easily have fit. The strong armor plate on the rear of the tank was severely deformed as if a shell had struck it. The concussion had torn off the engine's radiator. It is still unclear to me today what could have caused that. In any case, my tank was unserviceable and I had to change tanks yet again.

Our situation became ever more uncomfortable. We could hear tank and machine-gun fire at a short distance. Had the British already gotten as far as our position? It was impossible to establish communications with the battalion. So I set out on foot to try to accomplish that. Leaping from crater to crater, diving for cover at every on-rushing salvo, I reached the route to Emieville. Fewer bombs had fallen there and I was able to make better progress. Around a curve in the road Tiger "I" approached me with the commander in it. The bomb carpet had also hit the area of the battalion command post, but the attack had not been as intense there as it had been at the 3rd Company. The battalion commander, Hauptmann Scherf, and the officers and soldiers of the battalion staff survived the carpet bombing packed tight together in the narrow winding staircase in the turret of the building. The house, itself, was demolished, but the tower remained standing.

I received orders from the battalion commander to set out with the 3rd Company as rapidly as possible and form a defensive front on the left flank of the attack corridor at the buildings of the stud-farm at Maneveille. It might have been 1000 hours, perhaps even later, when we finally had six tanks ready. They were ready for a maintenance facility, but at least they could move and bring their weapons to bear. It was difficult to find a route through the sea of craters without having a tank slip into a gigantic crater. But we succeeded and, after a 1.5 kilometer move along the park wall, we took position southwest of Maneville. (End of von Rosen's report.)

What was the situation with the other companies? The 1st Company was able to get a portion of its King Tigers operationally ready by noon. Oberleutnant Oemler's Tiger 100 slipped into a bomb crater and could not be recovered. The 1st Battalion of the 22nd Panzer Regiment also worked feverishly to dig out its tanks and get ready for action. Commitment before 1200 hours was impossible. Between 1200 and 1400 hours, on orders from the 22nd Panzer Regiment, the 503's 1st Company and the 22nd Panzer Regiment's 1st Battalion carried out a counterattack along the

Troarn-Caen road toward Demouville. It is no longer possible to determine how many King Tigers were actually serviceable. The 1st Battalion of the 22nd Panzer Regiment had a total of about eight Panzer IVs ready for action. A total of four tanks must have reached the village of Demouville. However, they had to pull back again because of strong pressure from the enemy. (Report by Major von Gottberg, commander, 1st Battalion, 22nd Panzer Regiment, 15 August 1975).

The 1st Company had heavy losses. Tiger 111 was penetrated by a round. Leutnant Schröder and Gefreiter Schulze were killed. Tiger 101 was also knocked out. The attack was broken off.

The 2nd Company and its Tigers, along with the training battalion of the 16th Luftwaffe Field Division and Anti-Tank Battalion von Obstfelder of the 346th Infantry Division, were committed by the commander of the 16th Luftwaffe Field Division, Generalmajor Sievers, in a counterattack northwest of Troarn. That counterattack brought the enemy advance toward Troarn to a halt.

Tiger Tank Battalion 503 withdrew its 1st and 2nd Companies in the late afternoon and assembled at Maneville. By order of the 21st Panzer Division, the battalion moved to the south to the Frenouville area on the Cagny-Vimont road. There it prevented a further advance by the enemy to the southeast. Cagny had fallen to the British in the late afternoon. The 1st Company lost Tiger 122 in a somewhat unusual fashion during its operations in the area east of Cagny. There are two reports of that, one by Lieutenant Gorman, platoon leader and commander of a Sherman tank of the Irish Guards, and the other by Hans-Joachim Thaysen, at that time gunner in Tiger 122.

The Gorman Story

[Editor's Note: With the exception of the first and last paragraphs, which were not available, this passage is taken from the account in Alexander McKee's *Caen: Anvil of Victory*.]

My name is Gorman, and at the time of Goodwood, I was a platoon leader in the 21st Irish Guards Armored Regiment, which was equipped with Shermans. During the afternoon of July 18th we fought in the hedgerow country northeast of Cagny. Two or three groups, each with four or five Tigers that were making good use of the cover, seemed to be opposing our 5th Guards

Armored Brigade. They would suddenly emerge from their cover, fire, and cost us several losses. We attempted to attack with the company closed up, whereupon the Tigers again disappeared in their cover, only to appear again and repeat the whole process anew.

This was my first time in action and I was excited. I had got across the little stream running into Cagny from the northeast, but the rest of my troop got stuck. However, I pushed on alone for a bit and found plenty of targets and was beginning to think this war business was not too bad after all; in fact, I was beginning to enjoy myself. But this didn't last long for, on glancing to my left, I saw to my horror the unmistakable shape of a Royal Tiger coming through a hedge under 200 yards away. I ordered my gunner: "Traverse left—on—fire!" He fired and I saw with dismay the 75mm shot hit the front of the Tiger, bounce off and go sizzling up into the air. I ordered the gunner to fire again, but a hollow voice came up from the bowels of the tank, saying "Gun jammed, sir." This was a situation for which I had not been trained and I did not know what to do. Glancing anxiously at the Tiger, I saw with horror that his long gun was slowly swinging around in my direction. Someone had once told me that when in doubt the thing to do was advance, so I ordered my driver to advance at full speed and ram the Tiger. We lurched forward, gathered speed, and hit him amidships with a terrific crash, just before he got his sights on to me. Both crews bailed out on impact and, since there was quite heavy shelling, both crews dived for cover. My wireless operator saw a convenient slit trench and, jumping into it, found it already occupied by the Tiger's crew. However, they both stayed there together, keeping their heads down. I crawled back, brought up my 17-pounder Sherman and managed to brew the Tiger. I then collected my crew and the Tiger's crew, and we went back and got another tank.

I recount this little story because it may well be the only example in the late war in which an army unit used the old naval tactic of ramming.

Sources

1. Staff College, Camberly: *Battlefield Tour* (1956), p. 44 (first and last paragraphs).
2. Alexander McKee, *Caen: Anvil of Victory* (1964), p. 273 ff. (remainder of narrative).

The Thaysen Story

As I remember it, the English attack started at 1500 hours. Up until that time we kept ourselves busy wiping away sweat. It was a blistering hot summer day. We could scarcely keep the hatches open because of the on-going artillery fire. The attack that started at about 1500 hours was supported by a tremendous number of British tanks. The main line of resistance was overrun in a few minutes. Only the 1st Company and a few anti-tank guns held for a little time. Soon the British were between, in front of and behind us. That had as a result that neither we nor the English knew who or what was where. In the meantime, both the German and English artillery fired wildly into the midst of it all. And, of course, the British and German infantry were right in there, too.

Tiger 112, the tank in which I was gunner, was engaged with one Englishman while we were fired on by others. That caused my tank commander (a newcomer, without combat experience), to well, let's say . . . to have the tank put in reverse, almost in a panic. We lunged back, right through a hedge, the type you usually found there.

Obviously, the commander was a bit out of it, since he must have seen that another tank was behind the hedge. In any case, there was a jolt, and we were hung up with an Englishman. There was no way that we intended to ram the enemy, the more so since we ran into him with the rear of the tank and I was still at 12 o'clock, busy with the Tommy that was firing at us.

Scarcely had we run into the Englishman when, apparently, a 75mm PaK firing at the Englishman hit us instead. It hit us in the left between the track and the running gear. The round penetrated and sliced the seat right out from under my backside. I found myself on the turret floor. At the same time, the round tore open a shell casing and the propellant charge ignited in a jet of flame. There was nothing for us but to bail out. The radio operator, loader and tank commander were the first ones out. The driver, Horst Becher, who lives today in Braunschweig, was able to grab his pistol and, after bailing out, did target practice at the Englishmen who were around the tank. And that was quite a sight, since he still had his headphones with the ripped-out cords dangling on his ears.

On dismounting through the turret hatch, I landed on a member of the English crew who, presumably, was also somewhat out of it. Apparently he thought I was one of his crew. For a moment, we looked at each other in a daze. Then a rush of heroism awoke in both of us. Each grabbed for the place where he'd usually find his pistol. Heroism failed from a lack of lethal materials. Since our tank started to burn, both of us started to crawl away from it and, since things were lively all around, we both sought cover in a hole behind the Tommy's tank. With one of us in the left corner and the other in the right one, we eyed each other and each tried to convince the other, with hands and feet, that the other was his prisoner. Since it turned out that each of us had opposite opinions about that, both of us shrugged our shoulders, grinned at each other and bolted for our own sides.

So that was that. It would be nice if I could meet one of the Englishmen. (Hans-Joachim Thaysen)

And so ended 18 July, the day that brought the greatest losses in personnel and equipment to the battalion. The 3rd Company alone had fourteen dead to mourn. On 20 July the company turned its last serviceable tank over to the 2nd Company and, by order of the OKH, was pulled out in order to receive new tanks from Germany at the Mailly-Le-Camp training area. On 22. July an advance party was sent with Feldwebel Müller, which, after a two-day stay in Paris, arrived in Mailly on 25 July. The company followed a few days later and was quartered in a bivouac area near the village of Sompuis until it could receive the tanks that were coming from Germany at the beginning of August.

But back to the battalion:

On 19 July the battalion moved through Argences and St. Pair to Troarn and secured there on the western outskirts of the village. Several enemy advances were repulsed. On 20 July the enemy renewed his attack on Troarn with armored support, but that attack also failed. Five enemy tanks were knocked out. The 21st Panzer Division was pulled out, but the remnants of the 22nd Panzer Regiment remained at Troarn. The battalion remained under the operational control of that regiment.

The British broke off Operation Goodwood on 21 July. In spite of the greatest fire preparation of all times, an English armored corps with three armored divisions was only able to penetrate to a depth of 12 kilometers and was, thus, unable to achieve a breakthrough. During that time period, the British lost 437 tanks, many of which were due to the actions of Tiger Tank Battalion 503.

DEFENSIVE FIGHTING ON THE ORNE: THE END OF OPERATIONS IN FRANCE

While the situation south of Caen was stabilized, things became increasingly critical south of St. Lô. The front was torn open on both sides of St. Lô. Panzer-Divisionen had to be pulled out of the Caen area and thrown into the area of the breakthrough. Between 23 and 25 July Tiger Tank Battalion 503 moved with its armored elements out of the Troarn area to the southwest into the Orne valley and crossed that river at Thury-Harcourt. It is no longer known how many tanks the battalion had when it reached the Orne Valley. It is certain, however, that the combat trains and the maintenance company did not accompany the tanks and the supply lines became longer. The replacement parts situation became more precarious. On 30 July the British 8th Corps broke through the weakened German front. A counterattack by the remnants of the 22nd Panzer Regiment and Tiger Tank Battalion 503, led by Oberst von Oppeln-Bronikowski, was unable to make any progress.

At that point in time, the battalion still had thirteen tanks in service. Sixteen tanks were in the maintenance facility for short-duration repairs. Up until 30 July, two officers and thirty noncommissioned officers and enlisted personnel had been killed in Normandy; one officer and thirty noncommissioned officers and enlisted personnel had been wounded; and eighteen soldiers were missing. Regarding battalion morale, the commander wrote:

In spite of the enemy's absolute air and artillery superiority, the morale in the unit is good. It is depressing that the losses suffered have a very unfavorable relationship to successes gained due to the farming out of the unit during operations—due, in part, to the terrain. Uniforms and equipment: Good. Rations could be far better in an area such as Normandy. (Monthly Report of Tiger Tank Battalion 503 on 1 August 1944).

That monthly report also makes it clear that the battalion was still under the operational control of the 21st Panzer Division.

During the first days of August, the tanks of the battalion were also involved in the fighting at Mont Pincon and Plessis-Grimoult. It was unusually hard fighting, in which the defense was favored by the hilly landscape of "Normandy's Switzerland." The limited fields of observation in that terrain repeatedly forced the enemy armor to move at the speed of the dismounted advancing infantry.

On 10 August the British crossed the Orne slightly south of Thury-Harcourt. On 11 August Hauptmann Wiegand provided cover in the southeast portion of St. Pierre with the last two serviceable tanks. That day, at about 1130 hours, the English attacked east with thirty tanks and strong infantry support past the village. Hauptmann Wiegand counterattacked with his two Tigers, set the three leading enemy tanks on fire with gunfire and forced the British to break off their attack for a time. However, both Tigers also took such a beating that they were no longer mobile. That day, 11 August, was the last day the battalion was employed on the Normandy front.

On 14 August, the Canadians began an offensive and pushed forward on both sides of the Caen-Falaise road to the south. By that evening, they were already 8 kilometers north of Falaise. American forces, coming south after their breakthrough at Avranches, were directly south of Argentan. The spearheads of the two arms of the Allied attack stood barely 28 kilometers apart. An encirclement of the German forces in the Falaise-Trun area appeared imminent.

The battalion succeeded in getting all of its wheeled elements, which included the Headquarters Company and the Maintenance Company, as well as the company trains, promptly on the march to the Seine at Elbeuf. It was ordered that priority in crossing was for armor, SS, Flak and artillery formations. As a result, all of the battalion's wheeled elements were able to make it to the other bank of the Seine in time. If they were no longer needed, they moved as far as possible to the north.

There was no chance for the tanks of the battalion to cross the Seine. There was no bridge that could be reached and ferries were not available for 60- or 70-ton vehicles. Therefore, if the tanks had to be left behind due to enemy action, mechanical problems or lack of fuel, they were blown up. The tanks that were engaged at Thury-Harcourt were able to escape the pocket that was forming at Falaise. All tried to get to the Seine at

Rouen. Even the tanks which had been made mobile again during the last few days at the maintenance facilities tried to reach that destination. Fate took its course, however, when they ran out of fuel; resupply was no longer conceivable. Thus, everyone tried to get as close to the Seine as he could with his tank. They wanted to reach the river, even if it meant on foot.

Hans Welsch, of the 1st Company, wrote of that in his diary:

13 August: We towed Tiger 113, which finished off our Tiger 112. Tiger 124 towed us further through Trun. Artillery fire.

14 August: Halt on the highway. Three aerial attacks on our tank. Oberfeldwebel Fendesack was severely wounded and died the next day.

16 August: In Ticheville in the evening. Civilians blocked the exit from the cellar where we had stayed. We shot our way free and ran to the tank. Tiger 124 went kaputt.

18 August: Tigers 113, 111, 100 and 122 were blown up shortly before the pocket was closed. Feldwebel Tessmer, Gefreiter Fiedler, and I stayed with Tigers 112 and 124 as demolition party.

19 August: The pocket of Falaise was closed.

20 August: I blew up Tiger 112 at 2200 hours. Gefreiter Fiedler did the same to Tiger 124. Back through Ticheville, Le Sap and Monnai.

21 August: Rainy weather. Thank God. Onward on foot, about 10 kilometers. Then Leutnant Witt took us along with him through Broglie and Bernay to Elbeuf.

22 August: We crossed the Seine at Rouen by barge in the morning. Ten kilometers by staff car, then on foot. Rest in Sotteville and wait for vehicle. Continued the journey with Leutnant Brodhagen to Fleury.

So much for the diary excerpt.

The 1st Company assembled at Pontoise and, on 28 August, headed for Germany. The tank crews moved in requisitioned automobiles. On 31 August the company arrived at Paderborn.

Less is known of the fate of the Tigers of the 2nd Company. Several tanks, coming from the maintenance facility, reached the Seine at Bourgtheroulde/Rouen. There was no possibility of crossing, however. There are several photographs of Tiger 213 wandering along the Grande Rue of Bourgtheroulde, searching for access to the Seine. A number of Tiger Is were abandoned at Vimoutiers. Several Tigers of the 2nd Company were stranded without fuel on the Route Nationale 179 between Vimoutiers and the Elloard farmstead. Others were abandoned on the road from Canapville. A Tiger II of the 1st Company also gave up the ghost there.

One of those tanks still stands today as a last witness to the fighting in Normandy. During those days of flight in August 1944, a Tiger I was left in the middle of Route Nationale 179 at Vimoutiers. The crew had set demolition charges on the turret ring and engine, leaving the turret somewhat tilted and the engine cover torn off its mountings. Later, American bulldozers shoved the heavy colossus to the side. The Tiger lay in that condition for thirty years, each year sinking deeper into the earth and increasingly overgrown by vegetation. A scrap dealer bought the wreck, from which the valuable items had been removed over time. Children played on the tank and did gymnastics on the long gun barrel. Gradually the Tiger at Vimoutiers became, first a local, then, a national curiosity that drew sightseers from near and far. In October 1975 three men got together who had particular interest in that tank. One was a former member of the Division Leclerc, who knew the significance of the Tiger. The others were a young historian and a weapons collector. They were able to convince the municipal council of Vimoutiers that the tank should be preserved. They collected money and set in motion the recovery and external restoration. Today that Tiger I, its exterior fully restored, is located at the same place as a memorial and witness to its time.

It remains to report on the 3rd Company:

On the evening of 18 July, the company assembled at the location of the trains at Rupiere. The only tank that was still fully operational was turned over to the 2nd Company.

The order arrived on 20 July to move to the training area at Mailly-le-Camp and receive new tanks. On 22 July an advance party left Rupiere and, after a two-day layover in Paris, arrived at the training area on 25 July. On 29 July the entire company followed. It was quartered in a bivouac area at the village of Sompuis. The new tanks arrived at the beginning of August—Tiger IIs, twelve with Porsche turrets and two with the new production (Henschel) turrets. The days were filled with getting the tanks operationally ready.

While that was going on, a propaganda film crew arrived and photographed "a day in the life of a tank company in combat," in the course of which Feldwebel Seidel's and Unteroffizier Jäckel's tanks dropped out with transmission problems.

On 11 August the 3rd Company left Mailly-le-Camp by rail. The two damaged tanks stayed behind. The first train, led by Leutnant von Rosen, was attacked by five Thunderbolts early in the morning on 12 August between Esternay and Sezanne. A portion of the carloads of basic-load ammunition that had been brought along immediately burned. The locomotive was shot up and Tiger 311 also burned. In the attempted emergency unloading, the tank came off the rail car and tipped over. And, again, the company had losses to mourn. Unteroffizier Wehrheim lay dead beside the tracks and was buried on the spot by the company. Feldwebel Bornschier died during transport on the hospital train. The company had five severely wounded and five with minor wounds, including the train commander, Leutnant von Rosen. The railroad line to Paris was blocked. It took three days until that and the following train could resume the journey to Paris. Leutnant Rambow had relieved Leutnant von Rosen, who went to a field hospital at Reims. Two days later, Tiger 311 was recovered by a railroad crane and towed to Route National 4, which was close by. That was as far as the salvage operation got, since the Americans got to the tank before the prime movers that had been made available by OB West could arrive on the scene. As a result, three of the crew members were captured by the Americans.

In the meanwhile, the 3rd Company got to Paris, unloaded its tanks and was quartered in the Bois de Vincennes. Hauptmann Scherf wrote:

The local-area commander for Paris ordered the company to stand by for possible commitment in the city, since the French resistance was already actively fighting there. When the situation intensified and Hauptmann Scherf went to Paris to find the command post of the local area commander, he could not find it. Everyone had disappeared without a trace. According to information previously received from the local area commander, the battalion was supposed to be positioned somewhere along the Seine to the north of Paris. After an additional two days of waiting—without hearing anything from the local area commander—

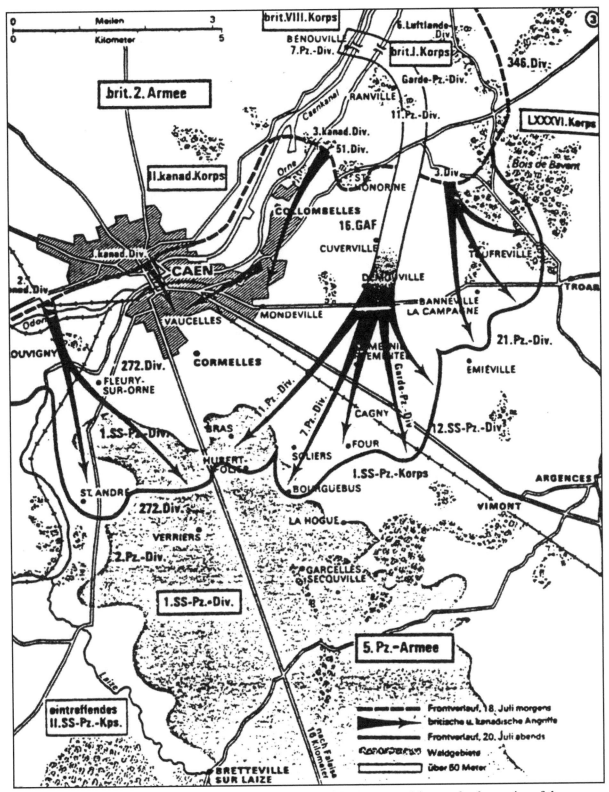

The breakthough at Caen began to take shape starting 20 July 1944. Its prerequisite was the destruction of the German armor forces (the 21st Panzer Division and Tiger Tank Battalion 503).

Hauptmann Scherf considered that he was no longer obligated to remain under the control of the local commander. The 3rd Company set out through Paris to reach the northeastern bank of the Seine and locate the battalion.

The company marched from Vincennes along the Boulevard de la Chapelle to the Gare St. Lazaire and from there along the Madeleine to the Place de la Concorde. The march continued along the Champs Elysées and the Place de l'Étoile-Maillot-Pont de Neuilly and, from there, on the right bank of the Seine toward Pontoise.

The company had scarcely left the northern part of Paris behind—about 10 to 15 kilometers—when it was obligated by a Luftwaffe field division that was committed on the Seine to occupy positions there. Under impossible employment conditions, the majority of the Tigers were knocked out by fighter-bomber attacks within a week.

OPERATIONS OF THE 3RD COMPANY AGAINST THE AMERICAN BRIDGEHEAD AT MANTES (22–30 AUGUST 1944)

The fact that Hauptmann Scherf did not receive specific orders as the commander of the 3rd Company in the last days of Paris is a sign of the complete confusion which reigned there. In fact, the local area command simply forgot about the company. It demonstrates the discipline of the company commander that he waited for days for orders, even though the situation in Paris became ever more obtuse. His decision to try to link up with the battalion—at whatever cost—demonstrates his initiative.

Coming from Vincennes, Hauptmann Scherf and the company marched through Paris on 31 August 1944. He wanted to reach the battalion which was rumored to be north of Paris. Scherf knew the battalion had crossed the Seine with all of its elements after having lost or turned over all of its tanks. It was on the move to the Belgian border. There had been no opportunity to cross the river with the remaining few operational tanks.

The 3rd Company had eleven Tiger IIs at its disposal at the start of the march. The organic supply elements of the company were also with it. As a result, the company had a certain amount of ammunition and fuel. It was autonomous for a few days. It only had the company maintenance section to perform repairs, however. It did not have

any maintenance elements from the battalion, so that major tank repairs were not possible.

Tiger 334 became disabled with transmission problems during the march through Paris at the Porte Maillot. Another tank became disabled at Théméricourt. It is not known whether additional tanks became disabled. The company maintenance section under Oberfeldwebel Großmann worked around the clock and made the impossible possible.

Hauptmann Scherf was unable to get information on the "big picture." It was hard to differentiate what was fact and what was rumor. The first American troops reached the Seine at Mantes on 19 August. By the evening of 20 August, they had constructed engineer bridges at Tosny and Mantes. Between Vetheuil and Porscheville there was a solid bridgehead. Ten thousand soldiers had taken the right bank. Numerous artillery formations were in position and reconnaissance was being conducted in depth. Initially there were no German combat-capable formations in place, at least nothing which could have opposed the Americans.

All available troops were assembled under the command of Group Schwerin as quickly as possible. It was placed under the operational control of the 1st SS Panzer Corps effective 23 August. Group Schwerin was given the mission to form a cohesive defensive front and contain the U.S. bridgehead. This was particularly urgent. Containment was needed in order to prevent German units, staffs and installations flowing back from Paris and the area north of it from being cut off or even surrounded and to give them time and space to conduct the withdrawal.

The 18th Luftwaffe Field Division, the remnants of the 17th Luftwaffe Field Division, and a parachute division were brought up. All of them were formations which were not motorized and had hardly any long-range antitank or antiaircraft weaponry. The 18th Luftwaffe Field Division assumed the sector between Vetheuil and Meulan on 21 August with its 35th and 36th Jäger Regiments.

Hauptmann Scherf moved ahead of the company to the command post of Group Schwerin at Magny en Vexin. He wanted to get information on the overall situation and find out the location of Tiger Tank Battalion 503. He was immediately pressed into the service of Group Schwerin and placed under the operational control of the 18th Luftwaffe Field Division. The company was turned off of its route of march. Late in the evening it reached an assembly area at Gaillonet (east of Oineville) after reporting at the command post of the 18th Luftwaffe Field Division.

The company was divided among both the 35th and 36th Jäger Regiments for employment. The supply elements of the company set up somewhat to the rear in the park of the castle at Marines. It appear seven tanks were operation on that evening of 21 August. It is possible that one or even two tanks that had become disabled during the move reached the company that night or on the following day. With the exception of the headquarters tanks—Tigers 300 and 301—the remaining tanks were divided into two platoons under the leadership of Leutnants Koppe and Rambow.

After establishing contact with both of the Jäger regiments, the terrain and the approach routes into possible areas of operation were scouted by the platoon leaders and tank commanders on 22 August. The terrain between Fontenay-Guitrancourt-Garganville sloped down to the Seine. It was difficult for tanks, since it was full of cliffs. Defiles and partially wooded high ground with long lines of sight, as well as several quarries, made employment of the entire company impossible. The regimental commanders wanted to split up the tanks down to company level, in order to provide corset stays along the front to which the light infantry could cling and have some antitank defense. Of course, that contradicted the tanker's maxim of *Klotzen nicht Kleckern*, but the situation and the terrain necessitated compromise.

The only source for the operations conducted that evening comes from an American report: "2040 Hours. Attack in battalion strength supported by 5 Tigers against the 314th Infantry Regiment at Fontenay." The American advance guard was forced back. Prisoners were taken. The Americans were fearful of a night attack. The loud armor noises the Americans reported during the night referred to the tanks of the 3rd Company which were moving into jump-off positions for the attack planned against Guitrancourt early on 23 August. Two things were expected of the Tigers: (1) spur on the attack of the 35th Jäger Regiment

on Limay over the wooded and difficult-to-approach high ground of the "Bois des Blancs Soleils"; and (2) following that, support the attack of the 36th Jäger-Regiment at Fontenay.

To accomplish that, the two platoons of the company were deployed so that each platoon enveloped the wooded high ground from the right and the left. Both platoons attacked at 0700 hours with light infantry mounted on the Tigers. The platoon attacking on the right reached the farm at Mélier where it received heavy defensive fire from US tank destroyers which had terrific positions on the high ground at Les Rues. The four Tigers of the left-hand platoon reached the high ground at "Bois des Blanc Soleils." They knocked out one tank destroyer there and then went into position on the southern edge of the woods where they received heavy defensive fire from the tank destroyers posted on the outskirts of Limay. The Americans reported the following at 0845 hours: "Tigers broke though the I Company positions; the company moved back to Limay."

At the same time, one company of 33rd Luftwaffe Jäger Regiment, supported by a Tiger, attacked south from Guitrancourt through the "Vallée aux Cailloux" in the direction of the N90. At the road, it swung west and reached the eastern outskirts of Limay after knocking out a Sherman.

As a result of the direct fire, the position of the Tigers on the edge of the woods at the "Bois des Blanc Soleils" became untenable. 155mm artillery had registered; two or four Tigers received considerable damage to their running gear and had to be towed out of the impact zone. As a result, the left-hand platoon was temporarily out of action. The Tiger at Limay also received a hit on its running gear, however, it was able to reach friendly lines at Guitrancourt under its own power.

All of the operations recounted here were met by the Americans with heavy artillery fire and massed attacks by fighter-bombers. The light infantry of the Luftwaffe suffered severe casualties, first mounted on the tanks and then while attacking dismounted. After the corset stays provided by the Tigers were removed, the Luftwaffe light infantry was no longer able to hold the line and large portions of the captured terrain had to be given up.

The attack of the 36th Luftwaffe Jäger Regiment at Fontenay also began at 0700 hours. It started without Tiger support. After the "Bois des Blancs Soleils" had been taken by the light infantry, the right-hand platoon at Mélier received the order to support the attack at Fontenay. The Americans reported the following at 1130 hours: "Tigers outside Fontenay." At 1350 hours there was a new attack with Tiger support as far as the water tower and at Le Mouchel, a part of Fontenay. There was also heavy fighting at the Prieu farm. The Tigers were pulled back at 1610 hours.

It was a hard day for the company. Although it did not have any total tank losses or casualties, it was difficult for the company to get its disabled tanks operational again with the means at hand.

The operational tanks established security at Guitrancourt and Fontenay on 24 August. Enemy close air support was constantly in the air. It attacked everything that wasn't under cover or was moving. Hauptmann Scherf was able to establish contact with the battalion. It can no longer be determined how the contact was established—whether by motorcycle messenger or by keyed transmission. There was a medium-wave radio in both Tigers 300 and 301. They were capable of covering greater distances. Hauptmann Fromme and Leutnant Heerlein came to the company on 24 August. They discussed how the battalion might be able to help with supply. It was not possible to release a maintenance platoon because it was foreseeable that the front in this sector would soon become fluid. Superfluous personnel were supposed to be sent back to the battalion. Because the company did not need two lieutenants after the recent losses of tanks, Hauptmann Scherf agreed to detail Leutnant Koppe to the headquarters company of the battalion to lead the supply section. Koppe had already proven himself once before in that area. In the current situation, fuel was an extremely rare commodity and absolutely necessary for the company to get back to the battalion.

25 August. The Americans continuously strengthened their bridgehead. Except for local attacks there were no offensive operations. Just like every other day, the enemy air forces were constantly overhead. The Tigers were once again the fire brigade. They made an appearance at Guitrancourt and Fontenay. Over the past few days reinforcements arrived: remnants of the 49th Infantry Division as well as the 6th Parachute Division. Among the reinforcements was also the 1st Company of Tiger Tank Battalion 101, which had four-

teen Tiger IIs. After being refitted in Germany, it was unloaded north of Paris and arrived in the area of operations of the 1st Battalion of the SS Panzer Corps after a long road march. Seven Tigers had become disabled during the long march. The situation of the 1st Company of Tiger Tank Battalion 101 was similar to that of the 3rd Company of Tiger Tank Battalion 503: organic supply elements but no maintenance facility.

Tiger Tank Battalion 101's 1st Company was assembled at Arthies. It went into action for the first time on 25 August at Drocourt. The company was outfitted with the Tiger II with the Henschel turret. In contrast, the 503's 3rd Company had the Porsche turret (with the exception of Tigers 300 and 314). As a result, it is possible to determine from photographs of knocked out or disabled tanks which company they belonged to. It is also possible to determine the built-up areas where the companies were employed.

On 26 August, both Tiger companies attacked together through the woods at Montgison towards Fontenay. American sources reported about fifteen Tigers. It can be assumed that the 503's 3rd Company and the 101's 1st Company each employed about seven Tigers. Exploiting the protection offered by the armor and the support of artillery and Nebelwerfer, the Luftwaffe light infantry battalion was able to advance into Fontenay.

Hauptmann Scherf's Tigers—employed on the left—attacked the water tower and the outskirts of Fontenay at Le Moucel. Around 1625 hours, U.S. fighter-bombers dive-bombed the Tigers and the accompanying infantry. A hail of lead poured over the attackers, who were now also being shelled by American artillery. The Tiger of Feldwebel Weiland received a hit outside of Le Moucel. While bailing out of the tank, Feldwebel Weiland was hit by a burst from a machine gun and was killed immediately. The Tiger was still capable of moving and was evacuated. Tiger 322 of Unteroffizier Schmidt was disabled by a hit at the water tower at Fontenay. Tiger 112 of the 101's 1st Company came to help in order to pull it out of the impact area. American sharpshooters forced the crew under cover again and again, so it was impossible to attach the tow cable. Tiger 301 of Feldwebel Neeb received five direct hits from the front; none of them penetrated, however.

American sources have reported the following concerning these engagements:

1430 hours. Tank noise in front of the 314th Infantry regiment in Fontenay.

1625 hours. Tanks in front of the positions of the 1st Battalion in Fontenay.

1646 hours. The U.S. Army Air Corps attacks with Thunderbolts. The aircraft strafe the Tigers and the infantry.

1650 hours. Two additional Tigers approach; 1 tank destroyer destroyed and 2 Tigers hit.

1700 hours. German artillery and Neberwerfer step into action.

1755 hours. Tigers approach C Company in front of the water tower at Fontenay.

1840 hours. One Tiger hit at the water tower.

1905 hours. Three Tigers break into the L Company positions.

1915 hours. Three Tigers pull back outside of Fontenay on the road to Meula. Artillery shells them but they are able to flee into the woods.

1920 hours. Tiger in front of B Company. The 155mm cannon shell it.

The fighting was broken off when it turned dark. The Tigers pulled back. Hauptmann Scherf and the rest of the company went to Gaillonat, the company assembly area. The company maintenance section was fully engaged one more time. Tanks rendered combat ineffective but still mobile towed immobile tanks to Marines. It was thought there might be somewhat more time to repair them there.

The U.S. XV Corps initiated its offensive to break out of the bridgehead on 27 August after having received additional reinforcements. It had been contained in the bridgehead for almost a week and had to fend off vigorous German counterattacks against it. Two armor divisions and two infantry divisions were ready to be committed to battle, about 40,000 men and 500 tanks. In addition, there was a monstrous number of artillery of all calibers and air supremacy above.

On the night of 27 August, a barrage of artillery pounded the forward-most German lines starting at 0145 hours. By the light of dawn, the fighter-bombers started their daily work: Everything that moved on the ground became their target. It was easy to see that big plans were in motion.

The operational Tigers of the 503's 3rd Company were under cover at Sailly in expectation of what was to come. The entire front exploded at 1600 hours. The Americans started to storm the German positions under the cover of artificial smoke. At 1700 hours, the Allied air forces joined in. American losses at Fontenay were high and the amount of terrain captured small. Guitrancourt, on the other hand, was lost towards the evening after see-saw fighting. By then the Tigers were in position. They had been identified by the Americans, however, and were under extremely heavy artillery fire. Two Tigers had been "made a mess" according to a note written by Gefreiter Liedtke that day. After darkness had fallen, the Tigers pulled back to Sailly to resupply so they could occupy defensive positions again on the morning of 28 August.

Tiger 301 of Feldwebel Neeb and Tiger 123 of the 101's 1st Company, which had lost contact with its company, were immediately taken under fire when they left the cover of their positions by fighter-bombers and tank destroyers. Walter Jung, the driver on Tiger 301, reported:

We were the last tank to pull out of position. We were under strong enemy pressure. The only option available was to move through the woods, where we created our own path. After a considerable amount of time we got to a road, but I am unable to reconstruct everything in much detail any more. In any case, we wanted to get to our support area at Gaillonet. I do not know where the other three tanks got to. I also don't know whether they were tanks from the company or from the SS.

It is known through photographic evidence that Tiger 300 was disabled at the outskirts of Oinville with running gear damage. The left-hand final drive seized and the left track broke. The Tiger slipped into a ditch on the side of the road and was no longer capable of moving under its own power. It had to be towed. Hauptmann Scherf went into the village on foot to arrange for recovery. The gunner, Unteroffizier Heider, and the loader, Gefreiter Deutsch, were sent back to get to the company somehow. The situation was very eerie, since there were no soldiers or civilians to be seen any more. The village appeared to be clear of humans but the tack-tack-tack of machine-gun fire could be heard not too far away.

After waiting for a fairly long time, during which nothing happened, a SPW of the SS came roaring down the road. The soldiers in the SPW called out: "We're the last ones. No one else is coming after us!" Unteroffizier Wunderlich and Unteroffizier Schneider, the radio operator of the commander's tank, prepared the two demolition grenades which were found in the tank. When they saw the first enemy tanks on the high ground, they set the charges. Both were able to make it back to German lines, but they did not see the company again until they were in Germany.

That was the final operation where the company was employed as a whole, even though it had been strongly decimated. What followed then was only a series of individual actions in which the tanks formed a rear guard again and again against the hotly pursuing enemy. On 29 August three Tigers under Leutnant Rambow were employed with 200 or 300 paratroopers of the 21st Parachute Demonstration Regiment in defensive fighting along the road from Vigny to Gadancourt. During that fighting one of the Tigers was so severely damaged between Avernes and Gadancourt that it had to be abandoned.

The supply elements of the company, located on the castle grounds at Marines, moved that night towards Beauvais. Tiger Tank Battalion 503 was supposed to be assembling somewhere north of the Somme. It didn't have any tanks at that point. The tank of Feldwebel Müller was blown up during the departure of the supply elements. It was no longer able to be repaired. The same fate befell a Tiger near the village of Santieuil, five kilometers south of Marines. It had become disabled shortly before reaching Marines. Two additional Tigers that were also in Marines with the supply elements became disabled between Marines and Auneuil during the pull back. When the Americans approached the next morning, they also had too be abandoned. At 0830 hours on 30 August, the 314th Regiment of the U.S. 79th Infantry Division occupied Marines.

On the previous evening, Unteroffizier Reitz, the senior medic of the 503's 3rd Company, was suddenly surprised by Americans when he was making his way forward from Marines to the tanks engaged at the front. In spite of the Red Cross, shots were fired. Unteroffizier Reitz was wounded and captured.

Leutnant Rambow passed through Beauvais on 30 August with two Tigers during the withdrawal. One tank became disabled with a broken track in the vicinity of the prison on rue Antoine Caron. The crew was in the process of repairing the track when the first British tanks from the 4/7 Dragoons advanced into the city. The third round from a Firefly hit home. The surprised crew fled through the residential rubble and was able to make it back to the battalion. Leutnant Rambow was able to fight in his Tiger as far back as Amiens. The Tiger had to be abandoned there due to a lack of ammunition and fuel after it had fired its last round.

One Tiger of the 503's 2nd Company was able to cross the Seine, contrary to previous reports. Together with Tigers of the 2nd and 3rd Companies of Tiger Tank Battalion 101, Tiger 222 crossed at Elbeuf on 25 August. The Tiger was abandoned by its crew at Saussay la Champagne northeast of Les Andelys. There is a photo of that tank in the museum at Les Andelys nowadays.

The battalion staff intercepted the remaining retreating elements of the 503's 3rd Company north of Beauvais. It used elements of the reconnaissance and scout platoons to guide the retreating vehicles—some in groups of three or four, others by themselves—immediately on to Lille. The battalion staff was at Lille; the battalion was assembling in Saclin, a suburb of Lille.

Gefreiter Blunk was killed by a close-air attack on the march column on 31 August. He was the nineteenth soldier to be killed during the eight weeks of operations in the west.

Over the course of several night road marches, the battalion moved to the area around Maastricht. The battalion received the order to move to Paderborn to be refitted at Sennelager. The battalion reached Sennelager on 8 September, moving by rail from Düren.

This concludes the report of Alfred Rubbel. Helmut Klein, gunner in Tiger 334, remembers:

After passing the Arc d'Triomphe, we had transmission problems at the crossroads on the near bank of the Seine. It took quite a long time until the company maintenance section arrived in its 1-ton prime mover to repair the damage. The Parisian populace stood in crowds at the edge of the road and followed the progress of our evacuation with grim countenance. There was firing everywhere in the surrounding streets. Cries and muttered threats were constantly getting louder and more numerous. The crowd pressed ever closer to the tank. At that point, Heinz Gärtner (commander of Tiger 334) ordered the turret cleared for action. I took the main gun out of travel lock, cranked the elevation down and traversed the turret through 360 degrees. In moments, the square was empty. Only caps, walking sticks and umbrellas lay around.

After the damage was repaired, we moved on behind the company. The steering mechanism finally gave up the ghost in a suburb of Paris and we could only drive straight ahead. They wanted to install a new transmission. We were in a patch of woods to the left of the road. For days we waited in vain for the crane and the maintenance company. From day to day, the stream of refugees increased and more and more German troops moved eastward. Waffen-SS troops took up positions at a stream about two kilometers in front of us. By then the Wehrmacht had already evacuated Paris for some time, but the Allied troops had not yet arrived in the city. So we roamed through the suburbs during the day. We mounted a tank machine gun on a captured automobile and thus provided cover for our patrol activity. On one of those expeditions with Heinz Gärtner, we visited a motor-vehicle repair shop and saw two Frenchmen spraying blue paint on a Wehrmacht vehicle that had been abandoned.

We secured the Wehrmacht property and, in addition, found an American Packard automobile that we later used to flee in and which then did long service in the 3rd Company. (It finally gave up the ghost in November in Budapest.)

We learned from the SS that they were going to withdraw on the next day after blowing up the bridge. At that point there would no longer be any German units in front of us. The commander of the SS unit ordered us to destroy our tank. We removed the machine guns and the radio equipment and put one demolition charge each in the fighting and engine compartments.

When we heard tank noises on the road and the last refugees confirmed that enemy units were at the bridge, Heinz Gärtner ordered the destruction of the tank. The driver, radio operator and loader waited in the Packard around the next bend in the road. After lighting the fuses on the demolition charges, Gärtner and I left the tank, ran to the nearest cover and waited for the detonation. Sixty seconds are a long time. They seemed like an eternity to us. We wanted to run directly back to the Tiger because we thought we had done something wrong. Then there was a rumble and the hatch flew off the commander's cupola. Flames blew out of the engine compartment and cupola. And that was how our good Tiger 334 went to the final hunting grounds. Then we went back and forth across France until we again found the battalion and crossed the Rhine at Aachen.

So much for Helmut Klein's report.

It remains to pick up the story of the two disabled tanks that had been left at Mailly-le-Camp. On 24 August Leutnant von Rosen, returning from the hospital in Reims, succeeded in arranging with the transport commander at Chalon for Ssyms rail cars to transport the two Tigers. On 25 August the railroad cars arrived at Mailly with a locomotive.

Gerhard Niemann, Feldwebel Seidel's gunner, reports:

25 August: The front was drawing nearer. The two tanks crept at a snail's pace toward the loading ramps. There was a low-level air attack during the loading operation. The locomotive was put out of action with a shot-up boiler. Even worse, it blocked the tracks. It was not until the next day that a new locomotive arrived. First the shot-up locomotive had to be cleared from the way. Then, finally, the train could get moving. The objective was to reach the depot maintenance facility at Tilleur in Liege. In Epernay, Reims and Charleville there were difficulties with the local commanders and the Reichsbahn since the train was not being fully utilized. It was only pulling twenty axles. Feldwebel Seidel was able to arrange for the movement to continue past both of the first stations, but in Charleville the engine was simply uncoupled and switched to a train loaded with wounded. There was hopeless confusion at the railroad station. They had stopped forming up trains. Feldwebel Seidel took over the still intact telephone switchboard and, after several telephone calls, received the promise that a locomotive would be sent out.

28 August: The locomotive actually did arrive, and the train rolled on in the afternoon.

29 August: Due to the lack of replacement parts, it was not possible to repair the tank at Tilleur. The tank was loaded again.

3 September: We reached Paderborn by way of Aachen and Cologne.

9 September: The main body of the 3rd Company arrived at Sennelager.

So much for Gerhard Niemann's report.

Both of the tanks were repaired and returned to the 3rd Company. That was why, in many of the photographs from the upcoming employment in Hungary, two Tiger IIs with Porsche turrets are to be seen alongside the newer models with "production turrets."

Tiger Tank Battalion 503 was refitted at Sennelager. Hauptmann Scherf was scheduled for the next battalion commander course and, by then, was only a guest with Tiger Tank Battalion 503. On 30 September, Leutnant von Rosen also officially took over command of the company.

CHAPTER 29

Recollections of a Panzer Soldier (Part III)

Dr. Franz-Wilhelm Lochmann

KING TIGER

After my leave I returned to Ohrdruf. The battalion had received new tanks. The 2nd Company was equipped with the Tiger I. The 1st Company got the new King Tiger. A tremendous vehicle. We certainly had little to worry about regarding rounds penetrating the front. Hopefully, the vehicle could deal with the heavy weight. The first King Tigers were equipped with the Porsche turret. The front of the turret was very rounded and could prove problematical with a direct hit to the turret. Turret jams and, in a worst case situation, penetration through the upper deck of the hull were conceivable. We did test runs and made ourselves at home in our new companions, meaning that we removed unnecessary racks so as to make optimal use of our storage space.

FRANCE

Early in the morning of 28 June 1944 we were loaded by rail and moved out toward France. Our move was overshadowed by a terrible accident. Unteroffizier Otto Oelsner was fatally injured when he climbed out of the hatch of the commander's cupola during the journey while the train was under a bridge. We bypassed Paris and were unloaded somewhere in Normandy. Everyone was extremely nervous for fear of possible aerial attacks. The combat tracks were put on in a feverish manner, and the vehicles were assembled in an adjacent patch of woods.

For the first time I was able to marvel at the new vehicles of the antiaircraft platoon. They were quad 2cm and 3.7cm guns on tank chassis. The quad 2cm vehicles had rhomboid turrets that gave the gun crew quite good protection from gunfire.

We started the campaign with a really long road march, which we continued in the days that followed. Our assembly area was south of Caen. On the way, we passed a totally bombed-out village during the day. That gave us an idea of what we could expect from the air. Our column moved so that there was an antiaircraft vehicle between every three Tigers. That made us feel completely secure. Suddenly the *Amis* [German slang for Americans] were there with their *Jabos* [German slang for fighter-bombers]. Because they did not have a good firing position they flew in a wide circle so that they could then attack us, four at a time. The column halted. We looked curiously out of the hatches. Then our antiaircraft vehicles let loose with a storm of fire. The Jabos veered off. They certainly had not expected that sort of reception. For them, the idea that a column would drive in broad daylight was unthinkable.

The company positioned itself well camouflaged and widely dispersed on a field road. Almost every tank was under a tall tree. Otherwise, the landscape was similar to that in Schleswig-Holstein. There were fields with breaks in their slope and, at large intervals, one might see a farmstead with red-tile roofs.

The company trains were a few kilometers away at the Château de Canteloup. We sat around the vehicles, idle. What did the waiting mean? Every day the Allies filled their bridgehead with troops and equipment. Attack! That was our idea. The closer we were to the enemy, the less danger the fliers offered to us. On 17 July our tank went to the Château de Canteloup. There was gasoline in the hull. The maintenance section was busy all night and the following day getting everything straightened out. In the morning of 18 July we saw an immeasurably vast armada of four-engine bombers and heard the never-ending thunderous roll of bomb impacts near our assembly area.

When we got to the company in the evening we were faced with an unimaginable spectacle. All of the once-green landscape was now gray-black. The air was hazy, as if it had never really got light the entire day. The greatest carpet bombing of World War II had dealt with our company relatively lightly. Several of the company's tanks were able to make it through the tortured landscape and stop the enemy, who was then launching a massive armored attack. The Allied armored formations had heavy losses and had to fall back again behind Caen. The other companies suffered substantially more from the carpet bombing. They had heavy losses. There were Tigers that had tipped over and lay in deep craters.

We remained near the water tower at Troarn and were worked over by extremely heavy artillery fire for two entire days. Oberfeldwebel Fendesack was our tank commander. The heavy rounds literally plowed up the entire landscape. At first we still made occasional position changes, sometimes a hundred meters forward, sometimes a hundred meters to the rear. But that was pointless. Finally we gave it up. We were totally done in and stoically let everything fly over us. Oberfeldwebel Fendesack got stomach cramps, and everyone in the tank took note: Even that man had nerves. When someone asked what time it was we had to take a vote on whether it was morning or evening.

During the days that followed we moved north from Falaise to St. Malo. Our tank dropped out of the attack on 1 August with engine trouble. All day long we were towed east in small increments. The maintenance section had it rough. Besides us, there were other tanks that were immobile and had to be evacuated out the of the danger zone one at a time, usually at night. At that time the

company lost Obergefreiter Marat, Feldwebel Vogt and also Oberfeldwebel Fendesack, who died after being severely wounded. Oberfeldwebel Hörnke was also severely injured. On 18 July Leutnant Schrîder and Gefreiter Schütze were killed.

Daily we were plagued by the damned *Jabos*. Once, the prime movers left us standing next to the road between a few trees. In our own interest we had camouflaged the vehicles very well. Nevertheless, a short time later they discovered us. Four *Jabos* dived down on us, one after the other. Sometimes they only strafed us, but then they hit us again with their rockets. Apparently they had selected us as a rewarding target. In the meantime, three additional flights arrived. Without a break, the four groups, each consisting of four Jabos, dove on our tank. All hell broke loose.

Werner and I sat way forward under the front slope. It was quite a racket when the planes strafed us on all sides of the tank. In between the strafing runs, they favored us with their rockets over and over again. The things seemed to have very sensitive impact fuses. In all truth, we were of the opinion they were not necessarily a lethal danger to us, but it was hard on the nerves. We cursed a blue streak and swore if we ever got hold of any of them we would extract our revenge in a most horrific manner. When the ruckus was over, we saw an ammunition truck burning nearby. The truck had caught fire right at the beginning, and the exploding shells had torn away our good camouflage completely. As we continued to be evacuated that evening we ran into some captured Tommies in the next village. The kids looked completely worried and upset. Our rage had blown over. We gave them something to eat and offered them cigarettes.

THE END OF TIGER 100

The last stop during our evacuation was in a narrow road. On the one side of the road it dropped steeply into a valley and, not far from our tank, there was a house. On the other side was tall vegetation and sharply rising terrain. We were told we had probably gotten safely out of the jaws of the pocket of Falaise and we would soon be looked after. We had camouflaged the tank well and gone down into the valley where the farmhouse offered the prospect of good quarters. The road was generally peaceful during the next twenty-four hours and there was hardly any traffic. From overhead, the ground-attack aircraft left the isolated farmstead in peace. The following day, a high-ranking officer showed up and ordered me to hold that road against expected strong Allied armored forces. In the village behind us a new blocking position was to be set up along a stream. The Allied attack was expected the following morning.

I went down to the house and outlined the situation to the crew. Hannes Berger, Walter Fischer and Piepel Grasse were enthusiastic. Unteroffizier Willy Fischer, who had been assigned to us to complete the crew, said that, for once, he wanted to get a good night's sleep. Late in the afternoon, Leutnant Piepgras came and we were happy to finally hear something from the battalion. The situation was catastrophic. Infantry fire rapidly drew near from the west. It was coming from the quite weak forces of the 12th SS Panzer Division "Hitlerjugend." In the distance we were already hearing the massive sounds of armor. The Leutnant gave me the task of remaining at the tank with one man from the crew and waiting until the last German troops were past. Then I was to blow up the tank. After that was done we were to fall back to the east, reach the Seine somewhere and attempt to regain contact with the battalion at Rouen. All units were exhorted to unconditional resistance. Only Tiger Tank Battalion 503 and units of the Fallschirmjäger were permitted to withdraw through the German lines since, as was said, we had been chosen to defend the V-2 launching sites. I stayed at the tank with Willy Fischer.

Left to ourselves, we started on a good bottle of circa 1923 Chablis and the preparations for the demolition. Since we had three Z85 demolition charges available, we wanted to do a really good job. The road took a sharp bend about 150 meters west of us. That was where the first enemy tank would have to appear directly in front of us. We planned to knock out the lead vehicle and hoped that we would then be able to have the demolition

blow the turret off the tank so it would land directly next to it.

We relished our last Chablis and also supplied the last two squads of the Waffen-SS that were moving past us with the precious fluid. Half an hour later it was time. The first Sherman tank suddenly rolled around the curve. He wasn't paying much attention. The tank lived up to its nickname of "Ronson lighter"—one strike and it lights up! Only after Willy Fischer had rescued his last carton of Wilhelm II cigars did I light the fuses on the charges and we bolted. We had used a fairly long fuse so we could get into cover as far as possible from the tank.

Then it went up, that unlucky tank. The tank had been only ballast for us and the battalion in Normandy. The turret landed exactly where we had planned it, right next to the hull. The Sherman we had knocked out blocked the road for his people. The tanks that were following had no chance to get around it, with the valley on one side and the hill rising on the other. As a result, we had at least brought the Tommies to a standstill. During the days that followed, Willy Fischer and I made our way to Elbeuf on the Seine. A little downstream from there we crossed the river in a rowboat and continued our journey to Rouen. Purely by accident, we encountered a mess vehicle from the battalion. Somewhere behind Fleury we reached the company. Three days later we traveled by truck through Cambrai to Germany and reached Aachen in the evening. At the end of August we were quartered in a barracks of Panzerersatzabteilung 500 at Paderborn.

The 3rd Company had been pulled out of the lines in France in the meantime. It was outfitted with the King Tiger at Paderborn. It turned over its remaining vehicles to the 2nd Company. While we were in Paderborn, the 3rd Company was still employed in France.

Refitting at the Ohrdruf Taining Area in June 1944. It was here that the battalion received its first King Tigers. While there, the battalion also had the opportunity to allow its soldiers to participate in excursions to local areas of interest.

Tankers visiting the Wartburg in beautiful Thuringia, the "heart" of Germany.
Left to right: Obergefreiter Albers, Leutnant Rubbel, Obergefreiter Dahlmann, and an unidentified soldier.

Tiger 322 of the 2nd Platoon of the 3rd Company, Tiger Tank Battalion 503, with the Porsche turret. Ohrdruf, June 1944.

Initial gunnery exercises with
the new King Tiger.

The period of refitting nears
its end. The 1st and 2nd
Companies of Tiger Tank
Battalion 503 were issued the
King Tiger. The 3rd Company
had to deploy with the Tiger I.
Transport tracks are being
fitted at the home base of
Panzer Regiment 2 at
Eisenach.

Camouflage is being applied
to the new King Tigers.

The officers and noncommissioned officers of the 1st Company, Tiger Tank Battalion 503, during a NCO night out at Waltershausen, Thuringia, on 14 June 1944. First (top) row, right to left: Feldwebel Graumens, Unteroffizier Schwarzmann, Unteroffizier Michaelis, unknown, unknown, Unteroffizier Ellerbrock, unknown, unknown, Unteroffizier Sroka, Unteroffizier Sepke, Unteroffizier Johannsen, Feldwebel Vogt, and Unteroffizier Höppner. Second row: Feldwebel Tessmer, Unteroffizier Warms, unknown, Feldwebel Martach, unknown, Feldwebel Moscardini, unknown, Feldwebel Mewes, Feldwebel Wolf, unknown, Feldwebel Trenka, Unteroffizier Kuhtz, Stabsfeldwebel Ehrentraut, Stabsfeldwebel Schmidt, and Unteroffizier Zaic. Third row: Unteroffizier Vogel, Oberfeldwebel Hörnke, Oberfeldwebel Fendesack, unknown, unknown, Leutnant Linsser, Oberleutnant Oemler, Leutnant Schröder, and Hauptfeldwebel Wendt. Fourth row: Unteroffizier Schälke (?), Unteroffizier Eschrig, Unteroffizier Wilde, Unteroffizier Grasse, Unteroffizier Weidenkaff, Unteroffizier Knispel, Unteroffizier Scharf, Unteroffizier Kück, and Unteroffizier Manthei.

The tanks are zeroed in.

Fighter-bomber attack on the rail movement of the 3rd Company, Tiger Tank Battalion 503, at Esternay. Tiger 311 toppled over during the emergency unloading.

The tanks are ready to be loaded by rail. The transport tracks have been mounted and the skirt guards removed. The tanks are moving out to the rail station at Ohrdruf.

Another view of the approach march during the night to the invasion front.

During the night road march to the invasion front in the Caen area on 7 July 1944. Soldiers of the 16th Luftwaffe Field Division, to which the 503 was attached, marvel at the Tigers.

Tiger 123, commanded by
Feldwebel Seidel, rolls
towards the front.

And here it is after its fall.

18 July 1944, northeast of
Cagny: The Sherman of
Lieutenant Gorman of the
21st Irish Guards Armour
Regiment rammed Tiger 122
of Feldwebel Gerber of the
1st Company, Tiger Tank
Battalion 503. The course of
events is portrayed differently
by Gorman and Gerber in the
text of the book. This photo,
coming from French sources
and only recently discovered,
shows that the Tiger had not
pointed its cannon at the
Sherman. In addition, the
German crew was not
captured by the British.

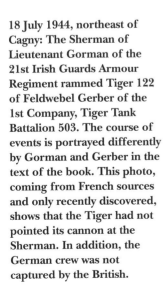

Assembly position of the 1st Company, Tiger Tank Battalion 503, on the grounds of the Chateau de Canteloup, 16 kilometers east of Caen, mid-July 1944. One can see two British prisoners of war (with guard) who are transporting two food containers. They did not belong to the 503.

Unteroffizier Gärtner, 3rd Company, Tiger Tank Battalion 503, was awarded the German Cross in Gold in July 1944. To his right is the company commander, Hauptmann Scherf.

July 1944, from left to right: Leutnant Heerlein, Hauptmann von Eichel-Streiber (company commander of the 503's 2nd Company) and Hauptmann Fromme (battalion commander).

Elements of the supply company in Normandy. Note the widespread use of the reed-green panzer uniform.

Battalion officers, left to right: Leutnant Heerlein, unknown, and Hauptmann Wiegand.

A break in the action in Normandy. Left to right: Hauptmann von Eichel-Streiber (commander of the 2nd Company, Tiger Tank Battalion 503), Hauptmann Wiegand (commander of the supply company), Oberarzt-Doktor Schramm (battalion surgeon), and Hauptmann Scherf (commander of the 3rd Company).

Oberfeldwebel Rondorf and Hauptmann Scherf of the 3rd Company. The battalion insignia can clearly be seen on Scherf's field cap. No reason is known for the presentation of the "adult beverages."

The battalion command post at Emieville prior to the carpet bombing on 18 July 1944.

After the carpet bombing at Maneville on 18 July 1944.

Tiger 313 was flipped upside down. The tank commander, Feldwebel Sachs, and another crew member were rescued alive.

Tiger 322 did not fare well either as a result of the carpet bombing.

Leutnant Heerlein, the battalion adjutant.

The dramatic situation at Falaise-Trun can be read on the faces of these soldiers from the 2nd Company, Tiger Tank Battalion 503.

Left: Tiger 213 moves along the Grand Rue Bourgtheroulde at Elbeuf in search of a Seine crossing.

Tigers of the 2nd Company of
Tiger Tank Battalion 503 take
a break on the move east to
the Seine.

On the west bank of the Seine
at Rouen. No bridge, no
ferries. Waiting for a miracle,
but first a bit of sleep. Who
knows when there may be
another opportunity? The
vehicles do not belong to
Tiger Tank Battalion 503.

Unteroffizier Heier, 1944.

In the bivouac area at Sompuis near Mailly-le-Camp. The 3rd Company, Tiger Tank Battalion 503, awaited new tanks there after its complement was destroyed during the fighting in Normandy.

Orders being issued to the 3rd Company. Standing in front of the formation, left to right: Feldwebel Schad, Feldwebel Grohmann, Leutnant Koppe, and Hauptmann Scherf. The battalion insignia can also be seen on Leutnant Koppe's cap.

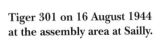

Tiger 301 on 16 August 1944 at the assembly area at Sailly.

British soldiers investigate a knocked out Tiger II of the 1st Company, Tiger Tank Battalion 503, which was abandoned at Plessis-Grimoult on 10 August 1944.

Two Tiger IIs of the 1st Company which became disabled at Vimoutiers and were blown up by their crews. The photos were taken by British soldiers between 13 and 20 August 1944.

The 3rd Company road-marches through Paris in August 1944.

On the Boulevard de la Chapelle in Paris. This photograph of Tiger 311 was reputedly taken by a member of the Resistance.

Two views of Tiger 300 at Oinville on 26 August 1944. This was the company commander's vehicle. Hauptmann Scherf's Tiger was later recovered.

King Tiger of the 3rd Company at Beauvais on 30 August 1944. This tank was knocked out by a Sherman Firefly after it had become mechanically disabled.

Gefreiter Walter Junge of the 3rd Company, Tiger Tank Battalion 503, points out battle damage on his tank, Tiger 301, at Sailly on 26 August 1944.

A demonstration conducted for the weekly newsreel at the Senne Training Area near Paderborn in September 1944. The 3rd Company was reinforced with tanks from the 1st Company for the "show." In the photo, Leutnant von Rosen passes in review. At the time, he was the acting commander of the company.

Tiger 313 (?) takes the lead in a company march formation. The commander is Feldwebel Kuhnert. The driver is Unteroffizier Runge.

In the foreground—still without a turret number—is a tank from the 1st Company. The tank commander has not been identified; Obergefreiter Schlenzek is in the loader's hatch. The newsreel wanted eight tanks in line to create a more dramatic effect.

The 3rd Company road-marched to the entraining station at Paderborn on 9 October 1944. The 80-centimeter-wide combat tracks were exchanged for the 60-centimeter loading tracks for the rail movement, since that reduced the overhang when the Tigers were loaded on the special railroad cars (Ssyms).

IN HUNGARY, AUSTRIA, AND CZECHOSLOVAKIA, 1944–45

CHAPTER 30

Employment in Hungary

Richard Freiherr von Rosen

TIGER TANK BATTALION 503 IN BUDAPEST: THE HORTHY CRISIS

The battalion assembled in the Paderborn area. The staff was at Neuhaus; the companies in the surrounding villages. The 1st Company was billeted at Bentfeld, the 2nd at Elsen, and the 3rd at Hövelhof. As many soldiers as possible were sent on leave, since there was no question the time in Germany would be short. However, the next area of operations was not known.

The companies were again filled out with personnel. The new men came from Panzer Replacement Battalion 500 at Paderborn. Leutnant Wagner was transferred to the 503's 3rd Company to become the third platoon leader. The number of wheeled vehicles was also increased to the extent that replacements were available. The civilian automobiles that had been brought along from France were turned in. Between 19 and 22 September 1944, forty-five Tiger IIs were rapidly issued to the battalion, bringing it back to its full complement of tanks. Time remained for instruction of the new personnel, preparing the tanks and zeroing the weapons until 9 October. The tanks were loaded in pouring rain at Paderborn, a few days after the 3rd Company, reinforced with tanks from the 1st Company, had to perform some "dog and pony" shows for the *Deutsche Wochenschau*

[*German Weekly Newsreel*]. The pictures are still in existence and repeatedly show up in various German and foreign publications.

Where were we headed? We soon confirmed that we were undoubtedly headed east: Halberstadt-Halle-Eger-Pilsen-Prague-Brünn-Pressburg. On 13 and 14 October the trains arrived at Budapest. The tanks were unloaded at the East Railroad Station.

13 October 1944: The battalion command post was set up in Dunaharaszti. The 1st Company moved to Czonemedi.

14 October 1944: The 3rd Company occupied billets at Taksony, 15 kilometers south of Budapest. During the move from the East Railroad Station, the company received an enthusiastic greeting from the populace. The soldiers were given apples, pralines and cigarettes. However, we also saw street barriers occupied by the Honveds [Hungarian army]. Antitank and antiaircraft guns were positioned with their barrels all directed threateningly toward the streets. What did that mean?

Something was in the air. During the course of the day rumors also reached us of the possibility of a Putsch. Heightened precautions were ordered. The soldiers remained in the local pubs with the villagers until late in the night.

15 October 1944: Leutnant von Rosen was ordered to the battalion command post at 0200

hours. New orders: "At dawn the 3rd Company moves with all of its elements to the other side of the Danube at Budakeszy."

A putsch by the Hungarian regime and military was clearly a possibility to be reckoned with. That necessitated that the few German units there draw closer together so as better to meet any eventuality. Therefore, all available units of Tiger Tank Battalion 503 were ordered to Budakeszi, a suburb on the edge of the Budapest Hills. That movement also negated the possibility that the tracked and wheeled units of the battalion might be cut off by a possible demolition of the bridges over the Danube.

The company marched at 0500 hours in the early morning—ready for combat—through Budapest. It set up under tall trees to the right of the Budapest-Budakeszi road. The battalion command post and the wheeled elements were in Budakeszi.

The situation cleared up at noon on 15 October. After the Red Army had also advanced into Hungary, the imperial regent, Admiral Horthy, instituted negotiations with the USSR and the Western powers. On 15 October he declared he had asked for a cease-fire with the Soviet Union: "I informed a representative of the German Reich that we were about to agree to a military truce with our former enemy and halt all military operations. . . . The commanders of the Honved have received corresponding instructions from me" (Nikolaus von Horthy, *Ein Leben für Ungarn*, Bonn: 1953, p. 325).

That proclamation, which was announced at 1300 hours over the radio, spread like wildfire. The attitude of the Hungarian units toward the German units deteriorated rapidly and took on a hostile character in some cases. The Honveds had erected barricades in Budapest. The majority of the Hungarian civilian population viewed it all uncomprehendingly. Resignation set in because there was a significant fear of the Russian troops.

The battalion was ordered to prepare for operations!

In the meantime, the pre-planned measures and actions of the opposition on the right proceeded. The "Arrow-Cross" men [Ferenc Szálasi's Hungarian Fascist Nyilas movement], who had seen in the radio proclamation the signal for their long-awaited hour of seizing power, occupied the radio station and proclaimed a counter-order. The Arrow-Cross organization, along with numerous Honved and police units and officers, spontaneously placed themselves on the German side. In the city gunfire erupted in places. (Nikolaus von Horthy, *Ein Leben für Ungarn*, Bonn: 1953, p. 325)

The battalion's Tigers moved to all the bridges over the Danube and blocked all traffic between the city halves of Buda and Pest. Hungarian units that were not known to be loyal to the Germans were disarmed.

The military action that had been planned for the 22nd SS Cavalry Division, Tiger Tank Battalion 503, and the forces available to the senior SS and police commander had to be postponed until the morning hours of 16 October, since all of the tanks had not yet arrived. (Friedrich Husemann, *Die guten Glaubens waren*, Osnabrück: Munin-Verlag, 1973, p. 424)

16 October 1944: At 0430 hours the Germans promised a cease-fire, with the condition that the Hungarians did the same.

At 0535 hours Admiral Horthy, under pressure from the German countermeasures, gave his bodyguard the order to offer no resistance.

At 0555 hours Admiral Horthy left his residence.

The military action started at 0600 hours. Admiral Horthy's order had not reached one battalion of the bodyguard in the park next to the residence, which resulted in a skirmish that left four German soldiers dead. The residence was occupied. The 503's 2nd Company took part in that operation. Elements of the 3rd Company stood by in readiness at the bottom of the hill where the residence was located. "In the city there were only insignificant skirmishes. The German units could therefore be pulled out in groups. The Honved and armed Arrow-Cross men took over security duty" (Kriegstagebuch des OKW, Band IV/1: 1. Januar 1944–22. Mai 1945).

With that, the mission of Tiger Tank Battalion 503 in Budapest was ended.

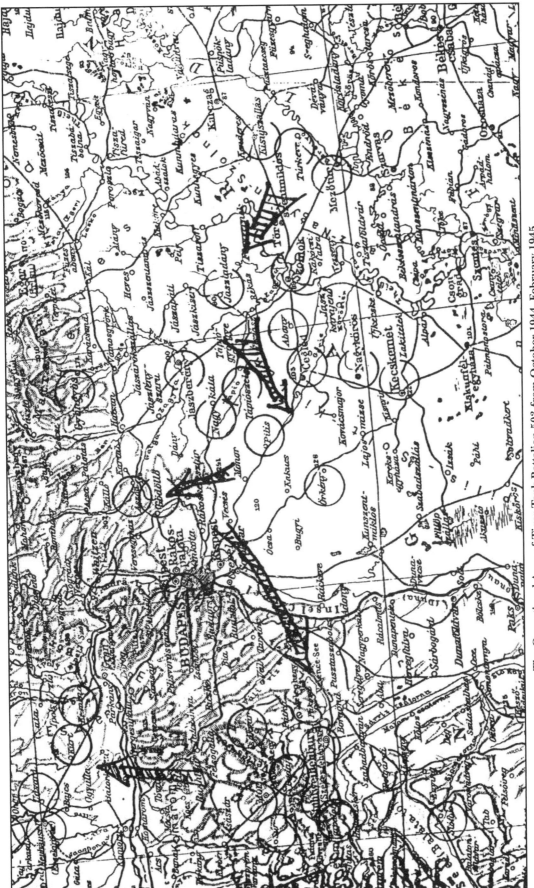

The Operational Area of Tiger Tank Battalion 503 from October 1944–February 1945.

THE ATTACK ON THE SZOLNOK BRIDGEHEAD AND THE FIGHTING ON THE THEISS

17 October 1944: What was the situation?

The immediate consequence of the call by the imperial regent, Admiral Horthy, for a cease-fire was that the Second Hungarian Armored Division, by order of the Commander-in-Chief of the Second Hungarian Army, Colonel General Verres, abandoned its positions in an extremely important sector and pulled back to the Theiß. The withdrawal took place without any consideration of its consequences for the neighboring formations which were still fighting. (Friedrich Husemann, *Die guten Glaubens waren*, Osnabrück: Munin-Verlag, 1973, p. 424)

The IV Panzer Corps—commanded by Generalleutnant Kleeman and assembled from the remnants of the staff of the IV Army Corps that had been smashed at Jassy—had been given the mission to break through the enemy on the east bank of the Theiß River east of Szolnok as soon as possible—but by 19 October at the latest—with the 24th Panzer Division and the 4th SS Police Division. It would then advance in a generally eastward direction into the deep flank of the Russian armored forces that were engaged with the III Panzer Corps at Debrecen.

That mission involved a relief attack as much for the weak German defenses along the Theiß River as for the hard-fighting German armored formations in the Puszta. As part of that operation, the 24th Panzer Division had to cross the bridge over the Thei· that was still available at the edge of Szolnok. It then had to assemble on the extremely narrow meadow area on the east bank of the river and, after a short artillery preparation, set out at first light to break through the enemy positions on the high bluffs. Following that, it had to turn toward the city of Mezötur, which was about 25 kilometers away. The division had to capture Mezötur and then, proceeding through Thurkeve, take the high ground southeast of Kisujszallas and later establish contact with the III Panzer Corps.

The 4th SS Police Division was to follow the 24th Panzer Division initially, then advance along the Szolnok-Debrecen road and thus cover the deep left flank of the 24th Panzer Division. As a result of the operation in Budapest, the units of that division did not arrive in and around Szolnok until sometime during the course of the day of 18 October. Therefore, the leaders' reconnaissance for the assembly position and attack had to be extraordinarily brief. Practically nothing was known about the enemy positions, not even the fact that a Rumanian infantry division was in the opposing positions. (F. M. von Senger und Etterlin, *Die 24. Panzer-Division, vormals 1. Kavallerie-Division, 1939–1945*, Neckargemünd: Kurt-Vowinckel-Verlag, 1962, p. 266 ff)

Tiger Tank Battalion 503 was placed under the operational control of the 24th Panzer Division and was to support the impending attack of that division at Szolnolk. As it turned out, a part of the battalion went to the 4th SS Police Division for the attack.

The tanks were entrained in Budapest. The wheeled vehicles moved by road march. Because of a shortage of the special Reichsbahn railroad cars (Ssyms), the companies could only follow each other, entraining when the train returned with the empty cars.

18 October 1944: The entire 1st Company unloaded at Abony. As evening approached two trains carrying the 3rd Company were sent to Cegled. The operations order for the coming day's attack arrived.

The 2nd Company and a platoon of the 3rd Company (Leutnant Wagner) did not arrive until the next day at the new area of operations and, by order of the IV Panzer Corps, were placed under the operational control of the 4th SS Police Division. As a result, Tiger Tank Battalion 503 was split into two parts. Hauptmann Fromme, the battalion commander, found himself with his command tank, Tiger "I," with the half of the battalion that was with the 24th Panzer Division. It had been given the mission of leading the thrust into the Russian flank as spearhead of the division.

19 October 1944: In pitch-black night, the 1st and 3rd Companies moved into the attack positions in the tiny Theiß bridgehead in the southeast portion of Szolnok. The commanders were briefed in the last calm before the storm. Leutnant Rambow received the Iron Cross, Second Class he had earned in France. The attack was to start at 0500 hours. The 1st Company was to be in front, led by Leutnant Piepgras. It would be followed by the 3rd Company. Von Rosen wrote the following in 1946:

Shortly after the lead tank had crossed the main line of resistance, the first Rumanians—they were the ones who held the positions in that sector—approached the tanks with their hands raised. It was possible to cross an embankment that ran across the direction of the attack and which had been a serious concern for the armor commanders during their map studies. The next village was rapidly reached, from which the Rumanians tried in vain to flee. They were waved to the rear since the tanks had no time to concern themselves with prisoners. An antitank belt facing the direction of the attack was overrun. As it turned out, the entire depth of the defensive position had been penetrated. Mines were discovered twice on the avenue of advance, but it was possible to drive around them. As a result, the Tigers thrust ever deeper into the hinterland. Enemy trains were surprised; entire columns swept from the road. Nothing could halt the forward advance. The tanks appeared like ghosts, a total surprise for the enemy.

At about 1000 hours, after advancing about 20 kilometers, the 3rd Company crossed a railroad line just as a long freight train approached the rail crossing with much steam and smoke. Tigers were rapidly brought into position both right and left of the rail crossing. One round and the locomotive disappeared in a cloud of smoke and steam. The train came to a standstill. It was an incomprehensible scene. Hundreds of Russian soldiers streamed from the cattle cars, all attempting to reach the safety of a small patch of woods. Riderless horses galloped in all directions. Rail cars loaded with vehicles and equipment were set ablaze by gunfire. The tanks had encountered a train carrying elements of a Russian guards cavalry division. However, there was little time to spend there. The 1st Company was already moving forward and the 3rd Company had to follow.

The city of Mezötur, the first intermediate objective of the battle group, was reached late in the afternoon. Forty kilometers had been covered. It was high time to refuel. The battalion went into a hedgehog position outside the city. The combat trains were brought forward. Mezötur, itself, was cleared by the 24th Panzer Division. That developed into localized fighting in several parts of the relatively large city. During the night, elements of Russian units that apparently had been unloaded on the open tracks southeast of Mezötur also became involved.

For Tiger Tank Battalion 503, the night in the hedgehog position was not quiet. Russian ground-attack planes attacked for a while in the evening. They dived on the battalion's tanks without causing significant damage. During the night, a Russian patrol was able to approach the commander's tank. The patrol was driven off by fire from machine pistols and several hand grenades. (Freiherr von Rosen, personal notes, 1946)

20 October 1944: It had already been determined the previous evening that the enemy had drawn strong forces from the Debrecen area to throw against this advance that endangered his flank. As a result, stronger enemy opposition had to be reckoned with that day.

In the gray light of dawn, the 3rd Company took over the point of the attack. Whereas the tanks had, until that point, advanced to the southeast, they then made a 90-degree turn and attacked toward the northeast. Orders gave the city of Turkeve as the new objective of the attack.

From there the attack was to continue as far as Kisujszallas. The lead tanks were already being fired on by antitank guns after the first 500 meters. The enemy had worked his way that close during the night. The situation was serious, since the route of the advance there ran along a causeway with marshy terrain on both sides. The 3rd Company could not deploy. Only the lead tanks could engage the enemy. Six antitank guns on both sides of the road opened fire on the Tiger by surprise. They were eliminated in less than ten minutes, but the Russians had additional antitank guns organized in depth. They defended themselves bitterly and with stubborn determination.

The tanks of the 3rd Company took many hits. If the Panzer IVs of the 24th Panzer Division had been forced to take the lead, not a single one of them would have made it through. The strong frontal armor of the King Tiger withstood the antitank rounds. Nothing could stop them and the tanks at the point chewed their way right through the strong antitank defense until they could gain open and negotiable terrain. However, the satisfaction at the success did not last long, for within a few kilometers they came up against the next antitank gun belt. Again, the lead tanks were hit dead on. Again, several tanks were disabled with damage to guns or tracks. That defensive belt was also penetrated. Within a few kilometers the company found itself in the midst of an infantry position with tank hunter/killer teams. They attacked the Tigers with satchel charges and Molotov cocktails. There was only one way to deal with that: Blast through at full throttle and with all machine guns blazing.

The battle group approached Turkeve. We had planned to bypass the city on the left and then attack it from its rear. But that was easier said than done, since the entire outskirts of the place were thick with antitank guns. The tanks again took frontal hits, with the result that, gradually, almost all of the tanks were disabled. Leutnant von Rosen's tank received a hit directly beneath the main gun, preventing the tank from firing. However, he continued to lead the attack. Finally, there were only three King Tigers from the 3rd Company left in the attack. The company commander covered the last 1,000 meters to Turkeve with them. He then reached the northeast outskirts of the city and advanced into it from there. The Russians began to clear out.

During the nearly five hours of attack, the 3rd Company had destroyed thirty-six antitank guns, thereby chewing its way kilometer by kilometer through the enemy in uncommonly tough and bitter fighting. The company had several wounded, but no men were killed and none of the tanks were total losses.

During the hours that followed, individual tanks that had succeeded in repairing their damage linked up with the company. As a result, the company had six tanks operationally ready. That was a particularly praiseworthy accomplishment for Feldwebel Gro·mann, who was always at the very front with his maintenance section and accomplished miracles of repair.

As noon approached, the division commander came forward with praise for the company and a short discussion of the continued attack. The second intermediate objective was the city of Kisujszalla. It was important the success should be rapidly exploited and the enemy denied further time for renewed defensive measures. Apparently, the King Tigers had had a significant effect on his morale and he slowly began to soften up.

The attack initially continued well the next afternoon. After moving about 15 kilometers, the tanks turned off the main road and slowly approached the city. They reached the Kisujszallas-Devavanya road. From there, they had a good view of the improved road from Debrecen to Kisujszallas a few kilometers away. An unbroken line of tanks, trucks and, above all, antitank guns rolled along it into the city. Between fifty and seventy antitank guns were counted in a very short time. There was no way to take the city in a coup de main against that sort of superiority and even less chance of holding it if it were captured. The battle group assumed a hedgehog position not far from the city. Supplies came during the night without any serious interference. Reconnaissance efforts revealed early in the morning that the enemy had reinforced his armor forces to the northeast.

21 October 1944: During the morning of 21 October, the battle group received orders to pull back to Turkeve. The Russians had recaptured the city of Mezötur behind the battle group. Hauptmann Fromme and the 1st Company rolled back to Mezîtur and were immediately involved there in heavy street fighting. During the short time that the Russians had been back in the city they had even been able to position a 7.62cm antitank gun in a church steeple. For the first time, the battalion encountered the American 5.7cm antitank gun. It was capable of penetrating even the frontal armor of the Tiger. Leutnant Beyer was wounded by just such a round that penetrated his tank. Oberfeldwebel Markus and Unteroffizier Schielke were killed.

As ordered, the 3rd Company remained at Turkeve. Fighting developed at Turkeve with Russian tanks attacking from the northeast. The combat trains, which were following the combat elements during the attack, were attacked by the Russians. The company lost its first soldiers killed in Hungary. A prime mover and a truck were lost. The maintenance section worked feverishly to prepare disabled tanks and wheeled vehicles for towing. As evening approached, the company received orders to pull out. They were to reestablish contact with the battalion staff in the Mezötur area.

Since enemy pressure, particularly on the neighboring formation to the left, the 4th SS Police Division, had markedly increased along the Debrecen-Szolnok road, the attack was completely broken off on 21 October. The 24th Panzer Division had to make possible the formation of a new Theiß bridgehead by defending the village of Törökszentmiklos. (F. M. von Senger und Etterlin, *Die 24. Panzer-Division, vormals 1. Kavallerie-Division, 1939–1945*, Neckargemünd: Kurt-Vowinckel-Verlag: 1962, p. 266 ff.)

The 24th Panzer Division and the lead battle group of Tiger Tank Battalion 503 were to execute the withdrawal to the hill at Törökzentmiklos during the night and following morning. They would link up there with the formations of the 4th SS Police Division and the trail battle group of Tiger Tank Battalion 503 under Hauptmann Wiegand. Battle Group Wiegand consisting of the 2nd Company and one platoon of the 3rd Company under Leutnant Wagner didn't arrive at the offload station until 19 October. By that point, the battalion (minus), consisting of the 1st Company and two platoons of the 3rd Company, had already been attacking with the 24th Panzer Division. Contrary to prior plans, Battle Group Wiegand was not sent by the IV Panzer Corps to the 24th Panzer Division. Instead, it was committed with the 4th SS Police Division. That division's mission read that it was to advance from Törökszentmiklos through Kenderes to Kisujszallas and attack that city along with the 24th Panzer Division.

On 20 October Hauptmann Wiegand set out with his battle group from Törökszentmiklos. His mission was to advance 35 kilometers deep into enemy territory while braking any opposition. He was to capture and hold Kenderes as his day's objective. When the battle group got to Szaparfalu, it ran into a strong antitank and armor defenses which brought the attack temporarily to a standstill. The situation became critical when the enemy fired on the tanks from the front and flanks of the battle group. Hauptmann Wiegand advanced into the middle of the antitank belt with his tanks, overran two antitank guns, and then rolled up the entire defensive belt from the flank, even though he took direct hits on the turret and gun. The battle group was able to destroy twenty heavy antitank guns and artillery pieces as well as knock out an enemy tank and break the enemy resistance. The day's objective, Kenderes, was taken as ordered (Tiger Tank Battalion 503 "Feldherrnhalle": Award Recommendation for the German Cross in Gold for Hauptmann Wiegand, dated 18 March 1945).

The 503's 3rd Company suffered a painful loss in the process: Leutnant Wagner was so severely wounded that his left arm had to be amputated.

On 21 October that attack also had to be broken off because the forces of the Russian 6th Guards Tank Army that had been brought up were too powerful. Battle Group Wiegand then made its way back to the hill at Törökszentmiklos, as ordered. It then linked up with the main body of Tiger Tank Battalion 503.

Until that happened, however, the 24th Panzer Division with the lead battle group of Tiger Tank Battalion 503 first had to fight its way there. What made the situation bad was the fact that the enemy situation was totally unclear and that, by then, any immobile tanks had to be towed there if they hadn't already been repaired. Since the majority of the operational Tigers were needed for the towing, the motorcycle soldiers [*Kradschützen*] of the 24th Panzer Divsion had to take over the lead.

The Tigers moved in the first third of the long army column. In an emergency, they would be quickly available. There was a row of tanks, each with a second in tow. Since the march could only be conducted at night, the distances covered were quite limited and everyone hoped that the Russians would not be active.

22 October 1944: Early on 22 October, Hauptmann Fromme and his Tiger battle group were about 15 kilometers from Törökszentmiklos when the order was received: "Halt!" Friendly reconnaissance had reported strong enemy forces on the left flank. The hope of getting through to Törökszentmiklos without enemy contact was thus destroyed.

The battalion attacked. The 3rd Company, with five tanks, was in the lead. The 2nd Company followed. It was early morning, brisk and foggy. The attack sector was meadowland with fruit trees, scattered farmsteads and hedgerows, a highly unsuitable terrain for attacking tanks. Visibility was limited to 100 meters at best. Von Rosen wrote the following in 1946:

After about 2 kilometers we made out the first Russians. They fled head over heels in the fog, abandoning all their equipment. The company had dispersed, meaning it attacked in line with an interval of about 50 meters between the tanks.

All of a sudden, I saw a gun in position about 80 meters in front of me. In the same instant, we also had a direct hit on the turret which took our breath away. I could not even fire the gun. The gun had been put out of action two days earlier by a direct hit I received at Turkeve. I had not changed tanks since I did not want any other tank commander leading a tank that was not completely ready for action.

That hit was immediately followed by a second direct hit on the right final drive. It was followed by a third one on the left final drive. We sat, God forsaken, in a tank that was no longer capable of moving. We were waiting for the round that penetrated. The neighboring tank finally noticed my situation and knocked out the gun. Afterwards we saw that it had been a 10.5 centimeter howitzer that had plastered me over open sights. The front armor on the turret was torn and a deep hole had been bored in the armor, but the round had not penetrated. Leutnant Piepgras was wounded in that attack.

Leutnant Fürlinger, who had taken over Tiger 112, had continued to attack with somewhat too much zeal. Without paying attention to the other tanks, which was, indeed, difficult in the fog, he stormed forward and suddenly found himself in the rear of an antitank defensive belt that had not yet been eliminated. At first the Russians were stunned, but they then dragged their guns around and fired on Leutnant Fürlinger's tank at pointblank range from all their guns. It was a miracle that his tank remained capable of moving and could make it back to the German tanks. He had twenty-four direct hits on his tank. The tanks of the 3rd Company were also able to knock out several antitank guns. The resistance was broken. Two Tigers towed mine away and we were able to establish contact that afternoon with the units that were already in Törökszentmiklos. Tiger Tank Battalion 503 reassembled there. (Freiherr von Rosen, personal notes, 1946)

23 October 1944: The attack was broken off in the morning. It had been rendered pointless by changes in the overall situation:

The involvement of the two divisions with the attached battle groups of Tiger Tank Battalion 503 had been unable to affect the outcome of the fighting around Debrecen, which fell into Russ-

ian hands on 21 October. However, it was able to slow the Russians down and thereby contributed to preventing the Russians from advancing into the rear of Armeegruppe Wöhler, which was painfully fighting its way back to the Theiß. The continuity of the front had been assured. (F. M. von Senger und Etterlin, *Die 24. Panzer-Division, vormals 1. Kavallerie-Division, 1939–1945*, Neckargemünd: Kurt-Vowinckel-Verlag, 1962, p. 266 ff)

24–31 October 1944: During the days that followed, the operational elements of the battalion were committed in several small battle groups on both sides of Szolnok to secure the crossings at the Theiß. A bridgehead was able to be held at Szolnok. The damaged tanks were towed away. The maintenance facility at Jaszladany worked in high gear. From 23-26 October, a battle group of the 3rd Company, led by Leutnant Rambow, secured in the Theiß bridgehead. Another battle group, under Leutnant von Rosen, launched several local attacks. The Russians were hard to pin down and often disappeared as soon as the Tigers arrived. In the meantime, the rainy period had begun and it poured in torrents. The ground, especially at the banks of the river, was bottomless mud.

In several places the Russians had already crossed the Theiß. On 28 October, the 3rd Company was committed south of Szolnok on the west bank of the Theiß at Toszeg. Tiger 321 was disabled with a hit on the rear deck by a mortar round. Gefreiter Meß was killed on 27 October in a battle group of the 1st Company. The operations on the Theiß offered little satisfaction, since there was hardly any visible success and yet one had to remain ready for action and prepared for an enemy attack. It was wet and cold and totally depressing.

In the meantime, the Russians had strengthened their bridgehead over the Theiß. The Tigers could only delay its expansion.

At the end of October, the battalion assembled at Cegled, 35 kilometers west of Szolnok. Seven tanks of the 3rd Company were again operational. A new operation was imminent. The battalion moved to Nagykörös. The situation there was extremely uncomfortable. Russian ground attack aircraft fired on anything that moved on the ground. The companies suffered losses.

OPERATIONS IN THE CEGLED-KESKEMET AREA

1 November 1944: Jaszladany was evacuated. The maintenance facility had been there. The damaged tanks were towed to Cegled, or crept there on their own, to the extent that they were still somewhat mobile. The route from Jaszladany through Abony was already under artillery fire.

The situation outside of Budapest had dramatically worsened:

On 1 November 1944, strong Russian forces were advancing from Kecskamet toward Budapest. In so doing they went around the 24th Panzer Division on either side of Kecskamet. They temporarily split the 24th Panzer Division into three groups, as well as overrunning the forward division command post. In the early afternoon of that crisis-rich day, a Russian-Rumanian assault group got into the southeast part of Nagykörös, but was beaten back again a little later. (Ernst Rebentisch, *Die Geschichte der 23. Panzerdivision, 1941 bis 1945*, p. 434)

Tiger Tank Battalion 503 attacked at about 1500 hours together with the 21st Panzer Grenadier Regiment from the area southwest of Nagykörös to the east in order to cut a way clear for the units of the 24th Panzer Division that were encircled in Kecskemet. That time the 2nd Company led the attack. The 3rd Company, battalion staff, and the 1st Company followed. A little later the battalion encountered enemy troops that were moving across the front. They were following the Russian formations that had already broken through toward Budapest. They were completely surprised to again run into opposition. Up till then, no one had stood in the way of their forward push toward Budapest. Von Rosen wrote the following in 1946:

Our attack proceeded further along the road to Kecskemet. All of a sudden, the 2nd Company encountered strong antitank guns. From my position, I was unable to participate. The lead vehicle, commanded by Leutnant Brodhagen, went up in flames. The terrain on both sides of the road offered limited observation, consisting of vineyards and gardens with bits of meadow and fields in between. In the meantime, dusk was falling and the visibility got worse and worse. One could only pick out the enemy positions by the muzzle flashes of the guns as they fired. Those were the only aiming points available for fighting the enemy in the twilight. There was no way to frontally attack the Russians in this instance.

The lead elements came to a halt and Hauptmann Fromme ordered the 3rd Company to swing far to the right and attack from the flank. However, the Russians knew well why they had placed their antitank guns in position there. The terrain on both sides of the road was marshy. Two King Tigers of the 3rd Company bogged down, an uncomfortable situation to be in when in full view of the enemy. The marshy ground therefore made it impossible to go around the antitank gun position. As a result, assault troops of grenadiers were employed. They rooted out the Russian positions and pockets of resistance under covering fire from the tanks. When the Russians saw what was happening, they pulled out relatively quickly. After that, it was possible to establish contact with the units that had been encircled in Kecskamet with no further problems. That completed the mission. The Russians, however, were again unimpeded in their advance on Budapest.

During the night, the tanks that had got stuck in the soft ground were recovered. That is quickly written down, but how many bad breaks were suffered? How often did the tow cable have to be put back on? How often did it break? How often did a tank that seemed freed return to its starting point? That was the hardest of hard work. (Freiherr von Rosen, personal notes, 1946)

2 November 1944:

During the course of the night, Tiger Tank Battalion 503 was placed under the operational control of the 23rd Panzer Regiment of the 23rd Panzer Division, which was commanded by Oberstleutnant Prinz zu Waldeck. At the same time, the newly formed battle group, to which some Panzer IVs were added from the 24th Panzer Division, moved to Sashalom, 10 kilometers southwest of Cegled. Starting at 0940 hours, it would advance in the direction of the 1st Panzer Division, which had to move out at the same time from Örkeny. The intent was to sever the rearward lines of communication of the enemy who was advancing to Budapest. (Ernst Rebentisch, *Die Geschichte der 23. Panzerdivision, 1941 bis 1945*, p. 434)

The mixed battle group, consisting of Sturmgeschütze, Panzer IVs, Panthers, and King Tigers, as well as SPWs, encountered strong enemy resistance shortly after the start of the attack. The Panthers led the attack and had difficulty in engaging a skillfully constructed antitank gun position on the edge of marshy terrain among low-lying vegetation. The attack soon came to a halt. The cry rang out: "Tigers to the front!" Von Rosen wrote the following in 1946:

I attacked with the 3rd Company. The situation initially looked very sticky but, after a short time, we had knocked out ten antitank guns. Several antiaircraft guns, trucks and other equipment were abandoned; the Russians had quickly pulled out under the pressure from the Tigers. After that line of resistance had been broken, we then advanced as the spearhead, ever deeper behind the Russian lines. Our mission was to reach a designated point about 25 kilometers away and link up with the 1st Panzer Division which was advancing to meet us from Örkeny. That would cut the Russians advancing toward Budapest off from their supplies. However, that was not what happened. After we had advanced another three kilometers, the company encountered enemy tanks in difficult, uphill terrain. The enemy armor was well concealed in the edge of the woods and was not spotted until after it had opened fire.

After the first of the Russian tanks had been set on fire, the others took off into the countryside. Our attack continued. In order to advance more rapidly, the riflemen rode on our tanks. Only the two lead tanks of the company moved without infantry mounted on them. We put kilometer after kilometer behind us in that manner. The Russians could emerge from behind the corner of every patch of woods and, after a while, we encountered enemy tanks again. We spotted enemy tanks in an isolated farmstead at 1,500 meters and immediately opened a firefight. We noticed a particularly brilliant muzzle flash from several of the Russian tanks. That was our first encounter with the Stalin tanks with a 12.2cm gun and very heavy armor. What would be the outcome of that engagement? Then the first Stalin tank was in flames! Onward! The attack sector became increasingly marshy at spots.

Feldwebel Seidel and his Tiger 313 found a soft spot, and it was immediately buried up to the track guards. We couldn't stop then; we had to go on. It was already getting noticeably dark, and we had several more kilometers ahead of us. So I left Feldwebel Weigel and his tank to protect Tiger 313. However, it was easy to see that the terrain was too unfavorable. There was no firm ground for the recovery tanks to negotiate.

We made it to the objective of our attack by dark, a road intersection in the midst of the woods. Security was established in all directions. We established radio contact with the 1st Panzer Division, but they were still far away. A link-up with the 1st Panzer Division in the foreseeable future seemed to be ruled out. Our situation, therefore, was anything but rosy. Once again, we were in the midst of the Russians and deep behind their lines. We had used up half of our fuel. From near and far we could hear the typical sounds of Russian tanks.

The Russians seemed to have been thrown into confusion somewhat by our advance. After several hours, the order came from our corps to break off the attack and return to the previous start point. Our new order: "To the rear, march!" By order of the battalion, the 3rd Company remained as the lead company. We thus had to count on enemy contact during the return march. When we got back to Feldwebel Seidel and his Tiger 313, we broke off the march and again studied the possibilities for recovering the tank. Then Hauptmann Fromme gave the order to blow it up. It was the first total loss of the 3rd Company in Hungary. Leutnant Heerlein's tank set it ablaze with a main gun round. We reached our starting point, the village of Sashalom, as morning broke. (Freiherr von Rosen, personal notes, 1946)

With that, the first operations in Hungary came to a close. Several days followed in which the battalion was not committed. Only a few tanks were operational, and only for limited action, at that. In the last two weeks there had not been a single day we were not employed and no time at all for maintenance service. The tanks had put on between 400 and 500 kilometers and urgently needed service and maintenance. Since all of the tanks had held up well until that point, the moment arrived when all of them needed attention. The recovery means available were totally inadequate to deal with such a massive breakdown of tanks. Therefore, the few tanks not disabled had to tow the others. Top priority became restoring combat readiness as rapidly as possible. The maintenance facilities needed several days of undisturbed work for that.

The remainder of the 3rd Company moved through Cegled to Cegled Bercel, where the maintenance company had been for a short time. It was intended to tow the damaged tanks on to Budapest on the improved road. Rail loading would have taken too much time, which the Russians no longer allowed. They pressed from all sides and were even nearing Cegled Bercel.

At 2300 hours a column of about twelve damaged tanks, some of them in tow, moved from Cegled along the road toward Budapest. The column was led by Leutnant Rambow.

3 November 1944: Early in the morning the column passed Bercel. Between Albertisa and Pilis it was strafed by low flying aircraft. At Ullö, about 15 kilometers outside of Budapest, it encountered a Russian antitank obstacle, totally by surprise. The sector had seemed secure, but the Russians had succeeded during the night in breaking through that far. There were no German units available to seal off the breakthrough. Probably it had not yet been reported. For Leutnant Rambow, as commander of the march group, the situation was abominable. With the disabled and partially immobile Tigers, he could not defend himself. The leading tank, Tiger 300, was set on fire by the antitank guns. The crew bailed out. In spite of the enemy fire, Leutnant Rambow and his men were able to cut the tow cable and, finally, save the other tanks. (See also the report by Niemann.)

The march moved back to Pilis and from there through Kava, Gomba, and Uri to Tapiosüly. Two maintenance platoons moved there on 3 November and set to work in high gear. The third maintenance platoon moved to Totmegyer, almost on the Slovakian border, where it could work on the most serious damage without being endangered by surprise shifts of the front. The damaged tanks that were intended for that platoon were loaded at Tapiosüly onto the Ssyms rail cars that had been sent forward. The tanks with the most serious damage of all, which even the third maintenance platoon lacked means to repair, were sent to Vienna for repair at the depot.

With the breakthrough to Ullö, the Russians had reached the outskirts of Budapest for all prac-

tical purposes. In the days that followed, they were able to advance into the outskirts to a certain extent, but then remained where they were for a long time. For the battalion, however, the direct route to Budapest was blocked. It had to fall back to the north and, in the afternoon, it moved to the Aszod area. The 3rd Company was given billets in Koka.

4 November 1944: Cegled and Abony fell to the Russians.

5 November 1944: The battalion and the tank companies moved to the Gödöllö area. The corps staff was also there. The battalion was mentioned in the Wehrmacht Report.

JASBERENY AND GYONGOS: FIGHTING IN THE MATRA MOUNTAINS

The 3rd Company moved back to Koka. The overall situation was rather ticklish. A Kampf-gruppe was formed from the eight battalion tanks that had been made operational in the meantime. They included several tanks from the 3rd Company, which were led by Leutnant Rambow. Oberleutnant Oemler commanded the battle group, which was placed under the operational control of the 13th Panzer Division. It was employed until 13 November in the Jaszbereny-Nagykala-Tapioszele area.

9 November 1944: The battalion command post moved to Tura. The company trains went back to Gödöllö.

15 November 1944: Leutnant von Rosen took over command of the battle group, which assembled in the Hatvan area. Twelve Tigers from the tank companies were operational. In addition, the battalion's flak platoon was attached to the battle group with its vehicular-mounted quad antiaircraft guns. In order to maintain radio communications with the battalion over long distances, Tiger I of the battalion headquarters, which had medium-wave radio equipment, was provided to the battle group. The battle group was also given its own combat trains, which imparted a degree of autonomy in both supply and repair. Thus, in addition to a field kitchen, recovery elements and maintenance services under Werkmeister Späth belonged to the trains. The command and control relationship of the battle group was changed; it was then placed under the operational control of the 1st Panzer Regiment of the 1st Panzer Division.

18 November 1944: Until 18 November, the battle group had to cover a large sector, which

could only be guarded with difficulty due to unfavorable terrain conditions. The battle group then covered the withdrawal of elements of the 1st Panzer Division to a new line of defense at Gyöngyös. Again and again, it had to intervene as the "fire brigade" if enemy tanks appeared somewhere in the sector or if some other problem developed. On 18 November, the Russians surprised us with an intense raid by ground-attack aircraft. The bombs fell among the tanks which were getting ready to move out. There were several seriously wounded among the flak platoon, the open antiaircraft vehicles providing little protection. Late in the afternoon the battle group reached Gyöngyöspata in the Matra mountains where it initially served as the division's reserve.

19 November 1944: During the night of 18–19 November, the Russians advanced into Gyöngyös by surprise. Elements of an infantry division were in the city. With the surprise appearance of the Russians, they fled. Since it was feared that the enemy would break through the front between Budapest and the Matra Mountains, it was ordered "from above" that the city be retaken. However, the requisite means to do that were not on hand.

The battle group, which had been alerted in Gyöngyöspata in the early morning hours, immediately moved out to Gyöngyös. About 10 kilometers outside the city, the battle group encountered a confused mass of fleeing soldiery that blocked the entire highway with its vehicles. It was difficult to swim against that stream. In addition, an intense attack by Russian ground-attack aircraft stirred up the pot in that cauldron of confusion.

The battle group only made it to the outskirts of the city of Gyöngyös. German units had blown up a road bridge over a ravine just outside the city that could not be circumvented. As a result, the tanks took up position there for a while and raked the suspicious houses on the outskirts of the city. That soon stilled what had initially been quite lively enemy infantry fire.

Gradually the Panzer IVs of Panzer-Regiment 1 also arrived, accompanied by the regimental commander, Major D.

New situation: The armored units of the 1st Panzer Division—all commanded by Major D and including the Tiger battle group—were placed under the operational control of the infantry division that had just fled out of Gyöngyös. All units

were immediately to close up with that division, but the route led directly through the center of the city and was, thus, impassable. Von Rosen wrote the following in 1946:

Therefore, we had to go cross-country. That was difficult in the hilly terrain. We moved right through the vineyards. The Tigers, which sank deep into the soft earth, laboriously crawled up the steep slopes and down again on the other side. A stream had to be forded, but the last 50 meters, in particular, were the most difficult. In order to reach the hard-surface road on which we were to provide cover toward the city, we had to negotiate a steep slope.

The first tank climbed the slope, but then the soft ground was so chewed up that that tank had to tow the others up, one vehicle at a time. That was all further complicated by the fact that the Russians had set up an antitank gun on a water tower at the edge of the city with which they maintained an accurate fire on us. However, we then proceeded to take them out.

The Panzer IVs of the 1st Panzer Regiment did not make it on that route. The few tanks that the regiments still had got stuck back in the vineyards. Only Major D's command tank—towed by a Tiger—made it through the difficult terrain. Several of my Tigers were also disabled along the way, some early in the morning. Others hopelessly bogged down in the difficult terrain, so that my proud fighting force only consisted of five Tigers at that point.

I covered the approaches to the city with three tanks. Unteroffizier Gärtner (3rd Company) and Feldwebel Jakob (2nd Company) were with me. Feldwebel Bornschier and an additional Tiger covered another exit road about one kilometer away.

When darkness fell, I was ordered to Major D's command post. I drove there with the Kettenkrad. The order had come from the corps that the infantry division was to recapture the city with our help. Not a nice mission, but we could see the purpose. When I then learned the details, however, I was a bit shaken.

It was ordered that we were to attack in two attack groups on two different approach roads at night. The right-hand attack group, under my command, consisted of my three Tigers, six or seven SPWs that were armed with triple antiaircraft mounts and, in addition, about 100 infantry-men who came direct from a march company of returning convalescents. They had been hastily assembled as a company. They only had infantry weapons and lacked all drive and spirit. The spear point of the attack—if that's what you wanted to call it—was with my attack group. The left-hand attack group, with Feldwebel Born-schier's two Tigers, was about equal in its "strength." We were in mutual communication by radio.

Led by Major D, that fighting force was meant to force its way through the city starting at 0200 hours. It would then establish contact with the elements of the infantry that were on the far side of the city. However, those infantry units, for their part, were not to take part in the attack. That operation would have led through the houses and confused streets of a city that was not exactly small and that had been held by the Russians for twenty-four hours and who expected us to attack. What insanity!

I briefed my commanders. The old, experi-enced tank men knew what a night attack in such a city involved. At around 2200 hours I was called to the infantry division for a briefing on the oper-ation. A coordination meeting followed with the commanders of the SPWs and the infantry. My protests against the operation were rejected by the division commander. The corps had ordered the attack and no one dared to raise objections. The infantry division's conscience still twinged after it had been overrun by the Russians during the previous night and it had abandoned the city head over heels.

By radio I requested my supplies from Tiger Tank Battalion 503, as I did every evening. The supplies had to be brought to us over about 50 kilometers of deeply snow-covered roads through the Matra Mountains. The large trucks could not follow our cross-country path through the vine-yards. I then reported to the battalion command post regarding the operation ordered by the corps. I had an encoded, keyed transmission sent: "The corps has ordered a night attack on Gyöngyösch. Long live the Führer!"

That was no expression of special Nazi senti-ment. Instead, it alerted the battalion we had been sent on a suicide mission where the chances of sur-vival were slim. The battalion staff immediately understood that, and the commander sent Leut-

nant Heerlein to the corps command post to inter-vene. However, the decision of the commanding general remained unchanged.

19 November 1944: At 0200 hours on the dot, we set out from Major D's command post. He led the two attack groups by radio from there.

Unteroffizier Gärtner's was the point vehicle. Behind my tank came Feldwebel Jakob. The SPWs with the mounted grenadeirs followed the Tigers and the 100 infantrymen trotted along to the rear. They were supposed to be even, advanc-ing to the right and let of them. We got to the first houses of the city and fired in the darkness with everything we had, simulating a larger com-bat force. The antiaircraft SPWs with their triple mounts did the same. The Russians decamped. By the light of the flares we fired we could see their abandoned positions as we passed them. The muzzle flash of the first antitank gun blazed out on the left. It fired too high, which was easy to do at night. The tracers whizzed past us, over our heads. The lead tank fired and the antitank gun was silenced.

We slowly shoved our way forward and reached the water tower from which we had been fired on at mid-day. The pale light of flares briefly illuminated the street ahead of us. The darkness of the night was all the more impenetrable when they went out. I could not make out the vehicle in front of me. Only his exhaust flames shim-mered faintly. Slowly, we felt our way forward. There, blatsch, an antitank round impacted in front of us. Unteroffizier Gärtner, ahead of me, also reported hits by antitank rounds. If only the infantry would advance even with us and clean out the houses to the right and left. They were packed with Russians.

At that point, we had advanced about one kilometer into the city. Blam: A hit from the right. The Russians had antitank guns positioned in the doorways of the houses. They were pre-pared and had intentionally allowed us to get that far into the city. We fired high explosive round after high explosive round along the rows of houses. It calmed down somewhat. I was almost out of flares. A further advance, without having the infantry on line with us to clean out the houses on both sides was impossible.

Accordingly, I ordered: "Halt." I dismounted and, armed with a machine pistol, hastened back to the infantry. At last I found their leader, an

Oberleutnant. He was helpless and had no control over his men. A spirited Unteroffizier volunteered and went with me with his squad to clean out the houses on both sides of my three tanks. As the infantrymen entered the first courtyard with the Unteroffizier in the lead, he fell, fatally shot. At that instant the infantrymen vanished and I stood there, all alone. A flare hissed on high, fired from our first tank, and I saw that I was barely two meters from a Russian antitank gun. The crew had bolted. How easily that could have gone wrong! At that point, the grenadiers mounted on the SPWs had to get involved. And those men did, in fact, advance with machine pistols, hand grenades and Panzerfäuste. They cleaned out the houses and street to our right and left. We renewed our forward progress and soon reached a major intersection.

There, however, the grenadiers encountered such heavy Russian resistance that they could not move forward. The attack again came to a halt. As the day dawned, we knocked out two antitank guns at the intersection. There was no way to tell how many, however, lurked beyond that point. The Russians exerted heavy pressure from both sides and returned over roofs and through backyards. The situation got even more uncomfortable. We closely watched the street in front of us, the houses, doors, windows and roofs. The Russians were emerging everywhere. If you were so careless as to stick your head a bit out of the tank, then a shot zipped past.

Suddenly, I saw a man come out of a house and approach Unteroffizier Gärtner's tank quite calmly. He was a civilian, and I waved to him to come to me. Then he suddenly threw a satchel charge, which he had skillfully kept hidden. Before I could react he had again disappeared in the house. The grenadiers were then hit from behind with fire from machine pistol fire. They had to clear out of the houses. One could not deny the Russians a certain level of aplomb.

In the midst of that mess, I received a radio message from Major D who was still in his command tank outside the city: "Continue the attack." Was he totally insane? I let him repeat the message, then I acknowledged it. It would be lunacy to continue the attack by day. Therefore, I had all three Tigers at our location rev up their motors and we delivered another barrage from all barrels, so that the noise of the fighting could be heard back at the command post. I then reported by radio that an advance past the intersection was impossible. Our situation grew more dangerous. All of a sudden, Molotov cocktails hurtled down from the roofs and satchel charges were hurled from doors and windows. The enemy assault troops renewed their approach. In the meantime, Unteroffizier Gärtner's tank suffered damage to a track. Woe to us if a track broke here! And so we remained there for a few more hours.

Why did we have to hang onto that part of the city? Our thoughts regarding the higher levels of command were not exactly friendly! The Russians renewed their attack. Once again, they had slowly worked their way forward on our right and left and poured a sudden blast of fire on the poor grenadiers. They were on the receiving end of a veritable hail of bullets. They had to pull back, suffering substantial losses. Finally, the order also reached us to fall back. By then it was two hours past noon. We had held the positions for twelve hours. I covered the withdrawal with the Tigers. By then, however, the Russians had closed in behind us. It was high time to get out. Rolling slowly backwards, and firing on everything, we pulled back.

That was the end of the attack. It was the only attack I can remember where we failed to accomplish our mission.

I got new orders from Major D: The battle group was to move to Gyöngyöspata as the ready reserve of the 1st Panzer Division. In the meantime, the division had scouted out a route that was ostensibly negotiable for tracked vehicles. On that route, however, a Tiger that had been repaired by the company maintenance section got hopelessly stuck in a defile when it tried to get to the battle group. I got that report as evening approached, when I had already set out toward Gyöngyöspata with my tanks. At the same time, we received another piece of bad news. Leutnant Rambow had set out along that route in a Kettenkrad to get to me. He had an accident and had to be taken to a hospital. At that point, I no longer had any officers in the company. That made eight Leutnants that the battalion had lost.

Before it got dark, I borrowed a Schwimmwagen from Major D and drove to the spot where the tank was stuck. It is almost impossible to conceive of the state of the route. It consisted of deep, bottomless mud which even the cross-country Schwimmwagen barely navigated. We had to push the vehicles for whole stretches, so the trip took several hours. It was a pitch-black night. We had to drive in black-out conditions and did not know whether we were still ahead of the Russian spearheads or whether they had already passed us. There was no established lines, and no one knew where friend or foe was. Every now and then we stopped, turned off the engine and listened to see if we could hear the noise of tanks or vehicles. Finally, I got to the tank that was stuck.

In the meantime, unbeknownst to me, a second Tiger had arrived there. It had also been on its way to the battle group. With the help of that Tiger we tried to pull out the stuck vehicle, but a single tank just could not get it out. We disconnected the tracks and tried everything possible, but the tank would not stir from the spot. At about midnight, I returned to the unit to order up a second Tiger and also specialists from the recovery platoon from Gyöngyöspata. In the process, I scouted out a better route that led there. We moved downhill along narrow vineyard paths and then steeply back up the other side, forded little streams and went through villages in which there was no longer any trace of German soldiers.

20 November 1944: Early in the morning I was back at the recovery site. The recovery operation was gradually coming together and it could be assumed the tank would be recovered. I was concerned whether the Russians would give us enough time. The remaining elements of the battle group finally made it to Gyöngyöspata—along a different route. I left only two Tigers for the recovery operation. In order to be prepared for any eventuality, I had the tank that was stuck prepared for demolition. I went to the division command post again in order to report that a portion of my battle group was still out in front of the German troops and that, no matter what happened, they would need to hold the return route open for us. Therefore, the division could not yet withdraw from Gyöngyöspata. Then I moved forward again. I had several radio contacts with the tanks that were working at the recovery operation while I was en route. I had hoped that everything would go well. Then I got a radio message from up front that the recovery operation had to be

called off and the tank had been blown up. What had happened in my absence?

The tank that had been stuck had been pulled out and was being prepared to be towed when the first Russians appeared. With a "Hurrah" the Russians came on. The towing cable was attached under fire. The Russians had almost made it to the tank when it slid and became stuck more than ever. There was no more chance to save it. With great worry, the tow cable was released and the tank set ablaze by gunfire.

The tanks then pulled out. They had a 10-kilometer march through no man's land—or were the Russians already there? I moved toward the recovery group with two tanks so as to help them in an emergency. Finally, as darkness fell, we reached our own forward lines, which then lay roughly between Gyöngyös and Gyöngyöspata. Everyone there was expecting the Russians who were advancing. The battle group was quartered in Gyöngyöspata and the maintenance section immediately got back to work.

21 November 1944: Early in the morning, several tanks came back to us from the maintenance facility. My fighting force had grown to ten tanks. The battalion sent Leutnant Fürlinger to the battle group to give me some support. There was an alert in the afternoon. The Russians were attacking. We knocked out nine tanks. Some of them had gotten stuck in the boggy terrain.

22 November 1944: Two tanks moved forward to provide security. They gave me a situation report hourly. Everyone else was allowed to rest. There were several more tanks knocked out by the tanks up front. Our presence stabilized the situation.

23 November 1944: We were rudely awakened. The Russians shelled the place with Stalin organs. In our quarters, the windows came crashing in. Unpleasant! I sent four tanks forward to provide cover. Soon thereafter I received report from them that another eight Russian tanks had been knocked out. That made twenty-five in three days. In the afternoon Jabo attacks were added to the Stalin organs, another unpleasant appearance. The communications SPW—used to maintain radio contact with the battalion—in the courtyard of my command post took a direct hit that penetrated. Although I set the battalion flak platoon to work, the Russians kept up the pressure.

24 November 1944: Feldwebel Bornschier's tank was penetrated by a hit through the side of the hull. Thank God not much happened!

25 November 1944: Feldwebel Bornschier's tank was back in service. The hole in the armor was still there. It was stuffed with a rag, since it was very disturbing to have light penetrate inside the tank from an unexpected place. Unfortunately, we also had a personnel loss. Gefreiter Böhler was hit by a bomb fragment and had to go to the hospital. He was visibly anything but eager to be in the hospital, and I counted it to his credit that, even though still far from healed, he would flee the hospital and came back to us to avoid being moved to the rear.

The division command post of the 1st Panzer Division moved another 10 kilometers back that evening. I also sent my unarmored elements back.

26 November 1944: By order of the 1st Panzer Division we moved to the Panzergrenadierregiment 1 sector. The march was quite difficult. Once more we had to make detours through vineyards with their difficult terrain. After crossing the most difficult places, I had Leutnant Fürlinger lead the tanks to the designated place. I then moved back in the Kettenkrad. I wanted to give instructions to several tanks that had been left behind. In particular, I wanted to inform myself about the situation at the division command post. When I got back to the 1st Panzer Grenadier Regiment an hour later, I discovered that my tanks were already in action. After I was shown the situation on the map, I followed after them in the Kettenkrad.

I moved kilometer after kilometer along the highly visible tank tracks. Judging by the distance, the attack must have made good progress. In the meantime, night had again fallen and the ground got softer. Without exaggeration, the mud was nearly knee deep. I wondered how the tanks had ever made it through. I moved on additional kilometer after kilometer—at least that's the way it seemed to me in the dark. The situation got stranger and stranger. Nowhere was there a German soldier or even a sign of his presence. If I had not had the unmistakable Tiger track marks in front of me, I would have certainly believed I was well behind the Russian lines.

Suddenly, the Tigers emerged directly in front of me in the darkness. Leutnant Fürlinger came

over to me. He had just been wounded in the head and was bleeding heavily. He had been moving with the commander's hatch open. There was, indeed, no other alternative at night. Just at the moment he leaned over to say something to the gunner, his tank took a hit on the commander's cupola. He was hit in the head by a few fragments. He'd had extraordinary luck.

Leutnant Fürlinger reported to me that, without being allowed to wait for my return, the commander of the 1st Panzer Grenadier Regiment ordered him to attack as soon as his forces had arrived. In addition to the battle group, our armored flak platoon was also there. With its quad antiaircraft guns, it had perfomed admirably. The attack had driven forward about 10 kilometers to the present position. No grenadiers were available to help clear the terrain. Fürlinger considered it a miracle I had safely gotten that far on the Kettenkrad.

Fürlinger had to get back to a doctor as soon as possible and I had to arrange as soon as possible to get the tanks out of that idiotic situation. Without infantry, in the midst of the Russians— that was totally senseless and insane. We took up a hedgehog position with the tanks. I immediately received permission from the division to pull the tanks back. They obviously had a bad conscious about the asinine operation we had been ordered to execute.

In the withdrawal operation that followed, two of the Flak vehicles got stuck in the boggy ground that had been chewed up by the tanks. Another Tiger bogged down in the attempt to tow them out. The tanks could do little maneuvering on the soft ground, since any turning movement made them sink in deeply. On top of all that there was the total darkness and the proximity of the Russians, which we just had to ignore in that situation. We could hear Russian voices with frightening clarity from a neighboring small patch of woods. We freed up the Tiger again. We could scarcely move in the deep mud that sucked our boots down. The tow cables were hooked up; the towing tanks took up the slack. Then came the big moment when the two tanks pulled forward on a single command. The tank that was being towed moved several centimeters. The tracks of the tanks that were pulling spun wildly, but could not get a grip in that ground. They ground deeper into the earth. The recovery tanks came within a hairsbreadth of getting stuck themselves. Then, a metallic clang, shouts, motors were stopped and everything was as still as before. A tow cable had snapped. So that wouldn't work. Something else had to be tried. The next attempt was also fruitless.

27 November 1944: It was 0100 hours. I had the two flak vehicles prepared for demolition, but we did not give up. I moved back to the 1st Panzer Grenadier Regiment. They were already eagerly awaiting my return there. At 0300 hours the German withdrawal was to begin, including the evacuation of the village in which the regimental command post was located. It was impossible to get my tanks back by 0300 hours. Since the division had thrown us into such an impossible situation, it now had to suffer the consequences. The withdrawal would be postponed until my tanks were out. The final deadline, however, was dawn. For us, that meant we had little time left. When I got back to the Tigers—I got through with the Kettenkrad—the situation had not changed.

During my absence, another Tiger had bogged down. However, it had gotten free again. Fortunately, the Russians had remained quiet. If they had been a bit more aggressive they could have wiped out the entire battle group.

I saw no alternative to blowing up the two flak vehicles, and that is what happened. We reached the village with the regimental command post by dawn and there received the order to move to Jobbagyi, where I was to report to the command post of an SS division. After that night's activities, I was dog-tired. Such a night took more nerves than conducting a heavy armored attack. The battle group was temporarily back to being division reserve. It set up in quite nice quarters and immediately started technical service on the tanks. Leutnant Koppe, who had been moved a few days earlier to the 3rd Company as a platoon leader, came forward to me. I was pleased to again have help.

28 November 1944: It was a peaceful day. Feldwebel Grohman, my orderly-room NCO, came forward. There were after-action reports to write and the paperwork had to be disposed of, but the mail had also come through, including the official mail. That included, for the third time, a blotter report that had originated in Kassel against eight men of my company. On a detail

to Kassel before our transfer to Hungary, they had failed to see a Feldwebel of the street patrol service and had not saluted him. It was actually demanded that I was to punish my veteran men for such a thing! For the third time, the report found its way into the waste basket. I was certain, however, that another warning would arrive within the next eight weeks.

OPERATIONS LEFT OF THE DANUBE LAKE BALATON-STUHLWEIßENBURG-MOR-ZAMOLY

29 November 1944: I was ordered to move to a village that was 15 kilometers away. Terrible quarters, mostly with only one heated room that we had to share with great-grandmother, grandmother, mother and child.

30 November 1944: At 0200 hours a messenger arrived from the battalion with the written order: "The battalion is moving to a new operational area. Tracked vehicles will load on the railroad at Waitzen (Vac). Leutnant Koppe is to take the armored elements there. Move out immediately." I had to report to the battalion command post. (End of von Rosen's immediate postwar notes)

There I discovered the situation:

The Russians had reorganized after the costly fighting east of Budapest in the last ten days of November and redirected the spear point of their attack against the southern wing of Army Group South. In the meantime, the Soviets had succeeded in linking their two bridgeheads over the Danube south of Mohacs. Opposing them were only weak forces, mostly Hungarian. Fünfkirchen had been captured and nothing was available that could prevent a rapid advance toward Lake Balaton. On 1 December the Russian armored spearheads had already reached Dombovar and Kaposvark 80 kilometers west of the Danube. (Ernst Rebentich, *Die Geschichte der 23. Panzerdivision, 1941 bis 1945*, p. 436)

By shortening the front in the Hatvan area, the 23rd Panzer Division and 1st Panzer Division were freed up in order to be committed against the Soviet formations under the command of the LVII Panzer Corps (General of Panzer Troops

Kirchner). The 23rd Panzer Division, advancing ahead of the corps, had already reached the area south of Lake Balaton on 30 November. It covered the Pecs-Pecsvarad-Bataszek area and the roads leading north from there with motorized patrols. The mission of the 23rd Panzer Division was to delay the Soviet advance as much as possible. Tiger Tank Battalion 503 was placed under the operational control of the 23rd Panzer Division.

The battalion was faced with a difficult problem: fifteen damaged tanks were in the maintenance facility at Kürt. It would take at least fourteen days to repair them since replacement parts had to be brought from Germany in the unit's own trucks. The corps ordered that the maintenance company had to remain in Kürt until the tanks were repaired. For the time being, the enemy situation in that section of the front did not cause any concern. There was, indeed, no other alternative, since that number of tanks could not be towed the approximately 50 kilometers to a railroad station where they could be rail loaded. There were no prime movers available for that. As a result, the maintenance facility remained in Kürt. The third maintenance platoon was in Vagselly (Sala). Repair work that would take even longer was done there. Hauptmann von Eichel had been there for three weeks already. He maintained contact with the forward elements of the battalion.

1 December 1944: Leutnant von Rosen moved through Budapest with the commander to the new area of operations.

2 December 1944: Established contact with the LVII Corps and the 23rd Panzer Division. The division had a sector that was almost 100 kilometers wide. As a result, only a covering-force mission or a delaying action could be conducted. Farther to the rear, at Lake Balaton, it was intended to construct a blocking position. We wanted to stop the Russian steamroller there. The Russians were covering between 20 and 30 kilometers a day. In the afternoon, the wheeled vehicles arrived via road march. The battalion command post was set up at a manor house at Simontornya.

3 December 1944: The battalion's tanks arrived by rail transport and were unloaded at Balatonkenese. Security at Simontornya. The battalion moved towards Lake Balaton. One battle group led by Leutnant von Rosen remained behind.

4 December 1944: Immediate counterattack in conjunction with the 3rd Company of the 128th Panzer Grenadier Regiment. Order to withdraw arrived in the evening. Leutnant Koppe received the Iron Cross, First Class. The battle group was once again placed under the operational control of the 1st Panzer Regiment of the 1st Panzer Division. It moved to Lepseny. The command post of Tiger Tank Battalion 503 was in Polgardi.

5 December 1944: Two alerts. Employment 5 kilometers west of Siofok. The main line of resistance consisted of no more than isolated strongpoints. The Russians attacked again and again. They wanted a decisive breakthrough at Stuhlweißenburg at any cost.

6 December 1944: It was necessary to divide the battle group. Three Tigers, led by Leutnant von Rosen, launched a counterattack. They cleared a village, destroying six antitank guns in the process. The second part of the battle group, led by Leutnant Koppe, attacked at Siofok. It lost one tank. Oberfeldwebel Kitzmann of the 2nd Company was killed. The terrain was difficult, very marshy in places. The tanks of the battle group provided cover in vineyards. Heavy infantry attacks. The ground in front of the tanks teemed with Russians, as if an ant hill had been disturbed. Because of the machine-gun fire of the tanks, the attack came to a halt in a depression.

The 1st Panzer Regiment ordered both parts of the battle group to pull back at 1800 hours. It was intended to pull back the infantry at 2100 hours. During the withdrawal of one of the sections, two tanks got stuck in the total darkness. A third one bogged down while attempting the recovery. The place where that happened was barely 100 meters from the foremost Russian units. German infantry were not available to provide security. To make the catastrophe complete, a radio message arrived from the other section—led by Feldwebel Seidel—that two tanks were stuck fast in boggy ground. To have five tanks stuck at the same time was enough to drive you to distraction. The tanks of the second section were recovered within an hour. Leutnant von Rosen was able to coordinate with the regiment, ensuring the infantry would not withdraw to the new line until the recovery of the tanks had been completed. Von Rosen wrote the following in 1946:

I turned over command of my three tanks to Feldwebel Seidel and moved to Leutnant Koppe's section. There I found the following situation. Three tanks appeared to be hopelessly bogged down in the morass 20 to 30 meters from the road to Siofok. The road was almost impossible to recognize in the dark and the tanks had turned a few meters too soon to make it onto the hard road. As a result, they ended up in the marshy ground. The Russians were alert to everything and fired wildly whenever there were engine noises on our side. That increased the difficulty of the recovery operation immeasurably. Before any of the Tiger's engines were started, everyone had to take cover in the tanks. The Russians fired with everything they had at their disposal: Artillery, mortars, machine guns and antitank guns. They had the main road as a guide line and fired blindly along that "compass heading." We had to move on the road and start the recovery operation from it. Finally it was done. After hours of tiresome effort, we succeeded in getting at least the first tank onto the hard road. Another barrage. One man was wounded.

7 December 1944: It was past midnight. We had to hook several tow-cables together in order to reach from the improved-surface road to the tanks that were embedded in the mud. A second tank made it onto the road. However, our situation became ever more critical. There were no friendly units to the left or right of us. We were without any protection. Renewed hail of gunfire. The Russians again fired along the road. Then I was hit. I received a light blow from behind on the shoulder and my right arm immediately hung limp. Shot through the upper arm. It bled copiously. I gave instructions to Leutnant Koppe and, when a motorcycle messenger came to us from the rear to see how much longer the recovery operation would take, I returned to the command post and the doctor on the motorcycle. Leutnant Koppe was back with the tanks within another hour. The last tank could not be recovered. The Russians had worked their way up to the tank and had already made it onto the road behind. The tank had to be knocked out with our own gunfire. However, despite all the difficulties of that night, I was pleased we only had a single tank as a total loss.

I moved back to the battalion command post at Polgardi. The doctor said I had to go to the hospital. Leutnant Koppe was given temporary command of the 3rd Company. (End of von Rosen's immediate postwar notes.)

8 December 1944: Alert at 1000 hours at the battalion command post. The Russians were attacking Polgardi. Tiger 124 was knocked out. The staff moved to Stuhlweißenburg in the Varpalota area. A maintenance platoon had set up in Bodajk. At the same time, there was a catastrophe at the maintenance facility at Kürt. Naturally, the Russians had not been blind to the fact that numerous German combat formations were being withdrawn from the Hatvan area. It was hoped that those formations would be freed up as a result of shortening the front. What had to happen happened. The Russians immediately launched an attack on that weakened sector northeast of Budapest.

Hauptmann Fromme's concerns in connection with moving the battalion to the Stuhlweißenburg area were dramatically fulfilled. The Russians broke through the German front in a surprise attack with strong forces and poured into the open hinterland lying before them. Early in the morning of 6 December, Russian tanks were outside of Kürt. Anything that could still fire was brought into position. A large number of Russian tanks were knocked out. The recovery platoon was able to tow the immobile tanks out of the immediate danger zone. On 7 December, however, the Russians were back again. They advanced past either side of Kürt and caught up with the tanks that had already been towed out. Feldwebel Bornschier of the 3rd Company was killed in that fighting. There was no alternative left in that situation but to blow up eight Tiger II tanks. At least the crews and the maintenance platoon with its entire complement of equipment had been saved and sent back to the battalion.

9 December 1944: The battalion commander, Hauptmann Fromme, was moved to the armor school as a tactics instructor. Hauptmann Wiegand was given temporary command of the battalion until the arrival of Fromm's successor, Hauptmann von Diest-Koerber.

10–17 December 1944: The battalion command post was in Stuhlweißenburg. The Russians had not yet succeeded in breaking through the narrows between Lake Velence and Lake Balaton. Several tanks from the maintenance facility arrived in Vagselli. The battalion kept busy as "fire brigade". Wherever anything heated up, the battalion had to handle it almost single-handedly. Practically by itself, the battalion stabilized the front through its appearance. The front firmed up outside of Stuhlweißenburg. On 17 December, six Tigers led by Oberleutnant Oemler (1st Company) were in action at the front. Two tanks were knocked out by direct hits. The ordnance officer, Leutnant Rollik, brought the new commander from the command post of the III Panzer Corps. By then, the corps had taken over command in the Stuhlweißenburg area. The corps staff was in Fehervarczuro.

18 December 1944: The III Panzer Corps again placed Tiger Tank Battalion 503 under the operational control of the 1st Panzer Division. The order arrived by radio in the evening from the division that the battalion was to immediately move to Balatonkenese.

19 December 1944: Early in the morning, the battalion marched to Balatonkenese at the eastern tip of Lake Balaton. The intended attack was called off. Thirteen of the battalion's tanks were operational. It had rained for days. Once off the roads, the ground was bottomless, with deep mud everywhere.

20 December 1944:

At 0720 hours, the Soviet artillery fired an intensive barrage on the Lake Velence-Tac sector and to its east. For 25 minutes it pounded the main line of resistance and the depth of the main defense area. Heavy preparatory fire, though not as heavy as that in the eastern sector, also fell on the area as far as Lake Balaton.

At 0740, massively superior Russian infantry formations attacked, supported by several tanks. The Hungarian troops that had been newly brought forward abandoned their positions . . .

Simultaneously, other Soviet formations attacked the positions of the 271st People's Grenadier Division east of Lake Velence and broke through them . . .

A Soviet formation of about 2,000 men advanced through Dinnyes toward the north and northwest. The grenadiers and the flak artillerymen were unable to halt the vastly superior enemy. Kislafaludimajor and Pakozd were lost.

The Soviets advanced as far as the high ground 5 kilometers east of Stuhlweißenburg.

By doing that, the Soviets succeeded in breaking through the narrows between the lakes and into the deep flank of the German-Hungarian forces positioned yet farther south . . .

While the 1st Panzer Division held its line—it wasn't in the spear point of the offensive—its left-hand neighbor, the 23rd Panzer Division, only occupied strongpoints on the evening of 20 December. This line ran from the railroad embankment east of Alsosomiyo-railroad station at Szabadbattyan-Föveny-south of Stuhlweißenburg-high ground east of the city . . . (Ernst Rebentisch, *Die Geschichte der 23. Panzer-Division, 1941 bis 1945*, p. 459, 461–64)

One of the battalion's maintenance platoons moved to Varpalota.

21 December 1944: It was still relatively calm in our sector. Supply and technical service.

22 December 1944: The 1st Panzer Division intended to launch a local counterattack in the enemy's left flank. As ordered, the tanks moved at about 0100 hours to Nadasladany (40 kilometers). The local counterattack was to be launched against the village of Urhida during the afternoon. The attack would be led by the battalion commander. The line of departure for the attack was set in Sarkeszi, where there were still 200 friendly infantry.

Furious fire from antitank guns and mortars met our tanks as they attacked. Several antitank-gun and machine-gun nests were destroyed or overrun. As darkness fell, the majority of the village had been captured. The rest of the village would be taken in the dark. Five Tigers suffered significant damage from gunfire. The command tank had also been hit. Leutnant Koppe moved to Tiger 314 after losing his tank.

Shortly before the commander left the battalion command post in Berida at noon on that 22 December for the attack on Urhida, Leutnant von Rosen reported back from the hospital in Vienna. The commander interrupted his report: "Leutnant! Your report is incorrect! Effective 1 November 1944, you have been an Oberleutnant. . . . Congratulations." At the same time, the commander ordered another eight days of convalescence, since von Rosen's wounds had not yet healed.

23 December 1944: Urhida was completely cleared of the enemy in the gray light of dawn. Tiger 133 was knocked out by an antitank gun and burned out during the final clearing of the village.

While heavy artillery fire landed on Stuhlweißenburg, the Russian infantry prepared for attack south of the city. Shortly after midnight the last units of the 23rd Panzer Division cleared out of Stuhlweißenburg. The 126th Panzer Grenadier Regiment and the 51st Panzer Engineer Battalion moved into the Csormoha line . . . [5 kilometers north of Stuhlweißenburg] (Ernst Rebentisch, *Die Geschichte der 23. Panzer-Division, 1941 bis 1945*, p. 459, 461–64)

Urhida continued to be held. The tanks were pulled back to Nadasdladany that evening. At about 1900 hours a new order arrived from the III Panzer Corps: The battalion was placed under the operational control of the 4th Cavalry Brigade, commanded by General Holste. It immediately moved to Fehervarcsurgo. The departure took place at 2200 hours. At the same time the maintenance facility moved to Dudar.

24 December 1944: The tanks arrived at about 0500 hours in Fehervarcsurgo and, after a catnap, rolled on to Sakarestje at 0630 hours. From there, the 4th Cavalry Brigade intended to mount a local counterattack south. For that, the Tigers were attached to a battle group from the 23rd Panzer Division commanded by Oberstleutnant Weymann, which was also participating in the attack. Eight Tigers arrived from the battalion, but only six were fit for combat. At daylight, the Russians shelled Sakarestje from all sides with artillery, Stalin organs and mortars. The planned attack did not come off. The Russians had acted first. Instead of attacking, the German forces became continuously involved in fending off heavy Russian assaults. Leutnant Rambow knocked out seven tanks by noon with his tank. Obergefreiter Kühn stopped their progress. Exactly eight minutes were needed to knock out the seven tanks. Then the track came off that tank. Obergefreiter Leif and Hans Welsch put the track back on the tank under enemy fire while Leutnant Koppe and his tank provided covering fire.

On Christmas Eve the enemy pressure grew stronger and stronger. Sakerestje had to be abandoned. During the withdrawal, Leutnant Rambow's tank got stuck and had to be blown up. A sad Christmas. One positive event: Unteroffizier Gärtner was promoted to Feldwebel.

25 December 1944: The battalion was again placed under the operational control of the 23rd Panzer Division. It remained with Battle Group Weymann, which was providing cover immediately north of Sakerestje. The Tigers knocked out two enemy tanks. The flak platoon shot down a Russian Il 2. Heavy artillery and mortar fire.

26 December 1944: More security missions. The Russians penetrated deeply east of Sakarestje and were outside of Sakbereny. The command post of the 4th Cavalry Brigade was there.

27 December 1944: Five Tigers in action. Two T-34's knocked out.

28 December 1944: During the night the Tigers wiped out two T-34s and three antitank guns. The battalion was again attached to the 4th Cavalry Brigade. It was further placed under the control of the heavy battalion, commanded by Rittmeister Graf Plettenberg. Von Plettenberg's command post was in Mor.

29 December 1944: The battalion command post moved to Balinka. The battalion battle group consisted of only three tanks, which were posted at the western outskirts of Mor as ready reserve. Even more than enemy action, the weeks of continuous employment as "fire brigade" and the many kilometers in difficult and extreme terrain conditions had taken their toll. The number of tanks with technical problems was large. The battalion commander reported the following in his monthly report of 1 January 1945:

The primary difficulties lie in the following areas:

1. Lack of spare parts (including major end items such as power plants, transmissions, differentials etc.)
2. Lack of recovery means in a terrain ill suited for tracked vehicles, resulting in the use of tanks over and over again for that purpose.
3. Inadequate or no availability of Ssyms rail cars for transporting disabled tanks to the rear and bringing repaired tanks forward.

As a result of items 1–3 above, the battalion cannot be employed in the strength it should be able to muster.

Of great concern to the battalion was the number of disabled vehicles located all over the place; it was an impossible mission for the recovery elements at the time.

Heavy artillery and mortar fire on Mor.

30 December 1944: Reconnaissance in force along with the 2nd Troop of the 5th Mounted (*Reiter*) Regiment (von Mackensen) to Pusztavam. Four tanks employed.

31 December 1944: Oberleutnant von Rosen took over the battle group and reported to Rittmeister Graf Plettenberg in Mor. The "convalescence" was over. No action, but heavy mortar fire on the village starting at 2200 hours. The quarters of two tank crews were destroyed by direct hits. Fortunate that the men were in the tanks!

1 January 1945: The battalion command post moved to Sur. Aerial attack on Mor. Alert for the battle group in the morning. The Russians were exerting heavy pressure on the grenadiers. The tanks conducted a relief attack on Hill 128, five kilometers north of Mor, which was strongly held by the Russians. The heavy battalion of the 4th Cavalry Brigade and Mounted Regiment von Mackensen attacked from the southeast, the Tigers from the south. The two attacking groups were to meet on the objective.

Oberleutnant von Rosen lost his way with his Tigers on the approach march. In the snow-covered landscape, one hill looked like another. Where was that damned Hill 128? There—strong Russian antitank defenses on a hill. The battle group had already lost a great deal of time, so there was only one thing to do: Attack the hill without thinking about what might be to the right or left. The Russians fled, abandoning all their equipment. It was even the right Hill 128, and the tanks were on time and without losses on the designated objective of the attack. When the attack group of the 4th Cavalry Brigade arrived, the tanks had everything well in hand.

Then security at Felsödobos. Tiger 332 had engine trouble and had to be towed back. Since the route back led through no man's land, a tank from the 3rd Company accompanied it to Bodayk to provide cover.

2 January 1945: Local counterattacks in conjunction with the heavy battalion of the 4th Cavalry Brigade. Three Tigers in action.

3 January 1945 and 4 January 1945: The battle group was at Felsödobos again. Hauptmann von Diest-Koerber came to the battle group, as did General Holste, commander of the 4th Cavalry Brigade. In the afternoon, we were ordered to pull back to Mor. A night attack was ordered on Pusztvam. There were only two Tigers operational. A third tank dropped out shortly after crossing the line of departure. The heavy battalion had three Panzer IIs and grenadiers mounted on SPWs. After a 10-kilometer night march through the forests of the Vertes Mountains, the attack group appeared at Pusztvam, totally surprising the Russians and capturing the place in short order. The grenadiers advanced with the tanks; the Russians were completely overrun. In addition to a great number of prisoners, many hand-held weapons and vehicles and eleven antitank guns were captured. Back to Mor.

The battalion's tanks were ordered to Bakonyszombathely, one after the other, where the maintenance facility had moved the preceding day. Another post-manufacture modification. The turret races and the tracks were changed out.

5 January 1945: The redesignation of Tiger Tank Battalion 503 as Tiger Tank Battalion "Feldherrnhalle" was announced. We continued to think of ourselves as "five-oh-three"!

Leutnant der Reserve Rubbel of the 1st Company was moved to the 3rd Company and took over the second platoon.

6 January 1945: The battalion remained under the operational control of the 4th Cavalry Brigade; it was directed to coordinate with the brigade's heavy battalion under Rittmeister Graf Plettenberg. The tanks moved to Bakonycsernye in the evening. An attack in the Zamoly area was planned for 7 January.

The situation:

On 2 January, two German corps initiated an advance from Komorn to Budapest. The city had been encircled for fourteen days. On 5 January, after overcoming bitter resistance, the spearheads of the attack were only 25 kilometers west of Budapest. Newly arrived enemy forces, however, prevented further progress. The leadership thereupon decided on a rapid reorganization and a shift of the spear point of the attack to the area directly south of the Danube.

The I Cavalry Corps—with the 1st Panzer Division, 23rd Panzer Division, and 4th Cavalry Brigade—was ordered to advance toward Zamoly-Cesakvar. It would move east with its spear point on the left. While the 1st Panzer Division conducted limited-objective attacks toward Stuhlweiß-enburg and Gyulamajor, the 4th Cavalry Brigade would advance on Zamoly from the sector east of Söred. The 23rd Panzer Division was to cover the right flank of the 4th Cavalry Brigade with a simultaneous attack to the southeast and east. (Ernst Rebentisch, *Die Geschichte der 23. Panzerdivision, 1941 bis 1945*, p. 467)

7 January 1945: The battalion moved to Fehervarcsurgo. At about 1140 hours, the combat elements proceeded through Magyaralmas-Alsopuszta to Borbalamajor to launch its attack on Zamoly from there. Two battle groups were formed. One was to attack to the north, the other to the south. The battalion commander was with the southern battle group, which had six Tigers and ten Sturmgeschütze of the heavy battalion. Heavy snow squalls and extremely poor visibility. The Tigers soon encountered an antitank belt. The tanks were fired on from the front and, what was more unpleasant, from the side as well.

Feldwebel Gärtner of the 3rd Company had a round penetrate the side of his tank. Apparently, we were also dealing with Stalin tanks. Gärtner was brought back and bled to death on the way to the medical clearing station. Before he died, he had stoically removed the remnants of his pistol from the wound, doing it as if it were something trivial. His death was a very serious loss for the 3rd Company. The attack was broken off. The tanks were pulled back to Borbalamajor where they provided cover. It was an abominably cold, wet night in the tanks. Supplies did not arrive until morning. The southern battle group was ordered to link up with the northern one in Lajamajor. That was also the location of Graf Plettenberg's command post.

8 January 1945: It was evident on 8 January that the enemy still held the initiative. Orders and counter-orders competed with each other. The combat echelons and the battalion commander arrived at 0700 hours as ordered in Lajamajor. At 1100 hour the order arrived to immediately pull back to Borbalamajor. The tanks rolled there. As soon as they arrived at Borbalamajor, a new order came: Return immediately to Lajamajor. In the meantime, about sixty Russian tanks had been reported there. However, aside from artillery and mortar fire, it remained relatively quiet in Lajamajor.

9 January 1945: Alert in the morning. The battalion immediately moved to Alsopuszta in the area of operations of the 23rd Panzer Division. The battalion was split up again. The 503's 1st Company, with Leutnant Piepgras, remained with the 4th Cavalry Brigade, knocking out seven Russian tanks during the course of the day. The other part of the battalion was placed under the operational control of the 23rd Panzer Division. Led by the commander, that group attacked south and was able to restore the old main line of resistance at Sarkeresztes. At the start of the attack, Leutnant Rambow's tank was eliminated from taking a part in the engagement when a shell burst in the gun barrel. However, the tank and its amputated stump of a main gun remained for two additional days with the combat elements.

The battle group then turned to the east toward a vineyard village that had been lost. The infantry, a Luftwaffe unit that had been attached to the 23rd Panzer Division, was hesitant in following the tanks, bunching up behind the rearmost vehicles.

The Russians had dug a broad and deep antitank ditch outside the village that the tanks were unable to negotiate. We continued the attack. Then there was a heavy blow to the tank. As I was able to determine later, it was a round that penetrated the engine compartment from the right. Other tanks in my company also received direct hits. In conjunction with the other tanks of the battalion we reached the designated high ground from which we had an effective field of fire covering Zamoly. At the same time, Graf Plettenburg and his heavy battalion pushed into Zamoly. Graf Plettenberg was severely wounded in that operation and his adjutant, Graf Oberndorf, was killed. We had a good view from the high ground overlooking Zamoly and the area beyond it. Feldwebel Sachs and his tank destroyed three Russian liaison aircraft that were on a meadow at the edge of Zamoly just as they started to roll.

We had no time to lose and continued our attack. The successful penetration had to be broadened. We put an additional number of antitank guns out of action and then came to a sloping vineyard. It was difficult to identify, but it appeared to drop off quite steeply in front of us. Further movement in that direction was blocked. As a result, we set up security, spaced well apart from each other. In the meantime, we also survived an attack by ground-attack aircraft that also dropped bombs.

The enemy had very skillfully positioned SU-152 assault guns in the vineyard. We had not yet spotted them when, suddenly, the first of our tanks went up in flames. Three of its crew were killed and the others were severely burned. After another half hour, the same thing happened to a second tank. We pulled back a little. Apparently, the Russian assault gun crews had observed us initially while dismounted. When they had us spotted, they then fired a single, aimed round. Then they immediately moved back to their rear into cover. Thus, we had little chance to knock them out. We were unable to find any reverse-slope positions in that open terrain. However, it was important to hold our position on the rise and provide cover, since that was the only way to provide flank protection for Zamoly. In spite of small changes of position—a bit forward, then a bit back, a bit to the left, then again to the right—it was impossible to change the fact that the Tigers stood out like great big targets in the open terrain.

After another half hour, a third tank, the one to my left, was knocked out. Crew members were also killed in that tank. We could not identify the assault guns. I figured that my tank would probably be the next, since the Russians were systematically firing on one tank after another, working from left to right. I observed intently. It was a very nasty situation. Slowly it got darker. How I longed for the night! I was probably thinking just that when I saw a mighty streak of fire and there was an explosion in my own tank. We were all thrown around, and suddenly there was daylight in my tank. That was my first impression. We had been penetrated! Bail out! We all got out. Only the driver was wounded. The darkness that was then falling shielded us from further losses. I had two operational tanks left. The immediate next move was back to the commander's tank.

Armed with machine pistols, another member of our crew and I went back to our tank. We had to retrieve it. We prepared it for towing. That meant that the engine and final drive had

to be disconnected from each other in the tank. While that was being done, I stood guard against surprises with my machine pistol. That probably had more of a psychological value than any real one.

Under the noses of the Russians, we evacuated our tank using one from the 1st Company. I saw how lucky we had been. A large chuck of armor had been blown away. Despite that, we had had only one wounded soldier.

The Russians had positioned themselves under cover of the earth thrown out of the ditch. Behind the ditch the ground rose to a vineyard, which meant the Russians could not withdraw without being seen. They gave no sign they would surrender in their hopeless situation. We moved right up to the ditch with the tanks in order to enable our own infantry to advance and infiltrate. The Russians replied with satchel charges, hand grenades and antitank rifles. They aimed their fire at the vision slots of the tanks. Our own infantry remained behind our tanks and made no move to leave that cover. They suffered losses even though they were behind the tanks. Then I saw how Hauptmann von Diest-Koerber climbed out of his tank and, right arm gesticulating forward, tried to urge the infantry forward with him. A scene like something out of an old battle painting! I couldn't breathe. We tried to hold the Russians down with our fire and give him cover. The infantry, however, did not follow him. He was all alone in front of the trench. He hastened back again behind our tanks. He finally succeeded in approaching the ditch with a few courageous infantrymen. They brought a machine gun up into action and rolled up the entire enemy position.

When I think back to that attack I always have a second image before my eyes: A large Russian, apparently an officer or commissar, covered with blood. He stood upright behind his cover and with wrathful, hate-filled visage screamed something in our direction and then collapsed. You had to have respect for such brave individuals.

There were many dead lying in the ditch. About 300 Russians were captured. The tanks gathered in the village. We encountered no resistance there. After the infantry had reoccupied its former positions, the tanks returned to Alsopuszta to be resupplied. Snow continued to fall heavily. We spent the night in the tanks. It was cold. We used the blowtorches for heat, so we all ended up with black faces.

10 January 1945: At midday another attack was to start against Zamoly. However, it was then postponed to the following day.

11 January 1945: Oberleutnant von Rosen reported:

It was a thaw, slush. At 0600 hours we rolled out. The attack was to begin at 0640 hours after a short preparation. The battalion had a total of thirteen Tigers operational. I was with the tanks of the 3rd Company on the left flank. After a Nebelwerfer barrage, we overran the enemy positions. As the lead tank, I was able to cross the Zamoly-Stuhlweißenburg road, which the Russians had doggedly hung on to. Then we had to make a 90-degree turn. My left flank was uncovered. Ten to twelve guns were in position to my left, but the Russians bolted.

Of the thirteen tanks of the battalion that had set out in the morning, only three were still in service by evening. Tigers 121 and 122 were total losses. Feldwebel Kukla, Unteroffizier Höppner, Obergefreiter Woisin and Obergefreiter Walter of the 1st Company and two additional solders had been killed. The remaining tanks, some of which had taken serious hits, were recovered and brought back to the rear. Leutnant Heerlein was wounded during one of the towing operations. That day had brought heavy losses to the battalion. On the other side of the balance sheet stood the successes: Zamoly had been recaptured, thanks to the employment of the Tigers, which had established the prerequisites. During the course of the operation, the battalion had destroyed twenty-one tanks and assault guns, twenty antitank guns, three airplanes, and one multiple rocket launcher. Once more, we retired to Alsopuszta.

12 January 1945: In the morning, I moved back to the command post at Bodajk with the commander. There I was told I was officially the company commander; heretofore, I had only been the acting commander. In the meantime, Leutnant Fürlinger was with the five tanks in Alsopuszta which had recently been made operational again. The remainder of the battle group moved

to Magyaralmas. I was sent to the battalion trains for eight days. Hauptmann von Eichel came forward from the rear.

13–17 January 1945: The maintenance facility at Sur and the company maintenance teams worked full speed ahead at restoring the combat readiness of the damaged tanks. Leutnant Fürlinger was still in Magyaralmas with his battle group.

An attack toward Stuhlweißenburg was planned for 18 January. The battalion was to be committed along with the 23rd Panzer Regiment of the 23rd Panzer Division. At the same time, other forces were to carry out the main effort past Stuhlweißenburg.

18 January 1945: At 0645 hours eight of the battalion's tanks, together with the 23rd Panzer Regiment, set out for the attack. The attack originated from Margitmajor and was led by the commander. Very soon after the start of the attack, the lead Tigers ran into a minefield that was covered by antitank guns. While the tanks suppressed the antitank guns, the battalion's panzer engineers cleared the mines. West of the high ground at Point 153, the tanks were only able to cross an extremely marshy stream bed with difficulty. The tanks were raked with gunfire from all sides. Seven enemy tanks and ten antitank guns were destroyed. The Tigers could not avoid damage from the heavy artillery, mortar and antitank gun fire. One after another, four Tigers were put out of action. They had to be evacuated and then towed back to the rear. The commander's tank also took a direct hit that prevented the main gun from firing. As evening approached the enemy launched several local counterattacks that were repulsed.

The battalion was withdrawn and moved back to Magyaralmas. Two Tigers remained forward, providing cover for the grenadiers.

19–21 January 1945: The battalion stayed in Magyaralmas and repaired the battle damage or the mechanical problems. Oberleutnant von Rosen relieved Hauptmann von Eichel.

22 January 1945: The 1st Panzer Division moved out against Stuhlweißenburg. Together with the 23rd Panzer Regiment, Tiger Tank Battalion 503 was to advance east of the city to cut off the withdrawing enemy. At 1100 hours the battalion moved out east of Sarkeresztes with nine Tigers and several Panthers and Panzer IVs. The Gyulama-

jor farmstead was recaptured. Strong enemy anti-tank defenses. After that the advance continued south. Von Rosen wrote the following in 1946:

We were behind the Russian lines and no longer had strong opposition. We moved right along a depression. Suddenly we saw hundreds of Russian infantry retreating. Up to that point, they had been hidden
by a small patch of woods. We livened up the withdrawing troops. They had not expected us there. Then, all at once, seven assault guns appeared. Our appearance seemed to put them totally at a loss. Fire—target! Fire—target! Seven assault guns were ablaze. We reached the road from Stuhlweißenburg to Csala. The continuation of the advance had to be stopped as evening drew near, since most of the tanks had fired off their ammunition and half had become disabled due to damage from gunfire. The supplies did not get forward until nearly midnight. The roads were miserable and the Russian artillery was also very active during the night. Since only five tanks were still operational, the commander turned over the operation to me. It was the coldest night so far that winter and we froze horribly in the tanks. Sleep was out of the question.

23 January 1945: As dawn broke we continued the attack toward Csala. It went well for three or four kilometers. Then we ran up against a Hungarian farmstead that was well defended. We took a goodly number of hits. There was no way to get at it frontally. We pulled back again, went around the enemy and came at it again from the flank. After we had knocked out four tanks, the Russians pulled out. In occupying the Puszta, two of my tanks moved onto mines. We could no longer continue the attack. The defense had become too strong. We spotted five Stalin organs, as well as several guns, that were taking us under direct fire. That kept us busy. We were able to disengage from the enemy and then set up in the Puszta. In so doing we had to endure several artillery barrages. We were also aggressively attacked by ground-support aircraft. They flew at us in flights of four or five at a time and dumped heaps of small and very small ordance on us. Fortunately, they were not very accurate and the entire lot went into an open field about fifty meters away. That evening, Hungarian tanks and in-fantry

arrived to relieve us. We moved to Stuhlweiß-enburg and were able to get a good night's sleep there. (End of von Rosen's immediate postwar notes)

24 January 1945: The battalion was again placed under the operational control of the 4th Cavalry Brigade and moved to Magyaralmas. Plans were made to attack the Zamoly area again tomorrow.

25 January 1945: The battalion was only able to provide one small battle group with a few Tigers. It was led by Leutnant Beyer. The attack did not get off the starting blocks until the Tigers got involved. Two tanks were damaged by gunfire and mines. One of them, commanded by Leutnant Rubbel, lost both tracks in a minefield. It could only be towed out with the help of all the tanks in the evening, in a snowstorm. The battle group went back to Zamoly at night.

26 January 1945: The battalion moved to Borbalamajor. An attack with limited objectives was to be launched from there. Only three Tigers and several Hungarian Panzer IVs attached to the battalion were operational. The attack of the small battle group made good progress at first, but the Hungarian infantry intended to support it could not follow. The tanks became disabled by stronger and stronger tank and antitank gun fire and were withdrawn. Moved again to Magyaralmas. The snow switched over to rain and turned the paths and roads to slush. Later there was a hefty snowstorm.

27 January 1945: The battalion was not employed, since none of the tanks were operational.

28–29 January 1945: The battalion remained under the control of the 4th Cavalry Brigade. The maintenance facility in Fehervarczurgo had five tanks ready for action again.

30 January 1945: The battalion command post moved to Iszkaszentgyörgy; the combat elements moved to Sarkeresztes, where the heavy battalion of the 4th Cavalry Brigade was also located. Nine Tigers were operational.

31 January 1945: It was uncomfortable in Sarkeresztes. There was a lot of harassing fire from artillery. The Russians advanced everywhere along the front with strong forces and achieved a number of penetrations. Orders from the 4th Cavalry

Brigade: The battalion was to move out immediately with the brigade's heavy battalion to counterattack and take back Gyulamajor. Hauptmann Sonntag was the acting commander of the heavy battalion. The battle group, led by Hauptmann von Diest-Koerber, set out south from the vineyards east of Sarkeresztes. The attack started well. As usual, it ran into artillery and mortar fire. Then, however, the battle group was hit by fire from antitank guns and tanks. It was impossible to approach Gyulamajor from the front. The commander attacked Hill 214 with four King Tigers; the tanks enveloped from the left. There were enemy tanks there as well. Several were set afire by gunfire. The remainder withdrew. Friendly grenadiers occupied the enemy's positions—some of which were constructed very well—and hunkered down.

One King Tiger was hit by a round that penetrated the turret, probably from a Stalin II. Two members of the crew were severely wounded. Leutnant Koppe succeeded in advancing into Gyulamajor with three tanks. Since our own infantry forces were too weak, the village had to be given up again in the evening.

1 February 1945: Leutnant Koppe forced his way back into the village during the night with reinforced infantry elements while Leutnant Piepgras remained with two tanks on Hill 214 and provided cover. Gyulamajor was finally captured in its entirety. However, the Russians remained firmly in control of the improved road east of Gyulamajor.

An order from the 4th Cavalry Brigade arrived by radio in the gray light of dawn: "All units are to proceed immediately to Point 166 south of Gyulamajor." The Russians were said to be there with fifty tanks. Only four Tigers were available, since Leutnant Piepgras had to remain on Hill 214. In accordance with that order, the commander immediately set out from Gyulamajor with the available tanks. Shortly after moving out, one of Leutnant Koppe's tanks broke a track, which had to be repaired under artillery fire. The second Tiger then reported extremely high engine temperatures and was unable to follow the group. Shortly thereafter, the third Tiger ran onto a mine and was stuck.

There are days when nothing goes right.

The commander moved on alone to Point 166, calling en route for support from Leutnant Piepgras. It took a while, however, before he could get

there. At a road embankment, Hauptmann von Diest-Koerber spotted twenty to twenty-five enemy tanks. At that point he was all alone, but he still opened fire. After the first round, which was a hit, the enemy tanks came to life. The commander's tank was then covered with fire from the enemy tanks and received numerous hits that made it unfit for combat and incapable of moving. Thank God that Leutnant Piepgras arrived at that juncture with his two Tigers and knocked out three enemy tanks, whereupon the others decamped to the south. It was possible to restore limited mobility to the commander's tank and bring it back. Leutnant Piepgras remained forward and continued to engage individual enemy tanks.

Several tanks that had been repaired came forward from the rear. One of those tanks got into a marshy spot at Gyulamajor and became hopelessly stuck. The village was evacuated in the evening and the tank had to be blown up. Two tanks stayed forward to provide cover. All of the others were brought back for repairs at Sarkeresztes. On the plus side, the battalion could count seventeen tanks or assault guns knocked out that day.

2 February 1945: The situation remained unchanged.

3 February 1945: Five of the battalion's tanks were at the front. Leutnant Fürlinger led the battle group, which was again to attack at noon along with units of the newly brought up 5th SS Panzer Division "Wiking." At the same time, the Russians attacked from several positions. Gyulamajor was finally captured that evening. In the course of that operation, five antitank guns were captured. The tanks had to remain in position during the night. Heavy fog.

4 February 1945: The Russians attacked Gyulamajor with tanks as dawn broke. Battle Group Fürlinger knocked out eight Russian tanks and overran five enemy antitank guns on a hill south of the village. As evening approached, the battle group was pulled back to Sarkeresztes.

5–10 February 1945: The battalion was not committed. The maintenance facility and the company maintenance sections worked like madmen. At the front, nothing but artillery duels. Rain and thaws.

9 February 1945: The battalion was to be withdrawn from the sector. The destination was not yet known.

THE BATTLE OF THE GRAN BRIDGEHEAD

12 February 1945: Loading the Tigers began at Mor. The battalion became part of Panzer Corps "Feldherrnhalle" and was to take part in the planned elimination of the Gran bridgehead. The battalion was placed under the operational control of the Reich Grenadier Division "Hoch- und Deutschmeister." The start of the attack was set for 17 February.

13 February 1945: The first trains arrived and unloaded at Perbete. The battalion was quartered in Csuz. Since not enough Ssyms rail cars were available, the 3rd Company had to wait until empty cars returned to Mor from Perbete. As a result, that company did not load until 15 February.

15 February 1945: The commander went with the company commanders through Kürt for a leaders' reconnaissance and to establish liaison with the grenadiers occupying the main line of resistance. The front lines ran from north to south at the eastern outskirts of Kürt.

The battalion was to launch its attack from there on 17 February. The tank commanders were then briefed on the attack sectors lying directly in front of them by the company commanders. Those briefings were done individually, sneaking along concealed paths with great care.

16 February 1945: The attack was to proceed through rising hilly terrain north of the road that ran east from Kürt. Because of the difficult terrain, the Russians did not expect any attacks there. At the road itself, on the other hand, well fortified antitank positions and mine fields had been spotted. The problem was how the tanks were to get to the high ground. The battalion's combat engineer platoon was put to work and constructed a firm route that was negotiable for Tigers. By night, however, the climb would still be a risky venture for the Tigers.

17 February 1945: We awakened at 0200 hours. At 0230 hours the battalion moved out. In the meantime, it had again grown to twenty-two Tigers. With six or seven Tigers in each company, two staff Tigers, SPWs and the combat trains, the battalion moved forward through Für and Kürt. It was a very difficult approach march, since it was pitch dark and the driving had to be done without any lights at all. There was an extremely risky ascent for the tanks on the steep climbing route that the engineers had constructed through a rock quarry to the otherwise inaccessible high

ground from which the attack was to be conducted. Not a single tank got stuck.

At 0420 hours the attack began. The 2nd Company went forward on the left, the 1st Company forward on the right. Behind them, in the center, were several tanks of the 3rd Company. The Tigers rolled forward through our own positions during an artillery barrage. When the tanks then made their way into the midst of the Russian positions, the enemy defense woke up. In the Russian barrage that ensued, the grenadiers of "Hoch- und Deutschmeister" who were following suffered significant losses. Leutnant Piepgras had crossed an enemy trench and was then left, immobilized, in a mine field. The battalion's engineers came forward in SPWs and cleared a gap. The Tiger that was moving alongside the battalion headquarters tank—Tiger "I"—on the right was set on fire by a direct hit. The fire illuminated the battlefield, making the tanks into good targets for the Russian antitank guns.

The grenadiers closed up to the tanks and the commander gave the order for the advance to continue. As his tank was on the verge of crossing a second Russian trench, it was hit on the turret by a round from an antitank gun. Since the commander was driving with the hatch open, as all tank commanders had to do at night for purposes of orientation, he was gravely wounded on the back of the head by a round fragment. He only had time enough to inform Leutnant Heerlein to take over command, before he was loaded into a medical SPW and taken to the rear. Immediately after the commander had been wounded, the attacking Tigers came up against an extremely cleverly emplaced battery of large-caliber long-barreled guns. The tanks shot them to pieces or overran them. After that happened, the Russian resistance in that sector quickly collapsed. Hauptmann Wiegand came up from Tardosked and took over temporary command of the battalion.

18 February 1945: Von Rosen wrote the following in 1946:

I did not take part in the attack on 17 February, since the main body of the 3rd Company had not arrived at Perbete in time. On 18 February I had all of the available operational tanks.

As day dawned, we attacked along the railroad line toward Kis-Ufalu, again as part of the battalion. After three hours and breaking through a strong position consisting of antitank guns and tanks, we captured the village. We received outstanding support from our artillery, whose forward observer rode in my tank as the sixth crewman. We broke through the wall of smoke created by the steadily advancing artillery barrage and rooted the Russians out of the place. The Russian Gran bridgehead defenses were buckling. After cleaning out the village we started a further advance into the depths of the Russian position. Suddenly, we were faced with a hasty minefield; the mines had been laid on the surface.

In order to save time, I dismounted and cleared a gap for the tanks, disarming wooden-cased and tar mines as we had been trained to do in 1943 at Tolokonoje by engineer Oberfeldwebel Baumann. In half an hour I had disarmed fifty mines. We passed the minefield without damage. We reached our first intermediate objective and found only light resistance. In the meantime, we had got well behind the Russian lines. A new order arrived by radio from the division. When we deciphered it, our first thought was that there had been a mistake. We queried the division. No, there was no mistake. We had been given a new objective that was about 20 kilometers from the location we were at then. And it was already getting dark.

We continued our attack, always cross-country. From time to time enemy tanks appeared in front of us. A brief exchange of fire, knock the tank out, and forward again. The most difficult thing was orienting ourselves in the pitch-black night. As midnight approached we got into a marshy place that gave us difficulties. At some distance we saw white flares go up to our left, the sign for "friendly troops" and we also heard the typical noise of German tanks. After about another hour we were able to establish direct contact. It was the 1st SS Panzer Division "Leibstandarte," which had attacked from the north with forty to fifty tanks. We closed up with them for a time, but then were halted by order from the division. That was in the Muszla area.

19 February 1945: Hauptmann Wiegand moved to the division to establish contact and report. I waited several hours with the tanks for our supplies, which arrived at about 0400 hours in the morning. With them came the much-desired field kitchen. The food was cold, but at least the coffee was warm. At about 0700 hours, I went to Köbölkut with the tanks. Hauptmann Wiegand was already waiting there for us. He had received new orders in the meantime. We were to clear two villages, but the Russians appeared to have got wind of the advance of the Tigers. They pulled out and we were able to complete that mission without much opposition. We would have liked to have a bit of a break at that point, but a new order by radio sent us off on a new mission. That time the mission led us into hilly terrain. It was a strain for us; we had not shut our eyes for forty-eight hours.

The beautiful early spring sunshine was some compensation. By evening we got to our new objective. We were eagerly anticipated there. We were to immediately take part in a night attack on Kemend. Therefore, again, no sleep. The terrain of the attack was difficult; numerous deep ravines had to be crossed. In the darkness—possible enemy contact at any moment—it was doubly unpleasant. We had already crossed the Russian lines. They had been abandoned. That did not seem right to us. After a very difficult crossing over a bad ravine, we got to a broad, gently falling plateau. We could only guess at the direction of our attack. We advanced slowly. It was clear to me that the most difficult part would come at daybreak. If we were actually able to get to Kemend during the night, then we would be on our own during the day. All of the terrain was under good observation from the Russian positions from the superior elevation of the far bank of the Gran. No sort of supply or replacements would be able to get forward to us during the day. That, however, would have to wait. For the present, the attack was still in motion, but the silence of the Russians was disturbing.

Suddenly we ran into mines: To our right, to our left, and in front of us, mines. Some of us were already in the midst of the minefield, whose boundaries could not be discerned. Thousands of mines must have been laid there. We attempted to clear the mines. They were carefully laid and completely frozen to the ground. We moved slowly forward. Then we saw that such an approach just would not do. We worked feverishly to replace the damaged track links. While we did that, several more mines went off. It was a loathsome situation. Something had to happen. We could not get through that minefield. Therefore: Pull out. It was already beginning to get light.

20 February 1945: We fell back again as far as the ravine. As day broke we already had the Russians at our throats. They made an extremely spirited attack with tanks, but we were superior to them in that situation. As noon approached we got a bit of a break. Hauptmann Wiegand moved back to the command post. I left two tanks up front to cover us and pulled back about 2 kilometers with the others to give the crews a little rest. The ones out front were to be relieved every two hours.

I lay on the rear deck of my tank in the warm sun and immediately fell asleep. Shortly thereafter we were shelled by artillery. My left elbow was smashed by a shell fragment. I was barely aware of it in my half-asleep state and did not really come to until the surgeon was already working on my arm. I turned over the leadership of the company to Leutnant Koppe and was brought back to the command post at Köbölkut in a SPW. Dr Büry cared for me there. I took leave of my soldiers, saying: "I'll be back in three months!" (End of von Rosen's immediate postwar notes)

Three months later the war was over.

CHAPTER 31

After-Action Reports of Hauptmann Fromme and Oberleutnant Oemler

AFTER-ACTION REPORT OF HAUPTMANN FROMME

Tiger Tank Battalion 503 Command Post
25 November 1944
Ia 371/44
Secret

The battalion was entrained on 9 October 1944 for Hungary to complete its refitting in the Budapest area. The crisis in Hungary made it necessary for the battalion to be committed on 16 October to occupy the castle at Budapest, an employment that was almost entirely a demonstration, but which was a decisive success.

An intensification of the situation east of the Theiss and at Debrecen required immediate action. The armored units entrained in the Szolnok area. However, due to the shortage of Ssyms rail cars, which had to operate in shuttle service, not all were able to arrive at the assembly position in time. The units marched directly to the assembly area on unloading, starting the attack a few hours later. The tanks that arrived the next day were, likewise, formed into a battle group and placed under the operational control of another division, so that the battalion went into action in two battle groups with two different divisions on two different days. Provided the assault was successful in penetrating into the enemy rear, the battalion would then reunite.

Both groups were extraordinarily successful. From 19–23 October 1944, 120 antitank guns and 19 guns were destroyed. The extremely tough and steadfast enemy (penal battalions) was shaken to the core by the energetic assault and his communications to the rear thrown into total confusion by the destruction of various columns and a transport train which, in the final analysis, forced the Russian Sixth Army from the Debrecen area. The total distance of about 250 kilometers covered during the operation was accomplished essentially without mechanical failure. The Tiger II proved itself extremely well, both in its armor and from a mechanical perspective. Vehicles which received up to twenty hits without becoming disabled were not uncommon.

The follow-on operations were limited in scope, in particular counterattacks with weak friendly infantry against the enemy crossing the Theiss northeast of Szolnok. Those operations, however, as already reported by SQ-messages, had the successful outcome that, wherever the Tigers were employed, the Russians were prevented from major combat operations.

During that time and continuing up to now, the battalion has not been given any time at all for technical servicing, in spite of continual requests. That has been due, in part, to the situation. However, that has also been due to inadequate understanding on the part of the superior commands, which have always had just two questions: "How many are operational?" and "How many will be ready for action tomorrow?" In spite of that, there has been an average of twenty-five to thirty tanks in service through 30 October.

On 31 October the battalion moved to a new operational area near Kecskemet, where it was to be employed as part of the LVII Panzer Corps. Its mission was to intercept the Russian assault groups advancing to Budapest. Damage appeared almost immediately in the extremely difficult, partially swampy terrain that was decidedly unsuitable for armor; in particular, there was damage to the drive sprockets, tracks, track-tension adjusters and ventilators. Within a few days, due to a shortage of replacement parts, which had been requisitioned in timely fashion but had not been promptly or completely provided, that damage led to the majority of the battalion's tanks being disabled.

As a result of insufficient means of towing, the battalion was faced with the decision of either blowing up the damaged tanks that were in front of the main line of resistance or recovering them with those Tigers that were still operational. Naturally, that also caused mechanical damage to the Tigers that were employed for towing. Only timely and pre-planned loading of the tanks at the last moment on the railroad allowed the battalion to avoid greater losses of armored vehicles.

The few remaining operational tanks were shunted from division to division and assigned missions that were inappropriate, that were incapable of being carried out and that were intolerable. (See after-action report concerning Battle Group Oemler for 15 November 1944.)

Since 18 November the battalion has been employed in the Gyöngyös area. The unceasing bad weather has made it impossible to leave the roads. Since the mechanized infantry and light infantry regiments are too weak, the Tigers and also the self-propelled antiaircraft vehicles have to provide cover in the front lines without any dismounted protection. Attacks in pitch black night in terrain which has not been reconnoitered with far too weak infantry forces are not uncommon, e.g., a night attack with 120 convalescing infantry and a SPW battalion (strength forty men) to capture a city that was strongly held with antitank guns and infantry. Such attacks can only be successful if the grenadiers also actually take part in the attack ahead of and to the sides of the tanks, destroying the antitank guns that are massed in the doorways of houses and gates, where they can not be knocked out by the tanks. The infantry cannot crumble at the first sign of resistance and leave the Tigers all alone so that it is easy for enemy hunter/killer teams to engage them.

Experience has confirmed that the Russians construct strong antitank defenses immediately behind their foremost units. The employment of American 9.2cm and conical antitank guns (7.5 down to 5.7cm) has, fortunately, only led to two total losses so far. Those weapons even penetrate the gun mantlet at ranges under 600 meters. Hits that penetrate the back of the turret cause explosion of the ammunition stored there and generally have resulted in total losses of the vehicles.

In armor versus armor engagements, the 8.8 KwK 43 has proven effective in destroying all types of enemy armor, including the Stalin tank at ranges up to 1500 meters. T-34 and T-43 tanks could be knocked out in favorable firing conditions at ranges up to 3,000 meters. Frequently, as in the West, the Russian tanks avoided combating Tigers or turned away after the first tank was knocked out. The same holds true for assault guns as for the Stalin tanks. Assault guns have not yet been knocked out at ranges greater than 1,500 meters.

In summary, the Tiger II has proven itself in every way and is a weapon that the enemy fears. When the formation is used as a single, unified entity and is employed in accordance with proper tactics, it always brings decisive success. However, most of the higher-level commands do not look out for the technical and tactical needs of a Tiger-Abteilung.

Armored Antiaircraft Platoon
In the armored flak platoon, the quad guns have proven themselves the best. In both armored protection and cross-country performance, they are immediately in a position to provide adequate protection against aerial attack and also to perform an impressive role in ground engagements. In an extremely short time, the quad-gun section achieved three confirmed and two probable aircraft kills. The 3.7cm guns are unsuited to accompany an armored attack. The crew is totally unprotected whenever the gun is ready to fire or the time taken to ready the gun for action is excessive. In addition, no 3.7cm explosive ammunition has arrived since the battalion has been committed in Hungary.

The Combat Reconnaissance Platoon
The combat reconnaissance platoon has not yet been committed because it only just arrived from Germany. The one exception was the detailing of

the medium-wave radio SPWs to the combat elements due to the loss of the command vehicles.

Scout and Combat-Engineer Platoons

The scout platoon has completed all tasks assigned to it. The Kettenkrad has particularly proven itself in this terrain. The combat engineer platoon was primarily used in construction of provisional crossing ramps, in reinforcing bridges and for improving routes.

Signals Platoon

An additional Fu2 set (second receiver) is an absolute necessity since, when working with other units, the ultra-short wave traffic so exceeds the present capabilities that an Fu5 is inadequate. Moreover, it is impossible to maintain radio communications with superior or sub-units on one and the same frequency.

The GG 400s in the vehicles have generally proven inadequate as a result of the ongoing demands and the resultant constant repairs. Type Cs are preferable.

It would likewise be desirable to use the back-pack "b" receiver in lieu of the medium-wave "c" receiver, since the "b" could be fed by either a vehicular battery or a plate battery and 2 b 38 batteries. Doing that would lead to a considerable improvement in guaranteeing the electrical supply.

(signed: von Diest-Koerber)
Hauptmann and battalion commander

AFTER-ACTION REPORT OF OBERLEUTNANT OEMLER

The Battle Group Leader
1st Company, Tiger Tank Battalion 503
In the field
15 November 1944

On 11 November 1944 at 1430 hours the battle group received the order from the 13. Panzer-Division via a battalion officer to move to Szentmartlós. The battle group was placed under the operational control of Armored Battle Group Künzel. The Tiger battle group arrived at 1530 hours in Tápiószentmartlós (coming from Pápióbicke) and reported to Hauptmann Frondseck at the regimental command post. New orders arrived from the division at 1530 hours: "Battle group is to be placed under the operational control of Grenadier Battalion Seidel." It moved with two companies of Grenadier Battalion Seidel mounted on its tanks by way of Point 108 to Farmos. The 1st Company of Grenadier Battalion Seidel—outfitted with SPWs—moved through Nagykata to Farmos. The battle group moved out from Farmos with Armored Group Battalion Grün, which had, in the meantime, been ordered to that location. The elements advanced on Tápió Szele and set up south of the city.

Departure took place immediately after the arrival of the mechanized grenadier company. The division commander of the 46th Infantry Division informed the leader of the battle group that the route ordered for the Tigers was good. However, the Tigers were not able to follow that route and the tanks bore off to the southeast so as to get to a parallel route 2 kilometers away. That route also proved unusable, since the bridges were too weak and the terrain completely softened and swampy. The Tigers bogged down and had to turn around.

At 1730 hours the leader of the battle group arrived in Farmos in a staff car with Hauptmann Seidel and Hauptmann Grün. Since it had become completely dark in the meantime, Battalion on Seidel and the Tigers did not arrive, Tapio Szele was already held by the enemy and the terrain was not even negotiable for a SPW, Hauptmann Seidel did not start the attack.

Because there would be no getting through on the routes that the Tigers had to follow, Leutnant Fürlinger immediately moved on the road through Nagykata to Tápióbiske to inform the division regarding the situation, to get new orders and to direct the Tigers through Nagykata. At the division, a state of total confusion reigned regarding the situation of the battle group. The division halted the Tigers and, by order of the corps, ordered them to Nagykata. Effective 0430 hours on 12 November, they formed the corps reserve at Nagykata, together with Battalion Grün, an SPW-equipped panzer-grenadier battalion.

Leutnant Fürlinger reported the situation regarding Battle Group Seidel, took new orders for the withdrawal of Battalion Grün and, after they had refueled, guided the Tigers to Tápióbiske. On 12 November the battle group was corps reserve at Nagykata.

1230 hours: An order from the 23rd Panzer Regiment arrived by messenger-Tiger battle group is placed under the operational control of the 23rd Panzer Regiment and moves through Jasbereny to Jakohalma. The leader of the Tiger battle group immediately moved to the 13th Panzer Division for a situation brief. A new order was awaiting him at the division: Tiger battle group—attached to a battle group of the 23rd Panzer Division—and Armored Battalion Grün had the task of clearing the Nagykata-Jasbereny road of enemy, advancing through Jasbereny and establishing contact with the 23rd Panzer Division. It would have been impossible to carry out the initial order because the road was held by the enemy on a broad front.

The Tiger battle group set out at 1400 hours toward Jasbereny with the first objective of the attack being a road intersection 2 kilometers southwest of Jasbereny.

800 meters before the intersection, the Tiger spearhead encountered enemy tanks, assault guns and very strong infantry forces. One assault gun and three enemy tanks were knocked out. A further advance was impossible since Battalion Grün had been attacked on its right flank. It had not advanced with the tanks and was stuck five kilometers behind them. It was not feasible for the Tigers to fight alone on the road through the woods. Further, it would have been impossible to leave the road in terrain that was very marshy in areas. In spite of support from heavy weapons, the SS Battalion that had been committed in the woods to provide cover was unable to stop the attacks of the enemy who had advanced to within extremely short range in the thick underbrush. It pulled back after blowing up the ammunition point located in the woods.

At 1600 hours the battalion also ordered the Tigers to pull back as far as its command post, about six kilometers to the rear.

At 1900 hours the leader of the Tiger battle group received the order to contact the commander of the 13th Panzer Division by land line.

At 1940 hours the commander of the 13th Panzer Division gave the following order to the Tiger battle group by phone:

Three Tigers are to move through the woods again to the road intersection, 800 meters from the edge of the woods near the intersection. Three Tigers move to the to the entrance to the woods, two kilometers behind the first Tigers and provide cover there, preventing the Russians from infiltrating through the woods. Two Tigers are to spend the entire night driving back and forth between the two strongpoints and maintain

contact. Each tank strongpoint was to be secured by fifteen infantrymen.

The Tiger leader immediately reported that:

1. The woods, particularly in its eastern portion, was strongly held by the enemy. It would be impossible for a Tiger to enter it, even by day, without extremely strong close-in protection by infantry.
2. The terrain was extremely marshy and it would not be possible to leave the road (especially at night).
3. Because of the trees, a Tiger on the road would not even be able to traverse its gun, let alone turn. Further, if one tank were knocked out, the others would be unable to pass it.
4. The Tigers could not move around at night in terrain that was unsuitable for armor about five kilometers in front of the German main line of resistance.
5. As a result of the forced march of the previous night, only six Tigers were fully operational and one was only conditionally operational.

In spite of those objections, the division insisted on the execution of the order. The only change being that two SPWs were to replace the Tigers for maintaining contact.

After the initial infantry units arrived at 2200 hours, the first three Tigers set out. The infantry first had to be pulled out of the lines. The group, led by Leutnant Fürlinger, consisted of two Unteroffiziere, twelve men and two SPWs. The departure of the other three Tigers was delayed, since the infantry was not yet there. The first three Tigers moved forward with mounted infantry (four to five men on each tank). The night was pitch dark, the sky overcast. It was raining and visibility was generally zero.

The security group halted two hundred meters ahead of the spot that had been reached during the day and had been designated by the division. The leader sent two of the infantry from his vehicle forward. Ten meters in front of the tank they were fired on from all sides from the woods and the road. The Tigers formed a hedgehog on the road. The enemy slowly infiltrated past on the right and left. On several occasions, Russian hunter/killer teams that had approached the tanks were chased off. Since it had not been possible to prevent the Russians from infiltrating

s.Panzer-Abteilung 503
Abt. Ia   465/44 geh.   **Geheim**

Meldung vom 1. Januar 1945

Verband: s.Panzer-Abteilung 503
Unterstellungsverhältnis: Gen.Kdo. HHh.Pz.Kp.
I.Kav.K.

Nr.: 58/45 g   Akt: Ia   Eing: 4 JAN 1945

1. Personelle Lage am Stichtag der Meldung:

a) Personal:

	Soll	Fehl	Krank u. Verw.innerh. v. 8 Wochen	c) in der Berichtszeit eingetroffener Ersatz:	
				Ersatz	Genesene
Offiziere	28 + 5 Beamte	1	1		
Uffz.	279	–	14	Offiziere 3	1
Mannsch.	598	–	37	Uffz. und Mannsch. 1	–
Hiwi	31	12	–	7	6
Insgesamt	941	14	52		

b) Verluste und sonstige Abgänge in der Berichtszeit vom 1.12. bis 31.12.44

	tot	verw.	verm.	krank	sonst.
Offiziere	1	–	–	–	–
Uffz. und Mannsch.	2	4	–	5	1
Mannsch.	1	4	–	12	–
Insgesamt	4	8	–	17	1

d) über 1 Jahr nicht beurlaubt:

insgesamt: 20   Köpfe 1,8 % d. Iststärke

davon:

12-18 Monate	19-24 Monate	über 24 Monate
20	2	–

Platzkarten im Berichts-monat zugewiesen: 12

2. Materielle Lage:

		Gepanzerte Fahrzeuge						Kraftfahrzeuge				
		Stu. Gesch.	III	IV	Berge V	VI	Schü.Pz. Pz.Sp. Art.Pz.B. (leFz.Fu.Wg.)	Pak SF	Kräder			Pkw
									Ketten	im.angetr. Bwg.	sonst.	gel.	O
Soll (Zahlen)		–	–	8	5	45	11	–	14	–	6	38	1
einsatzbereit	zahlenm.	–	–	2	–	10	5	–	5	–	2	7	2
	in % des Solls	–	–	25	–	22	45,5	–	36	–	33	18,5	200
in kurzfristiger Instandsetzung (bis 3 Wochen)	zahlenm.	–	–	2	1	8	4	–	4	–	1	8	2
	in % des Solls	–	–	25	20	18	36,5	–	29	–	17	21	200

		–noch Kraftfahrzeuge				Ketten-Fahrzeuge		Waffen			
		Lkw				Zgkw.	RSO	s Pak	2 cm	MG. ( )	sonstige Waffen
		Maultiere	gel.	O	Tonnage						
Soll (Zahlen)		6	84	34	397,5	*)7 **)13	–	–	3	136	876
einsatzbereit	zahlenm.	3	29	41	242	1	3	–	–	3	103(19)	854
	in % des Solls	50	60		61	14	23	–	–	100	75	97
in kurzfristiger Instandsetzung (bis 3 Wochen)	zahlenm.	2	8	7	61	1	2	–	–	–	–	–
	in % des Solls	33,33	10	20	15	14	15	–	–	–	–	–

*) Zgkw. mit 1–5 t, **) Zgkw. mit 8–18 t
( ) davon MG. 42

3. Pferdefehlstellen:

Anl. zu Nr. H777/45 geh.
Gen. Insp. d. Pz.Tr.

Monthly status report of Tiger Tank Battalion 503, dated 1 January 1945. *Personelle Lage* = Personnel Situation; *Materielle Lage* = Equipment Situation; *Soll* = Authorized; *Fehl* = Missing/Short; *einsatzbereit* = operational; *Kraftfahrzeuge* = vehicles; *Waffen* = weapons; *in kurzfristiger Instandsetzung (bis 3 Wochen)* = short-term maintenance (less than 3 weeks).

through the woods during the day, it was totally impossible to do so at night. Only ignorance of the strength of the security group prevented the enemy from completely wiping it out.

As for the SPWs, one dropped out at the start. The lead Tiger of the second Tiger covering force threw a track three kilometers before reaching its designated position. The terrain prevented the two other tanks from moving past.

When the pressure from the enemy became too strong, the Tigers of the first security group slowly pulled back 400 meters. Enemy tanks had been approaching from the south (and, apparently, the T-34s also got stuck on the woodland paths). The SPW was sent back to establish contact, was fired on, and did not move forward again.

Hauptmann Grün and the Tiger leader were continuously kept abreast of the situation by radio. At about 2300 hours, the Tiger leader telephonically reported the enemy situation to the operations officer of the 13th Panzer Division from Grün's command post. He inquired whether the Tigers, in spite of the strong enemy pressure, were to hold their strongpoint under those conditions. The danger existed that the Russians would cut the Tigers off from supplies and mine the road. Nevertheless, the order was not rescinded.

At 0200 Hauptmann Grün received the order to link up with the Tigers that were providing cover and advance to Jasbereny that night. The battalion moved out with the second trio of Tigers at 0500. It first had to be withdrawn from the lines. After reaching the lead Tiger strongpoint, the battle group deployed. The lead Tiger started by knocking out five 7.62cm antitank guns when it had only gone 150 meters. It then attacked 200 meters through the edge of the woods. At that point, the battle group encountered a strong antitank-gun defensive belt and well concealed assault guns. Leutnant Bielefeld was killed by a short-range antitank gun hit in the attempt to outflank the antitank guns to the left through an open field.

German Panzerfäuste, sticky bombs and other close-combat antitank materials lay scattered about in the abandoned Russian positions alongside the road. A Russian infantryman with a Panzerfaust was shot down within 20 meters of the tanks as he tried to sneak up to the side of the Tigers. Since the infantry had not advanced as far as the tanks, the enemy in the woods counterattacked with an "Hurrah!" from his old positions in battalion strength. They forced the infantry that

were following back from the road to the left, with the result that the Tigers had to fall back. The Russian attack was brought to a halt and the battle group formed a hedgehog defense.

The leader of the battle group recommended an enveloping move to the north. By doing that, the battle group could establish contact with the 23rd Panzer Division. At 1300 hours the order arrived to execute that maneuver. At 1500 hours, the battle group reached the command post of the 2nd Battalion of the 40th SS Regiment without further contact with the enemy. The Tigers then moved out from the north toward the intersection. They turned to the west south of the Jasbereny-Nagykata road. They established cover at the designated point. By the time darkness started to fall, the battle group withdrew toward Grün's command post. At a distance of one kilometer from the command post, the entire group of Tigers got stuck on the road and the laborious recovery lasted until dawn.

As a result of totally improper employment, four Tigers were disabled (as could only be expected) with damage to tracks, drive sprockets or transmission trouble. The relationship with the division was most unpleasant. Practically no attention was paid to the fundamental principles of employment of Tigers. Due to the various types of operations and the ongoing changing command and control relationships, it was not possible to bring forward supplies. When the radio vehicle became disabled, the request to borrow a vehicle for a few hours to guide the supply vehicles forward was rejected by the division O1 [special duty staff officer] with the words, "You see to it how you get your fuel forward! I am not here to get your fuel to you !" When the attack did not move forward on 13 November, the operations officer of the division told Hauptmann Grün that he did not have any information on the enemy situation. In contrast, the leader of the armored group and the Tiger leader were constantly in contact with the Tigers providing cover. They kept the divisional operations officer constantly informed during the night of 12–13 November and personally orientated him around 2400 hours concerning the situation and their impression of the enemy.

The leader of the battle group:

(signed: Oemler)
Oberleutnant and company commander

Recollections of a Panzer Soldier (Part IV): The Reorganization of the Battalion

Dr. Franz-Wilhelm Lochmann

Having a tank company at the same place as the replacement battalion was located did not bode well. Whenever we painted the town red in the evenings, we had ourselves picked up by a staff car. That was not a good thing, since there was fuel rationing and even the battalion commander of the replacement battalion, Oberstleutnant Hoheisel, rode around Paderborn on a bicycle. (Oberstleutnant Hoheisel had succeeded our first battalion commander, Oberstleutnant Post, as battalion commander.) We were banished to the countryside near Bentfeld. The battalion and its staff were quartered in Neuhaus. At the end of September and beginning of October, new Tiger IIs were issued to the battalion at Sennelager. At that point, we were the first Tiger battalion that was entirely equipped with King Tigers. Those vehicles were equipped with the so-called production turrets by Krupp. Several Tigers had the Porsche turret.

BENTFELD

In Bentfeld, once more, we not only led a relatively peaceful, but also a very cheerful life. There were abundant Marketenderwaren and Unteroffizier Höppner took over the village pub. One time, when we were expecting a particularly high-level visit at the battalion in Elsen, the 1st Company was designated to post a particularly snappy

guard. I was given two days to prepare for that operation. With the collection of senior privates detailed to me one could, indeed, take on any combat situation or clean out a supply dump, but mount a snappy guard—no, that remained to be seen. We moved to Elsen. Then came our great moment. With great timing, the entire guard piled out of the vehicle and fell in. It was a magnificent guard. "Attention! Shoulder arms! Present arms! Eyes right!" Hauptmann Fromme beamed. The guest was visibly impressed. They slowly rolled past and we followed them with our eyes. While presenting arms, I softly said, "And now to beat a hasty retreat." Out loud, I bellowed, "Guard dismissed!" We had a great time. As a reward, I got a four day official trip to Hamburg. That was the last time I got to go home. Then the final phase of the war swallowed us up.

HUNGARY

As the general military situation in Hungary had become hopeless, Imperial Regent Horthy resolved to arrange a cease-fire with the Allies. Tiger Tank Battalion 503 was set in motion from Sennelager to Budapest. After detraining, we moved to Budakezy. On 15 October we took over the security of the city. In the meantime, our vehicles repeatedly moved around the streets of the city as a demonstration of military might. Skorzeny took care of the rest with a small SS troop. The potential catastrophe for the southern front was significantly ameliorated by that.

On 18 October our commitment in the Szolnok area began. The battalion succeeded in forcing back strong Russian forces. On 20 October we formed a hedgehog position in the Turkeve area. The vehicles formed a great circle, about 60 to 100 meters apart. We granted the infantry who had been assigned to accompany us a break for the night. The battalion commander, Hauptmann Fromme, took position at the edge of a road that led to the east. He had "remounted" in a tank from the 1st Company. To his right, and offset a good 60 meters, was Tiger 100.

At 0200 hours the radio operator of Tiger 100 took his watch in the turret. In front of him lay a ready-to-fire machine pistol and a loaded flare gun. He peered out into the peaceful night. The landscape was, indeed, very open, but it was totally dark. At about 0300 hours he heard a soft metallic clattering approaching on the road. It was a very typical sound, the noise of carefully moving infantry. The radio operator concentrated on watching the street. Then he identified what it was. Moving quietly on both sides of the street, about twenty men on each side, they were approaching the commander's tank. They were still about 40 meters away and did not seem to have noticed the colossus. Nobody stirred on the commander's tank. Were they blind? Were those our own troops? Damn, I thought. They must be asleep over there. I sent up a flare. It slowly swayed from the parachute and illuminated the entire scene. They were Russians. A combat patrol. Alert. The machine pistol fired on full automatic. Machine gun fire slowly opened up from the Tigers nearby. The disturbers of the peace were driven off. In the future, the youngsters then knew the drill. Even when the commander took his place in their tank, the crew could not turn over the guard to the others, especially when it was Hauptmann Fromme.

FIGHTING AT MEZÖTUR

During the days that followed, we were continually busy. Our concern was less the Russian tanks and assault guns than the Russian antitank guns. The Russians skillfully constructed deeply echeloned antitank belts. We broke through them and moved into Mezîtur. Slowly we rolled along the main road into the place. Suddenly, a 7.62cm round whizzed overhead, barely clearing our turret. It came from the left. We paid better attention at the next gap between houses. But we still were unable to discover them. Another round barely missed us. The thing must be in a very elevated position. Between the houses we got a break. At the next side street we were even more attentive. The turret was traversed to the left. And that was where we spotted the muzzle flash. It was unbelievable. It came from the lower part of the church tower. We could not identify the antitank gun, but we let loose with a high-explosive round. We scored a direct hit. We could see the barrel and wheels of an antitank gun through the destroyed section of the wall. That one would leave us in peace.

After we had already wiped out twelve antitank guns that day, the thirteenth got us on the commander's cupola. Leutnant Piepgras was wounded. Thank God, the injury was not severe. Leutnant Fürlinger was in another tank of the company. He moved in the vehicle on the left flank. He was incredibly impetuous in advancing. Again and again he overtook our point. How would that turn out? Not only did he endanger himself, but he also interfered with our field of fire to the left. A little later he was stopped by the Russians. His vehicle took an extraordinary number of hits. Thank God none of them penetrated. Hopefully, he would start to pay better attention. On the same day, Feldwebel Markus' tank received a direct hit from an artillery round. The Feldwebel and his gunner, Unteroffizier Schielke, were killed. The other members of the crew got away with hardly a scratch.

LEUTNANT BIELEFELD

We were employed further south during the next few days. We arrived at a division command post with a total of three tanks. Our company commander, Oberleutnant Oemler, was with us. They were expecting strong Russian armored forces. Leutnant Bielefeld and another of our tanks were to provide cover far to the east. The terrain was not favorable for the employment of armor. The situation was totally confused. Our commander tried to put a stop to that nonsense. He was unable to prevail. When Leutnant Bielefeld went beyond radio range for a tank, I climbed into a command SPW. After an hour, I made contact with the radio operator, Hans-Jürgen Fiedler. The Russians had cut off the tanks. Leutnant Bielefeld had been killed in the meantime.

While my crew fought off a strong Russian armored attack on the command post, I sat with the map in the SPW and attempted to guide the two tanks out of the miserable situation. Jürgen Fiedler kept giving me a description of the terrain in front of the vehicles. I tried to match it with the corresponding point on the map. I was able to direct them around a marshy area to the north of us. They made it past the strong Russian forces, and I was then able to guide them out of the danger zone and well behind us.

I was happy to again climb into Tiger 100. We all pulled out. A few days later, Leutnant Fürlinger came back to our tank. In the course of attacking a village, we knocked out all of the antitank guns. We were on the outskirts of the village and were waiting for the infantry coming behind us. Leutnant Fürlinger spotted a few tanks disappearing into a hollow on our left flank. He set us in motion, driving across the village. Then the vehicles reappeared and Werner and I cried out at almost the same moment: "They're friendlies!" At that moment we were hit by a round from an antitank gun in the village. The gunners had probably returned to the gun after they had initially taken flight. They had taken good aim. The 7.62cm hit the hull where it was welded together on the bottom.

Werner whipped the tank around. The turret crew showed them who was the boss here. The weld seam had been torn open about 30 centimeters in front of me. That would have consequences for us. The hull was bent somewhat, and we would have incredible wear and tear on the final drive in the immediate future. And that came at just the time when the operational tanks were continually forced to do long road marches.

LAKE BALATON
Our track was damaged by heavy artillery fire while we were in the vineyards. The turret crew was busy. Werner and I were outside. The air was damned full of lead. For lack of a sledge hammer, we tried to pound the connecting pins back through the track with an axe. Werner hit the ball of my thumb with the edge of the blunt side of the axe. I yelled: "Can't you aim right?" Werner replied: "Can't you hold the pin right?" We were back in a good mood in the tank. Later, when it

quieted down a bit, I fixed him a slice of bread with processed cheese in a tube. "Do you have anything else?" I opened a can of smoked sausage. Werner chewed in contentment. Promptly from the turret: "Are you chowing down again?" I passed the slice of bread and cheese up into the turret to Richard Schwarzmann, who had joined our crew. He exploded: "I like that! You eat the smoked sausage and offer us the crummy cheese!"

POLGARDE (8 DECEMBER 1944)
Long before daylight we arrived at the attack position. The tank regiment to which we were attached wanted to start things off with a feint on the right flank as soon as it was light. Our battle group would then make a frontal attack across a bridge. There were five Tigers available. Leutnant Koppe got into Tiger 100 with us. Feldwebel Mewes and Unteroffizier Bieske and their crews were with us from our company. We had great support from Feldwebel Weigel and Feldwebel Seidel and their crews from the 3rd Company. In addition, we still had a few self-propelled Flak vehicles from our battalion and a bunch of very well equipped SPWs. We were supposed to press through to the middle of the village. As soon as things really got stirred up with us, the tank regiment would roll up the relatively long, stretched-out village from the left.

We made a frontal attack on the village in a broad, shallow wedge and were able to silence all the antitank guns. Everything went a lot faster than expected. We crossed the bridge and found ourselves on a broad road. With Mewes on the right and Bieske on the left, we pushed into the village. Tiger 100 followed a little behind the two lead Tigers. Seidel and Weigel followed behind, leaving a gap. We reached the church. I gave our location to the regiment, according to the map grid superimposed on the Hungarian map. We were told, "Roger—wait." The Russians fled before us. We had to keep going. Finally we noticed that the coordinates on the maps in the command vehicle did not agree. We moved on. The village was jammed full of vehicles. Everywhere there were Russians with their hands raised. One of our tanks bagged an airplane. It was the kind known as a "sewing machine" or the "duty NCO."

We halted a 100 meters before the end of the long village. We could hardly believe all the precious items Ivan had blessed us with. We loaded up with canned rations. I happened to find a cheap camera in one vehicle. It was an Agfa box camera with film in it. It had not yet been exposed. The infantry behind us collected endless columns of prisoners. Suddenly it felt kind of strange. There was nothing happening on the left flank. The Russians were offering tough resistance there. There was a road running perpendicular to the end of the village. We slowly crept forward. Moving by bounds, the two lead tanks covered each other.

We kept an eye on the center. When Unteroffizier Bieske's tank which was moving on the left shoved its front slope past the last house, a round penetrated the hull at the driver's position. It came from an antitank gun only a few meters away next to the house. The tank caught fire immediately. The driver and radio operator were killed. The crew in the turret made it safely out of the burning vehicle. The following infantry immediately moved up to take out the antitank gun. Those guys didn't need to attack. The Russians had only a few moments to rejoice at their success. The tanks of the armor regiment with which we were meant to capture the place wiped out the gun crew before they could swing the gun around. The regiment was now advancing on the village. We lost our comrades Wagner and Bohn.

Our commander, Hauptmann Fromme, was transferred in mid-December. He was replaced by Hauptmann von Diest-Koerber. At that time the battalion was still fighting around Lake Balaton.

MOR

Shortly before Christmas was when it happened. Our right final drive gave up the ghost and we were towed to Mor. The tank was positioned outside the church, deep in the mud. At that time our recovery vehicles and the maintenance personnel were working near miracles. They were on the go day and night. Welcomed everywhere, they had to concern themselves with the vehicles and work day and night in the maintenance facility. Several damaged tanks were rail loaded and transported to the rear. Then frost set in. Our tank, which had sunk deep in the mud, froze completely to the ground. On Christmas Eve we were alone in Mor. That night the Russian infantry reached the outskirts of the town. They were thrown back out. The recovery platoon appeared on Christmas day. They couldn't pull the tank out of the frozen mud. We poured liters of gasoline

around the tank and started a lively fire. Finally we were successful. They towed us a good bit back toward the rear. Then the prime movers had to go back to the front to look after other vehicles that were in greater immediate danger than we were. The Spieß found us in a railroad watchman's shack on New Years. The prime movers were there the next day and they patched us up again somehow.

As February began, Tiger 100 was constantly in action. It was surprising how long our final drive held up. Leutnant Piepgras was our tank commander. Then Leutnant FÅrlinger took over our tank as acting company commander. I was able to spend a few days with the trains to get rid of a tapeworm infection that had been troubling me for weeks. There I had a great piece of luck and got to go to Vienna.

VIENNA

A large number of our vehicles that required overhaul from the ground up had been transported to Vienna with their drivers. Along with Unteroffizier Kück, I was to go and bring those tanks back. We were able to go to Vienna. Those were a few glorious days.

In a hospital we visited my great mentor, Pan Vogel. His arm had been mangled by a round that penetrated the turret and his gunner, Hanjo Thaysen, had lost an eye. Pan's home was in Schweinfurt. Why was he there in Vienna, where he was only waiting for the Russians to march in? We decided to look after him and get him out of the hospital.

We convinced the doctor who was responsible for his case that we were on our way to Schweinfurt on official duty. (By the way, Pan had been promoted to Feldwebel—again.) The doctor was happy to get rid of one of his patients. Pan was given marching orders to Schweinfurt which, of course, was not a ticket for the Reichsbahn [the German railroad]. We then sought out a suitable train and waited with Pan at the barricade until the train had started moving very slowly. Pan had a conspicuous arm and shoulder cast, which we had christened a "Stuka." The barrier to the railroad platform was manned by Feldjäger [military police]. There was no getting through there without a ticket. They were on the watch for deserters.

As the train started moving, we dashed up to the barrier and called out: "Help us—a severely wounded man—he must get onto the train, immediately!" And the Feldjäger helped us get our severely immobilized comrade rapidly onto the moving train. Pan looked after himself en route and landed safely in Schweinfurt. They patched him up in the hospital there. For him the war was over.

THE FINAL OPERATIONS

While we were in Vienna, the battalion eliminated the Gran bridgehead. Then it was moved to Verebely in Slovakia. There we had a few days of quiet. An unfortunate accident occurred during a training session on mines. Unteroffizier Böhme was mortally injured by a hand grenade. He was buried in the village.

From there we moved north, roughly parallel to the Austrian border and into the lesser Carpathians.

A MISSED OPPORTUNITY

We were all by ourselves with two King Tigers covering to the east. The maintenance elements units and battalion staff were four to five kilometers behind us. Both tanks were without infantry protection. It was night. As usual, the radio operator of Tiger 100 took the unpopular middle watch in the turret. From the east he heard a slowly approaching armored formation. As time went by, it became clear that there were at least forty enemy tanks.

However, it was also clear that they were not approaching us directly. They would pass farther to our south. The radio operator awakened Leutnant Rambow and told him about the rare opportunity. Unfortunately, we would not have any radio communications with the battalion until 0600 hours in the morning. The Leutnant could not make a decision to change positions to the south, especially since a neighboring division had taken over the sector there.

As day broke, forty Russian tanks that we could have easily held off broke through south of us. They significantly endangered our formations, but eventually were boxed in and destroyed in a wooded area.

We then had to move to the Brünn area [current-day Brno in the Czech Republic], during which we had to cross a pass in the lesser Carpathians. At the southern foot of the mountains we were stopped by a Major. He demanded that we show him our march orders. Oberleutnant Oemler told him what our mission was and refused to

be "drafted" by the officer who was apparently trying to round up forces to support him. In a rage, the Major snarled, "I am Major X and order you . . ." The Leutnant only said, "Panzer, Marsch!" and we moved on.

There were numerous Feldjäger employed in that area to snap up retreating infantry and force them into their positions. We were drawing near the final phase of the war in Czechoslovakia. It was, indeed, true that the retreat had to be controlled, but the methods of the Feldjäger appeared dubious. In the northern foothills of the lesser Carpathians we ran into another bunch of them, with a dying infantryman. When I started to help him, I was told: "There is nothing here that requires your help. This is a deserter." I was shaken. He was an Obergefreiter, decorated with the Iron Cross, First Class, and two *Panzervernichtungsabzeichen* on his arm. Probably all he wanted to do was to make it back to his unit that was assembling to the rear, and the Feldjäger had shot him.

At a small railroad station we waited for a locomotive that was to transport us toward Brünn. That stretch of railroad was already under Russian fire. I visited the neighboring village along with our loader. When we returned, the transport had already departed toward Brünn. An elderly communications officer was there to tear down telephone equipment in the railroad station. He told us that there would be no more trains coming through. At that point, good advice was, indeed, priceless. How were we to get to our unit? Since the Oberleutnant was to fall back to the west after completing his work, he did us yet another favor before he finally put an end to the telephone service to the Brünn railroad station. He requested a railroad motor car be sent from Brünn to fetch a courier from Panzer Corps "Feldherrnhalle." Two hours later, the railroad motor car arrived and Wolfgang Speckin and I could follow the tanks. At Brünn we were able to get out of the affair relatively unscathed and continued our journey to Klein Wartenberg, where we rejoined the company. Once there, I was (after the fact) awarded the *Panzerkampfabzeichen* for having participated in seventy-five armored engagements. By the end of the war, I had been in ninety-five engagements.

We were employed in the Nikolsburg area of operations after our tank had been quickly made operational again. We covered the final withdrawal movement of our units from Czechoslovakia. We performed that task with only two tanks and without significant infantry support.

We were positioned with Richard Schwarzmann in moderately hilly terrain. Perpendicular to us, we could see a road on a ridge, about 2,000 meters away. Early in the afternoon, a number of Russian tanks rolled along across our front as if they were targets in a shooting gallery. We waited until the first vehicle threatened to disappear from our view among trees and bushes. Then: Fire at will! The lead vehicle, a T-34, burned. The column stopped. Then it was the turn of the last visible vehicle. After that, it was child's play. Before the Russian tanks could save their skin, we had shot the entire column into flames.

We had a similar covering-force assignment the next day. It was quiet for almost all of the day. Then while the infantry pulled out, we heard an amazingly fast round pass overhead. That was no "Ratschbumm." That was a big round. In a state of extreme tension we searched the terrain. A few minutes later another round like the first one whizzed over us. We had not spotted any muzzle flash. Nevertheless, it had to be a Joe Stalin or a new heavy Russian antitank gun or assault gun. We moved forward about 200 meters and then observed from really good cover. We still could not spot anything. When the order finally came for us to also pull out to the west, we took the safe approach and pulled out by moving in reverse. We mistrusted the apparent quiet and wanted to keep our heaviest armor toward the enemy. After 400 meters we took a brief halt and another large caliber round whizzed over our turret. Only after another 200 meters, when we were safely in some low ground, did we turn the tank around and drive back to the new designated position. We had not been able to spot our opponent. It had probably been a heavy antitank gun.

On Easter we were ordered to a bridge with two tanks. A small squad of engineers were preparing the bridge for demolition. Four hundred meters southeast of the bridge was a village. We moved into the village and hoped for a break in the fighting. People were baking in all of the houses. It smelled of onion tarts and meat pies. White flags already hung from most of the houses. The Czechs were expecting the Russians. I went into a house along with the loader. We wanted to wash up. Without our requesting it, a friendly old lady brought us warm water to wash and shave. After we had finished our personal hygiene, she served us onion tarts.

Unfortunately, each of us could only take a small piece along with us; both tanks had been ordered back over the river. The engineers had completed their preparations for blowing up the bridge. And then we saw them coming at us. We were attacked by a very large cavalry unit at full gallop. I felt like I was back in the time of Frederick the Great. That had to be at least an entire troop at peacetime strength and it had only one goal in mind—the bridge. Apparently, they did not notice us. At first we didn't think it right to greet the cavalry with high-explosive rounds. However, when they were not discouraged from their intention by a few machine-gun bursts, we got serious and let the 8.8cm guns do the talking. The effect was horrendous. Somehow, we took no pleasure in repulsing the cavalry attack. We were happy when the bridge was blown and we could withdraw as ordered.

On 30 April Hitler committed suicide. The last rats left the sinking ship. Everyone was talking about the end of the war. We were all agreed that we had no intention of falling into the hands of those Russian bastards. The war was over for us, not when Schörner capitulated, but when we got home.

CHAPTER 33

The End of Separate Unit Status: Incorporation into Panzer Corps "Feldherrnhalle"

Alfred Rubbel

It cannot have escaped the reader's attention that in spite of redesignating Tiger Tank Battalion 503 as Tiger Tank Battalion "Feldherrnhalle" (FHH), the new designation really never took hold. The redesignation coincided with the incorporation of the battalion into Panzer Corps "Feldherrnhalle" on 19 December 1944 by order of the OKH. At that time, as today, we held fast to 503.

It is perhaps necessary to recapitulate why our battalion was chosen out of ten separate Tiger battalions to give up its separate status and be incorporated in a newly formed and, in our opinion, insignificant, large formation whose name had a Nazi air about it.

It is well known that, the more improbable a German "final victory" became, the more Hitler held the army responsible for the failure. After the 20 July 1944 assassination attempt, his distrust of the army increased. One result was that the Waffen-SS formations were increased and enlarged. That created a situation that allowed shifting military power from the army. As we all know, that intention of the Nazi regime had no effect on the relationship between the army and the Waffen-SS among the frontline troops. The courage and toughness of the Waffen-SS soldiers commanded our great respect.

In carrying that out, it was also decided by the highest levels of the political leadership to include special fighting formations in the army that formed a part of this "Praetorian guard." In this case, they originated from the SA-Wachstandarte "Feldherrnhalle." The prerequisites were different here, however. The Waffen-SS was the fourth element of the Wehrmacht. "Feldherrnhalle," on the other hand, belonged to the army as a regiment during the campaign in France and as a division in the Russian campaign.

It is an absolute certainty that the newly formed Panzer Corps "Feldherrnhalle" experienced no ideological alteration as a result of its renaming. Only a very small number of the remnants of the shattered formations that had originally born the name "Feldherrnhalle" were incorporated into the corps. The increase to corps strength was accomplished by taking in the remnants of other formations that were in the area where the Panzer Grenadier Division "Feldherrnhalle" was employed. For example, the 13th Panzer Division and Tiger Tank Battalion 503 were "incorporated" and placed at the disposal of General Command (*Generalkommando*) IV which was redesignated Panzer Corps "Feldherrnhalle." The commanding general was General of Panzer Troops Kleeman. The commander of Panzer Division "FHH" 1 was Generalmajor Pape. The commander of Panzer Division "FHH" 2 was Generalmajor Dr. Bäke, who was already well known to us as the commander of Tiger Tank Regiment Bäke, to which our battalion had belonged. Dr. Bäke died in 1978.

For us, there were no fundamental changes. We did not wear the "Feldherrnhalle" cuff titles or the *Wolfsangel*, the stylized SA symbol on the shoulder boards. After January 1945 we only included "Feldherrnhalle" in parentheses alongside the designation Tiger Tank Battalion 503 in written correspondence. The results of an ordered elevation of our battalion to membership in the SA found scant official notice.

I also don't recall the officially designated *NS-Führungspersonal* [Nazi party political leaders] hav-ing been any more active than they were prior to 20 July 1944. For us in the front lines, they had a purely "token" function. The concern that with the impending end of the war, the enemy powers who took custody of our soldiers would rate membership in the "Feldherrnhalle" as equivalent to the Waffen-SS proved unfounded. The arrival of the chief of staff of the SA, Schepmann, in April 1945 at the corps staff in order to take part in the "final battle with his troops" remained a barely noticed episode.

CHAPTER 34

Diary Entries from 14 December 1944 to May 1945 as Commander of Tiger Tank Battalion 503

Dr. Nordewin von Diest-Koerber

14 December: Dawn in Bohemia. Mountainous landscape. Some snow at the higher elevations. Otherwise, mild and hazy. In Brünn (Brno) at 0830 hours. Waited there for hours since a passenger train was derailed on the stretch ahead of us. Endless detours. Instead of arriving at 0100 hours, we did not get to Vienna until 1200. In Vienna (with luggage) from one place to another. Finally, that evening I got to a personnel movement center since there were no more trains going to Budapest. I slept well. Vienna is still amazingly intact.

15 December: 1015 hours, departure from the west train station. Moved via Bruck (destination Komorn—65 kilometers from Budapest). Progress was slow, stopping every few kilometers. However, I had a very good seat in the train, also pleasantly heated. At about 2400 hours we were in Raab (Györ). The train was dark. It got colder since there was no more heating after we crossed the Hungarian border. Hungarian border railroad station had been heavily bombed (Americans). Bedbugs in the train.

16 December: We arrived in Komorn (Komarom) at about 0200 hours. Pitch dark, no one knew anything. We stumbled through the little city (with heavy luggage) at night (slush, formerly snow, since it was at the freezing point. Black ice on the streets). We found a personnel movement center at about 0330 hours where, again, no one knew anything. However, we found several dirty mattresses and slept there until about 0800 hours. After breakfast (unwashed) continued by truck to Kisber, since the LVII Panzer Corps, to which my Tiger Tank Battalion 503 (King Tiger) was attached, was supposed to be south of there at Fehervarcsugo.

The roads were slick, terrible (at the freezing point), torn-up and blocked with columns. One element of the Hungarians was disarmed by the other Hungarians (Arrow Cross men) because it would not fight. That element was driven to the rear. In Kisber (a small city) at noon. It did not make a very good impression. Many civilians, in part refugees, some of them digging positions, some working on the roads. Mediocre impression. Some not very attractive women in very beautiful furs.

Noon meal in a rather dirty spot, quite good, but a lot of paprika. Then on with several vehicles through Mor (headed toward Stuhlweißenburg) until we were near Fehervarczurgo. Then, on foot, about 3 kilometers with heavy luggage through ever-worsening mud! Totally exhausted, I arrived in Fehervar. This afternoon the corps was withdrawn (to the Budapest area)! However, I ran into an advance party of the arriving III Panzer Corps and found quarters in the immense Castle Fehervar (Count Esterhazy). I occupied a room, little furniture, but still heated. Bed (without covers, etc). I could not find out yet whether "503" went with the LVII Panzer Corps or stayed in the area. More information will be available in the morning from the army.

17 December: I slept well. In the meantime, news arrived that "503" will, for the present, remain in Stuhlweißenburg (15 kilometers away). I called there. Ordnance officer (Leutnant Rollick) will pick me up. I went with him 3 kilometers to the village of Bodajk, where I met Dieter Diest (in approach march with I./130 there). Then on to the battalion, which was in Stuhlweißenburg. Adjutant Heerlein (good). The commander of the supply company is Hauptmann Wiegand (he led the battalion for the past eight days after my predecessor, Hauptmann Fromme, left; he made a very good impression). Quarters in a immaculately clean little middle-class house. I had a proper bed with white sheets. Six Tigers employed at the front.

Sixteen more Tigers under repair or on their way forward. In the evening various battalion officers visited me.

18 December: During the morning I went with the Ordonnanzoffizier to the III. Panzer-Korps (in Fehervarcsurgo). Commander: General Breith; Adjutant: Major Düwel (whom I already knew from the regulations writing staff at Wünsdorf). We were immediately placed under the operational control of the 1. Panzer-Division; the six Tigers in the main line of resistance (two of which were disabled yesterday as a result of hits they received). Returned immediately.

Back to 1st Panzer Division in the afternoon. The operations officer was not there, so back again. Operations at present appear very unfavorable. More rain showers, the entire terrain impassable and like a sponge. Several enemy ground-support aircraft.

To Stuhlwei·enburg again in the evening, more visiting with various officers of the battalion, and also Dieter Diest was there. He is in Bodajk at present, where our First Maintenance Platoon is (led by Werkmeister Neubert—Knight's Cross of the War Service Cross with Swords). News today of a strong attack by us in the West (starting 16 December).

Order from 1st Panzer Division by radio at 2345 hours that we are to move tonight about 50 kilometers to Lake Balaton, to Balatonkenese. However, we will not move out until early in the morning.

19 December: 0500 hours company commander's meeting; 0600 hours departure of tanks etc. I moved to the 1st Panzer Division (to which we are currently attached) at 0900 hours for a commanders meeting. Thorough discussion of a planned operation. 1300 hours, call from corps that the operation is cancelled. Back again to Balatonkenese. Passable quarters. Thirteen tanks there. Various official duties.

20 December: During the morning, various official duties. With Leutnant Koppe (acting commander of the 3rd Company) at 1000 hours, moving along our sector of the front in the SPW (eastern edge at the eastern edge of Lake Balaton). Routes very muddy. It was at the freezing point but felt colder. Roses were blooming in Balatonakarattya. I picked one for a letter home to Jutta.

Several enemy ground-attack aircraft. Flak filled the skies. Several German fighter planes.

Then to the command post of the grenadier regiments positioned in front of us, but the commanders were not there. The terrain in front of us is mostly very muddy and impassable for tanks. At present, the Russians are very quiet here. Back at 1415 hours. I got a lot of official duties out of the way in the afternoon.

21 December: Frost. A few clouds. Heavy Russian attack with many tanks against the division on our left (Stuhlweißenburg and farther to the east) that led to deep penetrations. It was quiet where we were. At noon I moved to the corps through Stuhlweißenburg, on whose outskirts our troops were still holding. Strong rearward movements, especially by the Hungarians. Heavy enemy air activity over the city. Also our own fighters. I took care of various business at corps. Briefed on situation (rather tense!). Returned in the dark, arriving at the battalion at 1800 hours. Call from the 1st Panzer Division operations officer at 2400 hours: The battalion must be in Nadasladany (toward Stuhlweißenburg) at 0600 hours for the planned local counterattack. Distance of 40 kilometers, very dark, immediate alert of the battalion!

22 December: Tanks rolled at 0100 hours, staff around 0400 hours. We were supposed to find Oberstleutnant Huppert (leader of the battle group) in Nadasladany (castle). However, no one was there. We waited around in a cold, dirty room

(the castle was fully occupied). At 0600 hours (the time were supposed to cross the line of departure) still no one was there. Huppert finally arrived at about noon. Discussion: Village of Urhida, which had been lost was to be recaptured (cornerpoint of the position). Seven Panzer IVs were attached to me. Rolled out as far as Sarkeszi. There, about 200 infantry were brought along. Attack on Urhida. Difficult, rolling terrain; vineyards, thickets, houses, barns, great expanse. Heavy opposition (antitank guns, mortars). In spite of it all, we advanced into the village after I had taken over the point. My main gun was knocked out (7.62cm antitank guns). Destroyed about eight or ten antitank guns, as many mortars, machine guns etc. Five of my Tigers were damaged by enemy fire. We had two thirds of the village by dark, then pushed on through the remaining third in the darkness. Established contact with a small battle group to our east. Most of the Tigers remained in Urhida for the night (Leutnant Rollik in charge) and knocked out a lot of Russians. The other Tigers pulled back about one kilometer to a farmstead (Livia Puszta). I moved back and forth several times during the night between the farmstead and Huppert's command post (Nadasladany) by SPW. Very tired.

23 December: In Nadasladany for rest at about 0200 hours. Disturbed frequently by telephone conversations concerning supplies, the maintenance sections and the like.

One Tiger was knocked out by a 7.62cm gun some time near morning in Urhida during a clearing operation. Burned out. A lot of work taking preparatory measures. Today Stuhlwei·enburg was evacuated. We also pulled back a bit as evening approached. Urhida is still being held. My Tigers and, in addition, eight Panzer Vs and seven Panzer IVs were attached to me for purposes of supply. Three Tigers and four Panzer IVs are placed under the control of our neighbor (Oberst Bradel). Practically everything is split up into small groups. Barely able to maintain communications, particularly since my tank also had to go to the maintenance shop (the main gun).

At about 1900 hours news came from III Panzer Corps through the 1. Panzer-Division that the battalion is to pull back today through the mountains (through Inöta) to Fehervarczugo, turn south from there and attack south with the 4th Cavalry Brigade (Holste) in the morning. Crazy excursion! We drew back to Nadasladany with our tanks. By doing that, the 1st Panzer Division sector, which was only held by a few weak strongpoints, would collapse in short order. Took leave of Oberstleutnant Huppert, who is a very decent fellow. Departed around 2200 hours.

24 December: Marched the entire night. Got to Fehervarczurgo (castle) at about 0200. Meeting there that we would be attached to Oberstleutnant Weymann's battle group (the armored units of the 23rd Panzer Division). It was to launch a counterattack south early today within the framework of the 4th Cavalry Brigade. The line of departure for Battle Group Weymann: The village of Sarkeresztes. In the meantime, our tanks also arrived (eight vehicles, two with damage). I had the crews position themselves near the houses in Fehervarczurgo so that they could get a few minutes sleep. The Russian "sewing machine" flew like crazy, continually dropping bombs among us. However, nothing happened.

I took the Volkswagen to Weymann's command post in Sarkeresztes and discussed the operation. Then, back to Fehervarczurgo, where our battalion had set up its command post in an outbuilding of the castle.

Caught a few hours of bad sleep. The tanks rolled at 0630 hours. I left at about 0800 hours in the SPW for Sarkeresztes. There was a great hullabaloo there, Russians firing from all sides (artillery, mortars, Stalin organs). After the commitment of the tanks had been arranged, I moved back. There I found a great crush of every conceivable officer (supply, maintenance company, recovery platoon, etc.). A thousand things to do (especially getting damaged Tigers safely to the rear because of the threatening situation), written traffic and the like. In between all that, a little Christmas celebration for the close staff (clerks, messengers) with sharing of a lot of beautiful material pleasures. Then, again, with the Volkswagen forward to Sarkeresztes. Leutnant Rambow had knocked out seven tanks. As for the planned attack, it had turned into a defensive operation against a massive Russian assault. Sarkeresztes was, again, a rowdy scene (mortar fire!). I ran into the commander of the 6th Panzer Regiment, Major Graf Schulenburg, and several members of my former headquarters company. The enemy disturbed the Christmas festivities a bit! At about 1900 hours, back, again, to Fehervarczurgo. A few more things accomplished, ate a bit, then heard a bit of Goebbels' "Christmas Speech," which put me to sleep. During the night, the usual "sewing machine" bomber.

Unfortunately, Sarkeresztes was lost during the night, in the course of which one Tiger that had gotten stuck had to be blown up.

25 December: As in the previous days, beautiful sunny weather. Frost (no snow) and intense Russian activity in the air. Corps moved back from Fehervarczurgo. We were attached to the 23rd Panzer Division (as before with Battle Group Weymann). For the time being, everything remained where it had been. Battle Group Weymann just north of Sarkeresztes. All sorts of things to do or discuss. Moved to 23rd Panzer Division (it was in the village or in the castle; commander was General von Radowitz. Not inspiring.) To Major Graf Schulenburg's command post (commander, 6th Panzer Regiment). 17.2cm artillery fire there (a regular barrage!) Then, up front to our Tigers, where we were showered with artillery and mortar fire so that I finally got out of there with my Volkswagen.

Frost, clear, "sewing machines" active in the night, dropping bombs. Our tanks knocked out two Russian tanks today. Our antiaircraft vehicles shot down an Il-2.

26 December: The night was relatively quiet, as was the day. All sorts of official business. At 23rd Panzer Division—1500 hours, headed toward Chakbereny in the Volkswagen where the 6th Panzer Regiment (and 4th Cavalry Brigade) command posts are located. Ran right into Major Graf Schulenburg (with Rollick). Ever thicker fog set in. Suddenly: Wild shooting, alert, vehicles and horses fleeing every which way. Russians in the place (with mortars, tanks, etc.)! Since there were enough officers on the spot (including a SPW battalion and its commander who were being held in reserve), I had nothing to do. I moved back to the next village (already lots of fleeing vehicles!) and alerted the Flak battalion there (in Sõred) to construct a covering position and turn the guns toward the east. The fog, which was thick as cotton wool, was truly horrible. Then to the 23rd Panzer Division at Fehervarczurgo. It did not know anything and had no more communication with the

4th Cavalry Brigade (naturally, since everyone had bolted). We took appropriate measures.

A counterattack on Chakbereny was to be launched in the evening, but it was called off, since the main line of resistance was pulled back a bit. Fog and a few degrees below freezing.

27 December: Fog, hoar frost, not very cold. At the division, with Major Graf Schulenburg (Panzer-Regiment 6), in whose sector our five Tigers are now positioned. Heavy Russian 17.2cm fire in his village.

An assortment of reading and writing chores.

Since the front has generally been pulled back (Budapest is now surrounded) there is much concern for our damaged vehicles (Tigers, SPWs, Flak vehicles, etc.) that are scattered everywhere—the same with the 23rd Panzer Division—our Tigers knocked out two T-34s today.

28 December: At the 23rd Panzer Division—official duties. Up front with the tanks. In Sõred with Hauptmann Voigts (old comrade from Neuruppin), commander of the 2nd Battalion, 6th Panzer Regiment.

17.2cm artillery fire.

Our tanks knocked out two T-34s and three antitank guns. A call reached me at Voigt's location that we were again attached to the 4th Cavalry Brigade. Directed to coordinate with Rittmeister Graf Plettenberg, commander of the heavy battalion (located in Mor).

I moved to Mor, connected with Plettenberg and Oberstleutnant Sauer (commander of the cavalry regiment). Early in the morning we were to move again to the north.

A night under abundant artillery fire.

29 December: 0730 hours with the Volkswagen on concealed routes to Mor (small city). In the meantime, the staff moved through Bodajk in the Bakony mountains back to Balinka (at the right moment, since significant artillery and Stalin organ fire was already falling on Fehervarczurgo). I returned to Mor by a very poor route (there was no more proceeding through Bodajk, since the roads were under observed artillery fire). There I was with Oberstleutnant Sauer and Rittmeister Graf Plettenberg, with whom our three tanks were serving (the others had been taken to the rear with damage). The Russians laid down (heavy) artillery and mortar fire in the village and attacked with heavy infantry forces. Our tanks are in position on

the west outskirts of Mor as ready reserve. Back through the mountains to Balinka. Pretty area, sun, light frost, a nice picture. Assorted official duties and at 23rd Panzer Division (now at Bakonyczernye).

30 December: Through Bakonyczernye with the Volkswagen in the morning to Dudar (1st Maintenance Platoon), then to Zirc (where several of our vehicles are waiting to be loaded at the railroad station). Then on good roads through the Bakony Woods (very beautiful area with old ruined castles, mountain forests, light frost—unfortunately, substantial fog overhead) to Veszprem-Varsany, where our engineer platoon was in the process of constructing a loading ramp for two of our Tigers (which we towed there from Mor for reasons of security).

Then with III Panzer Corps where I reported to the chief of staff (Oberstleutnant von Weberstädt). Visited the adjutant, quartermaster, etc. Back through Sur (through the Bakony forest), another good road. Back to Balinka in the evening. Call during the night that I should go to the I Cavalry Corps, to which we are now attached.

31 December: Awakened at 0630 hours, set out to I Cavalry Corps (located in Zirc) at 0730 hours. Reported to the commanding general, General Harteneck. We are, for the present, to be corps reserve (therefore move to Sur).

Back through Dudar; discussed the move there with the First Maintenance Platoon. Then through Bakonycsernye to the III Panzer Corps, where I did some arranging for quartering the maintenance platoon. On the return to Sur, I arranged for our billeting (local area commander and the logistics officer of the 23rd Panzer Division). On the return to the 4th Cavalry Brigade, somewhere in the mountains in Aka. The route was awful. I had to go the last kilometer on foot. It snowed. Waited for hours at the 4th Cavalry Brigade, since the brigade commander, General Holste, who wanted to talk to me, was not yet there. He arrived at about 1700 hours. I sat with my fraternity brother, Leutnant von Senden, who is the operations officer there. Meeting with the General, who made a good impression (oak leaves). I got a cup of real coffee. Back through the mountains (terrible defiles, jammed with horse-drawn vehicles) through Sur to the command post. The officers of the staff and several

others assembled there. Evening meal, little speech, grog. 2400 hours: "Führer speech."

1 January 1945: Heavy fire from Russian artillery and rocket launchers started early and kept up long. On our front, the Russians attacked heavily north of Mor in our vicinity.

Thorough personal hygiene, new underwear.

Then to Sur, preparations for our quartering there. Back to Balinka, lunch, then everything to Sur.

1500 hours to III Panzer Corps, meeting there with chief of staff about quartering our rearward maintenance platoon.

1800 hours, meeting with chief of staff in Sur, then supper.

Oberleutnant von Rosen was in action at Mor with four tanks today. One was disabled with engine trouble and had to be towed back out of the main line of resistance during the night (very difficult!). Two repaired tanks went forward to von Rosen. Three more arrived from the maintenance facility during the night.

Quarters in Sur with the parish priest (electric lights and bed).

2 January: In the morning through Dudar (with the 1st Maintenance platoon) to the I Cavalry Corps at Zirc. Then by way of Varsany-Veszprem (where two Tigers were loaded) Bakony-Szombately (talked there with quartermaster of the III Panzer Corps regarding fuel) and back to Sur. Quite a lot to do there, meetings with various officers, etc.

Three Tigers in action today with von Rosen. Good results. Took care of mail in the evening.

3 January: Disposed of an assortment of official business. Five tanks arrived today in Kisber from Vagsellye. During the morning, through Aka (with the 4th Cavalry Brigade) to Felsödobos (southeast of Kisber), where our tanks are located, attached to the heavy battalion (Rittmeister Graf Plettenberg). General Holste (4th Cavalry Brigade) also there. Back to Sur in the afternoon, scouting the route (bad!). Took care of a lot of official business and mail.

4 January: In the morning, through Bakonyszombately to Patateszey to our trains and supply company. Talked with the troops, visited in the quarters. With Wiegand at noon.

In the afternoon, back with the 1st Maintenance Platoon (which is now in Bakonyszombately), then in Sur. Lots of the kind of stuff that keeps officialdom busy. Then to Bakonyszombately where a film and newsreel were running (film: *Journey in the Past*). There I learned from the assistant operations officer of the III Panzer Corps that, as of today, we belong to Panzer Corps "Feldherrnhalle."

Thirteen Tigers operational today.

5 January: To the III Panzer Corps in the morning to get back our two quad Flak vehicles that were attached there. However, hours of discussion regarding the 7 January attack prevented me from getting to the chief of staff.

With the 1st Maintenance Platoon.

Back to Sur. Brief lunch, then to Zirc to corps. We are attached to the 4th Cavalry Brigade again.

Back to Sur by way of Veszprem-Varsany-Bakonyszombately. Lots of official business at Sur. Then over to the 4th Cavalry Brigade at Aka where I conferred with the commander etc. regarding the attack. Evening meal with the staff with the family of the local count (good!). Meetings ran until 2300 hours. Only then did I drive back. Bombed en route by the "sewing machine," since I had to use lights due to the extremely bad road.

6 January: Lots of official stuff and meetings regarding the attack. Then to III Panzer Corps, where I got our flak vehicles back. Guderian was there today. Back. Preparations for the move southeast.

In the evening to Bakonycsernye with all of the tanks. I, myself, back again by car through Isztimer (through the mountains) to Fehervarczurgo to the 23rd Panzer Division. Plettenberg, was also supposed to be there. I was supposed to move out together with him tomorrow. He could not be found, however. Stalin organs fired into Fehervarczurgo. Back through Isztimer-Balinka (roads terribly packed), arriving at Bakonyczernye about 2400 hours.

7 January: Awake at 0500 hours. Departure at 0600 hours. Roads totally jammed. Forced my way as far forward as Fehervarczurgo with a SPW; discussed the operation with Plettenberg. The tanks showed up at 1130 hours. Things finally got moving at 1140 hours, with Plettenberg near Borbalamajor in order to capture Zamoly from there. Half of the battalion moved to the north. I went with the southern group. We encountered a strong antitank belt. One Tiger knocked out

(commander killed). Since it got dark too quickly, Zamoly could not be captured.

We set up security around Borbalamajor in the darkness. Then the order came that we should join Plettenberg and the northern group, so we departed in the night.

Supplies did not arrive. Spent hours in Felsî-puszta, then with Oberleutnant von Rosen to Magyaralmas, where we finally connected up with our supply elements. With that, the night was over.

8 January: Arrived at about 0700 hours in Lajamajor. Plettenberg and the northern group also there. But another order arrived at 1100 hours: Everyone back again to Borbala-Puszta, from which we were to attack to the south.

All sorts of mortar fire etc. in our vicinity during the morning.

We rolled again to Borbala-Puszta. Arrived there to be greeted with a call from the 4th Cavalry Korps sending everyone back immediately to Lajamajor. Sixty enemy armored vehicles were reported there. Back again to Lajamajor where there was all sorts of confused flight. In the meantime, various telephone calls with General Holste and others. Assorted vehicles drew near to Lajamajor, cross country, as darkness fell. They turned out to be German SPWs. Other than that, everything remained quiet (aside from artillery and mortar fire). I was with Oberstleutnant Rojahn (an old acquaintance from Radensleben) who commanded the 41st Mounted Regiment. He was situated a little south of Lajamajor in an earthen bunker in a defile. There I had direct telephone connection to higher levels of command. Finally got a good night's sleep in the earthen bunker, where it was warm.

No end of hares and pheasants around. It snowed continually, at times with heavy squalls.

9 January: Alert at about 0900 hours—battalion to immediately move to the 23rd Panzer Division, horrendous mess! Immediate objective: Also Puszta (remnants of a totally destroyed estate). I preceded the battalion with the SPW. I called the 23rd Panzer Division, which claimed we were attached to the 4th Cavalry Brigade. Call to the I Cavalry Corps: One company of ours is attached to the 4th Cavalry Brigade, the other units are with the 23rd Panzer Division. So, split up again! The 1st Company, Tiger Tank Battalion 503 (Leutnant Piepgras), remained with the 4th Cavalry Brigade and knocked out seven enemy tanks.

We set out to the south from Also Puszta (less infantry), pushed the enemy to the south in terrain that was favorable for armor and reached the main line of resistance at Sarkeresztes (which was still being held). Then we turned to the east toward a vineyard village. The infantry, a Luftwaffe ground unit that was attached to the 23rd Panzer Division, followed—terrible. There was a deep ditch just outside the village that was full of Ivans. Tough fighters (a new mechanized corps). We moved right up to the ditch and fired wildly into it with everything. The Russians defended themselves with satchel charges, antitank rifles and the like. The infantry behind us did not advance a single step. I got out of my tank and, running upright, brought them to within 50 meters of the ditch (still behind our tanks!). Cowardly behavior, not one Unteroffizier visible (Leutnant killed).

Significant losses among the infantry. I tried to get the men to follow me forward with a "Hurrah" while my tanks held down the Russians with gunfire, but I was the only one who advanced to the ditch. The infantry stubbornly remained lying where they were. Finally (after two hours!!) I succeeded, with the help of three decent Obergefreite and a machine gun, in getting to the ditch and eventually taking about 300 prisoners. About 100 dead or wounded lay around in it. I moved to Sarkeresztes with wounded and prisoners and established contact with the commander of the infantry battalion (Hauptmann von ôhmichen). In the meantime, Oberleutnant von Rosen advanced into the vineyard village with the infantry (no resistance). I then collected my tanks after the lines had been reestablished there. Back to Also Puszta where we were resupplied during the night. We were housed in our tanks or in makeshift quarters in stalls on stinking straw—constant snow squalls. An extraordinary number (hundreds!) of hares.

10 January 1945: A cold night in a shot-up hovel. Spent the morning in Magyaralmas with Major Huck. Maintenance and similar activities.

An attack order arrived at noon for an afternoon attack on Zamoly. However, due to lack of time and preparation, it could not be carried out. Unending command conferences during the evening in Felsö-Puszta regarding the impending attack (now for early morning).

The night was rather cold and sleeping quarters cramped.

11 January: Awake at 0445 hours. Preparations. We attacked as part of Battle Group Weymann (our tanks in the lead). Battle Group Weymann arrived. Thawing weather, slush. Organized, rolled out at 0600 hours. Short attack position. Departure set at 0640 hours. After crossing our own main line of resistance, we pushed the main body of the enemy—infantry with heavy weapons—out of their positions. Then several hours of heavy fighting with numerous enemy tanks (including "Joseph Stalin" types with 9.5cm guns), assault guns, heavy antitank guns and antitank hunter/killer teams. We suffered three total losses (including the two Tigers on either side of me) and numerous additional losses (six dead, ten wounded). Bit by bit, seven more tanks were more or less severely damaged by serious hits (including one hit by a bomb), so that I was finally left with a total of three tanks (having started the day with thirteen).

Nevertheless, we did reach the high ground as ordered. Behind us, the village of Zamoly was captured (during which Graf Plettenberg was wounded and his adjutant killed). We were constantly attacked by strong enemy air forces. Among others, my own adjutant, Leutnant Heerlein, was wounded by a bomb fragment while towing a tank. I remained forward until dark where, with the help of the two other tanks, a knocked out Tiger was hauled practically out of the Russian lines. It was a very difficult task. Forward with one Tiger in the dusk with a towing cable already hooked up on the front. Get close to the damaged tank. Then, two men leapt out under fire from the enemy. One hooked the towing cable to the back of the damaged tank and then climbed back into the towing tank while the second man scrambled into the knocked-out Tiger through the open hatch. He disconnected the engine and final drive inside the tank. Then, slowly, a centimeter at a time, the disabled tank was towed back while the other two Tigers gave covering fire.

We then pulled back, as ordered, and moved behind our own main line of resistance. Pouring rain. Spent the night in Also-Puszta again, where the rain soaked through everything (the roofs were burned off). No straw. I took the Volkswagen over to Felsö-Puszta from where I was able to telephone the brigade and corps. Everyone congratulated us on our success: twenty-one Russian tanks and assault guns knocked out and more than twenty antitank guns, one Stalin organ and three aircraft (destroyed before they could take off by several Tigers on my left flank, which I had not been aware of during the fighting), numerous enemy dead. But it had also been a difficult day for us, especially difficult for our recovery and maintenance elements that had recovered all of the disabled Tigers in the zone of enemy artillery fire behind us.

I did not get back to Also-Puszta until midnight.

12 January: Back to Bodajk in the morning. Leutnant Fürlinger formed a battle group in Also-Puszta with the three other Tigers and two that had been brought forward from the maintenance facility.

Cleaned up thoroughly and changed underwear at Bodajk. Passable little quarters. To the brigade in the afternoon where General Holste gave us his compliments. I managed it so that our battle group could move out of the filthy hole of Also-Puszta to Magyaralmas.

13 January 1945: To the III Panzer Corps in the morning where I talked to the chief of staff. Moved back. With the maintenance facility at noon. Then, paper work and the like from 1400 to 2200 hours. It had piled up beyond belief. To the brigade in the evening regarding naming of Leutnant Linkenbach in the Wehrmacht honor roll.

14 January: Company commander meeting in the morning in the battalion, among other things. Lunch. Then to the battle group, which is now attached to Oberstleutnant Weymann. Also saw Weymann. Then back to the brigade again regarding Leutnant Linkenbach and the German Cross in Gold for Oberleutnant von Rosen. Then writing after-action reports and other correspondence.

More thaw weather, but colder at night; frost.

15 January: Took care of a pile of paperwork. At noon, by way of Sur (with the maintenance facility) to Bakonyczombathely to the III Panzer Corps. With the operations officer and the adjutant there. Then back, official duties. It was colder, with black ice at times. Cold and clear at night.

16 January: Beautiful weather, but cold.

To Battle Group Fürlinger in Magyaralmas, where I awarded several Iron Crosses, First Class. Then to the 23rd Panzer Division (in Fehervarczurgo), to which we are now attached. All sorts of official duties, haircut, wash, mail.

17 January: Cloudy, cold. Quiet. Noon with Leutnant Fürlinger, then to the 23rd Panzer Division. Commanders conference for tomorrow's attack. We will participate in an attack to pin the enemy in the direction of Stuhlweißenburg while, at the same time, larger attacks are to be launched past the city to the east. We are to work with the 23rd Panzer Regiment and grenadiers.

Still in Bodajk in the evening. Birthday celebration for Leutnant Rollik.

2030 hours: The battalion moved to Magyaralmas. A short meeting there with the commander of the 1st Battalion, 23rd Panzer Regiment (Hauptmann Kujacinski).

18 January: 0430 hours: Departure from Magyaralmas. Attack position at Margitmajor with eight Tigers. Move out at 0645. Crossed friendly lines. Breached a Russian minefield with help from panzer engineers. Strong enemy resistance with heavy weapons while the enemy infantry began to flee. Difficult crossing of a broad stream with soft banks. Intense fire from all sides. Hard fighting all day. Over time, four of my Tigers became disabled through enemy fire They had to move back on their own or tow each other. I was hit on my main gun so that the weapon was unserviceable; but I stayed up front. The accompanying Panthers also melted away until only two were left. The Panzer IVs and Sturmgeschütze following us suffered significant losses. We destroyed seven enemy tanks and about ten antitank guns. Unusually heavy enemy artillery fire, including flat-trajectory weapons from all sides. As evening drew near there was a local enemy counterattack to our left that was quashed with our help.

As it grew dark we got the order to pull out, after the grenadiers had firmly established themselves. Two Tigers remained up front in the main line of resistance to provide cover. We moved back to Magyaralmas.

A very wearying day, everyone pretty well exhausted. I still had to go to the 23rd Panzer Division for a short meeting. The general thanked us. Then back to Magyaralmas, dead tired. Sleep.

19 January: Piles of paperwork. Mail. With the 23rd Panzer Division in Fehervarczurgo in the evening. The assault past Stuhlwei·enburg should go well. Wehrmacht report very bad: The Russians are at the German border everywhere.

20 January 1945: Heavy snow in the morning.

In Fehervarczurgo with the division and with our surgeon (due to intense pain in my shoulder). Bitter fighting with our everlastingly smoking stove!

Wehrmacht report very serious: The Russians are in East Prussia (Insterburg, Neidenburg, Gilgenburg) and in Silesia. They are also well into Warthegau. There is no way it can be fixed.

In the evening, the very decent Hauptmann Kujacinski (commander of the 1st Battalion, 23rd Panzer Regiment) was with us for supper.

Mail.

21 January: At 0815 hours an alert came from the 23rd Panzer Division—some "Joseph Stalin" tanks had been sighted. However, it remained quiet in the morning. With General Holste, 4th Cavalry Brigade, in the afternoon. He wanted to know all sorts of things concerning the ordered incorporation of Hungarian tanks in his brigade. After that with the 23rd Panzer Division.

Wehrmacht report: The Russians are at Oppeln, Thorn, Deutsch-Eylau. Germany will soon be completely lost.

Official paperwork and mail.

22 January: With Hauptmann Kujacinski (23rd Panzer Division) at 0800 hours. The 1st Panzer Division will advance into Stuhlweißenburg today. We are to advance east of the city to encircle the withdrawing enemy. We started without any great preparations with nine Tigers and a few attached Panthers and Panzer IVs. We crossed the German lines east of Sarkeresztes, overran enemy positions, captured the farmstead of Gyulamajor, where there was a lot of resistance from antitank guns. Then we pushed on over rolling land to the south along a large, shallow depression. We ran into the midst of a Russian withdrawal movement, destroyed seven 7.62cm guns on self-propelled mounts, two tanks, vehicles and numerous antitank guns (fifteen of them). In addition, we fired with all our weapons to very good effect on the Russians who were streaming to the rear. As evening approached we reached the road that runs northeast from Stuhlweißenburg. Heavy enemy tank gun fire came from somewhere. Hungarian infantry closed up to us. We provided cover to the east until night. Indeed, it was intended for us to move out again, but we had practically run out of ammunition. Because of the bad routes and heavy enemy artillery fire, supplies did not arrive until midnight. We resupplied in extreme cold.

Oberleutnant von Rosen took command of the remaining five Tigers until morning.

23 January: I led the supply vehicles back through the night—very difficult. We did not get back to Magyaralmas until 0500 hours. Telephone call with the division: The battalion was to move into Stuhlwei·enburg early in the morning. Got a few hours sleep. Briefly with 4th Cavalry Brigade (currently in Magyaralmas).

To Stuhlweißenburg in the afternoon. It has suffered greatly. The Russians had run wild among the civilian population.

24 January: Spent the morning at corps. We have been attached to the 4th Cavalry Brigade again, so back to Magyaralmas with the battalion!

To the maintenance shop, briefly, then to Stuhlweißenburg, clear out.

Leutnant Heerlein departed on leave today.

Back with the battalion to Magyaralmas. Immediate meeting with 4th Cavalry Brigade regarding an attack planned for tomorrow morning. The Hungarian tanks were attached to me. I had nothing but problems with them the entire night (no competence with the vehicles, weapons or German language; dapper Leutnants and unwilling enlisted men). Hardly fit for serious operations!

25 January: We can only provide a small battle group with a few Tigers led by Leutnant Beyer for the attack. At 0500 hours I moved with the battle group to Zamoly, where the attack was launched. I remained in the village, into which the Russians were firing like mad. The extremely costly attack only got moving when our few Tigers became involved, whereupon we broke through four enemy positions, one after another. Two Tigers were disabled due to damage from gunfire or mines. One of them lost both its tracks in a minefield. Leutnant Rubbel was not able to tow out all the tanks that were recovered until evening, thanks to the onset of snow squalls. Then back to Zamoly in the night. An extremely difficult operation!

I spent the entire day in Zamoly in a lousy potato cellar. However, we installed a stove, carpet and furniture and made it comfortable. General Holste sat in a cellar bunker on the other side of the street. The village was totally destroyed by the enemy artillery fire that continued into the night.

26 January 1945: During the night the area that had been taken on 25 January had to evacuated due to the lack of an overall success. The Russians continued to shell Zamoly.

I had to move to Borbalamajor with the remaining tanks and the battalion staff after recovering our trackless Tiger. A limited-objective attack was to be mounted from there early in the morning. We put together a small battle group with three Tigers and several Hungarian Panzer IVs. The 23rd Panzer Division attacked to our right, but it made no forward progress. The attack of our battle group, however, went quite well, though the Hungarian infantry did not follow as planned. The attack lasted into the night. Then it started to rain. I spent the entire day with Oberstleutnant Sauer in Borbalamajor. He was leading the attack. Because of the intense enemy artillery fire, he remained in a potato cellar. Finally, in the dark, our three Tigers were rendered unfit for combat by the continually strengthening resistance from Russian antitank guns (tanks?) and brought back with the entire battle group. At about 2200 hours they all got back to us. I headed back with the Tigers to Lajamajor where the trackless Tiger that had been so painfully recovered yesterday had slipped into a bomb crater. The rain turned into an ever wilder snowstorm. The recovery did not work, since the ground was ice covered and too slippery. I broke off the attempt. We all moved back to Magyaralmas, where we arrived at about 0200 hours.

27 January: Snowstorm, wild snow squalls, very cold. All the roads contain snow drifts. I pushed my way through to the III Panzer Corps with a SPW. The storm let up in the evening.

For the first time in a while, the battalion cannot be employed due to inoperable Tigers. In the evening I received the order to move to Moha with the battalion. As a result, we would be more in the center of the entire, giant sector that the 4th Cavalry Brigade had now taken over.

Shocking Wehrmacht report: The Russians are in upper Silesia, on the Oder, west of Posen, at Schneidemühl, northwest of Bromberg, in Wormditt, Gerdauen, etc.

28 January: Cold.

Still in Magyaralmas, somewhat quiet. I wrote letters but most of the intended recipients are probably fleeing before the Russian advance. In the meantime, at the III Panzer Corps and with the forward maintenance platoon in Fehervarczurgo.

We remain attached to the 4th Cavalry Brigade, which has moved to Iszkaszentgyörgy. Since we finally had five Tigers operational this evening, I

got another chance to make the attempt to recover the Tiger stuck in the bomb crater at Lajamajor. The combat engineer platoon worked last night and all day on preparations and blasted a kind of sloping ramp. Unfortunately, a nasty, icy snowstorm set in. Nevertheless, after hours of strenuous effort and to our great delight, the recovery operation was a success around 0400 hours. We also towed four immobilized Hungarian Panzer IVs with us from Zamoly (to the maintenance platoon).

29 January 1945: The wild, icy snowstorm kept up in extreme cold. Unbelievable snowdrifts. Taking a SPW I laboriously made it to Sarkeresztes where our tanks are to be repaired. The heavy cavalry battalion was also there. It is now commanded by Hauptmann Sonntag. Limited possibilities for billets in that totally destroyed village, but it will have to do. Then checked out the road to the brigade from Moha-Iskaszentgyörgy. It lacks two bridges capable of supporting tanks. The brigade can only be reached by a long detour to the north. Back to Fehervarczurgo. I then wanted to go to the brigade, but gave that idea up due to the cold and the unimaginable snow drifts. The ice storm rages so intensely that it is impossible to see in front of oneself. Imagine what our people fleeing from eastern Germany have to go through! The Russians are pushing inexorably forward there.

In the afternoon I fought my way to the III Panzer Corps and to the maintenance facility. Then back to Magyaralmas. One the way, my SPW slipped into the roadside ditch and stuck fast on a hill where the ice storm raged the worst. By a miracle it worked out that, after a while, a Hungarian prime mover emerged from the blinding snow squall and helped free us. In Magyaralmas we were in an ice cold hovel where we could not get the stove to work. It smoked like mad because of the storm. We provided a bit of warmth with blowtorches.

30 January: The snowstorm let up a bit. In the afternoon the battalion staff moved to Iszkaszentgyörgy (billeted with the parish priest). The armored elements, to the extent they were ready, went to Sarkeresztes. A "Führer speech" in the evening.

31 January: To Sarkeresztes in the morning. The heavy battalion of the 4th Cavalry Brigade and our nine operational Tigers are there. On the return trip by Volkswagen we got stuck in the

snow. So the last stretch to Sarkeresztes was on foot under brisk Russian artillery fire. Obviously a great hullabaloo on all fronts, the Russians attacking everywhere with strong forces. A call from the brigade reached me in the village: The Russians have broken through at a number of places. The Tigers were to mount an immediate local counterattack with the heavy cavalry battalion and recapture Gyulamajor as the first objective.

The Tigers rolled immediately under my command as far as the vineyards east of Sarkeresztes. From there we headed south. Under artillery and mortar fire at first, then antitank guns everywhere and numerous tanks. We made no progress in a frontal attack on Gyulamajor. I therefore shifted four tanks a bit to the left against the enemy-occupied Hill 214. With a few grenadiers following, we made better progress there. Russian tanks put up significant resistance. After we had set several on fire with gunfire, the others pulled back. The grenadiers were able to establish themselves—with several heavy weapons—in quite good positions that had been recently constructed. One of my Tigers was hit by a heavy round (9.5cm?) that penetrated the turret. Two seriously wounded. To our right, Leutnant Koppe advanced into Gyulamajor with three Tigers. However, the weak infantry forces accompanying him were tossed out by the Russians. It became pitch black with freezing rain and snow, horribly cold and uncomfortable. We slugged it out with some enemy attempting to advance in the dark.

1 February: The night continued to be miserable and filled with fighting. Leutnant Koppe forced his way into Gyulamajor again with stronger infantry forces. I also pushed in from the east side with my tank in the morning, while Leutnant Piepgras remained on Hill 214 with two Tigers. Finally, Gyulamajor was completely in our hands. However, the Russians remained with strong forces on the paved road directly east of Gyula. In the gray dawn of the morning, the radioed order from the brigade reached me to immediately take all available tanks—there were, however, only three, since Leutnant Piepgras was still engaged on Hill 214—to point 166, south of Gyula, where the Russians were attacking with many (said to be about fifty) tanks. I immediately headed south from Gyulamajor. However, at that very moment, one of Leutnant Koppe's Tigers broke a track (mines?). It had to be repaired with

a lot of hard work in the midst of artillery fire. The second Tiger's engine temperature remained at more than 100 degrees Celsius, so it had to go back for repairs. The third Tiger ran onto a mine after leaving the village and was immobilized. I ended up by moving by myself to Point 166 and calling Leutnant Piepgras forward on the radio which, however, took a long time.

I spotted numerous (perhaps about 25?) Russian tanks on and behind a road embankment ahead of me and opened fire while in the open. After my first round—apparently a direct hit—a lot of confusion set in on their side. I was immediately covered with heavy tank fire from the Russians, so much so that my Tiger was soon combat ineffective and immobilized by heavy damage to the running gear. In spite of the gunfire, I leaped out and, with a tremendous amount of physical effort while lying down, was able to disentangle a road wheel that had been knocked off and become jammed in the track so that the Tiger was again mobile. In the meantime, Leutnant Piepgras, had arrived along with his two Tigers. He knocked out three more Russian tanks, whereupon the rest of the enemy tanks slunk off to the south. My Tiger headed to the rear for repairs, driving with extreme caution so as not to throw its track. I spent the afternoon at Rittmeister Sonntag's command post (heavy cavalry battalion) in the vineyards. Leutnant Piepgras continued to engage individual enemy tanks up front.

I succeeded in spotting the Tigers that stayed forward in resupply by bringing them back individually. One of our Tigers that was moving forward again got into a soft spot at Gyulamajor and got hopelessly stuck. Since we had to clear out of Gyula in the evening, that Tiger had to be blown up after we had made every effort to recover it. I had even gone back another time to Sarkeresztes in the hope that I might be able to get another tank for towing that might have come forward from the maintenance shop. Two repaired Tigers were not available until 0200 hours, when it was too late. They remained forward for the night to provide cover while the other tanks went back to Sarkeresztes for repairs. All of the crews were totally exhausted.

I moved through Fehervarczurgo to the brigade at Iszkaszentgyörgy, where I was congratulated on our successes (17 tanks and assault guns knocked out). I did not get back to quarters until about 2300 hours, where I immediately fell dead asleep.

The Russians were in Küstrin today.

2 February: Finally a little quiet. With the commander of the 4th Cavalry Brigade. Took care of all sorts of official business. After-action reports. Award recommendation for the German Cross in Gold to Leutnant Beyer, among others.

At 1700 hours I started off by staff car (with Oberleutnant Brandt and Leutnant Gille) to Sur, where we had been invited to supper with Oberleutnant Barckhausen at 1900 hours along with all the company commanders. Very heavy fog. The stretch of road to Fehervarczurgo was very narrow due to the snow that had been shoveled to both sides. The road was completely blocked with Hungarian traffic, some of it Panzer IVs (several towed) and traffic in the other direction. We remained stuck in one spot for an hour. Only with the greatest of energy and lots of sign language were we finally able to get through, since the Hungarians did not understand a word of German. We finally made it to Sur at 2030 hours. Good food, wine, a nice evening. We didn't want to think about our families, mostly in eastern and central Germany. Moved back at 2400 hours, getting to Iszkaszentgyörgy at about 0200 hours.

Thawing weather, slush.

3 February: I was with the brigade in the morning in a pretty little baroque castle of a Graf Pappenheim in Iskaszentgyörgy. The engaging, cultivated old Graf, who had filled his little castle with a most beautiful collection of antique books, weapons and the like, has chosen the await the further advance of the Russians and die there.

Today we had a battle group forward with five Tigers. It was led by Leutnant Fürlinger. Along with elements of the newly arrived 5th SS Panzer Division "Wiking," it was to take part in an attack that was to start at 1130 hours to establish a sane defensive line. I stayed in radio contact with Fürlinger. The attack, however, did not really get started since the Russians launched their own attacks at several locations at the same time. I spent part of the time with the brigade to get orientated on the big picture and part of the time monitoring the radio traffic of our battle group so as to be able to get involved if needed. Thanks to the effectiveness of our Tigers, Gyulamajor was finally captured in the evening, in the course of which five heavy antitank guns were captured.

Unfortunately, our Tigers had to remain in the main line of resistance throughout the night to provide cover (only being resupplied in rotation). Thawing weather, fog so heavy that you could no longer see your own hand in front of your face!

4 February: Back in radio contact with Fürlinger. As the fog lifted, the Russians attacked Gyula at dawn with tanks. Our Tigers knocked out eight enemy tanks and occupied some high ground south of the village, overrunning five Russian antitank guns in the process.

Thawing weather, glorious sunshine. Heavy Russian aerial activity, bombing attacks, including one on Sarkeresztes, where one of our company maintenance sections was hit (loss of vehicles and equipment).

As evening drew near we were able to pull our Tigers out of the lines to Sarkeresztes where they could be quartered in the more-or-less demolished houses.

5 February: For a change, there was no action for us. I made another trip to Iskaszentgyörgy and moved to the brigade. There I discovered that we were now attached to the 4th SS Panzer Corps. I immediately went to Inota to look for it. Briefly established contact. The roads were already very soft and slushy due to thawing weather, rain and fog. Finally there was an opportunity to dispose of official business. Movies in the evening in Castle Iszkaszentgyörgy ("Zirkus Renz," lots of technical problems).

6 February: Paper work.

More thawing weather, rain.

Movie showing at the castle in the evening.

7 February: Spring weather. At the front, only artillery fire. No tanks employed. Feverish activity at the maintenance facility.

8 February: Continued quiet. Fog and slushy weather.

In the afternoon in Inota with the IV SS Panzer Corps. We will receive an order in the morning to move to its area.

Evening with the 4th Cavalry Brigade.

9 February: Continued quiet, mild weather.

Order in the evening to submit a transportation request: The battalion is to be rail loaded, but with an unknown destination!

10 February: Still quiet. Took leave of the 4th Cavalry Brigade and General Holste, Oberstleutnant Rojahn, Rittmeister Sonntag, and other officers—a thoroughly splendid and reasonable

bunch who were sorry to have to let our battalion go.

Official business.

11 February: To Mor in the morning, where our Tigers loaded on the train. On to Kisber, where the maintenance shop entrained with the repaired vehicles. In the course moving there, I lost a wheel from my staff car—no apparent reason. However, nothing happened. In Kisber I saw the commander of the railroad station regarding the loading, then to Bakonyszombately to the supply company (lunch with Hauptmann Wiegand, questions about entraining). Then on to 6th Army High Command (the operations officer and the movement control officer) at Györ-Szent-Marton. On through Raab (Györ) and along the Danube, which we crossed at Komorn. Continued north to Neuhäusel (Ersekujavar). From there to the east as far as Nagy Surany, where our new corps (Panzer Corps "Feldherrnhalle") is located. General orientation with the operations officer and directive on the area we are to occupy. Good supper (roast hare) at the "Officer's Club," which is in a large sugar factory. Spent the night (with Leutnant von Hagemeister and Leutnant Gille) in the adjoining "guest quarters."

12 February: Morning discussion with the chief of staff, Oberstleutnant von Plato (good!), regarding our impending commitment (elimination of the Russian Gran bridgehead). Lunch with the commanding general, General Kleemann. Then back south through Neuhäusel to Ogyalla to division "Hoch und Deutschmeister," with which we are to cooperate. Spent the night there with the commander of the Panzerjäger Battalion, Hauptmann Sloot.

13 February: (My birthday). Moved in the morning to our new billets at Csuz. Good quarters at the rectory but the other billets were not so good (cramped and dirty). The priest speaks German well. Up front with the Volkswagen through Für to Kürt. The main line of resistance runs from north to south along the eastern outskirts of Kürt. Careful study of the terrain, particularly from an observation position in a haystack. We are to launch a night attack on 17 February from here to push in the Russian bridgehead. At the moment, the Russians are quiet. Several mortar barrages on Kürt. The ground is already very soft. In Kürt civilians invited us to lunch (scrambled eggs and sauerkraut).

Moved back to Csuz. The first battalion train arrived and was unloaded at the nearby railroad station at Perbete. Additional trains followed. Leutnant Heerlein and Leutnant Rollik arrived back from leave. All sorts of birthday congratulations from the battalion arrived, along with birthday cakes. We had a good time over it and emptied a gift bottle of champagne.

To Division "Hoch und Deutschmeister" in the evening, at Ogyalla. Roads severely flooded, very dark night. There was a meeting at the division regarding the results of our leaders' reconnaissance: Direct attack on both sides of the improved road from Kürt to the east appears unlikely to succeed due to the identified extensive Russian minefields and antitank positions. We have to somehow advance east with the tanks onto the steep, hilly terrain to the left (north) of the road and upward from there, where an armored attack is certainly not expected. The division agreed. By then it was about 2200 hours, so I did not get back to Csuz until 2300 hours. The battalion's officers—those who had arrived by then—were assembled. We had a very good time together with cake and a little bubbly until 0100 hours.

14 February: I spent the morning in the sector near Kürt with Leutnant Heerlein and Leutnant Fürlinger. We scouted the possibilities of negotiating the ridge paralleling the road out of Kürt on the left at night (departing from Kürt). The ground was already muddy. The Russians are quiet.

Hauptmann Sloot came to a meeting discussing the attack at noon in Csusz. Our engineers went to Kürt to build a solid route up into the high ground from Kürt.

15 February: All sorts of paperwork. I moved to Kürt with the company commanders to coordinate with the grenadiers who are in the main line of resistance. The tank commanders were then individually briefed by their company commanders on our prospective attack sector (using concealed paths and every possible precaution).

16 February: Very beautiful weather, but the countryside is muddy.

In Für at 0900 for a meeting with the grenadiers. Meeting concerning the attack with Division "Hoch und Deutschmeister" took place at 1400 hours.

Meeting with all the battalion officers and supper at 1900 hours in Chuz.

17 February: Up at 0200 hours. Departed with the tanks at 0230 hours along with the SPW's, combat trains etc. into the vineyards north of Kürt. (Added note by the author: As I remember, about twenty-two Tigers, six or seven in each company and two command tanks.) The approach march was extremely difficult, since it was pitch black and all the vehicles left Für in complete blackout. The move up the steep road that our engineers had built was quite risky. It led up through a stone quarry to the otherwise unattainable high ground from which the attack was to begin. Fortunately, none of the tanks got stuck!

Once up there, we assembled in the already familiar terrain (two companies forward, the third in the middle to the rear). The attack began at 0420 hours in complete darkness. Even though we are already familiar with the terrain, orientation was extremely difficult. During a heavy barrage from our own artillery, we rolled forward between the positions of our infantry. We were already among the first Russian rifle positions when the enemy defense woke up. The Russian artillery soon fired final protective fires, which caused significant losses among the grenadiers of Division "Hoch und Deutschmeister" following us. After crossing an enemy trench, Leutnant Piepgras ran right into a minefield and was immobilized. I called forward our engineers who were following in SPWs and—between the Russians(!)—they cleared a gap through the minefield. The Tiger moving beside me took a direct hit (antitank gun?) and burst into flame, illuminating a portion of the battlefield. For a while, that made us good targets for the enemy defense. I crossed a second Russian trench and ordered the attack to continue forward, since our grenadiers had closed up to the Tigers. I was then hit—apparently from short range—by an antitank round on the right side of my turret. Since, necessarily, I had my head out of the hatch to better orient myself, I was hit by a substantial number of fragments in the back of my head. I lost a lot of blood, my earphones filled up with blood and I lost consciousness. I was only able to only transmit the message that Leutnant Heerlein was to take over leadership of the battalion. My Tiger dropped back a bit and I was transferred to the medical SPW that was back there. It moved me back into the vineyards where the surgeon was set up in a wine cellar. He took out a number of bone splinters, bandaged me and

sent me on back by way of Für in a staff car (brief report to division there) to Chuz. There, I took care of the most pressing items while lying down and had myself taken to Hauptmann Wiegand (supply company) at Tardoskedd. He immediately moved up front to take over command of the battalion. I was taken back to Pressburg by way of Totmegyer and Glanta. In Pressburg I was operated on that afternoon in a Luftwaffe special skull hospital. It was pretty horrible. That night, with the help of medicine, I got a few hours of sleep.

18 February: Things were tolerable. My head hurt a bit. A bit of fever.

19–24 February: Speedy recovery. Oberleutnant von Rosen was brought to us on 20 February. (Pretty bad arm wound in the evening of 17 February. Elbow joint smashed.) He was placed in my room and I learned from him that our night attack had led to considerable success under Heerlein's leadership. Right after I was wounded, a carefully emplaced battery of the most modern, large caliber, long-barreled guns was overrun by the Tigers about a thousand meters beyond where I had been hit. With that, the Russian resistance collapsed in that sector. The entire Gran bridgehead was eliminated in a day and a half, freeing an SS division that was attacking directly on our left from a desperate situation. On 23 February I was able to get up for a short period and get around. There were air raid alarms almost daily (American bomber fleets flying to Vienna). Russian bombers bombed Pressburg several times.

25 February: I checked out of the hospital with a bandaged head, over the protests from the doctors who wanted to hang onto me and then send me on hospital leave (where?). Since I was not able to get a telephone connection, I took a train to Tardoskedd (1430–1800 hours), where I happened into a birthday party thrown by the supply company and the trains for Oberfeldwebel Hensel.

26 February: Reported back to the corps at Nagy Surany. Then on to the battalion, which had just been moved back to Csuz again after the battle of the Gran bridgehead had been successfully concluded. Quiet; time for maintenance.

27 February–6 March: The battalion remained in Csuz. The repair of the Tigers proceeded well. Polished off an incredible amount of official paperwork. An incredible mud period set in. Even the paved roads are in horrendous condition. We

are almost completely isolated and can only get around with Kettenkräder and the like, since the roads have been almost completely destroyed by the SS formations that have been withdrawn. The conditions are like those during the mud period in Russia. Our quarters continue to be in the rectory at Csusz. On about 3 March we were placed under the operations control of the 4th Panzer Regiment.

On 4 March the Wehrmacht report stated that the Russians had also occupied central Pomerania and our hometown, Zeitlitz.

On 6 March there was a meeting for all officers of the battalion in Csuz. There is an extreme scarcity of fuel, since the supply is no longer assured (the local refinery in Komorn has been destroyed by American bombing). At noon we discovered that we are to move farther north to the area of Verebely (east of Neutra) on 7 March.

Received a postcard on 7 March from my sister-in-law, Hertha Bernuth in Munich, mailed on 20 February, saying that brother Wilfried was severely wounded at Stargard and transported out. My mother had suffered a broken hip in Zeitlitz. Was she able to get away from there in time?

7 March: Moved with the entire battalion through NeuhÑusel to Verebely and there attached to the 4th Panzer Regiment. We found quite nice quarters in that clean little city (not much furniture). The electric lights function—15 kilometers behind the main line of resistance.

8 March–24 March: 8 March: all sorts of official duties.

9 March: Numerous trips with the officers of the battalion to reconnoiter terrain as far as the Gran. Moderately cold. More scouting of terrain on the next day. Then a total ban on driving motor vehicles due to the loss of Komorn.

Slowly it is becoming spring. Several beautiful, warm days.

The military situation on the western borders of Germany has now become critical. At Stuhlweiß-enburg the situation is also obviously critical. A great deal (certainly unnecessary!) of work with the reduction in size of the battalion. Strength reduced to thirty-one Tigers and a corresponding reduction in the trains and the maintenance capabilities. We're never that strong anyway!

Finally got mail from my wife and sisters on 18 and 23 February. All of them are now in Brandenburg-Mecklenburg-Rügen. News is only lacking from my mother and the ones living in Zeitlitz. Brother Wilfried (lost one eye) is in Münster.

Several nice birthday celebrations. It was warm and spring-like. There is still a deceptive quiet on our front. However, the Russians are continually getting stronger. Serious business, all of it bad, going on at Stuhlweißenburg and Komorn. Leaders' reconnaissance, visit from Oberst Bäke (commander, 13th Panzer Division). Went to the maintenance facility at Neutra (otherwise, all motor vehicle trips are still banned). On 22 March a nice company get-together in the evening with the 1st Company. We did a sand-table exercise with all the officers (Oberst Bäke was there). Strikingly warm summer weather. The Russian offensive that was expected on 23 March and then on 24 March still has not taken place.

25 March: The Russian offensive on the entire Gran front was launched. The enemy formed numerous bridgeheads west of the river from which he pressed forward. Our battalion rolled to Töhöl and launched a counterattack against Nagykalna, which was held by strong Russian forces. Although we continued our attack for the entire night—lacking any sort of other supporting units (!)—we did not make it into the place, especially since enemy attacks took place on both the right and left.

26 March 1945: In the morning we were ordered back to Töhöl, where defensive fighting was already in progress. We were to launch local counterattacks which, in my opinion, were senseless since the Russians had already pushed through on our right and left as far as the Verebely line. In Tîhîl the other units have already disappeared. Under heavy artillery and mortar fire, we slugged it out with the enemy who was not pressing hard there. I have already ordered our trains back out of Verebely.

27 March: During the night the battalion was ordered back out of Töhöl to Verebely. It was to get ready for further ominous counterattacks. We formed a sort of bridgehead with our Tigers at the eastern outskirts of Verebely while the front crumbled completely in front of us. Indeed, I had to pull back a portion of the Tigers through Verebely to the west to secure our rear communications to Neutra (where the maintenance shop is) and the villages to the left and right of that road. The enemy has already been reported all around there. Our Tigers held the eastern outskirts of Verebely for the entire day. The enemy did not

feel confident enough to attack where we were. Infantry streamed back through the countryside to the west, completely scattered and in small groups. Without having received any orders from above, I went back during the night with the battalion staff, some of the tanks and the combat trains to Kalasz, where we formed a hedgehog and secured. Leutnant Fürlinger was killed by artillery fragments during the evening. He was with the Tigers in Verebely.

We are all quite depressed by the death of that splendid man. During the night, I ordered our Tigergruppe in Verebely back to Kalasz.

28 March: Fell back further to Neutra, which our maintenance facility had already left on the previous day. Obviously, there is no longer any proper front line. With great effort, along with other units, we held a "bridgehead" at Neutra throughout the day. The line was only held by our Tigers, since the Russians did not venture one step forward wherever they encountered our tanks. They immediately pulled back and went around to the right and left of us.

I got hold of the corps in the rear area. Heated discussion with the commanding general, who demanded constant local counterattacks from me to the east "in cooperation with the other units of the corps located at Neutra." His situation map, in fact, was filled with notations of all sorts of units. I energetically informed him that my tanks were practically all that was left in the so-called front line, and those were close to collapse as a result of the long commitment without any maintenance. He could observe his other units flooding past through the countryside on both sides of his command post. He snapped back at me that I could not make assertions that made lies of the reports of his unit commanders. I requested that he relieve me as commander of the battalion if my portrayal of the situation was incorrect. Oberst Bäke, the commander of the 13th Panzer Division, confirmed my reports. That quieted the General down a bit. He let up on the "counterattacks." I spent the night in a dirty, little house on the road out of Neutra. By radio that night, I arranged with the maintenance facility to recover several Tigers that had broken down at Neutra. I also arranged to resupply the tanks remaining at the front.

29 March: The Tigers, as the last fighting unit, were pulled out of the "bridgehead" at Neutra, since the Russians had already pushed far past to the west both north and south of us. We were quite concerned about recovering the Tigers that had been disabled but, thanks to exemplary work of the rear-area services (maintenance teams and prime movers), all the tanks were successfully recovered despite enemy artillery fire. I brought up the rear in the Volkswagen through the uncomfortably still and abandoned city of Neutra. I followed the Tigers, which constituted the rear guard. Enemy artillery and Stalin organs fired ceaselessly into the little city. Here and there blocks of houses blazed. Collapsing walls interfered with our movement. There was no trace to be seen of the populace.

As has become usual, there were numerous bombing attacks and strafing runs by Russian aircraft on the withdrawal route. Every few moments we found ourselves in the roadside ditch.

Since all of the remaining Tigers became disabled en route with mechanical problems and had to be towed, the battalion moved "for refitting" to Sered. Spent the night with the supply company and got a few hours of sleep.

30 March 1945: At the corps early (where?). We agreed to send a portion of the more seriously damaged Tigers and the maintenance facility (heavy maintenance platoon) by rail to the west. That would have to take place without much preparation, depending entirely on the initiative of the maintenance leadership with improvised means. It worked. The other Tigers were hastily repaired [most likely about 12?].

The Russians are pushing forward everywhere. South of Vienna they are already in the Reich. Things are also collapsing in the West: The end of Germany.

The only course left for us is to offer the maximum possible resistance in conducting a fighting withdrawal. This allows as many German units as possible to get to the west and also hold the way open for the perpetually increasing number of civilian population (women and children!) who were earlier evacuated from western Germany and who are now fleeing on the roads. Our men, as I have repeatedly said, totally understand that. The discipline, the combat readiness and the fighting spirit of the officers and men of the battalion is, with very few exceptions, amazing. It is sometimes almost beyond belief where our supply company still comes up with rations, fuel (frequently from abandoned flying fields) and 8.8cm ammunition (often reworked ammunition from heavy flak). One also has to realize that, on their runs, they often encounter enemy units that have pushed forward!

Special details from the maintenance company even get new Maybach engines for our Tigers from Friedrichshafen, even though French forces are already in the area around the city. What a temptation it must be for the members of the maintenance company, some of whom come from southern Germany, not to return to the unit! There has not been a single case of that happening.

31 March: The battalion formed a blocking position with the few repaired Tigers at Castle Bab. Throughout the day, Russian attacks failed against the barrier. The battalion staff remained in the little Wag bridgehead, but moved at night to Gerenscker (west of Sered, south of Tyrnau).

1 April (Easter): Heavy fighting all day in and south of Tyrnau. Other than our Tigers screening the eastern outskirts of Tyrnau, all that I saw were retreating groups of German infantry, mostly leaderless. Since the Russians were advancing into Tyrnau from the flanks, I ordered the Tigers to fall back. They had to fight their way back through the city. Fortunately, not a single vehicle was lost in the process. Then further retreats to the west toward the lesser Carpathians.

2 April: The Russians kept up their attack. As always, we were alone in the front line. Somewhere I ran into a newly organized SPW company with vehicular-mounted, super-heavy twin machine guns. It was led by an able Leutnant. For the immediate future, I impressed the unit into my service. With its weapons, it represented a major source of support for us. We can temporarily block the Russian attack in a sort of bridgehead at the eastern edge of the lesser Carpathians, where we are defending the Nadas-Boleraz area.

My command post is in the nearby church at Binowce, where we remained throughout the night. The road from Nadas over the pass crosses the mountains by us.

3 April 1945: There was heavy fighting throughout the day around Nadas, which our Tigers and SPW's were holding. They were under heavy enemy fire that forced changes of position. However, here, as in most cases, the Russians avoided direct attacks. Instead, they pushed along undefended byways through the mountains and fired on us from the flanks. Therefore, the battal-

ion command post was moved two kilometers farther to the west over the pass into a patch of woods. During the night, we supplied the tanks and recovered damaged vehicles.

4 April: The few Tigers and SPWs still held Nadas in the early morning. I heard from corps that the enemy had already broken through far to the west of us on our right at Pressburg (at the southern end of the lesser Carpathians). An awful mess there!

As ordered by radio, the Tigers pulled back on the road over the pass as far as Apfeldorf. Unfortunately, a Tiger that got stuck in soft ground and had been hit by a heavy antitank gun had to be blown up. The remnants of the battalion spent the entire day, ready for defense, at a farmstead west of Apfeldorf. It was already under heavy enemy artillery fire. The breather was short and the Russians took the opportunity to attack from the air. In the evening we were ordered to pull back a few kilometers to the west along the main road.

5 April: With our few fighting elements, we were positioned on the road leading west out of Apfeldorf. A radio order reached us at noon to move west/southwest as fast as possible through Senitza to the Sastin (Schloßberg) area, where an enemy breakthrough was expected from the south through Marvaör. We reached Marvaör. The Russian leading units evidently cleared out when we showed up. We stopped the attacks of fairly strong enemy forces at the outskirts of Marvaör, although I only had four Tigers to commit. We secured the village throughout the night under substantial enemy artillery fire.

6 April: All day long we held the village under increasing enemy artillery fire. Nothing was to be seen of the German infantry that had been announced over the radio. The remnants of the other German units had abandoned the place during the night. While I was outside of the tank, I was slightly wounded in the back by a mortar round fragment. An order arrived in the evening to move to a farmstead, Novy Dor, where we found a few hours of rest. Unfortunately, two Tigers became disabled with mechanical problems during the withdrawal. I was on the road all night recovering the two tanks with prime movers in front of the advancing Russians. The recovery was a success.

7 April: Strong enemy pressure on all sectors of the front. I defended two major retreat routes with two battle groups, each with two Tigers and a

Homemade birthday congratulations to Leutnant Erich Fürlinger on the occasion of his twenty-fifth birthday. This was presented from the combat elements of the 3rd Company to Leutnant Fürlinger, who was assigned to the 1st Company.

few of our Flak vehicles. I directed the operation by radio and by visiting them in the staff car. Unfortunately, we had a total loss of a quad Flak vehicle. (Hit by a round from an antitank gun!) The command post was in Petrova Ves for several hours but was seriously disrupted by Stalin organ fire and Russian ground-attack aircraft. I was totally exhausted. In the evening, we received the order to fall back to Hulicz with the remnants of the battalion, where we were to form and defend a bridgehead on the March River. That took place (in a very makeshift fashion!) in the dark.

8 April: Finally a bit of sleep and a chance to wash. Our remaining tanks launched a few limited counterattacks from the eastern outskirts of Hulicz. Low-level aerial attack at Hulicz. Sunny. Cold nights. Took care of the most pressing paperwork.

9 April 1945: Still in Hulicz. After an artillery preparation, the enemy attacked the Hulicz bridgehead in several places with strong forces. Fortunately, a few repaired Tigers arrived from the maintenance shop. Our few tanks held off all the Russian attacks throughout the day. During the night, the battalion was ordered to move to the west bank of the March in the Lundenburg area to Lanstorf.

10 April: We got to Lanstorf in the morning. Magnificent spring weather. The corps was in Eisgrub (a prince's castle like those in Liechtenstein). Repairs. Sleep. Early in the evening the Russians felt their way forward across the March toward Lundenburg.

11 April: During the night I attended a meeting at the 13th Panzer Division. It was supposed to defend Lundenburg. At dawn, our few Tigers were ordered to Lanzhof (south of Lundenburg) to stop a Russian attack. They stayed there under heavy fire from all sorts of weapons. I accompanied them in the Volkswagen (not much fun!). The Russians then attacked with eleven tanks. One Tiger was knocked out, a total loss. The other Tigers knocked out ten of the eleven attackers. (I, in the meantime, retired with my Volkswagen.) The Tigers remained there for the night as security.

12 April: Early orders—the battalion is to move south from Lanstorf into the Zistersdorf oil region, since a new mess was about to happen. Two Tigers had to remain as corset-stays with a battle group at Lundenburg. My other tanks

became disabled with major mechanical problems during the long march south, so that we reached the barracks at the Windisch-Baumgarten oilfield at Zistersdorf without any tanks. By "Führer order" we were to defend that oilfield to the last drop of our blood. It had already been abandoned by the technical personnel and partially destroyed. A pretty senseless order for a battalion staff without tanks or heavy weapons!

13 April: After radio traffic with the corps, we moved to the west without spilling our last drops of blood. I concerned myself with towing and repairing our tanks. Thanks to the unceasing efforts of our rear-area services, it was going fairly well. The front continued to crumble everywhere. Our little battle group at Lundenburg had an extremely difficult day today. A very heavy Russian attack on the place fell apart after our Tigers knocked out sixteen enemy tanks. In the evening I was with the maintenance company. It is still relatively intact in spite of numerous moves and unannounced departures. It is now in Bergen (near Nikolsburg) and working at full tilt. Paperwork, wash, sleep.

The battalion staff remains just west of Zistersdorf, where it is still quiet.

14 April: The corps front lines continue to fall back. Our tanks still aren't operational or become disabled again with new problems whenever they are finished. Very disappointing! In the evening, the remnants of the battalion move from the Zisterndorf area to Wilfersdorf.

15 April: The battalion moved to the east into the area of operations of the 357th Infantry Division, with which we are to form a new defensive front. In actual fact, however, our Flak vehicles are the only ones forming the front. We can find no more than fragments of the 357th Infantry division. I remain with the SPW and two quad flak vehicles in Rabensburg, where we hold the shattered front all by ourselves. Wild mortar barrage from Ivan. I did not get back to our new command post in Alt-Höflein until nightfall.

16 April 1945: A bit of peace and quiet in our Alt-Höflein command post. Only a few Flak vehicles are employed from the battalion (blocking positions on the retreat routes). I could finally report four Tigers operational to the corps in the morning. However, they were not employed, so that everyone had a bit of rest in the beautiful weather at Alt-Höflein.

In the night, however, we suddenly had to move with the battalion to Wilfersdorf, where some sort of mess is brewing (Russian breakthrough in the deep right flank). We reached the village in the dark and set up there.

17 April: Our few Tigers and Flak vehicles were engaged in defensive fighting at Wilfersdorf and Hobersdorf. Heavy Russian artillery fire, but no more than small-scale, scattered and cautious Russian advances in our sector. We stayed in the village for the night. Resupply worked.

18 April: The battalion moved to Erdberg early in accordance with a radio order from the corps. The enemy is advancing alongside us. A difficult recovery of a Tiger that had broken down at Wilfersdorf was successful.

19 April: A radio order from the corps sent us rolling early as fast as possible from Erdberg to the north, where another mess was in progress. The enemy was already at Klein Hadersdorf and Poysdorf with his tanks. I divided the combat vehicles into two little groups and led them from the SPW. The fighting became heavy. We saved the situation by knocking out thirteen Russian tanks without any losses to ourselves. We rolled through burning Hadersdorf to the west during the night.

20 April: A corps order occasioned further movement to the west into the Föllin-Alt-Ruppersdorf area. Along the way we knocked out two enemy tanks that were chasing us. In the evening we were in Alt-Ruppersdorf, which was already under fire from enemy artillery. During the night, a surprise Stalin organ barrage descended on our command post, making our quarters totally unliveable. We had telephone contact with the 13th Panzer Division.

21 April: A crazy day! I phoned at dawn—thick fog outside, even at the 13th Panzer Division, which was about four kilometers behind us. A sudden cry in the telephone ear piece: "The Russians are coming"—then a great crash, shots and silence. I did not learn until evening that the Russians had broken through to our right in the early-morning fog with twenty-five tanks and mounted infantry. Of all places, they overran the division command post and then advanced farther to the west. At the same time, an additional Russian armored attack started to the north of us. Wild gunfire in the fog both to the right and left of us. I was only halfway filled in on the situation by motorcycle riders who had become separated

from their units. I alerted everyone, had the tanks get ready for combat (still five Tigers) and, after a quick meeting of the tank commanders, dashed off in the SPW toward the west, following the enemy who had broken through (in radio contact with the Tigers).

I reinforced my "pursuit" with several small tanks [Wasps—10.5 cm light howitzers on self-propelled mounts] that had halted in a village, then with three Tigers that met me on their way back from repairs at the maintenance shop. It turned into a wild chase! After going several kilometers to the west, I spotted the enemy armored force through a break in the fog in the terrain to the right of the road I was on. I approached to within 400 meters, whereupon Ivan opened fire on me. We were able to duck into a depression. Our Tigers then emerged. The Russians dashed past us and the farmstead until a river course (the Thaya) brought them to a halt. They formed a hedgehog defense in the patch of woods there. I mounted my Tiger and deployed the tanks in the terrain to the right and left of the farm courtyard so we could observe the entire patch of woods.

I had the two left-hand Tigers carefully approach the woods. They were immediately met with a hellish fire from the tanks (possibly also including heavy caliber fire? 9.5 cm?). We also fired into the woods at the same time. An attempt to get at them on the right side also miscarried. The corps demanded an immediate attack on the enemy over the radio. I had no desire to do that— attack across completely open area. I pondered for quite some time whether we might succeed with a simultaneous attack from all sides (with six or seven Tigers). At that moment, the entire Russian armored group, with mounted infantry, broke out of the woods, but toward the east. It developed into a wild armored engagement which, of course, affected the mounted infantry first.

A portion of them then attempted to get away to the east on foot. We knocked out ten enemy tanks outside of the "Mitterhof" farm and eight more during the pursuit. We suffered no losses. Of the remaining tanks, two more were taken out by PaK as they crossed the thin German lines. I pursued the infantry with the SPW and the small tanks. Under fire from our on-board weapons, the infantry quickly gave up the attempt to escape and became prisoners. In spite of our overwhelming success at that place, our entire front was pulled back today all the way to Laa. I spent the night in Laa with all the units of the battalion.

Unfortunately, Leutnant Linkenbach was hit in the head and severely wounded today.

22 April 1945: The battalion command post was moved to Zwingendorf, southwest of Laa. The Tigers set up at Stronsdorf. A small battle group with two Tigers was employed farther north at Dürrnholz-Neuprerau. The enemy did not attack us today. I put in a recommendation at corps for the Knight's Cross for Leutnant Linkenbach, who was transported to the rear yesterday. Unfortunately, our rear area services have not determined his location. [Leutnant Linkenbach died soon after he was wounded.]

23 April: The battalion is in Zwingendorf; the Tigers remain where they were employed yesterday. Quiet in our sector. April weather, hail showers and cool.

The Russians have already advanced into parts of Berlin.

24 April: We remain in and around Zwingendorf. Nothing special happening. Paper war.

25 April: Still at Zwingendorf. Then to corps where I received orders to move the battalion north with the Tigers to the left wing of the corps. New location: Socherl. We reached it in the evening with all combat units. Good quarters, very friendly people. I was invited to spend the evening with Oberst Bäke at Aschmeritz.

26 April: The battalion is in Socherl. One of our battle groups with a few Tigers was a bit farther south at Wulzeshofen, another committed in the front line directly in front of us at Wostitz. The Tigers at Wostitz knocked out an enemy tank.

27 April–30 April: We continued to remain in Socherl. It was quiet at the location of our southern battle group. On the other hand, there were several enemy attacks in front of us at Wostitz. We were able to repulse them with the help of our Tigers. In the course of that engagement we knocked out six enemy tanks. The battle group had to execute an unpleasant night operation to eliminate an enemy penetration. For the most part, the main line of resistance was held. The nightly supply run ran smoothly. Unfortunately, we lost two of our best tank commanders: Feldwebel Knispel [German Cross in Gold] and Feldwebel Skoda [Iron Cross, First Class].

The heavy fighting in Berlin approaches its end.

1 May: Adolf Hitler dead in Berlin.

My brother Achim is also in Berlin as a special duty officer with the local area command: General Ritter von Hauenschildt.

In the afternoon, I—along with my adjutant and all sorts of supporting documents—was called to Panzer Corps "Feldherrnhalle" regarding awarding the Knight's Cross. Since there was no longer communication with the OKH, the corps and armies are now acting on their own. Meetings with General Kleeman and the other gentlemen.

2 May 1945: Visited all the units of the battalion (including the maintenance and supply companies, battle groups, etc.) and discussed Hitler's death. Drew attention to his capable successor, Admiral Dönitz. The corps adjutant was with us in the evening.

3 May–6 May: Remarkable, uneasy quiet on our sector of the front. Battalion in Socherl. I was able to dispose of all possible written and administrative work. One does everything with the conviction that it is meaningless.

The maintenance shop was able to repair a great number of Tigers, which were brought forward. The corps reported energetic Russian attack preparations on our front sector. Our Tigers [probably about 12] were distributed on the most important roads in the 50-kilometer-wide corps sector as corset stays. On the lesser roads there were several supply vehicles, maintenance sections, motorcycle messengers and the remaining flak vehicles. The battalion staff, in the center of the sector, had contact with the battle groups by medium-wave radio and, thus, a degree of oversight over the entire sector. The order went out that vehicles which became disabled during future withdrawals were no longer to be recovered, but were to be blown up. Sad end!

The entire Western Front (including Italy) has surrendered. The Americans are advancing north of us toward Prague. We have all sorts of doubts whether we can still make it into the American zone.

7 May: The Russian attack began this morning with a level of aerial activity that we have not yet experienced along the entire corps front. The front rapidly collapsed, even though our three battle groups acquitted themselves well defen-

sively. I could report knocking out sixteen tanks, twelve antitank guns on self-propelled mounts, seven guns, and one airplane. The Russians, however, moved west on secondary roads past both sides of our battle groups. For the most part, they were motorized. I maintained radio contact, going to several sections in the Volkswagen (during which we were repeatedly flat on our faces in the roadside ditch due to aerial attacks). For the first time in our experience, the Russians committed larger massed groups of thirty or more bombers against the villages and the retreat routes, which were frequently densely packed. In between those bombing raids, low-level ground attacks. Naturally, there was no more German air activity.

As evening approached, we had to leave our friendly Socherl pretty rapidly. Within it were the graves of our comrades who had fallen in the last few days.

Overall, there was a rapid retreat of the front. The Russian pursuit was only slowed by a few battle groups. We remained with the battalion staff throughout the night in the retreat march on the often totally jammed roads. Frequently, progress was only measured in meters.

8 May: Early in the morning we reached Schidrowitz. We were able to make contact with Panzer Corps "Feldherrnhalle." No further orders: Retreat to the west, if possible by way of Budweis. Then possibly hope for being taken over as a unit by the Americans. Battle groups should, if possible, block along the main roads for as long as possible. No more tank recovery. The corps apparently knew less about what was going on in the zone of its retreat than I did, since I still had radio contact over the entire breadth of the front. I gave the order to the rear elements of the battalion (by radio or motorcycle messenger) to pull back as quickly as possible by way of Budweis farther to the west.

CHAPTER 35

The Final Engagements of the Battalion with Army Group South

Alfred Rubbel

As 1944 ended and 1945 began, no one could seriously continue to believe that Germany could avoid an ending to the war that appeared to be only weeks away and would be a catastrophe such as our history had never known. There was no longer any military way to prevent the advance of our enemies against Germany from the east and from the west. In the west as in the east, the enemy had started to cross the German border. Unimaginable deeds of cruelty by the Red Army in East Prussia–Nemmersdorf was the first locality exemplifying that—portended what lay ahead for the Germans in the east. The declaration by our enemies that their war objective was unconditional surrender and the total occupation of Germany ruled out a political solution. The hope that the western enemies would break with the Soviets and make a common front to the east with the Wehrmacht was, admittedly, faint. That illusion, however, and the anxiety over falling in Russian hands, were ground enough for the combatants on the Eastern Front to fight on to the final hour, against all logic—as the Monday-morning quarterbacks are so clever in pointing out with their 20/20 hindsight.

BACK TO THE BATTALION

18 December 1944. I was at the officer candidate school [*Oberfähnrich-Schule I*] of the armor school at Krampnitz (in Potsdam). The course of instruc-

tion, which I had to repeat due to a recurrence of Malaria, was finally at an end. In April of 1944 I had left the battalion. The bus with about thirty others, also promoted to officer candidate, left the school grounds to take us to the Potsdam railroad station. From there we were to go to the responsible replacement troop units. A further eight week course of instruction awaited those of us who were classified as professional soldiers. Those of us like me who were reservists received an immediate assignment to the front. I hoped that the promise of returning to the battalion would be honored.

However, we were still at Lanzentor. It was deep winter. The windows of the buses were frozen up since there was no heating. The door of the bus was torn open and a Panzer Major, decorated with the Knight's Cross, stood in the door and called out my name. Sitting way at the back, I only then recognized our "visitor". It was our commander, Major Fromme. I stood up, went to the front of the bus and reported. The Major returned the salute and, in front of the occupants of the bus, informed me the paperwork for my impending promotion to Leutnant was at the 500th Replacement Battalion in Paderborn. Further, he told me about my return to Tiger Tank Battalion 503. At that time, the battalion was presumably at Stuhlweißenburg in Hungary. I was rather proud of that meeting with my commander, who was on his way to the school to take up his new duties as tactical instructor. Of course, I was also proud about the doubly good news of my promotion and my return to the battalion.

On arrival at Paderborn, there were a few days of leave for Christmas and New Year's. Unfortunately, two thirds of the time was uselessly expended in an arduous railroad journey to East Prussia to see my family, only to find that they had already fled. I finally saw them in Saxony but, unfortunately, I was already overdue for the date I was to report to the personnel movement center at Vienna. After a few bumps along the way, I finally made it, a bit late, to Vienna on 3 January. No one there made a big thing of my lateness. It seemed to me that all the bureaucracy there was predominantly occupied by Austrians, and the comrades seemed to understand that, in January 1945, the desire to get to the front was limited. A not so ineffective regulator of the desire to linger in Vienna was that each night one was assigned to a different hotel, and with each new hotel, the quality continually sank.

I sought out Tiger Tank Battalion 503. All that I could learn from the personnel movement center was that no one could tell me where to find it. It was not known that it had now become Tiger Tank Battalion "Feldherrnhalle," and I did not know that either. On a stroll around Vienna I suddenly saw a truck from the battalion. I stopped the truck and asked where the battalion was. It was hauling replacement parts from the depot and was to take them to the maintenance company at Bakonyszombately. Adieu, Vienna, adieu Ankerhof, on to Hungary! On 6 January I was able to report back at the battalion. I was employed as platoon leader of the second platoon in the 3rd Company. It was understandable that my desire to return to the 1st Company, from which I had come, could not be met.

Since the tank complement in January 1945 consisted of only ten operational Tigers and eight more in for short-term repairs, the organization according to tank platoons and tank companies was suspended. There was only a single Tiger combat element which included the members of all the tank companies. As a result, I had the opportunity again to be with "my" 1st Company. That made me feel good, but also caused irritation, since it also eliminated the distance between officers and men, that I was warned was required between myself and my former comrades in the

company. I was of a different opinion. I felt it was wrong to distance myself from my comrades because I had been promoted to a different rank category with different tasks. And I would not dare to write about it here, today, if there were not other living witnesses to attest to the fact that the interaction that developed depended exclusively on mutual respect and, therefore, occasioned no problems.

THE BATTALION IN JANUARY AND FEBRUARY 1945

From the middle of December 1944 until the middle of February 1945 the Schwerpunkt of the defensive fighting for the still relatively intact Army Group South (Wöhler) was with the 6th Army (Balck) in western Hungary. The strategic intention of the Second Ukrainian Front (Malinowski) was to advance out of the eastern Hungarian low plains, bypass the Slovakian mountain range to the south with the main body of its troops, capture Budapest and advance through the western Hungarian low ground to Vienna. The Wehrmacht report at that time repeatedly mentioned the bend in the Danube, Budapest, the Pillis mountains, the Vertes mountains, the Lake Velence, Bakony Woods, Lake Balaton and the Gran River. Our battalion, even though it had belonged to Panzer Corps "Feldherrnhalle" since the turn of the year, was also committed with the III Panzer Corps (Breith) and the I Cavalry Corps (Harteneck).

Budapest was encircled. One attack in January 1945 from the southwest through Stuhlweißenburg and a new attack in the Vali sector near Zamoly with strong armored forces, including the 1st Panzer Division, failed to break through. Reduction in the pressure on Budapest, to say nothing of its relief, failed. Therefore it was clear that the days of "Festung" Budapest were numbered. Budapest fell on 14 February 1945. North of the Danube, the Russians formed a bridgehead over the lower Gran, thereby threatening capture of the oilfields at Komorn.

We moved to the area north of Komorn, the tracked units transported by rail. On 17 February 1945 the attack on the Gran bridgehead began. We were placed under the operational control of the Division "Hoch und Deutschmeister," a formation given the honorific after old Austrian traditions. To our north, the 12th SS Panzer Division "Hitlerjugend" attacked. On 23 February the bridgehead was crushed. That was the last combat operations of the battalion that deserves the designation "attack." That successful operation exacted no more than limited losses in men and equipment.

The commander was wounded, but returned to the battalion on 26 February. The commander of the 3rd Company, Oberleutnant Freiherr von Rosen, was also wounded that day but did not return again to the battalion. Leutnant Fürlinger led the 1st Company, Hauptmann von Eichel-Streiber the 2nd Company, and Leutnant Koppe the 3rd Company. February 1945 ended with ongoing small operations between the Danube and the foothills of the Carpathians.

THE SECOND ENGAGEMENT AT ZAMOLY ON 25 JANUARY 1945

Of the series of engagements in that area (see the personal diary of the battalion commander), the fighting at Zamoly is particularly memorable to me for several reasons, even though that fighting has no significance when viewed from the overall situation. The Wehrmacht report for 25 January 1945 reported for that sector of the front: "In Hungary, our attack formations broke through strong enemy antitank positions between Lake Velence and the Danube and advanced as far forward as the Vali sector . . ."

We were temporarily attached to Generalmajor Holste's 4th Cavalry Brigade. Together with units of the 5th Cavalry Regiment, we were intended to Zamoly at first light on 25 January. The leader of the attack group was Rittmeister Graf Plettenberg. On 24 January at 2300 hours all officers, including the tank commanders, were present when Plettenberg issued his order. Three or four King Tigers led by Leutnant Beyer were detailed from the battalion. We had an exceptional orders session. I have seldom seen one as good and tailored to the circumstances.

Plettenberg was a persuasive personality. He knew how to present the mission in the shortest time possible and in an impressive manner. After asking for input from the participants, he would develop the concept of the operations.

It was extremely cold, I would estimate about minus 14 degrees Fahrenheit. In the last two weeks about 20 or 30 centimeters of snow had accumulated on the ground. It was important to keep the engine, transmission and batteries warm. It was also important to remember that in an attack on a position held by a static armored enemy, there would not only be antitank guns, but also mines, which are easy to lay in snow.

That was what happened to me. An antitank gun belt opened fire from head on with 7.62 centimeter guns out of the cover of a maize field. It had no effect on us. As we pressed forward at full speed, we moved right into the minefield that had been laid to protect the antitank guns. Both tracks were blown off. The Russians were masters in the use of mines in combat. They used inexpensive products, wooden-cased mines and mines in paraffin paper, both with no metal parts. They employed them without regard to the human effort required. That type of weapon could not be engaged by a tank. Even the Tiger, though almost immune to antitank guns and tanks, was relatively helpless against mines. Due to neglecting combat reconnaissance, which was my own fault, I learned a lesson with painful consequences. Anyway, back to the attack at Zamoly . . .

We made our way in the night to the jump-off position and waited for hours there for the attack to begin at 0700 hours. It was always a mistake to underestimate the enemy. To consider him stupid, however, is culpable. Antitank fire and mines, as outlined above, brought us to a halt when we set off for the attack at first light. We had moved out with no cover in our giant tanks in a snowfield as it increasingly grew brighter. During the night the Russians had brought forward massive amounts of antitank guns and laid mines in front of them. If we had given any consideration to the enemy situation, we would certainly have expected that or similar measures. To attack there—after noisy preparations on a clear, still winter night where every noise carries far—was a serious mistake. If it was not possible to conceal our intention, a redeployment shortly before the start of the attack and movement from another, unexpected direction would have been better. Antitank guns and mines don't move. Only tanks could have approached us and those would have neither surprised nor endangered us. The responsible leader of the Tigers should have thought that out. Another solution would have been to pin them from the front with one element while going around a few hundred meters with the rest.

Our situation in the immobilized Tiger was a classic for the enemy. It had rolled off of its tracks and was alone in the middle of a minefield and covered by fire from antitank guns. Things happened just as he had planned them. We wanted to make them pay dearly, however. We did the best we could with our 8.8 cm L71 gun to get at Ivan in between the impacts from the 7.62cm antitank guns. There were four or five antitank guns, less than 1,000 meters away at the edge of an unharvested maize field.

In the meantime, the driver was wounded. The crew in the turret was still active. When our gun fired, it was coupled with a strange sound. A look through the vision blocks of the commander's cupola revealed an extraordinary picture. Our gun was no longer as long as it used to be. Moreover, the barrel was spread out, symmetrically, like a palm, right back to the mantlet. In the plethora of hits we had taken, we had not noticed one that had hit the gun and dented the barrel. The next round we fired destroyed the barrel.

Our situation was not pleasant. We needed to bail out. However, in the fire we were receiving—and Ivan was shooting at us with everything he had—that was impossible. I do not remember how long the hail of gunfire lasted. Suddenly, we realized there were no more hits. It had started to snow so heavily that visibility was under 50 meters. Get the wounded out and move to the rear. By the time we had made it to our two comrades who had sought cover in a depression, the snow squall was over. We had made it one more time!

During the night we succeeded in recovering the Tiger, complete with its tracks, and making it provisionally operable. However, just to complete our miseries, it then slipped into a deep bomb crater and required several days of labor to get it out again.

THE BATTALION IN MARCH 1945

At the beginning of March we moved to Verebely in the border area between Slovakia and Hungary that the Hungarians had annexed. It was so peaceful there that garrison routine set in. Training schedules were drawn up; training was instituted for the company in antitank defensive measures tanks and tactical training for the officers. We younger officers did not take this entirely seriously at first, for example, arriving late at a planning exercise in which Generalmajor Dr. Bäke took part. When, at that exercise, the battalion commander asked one of us about the meaning of Hungarian place-name prefixes like "Kis" and

"Nagy" and the one questioned answered with a cheerful "Nem tudom"—I do not know!—Hauptmann Dr. von Diest-Koerber did not seem particularly pleased, especially with such nonchalance in a public forum.

During our days at Verbely we celebrated Erich Fürlinger's birthday. Shortly thereafter, he was killed. The opportunity was taken to send a congratulatory card to Richard von Rosen, in the hospital at Pressburg, on the occasion of his being awarded the German Cross in Gold. It was a "situation report" of the achievements of the 3rd Company in March 1945. It was sketched by Helmut Linser and is presented in the book along with the one presented by the 3rd Company to congratulate Leutnant Fürlinger.

The Russian attack began across the breadth of the Gran front at the end of the month. The overextended front fell back. But the time of being able to stand firm was past—not surprising considering the onrushing masses. We pulled back to Verebely and held a position on the eastern outskirts for two days. The German units had pulled out and there was no more support from our artillery. The Russian infantry columns, deployed into skirmish lines, flowed on past us at a distance of 500 meters to our right and left. They could not be stopped. There was not enough ammunition to put a lasting halt to the movement. In spite of visibly effective fire, new brown columns kept right on coming from the depths of their positions. The concept of "stepping out" certainly applied there. The Russians were already behind us. They waded through the river that we had hoped would be a barrier. They were already in our rear. Strong enemy artillery fire on our tanks' positions. It killed Erich Fürlinger, the leader of the battle group. Before the Russians blocked the bridge and the route of our retreat, I ordered that we should pull back. Our position had been "neutralized." We would form a new barrier to the attacker farther to the west.

The fighting at Verebely and that which followed in the Neutra area show that there was no longer a coherent front. At the corps and divisional level, they were no longer in a position to command. They had increasingly lost the ability to analyze the German and enemy situations. The war disintegrated into individual engagements predicated on self-defense.

THE BATTALION IN APRIL 1945

The battalion continued to fight with small battle groups east of the lesser Carpathians in the Tyrnau area. They were on their own. The battalion command managed to keep a handle on things, in spite of the fragmented commitment; at least we still had leadership. Our commander had to continually stand up to the higher levels of command in order to prevent our soldiers from being squandered. That was something he could not do from his own command post. Instead, he had to go to the divisions and regiments to which we were attached in ever-changing command and control relationships. There he would argue our case in person. Since March I had been on the battalion staff as a special staff officer. Therefore I experienced from first hand what a restless existence the commander led in fulfilling his mission. Often we did not see him for a full twenty-four hours. He did not spare himself, even though he was a full ten years older than the officers of his staff. He earned my highest respect for his outstanding fulfillment of duty.

At the beginning of April—it was near Easter—I was given the task of arranging quarters for the battalion at Nikolsburg. Presumably the intention was to improve the striking power of the battalion by bringing together the scattered fighting units and put a powerful combat formation in the hands of the command. That was not to be. The enemy crossed the lesser Carpathians faster than expected and pushed on to the Zisterndorf oil region. There was hard fighting for almost the entire month of April. It brought us local successes, but they did not prevent the Russians from achieving their intentions. In the meantime, the Russians had advanced into the southern outskirts of Vienna.

At month's end, Panzer Corps "Feldherrnhalle" ordered the combat elements of the battalion to Socherl, south of Brünn. Several Tigers were back in action but, otherwise, things were quiet for us. The units of the Second Ukrainian Front were also exhausted after the offensive out of the Gran sector. It had taken place four weeks previously and their supply situation had also become difficult. As a rule, such a period of quiet boded ill. It almost always led to preparations for an offensive. In view of the overall situation, which brought the end of the war closer to us daily—and, with it, an uncertain fate for each of us—we could only subscribe to the thought: Enjoy the war, the peace will be frightful!

THE WAR IS OVER

We had quite pleasant days in Socherl right up until 7 May. The war appeared to have "fallen asleep." In spite of the quiet that the Russians allowed us, our few tanks (by my estimate, ten to twelve Tigers) established positions and blocked the enemy, and there were losses. Two of our most experienced tank commanders, Knispel and Skoda, were killed at the end of April.

The Russian attack broke out to the west on 7 May with enormous power. We had nothing with which we could oppose it. The only possibility remaining was to fall back. The operational area was to be the still unoccupied area of western Czechoslovakia. The Russians were still on the march in the eastern portion of the country; the Americans were about to cross to the east as far as the Bohemian Woods. We—along with other troops and civilians—made our way to the west. Objective: Protection of the U.S. Army! The Russians did not press particularly hard and did not overtake us. We no longer engaged in combat and, in forty-eight hours of unbroken marching, crossed Czechoslovakia. We were at the Bohemian Woods west of Budweis on 9 May, the day of the capitulation. The war was over!

The battalion had broken into two approximately equal halves. Four to five hundred men road marched together with their vehicles. The tanks were blown up. Most ended their westward journey on bridges that were too weak. The other half of the battalion moved west in several groups of varying size under individual unit leadership. We were not entirely successful in finding those units and passing on the order dissolving the battalion. Thus, the poor communication was also responsible for the fact that the danger of being turned over to the Russians by the Americans was either not known or was underestimated.

The commander personally gave the final order dissolving the battalion to the main body that had made it to Dobrusch, a forest town 20 kilometers west of Budweis. The men were to infiltrate the U.S. blocking line in the Bohemian and Bavarian Woods in the smallest of groups. We hoped to avoid capture in that area and being handed over to the Russians. The bulk of that group succeeded in so doing. The other comrades—about 400—moved south of us and, for a time, were innocuously directed by the Americans to Wallern. Later they were handed over to the Russians—broken promises—and paid dearly with years of imprisonment for the fact that we made it to freedom.

As I have evaluated the situation and pondered which measure was more correct at the time—to dissolve the units and scatter them, thus leaving the individuals to make it on their own, or to keep the "bunch" together in order to maintain unit cohesion as long as possible—I am unequivocally led to the conclusion that our commander's decision at that time was the only correct one. It was a tragedy that, in spite of the fact that Leutnant Hans von Hegemeister's scout platoon was unceasingly on the move to fish our folk out of the columns and divert them away from Wallern, it was impossible to inform more of our comrades and save them from Russian captivity.

Everything was handled in the best professional manner right up to the final minute. The battalion did not burst apart; everything followed due course. All possible measures were taken: Issuance of rations, promotions, discharge entries in and issuance of military record books, exchanges of addresses and terrain orientation (since not enough maps were available). After that, there was nothing left but to take leave of each other.

How did we feel? The end did not come as a surprise. Only the when and where had remained open until the final moment. Thus there was no shock and, considering the situation, no doubt as to what needed to be done next: Namely, to move as far as possible into Bavaria so that it would no longer be immediately obvious whether one came from the eastern or the western front. Above all, don't be captured near the border. That was my final mission of the war and I was able to complete it successfully, as planned.

October 1944: Rail movement of the King Tigers to Hungary.

During a break in the rail movement to Hungary. Left to right: unknown, Feldwebel Berger, Oberleutnant Brandt (commander of the headquarters company), and the Spieß of the headquarters company.

The 503's arrival in Budapest, 14 October 1944. They were warmly welcomed by the local populace.

The battalion command post in Turkeve, October 1944. The commander of the 24th Panzer Division is visiting. Left to right: Stabsarzt Dr. Schramm, Leutnant von Rosen, Leutnant Piepgras, General von Nostiz, and Hauptmann Fromme.

Leutnant von Hagemeister of the scout platoon.

The mess section of the 1st Company.

The appearance of the mighty King Tiger on the streets of the Hungarian capital—previously unknown there—was a well calculated measure which certainly contributed to the rapid and bloodless Szálasi coup. The employment of the battalion lasted only four days. Fortunately, the battalion did not have to use its weapons. The 2nd Company was positioned at the seat of the government, the Burgberg. The 1st and 3rd Companies were posted at critical points where they would make the desired "psychological impression." The populace was friendly and took care of German soldiers. This sequence of photos shows Tigers of the 2nd Company in the government quarter.

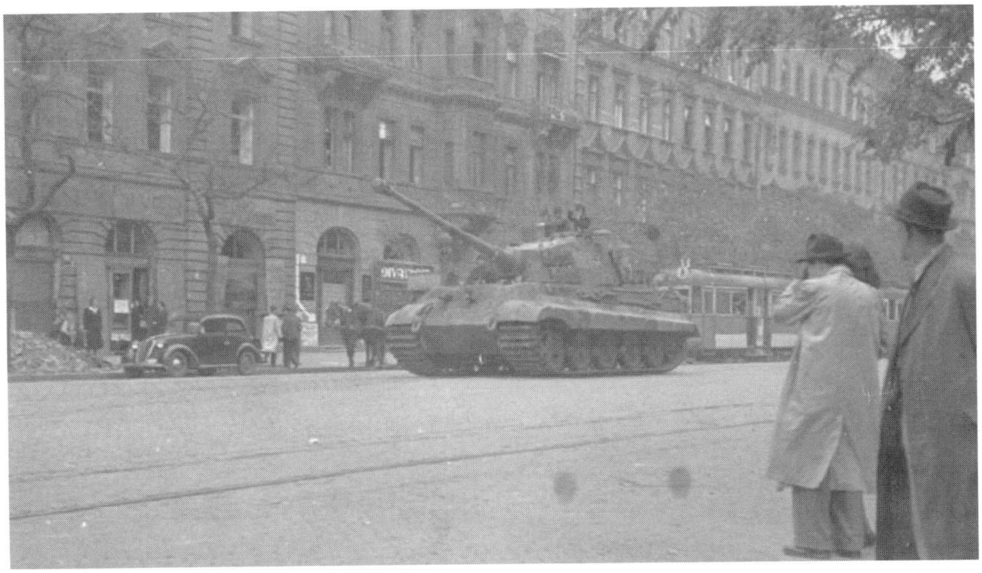

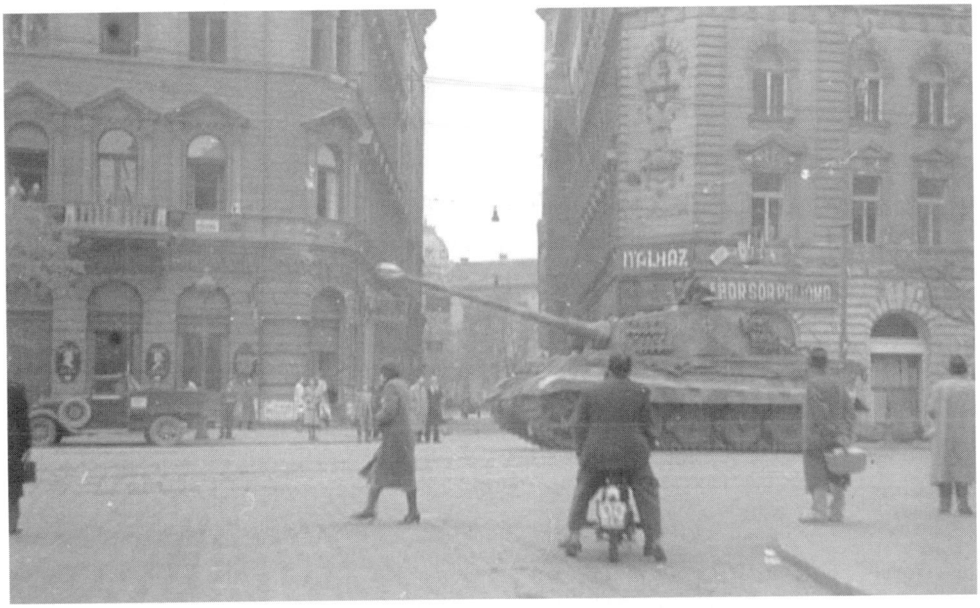

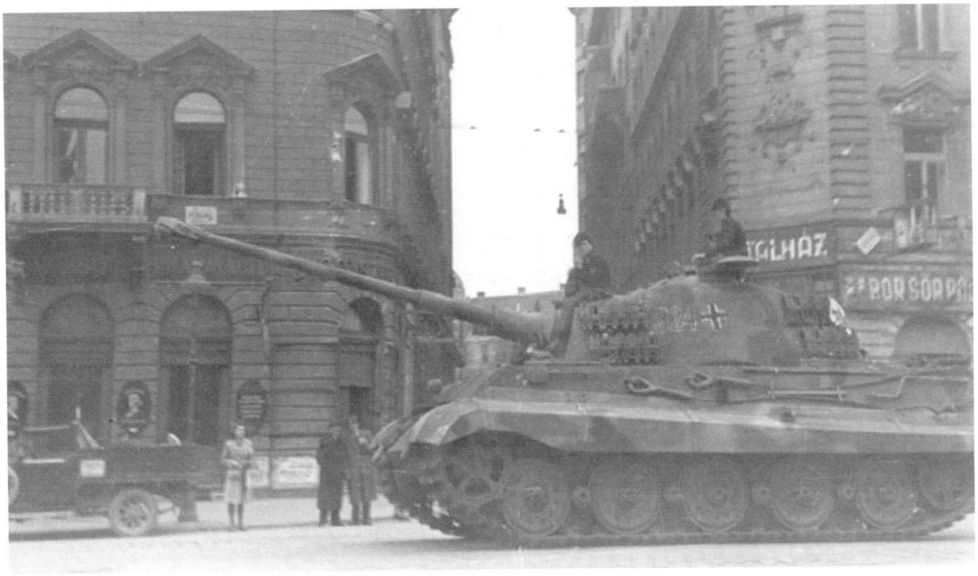

A Wirbelwind of the battalion's Flak platoon also adds to the intimidation factor in the streets of Budapest. These vehicles proved effective not only in their intended role, but also against ground targets.

Tiger 200 rolls over a barricade on the Burgberg.

Szálasi appears on Kapistvan Square in the government quarter, conducting initial discussions with the Hungarian military, who wore arrow-cross armbands to show that they would cooperate with the Arrow-Cross Movement. In the background is a German paratrooper sentry at the gate.

The commander of the bodyguard battalions of the former Hungarian Imperial Regent, Admiral Horthy, reports to the new head of the regime, Szálasi.

Admiral Horthy's riding horses follow him into captivity to Germany.

Tanks of the 3rd Company, Tiger Tank Battalion 503, at the foot of the Burgberg.

The "Horthy Crisis" is over. The battalion's Tigers road-march to the East Railroad Station in Budapest to entrain for operations on the lower Theiß.

A crew prepares its King Tiger for the movement. The soldier on the main gun affixes a muzzle cover to protect the gun tube from the elements.

Tanks line up in preparation for another move.

A field-expedient way of preparing a pig after the train has been loaded.

Tiger 333 has another King Tiger in tow near Bercel, Hungary, 3 November 1944.

On 8 December 1944, Tiger 124 was knocked out at short range by an antitank gun positioned in the houses on the left. Tiger 124 was part of an improvised battle group made up of tanks from the 1st and 3rd Companies. The 80-millimeter thickness of armor on the forward hull was penetrated completely. The driver and radio operator were killed. The Tiger burned out.

Feldwebel Gärtner of the 3rd Company, Tiger Tank Battalion 503, a particularly successful tanker and well-loved comrade, with his gunner, Obergefreiter Klein. Gärtner was killed in the Zamoly area on 7 January 1945.

The final two views of the
destruction of Tiger 123.

The 1st Company will eat well
tonight. Hungary at the end of
January 1945.

Tiger Tank Battalion 503 gets ready to move by rail again. Note that the normal tracks have not been replaced by the special transport tracks for rail movements. Hungary, January 1945.

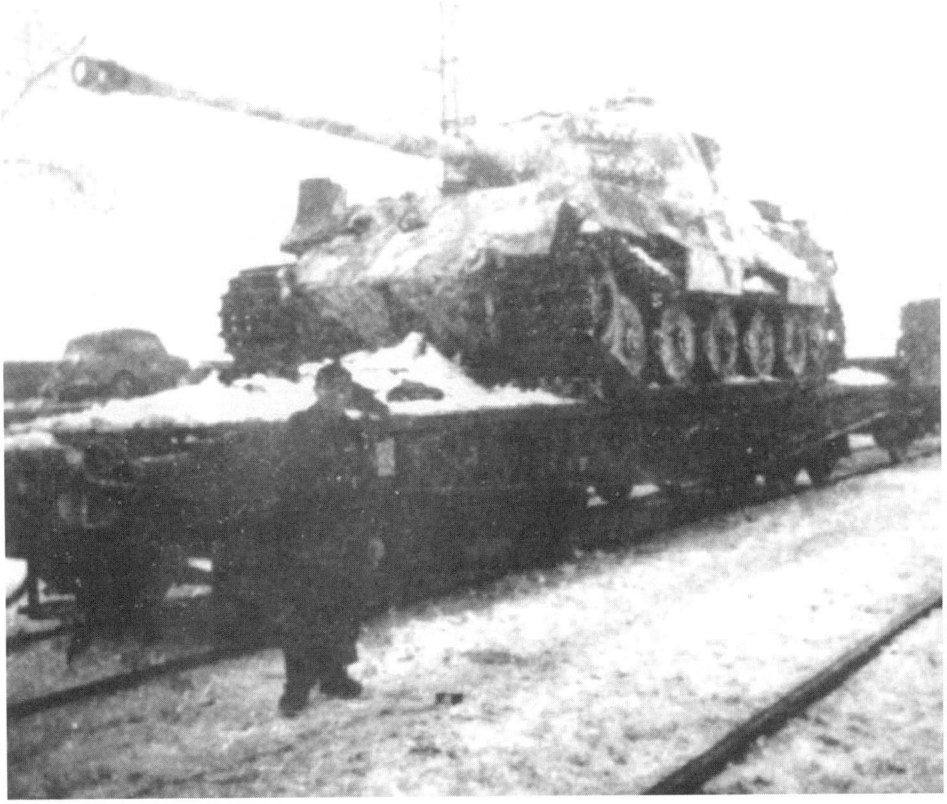

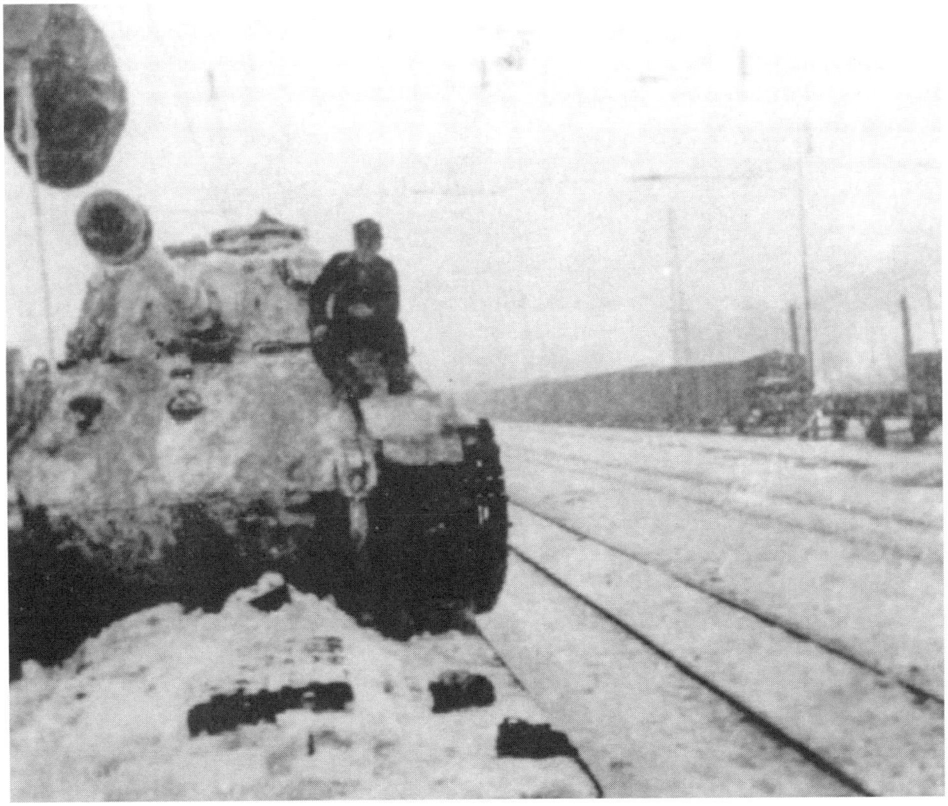

King Tiger 314 "Anneliese" of the 3rd Company at the maintenance facility at Sarkeresztes in January 1945. It was one of the two Tigers which had become disabled with transmission problems at Mailly-le-Camp in August 1944. They were repaired there and returned to the company before the move to Hungary.

King Tiger 131 in Hungary, January 1945.

King Tiger 131 is off-loaded from the Ssyms car in order to move to an assembly area. This photo was taken at the Gran Bridgehead in February 1945.

King Tiger 233 of the 2nd Company in March-April 1945. The commander cannot be identified.

Russian T-34 85s await orders to advance once again.

The school in Erdberg where the battalion had its command post on 18 and 19 April 1945. This photograph was taken in 1933.

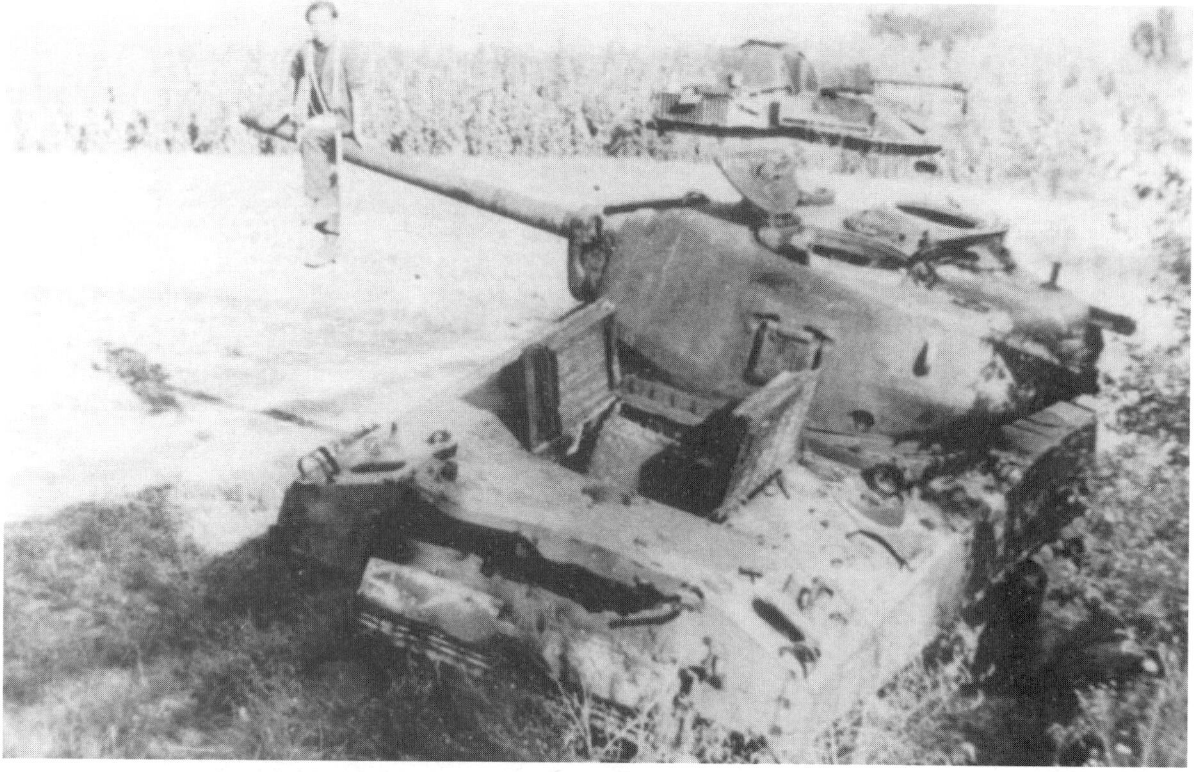

Two of the thirteen armored vehicles knocked out by the battalion on 19 April 1945 at Kleinhadersdorf. In the foreground, a M4 Sherman; behind it is a SU-76. The photo was taken in 1945 or 1946 at the vineyards on the Goldberg.

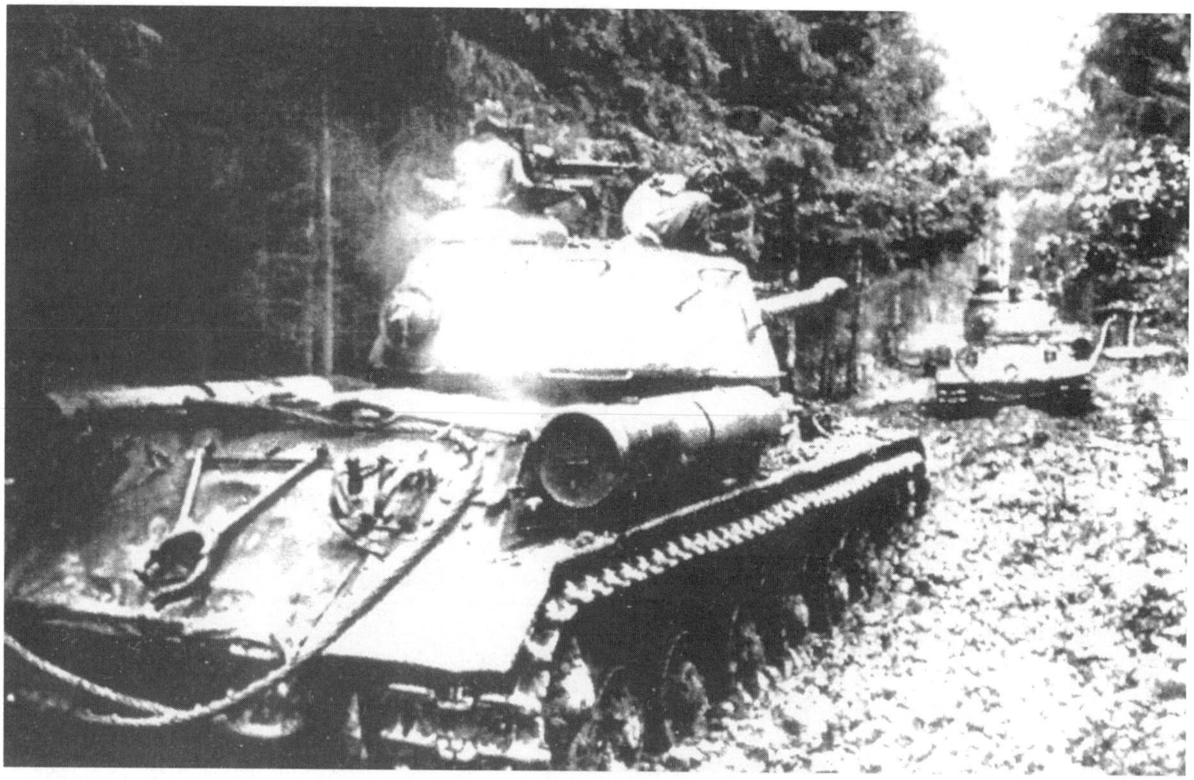

KV-85s advance along a wooded trail.

Hauptmann von Eichel-Streiber, company commander of the 2nd Company, Tiger Tank Battalion 503, in the Ukraine in 1943.

Oberstleutnant der Reserve Dr. Franz Bäke in the spring of 1944 at Tscherkassy.

Two views of Alfred Rubbel. On the left, Rubbel in his panzer uniform at Potsdam in December 1944; on the right, Rubbel in a walking-out uniform in Vienna in January 1945.

Hans Fendesack (left), the well-liked and respected tank commander and platoon leader in the 1st Company. He is sitting next to his gunner, Kurt Knispel, arguably the best tank gunner in the Wehrmacht. Neither of the men survived the war. Fendesack was killed in Normandy and Knispel was killed in action in Austria just before the war ended.

Hans Fendesack's gravesite.

Hungary, 1945: On the train to Totmegyer with damaged tanks. Transport tracks are visible on the Ssyms cars in the background. The battalion insignia is clearly visible on one of the overseas caps.

Feldwebel Seidel, the commander of Tiger 313.

Survivors of Tiger Tank Battalion 503 in 1955.

PART SIX

THE END, 1945

CHAPTER 36

The Final Hours of the Battalion

Dr. Nordewin von Diest-Koerber and Others

It was the end of April in the area west of Nikolsburg. We continued to fight, although the war was lost. The Russians could not be stopped on their drive to Berlin. The section of Czechoslovakia east of Prague had been occupied by the Red Army, as were the southeastern Balkans as far as the Prague—Adria line. In the West, the enemy had reached the Elbe. There were only isolated pockets of resistance still fighting in Germany. While the Russians stormed westward, the English and Americans advanced with extreme caution. The two army groups in Czechoslovakia, Army Group Center (Schörner) and Army Group South (Wöhler), were exhausted, to be sure, but they were still intact bodies of troops in the hands of their commands.

The battalion had about twelve to fifteen Tigers operational. Some of them were organized in small battle groups around which all types of units rallied. They felt secure near our Tigers and also fought along with us. Orders from above read: Withdraw slowly or conduct a delaying action to the German border in order to save troops and German civilians from the Russians.

In general, the local commander decided what was necessary based on his personal impression, on radio news reports that were often confusing and on the developing situation. The knowledge that there had been consultations between the Russians and Americans to the effect that all members of the 6th and 8th Armies would be turned over to the Russians after they were captured by the U.S. Army mobilized willpower to fight to the last. So much for the big picture.

The situation of the battalion as of 25 April 1945 was about as follows:

The battalion staff moved from Zwingenberg to Socherl. Our combat units, Tigers and Flak vehicles, were employed across the entire width of Panzer Corps "Feldherrnhalle." We could do no more than react. In front of us were the Russians, behind us the Americans who had crossed the Bohemian Woods to the east. Between them were the Czechoslovakian partisans and the Vlassov Army, which was becoming increasingly hostile to us in hopes of saving itself by renouncing us. The ethnic Germans were friendly.

It was unusually quiet at Socherl, where the battalion staff remained until 7 May. In spite of ongoing skirmishes in which they repulsed local Soviet attacks, our three battle groups also finally got a bit of a breather. Unfortunately, my friend, Kurt Knispel of the 503's 1st Company was killed during that period. He had been my gunner at Leningrad in 1941 and was probably the most successful tanker in the Wehrmacht, with 162 kills. Feldwebel Skoda of the 3rd Company was also killed.

It remained as quiet as ever in Socherl. The commander hosted a dinner to which the corps adjutant was invited. We celebrated Leutnant Hans von Hagemeister's birthday. Dr. Bury took care of athlete's foot infections and boils. We buried Feldwebel Skoda almost as if it had been peacetime at the village cemetery with the pastor, a coffin and participation by the local populace.

On 7 May the Russian offensive was launched. Its preparation had allowed us a rare period of quiet. A hitherto unknown level of Russian ground attack plane activity prevented movement behind the front. Conducting a fighting withdrawal prevented breakthroughs and outflanking maneuvers. As far as possible, we relieved the units while leaving rear guards in contact with the enemy. We moved the units to the west toward Budweis; the German border was our objective. Discipline began to break down. Columns of troops, mixed with refugees, flowed toward the rear. Traffic regulation was meaningless.

We discovered that unconditional surrender had been agreed on between the Wehrmacht command and the Allied military. According to that, all combat operations and movements were to cease and destruction of weapons, equipment and records was forbidden and threatened with punishment. There was no way that we were going to remain where we were and wait for the Russians.

It appeared logical to us that the U.S. Army would advance to the former German border, which lay somewhere in the Bohemian and Bavarian Woods. Unfortunately, our maps did not show just where. We could not or would not believe that the Americans would hand us over to the Russians; as a result—"Westward, ho!" In the meantime, 9 May had dawned. We had covered 150 kilometers toward the rear since leaving Socherl two days ago—in spite of the catastrophic state of the traffic. We got stuck again just outside of Budweis. There was no going forward. The Czechoslovakian partisans had armed themselves and attempted to put an end to the westward movement. We still had two King Tigers with us. Although the Czechs also had German 88mm flak guns in their possession, they avoided a really serious confrontation. Our journey resumed. Hans Welsch, of the 1st Company, described it in his diary:

9 May: In Budweis. The Czechs are not allowing the German soldiers to pass. We move forward. Our commander, Leutnant Rubbel, dismounts and approaches the Czechs. We move along behind him. The Czechs throw away their weapons and take off. The last round is fired

from the main gun. Then the tank is driven into the marsh. Discharge from the battalion.

The first Americans appeared at Budweis. There were still about 70 kilometers to the Bohemian Woods and, thus, to the border. At some point the rumor surfaced we were to assemble at Wallern, in the middle of the Bohemian Woods. That seemed quite reasonable since it corresponded to our hope that there, under the protection of the U.S. Army, we would be safe from the Russians. Indeed, it was obvious! Unfortunately, events took another course. Our battalion commander, Dr. von Diest-Koerber, described it in his personal diary:

9–10 May 1945: We kept up the retreat without pause on the road toward Budweis. The battalion staff and one of our battle groups moved near the end of the giant snake-like columns of vehicles rolling to the west. Everything frequently got into traffic jams. It was a miracle that the Russians did not appear right behind us. Disorganized groups of German vehicles pushed out of side roads onto the retreat route. Radio contact broke down with our battle groups operating to the south.

During the march we linked up with another of our retreating battle groups. One Tiger that had severe mechanical problems was driven off into a field and blown up so as not to endanger the march column. We kept one of our heavy prime movers with our group for any emergencies. Groups of fleeing civilians, sometimes with luggage and handcarts, moved everywhere on the road in between the vehicles. Among them were several hundred roughly fourteen-year-old youngsters, who had been "sent home" from a Nazi political school with heavy packs and in uniform. We overloaded our vehicles to the limit of their capacity with the unfortunate pedestrians. The prime mover was fully packed with women and children (including luggage) who had been evacuated from western Germany. Unfortunately, there were many vehicles in the column ahead of us that had not taken on any of those fleeing on foot.

We passed through a small town with a railroad station. The crossing guards were lowered!! A train full of men returning to the front from leave (!) had come from Germany. The men got off the train at the railroad station beside our road, just as in peacetime. Those who were lucky were able to jump onto one of our moving vehicles and move back again to the west.

As evening approached, we neared Budweis. A few kilometers outside the eastern outskirts of the city everything came to a halt. I learned from motorcycle messengers that the Czechs in Budweis had taken several 8.8 cm antitank guns from the German troops in the city and were blocking our road with them, allowing no one to pass. I ordered two of our Tigers that were following behind forward cross-country. They reached the outskirts of the city, bypassing by the column. After the exchange of a few rounds, they headed directly for the Czechs with the antitank guns. The Czechs at the guns immediately abandoned them. The passage was then open through the city for the rest of the corps columns. Since our few remaining Tigers were distributed among the columns in small groups, the route remained open.

We were moving further west at a walking pace—with the last two Tigers between us—when two vehicles from Panzer Corps "Feldherrnhalle" caught up with us. They were driving at high speed, mostly across the open ground. I recognized the corps special-duty officer who called out to me that he and General Kleeman were on their way to the quarters of the commander of the American Army that was facing us in order to negotiate the surrender of the entire corps.

We slowly pressed our way forward with mixed feelings. At the same time, American armored vehicles (with the first black soldiers) approached us. At about 1100 hours a German side-car motorcycle dashed back towards us: The same corps special-duty officer. I was able to stop him. General Kleeman had been immediately arrested by the Americans. All negotiations had been denied. No surrender to the Americans since we were in the Russian sphere of interest. All troops were to remain where they were. Weapons were to be turned over and collected. Wait for surrender to the Russians. Attempts to force a breakthrough through the three American blocking positions that had been set up in the meantime would be prevented by force of arms. Whoever fell into American hands would be turned over to the Russians.

With that, our fate was clear. I was able to reach most of the units of the battalion that were in the march column with the aid of the company motorcycle messengers who were with me. I

ordered all the companies: Immediately turn off to the right; exfiltrate the column in vehicles, if possible; and, assemble in the clearing in the woods just off to the right. In about an hour a major part of the battalion assembled—probably about 400 to 450 men (three line companies, the supply company, several company maintenance sections and the battalion staff). There were also about ten to twelve officers there.

I briefly said a few words of farewell, awarded all the Iron Crosses that had been put in for (the officers and Feldwebel provided them), made all requested promotions and recognitions. Brief remarks on my intent: Deactivation of the battalion into small groups of five to twelve men. After disabling all vehicles (both of the last two Tigers were blown up nearby), the men were to make their way the best they could through the Bohemian Woods in a southwest direction to Bavaria. Don't stay in built-up areas! Also avoid being taken by Americans because of the danger of being handed over to the Russians! In Bavaria, maintain that you were already in that area on 8 May!

Those were the last orders to the battalion. They ended with thanks for the years of unwavering comradeship.

Each man then received a rucksack. Several days earlier, the men in the trucks of the supply company had found them in an abandoned Luftwaffe camp. In addition, each man received a fresh loaf of army bread and a big can of butter as emergency rations. The company orderly rooms gave out the *Wehrpässe* [military identification booklets] (with discharge dates of 9 May 1945 and promotions, etc. properly entered). I took personal leave of all the officers, and they, in turn, shook the hands of the members of their companies. The vehicles were destroyed in the surrounding woods, except for those used to move a few kilometers through the woods and paths to the southwest and then abandoned. The clearing emptied by about 1700 hours.

I went with a ten-man group (the adjutant, Oberleutnant Heerlein, a tank crew, several motorcycle messengers and noncommissioned officers of the battalion staff) on the march which led through the great forest that started there. Our equipment: A map of the Bohemian Woods (unfortunately, a large scale!), our rucksacks, one pistol, and a compass—the most important assistance, since we did not want to use roads and lanes). We marched through the entire cold but clear night.

11–12 May 1945: The thickly wooded hills got steeper. Our progress became ever more arduous since we avoided even the paths in the woods. At some point during the night we ran into a road crossing our path. Americans were on it. They fired like crazy into the underbrush but did not dare go into it themselves. Armored vehicles moved back and forth on the road with headlights on. Probably one of the American blocking lines we had been told about! We dashed over the road individually at favorable moments. The march over the increasingly higher hills went a bit better by daylight. Where the woods were thinner, one could spot numerous other groups of German soldiers hastening to the southwest.

In the vicinity of Dreisessel Hill we encountered another group of the battalion staff, but soon separated again. Scattered groups brought horses with them. Without stopping to rest, we kept up the march and, by nightfall, crossed an American main supply route which was full of U.S. vehicles. In between them were entire German medical columns and vehicles with German prisoners. At a favorable spot I opened the door of a German medical vehicle that had stopped. If possible, I wanted information on the road and the upcoming built-up areas. I stared directly into the face of a black noncommissioned officer who was escorting the vehicle. I slammed the door in his face, and we quickly disappeared into the darkness.

Following the compass, our path led over a thickly wooded ridge. Then open land descended in front of us into a mist-filled valley. In the fog, we tumbled over several man-made terraces on the slope. Then, after pushing 200 meters through marshy ground, we came to an embankment with a paved road across it. It was the Moldau levee, which another American blocking line followed. American vehicles patrolled at close intervals, but the fog blocked their view.

We crossed the embankment and were in the process of binding together several pieces of wood that were lying about to make a raft when a few Landser emerged from the fog. About 200 meters away they had discovered a boat, but it still had to be dragged over the levee, which required at least thirty men. We ran over and actually succeeded,

with all of our united strength, including that of two *Wehrmachthelferinnen* [women in military service]. With burning lungs, we managed to heave the heavy boat over the embankment, using the brief opening right after an American vehicle went by. We then shoved it into the water. The crossing went quickly. Two men then took the boat back over the river for others to use.

We dashed over another raised stretch of road, then a double-tracked rail line with several railroad buildings with American sentries. We then immediately proceeded steeply upwards into the hills of the Bohemian Woods. The fog helped a lot of people.

After a short rest in the rising hills, we dragged ourselves onward, now thoroughly worn out. (It should be mentioned that it was only on this day that we finally passed Dreisessel Hill!) We had to offer a lot of encouragement to some of our party to prevent them from giving up the painful effort. During the following night we pushed on to a ridgeline with a hiking trail that crossed our route. A great boulder with a "C" on one side and a "D" on the other showed that we had reached the German-Czechoslovakian border! With renewed energy, we then started descending to Bavaria—although there were still several ridgelines to cross. As the sun rose we stopped in a clearing—now on German soil—and lay down, exhausted, and slept for several hours.

13 May 1945: At about 1100 hours, in more open hilly terrain, we encountered the first houses. We carefully sneaked up to a mill: German occupants! We were near the border crossing at Haidmühle. Hot coffee and rolls put us back in good spirits. The miller's family warned us of the Americans that were there, too, and of their hourly patrols. Above all, they told us about the large prisoner-of-war camp at nearby Freyung. They described the best way to get to Deggendorf on the Danube, which we were fortunately able to reach on foot on the following day after crossing all sorts of obstacles, barriers and American controls. That was where our little band that had become so tightly knit over the preceding days separated into little groups and headed for their various destinations in Germany or to relatives.

Note: About 120 members of the battalion succeeded in making it to their homes or to family members in such fashion. Several were captured by the Americans or the English but were not turned over to the Russians. A few members of the battalion were taken by the Czechs (or also by Russians) and went into Russian captivity. The greater part of the battalion (more 400 men and, perhaps, 12 officers) were caught by the Americans and collected in the prisoner-of-war camp at Zwiesel. They had not made it to Bavaria. Most of them had sought out houses and built-up areas. Because of exhaustion, they wanted to rest or obtain food. As a result, they fell into the hands of the Americans. Many of them had not believed they would be handed over to the Russians.

The 400 men were examined in the camp at Zwiesel. After fourteen days, they were loaded onto trucks that departed from the camp heading toward the west. They then drove on a side road through the Bavarian Woods to Pilsen and turned over all of the prisoners to the Russians. The first news of that extradition was brought to Germany by a Fahnenjunker-Unteroffizier who leaped from a truck during the trip through the Bavarian Woods and made his way through to West Germany. Those remaining on the trucks had to endure many years of bitter captivity as Russian prisoners of war, and it cost many of them their lives.

REPORT OF ALFRED RUBBEL

The clearing in the forest near the village of Dobrusch emptied in the afternoon of 10 May. After the commander's final muster and our discharge, each of us was responsible for his own decisions. In consideration of the advice to make it past the American interdiction lines in front of us in the smallest possible groups, it was advisable then to march on foot. This, despite the admonition to the tanker that his abilities decrease corresponding to the amount of time traveled on foot. Unfortunately, not enough comrades followed that advice. They moved farther to the west and were seized by the Americans in the broken hilly terrain and had to pay for their carelessness with Russian captivity.

With a small group of soldiers, I made my way on foot. With marching rations, binoculars, map, compass and pistol as my only baggage I was light and mobile. As evening approached, but while it was still light, I saw the first blocking position, the Prachatitz—Christianberg road, running in a north-south direction. We waited for darkness in the Oberhaid cemetery and attempted to determine the number and locations of the sentry posts. The *Amis* [Americans] made it easy for us. They made their rounds in their jeeps with the lights on. At their guard posts, they engaged in loud conversations. In the best infantry fashion, we advanced in a line of skirmishers. We sneaked as far as the road embankment that, unfortunately, ran along a terrace. We made it over that obstacle, about one meter high, in a single, concerted leap. It wasn't entirely noiseless and, in the process, we almost ran over a U.S. sentry. In his fright he could only give a grunt and, after a little time had passed, he found the trigger of his submachine gun and futilely emptied his magazine in the direction we had gone. The first step toward freedom had been blessed by fortune. Unfortunately, I was unlucky enough to get caught up in a tree branch in the darkness at the edge of the road that my marching rations and my binoculars got lost in the fall as I broke free. Also, our group did not get together again. "Bubi" Böhler, of the 3rd Company, who had been given that nickname because of his youthful appearance, was with me.

The night, which we spent under a sheltering spruce, was bitterly cold. We had no warm clothing other than our mouse-gray light tanker coveralls. In the quiet days at Socherl I had read a bit in Stifter's "Hochwald" ["Tall Forest"]. Now I had the opportunity to get to know his portrayal of the Bohemian Woods first hand. We traversed the mountain massif of Kubany at an elevation of 1,100 meters, wading at times through slush. We were safe there in the woods. The Americans did not like to leave their jeeps and the road. Our stomachs started to rumble. Now and again we came upon farmsteads in the wilderness where we were modestly taken care of. One day we descended into civilized country and landed in the neighborhood of Zwiesel in Buchenau.

After a foot march of a good 100 kilometers, almost entirely on woodland paths, we had to take a break. The group had, in the meantime, grown through the addition of various soldiers who had joined up with me as the possessor of a map and compass. The little village was packed with refugees so we were able to mix inconspicuously among them. At Graf X's castle we were able to exchange our military outfits for civilian dress. When the Americans drove through the village with their patrols, we retired into the forest, warned by our alarm system.

It had gotten to be the middle of May and it was time to move on. In order to travel legally, one had to have an Allied certificate of discharge as a demobilized soldier in order to avoid the danger of ending up as some sort of prisoner of war. My destination was Hanover.

Because the group had become so large and also too careless, we set out to the west toward Regensburg. Böhler wanted to go to his parents at Schwetzingen. Somewhere we met up with a group of older children who had been sent to the country [to avoid the bombing in the cities]. They were with their guardian. Because "Bubi" Böhler in his short pants fitted completely into the picture of the group, I advised him to join it, the more so since it was going to follow the same route for a while. He did it, though with a heavy heart, and was home, safe and sound, at the end of June.

My next destination was Staffelstein. That was where the family of Hans von Hagemeister had gone. I hoped to meet up with him there. I made my way there alone.

One problem was food. The region between the Bavarian forest, the Danube and Regen in which my westerly route led me at that time was, like so many others, overrun with former members of the Wehrmacht, refugees and "displaced persons" (people who had been brought from the east and released prisoners of war). The "displaced persons" were well cared for by the U.S. Army or the UNRA, a United Nations organization. The other two groups, the German soldiers and the civilians, depended on the charity of the local people. I must say that I experienced a great readiness to offer assistance during those weeks. Granted, the local administration also issued food ration coupons to us "traveling folk," good for one day only, and one could also purchase food. But, without "documents" there were no ration coupons and one also had to have money. (I no longer remember whether I had any money.) My own source of supply was, thus, a friendly invitation to share a meal.

And so, on the second day of Pentecost, after a luxurious meal at a hospitable farmhouse near Nittenau we experienced a near disaster. More than satisfied in every way—it had been roast pork with noodles and, for desert, preserved plums—I made my way along a winding road through the woods, paying far less attention than was my wont. As if conjured from the earth, a U.S. Jeep with *Amis* was parked five meters in front of me.

They waved me forward and indicated "come on" to make me understand that I was to approach them. My leap over the roadside ditch and disappearance into the underbrush went so fast and, for the *Amis*, came as such a surprise, that they had no chance to grab their weapons.

I was safe. That day, which had begun so well, could have ended quite badly. As we discovered later, there were many US units that sought to make up for their lack of an opportunity to be in combat by doing "their part in the war." Their desire to capture German soldiers was intense; it bordered on competition.

Somewhere the forest came to an end. A sloping meadow, filled with glacial boulders scattered erratically, separated me from the next patch of woods. To the right rear in the valley, at a distance of 200 to 300 meters, was a road. About 100 meters before I got to the edge of the woods, I heard engine noise and a whistle. It was my American friends from the previous encounter. They were back again and waving with increased intensity. They had, in the meantime, picked up two Landser. What caused me concern, however, was the heavy .50-caliber machine gun pointed at me. As I dashed toward the woods I heard gunshots and impacts next to me. The bandits fired explosive ammunition and a splinter tore through my left ear. When I was safely under cover, I bandaged my ear with my sole possession, with my "multi-purpose cloth" (handkerchief, shawl, mosquito-screen, sun shade—now bandage). I came to the conclusion that this could not go on. After more-or-less surviving six years of war I was not about to become a target for any trigger-happy Amis. A new strategy was in order!

In Weiden, Amberg, and Grafenwöhr, the U.S. Army had set up so-called "discharge camps." After the transfer of those solders of the 6th and 8th Armies who had been seized near the border came to an end, soldiers who were then caught were registered there. If there was nothing serious, such as membership in the SS, high party office or high military rank, you received a discharge certificate within a few days. At first I was uncertain how membership in "Feldherrnhalle" would be judged. After questioning men who had been discharged, I decided to surrender voluntarily at the camp at Weiden. My judgment proved correct. After four days, I had my "papers." For me, the war was finally at an end.

CHAPTER 37

Recollections of a Panzer Soldier (Part V)

Dr. Franz-Wilhelm Lochmann

THE FINAL ACT

We were loaded onto the rail cars with seven King Tigers. Led by Leutnant Rambow, we were, as it appeared, sent to Austria without a destination. At the Retz railroad station we heard that even Schörner had also capitulated. We were pleased that the commander had sent a VW-Schwimmwagen to us. We were supposed to get to Wallern by taking the back roads. The battalion was to be dissolved there.

There were many supply trains at Retz. We were able to outfit ourselves with an abundance of rations and cigarettes and also with items of equipment such as rucksacks, footgear, underwear and other practical things. We also found a railroad car with brownish-beige Luftwaffe coveralls that we put on over our black uniforms. We then set out and moved as far as our fuel took us. One King Tiger after another was blown up. The next-to-the-last was our Tiger 100. At the location where we would blow up the tank we found a truck with a defective cooling system. While the tank was prepared for demolition, we worked feverishly to make the truck road-worthy. The other crews moved on with the last tank.

Shortly before the truck was operable, Russian infantry emerged behind us. Leutnant Rambow advanced at them in the Schwimmwagen and held them off for a time. Then it was done. The truck started, we blew up Tiger 100 and drove off after our comrades. We caught up with them and

pumped the gas from the last King Tiger into the truck's fuel tank and were also able to fill a few spare cans. Then the last of the Tigers was blown up.

TOWARD BUDWEIS

We made only slow progress. We had a serious leak in the cooling system and had to stop every five kilometers to fill it. In the villages, Czechs approached us with flowers. They thought that we were Americans. We got to a place that was totally packed. All the Landser, no matter what compass direction they came from, reported they had encountered Russians. One group of Luftwaffe officers in a command car advised us that the Americans were in Budweis. We decided to get through to there. We "procured" yet another truck and decided to push on through to Budweis along with the Luftwaffe officers. Our group now included a few infantrymen, two motorcycle-messengers and several bicycle riders.

Before long we were under fire in a patch of woods. We had divided ourselves into groups and were determined to clear the hindrance from our path. It consisted of Czech partisans and we were able to speedily send them packing. We then moved on, continuing throughout the entire night. We only used back roads. The Russians were on all of the major arteries. Slowly we came to realize that we would have to expect something other than the Americans in Budweis. Battle Group "We Want to

Go Home to Germany" broke up. Those of us who were from Tiger Tank Battalion 503 wanted to stick together until we thought we were safe. Therefore, we drove west in our truck. We were very cautious and repeatedly avoided all the major arteries and villages. On the next day we encountered a French officer in a jeep. He escorted us to the Americans in Krumau (Moravia).

There we were put into a simply fenced prison camp. Despite our warnings, a crew from the 2nd Company separated from us and wound up in the local hospital. We soon realized that the Amis were getting ready to move out. They were only waiting for the arrival of the Russians. They were going to hand us over to them. With that, we made up our minds: "We have to get out of here". We risked the breakout shortly before midnight. Everything went like clockwork. There were only a few shots. We marched off through the night with thirty men from the battalion. We were exceedingly confident that we could do it. Along with our crew and that of Leutnant Rambow, I remember three other crews from the 3rd Company, among them those of Feldwebel Weigel, Feldwebel Seidel and Unteroffizier Spiekermann.

For the first part of the night I took the point with the crew of Tiger 100. I was only able to orient myself by means of the stars. The 1:300,000 map I had only offered rough orientation, especially since we were only able to proceed along dark woodland paths. For the second half of the night, Unteroffizier Spiekermann took over the point and I was the last man. We only moved ahead slowly. Again and again the point had to stop in order to decide on the most favorable route. During those short halts we sometimes sat down. I was dead tired. For three days and three nights I had had practically no sleep at all. And so what had to happen happened. I fell asleep during a short halt. The column did not notice I was missing for a long time.

As morning drew near I awakened and quickly grasped my situation. I got to a village that was occupied by Americans. There was a cemetery outside the village. I was still dead tired, so I crept into the bushes in the cemetery and slept there for most of the day. I had figured correctly. No *Ami* looked there. As evening approached, I strengthened myself with a frugal meal and studied my map. First I wanted to cross the "cold" and "warm" Moldau Rivers and then traverse the

Bohemian Woods in order to reach German territory on the other side in the Bavarian Woods, somewhere between Zwiesel and Grafenau. From there I thought I would head toward Nuremberg.

The weather in the spring of 1945 was splendid. I allowed myself time and was able to get past the really critical places quite well. I marched mainly at night and spent the day sleeping in thickets in the woods. The most time was needed for the crossing of the Moldau River, since American sentry posts were closely spaced on the west side and they ran regular patrols with jeeps. However, I also successfully got past that difficult sector during the night. In the Bavarian Woods I marched by day, avoiding contact with built-up areas. Now and again I was able to get advice from civilians who informed me about isolated hiking trails or Americans.

Actually, the Americans only patrolled the roads. The Amis were extremely cautious and still suspected that there were Werewolf resistance groups in the woods. Indeed, I had become a kind of wolf. Wolves are very cautious beasts. They are only dangerous in packs, and such packs are hunted without restraint. Therefore I never joined up with groups of Landser I met in the woods. They were too careless as they moved through the terrain and most of them had far more contact than I did with villages in order to get food. I was autonomous on that march since I was well supplied for all my needs.

One evening I got to a fairly large barn at the edge of the woods, behind which was a small field path. I decided to take advantage of that "hotel" for the night and made myself comfortable in the back part, but not before loosening a few sidings so I could slip out into the woods at any time. In the morning, an American patrol moved along the field path. The Amis stopped, and two of the soldiers entered the barn. Fortunately, they gave it no more than a superficial inspection. If I had been forced to bolt through the back wall I would have lost my entire set of goods.

At that time it occurred to me that my route along the border was not the best. I turned toward the Danube and kept my course to the north of the river, through the hills, maintaining some distance from the road leading to Regensburg.

Wörth was the first fairly large built-up area that I headed directly for. It was swarming with *Amis*. I heard from the civilians that there was a large prison camp in Regensburg where discharges were already being given. Further, Landser who were caught in Regensburg were no longer being turned over to the Russians. I took private lodgings there. It was a real experience to enjoy a bathtub once again.

I then resolved to bypass Regensburg to the east in order to then set off in the direction of Nuremberg-Würzberg to the north. When I crossed the same ridge line three times only to wind up again in the Danube valley, I decided to head to Regensburg, especially since I had encountered Landser who had been outfitted with discharge papers from the Americans there. In Regensburg I happened into an identity card control point run by the American military police. The guys were completely taken aback when I produced my military pay book. They took me to a military base where the Landser sat in the open, arranged behind barbed wire according to which military district the came from. Two days later I was given a questionnaire, had my hair cut, and was deprived of my decorations. On the next day we formed up to get our discharge certificates.

"AUTOMATIC ARREST"

My joy at being among the first twenty to be called up did not last long. We were driven into a special camp with clubs without first knowing what that meant. Slowly I figured out what the situation was. We had been separated as politically suspect. Why I was included was unclear to me. On the third day that camp was packed. 200 Landser were then dumped on us. For the most part, they had just been operated on.

As I learned from them, a German hospital had just been cleared out to make it available for the Amis and those soldiers, like us, had been given the notorious questionnaire. In the subsequent investigation of those Landser, two men who belonged to the Waffen-SS were discovered among them. Therefore all had been marked for further investigation as politically suspect.

A day later we were moved by truck to a barracked camp at the Grafenwöhr training area. I immediately busied myself as an interpreter and heard that after two days, the so-called disabled battalion, which was what the 200 Landser that had been pulled out of the hospital were called, would undergo a new screening. At the same time I heard that the previous questionnaires had not come along with those comrades so that they would all have to fill out those papers again.

When that battalion was called up, I attached myself to the bunch. This time I was more cautious in filling out the questionnaire. A similarity of names and my residence in Hamburg must have led to the so-called "automatic arrest." Therefore, this time, I gave Gîttingen as my residence. An ugly scar on my back that was still quite fresh served to lend credibility to my claimed stay in the hospital with a round that had lodged in my lung.

This time I easily passed the screening. I was discharged and transported to Erfurt by truck. Since the Russians were expected there any day I moved on to Eisenach as quickly as possible. From there I very quickly made it to the Werra River. In Eschwege the first thing I did was seek out Richard Schwarzmann's family. He had not yet got home. The rest of our group must have run into misfortune. I learned the truth later.

During the night that I fell asleep my comrades also slept later. Obviously, they posted sentries. Unfortunately, they failed to take armed Czechs they discovered seriously. An American battalion then surrounded the patch of woods. My comrades were taken prisoner and immediately turned over to the Russians. Only a few were able to save themselves. The others had to survive long years of Russian captivity. Richard Schwarzmann didn't come home until late, as did my loader, Wolfgang Speckin. My gunner, the good Hannes Berger, had an accident during captivity and, after surviving the entire war, died there.

I was in Hamburg with my family on 1 July 1945. I quickly found the first comrades of Tiger Tank Battalion 503. Leutnant Hans-Jürgen Haß and Feldwebel Gruteser from the staff, as well as Obergefreiter Karl-Ernst Koch from our company. In the search for missing and dead I made extremely quick contact, not only with the comrades of my own company, but also with those of the other companies.

The bonding and comradeship from those difficult years has remained strong right up to this day. In addition to many battalion get-togethers I see the former members of the 1st Company once a year. Most bring their wives along. We do not meet because we are living in the past or boundless militarists. We do so because we were welded into the bonds of comradeship in a time of trouble. We were fortunate to survive because each of us was there for the other. We did not want the war. History damned us to participate in it.

Let no one tell me that war is the father of all things. War is a terrible misfortune. Neither is war the continuation of politics with other means, as was so beautifully formulated. Politics and war are nothing other than the instruments of power, and we were misused by that power.

CHAPTER 38

Woe to the Vanquished!

Alfred Rubbel

Those words, which the Romans wrote nearly two thousand years ago, proved to have lost none of their historical reality as the power of the Reich collapsed with the surrender in May 1945 and the territory of the Reich was occupied totally by the victors in the war. In the East, in general, the German civilian population suffered under the abuses and atrocities perpetrated by both soldiers and also civilians. That is known and documented. Less well known and suppressed by interested parties is the fact that in the West, vast numbers of German soldiers had to suffer greatly under treatment that was in contravention to international law.

The U.S. Army in its zone of administration had planned and accepted as a part of its system—even if not as an intentional objective—conditions such that thousands of captured German soldiers died in the camps of hunger, exhaustion and disease.

There is a moral asymmetry that characterizes the issue. On the one hand, the Germans had committed war crimes to such an extent that all were collectively guilty. For a long time there was no contravening argument allowed; specifically, the fact that the other side also committed or allowed misdeeds that could be consider war crimes. The archives remain closed; discussion was unwelcome. One hoped that those who experienced such things would pass on and, with their departure, would be lost any interest in clarifying

the situation or setting things right. There is an obligation to combat that. It is due to every comrade who suffered or perished. Members of our battalion were also affected. Therefore, it is permissible to write about that in our book. It is not our intention to trivialize German war crimes, but neither is it our intention to trivialize those of the victors. Above all else, in that respect, it is important to bring forward information that has been withheld so long, particularly by former enemies who are, today, our allies. It is important to demand the truth.

When there were no more prisoners-of-war in German custody and, therefore, no reprisals could be feared, a shameful practice developed in regard to the adherence to or neglect of international law. The USSR, as everyone knew, was not sensitive in how it treated those in its custody. However, it was astounding to find that the French military, in part, rivaled the USSR in that regard. Both cases could possibly be explained by negative personal or national experiences. However, that the US Army should also be guilty of breaches of law and crimes in what was recognizable back then and provable today is not excused by anything. Captivity with the English, on the other hand, was like a stay at a health spa.

We, our battalion, had to deal with the Americans as well as the Russians. Here are a few experiences our comrades had with Americans:

- They broke their word. In spite of their promise not to hand personnel over to the Russians, they did just that.
- In many camps in the area of lower Bavaria the camp commanders competed in their unworthy treatment of German soldiers (head shaving), beating and feeding and quarters at a level that injured health that were a form of collective "revenge." The Auerbach (Grafenwöhr) camp held the "lead" in that respect.
- The use of guns against recognizably unarmed men who attempted to avoid captivity after the end of the war was not permissible according to the Hague Conventions on Land Warfare and therefore was reprehensible. (An almost parallel unlawful behavior can be seen in the use of guns by the former German Democratic Republic border police.)

One can search in vain for a comparable example from international law with regard to the secret directives of the U.S. regime immediately after the surrender. It attempted to remove the status of German soldiers as prisoners of war—entitled to protection under international law—and to replace it with that of so-called "disarmed enemy forces." That arbitrary action stripped them of the protection and control of the International Red Cross.

The unbelievable conditions in the U.S. prison camps in western Germany—camps that resembled concentration camps—and that were already becoming known in 1945 must be attributed directly to the "disarmed enemy forces" directive. The full extent of that crime of the U.S. Army—any other designation would be an additional scandal—first became really public with the appearance in 1989 of the book *Other Losses: The Shocking Truth behind the Mass Deaths of Disarmed German Soldiers* by Canadian author James Bacque. The author held the military commander-in-chief at the time, General Eisenhower, directly responsible.

The "collection" of soldiers and also other Wehrmacht members (of both sexes) amounted to a total of 3,700,000 "disarmed enemy forces" in U.S. custody. Billeting and care for them could no longer be guaranteed. Sensible troop commanders, such as General Patton, the commanding general of the U.S. Third Army, had ordered the quickest possible release of the Germans because of that situation. Eisenhower or his staff at SHAEF revoked that directive on 15 May 1946. Almost a million German soldiers died of hunger and illness in 1945–46 in the camps, according to Bacque.

The American camps at Dietersheim, Bretzenheim, Hechtsheim, and Bingen held leading positions in that respect. As a result, the U.S. moved into the same "bad" neighborhood as its ally, the USSR. The German Red Cross estimated that 1.6 million of the 3.2 million German prisoners of war died in Russian captivity. The difference between the two processes is in their origin:

- The Soviet Union, afflicted with well-known, ongoing difficulties with food supply—also affecting its own citizenry—could hardly do more for the prisoners, unless it had renounced taking prisoners.
- The U.S. or its expeditionary forces in Germany with its vast logistical capabilities, could have supplied the prisoners. If it was unable to do that, it should have taken appropriate measures to prevent this genocide..

We can hope and wish that James Bacque has given the impetus with his book to bring that dark chapter to the light of day to determine the truth: Is the U.S. Army guilty or not guilty?

CHAPTER 39

My Period as a Prisoner of War from May 1945 to October 1955

Ulrich Koppe

THE END OF THE WAR AND INITIAL CAPTIVITY (8–15 MAY 1945)

In the early days of the month of May 1945, I was employed with the combat elements as the acting commander of the 3rd Company in the area of southern Moravia (southwest of Brünn, north of Znaim). We supported an infantry division and had the mission of holding back the Soviet troops with about four to six tanks for as long as possible to cover the withdrawal of our own formations. We knew that American troops had already reached the area of Linz and the Bohemian Woods and were behind us. How far the Americans would continue their advance was unknown to us.

In addition to the tanks, the combat elements also included wheeled vehicles for supply and liaison. Fuel, ammunition and rations were still available. We maintained communications with the battalion staff by radio and with wheeled vehicles.

We still were in contact with the enemy up to 7 May. On 8 May it was noticeably quieter. Something was "in the air" that would soon bring the war to an end, at the latest when the Soviets and American troops linked up with each other in our area. During the course of the evening the news trickled in that the Wehrmacht had surrendered. A Soviet air-dropped leaflet confirmed the news. The leaflet demanded that we remain in our positions, stop all combat activity on 9 May at 0001 hours and wait for the arrival of Soviet troops. We

were to turn our vehicles and weapons over to them and become prisoners.

We did not follow the demands. A motorcycle messenger brought me the order to march west with the battle group to reach the American lines. In carrying out that order the combat elements moved west from the Budweis area in Moravia. Someone had told us that the American troops were at the Moldau River. Therefore, that was our goal.

On 9 May the march continued in beautiful, warm spring weather over intact Czechoslovakian roads. The tanks moved in the column. We were not impeded by the Czechs. We were allowed to move freely through the villages. Banners stretched over the streets read in English: "We welcome the victors." That certainly wasn't intended for the Soviet troops.

We were stopped by American troops near the city of Kronau on the Moldau. At that time we had only wheeled vehicles. The tanks had not made it through the march. We had destroyed every single one of them because of mechanical problems. One time during the march, an American airplane flew low over us without firing. For me, that was the proof that the war was finally over. We were the vanquished and were heading into an unknown future.

The U.S. soldiers at the roadblock allowed all German soldiers and civilians that came from the east to pass through. Naturally, the soldiers had to surrender their weapons, but we were allowed to keep our wheeled vehicles, particularly the trucks with rations. We drove on to the west and, after several kilometers, were directed into a large meadow near Wallern where the U.S. Army collected the members of all the units that had been committed on the Eastern Front.

The trucks and automobiles were parked in the meadow. The soldiers of the individual units gathered around them. The meadow was completely surrounded by American soldiers. There was no fence. A stream ran through the meadow. All in all, it was an undisturbed landscape with a view of the mountains of the Bohemian Woods.

We met other members of the battalion on the meadow who had come there in ways similar to ours. There were members of all the companies, a total of about 350-400 men, including about 15 officers. I cannot come up with an exact number, nor do I remember the names of all the officers. However, among them were Wiegand, von Eichel-Streiber, Ohnesorge, Piepgras. Rambow, Rollik, Schenk, Gille, Krettek, and myself. We kept the rest of the battalion together, as best we could, and looked after its organization, but turned the decision as to whether to "take off" over to each man to make for himself. It was unspoken but obvious that, for us officers, we would remain in captivity as long as our soldiers were prisoners.

The American soldiers more or less left us to our own devices during those days. They did a very superficial job of registering us, though they did question us as to our desired location for discharge. I no longer know whether they recorded that in writing. In any case, the opinion spread that all who were in the camp would be brought to Bavaria. Occasionally, promises were made to the officers of the units that we would not be turned over to the Soviet Army.

We were not given rations. We were fortunate in still having our field kitchens and rations for several days with us. Sick and wounded were cared for. However, a notable uncertainty lay over each and every one of us that could not be assuaged by the beautiful May weather and the peace in the air.

That uncertainty found a temporary end in the morning of 15 May in an American wake-up call and the demand that we prepare for departure with our vehicles. The meadow was cleared.

The only anxious question was: Where were they taking us?

American military vehicles were interspersed throughout the column. Armed soldiers sat on them. The move did not go toward the west, as we actually expected and hoped, but toward the east, approximating the route along which my battle group had marched westward a few days earlier. It gradually became clear to us what the U.S. soldiers intended, and it became quiet within and around us. After a three-hour drive, the U.S. soldiers turned us over to Soviet soldiers who led the column with their own guards past Budweis through Wittingau-Neuhas to a temporary forest camp at Neu-Bistritz.

IN SOVIET CAPTIVITY (15 MAY 1945–7 OCTOBER 1955): CAMP NEU-BISTRITZ, CZECHOSLOVAKIA (15–31 MAY 1945)

A patch of woods near the city of Neu-Bistritz was sealed off by the Soviet troops. No preparations had been initiated for billeting personnel. We lived in what tents were available, in shelters that we made ourselves and on trucks that we had still been allowed to keep. We were also allowed to keep our own field kitchens. The Soviets provided food, although not in adequate quantities.

The members of the battalion remained together. We set up our own "administration," cared for the sick and wounded and concerned ourselves with maintaining spiritual and bodily health. The shock of the imprisonment and the betrayal of their word by the U.S. soldiers in turning us over to the Soviets—which depressed each of us—was somewhat offset by the familiar unit cohesion within the companies. One could still speak of a military organization that now had the objective of returning in good health to the homeland. The Soviets had their part in that and continually promised us that we would "return home soon." Nobody fully believed that, but you clung to the positive things you heard.

For the first time, we learned to know officers' rations in that camp. In the Soviet Army, officers received better rations than enlisted personnel and noncommissioned officers. That was also true for German officers. We were given more sugar and tobacco and were probably given some butter. The officers decided unanimously to give the extra rations to the ill and wounded.

The Soviets were seldom seen in the camp. They carried out a registration of the prisoners. They recorded individual particulars and discharge locations. For the time being, abuses by Soviet soldiers were kept in bounds.

After about fourteen days, the first march unit was assembled. A medical examination was given to determine the suitability of each individual for transportation. The first transport included about 1,200 to 2,000 men, including about 100 officers. Our battalion was included in its entirety in that transport.

TRANSPORT TO FOCSANI (RUMANIA)

We marched in a heavily guarded long column. After spending the night in the open—fortunately it did not rain—we reached the Slabings railroad station, where we were meant to entrain. That was where the Soviets carried out the first strict personal and luggage inspection, along with an exact registration. All that I possessed by way of luggage was the clothing on my back and a small bag with a small number of necessary personal item such as toilet items. Rings and watches were taken from us, as well as sharp objects (such as knives and scissors), to the extent that we had not previously hidden them somewhere.

We were distributed among freight cars for the movement, forty-five men and one officer as officer-in-charge on each car. Slabings lay on an auxiliary stretch of railroad from Czechoslovakia to Austria, between Budweis and Brünn. The train left there on about 31 May 1945 with approximately 1,500 prisoners. A Russian officer was the movement officer.

The soldiers of the guard, who were either in a car of their own or in the brake houses on each freight car, reported to him. Whenever the train stopped, they formed a line of sentries around the train. A German officer was selected as representative for the prisoners. He concerned himself with the welfare of the prisoners to the extent that it was in his power and so far as the Soviet soldiers allowed it.

Interpreters made their first appearance on the train. From that point on, they played the role of "mediator" between the Soviet "lords" and the German "servants." We were dependant on them. Depending on their character makeup, some of them used their knowledge of the language shamelessly to their own advantage and to the disadvantage of their comrades. The Soviet soldiers behaved with restraint. They naturally continued to talk about an imminent journey home. As a result, most of the prisoners remained calm.

The question that concerned us on that train was the destination of our trip. One thing was clear: It wasn't taking us home. We were unable to get any detailed information from the Soviet guards.

During the journey the car doors remained closed. The doors were only opened to give us food and for the daily headcounts. The rations were meager: Bread, sugar and soup twice a day, along with something to drink. No one was actually able to satisfy his hunger. That was a state we would become accustomed to for a long time. The sanitary and hygienic situation was endurable. A doctor supervised the health situation. Those who were sick were taken to a hospital car.

With troubled hearts and minds, we traveled slowly past Vienna and Budapest and on through Arad (Rumania), Kronstadt, and Ploesti. On 10 June 1945, we arrived at Focsani, an unfamiliar mid-sized city in eastern Rumania (the Moldau region).

Immediately after our arrival, the officers were separated from the enlisted personnel and noncommissioned officers. I do not know where the members of our battalion went. We officers lost contact with them. During the long years of my captivity, I never saw any of them again.

TRANSIT CAMP AT FOCSANI, RUMANIA (10 JUNE–31 JULY 1945)

We arrived at Focsani on about 10 June 1945. The officers of our battalion came through the train ride in good health. We were all more or less fit.

Although several thousand German and Hungarian officers were in the camp, the German camp leadership included only noncommissioned officers and enlisted men. It included some quite bad people whose only concern was to harass the officers. The camp leader was, ostensibly, a Luftwaffe Stabsfeldwebel, an officer hater and martinet of the worst sort. He did everything he could to make our life hell and to "serve" the Soviets. He was supported by people who claimed to be some of the earlier prisoners of war, members of the National Committee for a Free Germany and from former communists who had emigrated from Germany. What they told us appeared to us to be extremely improbable.

The personnel of the Soviet guard remained aloof in the camp. Within the camp, a "camp police" was formed from ethnic Germans who behaved like the German camp administration so as to win popularity with the Soviets.

The camp was run strictly. Every morning and evening a muster was held that could last up to five hours. We were housed in great stone buildings that had been huge garages with concrete floors. Three-tiered wooden bunks had been constructed. There were no straw sacks or bed linens, there was no illumination and we received no replacements for tattered clothing. Footgear and clothing started to wear out and one had to do with makeshift repairs. There was a delousing station in the camp that everyone had to pass through about once every ten days. The washing facilities were terrible. There was a perpetual shortage of water, which was probably not unusual in that area. New latrines had to be built all the time. The food was "standard": 600 grams of moist bread, two broths with, for example, hard legumes in them and a bit of sugar daily.

Within the camp, we had to carry out the work required for maintaining feeding and hygiene ourselves. Therefore some of us were employed in the kitchen, others in the bakery, carrying water, cleaning latrines or building latrines. Other than that, we were left to ourselves. We had to come to terms with our fate. Debates over the past and future, stories about our homes and families, of whom we had known nothing for months, were extensive. We got our first news of the results of the Potsdam conference, the formation of zones of occupation and the start of the war crime trials from posted newspapers originating in the Soviet occupation zone.

The comradeship among the officers, and especially among us former members of Tiger Tank Battalion 503 was good. We all had to become accustomed to the feeling of the loss of freedom, the "imprisonment" and continuously living together. Each one tried to remain his own man, but everyone became a member of the camp community; an "escape" from that was difficult, if not impossible.

The poor and inadequate food and the lack of proper hygiene were burdensome in the long run. The first intestinal diseases set in, a result of the

hot, humid climate as well as the bad water. The sick were looked after by German physicians in a separate clinic. However, the doctors were limited in the scope of their decisions, since Soviet doctors or medics decided whether someone was sick and whether they needed to be moved to the hospital in the city. I did not see any cases of death in the camp but, certainly, there were some who died in the hospital. A general debilitation soon made itself evident.

We actually felt quite relieved when, one day, along with other officers and Hungarian and German soldiers, we were assembled for movement. We left the camp about the beginning of August 1945 and traveled farther to the east under the already discussed conditions of transport. That time, the whole gang of officers from Tiger tank Battalion 503 were in a single car, together with other officers.

At first, the trip headed north through Jassy, then to the east across the Soviet-Rumanian border. The destination was Kischinew, the capitol city of the Moldavian Soviet Socialist Republic. A prisoner-of-war camp had been set up there.

KISCHINEW CAMP (AUGUST 1945– FEBRUARY 1946)

In retrospect it seems to me that our stay in that camp was the best. The later camps were incomparably worse. The building that we occupied had earlier been an agricultural school. It had large rooms in which wooden bunks, tables and benches were set up. There were large hallways, toilets and washrooms. The grounds were, of course, fenced in and beset with guard towers. There was a large open square in front of the building in which the morning and evening musters took place. The guardhouse for the Soviet soldiers was at the main gate.

I no longer remember the Soviet guards. The senior officer, a Hungarian colonel, was the camp commandant. He honestly worked to make life endurable for all. We officers were appointed as leaders of companies or groups of a hundred soldiers and were meant to maintain order. After a few days of rest and getting accustomed to the camp, we marched out with the companies to work. I no longer know what kind of work the soldiers had to do.

Naturally, the interpreters had a particularly important function there. They gave us the orders and desires of the Soviet guards and vice versa.

Skilled craftsmen had a better position among the prisoners thanks to their knowledge and expertise. Our guards and the local "bosses" at the construction sites liked to keep the trained workers busy in all sorts of duties, including those of a private nature.

A core of camp workers (cooks, laundry, latrine, etc.) was formed, all of whom led a more pleasant life than those who had to go out every day to work.

The officers were housed in a special room and also got the first wooden bunks. I no longer remember whether there were straw sacks. We were also assigned a soldier who, for example, brought us the daily cold food. There was probably warm food as well; there were still special officer rations. In the course of time, we all came to have our own mess gear or similar containers and also spoons. All in all, we were happy to be able to be together with comrades. At the same time, we were all fully aware that we had a highly uncertain future ahead of us.

We were continually concerned with questions about when we would return home. No one could answer them. We no longer believed the familiar rumors that were spread, especially by our guards. Whether our guards actually knew anything more exact about our fate seems, in retrospect, unlikely to me. In the long years of imprisonment, I learned that all the measures affecting us prisoners were instituted from above, indeed, from far above, from Moscow itself.

I cannot say whether the soldiers guarding us in Kischinew were members of the Soviet Army. Later, in any case, all of the prisoner-of-war camps were under the NKVD/MVD (Interior Ministry) which had its own guard units (police units). The political commissars belonged to those units. I would later get to know them. In Kischinew we were spared them, so far as I could tell.

We experienced our first Christmas without mail at that camp. At that point, we weren't even allowed to write. As had been the case all along, our only source of information was the newspapers from the Soviet zone of Germany.

One day, about the end of February or the beginning of March 1946, Ernst Ohnesorge and I, along with nine other German and Hungarian officers, including the Hungarian colonel, were summoned to the guardhouse. There we were told to get our "gear" and be ready for immediate

departure. In addition to the six Hungarian officers, we consisted of one older Major, a Hauptmann from a tank unit, an Oberleutnant who was a jurist with a good knowledge of the Russian language, Ernst Ohnesorge, and myself.

We were just able to take leave of our comrades. They had to stay back at the camp gate. From there we were taken in custody by a guard detail consisting of an officer and three soldiers who shut us up in a prisoner transport vehicle (a kind of "Black Maria"). Everything had to move quickly and we were handled pretty roughly. The door of the vehicle was closed. The vehicle left the camp with destination unknown.

Naturally, each of us asked himself: Why we were treated like that? Was there something against us? What would happen to us? We got no answers to the first two questions. The third question was answered by the Soviet Union after our long journey as a prisoner.

My report on the captivity of the members of Tiger Tank B attalion 503 ends with the farewell from the comrades at the camp gate of Kischinew. After the officers had been separated from their enlisted personnel and noncommissioned officers in the Focsani camp, then came the separation from the officers that evening in 1946 at Kischinew. Ohnesorge and I never met any of them again as prisoners of war in the USSR. Only ten years later was I to meet several of them again in the Federal Republic of Germany.

JOURNEY IN THE PRISON VEHICLE THROUGH THE USSR

The "Black Maria" took us to the Kischinew railroad station. There, along with our guards, we boarded a waiting prison railroad car. For reasons that I do not know, such railroad cars were called "Stolipyn" in the Soviet Union. They only had small barred windows and were divided into enclosed compartments, each with two triple-tiered wooden bunks. Whether that referred to the minister of the same name in the Czarist empire or another inventive jailer I do not know. That railroad car was coupled to a regularly scheduled long-distance train. No one other than the guards knew where the journey ended.

We had to climb on board, accompanied by the constant cries of "Dawai, Dawai—Hurry up! Hurry up!" The compartments were already fully occupied with Russian civilian prisoners, who stared at us like vultures. They probably had their greedy eyes on our modest luggage. We quickly learned how to deal with them so that our possessions were kept firmly in hand.

A stove in the guards' compartment heated the railroad car. In those kinds of rail cars, it would be hot one time and then bitterly cold another during the multi-day trip. Our guards tried to get us our own compartment when we had to change cars but, thanks to the crowding, they were not always able to succeed.

The train left Kischinew sometime during the night. Nowadays I have trouble following the route on maps from the atlas. We changed trains several times on the trip. Often we remained for long times in freight yards and never knew when the journey would continue. As I remember, the journey led through Odessa-Kharkov-Moscow. At Moscow we were again taken by night in a "Black Maria." We went through the city from the one railroad station to another. At the second Moscow railroad station, which was to the east of the city, I read a sign on a railroad car that said "Wladiwostok." At that moment, my morale couldn't get any lower. I saw my comrades and myself dragged off to Siberia forevermore.

From Moscow we continued to the east, probably through Kasan-Swerdlowsk and then on to Petropawlosk. From there our route led over a single-tracked stretch to the southeast until we were ordered to get out at a stop. After ten days of travel we had reached our destination: Karaganda, a city that, until then, had been unknown to any of us in an unknown land, far distant from Moscow, from Kischinew and from Germany. We were in the midst of the Kazakh Steppe in the southeast Asian portion of the Soviet Union. What fate awaited us there?

KARAGANDA (1946–1950)

In 1946, Karaganda was no big city. The city was in a "banishment area." Since 1930 that meant people whom Stalin mistrusted or who were political dissenters—such as expropriated peasants (Kulaks), Volga-Germans and members of other groups with non-Russian national origins—had been banished there. Ordinary civil prisoners were also there. All of them could move freely in the city but could not leave the region.

Camps for prisoners of war had been set up in Karaganda as early as 1941, at first for German,

but later also for Hungarian and Japanese war prisoners. We eleven officers were brought to Camp 3, where we were received with curiosity and also with a little distrust by German prisoners of war who had already been in captivity from 1941 to 1944.

Encountering those "old prisoners" and living together with them was not without problems. For all of them, the war had ended sooner. They had difficult times of great privation during their imprisonment behind them. They had experienced the mass deaths of starved and sick comrades during the war years and had survived. In individual conversations, we gradually learned of their painful experiences of which we had no real conception. Right up to the end of the war, in delusional belief in the final victory, we had been informed that there were not any German war prisoners in the USSR.

We were the first officers to be incorporated into the camp community. There were no more privileges for officers. We had to get used to that, which went pretty quickly. With a few exceptions, the old prisoners soon accepted us as comrades in their community.

The prisoners in Camp 3 worked in a nearby mine and in another, more distant, mine. Each shift was driven there in trucks. Shaft 1 was probably the first in Karaganda. It had been built about 1930 by the exiled persons under inhuman conditions (climate, billeting and food).

Several days after our arrival in the camp I was assigned to a work brigade that worked in Shaft 1 as a transport brigade. From that time on, I and all former officers up to and including the rank of Hauptmann had to do physical labor. The first workplace in Shaft 1 was the most adventurous. The shaft had no elevator. You had to go straight down into the unlighted shaft on foot. You had to pay attention to avoid stumbling or hitting your head on cross-timbers and take care that the faint miners' lamps were not extinguished. There was no replacement during the shift. You had to work by the light of another comrade.

The work consisted in pushing mine cars loaded with coal or stone or the empties that were pulled out or returned by a cable in a special tunnel. The coupling and uncoupling of the cars was difficult and called for a special proficiency. Full or empty cars frequently broke loose from the cable and came crashing back down at breakneck speed. The only thing left to do was look for cover. Fortunately, during my time in the brigade there were no serious accidents. The local shift leaders spoke well of us prisoners. They probably appreciated our industriousness and our discipline. As an officer, they observed me closely initially. Later, I was treated like any other prisoner.

Life in the camp followed a set order, focused on the shift work (three eight-hour shifts: Morning, noon and night). There was also internal duty (kitchen, laundry, barbershop, infirmary with German doctors and medics, tailor shop, and clothing room). The internal duty was primarily staffed with skilled workers, then with prisoners who were not fully capable of working and, finally, with selected prisoners who had made themselves particularly "popular" with our guards.

In every camp, in addition to the German camp leadership, which included prisoners of varying qualities and character traits, there was an antifascist council. The council had the mission of politically influencing the prisoners with respect to socialism and the USSR. A chief "activist" was at the head of the council, with more "activists" at his side. All of them were exempt from work and received preference in food, clothing and billeting. They were in close contact with the Russian camp leadership and with the political commissars, for which the other prisoners held them in low esteem.

However, they were feared. One had to be particularly careful of what one said in front of them. Almost all the "activists" were released early. Several of them were employed as state and party functionaries in East Germany. They viewed us officers with suspicion that was concealed under false politeness. They may well have feared our influence on the former soldiers, though that was no longer great. Their attempts to politically influence the prisoners were not very successful. In truth, their efforts had effects opposite to those intended for many. After the release of all the "activists" by the end of 1949, no new antifascist councils were organized in the camps by the Soviets.

During all of the years of my captivity, I worked with former soldiers of every rank, at first underground, then, ostensibly for safety reasons, above ground, on construction, in quarries, and in night-time offloading of long tree trunks from railroad cars. I got along well with everyone. We not only shared our rations, we also went through the uncertainties and the difficult lot of imprisonment together. The only hostile feelings toward officers that I ran into came from fellow prisoners who had been influenced by false ideologies.

I was in three different camps in Karaganda until April of 1950. During those years an increasing number of former officers who had experiences similar to mine came to the camp. At the end of 1948 or the beginning of 1949 a group of officers, including three staff officers, came to our camp from the Dscheskasgan "silent camp." That "silent camp" had been disbanded. While we had been able to send mail home since 1946, that had not been allowed there.

In that year numerous civil prisoners also came to us from the Eastern zone from the former concentration camps of Buchenwald and Oranienburg. They were, on the one hand, higher officials and judges who had not been soldiers and, on the other, "officials" who had been placed in leading positions by the Soviets. The "officials" had been placed in leading positions by the Soviets because it was alleged the Nazis had imprisoned them unjustly in concentration camps. Some of the latter group had been removed again from their positions for criminal activities by the Soviets and imprisoned.

The rations remained the same for the entire time. In the morning we got 600 grams of moist bread, some sugar and coffee. At noon we received soup. At night, we were issued a porridge (Kasha) made from millet, buckwheat, barley or the like, or a cabbage soup with potatoes but no meat. We also received a bit of tobacco.

The state of the prisoners' health in the years from 1946 to 1949 was bad, although several of them were able to improve the rations by purchase of additional items. Not everyone could earn money. One first had to earn 456 rubles for the camp and could then get a maximum of 150 rubles paid out from anything over that. However, since the Russian work quotas were, as a rule, set very high and the prisoners were in quite weak health, it was very difficult to earn money. I did earn something in several of the months while I was working in the mine, but I never belonged to the ranks of the regular earners.

Several books have been written about life in the prisoner-of-war camps in the USSR that have described everything as I also experienced it. Granted, I was not with the authors whose books I mention at the end of this section, but each of them described that difficult time so well and thoroughly that I do not need to go into more detail.

In all of the camps we regularly received Soviet and East German newspapers. There were several comrades among us with good knowledge of the Russian language who translated the contents of the newspapers for us. As a result, we were more-or-less informed, even if in a one-sided fashion, about events in the world. In addition, we lived with continual rumors that originated from our guards, from the anti-fascist council and from the civilian population.

In Karaganda and also in the camps that followed, there was a limited range of books that were available. We could read German-language books that were printed in the Soviet Union. They were, primarily, books with political content (Marx, Engels, Lenin, Stalin) and classical as well as modern Russian novels (such as *Silent Flows the Don*). There were also books from German authors who had been banned by the Nazi regime (such as Heinrich and Thomas Mann and Ludwig Renn).

Of course, the most important question that concerned us continually was: When would we be released? We discovered that the Western Allies had promised to release all German war prisoners by the end of 1948. The Soviet regime had ostensibly joined in that decision. That date, however, was not adhered to by the Soviet Union. The trains from the Soviet Union to Germany until the end of 1948 consisted primarily of prisoners who were sick and therefore incapable of work. In 1947 I became ill with a serious lung inflammation and was unable to work for several weeks. Although I was given several medical examinations while I had this condition, I was not allowed to go on any of the trains. Instead, work-capable "activists" were allowed to go home.

TRIAL AND SENTENCING (CHRISTMAS 1949–APRIL 1950)

In 1949 we waited with a great deal of nervous tension for the date of our release. During the course of the year several trains set out from Karaganda to Germany. The last train with prisoners from the camp I was in left at the end of November. The camp, however, was not emptied. Well over one hundred prisoners remained in the camp, of which I was one. Those of us who were left behind

had an uncomfortable feeling, though we still hoped to be home before Christmas.

In the preceding years members of certain designated units of the army and the Waffen-SS had been constantly interrogated, imprisoned and, in part, sentenced for ostensible war crimes. After the departure of the final trains, a systematic interrogation began of all the remaining inmates of the camp, for which purpose the personnel (MVD officers and translators) were significantly increased.

During my first interrogation, a deposition from a fellow prisoner I knew of was read aloud after several questions. That person said I had taken part in a crime against civilians in the summer of 1943 in the Ukraine. My explanation—that I had not committed any such act—was indeed listened to and even written down, but that was of little help to me. The leader of the interrogation explained to me that, because of the facts of the case, charges would be made against me before a court. I was shaken and also full of despair, since I knew of nothing I had done that was a matter of guilt. I calmed down a bit when, after my interrogation, I learned from others in the camp who were in the same boat that they had gone through exactly the same experience.

On 25 December 1949, I was sentenced in the camp to twenty-five years of forced labor by a court-martial in oral testimony without a defender. No credence was given to my explanation. The testimony of the fellow prisoner, taken down in Russian, was proof of my guilt in the eyes of the court. It was a mockery of justice. The "witness" had already gone home several weeks earlier. That was how it went for me and for all the other war prisoners left in the Soviet Union at the end of 1949. We could register appeals against the sentence. All appeals were rejected as unfounded without any new oral testimony. It is not necessary to wonder whether those proceedings had been carried out according to the principles of jurisprudence.

We already had the feeling that the Soviet government wanted to show its people and the rest of the world that—and the fact is, today, incontrovertible—the Germans had perpetrated crimes against the Soviet Union during the war and that those responsible were going to be held accountable. Today I know that Stalin had set in motion those mass-sentences in 1949–50 on political grounds.

What sorts of people were sentenced? I shall cite four groups of people as examples:

1. Members of the Waffen-SS, Gestapo, and police.
2. Generals, general staff officers, staff officers and members of specific units of the army that had been employed primarily against partisans.
3. Higher officials and judges, party functionaries and members of the civil administration in occupied areas.
4. Other members of the Wehrmacht who had fallen afoul of the Soviets during their imprisonment.

I probably belonged to the fourth group because the false statement by the former fellow prisoner was a slight piece of evidence against me. I do not know whether that witness's declaration was pure chance or malicious intent. I had never talked about my military experience with that witness. The Soviets knew that I had been employed in the Ukraine in 1943 from my personal record, which I had been required to write before the sentencing. The unit, to which I belonged at the time in question, Tiger Tank Battalion 503, was never named in the record of the interrogation nor in the court judgement. The judgement was never given to me in writing. It was, indeed, not worth the paper it was written on.

As can be easily understood, our morale after those Christmas days was at the zero point. We saw ourselves delivered up to a completely unknown fate, alone and helpless in distant Asia. How could anyone help us or free us there after we were told, for example, that my sentence would not run out until 21 December 1974. We did not know, however, that our fate would soon become known to the German public, which reacted in horror. Nowadays, there is a comprehensive literature regarding the entire chain of events at that Christmas time in the camps of the Soviet Union. To that end, I will only cite the books by Lang and Lehmann at the end of this section. Exactly the same thing happened in Karaganda to Ernst Ohnesorge as happened to me. We met again as sentenced men in the same camp.

We were all sent back to work at the beginning of 1950, just as before the sentencing. Every day ran as it had before. Nothing had changed in the camp. Our treatment by the guards and the food were identical.

In April 1950 the unexpected occurred: About a third of the camp population was sent home! Ernst Ohnesorge was one of those released at that time. He informed my mother and several former comrades of my fate. They explained to my mother that, based on their knowledge and their acquaintance with me, they were convinced that I was not guilty of the crimes of which I had been accused in the Soviet Union. I would, in this place, like to thank all those comrades who stood up for me. They greatly helped my mother at the time, even though they could not do anything else to help me then.

The sudden and unexpected release of a third of the sentenced population of the camp had a dual effect on those of us who were left. On the one hand, it depressed us that we had been left behind. The uncertainty and inescapability of our fate strengthened its impressions upon us. On the other hand, it ignited a little spark of hope within us that we too might someday be released.

In April 1950, all the inmates of the camp were assembled for a movement. In tightly guarded and barred freight cars, the railroad journey headed west. However, we did not go home, nor, as several feared, were we delivered to East Germany. Instead, after several days of railroad travel through Swerdlowsk—Kasan—Moscow, we arrived in Borowitschi about the beginning of May. It was about half way between Moscow and Leningrad. We were housed in a camp there.

BOROWITSCHI (MAY 1950–JULY 1951)

Borowitschi is an unexceptional, typical small city in central Russia. I can scarcely remember anything about the city itself. The camp that the 400 to 600 of us who were from Karaganda came to was outside of the city, on a road, and therefore called a road camp. One could see a bit of the landscape. In that camp we were housed in several large barracks that each held 200 men. Prisoners from various camps of the Soviet union who had suffered the same fate that we had were there. Among them was the majority of the staff officers of Heeresgruppe Kurland. A portion of them had been sent home at the end of 1949.

We went from the road camp—with the exception, I believe, of the staff officers—to work at various construction sites in the city. Every morning, in columns "of fives," we went out the camp gate, then "shuffled off" to the work place. The work brigades were split up into skilled and unskilled laborers and set to work. I belonged to the latter. I had to mix and carry mortar, carry stones, unload lumber and perform other such unskilled laborer's tasks. There was a short lunch break. Food was brought from the camp. After eight or nine hours, we knocked off work, formed up "by fives" and were counted, departed for the camp and were counted again on entering the camp. That was how the work days monotonously continued throughout the year, broken only by Sundays when we did not work.

Material things remained similarly unchanged. Always the same food, the same clothing, though that, of course, was appropriate for the season. In winter there were quilted coats, fur hats, felt boots and, occasionally, gloves. Of course, none of it was top quality. It was particularly hard for the unskilled laborers to earn money at the construction sites in Borowitschi.

In 1950 a relief program began that was an immensely great material support for all of us and, at the same time, a real spiritual help. The packages and flow of parcels from the homeland—predominantly, of course, from the west—remained our greatest joy and aid. They increased steadily until our release in 1955. Thanks to the parcels, we knew that we were not forgotten. The parcels let us know that even more than the postcards and occasional letters.

In the summer of 1949 in Karaganda, to my great joy, I had already received several small packages from my mother. The postal connection, however, was severed before the sentencing. For several months the Soviets did not allow us to write. It was only when we got to Borowitschi that we could write again and again received small packages and parcels.

When we came through the camp gate in the evening the names of the fortunate recipients were read out and our joy knew no bounds. One dashed over to the place where the mail was handed out and received one's package. My mother took pains so that I was one of the first recipients of such loving gifts. We then received from home what we were not given in the camp: coffee, cocoa, milk and pudding powder, chocolate, butter and margarine, wurst and ham, as well

as other useful items such as soap and cloth. Not all of the inmates of the camp, of course, immediately got packages from home. The comrades from East Germany were far worse off than those of us whose relatives lived in the west. During the years that followed, however, that was balanced out by sharing among ourselves and also by organizations in West Germany. Everyone in the camp was well fed, thanks to the abundant mailings of parcels and small packages. As a result, they remained healthy.

CONTACT WITH THE HOMELAND

My mother saved my Feldpost letters from the years 1940 to 1945, in spite of the total damage from bombs in Berlin in February 1944 and the flight before the Russian troops at the time of the Oder breakthrough at the end of January 1945. She received my final letter as a soldier at 4 April 1945 on a relative's farm at Wittenberge in the Altmark.

All of the mail I received during the war has been lost. I do not know when I learned of my mother's flight from the breakthrough on the Oder. I wrote my first card to my mother on 3 February 1946 from the Kischinew camp. We received pre-printed reply cards from the Soviets which also contained reply cards. We could only write a few sentences. We were only allowed to write something very general: "In the present circumstances, things are going reasonably well and I am also in good health." Any reference to the location of the camp, its size, the fellow prisoners or the conditions in the camp and in the country were forbidden and were crossed out without comment. In addition, there was the danger that a card with such contents would not be sent. A photocopy of my first card appears later in this section. My mother received that card on 15 March 1946 in Berlin-Nikolassee.

The photocopy of a reply card that my mother sent me on 10 January 1951 is also presented on the following pages. I received the card on 11 February 1951 at Borowitschi. On it, my mother wrote: "Today I received two cards from November (1950), for which I am grateful. I can still scarcely believe it. After almost one-and-a-half years, the first direct sign of life from you." The censor crossed out a sentence. My mother also told me that two packages had been returned from Karaganda in the summer of 1950 and that she had written postcards to me during that time. Those, however, never got to me.

My mother preserved all of my cards and several letters from the time I was a prisoner of war. I only have the mail from home from February 1951 on. Mail prior to that time was either taken from me during the regular searches in the camp or I might have destroyed it before the date of the expected return home in 1949. At that time, no written-on pieces of paper could be taken back to Germany. Later that was changed.

In addition to that rather late-blooming postal connection, we were able to send news to our relatives with others who returned home. A train had already gone to Germany from Kischinew in the fall of 1945 with soldiers who were ill and no longer capable of working—no officers. The person detailed to assist the officers, Herr Bernau, also went in that train.

Like me, he was a Berliner and went back to Berlin. He had memorized the addresses of my relatives in Berlin and told them about me after his release. My mother and my relatives were, therefore, already informed before the end of 1945 that I was a Soviet prisoner of war in the Kischinew camp.

In April 1946 my mother got a letter from Feldwebel Spiekermann, who had been released to East Berlin from a Soviet prisoner-of-war camp. Spiekermann was the last radio operator in Tiger 300 and went into captivity with me. He wrote my mother concerning our captivity up to Camp Focsani, where we had been separated. He was of the rather optimistic opinion that I must already be at home or, if not, would soon return home. When he wrote that letter he could not have known that—separated from the former officers of 503— I had already made a long journey through the Soviet Union in a prison train and had arrived at Karaganda.

During the years from 1947 to 1949 my mother received additional personal reports about my fate from several returnees. As a result, she knew I was alive and where I was located. All the former camp comrades believed at that time that all war prisoners would be sent home from the Soviet Union by the end of 1949.

I owe all of my comrades thanks that they informed my mother of my fate and encouraged her hopes of seeing me again.

CAMP REWDA AT SWERDLOWSK (JULY–OCTOBER 1951)

The camp at Borowitschi was closed at the beginning of July 1951. Trains were assembled and, again, it was debated where "the journey" would lead this time. Rumors abounded, ranging from extradition to East Germany to being sent off to most distant Asia. The journey in the guarded, barred freight cars passed through Moscow-Kasan and headed east. The train traveled through the Urals. We were unloaded at the Rewda railroad station outside of Swerdlowsk.

In the Swerdlowsk area at that time there were six to eight camps, all filled with war prisoners. The prisoners started to be assembled there in 1951. Swerdlowsk was on the eastern edge of the central Urals, in the Asian portion of the USSR. The city was formerly named Jekaterinenburg. It was there, in 1918, that the Czar's family had been murdered.

Swerdlowsk is a major city (1981: 1,200,000 population), a transportation and industrial center of the Urals. I did not get to know the city itself. I was only in the Rewda camp for a short time. I have no particular memories of that period.

In October 1951 a portion of the camp population was assembled for movement. I was included. We were loaded on trucks and driven about 30 kilometers south to Dechtjarka, still in the Urals.

CAMP DECHTJARKA, NEAR SWERDLOWSK (OCTOBER 1951–7 OCTOBER 1955)

Dechtjarka was a small mining settlement. The inhabitants were mainly employed in mining. The place was built around the mines; it was not very attractive.

Camp life there resembled that at all the previous camps. At first we were housed in apartment blocks, but were soon moved to barracks. I would remain in those barracks for almost four years. Each barrack had four large rooms, each housing thirty to forty men. We slept on double-tiered wooden bunks with straw sacks, which were refilled occasionally. Two sets of double-deck bunks were placed next to one another with a table in between on which one could eat. One sat on the lower bunk to eat. The living space for the so-called free time of a prisoner was extraordinarily cramped.

In each room of the barracks were prisoners of every rank and occupation. There were also generals who had been sentenced. They had previously lived in a camp at Moscow. They integrated themselves into the camp community with no problems. All inmates of the camp, even the generals and staff officers, had to go to work daily to the extent of their physical capabilities. I lived with staff officers, generals, high officials and judges in the barracks and worked together with them at construction sites. We always had good conversations with each other, and each of them gave me a great deal for my later life. I was one of the youngest ones there, a college-prep graduate with frontline experience. Stimulated by books and newspaper articles, we discussed National Socialism, the resistance, democracy and politics, history and economics, the war and its end. I learned a great deal from the great treasures of knowledge and experience of those older fellow prisoners, and they paid serious attention to my ideas and opinions.

We had, by then, learned of the formation of two German states and knew, approximately, what were the differences between them. In addition, we knew of the Korean War and of the disagreements between the victorious powers, particularly between the Soviet Union and the United States of America. Naturally, all of that stirred us and occupied a major place in our discussions.

There were, of course, occasional disagreements among us, but they were not of great significance. There was some stealing at first, but it did not continue.

Thanks to the flow of parcels, the state of our health remained stable. There were occasional accidents at the construction sites. Unfortunately, I also saw deadly accidents.

A German dentist in the Dechtjarka camp put my teeth in order and built me a bridge that held up until my first examination by a dentist at Uelzen in November 1955.

From time to time our guards "feared" that diseases could result from the growth of our hair. As a result, our heads were shaven a few times, even though we were frequently searched and also deloused. Lice were an occasional occurrence in the early years. Later, we were totally free of them. Our hair was really only cut to humiliate us and put us on an equal footing with the Russian civil prisoners. In the final years, from about 1952 on, that was no longer done. We were able to let our hair grow, regularly went to the camp barber, and

several of us even had our own shaving gear (actually forbidden).

At some point our guards found out that a prisoner had received a written message from home in a cigarette. Sending written messages in parcels and packages was not permitted. Our guards were alarmed and instituted the following procedure: Packages and parcels were no longer handed out sealed. They were opened by MVD soldiers in a special room and the contents were examined. Cans were opened and emptied, coffee was dumped into containers that the prisoners brought in, cigars and cigarettes were slit open. Naturally, nothing was found. The guards had extra work and we were extremely angry. Where were we to find containers for coffee, butter, fat, marmalade and the like, and how were the foodstuffs to be preserved once opened?

There were strong protests. The German camp leadership had to search for a way out and, together with our guards, who were not pleased with all the extra work, came up with a solution. Cigarettes and cigars were no longer cut open. Chocolate was handed out in its packaging. Cans were repacked in a carton with the prisoner's number on it and stored in a special room. On designated days, each could get cans from his carton.

Since our guards did not want to do all that work themselves, helpers were assigned. I was selected from our barracks unit. From then on I was regularly present at the distribution of packages and parcels and when cans were handed out. I was able to untie and unpack packages and parcels so that everything could be given out as quickly and simply as possible, depending on which guard was at the counter. We learned our guards were also human. Many a package was handed out unopened. Naturally, one had to pay close attention and one could not say much about it.

During those years, the number of packages grew from month to month. I received packages, not only from my mother, but also from relatives, organizations and from former members of the 503 which, of course, made me particularly happy. Once again, I wish to express my special thanks to all former comrades. Your packages were a great, an extremely great, help.

Stalin died in March 1953. A certain uneasiness went through the entire land, and we in the camps also felt it. The news of his death spread quickly. During those days MVD officials appeared at the construction sites, since they expected some sort of rioting or the like among the war prisoners. Nothing of the kind took place.

The new masters in the Kremlin decided in May of that year to release some additional prisoners of war to the homeland. We were all surprised, one morning, when half of the camp population was called out and held back during the usual departure for work from the camp gate. I was not one of them. That evening we found out the comrades who had been held back had been taken to the Rewda camp, from which they were to travel home. We had a certain connection with the Rewda camp through the central hospital. In that way the first news trickled through about the delays in the transport home. The grounds for that were the events on 17 June 1953 in East Germany. A popular uprising had been bloodily put down by Soviet troops. The lords of the Kremlin considered it not a favorable time for the return of prisoners of war. The result was that the movement home did not actually take place until September 1953.

Once again, after an unknown and unexplained selection process, prisoners of war of all ranks had been sent home. And again, others, including me, were kept in the Soviet Union with no reasons given.

In 1953 the camps in the Swerdlowsk area were filled up again with German prisoners of war. Some came from the Stalingrad and Schachty areas. We assumed that now all, or at least the greatest portion, of the prisoners of war were collected in the Swerdlowsk area.

In 1954 we heard on the radio, which was controlled by the guards, and from the Russian and East German newspapers, that the German national soccer team had won the world championship in Bern. That, naturally, made us feel good, even though we knew no further details.

RELEASE AND RETURN HOME
(7–16 OCTOBER 1955)

In 1955 news trickled through that negotiations were in progress between the Soviet Union and the Federal Republic of Germany. We, of course, knew nothing more exact. We only noticed that our guards were a bit more friendly in their treatment of us. In the meantime, the generals were again assembled in a camp at Moscow. We later discovered that the federal chancellor, Dr. Ade-

nauer, was to come to Moscow with a delegation in September. We very much hoped that he would think of us.

We could only follow the course of his visit and the progress of the negotiations incompletely. Details were not known to us. Nevertheless, we found out they dealt with our treatment and our fate. I later learned the details and can refer to the books by Wilhelm Backhaus and Carlo Schmidt, listed at the end of this section.

The result of the negotiations were announced to us by the Soviet camp leadership at the end of September: Establishment of diplomatic relations between the Soviet Union and West Germany and the release of all German war and civil prisoners.

At a camp muster it was explained to us that we had been granted "amnesty" and would be returned to Germany. It began with the same little game: Individual groups were called out by name and transported out of the camps. Then 600 names, including mine, were called out according to the Russian alphabet and were assigned to railroad cars, forty men to a car. At the end there were about 100 prisoners left who then realized that they were not being released to go home. On the very evening of our departure, twenty-five of those were called to the gate by name and driven off in trucks. We soon discovered that twenty-five prisoners were coming to our camp in exchange for them. They were coming from the camp at Rewda. They departed the next day with us in the trains. On that day, several more prisoners also arrived in individual movements from all parts of the Soviet Union. They were also supposed to go home with us.

Finally, in the afternoon of 7 October 1955, everything was ready! That morning a freight train was shunted onto the tracks on the hillside across from us. We took leave of our comrades who, filled with doubt and pessimism, remained in the camp. (It should be noted that they all returned home in December 1955 and January 1956.) After yet another roll call, we marched to the railroad station and boarded the freight cars that had been assigned to us. Double-decked bunks with straw sacks were built into each freight car. There was a kitchen and food car, a medical car and a car for the train commander, a Soviet officer, but no additional guards.

As evening approached on 7 October 1955, our train started to move. The journey went from Swerdlowsk by way of Kasan, Moscow, and Minsk to Brest-Litowsk. The train stopped frequently on the open track and also at railroad stations. We could disembark and wander freely. However, as a rule, we did not stray far from the train; none of us wanted to remain in the Soviet Union. When the locomotive whistled, we climbed back on board the train.

In Brest-Litowsk we went through the last control. The inspection was harmless and we were free to board the freight cars from East Germany. The journey through Poland by way of Warsaw-Posen went smoothly. There was a longer stop before crossing the border into East Germany, since we were not supposed to arrive at Frankfort/Oder before dark. The train did not enter the railroad station. Instead, it had to remain outside. Men in leather coats (STASI men, the secret state police) positioned themselves at a discrete distance around the train. We had the feeling we were lepers and not welcome in East Germany. During the night the journey continued through Torgau and past Leipzig and then on through Weimar, Erfurt and Eisenach. People everywhere waved to us from the platforms. They knew only too well who we were.

Beyond Eisenach we reached Wartha, the last railroad station in East Germany. The train then stopped at Herleshausen! There we were received by an official from the federal government who, together with the Russian movement officer, now in civilian clothing, went from car to car and called each individual by name. On 16 October 1955 we walked on German soil for the first time in more than ten years.

We were driven in buses to the camp at Friedland and welcomed with heartfelt greetings by the populace of the cities and towns along the way. In the Friedland camp I ran into the comrades again who had been taken away from the Dechtjarka camp on the evening of 6 October. They had arrived in a train ahead of me.

I spent my first night in West Germany in a barracks of the federal border police. On the following day I was officially released from captivity at the Friedland camp. From the camp, I telephoned my brother in Munich and my mother, who had found a new home in 1945 in Barum, near Uelzen. On 17 October 1955 I drove to my mother's, together with my sister and the mayor of Barum.

AFTERWORD

I wrote this report to the best of my recollection almost thirty-five years after my release from captivity as a prisoner of war. As a result, it is certainly not complete nor is it representative of the experience of all the war prisoners in the USSR. I have described my own experience as a prisoner. The report could have been far more comprehensive, but that would have exceeded the scope of this book.

The period of captivity in the Soviet Union, which lasted more than ten years, was a difficult time for all. Life in the camps was, basically, monotonous and boring. The greatest burden was the uncertainly regarding our fate. I do not deny that the Soviet prisoners of war in Germany had a far worse time than what happened to us in the prison camps in the USSR after the end of the war.

My health came through the war and the long period of captivity in relatively good condition. After my release, I was still in condition both physically and mentally to begin an academic course of study and successfully complete it. For that I am thankful.

During the captivity and in the years that followed I have taken pains to discover the causes and bases for the initiation and the course of the war. I have read a great deal relating to that and also had many discussions. Today I am certain that, under Adolf Hitler's leadership in 1939, Germany started the war with Poland with a war of aggression that had no justification and waged war in the years that followed with additional European states. That war was broadened by Hitler into the Second World War.

The German people were led astray by Hitler and his followers. The mass of the people followed him without thinking. The same holds true for the Wehrmacht, above all for its leadership, even in peacetime. The opposition against the Nazi regime was too weak, poorly organized and came too late. Nevertheless, it brought honor to the men and women who gave their lives for it.

During the course of the war, things were done in all of the lands that were occupied by German troops that were outside the bounds of international and military law. The commanders responsible either did nothing or did not do enough against those war crimes.

The sentencing of the captured German soldiers in the Soviet Union was a result of those events. Those sentenced were sacrificial lambs for deeds in which they had not taken part but for which they have to carry a certain share of the responsibility.

SOURCES

1. *Der Neue Brockhaus*, Vol. 3, 1985, p. 84, 89.
2. Helmut Gollwitzer, . . . *und führen wohin du nicht willst. Bericht einer Gefangenshaft*, 3rd Edition, 1977.
3. Willy Kramp, *Brüder und Knechte*, 1965.
4. Alexander Solschenitzyn, *Ein Tag im Leben des Iwan Denissowitsch*, 1979.
5. Albrecht Lehmann, *Gefangenschaft und Heimkehr: Deutsche Kriegsgefangene in der SU*, 1986.
6. *Der Neue Brockhaus*, Vol. 5, 1985, p. 206.
7. Martin Lang, *Stalins Strafjustiz gegen Deutsche Soldaten*, 1981.
8. Wilhelm Backhaus, *Begegnung im Kreml, So wurden die Gefangenen befreit*, 1955.
9. Carlo Schmidt, *Erinnerungen, Goldmann Sachbuch 11316*, 1st edition, 1981.

This series of photos was taken fifty years after the war near the Austrian/Czech border.

Additional photos taken fifty years after the war near the Austrian/Czech border.

APPENDIX 1

Personnel Losses of the Battalion

Alfred Rubbel

By the end of the war, the German Army, without counting the Waffen-SS, had lost about 2.02 million men killed or missing. That was out of a total of 251 divisions and a personnel strength of 6.51 million men (as of 1944). The losses after the collapse of Germany and in captivity can only be crudely estimated. They approximated an additional 1.5 to 2 million men.

For our battalion, the only figures at hand for killed/missing are for the 1st, 2nd, and 3rd Companies of Tiger Tank Battalion 503. The losses cited above for the army in general and below for the tank companies themselves, can provide a basis for estimation of the battalions other losses. According to the battalion status report for 1 January 1945, the battalion had the following complement of personnel in December 1944:

28	Officers
5	Civilian officials
279	Noncommissioned officers
598	Enlisted men
31	*Hiwi*
941	Personnel on hand
+13	Short (1 officer, 12 Hiwi)
954	Total authorized personnel

By the end of the war, the headcount for the tank companies, with an authorized strength of 88 men, was

1st Company: 81 killed/missing = 92 percent
2nd Company: 69 killed/missing = 78 percent (up to 31 December 1944)
3rd Company: 56 killed/missing = 64 percent

As for the other companies—Headquarters, Supply, and Maintenance Companies— personnel on hand (not counting *Hiwis*) was 646; using a reduced loss rate of 50 percent brings it to 323 men. That estimate, though less certain, gives an estimate of killed/missing of

206	Tank companies (established)
323	Remaining companies (estimated)
529	Men killed/missing

With 910 soldiers (less *Hiwi*), that gives the battalion a loss rate of 58 percent. The overall losses of the army (*Heer*) amounted to 31 percent. For a combat formation that fought year in and year out at the hotspots of the fronts and therefore had to suffer higher losses, the form of estimation employed is reasonably in accord with probability.

Regarding other losses (wounded, sick, and other losses) there are only incomplete figures:

PERSONNEL LOSSES OF TIGER TANK BATTALION 503 DURING THE PERIOD FROM 1 JUNE 1943 TO 30 DECEMBER 1944 (INCOMPLETE)

Reporting Period	KIA	WIA	MIA	Sick	Other	Total	Operations
1–30 June 1943	—	—	—	7	4	11	Army reserve in Kharkov
1–31 July 1943	25	68	1	11	2	107	Citadel
1–31 August 1943	7	22	—	32		61	Fighting at Kharkov
1–30 September 1943	7	22	—	14	2	45	Defensive fighting west of Kharkov
1–31 October 1943	3	10	—	13	2	28	Fighting at Kiev, Pawlish
1–30 November 1943	3	7	—	11	—	21	Defensive fighting west of the Dnjepr
1–31 December 1943	5	7	—	21	2	35	Defensive fighting west of the Dnjepr
1–31 January 1944	10	13	3	17	—	43	Fighting with Panzer Regiment Bäke,
1–29 February 1944	4	8	—	12	4	28	Oratoff, Tscherkassy
1–31 July 1944	26	18	31	29	—	104	Defensive fighting in Normandy
1–31 October 1944	6	16	2	23	—	47	Defensive combat along the Danube
1–30 November 1944	5	11	—	9	—	25	Defensive combat along the Danube
1–31 December 1944	4	8	—	17	1	30	Defensive combat along the Danube
Total	**105**	**210**	**37**	**276**	**17**	**585**	

Theoretical monthly average: 45 lost (calculated on a basis of 13 monthly status reports; the battalion was in combat for 27 months).

We lost the following KIA:

- July 1943 (Zitadelle): 25
- January 1944 (Tscherkassy): 10
- February 1944 (Tscherkassy): 4
- July 1944 (Normandy): 26 and 31(!) missing

The Tscherkassy fighting in January–February 1944 was the most difficult for the battalion and lasted thirty-one days without a break. The modest number killed—a total of fourteen—is explained by the fact that only twenty Tigers went into action and only six were operational in the end. At Citadel and in Normandy, all forty-five Tigers was on hand. The large number of thirty-one missing in Normandy reflects the fact that those captured were counted as missing. The battalion was rendered combat ineffective in that fighting.

The "other losses" multiply the losses killed by a factor of five. The battalion losses due to wounds, illness and other losses can be estimated on the basis of the thirteen months of status reports at a monthly rate of about forty-five soldiers. That yields an estimated total of 1,500 over the three years of the battalion's existence.

The losses were made good by replacements and returning convalescents. Although each year about half of the battalion personnel were lost, the return of "former members" maintained a cadre.

The lists of losses for the 1st and 3rd Companies were compiled after the end of the war, based on personal notes, recollections and other sources. Their accuracy is not guaranteed. The 2nd Company is the only company for which there is an official source, the company newsletter for Christmas 1944. That newsletter only listed losses to 31 December 1944. Thus, in spite of an evaluation of all available records, errors cannot be ruled out. In particular, there is practically no information, with a few exceptions, regarding the fate of those comrades who were captured by the Russians at the end of the war. That included at least a third of the battalion personnel, approximately 300 men.

Inquiries to the search service of the German Red Cross and the Wehrmacht Information Office give the impression that both were faced with impossible tasks compounded by a lack of official interest.

In my research, I came upon two notable statistics that I wish to pass on to those who may read these pages:

1. Most tank crew members were killed outside of their tanks.
2. In the German Army, including the Waffen-SS, there were only 1,408 deserters, less than 0.02% of the personnel employed, from the start of the war until 31 December 1944. That was with a total personnel strength of 7.11 million soldiers. There were none from our battalion! There is truly no basis for the attempts by the radical left to cast doubt on the reliability of the German soldier and overturn historical reality with its demands for monuments to the "Unknown Deserter."

KILLED AND MISSING, 1ST COMPANY (FIELD POST NO. 21 346)

	Officers	NCOs	Enlisted Men	Total
Authorized Personnel	4	46	38	88
Lost	7	27	47	81

This determination, based on the numbers and names of losses that the company suffered between the time of its organization (4 May 1942) and its dissolution (10 May 1945), is complete. In the other lists errors cannot be ruled out. Judging by experience, the eleven listed as missing were probably killed in action.

Sequence Number	Rank	Name	Location	Date	Remarks
Manytsch (lower Don)					
1	Unteroffizier	Bleß	Stawropol	6 Jan 43	
2	Leutnant	Meller	Wesselij	9 Jan 43	Buried at Proletarskaja
3	Unteroffizier	Scheele	Wesselij	9 Jan 43	Buried at Proletarskaja
4	Unteroffizier	Griewald	Baraniki	14 Jan 43	
5	Unteroffizier	Dürrlich	Jekaterinowka	18 Jan 43	In Tiger 134
6	Gefreiter	Buck	Jekaterinowka	18 Jan 43	In Tiger 134
Rostow					
7	Leutnant	Detlef von Koerber	Sapatny	9 Feb 43	
8	Obergefreiter	Mau	9 Feb 43		
Kolchose 15					
9	Unteroffizier	Schulze	10 Feb 43		
10	Obergefreiter	Bobsin	10 Feb 43		

Sequence Number	Rank	Name	Location	Date	Remarks
Mius sector					
11	Unteroffizier	Dunkel		Feb 43	Drowned when their Panzer III broke through the ice on the Mius. Recovered in March and buried in Pokrowskoje
12	Obergefreiter	Gronau		Feb 43	As with Unteroffizier Dunkel
13	Gefreiter	Schult-Dargen		Feb 43	As with Unteroffizier Dunkel
14	Panzerschütze	Großmann		Feb 43	As with Unteroffizier Dunkel

Wilke and Gehrke (missing?); apparently belonged to the 1st Company.

Sequence Number	Rank	Name	Location	Date	Remarks
Bjelgorod area (Citadel)					
15	Leutnant	Jammerath	Michailowka	5 July 43	
16	Gefreiter	Kaneke	Korukow 1	2 July 43	Tank commander Tessmer
17	Obergefreiter	Beyer		12 July 43	Tank commander Tessmer
Fighting south of Merefa					
18	Unteroffizier	Neumann		2 Sept 43	
19	Feldwebel	Lehmann		2 Sept 43 (?)	
20	Obergefreiter	Krüger	Nowaja Wodelaga	7 Sept 43	
21	Gefreiter	Jokwer	Nowaja Wodelaga	7 Sept 43	
22	Gefreiter	Hornberger		8 Sept 43	
Glinsk-Tschigrin area					
23	Gefreiter	Dankert			ca. 28 Nov 43 Tiger 114 (Tank commander Rubbel)
24	Unteroffizier	Thome			ca. 10 Dec 43
Pawlisch area					
25	Unteroffizier	Rippl		Nov 43	Wounded; died in hospital in Germany in spring 1944
26	Unteroffizier	Leitzke		Nov 44	
Smerinka area					
27	Unteroffizier	Öls		12 Jan 44	Murdered by partisans; buried at Smerinka
28	Obergefreiter	Heider		12 Jan 44	As with Unteroffizier Öls above
29	Gefreiter	Mink		12 Jan 44	As with Unteroffizier Öls above
30	Gefreiter	Barton		12 Jan 44	As with Unteroffizier Öls above
31	Gefreiter	Djuba		12 Jan 44	As with Unteroffizier Öls above

Sequence Number	Rank	Name	Location	Date	Remarks
Smerinka area *continued*					
32	Gefreiter	Minek		12 Jan 44	As with Unteroffizier Öls above
33	Gefreiter	Wiesenfahrt		12 Jan 44	As with Unteroffizier Öls above
Winniza area					
34	Oberleutnant	Adamek		24 Jan 44	Buried at Winniza
35	Obergefreiter	Kubin		28 Jan 44	Buried at Winniza
Oratoff area					
36	Gefreiter	Bürger		31 Jan 44	
37	Obergefreiter	Wollmann		1 Feb 44	
38	Obergefreiter	Oppe			ca. 1 Feb 44 Traffic accident
Proskurow area					
39	Gefreiter	Schmähl	Fedorki	9 Mar 44	In Tiger 113
40	Panzerschütze	Schneider	Fedorki	9 Mar 44	
41	Oberfeldwebel	Erdmann		9 Mar 44	
42	Oberleutnant	Reutermann	Friedrichowka	10 Mar 44	Killed by partisans
43	Obergefreiter	Krause	Friedrichowka	10 Mar 44	Killed by partisans
Touste area (Huisatin)					
44	Unteroffizier	von Borries			ca. 15 Mar 44 Missing
45	Unteroffizier	Ritscher			Missing
46	Panzerschütze	Vorderbrügge			Missing
47	Panzerschütze	(?) (was the loader)			Missing
Scalat area					
48	Unteroffizier	Bausinger			ca. 15 Mar 44 Entire crew of Tiger 121 (Bausinger) missing
49	Gefreiter	Schulz, H.			Bausinger crew
50	Obergefreiter	Spatke			Bausinger crew
51	Obergefreiter	Wedler			Bausinger crew
52	Obergefreiter	Vorreith			Bausinger crew
Kamenez-Podolsk					
53	Obergefreiter	Zimmermann		March 44	Missing
54	Obergefreiter	Brück			Missing
55	Obergefreiter	Mundry			Missing
Tarnopol area					
56	Obergefreiter	Grütter		April 44	Killed with Battle Group Mittermeier
57	Obergefreiter	Werner		April 44	Killed with Battle Group Mittermeier
Ohrdruf Training Area					
58	Unteroffizier	Oelsner	near Gotha	June 44	Fatal accident during rail movement

Sequence Number	Rank	Name	Location	Date	Remarks
Normandy					
59	Oberfeldwebel	Fendesack		15 Aug 44	Killed in fighting in Normandy. Locations are difficult, mostly Caen and Falaise areas
60	Leutnant	Schröder		18 July 44	As above
61	Gefreiter	Gükl		19 July 44	As above
62	Feldwebel	Vogt		28 July 44	As above
63	Obergefreiter	Marat		25 July 44	As above
64	Gefreiter	Schütze		7 Aug 44	As above
Hungary					
65	Oberfeldwebel	Marcus	Szolnock	21 Oct 44	
66	Unteroffizier	Schielke	Szolnock	21 Oct 44	
67	Gefreiter	Meß		27 Oct 44	
68	Obergefreiter	Bohn	Polgardi	8 Dec 44	
69	Obergefreiter	Wagner	Polgardi	8 Dec 44	
70	Obergefreiter	Bîhm	Polgardi	8 Dec 44	
71	Feldwebel	Kukla	Zamoly	11 Jan 45	
72	Unteroffizier	Hîppner	Zamoly	11 Jan 45	
73	Obergefreiter	Walter	Zamoly	11 Jan 45	
74	Obergefreiter	Woisin	Zamoly	11 Jan 45	
Verebely area					
75	Unteroffizier	Bîhme, H.	Verebely	14 Mar 45	Accident during training
76	Unteroffizier	Schikarski	Verebely	25 Mar 45	
77	Gefreiter	Rauschenberger	Verebely	25 Mar 45	
78	Leutnant	Fürlinger	Verebely	27 Mar 45	
79	?	?	Verebely	Mar 1945	Truck driver killed by accident with hand grenade
Brünn area					
80	Feldwebel	Knispel		29 Apr 45	Buried in Urbau/Znaim
Area north of Vienna					
81	Stabsfeldwebel	Schmidt	Zistersdorf	?	May 45 Buried in Zistersdorf

Sources

First compilation 1950 by Lochmann/Rubbel
Various contributions by company members
Leutnant von Koerber Diary
Welsch Diary

KILLED AND MISSING, 2ND COMPANY (FIELD POST NO. 22 402)

	Officers	NCOs	Enlisted Men	Total (as of 31 December 1944)
Authorized Personnel	4	46	38	88
Lost	3	23	43	69

The particulars come from a newsletter of the 2nd Company for Christmas 1944. As a result, they can be considered absolutely reliable. The losses from 1 January to 10 May 1945 have not been compiled. During that time period the 1st Company had 11 losses; the 3rd Company had 3. It is likely that losses for the 2nd Company during that period were similar.

Sequence Number	Rank	Name	Location	Date	Remarks
1	Oberleutnant	Zabel, Fried.-Karl	Russia		Killed
2	Leutnant	Cüsow, Werner			
3	Stabsfeldwebel	Hammrich, Karl			
4	Stabsfeldwebel	Ruffert, Paul			
5	Oberfeldwebel	Porsch, Albert			
6	Feldwebel	Hennig, Franz			
7	Feldwebel	Heinl, Peter			
8	Feldwebel	Plum, Josef			
9	Unteroffizier	Behrens, Walter			
10	Unteroffizier	Drücker, Karl			
11	Unteroffizier	Klatt, Albert			
12	Unteroffizier	Nachbaur, Max			
13	Unteroffizier	Ramp, Waldemar			
14	Unteroffizier	Schälicke, Rudi			
15	Unteroffizier	Schmidt, Bernhard			
16	Obergefreiter	Klein, Paul			
17	Obergefreiter	Utesch, Lothar			
18	Gefreiter	Beckmann, Hans			
19	Gefreiter	Bendler, Erich			
20	Gefreiter	Braatz, Horst			
21	Gefreiter	Böge, Helmut			
22	Gefreiter	Dähne, Harry			
23	Gefreiter	Gergens, Walter			
24	Gefreiter	Hein, Hans			
25	Gefreiter	Hüneken, Hans			
26	Gefreiter	König, Friedrich			
27	Gefreiter	Reich, Gerhard			
28	Gefreiter	Schröder, Max			
29	Gefreiter	Tettenborn, Heinz			
30	Gefreiter	Williard, Heinrich			
31	Panzerschütze	Knapp, Alfred			
32	Panzerschütze	Pausewein, Willi			
33	Panzerschütze	Streetz, Günther			

Sequence Number	Rank	Name	Location	Date	Remarks
34	Obergefreiter	Bähr, Fritz	France		Killed
35	Obergefreiter	Degelow, Günther			
36	Obergefreiter	Rabe, Norbert			
37	Leutnant	Bielefeld, Walter	Hungary		
38	Gefreiter	Fink, Wolfgang			
39	Gefreiter	Wahl, Eugen			
40	Gefreiter	Blank, Paul			Killed in accident
41	Gefreiter	Lebert, Bruno			
42	Gefreiter	Porwol, Erich			
43	Panzerschütze	Pitz, Josef			
44	Unteroffizier	Beck, Josef	Russia		Missing
45	Unteroffizier	Dilly, Valentin			
46	Unteroffizier	Golder, Bernhard			
47	Unteroffizier	Keller, Johann			
48	Unteroffizier	Siebert, Walter			
49	Obergefreiter	Becker, Heinz			
50	Obergefreiter	Schlorke, Günter			
51	Obergefreiter	Brandt, Helmut			
52	Obergefreiter	Behm, Werner			
53	Gefreiter	Deringer, Hilmar			
54	Gefreiter	Paech, Eckard			
55	Gefreiter	Paulsen, Hans			
56	Gefreiter	Rohlfs, Henry			
57	Gefreiter	Stober, Robert			
58	Panzerschütze	Bartsch, Alfred			
59	Panzerschütze	Bohm, Dieter			
60	Panzerschütze	Heckmanns, August			
61	Oberfeldwebel	Kutzner, Walter	France		Missing
62	Unteroffizier	Damlaks, Gustav			
63	Unteroffizier	Messer, Otto			
64	Unteroffizier	Nowacki, Günter			
65	Unteroffizier	Panknin, Herbert			
66	Obergefreiter	Meyer, Max			
67	Panzerschütze	Mühl, Emil			
68	Obergefreiter	Golz, Bernhard	Russia		In captivity
69	Gefreiter	Besenhardt, Franz			

KILLED AND MISSING, 3RD COMPANY (FIELD POST NO. 30 628)

	Officers	NCOs	Enlisted Men	Total
Authorized Personnel	4	46	38	88
Lost	2	22 (?)	32 (?)	56

The list is based on Heinrich Hoffman's notes and contributions from Niemann and von Rosen. The listing of ranks is incomplete.

Sequence Number	Rank	Name	Location	Date	Remarks
Kalmück area/Ukraine					
1		Zahn, Fritz	Ilowajski	8 Jan 43	
2	Oberfeldwebel	Gerrels, Georg		8 Jan 43	Missing with Panzer III
3	Unteroffizier	Kunze, Walter	Osseerkij		
4	Unteroffizier	Jürgensen, Werner	Osseerkij		
5	Unteroffizier	Liebscher, Karl	Osseerkij		
6	Unteroffizier	Rummel, Sigmund	Osseerkij		
7	Leutnant	Taubert, Dr. Joh.	Osseerkij	9 Jan 43	
8		Baschek, Heinrich	Mius sector	21 Feb 43	
9		Brunswik, Alfred	Mius sector	21 Feb 43	
10	Feldwebel	Wunderlich, Heinz	Krutoj Log	6 July 43	Buried at Tawrowo
11		Essler, Adalbert	Krutoj Log	6 July 43	Buried at Tawrowo
12	Unteroffizier	Angerer, Ernst	Batrazkaja Datscha	6 July 43	Buried at Tawrowo
13	Unteroffizier	Petzka, Herbert	Batrazkaja Datscha	6 July 43	Buried at Tawrowo
14	Gefreiter	Stühler, Wilhelm	Batrazkaja Datscha	6 July 43	Buried at Tawrowo
15		Schmidt, Albrecht	Mjassojedowo	8 July 43	Buried at Tawrowo
16	Unteroffizier	Clas, Heinz	Scheino	11 July 43	Buried at Tawrowo
17	Oberfeldwebel	Tröger, Karl	Werchny-Oljschanez	15 July 43	Buried at Tawrowo
18	Unteroffizier	Miederer, Peter	Jakolewko	21 July 43	Buried at Tawrowo
19	Gefreiter	Pichler, Johann	Tawrowo	23 July 43	Buried at Tawrowo
20		Bierig, Herbert	Maximofka	20 Aug 43	
21		Riedel, Heinz	Scharowka	30 Aug 43	
22		Legath, Heinrich	Goluboff	31 Aug 43	
23		Schilling, Peter	Goluboff	31 Aug 43	
24		Will, Alfred	Goluboff	2 Sept 43	
25	Oberfeldwebel	Sauerkirsch	Goluboff	Sept 43	
26		Roth, Franz		4 Sept 43	
27	Leutnant	Weinert, Konrad		5 Dec 43	
28		Schubert, Leo	Bali (Winniza)	30 Jan 44	
29		Böttcher, Peter	Tschesnowka	17 Feb 44	Buried at Rubany Most
30	Unteroffizier	Rieschel, Hans	Frankowka	21 Feb 44	
31		Höhn, Walter	Czernowitz	26 Mar 44	
32	Unteroffizier	Rothemann, Kurt	Sloboda Zlota	30 Mar 44	Buried at Teofipolka

Sequence Number	Rank	Name	Location	Date	Remarks
France					
33	Unteroffizier	Dolk, Gebhard	Maneville	18 July 44	
34		Brendecke, Heinz	Maneville	18 July 44	
35		Ebert, Georg	Maneville	18 July 44	
36		Hinterpichler, Georg	Maneville	18 July 44	
37		Jäger, Anton	Maneville	18 July 44	
38	Unteroffizier	Mathes, Rolf	Maneville	18 July 44	
39	Gefreiter	Mühling, Josef	Maneville	18 July 44	
40		Peters, Willi	Maneville	18 July 44	
41		Pukownik, Josef	Maneville	18 July 44	
42		Radestock, Kurt	Maneville	18 July 44	
43		Schulte, Karl Heinz	Maneville	18 July 44	
44		Schuster, Willi	Maneville	18 July 44	
45		Thon, Horst	Maneville	18 July 44	
46	Unteroffizier	Westerhausen, Peter	Maneville	18 July 44	
47	Oberfeldwebel	Bormann, Ernst		12 Aug 44	During unit move; near Esternay
48	Unteroffizier	Wehrheim, Ernst	La Meix	12 Aug 44	
49	Feldwebel	Weiland, Josef	Sailly (Lille)	26 Aug 44	
50		Ricke, Klaus	north of Sailly	28 Aug 44	
51	Gefreiter	Blunk, Sigurt	Lille	31 Aug 44	
Hungary					
52	Oberschütze	Zäh, Alfons		1 Nov 44	Died at medical treatment facility at Jaszbareny
53	Feldwebel	Bornschier, Justus		10 Dec 44	Died at mobile field hospital 623
54	Feldwebel	Gärtner, Heinz	Zamoly	7 Jan 45	
55	Obergefreiter	Rauh, Nikolaus		22 Feb 45	Buried at Totmegyr (Tardosked)
Czechoslovakia					
56	Feldwebel	Skoda, Heinrich		30 Apr 45	Buried at Wostiz

APPENDIX 2

Short Biographies of the Contributors

The interest of numerous "outsiders" in our book as well as the likelihood that family members of our comrades will read it makes it appear desirable to say a few words about authors of the sections to those who have no personal familiarity with our battalion.

DR. NORDEWIN VON DIEST-KOERBER

Born 13 February 1912 in Koerberrode (Graudenz District), West Prussia (1919–1939 in the "Polish Corridor"), adopted in 1923 by his maternal grandfather with the double-name "von Diest-Koerber." Schooled in Bromberg and Stettin, receiving Abitur there in 1930. Trained in agriculture and forestry. Agricultural studies at Potsdam, Heidelberg, Munich, and Königsberg with final government-administered examinations and awarded diploma in agriculture; obtained doctorate in agriculture, 1939. At the same time, he performed one year of voluntary military service with the 4th Mounted Regiment, Potsdam, later the 6th Panzer Regiment at Neuruppin. After 1938 exercises, promoted to Leutnant der Reserve.

Took part in war in Poland with the 6th Panzer Regiment as a platoon leader, in France as company commander and in Russia as company commander until severely wounded in September 1941. After recovery in the fall of 1942, served as Oberleutnant der Reserve and special staff officer with the staff of the 3rd Panzer Army in Russia. Conversion training in 1943 to Tiger tanks and,

starting in the fall of 1943, served as company commander, then acting battalion commander of Tiger Tank Battalion 509. (At the same time all three younger von Koerber brothers went through the same conversion training as reserve officers on Tigers. Achim and Detlev went to Tiger Tank Battalion 503, Wilfried to Tiger Tank Battalion 505.) In November 1944, after attending the battalion commander course, he served as Hauptmann der Reserve and commander of Tiger Tank Battalion 503 in Hungary, Austria and Czechoslovakia until the end of the war. Received the Wound Badge in Gold after his seventh wound; the German Cross in Gold; the *Panzerkampfabzeichen* (3rd level, more than seventy-five engagements); and, the Knight's Cross (1 May 1945).

After the end of the war, occupied from July 1945 until 1954 in agriculture (farm manager, operation of a leased farmstead). Director of the Extension Station in Agriculture and Industrial Economics in Hanover. Then retirement.

CLEMENS GRAF KAGENECK

Born 17 October 1913 in Berlin, received the Abitur in March 1931 after six years of boarding school at Alloisiuskolleg in Bad Godesberg. Studied law, starting in the fall of 1931 (after four months riding and driving school in Schleswig) at Freiburg-Bonn. Law studies were interrupted by a period of voluntary service with the Potsdam 4th Cavalry Regiment from 1 April 1934 to 30 September 1935. *Referendar* (junior lawyer who has passed his first state examination) at Oberlandesgericht (regional court of appeal) in Cologne, April 1938. Also in 1938, after two field exercises, promoted to Leutnant der Reserve in the 6th Panzer Regiment at Neuruppin (successor to the 4th Mounted Regiment). Taken into active service in October 1938. Platoon leader in Polish Campaign. Signals officer of 2nd Battalion, 6th Panzer Regiment, in Western Campaign, regimental signals officer in Russia, 1941–42. In 1942 company commander of the 4th Company, 6th Panzer Regiment, during the campaign in the Caucasus. October 1942, O1 (first Ordonnanzoffizier) of the 3rd Panzer Division. April–June 1943, battalion commander courses at Putlos and Paris.

July 1943 until wounded on 30 January 1944 as commander of Tiger Tank Battalion 503. December 1944, class advisor at the armor school at Bergen. In 1950 joined the Dresdner Bank in Frankfurt and became director of its branch at Freiburg in 1952. Became Chief Executive Officer of the Hardy-Bank, Berlin-Frankfurt in 1962, and retired at the end of 1978.

ULRICH KOPPE

Born 1923 in Berlin. Attended school in Berlin from 1929 to Sept 1940. After Reich Labor Service in December 1940, joined the 5th Panzer Replacement Battalion as a volunteer. In 1941 with the 5th Panzer Regiment in North Africa. October 1942, Leutnant der Reserve. From August 1943 to May 1945, with Tiger Tank Battalion 503, finishing as acting commander of the 503's 3rd Company.

From May 1945 to October 1955 in Soviet captivity. After release, studied law and political science from 1956 to 1960 at the University of Göttingen. Referendar in circuit of Oberlandesgericht Düsseldorf from 1960 to 1963. Started in September 1963 as Reg. Assessor with the Regierungspräsident Düsseldorf. From May 1974 until retirement at the end of March 1988, department head with the Regierungspräsident Arnsberg. Married since October 1957 with three daughters.

FRANZ-WILHELM LOCHMANN, MD

Born 22 April 1923, Hamburg. Abitur 1941. Reichsar-beitsdienst in East Prussia. Volunteer to the 5th Panzer Replacement Battalion at Neuruppin. Tank radio operator in the 1st Company, Tiger Tank Battalion 503, from its activation until the end of the war. Final rank: Unteroffizier. In ninety-five armored engagements. After the war, studied medicine with several years of additional clinical training as specialist in internal medicine and general medicine. Settled down as practicing physician in Hamburg until 1986.

GERHARD NIEMANN

Born 1923 in Hamburg. Business training. 1941 volunteer. Attended the army infantry noncommissioned officer academy at Treptow/Rega in 1941; in 1942 at the armor noncommissioned officer academy at Putlos and Eisenach. April 1943: Tiger training at Paderborn. From May 1943 to May 1945 with the 503's 3rd Company.

After a short period of U.S. captivity in Czechoslovakia, commercial clerk in the wholesale textile trade. In the Bundeswehr from 5 April 1956 to 30 September 1977. In 1970: warrant officer. Final service position, warrant officer in charge of induction station for volunteers at Hanover. Author of articles on the military and on military history.

HERMANN RÖPSCHER

Born 1920 in Frankfurt/Main (Griesheim). After schooling and instruction, joined the 81st Rifle Replacement Regiment at Meiningen (Thuringia). In November 1940 with the battalion staff of the 2nd Battalion, 112th Rifle Regiment, at Ohrdruf (Thuringia). Russian campaign, June 1941. Frostbite outside of Moscow, Winter 1941. Hospital, Dresden. Replacement unit (signals) of the 81st Rifle Regiment at Meiningen (Thuringia).

June 1942, Neuruppin, Tiger Tank Battalion 503 (Maintenance Company and then the 1st Company). Unteroffizier up to February 1945. Transferred to the 211th Field Replacement Battalion. Employed as infantry in the lesser Carpathians and lower Austria. Wounded at the Thaya bridgehead at Laa. Hospital in Bohemia. Discharged by the U.S. Army in Germany. Professionally active since June 1945. 1949, examination for Master's degree (electrical engineering). Metrology and automatic controls technology, engineer in sales process engineering until 1983.

RICHARD FREIHERR VON ROSEN

Born 1922. October 1940: Fahnenjunker (officer candidate) in the 35th Panzer Regiment. With that regiment (4th Panzer Division) on the Eastern Front in 1941.

1942: Leutnant. Starting in July 1942 with the 2nd Company, Tiger Tank Battalion 502. Redesignated as 3rd Company, Tiger Tank Battalion 503, in January 1943. Platoon leader. Starting in September 1944, acting company commander of the 503's 3rd Company. Effective 1 November 1944: Oberleutnant and company commander. Eastern Front; Normandy; and, Hungary. Wounded five times. After a short period in U.S. captivity and activity in farming, joined the Bundeswehr in 1955 as a Hauptmann. General staff training at the Ecole Supérieure de Guerre in Paris. Troop and staff assignments. Final rank: Generalmajor. Retired 1982.

ALFRED RUBBEL

Born 1921 at Tilsit/East Prussia. After school, volunteer. After a short time in the infantry, to the 5th Panzer Replacement Battalion, then with the 29th Panzer Regiment of the 12th Panzer Division. In the central and northern sectors of the Eastern Front. 1942 with the 4th Panzer Regiment of the 13th Panzer Division in the Caucasus. 1943 conversion training on Tigers. March 1943 to May 1945 with Tiger Tank Battalion 503, with detailing to school to become a reserve officer in the summer/fall of 1944. Last duty assignment: special duty staff officer in the battalion. After a short period of U.S. captivity, professional training and agricultural activity. 1956 to 1978 in the Bundeswehr. Final official position: Class advisor at armored troop school. Following that, active in defense technology.

GERMAN ARMOR IN ACTION

Whether spearheading the blitzkrieg in 1939–40 or going muzzle-to-muzzle with Soviet T-34s in the East, German panzers thundered across the battlefields of World War II and revolutionized modern warfare. These heavily illustrated, large-format books place readers in the turrets of Tigers, Elefants, and other lethal vehicles.

TIGERS IN COMBAT
WOLFGANG SCHNEI
TIGERS IN COMBAT II
WOLFGANG SCHNEIDER

TIGERS IN COMBAT I

Wolfgang Schneider

$29.95 • PB • $8\frac{1}{2}$ x $11\frac{7}{8}$ • 416 pages
415 illustrations • 978-0-8117-3171-3

TIGERS IN COMBAT II

Wolfgang Schneider

$29.95 • PB • $8\frac{1}{2}$ x $11\frac{7}{8}$ • 368 pages
473 illustrations • 978-0-8117-3203-1

PANZER TACTI
GERMAN SMALL-UNIT ARMOR TAC
IN WORLD WAR II
WOLFGANG SCHNEIDER

PANZER TACTICS

German Small-Unit Armor Tactics in World War II

Wolfgang Schneider

$29.95 • PB • $8\frac{1}{2}$ x $11\frac{7}{8}$ • 368 pages
597 illustrations • 978-0-8117-3244-4

The Combat History of
GERMAN HEAVY
ANTI-TANK UNIT 653
IN WORLD WAR II
KARLHEINZ
The Combat History of
GERMAN TIGER
TANK BATTALION 503
IN WORLD WAR II
DR. FRANZ-WILHELM LOCHMANN,
RICHARD FREIHERR VON ROSEN,
AND ALFRED RUBBEL

THE COMBAT HISTORY OF
GERMAN HEAVY ANTI-TANK UNIT 653
IN WORLD WAR II

Karlheinz Münch

$29.95 • PB • $8\frac{1}{2}$ x $11\frac{7}{8}$ • 384 pages
474 illustrations • 978-0-8117-3242-0

THE COMBAT HISTORY OF
GERMAN TIGER TANK BATTALION 503
IN WORLD WAR II

Franz-Wilhelm Lochmann,
Richard Freiherr von Rosen, and Alfred Rubbel

$29.95 • PB • $8\frac{1}{2}$ x $11\frac{7}{8}$ • 384 pages
371 illustrations • 978-0-8117-3484-4

WWW.STACKPOLEBOOKS.COM

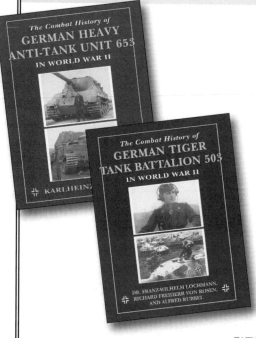